P9-APW-983

Explaining Crime

Explaining Crime

Second Edition

Gwynn Nettler
Professor of Sociology
The University of Alberta, Canada

McGraw-Hill Book Company
New York   St. Louis   San Francisco   Auckland   Bogotá
Düsseldorf   Johannesburg   London   Madrid   Mexico   Montreal   New Delhi
Panama   Paris   São Paulo   Singapore   Sydney   Tokyo   Toronto

87257

EXPLAINING CRIME

Copyright © 1978, 1974 by McGraw-Hill, Inc. All rights reserved. Printed in the United States of America. No part of this publication may be reproduced, stored in a retrieval system, or transmitted, in any form or by any means, electronic, mechanical, photocopying, recording, or otherwise, without the prior written permission of the publisher.

234567890FGRFGR78321098

This book was set in Times Roman by Black Dot, Inc.
The editors were Lyle Linder and Susan Gamer;
the cover was designed by Rafael Hernandez;
the production supervisor was Charles Hess.
Fairfield Graphics was printer and binder.

Cover drawing by Lorenz; © 1972 The New Yorker Magazine, Inc.

Library of Congress Cataloging in Publication Data

Nettler, Gwynn.
　　Explaining crime.

　　Bibliography:　p.
　　Includes indexes.
　　1.　Crime and criminals.　I.　Title.
HV6025.N46 1977　　　　364　　　　77-7585
ISBN 0-07-046306-9

To my students and colleagues
who can tell the difference between fact and fantasy

Contents

87257

Preface

"The seeds of every crime are in each of us," Leo Tolstoy believed. The point of Tolstoy's aphorism is to indicate a possibility common to all of us. The poverty of his statement is that it does not describe how the criminal seeds are germinated. On this, we dispute, and the victim in the cartoon on the cover of this book is no more confused in his response to crime than many of us.

Professional students of crime, like nonprofessionals, quarrel about which wrongs should be considered crimes. We vacillate between sympathy for the criminal and concern for the victim. We argue whether "the violence of conditions" justifies the violence of persons, and we debate whether crimes "understandably motivated" should be excused by the force of their circumstances.

Intellectuals—the occupationally thoughtful—as well as other citizens can be heard praising and condemning arson, theft, and murder depending upon their agreement with the political motives of the offenders and their approval or disapproval of the victims. On the right, the former Governor of California tells us that the Watergate burglars and their accomplices are not "really criminals." On the left, defenders of campus arsonists and urban guerrillas tell us that the goodness of their ends and the meanness of conditions transform their acts from crimes to "social banditry."

The general public, as usual, is in the middle. It thinks it knows what it means by "crime." Both its definition of crime and its sense of justice remain more universal and more historical than the current claims of political advocates. However, when nonprofessionals turn to professionals for explanations of crime and guidance in policy, they receive a potpourri of answers that leaves them as "balanced," or as muddled, as the citizen in our cartoon.

Criminologists dispute what should be called "crime," and how to count crime. We quarrel, too, about where to lay the blame. Some explanations of crime hold the actor responsible for his or her behavior and look for the causes of crime in the criminal's difference from lawful people. Other explanations blame the actor's circumstances; still others blame the "moral entrepreneurs" who have the power to define crime and to enforce their definitions through police and courts.

These explanatory efforts will be described and criticized. Our standard of criticism is how adequately an explanation answers the questions about crime asked by most citizens. Our critical standard is concerned, first, with the *clarity* of concepts and hypotheses; second, with the *evidence* for a theory of crime production; and third, with the practical *consequences* of applying a theory. It will be apparent that some theories of human behavior that appear plausible on paper do not work well with people.

All the explanations to be described contain some truth. The prices we pay when we believe one explanation rather than another vary, however. Our criticism concludes with a statement, a rare one, of the conditions that generate crime. This roster of criminogenic conditions provides a partial account of the costs of reducing crime.

ACKNOWLEDGMENTS

Fellow students have read portions of this work and have both corrected me and stimulated me. They are not to be blamed for my mistakes, of course, but they are to be thanked for their help. I am grateful to Douglas Cousineau, John Hagan, George Kupfer, and Leonard Savitz, who counseled me during the writing of the first edition.

This second edition has been revised and expanded. While my original counsellors continue to advise me, the present edition has also benefited from criticism by Donald Demers, Simon Dinitz, Michael Gillespie, Timothy Hartnagel, Lance Roberts, Jeff Schrink, Robert A. Silverman, Clyde Vedder, and George Weber.

Gwynn Nettler

Explaining Crime

Chapter 1

Crimes and Other Wrongs

"Crime" is one of the words used to describe the wrongs we do ourselves and others. The roster of conceivable wrongs is enormous, of course, and the word "crime" does not encompass all the damage done. In its legal sense, "crime" refers only to those injuries that receive the attention of government.

Because there are so many possible wrongs and because "crime" denotes only a select sample of all disapproved acts, the definition of crime varies from time to time and from place to place and there is controversy about what should or should not be called "crime." The laws and morals that dictate which wrongs are to be dealt with as crimes are themselves under challenge in changing societies.

AN ASSORTMENT OF WRONGS

The general idea out of which the notion of crime has developed is a moral idea, the concept of *sin*. Sin is a breach of divine law, an offense against the commandment of a god or gods. "Sin" is not a popular word among social scientists, but the moral motive that defines some acts as sins persists in the definition of crime.

Another conception of wrong that affects the definition of crime is the notion of *vice*. A vice is considered to be the wrongful use of one's appetites.

1

According to some observers, the harmful or degrading satisfaction of our desires is vice when we do not know we are acting "badly" and sin when we do (Brock, 1960, p. 34).

However uncomfortable, the notions of sin and vice may be to some modern thinkers, they both continue to underlie the idea of crime. Quarrels about which wrongs should be considered crimes and about the relative gravity of crimes remain *moral* quarrels. The idea of crime starts with some conception of proper behavior. The conception of proper behavior may be justified by reference to divine commandments or to naturalistic ethics, but a moral conception lies at the root of the idea of crime.

Shifting Morals and Changing Crimes

Morals change, whether or not we approve of this, and with the changes go variations in the content of crime. The broad boundaries of offenses against property, person, and "society"[1] remain fairly steady, but the criminal filling within these boundaries varies. In 1934, the American financier Samuel Insull expressed the point this way:

> If two men had walked down Fifth Avenue a year ago—that would have been March, 1933—and one of them had a pint of whiskey in his pocket and the other had a hundred dollars in gold coin, the one with the whiskey would have been called a criminal and the one with the gold an honest citizen. If these two men, like Rip Van Winkle, slept for a year and again walked down Fifth Avenue, the man with the whiskey would be called an honest citizen and the one with the gold coin a criminal[2] [from Schultz, 1972, pp. 135–136].

Despite such interesting variations in the definition of crime, all societies recognize some kinds of property appropriation as theft, whether the property is deemed to belong to the gods, the state, or individuals. Similarly, all societies

---

[1]"Society" is placed in quotation marks to indicate the vagueness of the term, a vagueness that characterizes much of sociological language (Lachenmeyer, 1971). The word "society" and associated terms such as "social order" and "social system" are useful but obscure. They may in fact be useful because they are obscure. At any rate, the lack of clarity of these terms can be verified by reference to dictionaries of sociology such as those edited by Fairchild (1944), Hoult (1969), and Mitchell (1968). The definitions found there justify the comment of the philosopher Ortega y Gasset that "the very name, 'society,' as denoting groups of men who live together, is equivocal and utopian" (1946, p. 24).

Unfortunately, "society" is not the only vague concept sociologists employ in thinking about social relations. Sociology is full of ambiguous language, and, as a consequence, a textbook such as this becomes pockmarked with terms enclosed in quotation marks. I can apologize for this early in the discussion and, at the same time, indicate the utility of words with fuzzy referents. The utility of obscure but emotionalized terms is that they can be employed as signals to stimulate partisanship without having to be submitted to the dull discipline of clear meaning. In short, it is possible to communicate ethicopolitical sentiment without saying anything definitive. It is this possibility that led Weil (1946) to argue that "the words and slogans which, throughout human history, have inspired the combined spirit of sacrifice and cruelty . . . turn out to be equally empty. Every empty abstraction has its faction" (p. 72).

[2]Gold hoarding was a crime in the United States from 1934 through 1974. During this period, keeping gold was not a crime in Canada or in many other industrialized countries.

define some kinds of killing of its members as murder and some kinds of disloyalty to the group as treason. However, the particular acts and circumstances that constitute theft, murder, and treason fluctuate, and in changing societies the meanings of these terms are contested.

Example: The Vocabulary of Homicide   The contest over whose wrong should be a crime is reflected in the names we give to the killing of other people. The word we use to refer to a homicide indicates whether the killing is justified or deplored. For example, "murder" is the name for legally unjustified, intentional homicide. The word has a *legal* meaning—homicide that the criminal law of our state calls "crime"—but it also has a *moral* meaning— homicide that is disapproved. Thus when terrorists kill their enemies or the symbols of their enemies in the form of innocent bystanders, they absolve themselves from blame for murder by calling their killing "execution." Elevating homicide to execution makes a claim for its justice; reducing homicide to murder denies the fairness with which death is dealt.

The quarrel in semantics is apparent also in the debate about abortion. Those who oppose the legality of induced abortion call it "murder." Those who favor legal access to abortion speak of "terminating pregnancy" or "removing tissue." Antiabortionists say that life begins with the fertilized egg. Pro-abortionists distinguish between stages in the development of human life. Thus they refer to a zygote (a fertilized ovum), an embryo (up to the last part of the third month of pregnancy), and a fetus (during the remainder of pregnancy). Some persons who favor the legality of the induced abortion of an embryo reject the legality of the abortion of a fetus. The point is that such different vocabularies reflect different moralities.

No facts will resolve such a moral debate because life and death are matters of definition, and definitions can be *chosen*, as Humpty Dumpty told Alice. In matters of right and wrong, morals, not facts, decide definitions.[3]

Being alive or dead is thus more than a matter of passing some physiological test. It is also a matter of social definition. Every society sets boundaries to what it considers life and death, human being and creature, justifiable homicide and murder. Ordinarily we do not notice that we have *defined* such issues. Our daily definitions are conventional, and the meanings to which we have become accustomed are part of us. However, there are occasions when a "decision rule" is required—that is, an official definition that permits action. For example, Sudnow (1966) reports that for an American hospital:

> An expelled fetus is either considered "human" or not . . . the dividing line is 550 grams, 20 centimeters, and 20 weeks of gestation. Any creature having smaller dimensions or of lesser embryonic "age" is considered non-human . . . and if "born" without signs of life, is properly flushed down the toilet, or otherwise simply disposed of. . . . Any creature having larger dimensions or of greater

---

[3]Indeed, this says little because morals are themselves defined as ultimates not to be influenced by such facts as consequences (J. Ladd, 1957).

embyronic "age" is considered human, and if "born" without signs of life, or if born with signs of life which cease to be noticeable at some later point, cannot be permissibly flushed down the toilet, but must be accorded a proper ritual departure from the human race [pp. 176–177].

To show that our morals *define* wrongs is disturbing, particularly when others challenge our morality and its preferred definitions. Each contestant in moral disputes likes to think that his or her preferences are divinely ordained, historically progressive, based on facts, or justified by some combination of these virtues. It is probable, however, that our morals, and hence our conceptions of crime, are learned preferences that define our ethnic and personal identity. Morals support self-interest, at least in the sense that a shared morality is valuable for personal identity, for knowing how to be. But apart from this grounding in self-interest, it is doubtful that concrete results, or other facts, affect morals as much as morals select facts to support ethical preferences.

Defining Victims

The grounding of conceptions of crime in conceptions of wrong means that it is easiest to define crime when there is an identifiable victim. Moreover, it is easiest to define crime when the identifiable victim is one of "our people" rather than an alien or an enemy.

It becomes more difficult to define crime, however, when the victim is a collection of individuals—a corporation or a university, for example. It is a commentary on our honesty that even "good" people find it easy to steal if the victims are not visible persons but invisible collections of anonymous others. Not only is stealing from organizations—such as the government or "Ma Bell"—a common practice, but it also does not appear like theft to many "noncriminal" people. If an organization is big enough, and distant, guilt about stealing from it diminishes (Smigel and Ross, 1970). Vocabularies shift, again, to express differences in our moral appreciation of such acts, and stealing is translated as "expropriation" or "ripping off." Euphemism relieves conscience, and, conversely, the words we use to describe the wrongs we do reveal whether there is a conscience to be relieved.

There is a further anomaly in our attitude toward crime. If the crime is carried off with flair and if the prey is big government, big business, or some detested victim like the stodgy rich—and if, in addition, the thieves are people with whom we can romantically identify, like Robin Hood, Robert Redford, or Paul Newman (for example, *Butch Cassidy and the Sundance Kid*)—then thuggery is less likely to be considered criminal and more likely to be thought of as belonging to some other category of sin or adventure.

A measure of this differential definition of some "big" crimes is that neither their perpetrators nor large segments of their audiences seem to regard them as criminal. Thus the first American skyjacker to parachute with an extorted fortune immediately became a type of folk hero, his name emblazoned on T-shirts, and his act imitated by others. Of course, when such acts are imitated frequently, they may come to be considered criminal.[4]

A similar attitude is witnessed in the recent case of a small-town banker who allegedly stole almost $5 million—probably the largest solo embezzlement in United States history. Many of his acquaintances felt, "Well, he got caught and should be punished, but he is still a good old guy" (Maxwell, 1972, 1973).

Bandits, ancient and modern, have always had their defenders as well as their prosecutors. In the public eye there have been "noble robbers" as well as monsters. Much depends on who the victim is and how the bandit handles himself or herself. Thus the poet dos Santos (1959) has eulogized the modern Brazilian robber Lampeo by claiming that, although he "killed for play and out of pure perversity," he also "gave food to the hungry."

It will be one of the recurring themes of this book that some crimes are rational; they achieve objectives. For this reason we look upon crime with a schizoid attitude, condemning it when we or our revered institutions are victims and praising it when the victims are despised and the villains are heroic. In short, when wrongs are done, victims are variously defined.

Some wrongdoers are themselves considered to be "victims of circumstance," pressured into their wicked ways and hence more to be understood than blamed. Yet other malefactors are deemed to be "persons" responsible for their decisions to do wrong and therefore blameworthy.

The injured, too, are variously evaluated. Some are held to be "victims," while others are not. Sometimes we believe that an injured person "deserved what she got" or "contributed to his own misfortune." A judgment like this makes such a contributory actor less innocent and hence less of a victim.

Spreading the Pain Reduces the Blame Defining a victim depends, then, on attributions of responsibility and conceptions of harm. If criminal damage is dispersed among us so that no one person seems to be injured, our sense of offense is diminished. If, in addition, everyone seems to profit in the short run, the wrong becomes difficult to discern. However, crime that lacks immediately apparent victims may still have high social costs—that is, we all pay for such crime "in the end."

An example: Automobile theft Automobile theft is a prime example of crime with reduced immediate pain, high profit, and long-term costs. No one seems to be hurt much by the stealing and fencing of automobiles and automobile parts. The victim is inconvenienced, but he or she is recompensed

---

[4]The hijacking of airplanes in North America was dramatically reduced by electronic surveillance of passengers and the application of stiff penalties to bandits. The reduction is another demonstration that some kinds of crime can be efficiently controlled by reducing the ease with which they are committed and by increasing the probability of a penalty when they are attempted.

Controlling crime by constructing technological barriers and increasing the celerity, severity, and probability of penalty goes against the grain of the criminological attitude that crime should be cured by removing its causes. It will be seen (Chapters 7 to 17) that locating causes and changing them are more difficult tasks than is often assumed. Measures to reduce skyjacking fortunately were not postponed until scholars had isolated the causes of this crime.

for the loss by the insurance company. Car thieves are seldom punished. Purchasers of "laundered" vehicles get a good deal, and the insurance companies pass the costs of this crime back to the consumers of automobiles in the form of higher premiums.

With the damage so distributed, victims are difficult to define, and automobile theft continues to be a profitable business. It is estimated that between $2 billion and $3 billion worth of cars and parts are stolen in Canada and the United States each year and that they are resold at a net profit of more than $1 billion (Plate, 1975, pp. 34–35). Since most legitimate businesses regard a 5 percent profit as a sign of success and a 10 percent profit as miraculous, the return from stealing automobiles—50 percent or greater—makes stealing automobiles a better business than manufacturing them.

Some New York police officers call automobile theft "happy crime" because everyone seems to profit and no one feels the sting (Plate, 1975, p. 48). The point of this example is, again, that crime can have high social costs without immediately apparent individual costs.

Crimes against Ourselves   Our difficulties in defining crime do not end here, however. If it becomes more difficult to "see" wrong where the victim is an unknown aggregation of individuals rather than an identifiable person, it is even more difficult to define injuries that we willingly inflict upon ourselves or upon that vague entity, society. Thus we debate whether licensing or ignoring pornography, sexual aberration, violent television programs, and dope hurts their consumers and the social order. We quarrel about the "right"[5] of individuals to harm themselves, and we are not certain how much self-inflicted injury constitutes a threat to society. We are far from clear whether people who damage themselves should be conceived to be persons or victims. However, no matter which definition is accepted, it will be a *moral* definition rather than a purely factual one.

The Notion of Victimless Vice

Since societies differ in terms of morals, the boundaries they draw between persons and victims also differ. A person is one who decides; a victim is one who suffers. A person chooses to act in the way he or she does; a victim is "caused" to act that way. A person imposes his or her will; a victim suffers from defective will or from what others decide. Alternatively, it is assumed that a person's choices are informed and therefore beneficial, while a victim's choices are ignorant and therefore harmful.

---

[5]"Right" is a word used to establish a moral claim upon a territory of behavior. It is doubtful that there are "natural rights," waiting somewhere out in Nature to be discovered. On the contrary, rights are only socially subscribed and competing claims for access to something of value.

The psychoanalyst van den Haag (1975a) puts it well: "I am not persuaded," he says, "of the existence of natural rights. . . . Rights are granted by governments, which also enforce them. Legislation—and only legislation—transforms individual claims . . . into rights by imposing them as obligations on others. . . . Unless individuals are tied together by affectional social bonds, rights can no more exist than societies can. Rights are but the rationalizations of these materially prior affectional ties."

These definitions are provided by morals, not by facts. They therefore change with moral changes and with the "side we are on." As we shall see (pages 165–168), our moral stance also affects the assignment of causation to human action.

Within this shifting boundary between rights and wrongs and between victims and persons, every society defines as criminal some acts that have no apparent individual victims. Every society condemns some violations of religious or ideological commandment, some offenses against public decency, or some threats to its welfare, even though no particular person is deemed to have been damaged by such acts.

Despite the universality of laws against offenses that do not immediately harm another person, Western criminologists, but not their Eastern counterparts, have been concerned to define categories of "victimless crime" that, it is believed, should be "decriminalized."[6] Thus Schur (1965) has questioned the advisability of legal penalties against induced abortion, homosexuality, and drug abuse. Some criminologists have recommended that these and similar offenses be taken off the books for both practical and moral reasons.

On practical grounds, the overloading of police and courts in Western countries urges that some crimes be differently defined, as has recently happened, for example, in the case of private homosexual acts between consenting adults.

Furthermore, the laws against so-called "victimless crimes" are difficult to enforce, and it seems practical not to spend so much time and energy on them. Such laws are difficult to enforce because many of these offenses are vices, and vices are pleasures. For the glutton, overeating is a pleasure; for the addict, smoking opium; for the gambler, risk; for the masochist, an encounter with a sadist. With the exception of induced abortion, the allegedly victimless crimes involve a self-inflicted injury or a voluntary exchange between a buyer and a seller—as in the drug trade or prostitution. Since victims of vice are not likely to complain about their pleasures, the police have difficulty finding a plaintiff, and the enforcement of laws against vice requires surveillance rather than response to citizens' complaints. Such enforcement is costly.

These practical reasons for challenging the criminalization of vice are seconded by moral doubts. When individuals choose to harm themselves, philosophers in free societies are placed in a quandary as to whether vice is wrong and, right or wrong, whether it deserves legal attention. By contrast, philosophers in totalitarian societies have no such doubts. Totalitarian regimes are bolstered by an ideology and managed by an elite with an unchallenged monopoly of power. The ideology includes moral conceptions of how people

---

[6]The words "criminalize" and "decriminalize" will not be found in dictionaries, although sociologists have been using them with increasing frequency. In sociological use, "to criminalize" means two things: (1) to bring an act or a situation within the scope of criminal law—that is, to make it a crime—and (2) to confirm a person in a criminal career, as when one says, "Prisons criminalize." "To decriminalize" has only one meaning—to remove an act from legal definition as a crime.

These terms seem useful neologisms and will henceforth be used without the defense of quotation marks.

should behave. Modern tyrants therefore have no hesitation about punishing activities they define as immoral, activities ranging from homosexuality and prostitution to drunkenness, absenteeism from work, the use of narcotics, and the expression of "wrong" ideas. There is no freedom in Cuba, the People's Republic of China, or the Soviet Union to be a "drag queen," a whore, an addict, or a dissident. Moreover, there is no public debate in these countries about whether people *should* be free to choose some forms of morally defined self-destruction or to criticize their social orders (Bassiouni, 1974; Blum, 1971; Blum et al., 1969; Connor, 1972; Solzhenitsyn, 1973, 1975; Tuchman, 1972; Zeitlin, 1967, p. 125).

In contrast, the very notion of a free society requires that individuals be responsible for their conduct and, therefore, that the state let them alone. In this tradition, the psychiatrist Thomas Szasz (1974) argues that self-damaging behavior is none of the state's business and that a person who chooses to commit suicide slowly with tobacco, alcohol, or heroin, or more quickly with a gun, should be free to do so. It is held that there are enough crimes of an interpersonal sort—the damage we do each other—for the state to attend to and that these wrongs are more deserving of official attention. It is also argued that the state that begins to protect individuals from themselves will be difficult to bridle and will progressively intrude upon private lives and restrict liberty.

Liberal Roots   Such doctrines in defense of liberty are historically rare. They have become more rare in recent decades as the number of democracies has decreased. In modern times Western intellectuals trace their debt to John Stuart Mill (1806–1873), whose famous essay *On Liberty* (1859) attempted to set the proper limits to state power. Mill objected to the state "pushing people around." He held that

> the only freedom which deserves the name is that of pursuing our own good in our own way, so long as we do not attempt to deprive others of theirs, or impede their efforts to obtain it. Each is the proper guardian of his own health, whether bodily, or mental and spiritual. Mankind are greater gainers by suffering each other to live as seems good to themselves, than by compelling each to live as seems good to the rest [pp. 75–76].

People who favor liberty, in this Millian sense, used to be called "liberals," but this fine label has been so stretched in the twentieth century that one who uses it has to specify which kind of liberal he or she is. Thus some nineteenth-century "small-l" liberals who live in the twentieth century have changed their political name to "individualist" or "libertarian" to distinguish themselves from other breeds of modern "liberals" who have less fear of state power.

The change of title indicates that it is difficult to believe in freedom and to practice consistently what one preaches. It is difficult for many reasons. One is that we cannot ask the state to do things *for* us without inviting it to do things *to* us. If the state is asked to guard our welfare, it will guard our welfare even when we have not asked it to—as when it protects our health against alcohol, fast cars, and other pleasures.

This is not the only reason why it is difficult to be consistently liberal, however. It is also tough to be a true believer in freedom because we have to live together as people with different tastes. We therefore cannot help intruding upon one another, and we are constantly redefining the boundaries—called our "rights"—of this intrusion. The issue in criminology is whether the criminal law ought to be used to define and defend these boundaries. It will be my thesis that no one can be consistently liberal. At some point all of us ask the state to defend *our* morals against *theirs*. Saying this recommends nothing. It is a description, not a prescription.

Difficulties in Being Liberal: The Myth of Victimless Vice   The idea of victimless crime has liberal roots. It is connected to the notion of victimless vice. Mill did not call purely personal wrongs by these titles, but he did try to define personally harmful actions that ought not to be anyone's business but the actor's. However, a difficulty with the liberal notion of victimless vice is that "victims," like "wrongs," are defined. Depending upon the definition, then, of vice and harm, there is often a victim of what seems to be a private act.

If our spouses wrong *their* bodies, *we* pay a price. If children harm themselves, their parents are victims. If parents are dissolute, their children are victims. If enough individuals harm themselves, society is the victim.

In brief, the notion of victimless vice requires that no one influence anyone. As long as someone pays a price for someone else's action, that action is not victimless. The prices paid can be offenses to one's taste or invasions of one's purse. They can vary from insults to eye, ear, and nose; to having to wend one's way on public streets through importunate prostitutes; to having to pay taxes in support of rehabilitation centers for sick addicts. Even our teacher, John Stuart Mill, got himself into this tangle and could not preach his principle with consistency.[7] For example, Mill believed that drunkenness and idleness were none of the state's business *unless* the drunk was violent or the lazy person was supported by the state, but he also believed that "there are many acts which . . . if done publicly are a violation of good manners, and coming thus within the category of offences against others, may rightly be prohibited. Of this kind are offences against decency" (1859, p. 153).

We can all agree with Mill as long as he remains general, but the minute our legislators become specific, as in their attempts to pass legislation concerning obscenity, we are aware that good manners and decency are themselves up for negotiation when we live as one tribe among many under the power of a single

---

[7]Mill's lack of consistency has recently been analyzed in detail by Himmelfarb (1974), who shows us that Mill's essay *On Liberty* contradicts other of his writings and that Mill himself did not foresee the consequences of his liberal prescription.

The historian Owen Chadwick (1976) seconds Himmelfarb's criticism of Mill's liberalism and argues that since "the state is based upon the moral health of its citizens . . . no society could put [Mill's principles] into practice and remain a society."

Debate about the right amount of state interference in citizens' morals has no end. The quarrel concerns whether the state *ought* to enforce morals and whether it *can* enforce them (Devlin, 1965; H. L. A. Hart, 1965).

state. For example, the liberal psychiatrist Szasz, who, we saw, believes that the state has no right to interfere with those who want to shoot heroin or otherwise kill themselves, at the same time believes that the state does have the right to prevent one person from injuring another. But, again, "injury" can be defined, as Mill defined it, to include offenses against public decency. Thus Szasz would not allow people to copulate in public (1974, p. 21). In a similar vein, Mill did not believe that allowing people to be free included the right to sell oneself into slavery, for "by selling himself for a slave, he abdicates his liberty. . . . The principle of freedom cannot require that he should be free not to be free. It is not freedom to be allowed to alienate his freedom" (1859, p. 158).

This argument—that freedom does not mean the freedom to choose slavery—can be extended, of course, to other ways of "abdicating our liberty." All that is required is a stretching of the word "slave." Thus moralists have used Mill's principle to oppose the freedom to be a prostitute or an addict. They extend Mill by defining whoring and addiction as forms of slavery. If, according to this liberalism, no one should be free not to be free, then the state has a right to intervene.

We are returned full circle to the theme with which we began: that conceptions of crime derive from conceptions of wrong and that the notion of wrong includes ideas of sin and vice. This means that there can be offenses committed against oneself, the gods, and society, as well as offenses committed against others.

Battling about Crime

Our discussion thus far leads to two conclusions: Not only is crime rooted in a conception of wrong, but it also seems inescapable that there will always be a shifting balance among the wrongs selected for nomination as crimes. It would require a heaven on earth, such as radical criminologists promise, before a society is "[created][8] . . . in which the facts of human diversity, whether personal, organic or social, are not subject to the power to criminalize" (I. Taylor et al., 1973, p. 282).

Demand for New Crimes In Western lands today the movement to decriminalize many acts that are now illegal is met with a demand that other acts that are presently lawful be made criminal. Thus there are advocates who

---

[8]The very idea of "creating" a society is a modern arrogance. It assumes a social science that we do not have. It sees social institutions as *instruments* of social existence enacted for specific purposes and subject to change according to plan. It views disputes about the design of societies as amenable to reasoned discussion and soluble in the light of facts. As I have argued elsewhere (Nettler, 1970, p. 206), "This is a fresh view, in more than one sense, and a probably incorrect one. In opposition, there is ground for agreeing with Rhees (1947) that social institutions are better described as *forms* of social existence rather than as their instruments, that institutions are crescive rather than enacted, that their reform does not control their development, and that arguments do not solve social conflicts nor experiments decide social issues."

We can do things to our social systems, of course. This means that insofar as we act in ignorance, we can make matters worse as well as better. The balance of good and evil results of acting upon good intentions is not known; and there is no science of societal engineering that allows us to build better worlds according to plan.

recommend that new categories of victims be defined and protected by the criminalization of such heretofore lawful acts as driving without a seat belt or polluting the environment by emitting noise, fumes, or liquid and solid waste—whether this is done by corporations, governments, or individuals and their animal pets. It has been urged, too, that the publication and dissemination of hate literature be made a criminal offense, as it now is in some jurisdictions. For example, the Canadian law against hate literature was recently applied in the arrest of persons in Toronto who were passing out leaflets to tourists urging, "Yankee, go home" (Canadian Press, 1975c).

The impulse to criminalize is apparent also in the rise of a "consumer advocacy" which demands that the manufacture, sale, and use of "harmful" products be penalized. These harmful products range from alcoholic beverages, aspirin, and tobacco to detergents, insecticides, some kinds of cosmetics, and "ill-designed" automobiles, bicycles, and tricycles (P. H. Weaver, 1975).[9]

Concern with rapid population growth has led some people to demand the creation of yet another kind of crime—that of bearing more than two children. Willing (1971), for example, would enforce laws against "excessive fertility" by tattooing and sterilizing offenders.

In addition to these advocacies, many styles of "discrimination"[10] are now criminal that once were not, and there is a demand that new forms of discrimination be punished by the state. In the United States in particular, it is urged that "unfair treatment" in housing, education, occupation, or any public service by reason of age, sex, race, creed, national origin, income, or tested traits of personality and intelligence be made criminal. In this vein, R. L. Williams (1974) would have

> a bold, Federal regulatory law, a truth-in-testing law . . . formulated and enacted . . . and vigorously enforced. . . . Sanctions, ranging from stiff fines, suspensions, dechartering of corporations, colleges, or universities, or even more severe criminal penalties should be leveled against the testing corporations, state departments of education, local school districts, colleges and universities. Black communities should file class-action law suits that demand an end to testing of black children for whatever reason [p. 41].

[9]A popular mistake in thinking about our lives is the assumption that what is *correlated* with some interesting event is the *cause* of that event. This fallacy runs like a red thread through much theorizing in sociology, as later chapters will illustrate. The error is apparent also in the attempt to protect consumers from products they enjoy. For example, the United States Consumer Product Safety Commission (CPSC), one of the government's most powerful regulatory agencies, has a research arm, National Electronic Injury Surveillance System (NEISS, pronounced "nice," of course). This research agency counts injuries *associated* with products. The assumption that is then built into many consequent regulations is that the injuries were *caused* by the product. This assumption may or may not be true, but it leads a Commission member to comment that the new standards for bicycles "may not reduce injuries, but [they] will improve the quality of bicycles" (P. H. Weaver, 1975, p. 138).

[10]"Discrimination" is a prime example of a politically useful vague word. The determination of discrimination in its *legal* sense requires agreement upon some standard of fair treatment. It also requires the assessment of *motive*, since, as the word is used by sociologists, to discriminate is to *intend* some unfair result. The difficulties of ascertaining the standard of justice operative when discrimination is charged and of inferring motive from result have led one criminologist to suggest that the term cannot be given an exact meaning for sociological use (Hagan, 1977b).

Similarly, A. E. Thomas (1972) would extend the penalties of the law to "certain acts committed by school people" which he believes can be linked as "accessory to whatever crime the child commits in later life as a result of a teacher's or administrator's cruelty" (pp. 179, 182).

In this vein, Loftus (1976) recommends that universities that discriminate against people "because of their race, color, religion, sex, national origin, or handicapped status" be penalized. She advocates penalties such as withholding research funds and accreditation "or, even . . . the university's tax-exempt status. Why not fine universities that fail to comply? Better yet, how about throwing the university's officers in the pokey along with other lawbreaking rascals!"

No end to crime The number of wrongs recommended for elevation to crimes seems endless, particularly in social environments that favor using the power of the state to improve our lives. Improving our lives includes righting wrongs, and, given the broad spectrum of injuries we can be deemed to inflict on ourselves and others, the tide seems to be running toward the invention of more crimes rather than toward a reduction in their number.[11]

Thus, in the Soviet Union, the State Sports Committee recently found "the passion for playing bridge to be socially harmful" (UPI, 1973). It is now illegal to organize bridge tourneys in that land.

In Canada it has been urged that physicians be charged with crime if they do not report children's wounds that could represent instances of child abuse (van Stolk, 1972), and others, concerned with "public apathy," have recommended that the failure of a citizen to report a crime be made a crime (CTV, 1974). The Canadian national sport, ice hockey, is also being examined for its possible criminal violence. The question being debated is whether athletic assault is "part of the game" or whether it should be criminally prosecuted (Canadian Press, 1975a, 1975d; Matheson, 1975).

The United States, with its passion for solving "problems"[12] by passing laws, is not surpassed in its production of crime through legislation. Thus, in the shadow of the burglaries, bribes, and frauds connected with several recent American Presidencies, Senator Edward Kennedy, in 1975, proposed a law that would make it a crime for government officials knowingly to lie to or mislead citizens. It is not clear from this proposed legislation whether unfulfilled political promises would qualify as crimes.

---

[11]No one has counted the claims made upon modern states to criminalize and decriminalize acts. It would be an interesting research to attempt to balance these advocacies.

[12]Apologies are in order for placing so many common terms in quotation marks. It is, of course, the words that are most used that get most abused. Think, for example, of the meanings of "love."

"Problem" is another word that has been appropriated to describe social concerns. The trouble with thinking about social issues as social problems is that the idea of a problem suggests a puzzle that has a knowable solution. Problems as they are given in mathematics, bridge building, or chess usually have solutions. However, we are deluded—and dangerously so—if we conceive of our difficulties in living together as problems that will be solved if only we think hard enough in the right way. By contrast, the idea of social difficulties suggests that we struggle with our hopes and fears and that we do so with imperfect knowledge. We respond more or less successfully to these difficulties, but we do not solve them as we do crossword puzzles (Nettler, 1976).

An Opinion   In Western societies, students of crime and justice are concerned with the overload of judicial systems. The American system in particular is embattled and is charged with being both unjust and ineffective, but these charges are also heard in Great Britain and Canada. It is believed that too many heavy crimes go unpunished and that too many light offenses are attended by an expensive tangle of attorneys, judges, juries, and social workers. In democracies the legal response to crime is itself directed toward conflicting objectives. For example, it has been proposed that the criminal law be used to reform offenders and, at the same time, to achieve justice by punishing them. In addition, the criminal law is used to protect society by restraining those who harm it and by deterring those who might be tempted to do so.

Chapter 17 will argue that one of these objectives should be abandoned— that of forcibly reforming offenders. Here it is pertinent to recommend that criminal justice systems be further relieved. My liberal preference is for less law, not more. Given this attitude, two steps seem sensible: (1) to decriminalize wherever the law is far behind public morals and (2) to lighten the judicial load by reducing some crimes to offenses and by divorcing some aspects of welfare, particularly juvenile welfare, from the attention of the criminal law.

The first step is illustrated by the continuing effort to get the criminal law out of our bedrooms. Many jurisdictions have had laws forbidding certain sexual practices between spouses—as well as other persons. Such laws are difficult to enforce, and they are now unpopular. However, some jurisdictions continue to pay legal attention to the private sexual practices of consenting adults. Such legal remnants can be removed without threatening public morals.

A second step toward lightening the judicial load is to redefine some crimes as "offenses" and to reduce them from indictable wrongs subject to trial by jury to summary offenses to be handled by a magistrate, in the way most traffic violations are now managed. In this vein an American attorney, Martha Kwitny, writes:

> Many actions now called crimes carry long potential sentences on the law books, but no substantial sentences in practice. In my experience as a public defender, appellate research aide, and prosecutor, I have observed that certain crimes are rarely treated by incarceration and therefore should be reduced to *disorderly persons offenses.*
>
> They include possession of drugs (marijuana, hashish, cocaine, heroin, pills) in quantities that sell for less than $2,000; sales of the so-called soft drugs (marijuana, hashish, pills) for less than $2,000; sales of obscene materials, even to minors; first offenses of cashing bad checks, or fraud or forgery or embezzlement schemes netting under $5,000; or first offenses of breaking and entering, larceny, receiving stolen property or other nonviolent crimes netting under $5,000 [1975, italics added].

This recommendation is a version of decriminalization, of course. It reduces selected categories of crime to offenses, but it does not ignore these wrongs.

LIMITING WRONGS: CRIMINOLOGY

Studies of quarrels about who should have the power to define wrongs as crimes and which wrongs should be considered crimes are interesting in their own right. They are a part of what criminology is about, but they are only a part. More questions are asked of criminologists than these. However, as professional students of behavior, criminologists can no more respond to every question all at once than other thinkers. The answers we get depend on the questions we ask, of course, but we can intelligently answer only a few questions at a time. The first maxim of a scholar should be: *Know your question.*

This maxim recognizes that there are many reasons for asking questions. Certainly many of our questions are "interested"; that is, they are motivated by an interest, by a concern to attain or maintain something of value. This is not the only reason for taking thought, however, and we also ask questions merely to satisfy our curiosity.

Whatever the motive for asking questions, each style of question directs our attention to different facets of life. Different consequences flow from this movement of attention. Part of the debate, then, about what criminology should attend to is stimulated by different desires. The revolutionary's questions are not the reformer's, and neither of these thinkers is apt to be intrigued by the conservative's questions.

Criminologists respond to these different styles of question by dividing their work. They turn their attention to three broad categories of question: (1) the sociology of law, (2) the study of social defense, and (3) theories of crime causation ("criminogenesis").

The Sociology of Law

The sociology of law tries to understand why some acts, but not others, are made the subject of the criminal law. It is concerned with how continuing social groupings come to define their expectations of behavior that shall receive formal, public attention. Among literate peoples, the sign of "formal, public attention" is codification in law. Within the field of criminology, only those laws are pertinent which describe the behavior of notice as an injury penalized by the state—that is, as crimes. Students of the sociology of law are interested in such questions as these:

1 What seem to be the determinants of definitions of behavior as worthy of, or irrelevant to, legal notice?
   a What factors seem to be correlated with changes in these definitions?
   b What consequences may be attributed to such changes? Concern with this question raises issues about the rationality of different modes of societal response to disturbing behaviors. These issues overlap with some of the questions asked about "social defense," but the attention here is to the consequences of criminal stigmatiza-

tion and the possibilities of reacting in more economical ways to crime and criminals.

2   How does the social group implement its criminal law? This question promotes study of courts, judges, and juries; of the differential administration of law; of the determinants of differential sentencing practices; and of the occupations concerned with processing the law (the police, lawyers, corrections officers, and others).

The Study of Social Defense

"Social defense" is a European term for what has also been called "penology" and "corrections." The study of social defense concerns the measures societies take in response to violations of their formal, public expectations. Researchers in this area are interested in the consequences of different styles of social defense, in the justifications given for these differing reactions, and in the determinants of both the reactions and their consequences. Inquiries in social defense address questions of the rehabilitation of offenders and the deterrent effects of punishment. Research also considers the economy of police systems, of mechanical surveillance equipment, and of the defensive possibilities in the physical arrangement of residences and businesses.

It is obvious that the research interests of students of social defense overlap the interests of students of "societal reaction." The difference is one of emphasis. Under the topic of sociology of law, students of societal response question whether the laws are themselves rational. Under the topic of social defense, scholars are less likely to question the law and more likely to consider how to implement its intent.

Theories of Crime Causation ("Criminogenesis")

Theories of crime causation are concerned with changes in crime rates and with the characteristics of individuals and groups that do or do not violate specific bundles of criminal laws.

The study of crime causation deals with the methodological issues inherent in finding out the characteristics of violators, victims, and nonviolators. It attends, also, to the theories constructed to explain both individual involvement in crime and historical and comparative variations in the rates of different kinds of crime. This is the part of criminology to which the following chapters are addressed.

Questions and Answers

Although a question-and-answer "division of labor" exists within criminology, the divisions are not sealed off from each other. What appears to be the same question can be answered under different rubrics. The purposes of the inquirer have an influence on where the answer will be sought. For example, some criminologists answer the question, "What causes crime?" by replying, in effect, "The criminal law." Such an answer calls attention to the politics of law making and law enforcing.

This kind of answer and its turn of attention are of interest principally to students of the sociology of law. If, however, we look at crime from the point of view of popular concern, this kind of response provides no answer. When the public and its representatives ask, "What causes crime?" they mean something like, "What produces the variations in those acts which have been universally condemned as 'wrongs in themselves'?" The quality of public concern with crime is the subject of the next chapter.

Chapter 2

Concern with Crime

Crime is a major concern of people in industrialized, rich countries, as both direct and indirect measures of this concern demonstrate.

Direct measures, such as public opinion polls and letters to political representatives, indicate a high level of public anxiety about crime and a belief that the number of serious crimes has recently been increasing. Polls of Canadian and American citizens consistently reveal crime to be among "the most serious problems [that they] would like to see the government do something about" (L. Harris, 1968). Fear of theft and of violence has risen steadily since 1965 among all segments of populations in Western lands, with such anxiety greatest among urban and suburban residents and among women. A recent Gallup poll reported that 60 percent of women respondents and 22 percent of men respondents were afraid to walk alone at night on some streets near their homes (Erskine, 1974b). In an American preelection survey, the Columbia Broadcasting System (1975) found that half the voters sampled considered crime a major election issue, third only after inflation and unemployment.

Canadians feel safer, and are safer (see pages 26–27), than their American neighbors; yet a poll of citizens in Toronto found that 28 percent considered crime a "very serious" problem in their city, while 61 percent considered the crime issue "moderately serious" (Courtis, 1970, table 1.1).

In both Canada and the United States, citizens believe that crime rates have been increasing during recent years. For example, almost three-fourths of the Canadians interviewed by Courtis assumed crime to have increased. This belief is prevalent among people of all educational and income levels, but it is most apparent among the less well educated, poor people, and blacks. As we shall see in Chapters 4 to 7, this variation in popular belief is justified by tallies of the more visible, predatory offenses.

In short, separate inquiries asking a variety of questions about people's attitudes toward public issues report similar results: Crime is a major domestic concern and political question (Erskine, 1974a, 1975; Field, 1973; *Life*, 1971, 1972; *Time*, 1968, 1972).

Indirect signs of concern with crime parallel these direct measures. For example, sales in Canada and the United States of protective devices, principally electronic burglar alarms, have increased over the past 15 years. The number of companies selling security services and equipment in Canada and the United States jumped from 100 to 900 during the late 1960s (*U.S. News & World Report*, 1970). Sales of such devices have also continued to grow in the 1970s in Great Britain and Western Europe. Design Controls, an American manufacturer of security systems, reports annual sales increases of 25 to 30 percent. ADT Security Systems, a company that operates almost 80,000 theft-alarm installations in Canada and the United States, "has shown a residential sales increase of 20 percent a year for the last six years" (*U.S. News & World Report*, 1975a).

Increased sales of security systems have been accompanied by an increase in private arming, particularly in the United States. Citizens have recently bought weapons in such numbers that one observer has termed the phenomenon the "urban arms race" (Seidman, 1975). Seidman's study shows that the tendency of citizens to purchase weapons is closely correlated with officially reported crime rates in their cities. This relationship is uniform in cities from coast to coast and is not associated with differences in political attitude.

An additional sign of public concern is the organization of citizens into self-help groups under such titles as "Helping Hands," "Block Parents," "Anti-Crime Crusade," "People against Crime" (PAC), "Turn in a Pusher" (TIP), and "Women against Rape" (WAR) (*U.S. News & World Report*, 1974a).

Organized self-help is being augmented by other resources. Private security forces in Canada and the United States increased by 150 percent during the 1960s and early 1970s (Malloy, 1972). The bodyguard business is also booming as a defense against the kidnapping and killing of business executives and political figures (Joseph, 1975). In Canada and the United States there are now two to three times as many private police officers as public ones (Skelly, 1974, p. 5).

THE QUALITY OF CONCERN WITH CRIME

The concern with crime is both personal and societal, but it is personal first and societal secondarily. It is a concern with protection of one's person and belongings and, after that, with the protection of those institutions and public properties which the citizen values. The concern is only slightly directed toward minor traffic violations, public drunkenness, and vagrancy. The interest is in those elements of public order which are perennial. The concern is expressed in the timeless desire to be able to move about freely without being robbed or beaten. It is witnessed in the universal wish to preserve one's property against theft and one's body against invasion. It is indicated by the shame and anger most citizens feel when their valued edifices—courthouses, government and university buildings, police stations, communications outlets, libraries, airports, department stores, and banks—are willfully damaged. It is measured, in part, by public opinion surveys that reveal the people's disapproval of attacks on their police and riots in their streets (Canadian Press, 1974; Erskine, 1968–1969; J. P. Robinson, 1970; Sornberger, 1974; *U.S. News & World Report*, 1974b).

Concern with crime seems relatively insensitive to the expensive, but less visible, crimes committed *against* governments and large corporations, and it is aroused *by* the crimes of corporations and governments only when their immorality is dramatized. Thus there has been widespread disgust with former President Richard Nixon and his aides, who were involved in a wider range of theft and deceit than even an American tolerance of political crookedness allows.

It has long been assumed that persons in politics are not to be trusted. This suspicion of people in power is not unique to the British or to North Americans. It is common in all Latin countries and on both sides of the Atlantic, and it has been recorded in such diverse places as Boulder, Colorado; Wellington, New Zealand; and Kyoto/Otsu, Japan (W. A. Scott and Rohrbaugh, 1975).

However, while some suspicion of persons in high places is normal, there is an ill-defined level of fraud beyond which citizens sense a corruption that threatens their social order. "Fish begin to stink at the head," says an Italian proverb. Citizens smell moral decay when their leaders are criminals. It is felt, with good reason, that heads of state should set examples of probity. It is believed that although they are subject to temptation, just as the rest of us are, they should nonetheless be more immune.

The concern with protecting person, property, and cherished institutions has recently been elevated in democracies by the spectacle of a corruption that ranges from government officials who take bribes and sponsor burglaries and assassinations to parents who help their children cheat in soapbox derbies (Woodley, 1974), and Boy Scout leaders who fake their membership rolls (Bridge et al., 1974). It is a concern that has been aggravated by reports of "consumer advocates" who mislead consumers with doctored statistics (de Toledano, 1975; Sanford, 1976; Tomerlin, 1972). It is an alarm stimulated by news of governments that systematically cheat their citizens in state-run lotteries (*Wall Street Journal*, 1975) and "cook the books" to conceal their financial shenanigans (see pages 183–184; see also Auletta, 1975a, 1975b; Canadian Press, 1975b).

This concern has been augmented, too, by a public sense that stealing and killing have become more prevalent in recent years, particularly in freer societies where populations have been moving from countrysides to cities and from traditional ways of living to modern ones (Clinard and Abbott, 1973).

RECENT INCREASES IN CRIME

Serious crimes have increased over the past decade or two in rich countries and in poor, "developing" lands. They have increased among societies with communist, capitalist, and mixed economies (Clinard and Abbott, 1973; Connor, 1972; Hollander, 1973). During this time, crime has probably declined or remained stable among two different categories of countries: (1) those under fresh totalitarian rule and (2) those that have been able to channel "Western influence" in such a way that primary group control is maintained. The second phenomenon has been suggested as explaining the relatively low crime rates in such diverse countries as Japan and Norway (McDowell, 1973; L. Ross, 1975).

Elsewhere, however, both official and unofficial tallies of crime indicate a real rise in criminal activity that parallels public concern with crime. There are defects, of course, in every measure of social phenomena. Chapters 4 to 6 describe deficiencies in attempts to count crime. It is concluded that all tallies of offenses in a population *under*estimate the true amount of crime and that the underestimation is greater for the more common, minor offenses.

Trends versus Levels

Measures that consistently underestimate the actual amount of crime do not prohibit assessment of *trends* within particular states. There is probably sufficient consistency within each jurisdiction in the definition and recording of crime to permit comparison of changes in crime rates within particular countries (Archer and Gartner, 1975). It is another matter, of course, to compare *levels* of criminal activity in different states. Modes of classifying and counting crime vary between countries. So too does the willingness to report crime officially. Thus in the Soviet Union, for example, "there are no published figures on crime (on a national basis), or [on] alcoholism, suicides, [or] the prison population . . ." (Hollander, 1973, p. 7). A comparison of the quantity of crime in different jurisdictions is therefore risky, but estimates of changes within a jurisdiction are possible.

Some Recent Trends   A survey of trends among countries with relatively reliable accounting systems indicates a recent upward trend in crimes against both person and property. For example, France and Italy have experienced increases during the 1970s in kidnapping, political terrorism, bank robbery, rape, street mugging, and a novel form of purse snatching practiced by nimble youths on motorcycles. Serious crimes known to the police have consistently increased in Italy since 1965 and in France since 1970 (*Annuario Statistico Italiano*, 1967–1973; *Annuaire Statistique de la France*, 1970–1974).

Although West Germany reports smaller increases in crime over the past decade, it too has felt the inflationary trend (*Statistischer Jahrbücher für die Bundesrepublik Deutschland*, 1965–1974). Switzerland and Sweden have recorded more stable rates of criminal activity, but there is concern in both countries with an increase in juvenile offenses (*Statistik Årsbok*, 1970–1974; Toby, 1969; *U.S. News & World Report*, 1975c).

England and Wales report more dramatic changes. Violations of property and of persons have increased steadily since World War II, with an acceleration in the rate of increase during the 1960s and 1970s. McClintock and Avison (1968, p. 38) calculate an increase in indictable offenses against persons of 82 percent between 1955 and 1965. This represents, in particular, an increase in indecent assaults on women and in malicious wounding. Even more striking increases are recorded for crimes against property. Robbery and breaking and entering, for example, increased 239 percent during this decade (McClintock and Avison, 1968, p. 42). Juvenile cases before the courts in England and Wales *doubled* between 1955 and 1968 (Power et al., 1972).

This trend continues in the 1970s. The year 1970 saw a rise of 6.0 percent over the preceding year in convictions for all indictable offenses among males and a slightly higher increase of 7.8 percent among females. The increase in convictions for crimes of violence was even greater than this overall rise. The proportion of convictions of males for violent attacks in 1970 increased 12.2 percent over 1969, and this increase was more than matched by a rise of 16.5 percent in convictions of females for violent crimes (Command Paper No. 4708, 1970, tables 13 and 15a). In London, crimes of all sorts increased 16 percent in 1974 over 1973. Robberies rose 31 percent; burglaries, 19 percent; and thefts from the person, 77 percent. Fraud, forgery, theft by employees, and shoplifting are all reported to have increased (*Annual Abstract of Statistics*, 1974; *U.S. News & World Report*, 1975c).

Criminal Ingenuity

Recent increases in old-fashioned crimes have been accompanied by advances in criminal inventiveness. New kinds of crime are keeping pace with technological change. Thus computers are being used as instruments of theft in a variety of ways. Technicians have stolen large amounts from their employers by feeding false information into their machines. In this manner a large British firm was recently defrauded of £43,000 by one operator (P. Hamilton, 1973).

Information and ideas are also being stolen. The customer files of the *Encyclopedia Britannica*, for example, were stolen and sold to a competitor. Similarly, the BOAC computer was tapped so as to give another airline an advantage in making reservations (P. Hamilton, 1973, p. 17).

Computers have also "gotten into the criminal act" as symbols of "the Establishment" to be attacked by revolutionary groups. Terrorists in Europe and in Canada and the United States have erased and stolen tapes and have destroyed computers. In one instance, the Angry Brigade, a British terrorist organization, tried to blow up police records stored in the London computer.

Criminal ingenuity has also turned to fire. It is sometimes difficult to separate fires started accidentally from those started maliciously, but insurance investigators have developed techniques for judging whether fires are deliberately set. In general, the greater the damage, the more likely that the fire is the result of arson.

The Fire Protection Association (1970) provides information from 15 large insurers in Europe, and according to its figures, arson has been on the increase. It is estimated that about 15 percent of all fires in these reporting countries are now deliberately started.

Crime in the United States

Like most other countries in the world, the United States is experiencing an increase in crime. The Federal Bureau of Investigation publishes annual Uniform Crime Reports for seven serious, or "index," crimes, subdivided into violent crimes and offenses against property. The violent crimes in the FBI Index are murder, forcible rape, aggravated assault, and robbery. The crimes against property are grouped as burglary, larceny-theft,[1] and automobile theft. All these index crimes increased during the 1960s at a faster rate than the population. Between 1960 and 1970 these crimes known to the police increased about 150 percent, while the population grew by about 15 percent. In more recent years, between 1970 and 1975, the total number of index offenses rose 39 percent, while the rate per 100,000 population increased 33 percent. During this period, violent crimes increased at the same rate (39 percent) as crimes against property. Figures 2-1 to 2-3 depict these increases. The increase in crime is apparent both in the number of offenses known to the police and in the rate of these crimes per 100,000 persons. The *rate* of increase in serious crimes has shown some recent fluctuations, some ups and downs, but the *level* of criminal activity in the United States has remained disturbingly high (FBI, 1974, 1975, 1976). In particular, the rates of juvenile crime and violent crime have risen dramatically.

Juvenile Crime   Arrests of juveniles for serious crimes increased by 1,600 percent in the 20 years from 1952 to 1972, according to FBI records. While arrests of adults, those 18 years of age and older, increased by 13 percent between 1960 and 1975, arrests of juveniles increased by 144 percent. Furthermore, as juvenile crime has increased, it has become more serious. Younger people are more frequently being charged with burglary, robbery, rape, and murder. In the United States in 1975, 9.5 percent of arrests for murder and nonnegligent manslaughter and 17.6 percent of arrests for forcible rape involved persons under 18 years of age (FBI, 1976, table 36). Official statistics

---

[1]Beginning in 1973, "larceny-theft" replaced the crime category "larceny $50 and over." This replacement reflects the rise in both prices and crime.

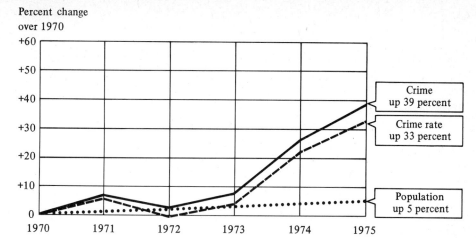

Figure 2-1 Crime and population, 1970–1975. "Crime" refers to index offenses; "crime rate" refers to the number of offenses per 100,000 population. (*FBI chart.*)

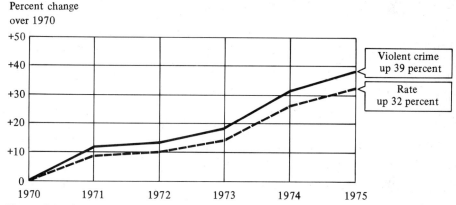

Figure 2-2 Crimes of violence, 1970–1975; limited to murder, forcible rape, robbery, and aggravated assault. (*FBI chart.*)

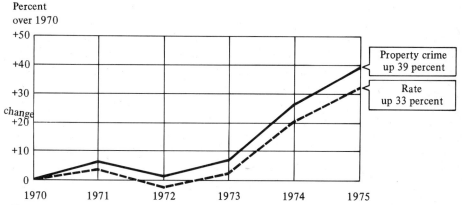

Figure 2-3 Crimes against property, 1970–1975; limited to burglary, larceny-theft, and motor vehicle theft. (*FBI chart.*)

report that nearly half (48 percent) of all persons arrested for burglary, larceny, and automobile theft in 1975 were juveniles (FBI 1976, table 36). During the past 15 years, the number of young girls arrested for murder increased by almost 300 percent (FBI, 1976, table 31; McNamara, 1975, p. 10).

The increase in the proportion of youthful offenders arrested for serious crimes has been accompanied by an apparent increase in casual violence. The callous nature of many of these attacks alarms both citizens and "youth experts" (Footlick et al., 1975). For example, six teenagers in New York City were recently charged with murdering three "old bums" by setting them on fire. At about the same time, two lads, 13 and 15 years old, were accused of murdering a 4-year-old boy "to have some fun," as they told the police.

Crime in the schools has led the National Education Association (1974) to conduct annual polls of its teacher members to ascertain their victimization. In 1974, 3 percent, or more than 63,000 American teachers, reported that they had been physically attacked by students. Another 11.4 percent, or about 240,000 teachers, said that their property had been maliciously damaged. The hazards associated with teaching, particularly in American urban high schools, moved the president of the American Federation of Teachers to protest to Congress that teachers have been doused with lighter fluid and set on fire, raped, beaten, and robbed (*U.S. News & World Report*, 1975d, 1976).

Violence is not restricted to juveniles, of course, and Americans have recently been murdering one another at a high rate, compared with citizens of other "civilized" societies.

Murder   Americans are killing one another at such a high rate that the psychiatrist Donald Lunde (1975) has called the situation a "murder epidemic." "More Americans were murdered from 1970 through 1974," Lunde says, "than were killed during the entire Vietnam war."

The most murderous people are young men, and it has been assumed that the postwar "baby boom" might account for the increase in homicide. However, a careful analysis of changes in murder rates between 1963 and 1965 and between 1971 and 1972 in the 50 largest cities in the United States demonstrates that "less than one-tenth of the actual rise in the national homicide rate since the 1960s can be explained by demographic changes" (Barnett et al., 1974, p. 23). These investigators show that homicide rates increased in every one of the 50 cities during the late 1960s and early 1970s. When these rates are adjusted to take account of variations in the age and ethnic composition of the cities—variations that make a difference in murder rates—it is found that the greatest increase in homicide has been in Detroit, Buffalo, and Honolulu. Detroit has been given the title "murder capital of the world" because of this dramatic increase in its homicide rate and because its 1971–1972 rate was higher than that of any other American city. Its rate of 39 murders for every 100,000 residents is among the highest in the world.

Barnett and his colleagues conclude that murder rates in American cities are higher than many people believe and that

at current . . . levels, a randomly-chosen baby born in a large American city has almost a two percent chance of dying by homicide; among males, the figure is three percent. Thus, an American boy born in 1974 is more likely to die by murder than an American soldier in World War II was to die in combat. With the reduction in auto fatalities because of lower speed limits and new safety devices, it is plausible that murder might soon surpass auto accidents as a cause of death in America [1974, p. 35].

Arson   Recent increases in juvenile crime and violence have been accompanied in North America, as in Europe, by improvements in some of.the older styles of crime such as arson.

The Insurance Information Institute (I.I.I.) performs the same function in the United States that the Fire Protection Association does in Europe. Its estimates show an increase in arson, paralleling that noted in the Old Country (see page 22). The I.I.I. estimates that losses due to arson in the United States in 1975 exceeded $1.4 *billion*, an increase over the estimated losses of $1.2 billion in 1974 and $845 million in 1973. Deliberately set fires are now believed to kill some 1,000 persons each year (D. Martin, 1976).

Arsonists have varying motives, of course. They range from pyromaniacs who derive sexual pleasure from setting fires to disgruntled but "idealistic" students (*Scanlan's Monthly*, 1972). Angry revolutionaries burn the symbols of their hated institutions, as do angry employees. In addition, failing business people set fires to defraud insurance companies (D. Martin, 1976). The business of arson is an example of rational crime (see Chapters 9 and 10), committed because it is easy, relatively free of risk, and rewarding.

Burning the Bronx   An interesting, but sad, case study in criminogenesis is provided by one of the boroughs of New York City, the Bronx, and, in particular, a section known as the South Bronx. Close to half a million people live in the South Bronx, an area that one investigator calls "the closest men have yet come to creating hell on earth" (H. E. Meyer, 1975, p. 141). The hell is characterized by high crime rates, many school dropouts (one-third of whom are unemployed), drug addiction, and the flight of business, industry, and those citizens who are able to move elsewhere. Anthony Bouza, commander of the Bronx borough police, describes the neighborhood as "the largest floating cocktail party in the world" (H. E. Meyer, 1975, p. 140).

Over the past 5 1/2 years, the Bronx has experienced nearly 70,000 fires—about 35 a night. Fire department officials estimate that at least a third of the fires are deliberately set. They are set by different people for a variety of reasons.

Some landlords have abandoned their buildings because rent control made it impossible to maintain them, rent them, or sell them. Arson has become a way of recovering loss by collecting on the insurance.

Welfare recipients are also alleged to set fires since being burned out makes a family eligible for a grant, "generally about $1,000. but sometimes as much as $3,090.—to cover the cost of new clothing, new furniture, and moving. In addition, burned-out families go to the top of the waiting list for public-housing . . ." (H. E. Meyer, 1975, p. 146).

A third motive for burning the Bronx is theft. Building strippers set fires and then move into the abandoned hulks to steal copper tubing, plumbing, and any fixtures they can sell.

Setting fires is also fun and a way for juveniles to make money. Half of those arrested for arson in the Bronx during the first nine months of 1975 were under 16 years of age. Meyer reports that torch services can be bought for as little as $3 (1975, p. 150).

Facts such as these explain public concern with crime. They do not, of course, explain crime, a task given to theories of crime causation.

Crime in Canada

As crime increased in many other affluent countries after World War II, Canada seemed a haven. Between 1950 and 1966 at least, the number of serious crimes (indictable offenses) did *not* increase, contrary to public notions that crime was on the rise (McDonald, 1969a). There had been an increase in the size of Canadian police forces relative to the population and an increase in police activity in the control of automobile traffic. However, while the Canadian public may have been premature in its perception of an increase in crime, official statistics for the remainder of the 1960s and the first half of the 1970s confirm the popular belief that rates of grave offenses have been increasing. Table 2-1 shows the rates of the more serious crimes per 100,000 population 7 years of age and over, year by year from 1965 through 1971. Most of these

Table 2-1   Crime Rates per 100,000 Population Aged 7 Years and Over, Canada, 1965–1970, 1971

Offense	1965	1966	1967	1968	1969	1970	1971
Murder (includes capital and noncapital murder)	1.5	1.3	1.6	1.8	1.9	2.3	2.2
Attempted murder	0.7	0.8	0.8	1.0	1.2	1.4	1.8
Violent rape	3.9	3.9	4.5	5.0	5.6	5.8	6.5
Wounding	5.0	5.8	5.9	7.3	9.0	8.8	9.7
Robbery	34.0	34.0	41.6	47.1	55.1	62.5	59.2
Offensive weapons	20.0	21.7	23.7	28.2	30.6	34.6	35.7
Breaking and entering	588.5	607.9	688.0	814.6	888.3	954.9	992.0
Theft—motor vehicles	232.2	236.0	258.0	290.7	327.1	337.5	346.8
Theft over $50	414.1	451.4	500.7	557.5	657.9	806.1	907.4
Frauds	197.5	225.0	239.1	272.0	317.5	361.5	358.9

Source: Summarized from *Crime Statistics,* 1967, 1970, 1971. Ottawa: Dominion Bureau of Statistics and Statistics Canada.

crimes have shown a steady recent increase in Canada, as they have in the United States. The *level* of criminal activity in Canada remains lower, however, than that in the United States.

Beginning in 1972, Statistics Canada changed its reporting base from crimes per 100,000 population 7 years of age and over to crimes per 100,000 population. As will be seen in Chapter 4, this is an inappropriate base, and it makes comparison with preceding years questionable. Furthermore, inflation produced a change in the definition of one kind of larceny, and "theft over $50" became "theft over $200" in 1972.

Allowing for these alterations, both the absolute number of different kinds of crimes known to the police and rates per 100,000 population have continued to increase in most of the categories reported in Table 2-1. Table 2-2 shows increases in all serious crimes between 1970 and 1974. Exceptions are sex offenses other than forcible rape and theft over $200.

COSTS OF CRIME

Public concern with crime involves more than the desire to protect one's person and property. There is also a concern for the social costs of crime, costs that are distributed throughout a society.

Crime is rewarding, of course, to some unknown, but considerable, number of rational thieves (see Chapters 9 and 10). But criminal activity does not *produce* wealth; it only *transfers* it against our wishes. Crime therefore represents a tax on every citizen. The tax is paid in the form of higher prices for products that are imposed by commercial theft and in the form of expenditures for private and public defense.

The social costs of crime cannot be calculated exactly because there are no scales on which to weigh the prices of the pain inflicted by criminal activity. Furthermore, there are no accurate figures on the costs of losses in production incurred by injuries to victims and by the conversion of potential producers into parasites who feed off the productivity of others.

We can only guess the cost of crime in terms of selected dimensions of criminal taxation. For example, insurance against theft itself represents a cost of theft. The increased prices of insurance due to rising rates of automobile theft and burglary of households and businesses are estimated in the millions of dollars in Canada and the United States. In addition, retail prices are increased to compensate for losses due to larceny. It is estimated that retail businesses lose 1 to 2 percent of the total value of annual sales as a result of shoplifting and theft by employees (President's Commission, 1967b, p. 32). Losses in discount (self-service) department stores are even higher—an estimated 2.6 percent of sales (*Newsweek*, 1973a). This criminal levy against retail business amounts to sums in the billions of dollars annually, and it produces price increases estimated at about $25 per family per year.

It is estimated that *unreported* theft from business and industry has a probable dollar value *double* that of all reported private and commercial theft. These commercial thefts, whether reported or not, have an interesting variety.

87257

Table 2-2 Crime Rates Per 100,000 Population, Canada, 1970 to 1974

Offence — Infraction	1970 Number — Nombre	1970 Rate — Taux	1971 Number — Nombre	1971 Rate — Taux	1972 Number — Nombre	1972 Rate — Taux	1973 Number — Nombre	1973 Rate — Taux	1974 Number — Nombre	1974 Rate — Taux	Percentage change, 1970 to 1974 — Variation en pourcentage, 1970 to 1974
Murder — Meurtre	433	2.0	426	2.0	479	2.2	475	2.1	545	2.4	+ 20.0
Attempted murder—Tentative de meurtre	260	1.2	335	1.5	412	1.9	483	2.2	521	2.3	+ 91.7
Manslaughter—Homicide involontaire coupable	34	0.2	47	0.2	40	0.2	66	0.3	53	0.2	—
Rape — Viol	1,079	5.0	1,230	5.7	1,285	5.9	1,594	7.2	1,823	8.1	+ 62.0
Other sexual offences—Autres infractions d'ordre sexuel	9,946	46.5	9,951	45.9	9,582	43.9	10,402	47.1	9,288	41.4	− 11.0
Wounding — Blesser	1,641	7.7	1,852	8.5	1,703	7.8	1,882	8.5	2,114	9.4	+ 22.0
Assaults (not indecent) — Voie de fait (sauf attentat à la pudeur)	77,338	361.8	83,015	382.9	85,135	390.0	89,696	406.0	94,750	422.1	+ 16.7
Robbery — Vol qualifié	11,630	54.4	11,239	51.8	11,832	54.2	13,166	59.6	16,955	75.5	+ 38.8
Crimes of violence — Crimes de violence	102,361	478.8	108,095	498.6	110,468	506.0	117,764	533.0	126,053	561.6	+ 17.3
Breaking and entering — Introduction par effraction	177,712	831.3	188,462	869.2	190,939	874.6	198,043	896.3	233,362	1,039.6	+ 25.1
Theft, motor vehicle — Vol véhicule à moteur	62,805	293.8	65,887	303.9	70,386	322.4	71,593	324.0	83,309	371.1	+ 26.3
Theft over $200 — Vol de plus de $200	150,010	701.7	172,386	795.1	149,356	684.2	63,383	286.9	79,745	355.3	− 49.4
Theft $200 and under — Vol de $200 ou moins	278,765	1,304.0	294,110	1,356.5	314,202	1,439.3	414,591	1,876.4	459,192	2,045.7	+ 56.9
Have stolen goods — Avoir en sa possession	11,956	55.9	12,353	57.0	13,842	63.4	13,945	63.1	15,312	68.2	+ 22.0

Frauds — Fraudes	67,271	314.7	68,181	314.5	68,743	314.9	71,774	324.8	75,873	338.0	+ 7.4
Property crimes — Crimes envers la propriété	748,519	3,501.5	801,379	3,696.2	807,468	3,698.8	833,329	3,771.6	946,793	4,218.0	+ 20.5
Prostitution	1,887	8.8	1,991	9.2	2,183	10.0	3,573	16.2	3,249	14.5	+ 64.8
Gaming and betting — Jeux et paris	1,838	8.6	2,267	10.5	3,126	14.3	3,011	13.6	3,264	14.5	+ 68.6
Offensive weapons — Armes offensives	6,440	30.1	6,788	31.3	7,516	34.4	8,949	40.5	10,812	48.2	+ 60.1
Other criminal code — Autres infractions au code criminel	251,641	1,177.2	248,691	1,147.0	262,130	1,200.8	336,312	1,522.1	366,714	1,633.7	+ 38.8
Other crimes — Autres crimes	261,806	1,224.7	259,737	1,198.0	274,955	1,259.5	351,845	1,592.4	384,039	1,710.9	+ 39.7
Criminal Code — Total — Code criminel	1,112,686	5,205.1	1,169,211	5,392.8	1,192,891	5,464.3	1,302,938	5,897.1	1,456,885	6,490.5	+ 24.7
Federal statues — Lois fédérales	36,494	170.7	39,667	183.0	39,779	182.2	42,786	193.6	44,394	197.8	+ 15.9
Addicting opiate-like drugs — Dérivés de l'opium causant abonnement	1,017	4.8	1,949	9.0	3,234	14.8	3,800	17.2	3,354	14.9	+210.4
Cannabis (marihuana)	13,054	61.1	16,951	78.2	20,606	94.4	42,651	193.0	49,676	221.3	+262.2
Controlled drugs — Drogues contrôlées	1,007	4.7	1,624	7.5	1,717	7.9	2,129	9.6	1,575	7.0	+ 48.9
Restricted drugs — Drogue d'usage restreint	3,711	17.4	3,483	16.1	3,259	14.9	4,212	19.1	3,980	17.7	+ 1.7
Provincial statutes — Lois provinciales	335,788	1,570.8	344,771	1,590.2	318,250	1,457.8	339,120	1,534.8	368,716	1,642.7	+ 4.6
Municipal bylaws — Réglements municipaux	73,086	341.9	73,915	340.9	73,580	337.1	76,282	345.3	81,306	362.2	+ 5.9

Source: Statistics Canada, 1974a:table 1.

They range from unprofessional to professional shoplifting—from "snitching" to "boosting"—and they include theft by employees who steal money, materials, and products from private and public corporations (*Esquire*, 1974; Jaspan, 1960, 1970; Mayer, 1972; *Wall Street Journal*, 1972). They range, too, from this sneak thievery to more forceful theft in the robbery of banks and warehouses and the hijacking of shipments.

In addition to theft from business and industry, which is popular because of the availability of things to be stolen, we have the more ingenious ways of taking other people's money. These are the frauds—the thefts by deceit. The cost of fraud is unknown, but the records of particular thefts give an idea of its enormity.

Stealing by deceiving has its own range of technique and grandeur. Fraud runs from small-time con games to elaborate deceptions that involve the sale of nonexistent commodities. For example, these more expensive frauds have allegedly included the sale of nonexistent cattle (minimum value of theft estimated at $3.2 million—Penn, 1973), empty anhydrous ammonia storage tanks ($6 million—*Time*, 1962), petroleum that was not there ($30 million—*Wall Street Journal*, 1973), imaginary business assets ($58 million—J. D. Williams, 1967), inventories of vegetable oil that did not exist ($219 million—*Time*, 1965), and insurance policies written on nonentities ($2 *billion*—Dirks and Gross, 1974).

Costs of Official Response

Loss of productivity and the direct and indirect costs to victims are only part of the levy imposed by crime. There is also the cost of official response to crime. This cost includes the prices of maintaining jails and prisons and the prices of services rendered by police officers, judges, juries, state-paid prosecuting and defense lawyers, and probation and parole workers.

The cost of official response is high, although it probably does not equal the cost of the crime it is designed to control. In the United States in recent years, for example, it is estimated that more than $12 *billion* is being spent annually on official response to crime. Of this sum, $104 million was recently spent on crime statistics and research alone (*Statistical Abstracts*, 1974, tables 262 and 263). Canada, with about one-tenth the population of the United States, spends a proportional amount—over $1 *billion* per year on police, courts, attorneys, and correctional workers (Statistics Canada, 1974b). Depending on the jurisdiction, it now costs between $10,000 and $15,000 a year to keep an offender in a "correctional" institution.

IN SUMMARY

This sample of the variety of costs of crime helps to explain public concern. The questions that the public asks of criminologists are, "What produces so much crime?" and "What can be done to reduce it?"

It will be seen that all explanations of criminal activity are partial. This does not mean that they are false, but only that they are incomplete. This means, too, that the explanations of crime point toward different causes of crime and toward different prices to be paid for the remedy. Chapter 17 will attempt to reconcile these partial explanations by describing some criminogenic conditions.

Before we explain crime, however, we have to know how our society defines the crimes that affect it. This is the task of Chapter 3.

Definition of Crime

"Crime" is a word, not a deed. It is a word that describes deeds, of course, but as long as it is used only to express moral condemnation, no one will be able to identify a criminal act with certainty. The meaning of the word varies with the morality of the user. Thus people use "crime" variously, as when they say, "It's a crime the way he treats her," "Private property is a crime," or "It's a crime to have to live like that."

Attempts to define crime more rigorously look to the law for help. Crimes, we have seen, are wrongs judged to be deserving of public attention through application of state power. It has been felt, therefore, that crimes are best defined as acts which are harmful to social welfare and which carry the possibility of a penalty imposed by the state. This definition helps a little, but not enough. It does not mark a clear boundary between criminal acts and other wrongs, since the state attends legally to many attacks on public welfare that are not considered criminal. Thus there is no clear line between those wrongs which are regarded as crimes, those personal injuries which are treated as civil actions (torts), and those numerous violations of regulatory laws to which penalties are attached, even though these violations are not called "crimes."

In short, *there is no essence of criminality*. No quality can be found in acts called "criminal" that distinguishes them from noncriminal injuries, breaches of contract, violations of regulations, and other disappointments (G. Williams, 1955).

The question, then, is why we should bother trying to define crime. There are, of course, different reasons for clarifying our terms.

Functions of Definition   Defining words serves several purposes. One purpose is to gain our audience's attention. When we define a term in a particular way, we are saying, "Look here. Attend to what I'm talking about."

Definition also has a personal function. Defining terms for ourselves helps us ascertain whether we know what we're talking about. We use many words automatically, and we often think we know what they mean until we are asked to define them. Defining a word tells us whether we are using it emotionally—to arouse a particular feeling—or denotatively—to refer to something.

A third function of definition is that of aiding communication. It derives from the second function, but here definition is an attempt to assure that two or more people attribute the same meaning to a word. If we are interested in communicating our ideas accurately, we need clear definitions. If, on the other hand, we wish to use words merely persuasively, we need be less clear about their definitions.

Legal Definition of Crime   The closest *approximation* to a clear definition is that given by law. As defined by law, *a crime is an intentional violation of the criminal law, committed without defense or excuse and penalized by the state* (Tappan, 1947).

Without further interpretation, this definition draws a circle. It says that a crime is a certain kind of breach of those laws called "criminal laws." However, we can use this unsatisfactory definition for the purposes of gaining attention and aiding communication if our questions are clear. We should keep at least the following questions separate so that we can think more calmly about their answers:

1   Why does this society treat certain acts, but not others, as crimes? This is a question for the sociology of law; it is beyond the scope of this book.

2   Why does a certain society have more or less of those wrongs universally regarded as crimes—those more serious wrongs such as treason, murder, forcible rape, assault, and theft? This is a question for theories of criminogenesis. It is the kind of question raised by *public concern* with crime; the attempts to answer it are the subject of this book.

Wrongs universally regarded as serious violations have been called *mala in se* (wrong in themselves). Public concern with such offenses narrows our attention. Such concern means that we need not ask why people commit those minor infractions which are crimes only because a local jurisdiction has prohibited them—crimes called *mala prohibita*. Social concern about crime is not with such sometime "delinquencies as that of a housewife who shakes her doormat in the street after 8 A.M., or a shopkeeper who fails to stamp a cash receipt, or a guest who fails to enter his name, nationality, and date of arrival in the hotel register, or the proprietor of a milk bar who allows his customers to play a gramophone . . . without an entertainment license from the justices" (G. Williams, 1955, p. 112). Few people want to spend time explaining why such ordinances are violated.

The context of the question asked about crime causation is that of public anxiety about the serious offenses as these have been widely regarded. In this context, it seems most reasonable to employ a legal definition of crime such as that cited by Tappan. This definition regards a "crime" as an intentional act that violates the prescriptions or proscriptions of the criminal law under conditions in which no legal excuse applies and where there is a state with the power to codify such laws and to enforce penalties in response to their breach. This definition says several things that require amplification. It holds that (1) there is no crime without law and without a state to punish the breach of law; (2) there is no crime where an act that would otherwise be offensive is justified by law; (3) there is no crime without intention; and (4) there is no crime where the offender is deemed "incompetent," that is, without "capacity." Each of these elements has its own history, its peculiar difficulties, and a range of implications.

NO CRIME WITHOUT LAW

The legal idea of a crime restricts its meaning to those breaches of custom that a society has recognized in either its common or its statutory law. As it is applied in Western countries, this restriction carries with it four characteristics that define "good" criminal law: politicality, penal sanction, specificity, and uniformity.

"Politicality" refers to the idea that there can be no crime without a *state* to define it. "Penal sanction" refers to the power of a state to punish violations of its law. This definition says that the legal meaning of crime requires a state, an organization with a monopoly of power, to enforce the law and to attach penalties to its breach. Laws that are not backed by force are less than law and more like agreements or aspirations. Laws without penalties are hollow. By this token, the term "war crimes" is a figure of speech, since such crimes are not legally constituted.

Law and Liberty

The conception of crime that places it within the boundaries of *law* has strong implications for civil liberties. The maxim that there can be "no crime without a law" means that people cannot be charged with offenses unless these have been defined. The protection of citizens against vague charges depends upon this ideal—that there must be a clear statement setting the limits of one's conduct in relation to others and defining the limits of the state's power to interfere in our lives.

This ideal has promoted other considerations having to do with the formulation of "good law" as opposed to "poor law," particularly as good and poor laws are conceived in the Anglo-American tradition. These additional ideals are that the criminal law must be *specific* and that it must be *applied uniformly.*

Good laws *specify actions* that are criminal and *specify penalties* for each breach. Poor laws are omnibus condemnations, such as one from a dead German code which prohibited "behaving in a manner contrary to the common standards of right conduct." This kind of phrasing lacks the specificity that is an ideal of Western criminal jurisprudence.

Similarly, it is an objective of modern jurisprudence that laws be framed and enforced so as to guarantee their *uniform application.* The ideal of uniform application does *not* require that each person and each crime be dealt the same sanction. People, and their crimes and circumstances, vary. Our law therefore allows consideration of individual cases and discretion in judicial response. The ideal of uniform application does require that *extralegal* characteristics of the offender not affect arrest, conviction, or sentence. Extralegal characteristics are those features of the offender that are *not* related to the purposes of the law—characteristics such as race and religion. As we shall see in Chapter 15, this ideal is easier to express in general terms than it is to assess in particular instances. It is easier to express than to assess because some extralegal factors are entangled with legally relevant considerations, as is the case when ethnic differences are associated with differences in patterns of criminal activity.

Not All Wrongs Are Crimes

The legal conception of crime as a breach of the criminal law has an additional implication. It narrows the definition of wrongs. Not all the injuries we give each other are recognized by law, nor are all the injuries recognized by law called "crimes."

For example, United States, Canadian, and European law recognizes *breaches of contract or trust,* so that people who feel themselves thus harmed may seek a remedy from the law. Similarly, the law acknowledges other injuries to person, reputation, and property, called "torts," which, while not breaches of contract, may entitle one person to compensation from another. There is an overlap between the ideas of crime and tort. The same act can be both a crime and a tort, as in murder or assault. However, we can distinguish between the wrongs defined by contract and tort law and the wrongs defined by criminal law in terms of the procedures employed in response to these different categories of wrong. The procedural difference lies in "who pursues the offense." A crime is deemed an offense against the public, even though it may have a particular victim and a particular complainant. It is the state that prosecutes crime, but it is individuals who "pursue" offenders against tort and contractual laws.

NO CRIME WHERE AN ACT IS JUSTIFIED BY LAW

A second category of "defense or excuse" against the application of the criminal law consists of legally recognized justifications for committing what otherwise would be called a crime. Both literate and preliterate societies recognize the right of individuals to defend themselves and their loved ones against mortal attack. The injury or death that may be inflicted against one's assailant in self-defense is thereby excused.

Similarly, all states accord themselves the right of self-defense. With the French philosopher Sorel (1908), states distinguish between *force*, the legitimate use of physical coercion constrained by law, and *violence*, its illegitimate use.[1] The damage that occurs through the state's application of force is excused from the criminal sanction. Thus homicide committed in the police officer's line of duty may be deemed "justifiable," and the injury defined as noncriminal.

NO CRIME WITHOUT INTENTION

As a result of our moral and legal history, the criminal law tries to limit its definition of criminal conduct to intentional action. "Accidents" supposedly do not count as crimes. As the American jurist Oliver Wendell Holmes, Jr., put it, the law attempts to distinguish between "stumbling over a dog and kicking it." If "a dog can tell the difference between being kicked and being stumbled over," as Justice Holmes believed, so too can judges and juries.

This assumption seems plausible, but it gets sorely tried in practice. It gets tested and disputed because, in real life, some "accidents" are still defined as the actor's fault. "Negligence" may be criminal.

All criminal laws operate with some psychological model of man. According to the model prevalent in Western criminal law, the "reasonable person" ought to use judgment in controlling his behavior in order that some classes of "accidents" will not occur. For example, the reckless driver may not have intended to kill a pedestrian, but the "accident" is judged to have been the probable consequence of his or her erratic driving. Persons licensed to manipulate an automobile are assumed to know the likely results of their actions. They are assumed, further, to be able to control their actions, and they are held accountable, therefore, regardless of lack of homicidal intent.

Western criminal law is based upon this changing, and challenged, set of assumptions. It therefore qualifies its desire to restrict "crime" to intentional breaches of the criminal code. This qualification is accomplished by distinguishing between classes of crime—impulsive rather than premeditated, accidental rather than intentional. Since the law wishes to hold able, but negligent, people to account, it includes the concept of "constructive intent," a term that stretches "intent" to cover the unintended, injurious consequences of some of our behavior. The penalties for doing damage through negligence are usually lighter than those for being deliberately criminal; yet the term "crime" covers both classes of conduct.

---

[1] People *do* use these words as Sorel said they did. Legitimate injury is called "force" or some other term less loaded than "violence." Injury that is deemed illegitimate is "violence." For example, Blumenthal and her colleagues (1972) studied the opinions of a representative sample of American men between the ages of 16 and 64. Among the findings were these:

(*a*) "Fifty-eight per cent of American men think that burning a draft card is violence, in and of itself."

(*b*) "Thirty-eight per cent think student protest is violence."

(*c*) "Twenty-two per cent feel sit-ins are violence."

(*d*) "Only 35 per cent of American men define 'police shooting looters' as violence."

(*e*) "Only 56 per cent define 'police beating students' [as violence]" (pp. 1300–1301).

Intention and Motivation

Motivation is sometimes used by lawyers to prove intention. The two concepts are not the same, however.

An intention is that which we "have in mind" when we act. It is our purpose, the result we wish to effect. The criminal law is particularly concerned to penalize illegal intent when it is acted upon.

A motive is, strictly speaking, that which moves a person to act. The word may apply to an intention, but it need not. Intentions are but one of the many motors of action.

Intention is narrow and specific; motivation is broad and general. A jewel thief may *intend* to steal jewels; the *motive* is to become richer. The motive is widespread and does not distinguish one thief from many others. His intention, to steal jewels, is more specific, and it is only one possible way of satisfying his motivation.

An intention may or may not move a person. It may remain a wish, a plot, a dream. *A criminal intention, without the action, is not a crime.*

Motives, on the other hand, may move us haphazardly, purposelessly, without the focus of intent. A motive may be purely physiological and variously gratified. It may even be "unconscious," if we believe the psychoanalysts. *An intention, however, is only something cognitive.* The word "intention" is reserved for thoughts, for verbalizable plans. It does not refer to those subterranean urges or those physiological fires that may have kindled the ideas.

Since "intent" is part of the definition of crime, prosecutors in Western countries must establish such purpose in the actor, and they sometimes try to do this by constructing "the motive." The strategy of demonstrating intention from motivation calls for showing the "good reasons" why a person might act as the accused is alleged to have done. The good reasons, the alleged motives, may all have been there, however, without the actor's having formed the criminal intent which the prosecutor is attempting to establish. This is simply because "good reasons" are not always the real ones.

The distinction between the movers of action and intentions becomes important as criminal law takes heed of another qualification in its definition of crime, the qualification that people shall be held responsible for their actions, and hence liable to the criminal law, *only if* they are mentally competent. The legal meaning of "intention" is embedded in the concept of competence.

NO CRIME WITHOUT CAPACITY

The condemnation that is implicit in calling actions "criminal" is based on moral premises. It is part of our morality to believe that a person ought not to be blamed for actions that are beyond his or her control. The notion that behavior is within or beyond one's control rests upon conceptions of "capacity" or "competence." These conceptions, in turn, are cultural. They vary in time and with place, and they remain disputed today. The dispute concerns the criteria of competence, but it does not challenge the legal and moral principle that people must be somehow "able" before they can be judged culpable.

Among modern states, the tests of competence are cognitive. They look to *mens rea*, the "thing in the mind," as definitive of the ability to form a criminal intent and as the regulator of one's actions. *Until* "the mind"[2] is sufficiently well formed to control the actor's behavior, and *unless* it operates in normal fashion, Anglo-American criminal law *excludes* the agent from criminal liability. Actors are considered "not responsible" or "less responsible" for their offenses if the offense has been produced by someone who is (1) acting under duress, (2) under age, or (3) "insane."

Crime under Duress

The first exclusion consists of criminal deeds performed "against one's will." The law recognizes circumstances in which a person may be forced into a criminal action under threat. Since intent and the capacity to act freely are diminished when this is the case, so too is legal responsibility.

Age and Capacity

A second application of the moral principle that people must have some minimal mental capacity before they ought to be held legally accountable has to do with limitations of age. Laws of modern nations agree that persons below a certain age must be excluded from criminal liability. The number of years required to attain legal responsibility varies by jurisdiction, but the legal principle persists in declaring individuals who are "under age" to be "incompetent" or "legal infants." They may be protected by laws, but they are not subject to the criminal law. In most Anglo-American jurisdictions a child under the age of seven years cannot be held responsible for a crime.

The Idea of Juvenile Delinquency   Above the age of 7 and below that of 21, young people in literate lands are variously categorized as to their legal responsibility for crime. In the common law of English-speaking states, it was assumed that a "legal infant," someone between the ages of 7 and 14, did not have the capacity to form a criminal intent, although in cases of serious crimes this assumption might be refuted by showing that the actor could distinguish right from wrong. Between the ages of 14 and 21 years, the common law assumed capacity adequate for legal responsibility, but this assumption, too, was open to legal rebuttal. Beyond 21 years, age was no longer a defense against liability for one's criminal acts.

As the common law became codified, these assumptions were carried into effect, with qualifications, of course, in particular jurisdictions. The statutory laws of the "developed" countries have come to define a special status of offender called a "juvenile delinquent." The upper age limit of juvenile delinquency is 18 years in most Western jurisdictions. Beyond this age, a person is treated as an adult in regard to the criminal law. This age limit varies, however, with the jurisdiction and and sometimes with the sex of the young

---

[2]Placing the word "mind" in quotation marks indicates its vagueness. Like many other useful terms, "mind" has many meanings. It may be interesting to consider how you use the word.

person. Until recently in Alberta, for example, the upper age limit for treating girls as juvenile delinquents was 18 years. For boys this limit was 16 years. This "reverse sexism" not only ignored the fact that girls mature earlier than boys but also produced some fascinating anomalies: ". . . one sixteen-year-old boy was convicted of *contributing to juvenile delinquency* and sentenced to a short term in the Fort Saskatchewan gaol. His 'offense' was that he was guilty of having sexual intercourse with his steady girl friend, a young woman who was nearly eighteen" (Cousineau and Veevers, 1972, pp. 246–247; italics added). A similar case has finally resulted in a court decision that Alberta's differential protection of girls and boys is in violation of the Canadian Bill of Rights. This interpretation resulted in a dismissed charge and in instructions to the police to treat both females and males as adults at age 16; however, this decision may be appealed (*Edmonton Journal*, 1976; *Edmonton Report*, 1976).

The tendency in most industrialized countries has been to *raise* the age limit so that more young offenders might be treated as delinquents rather than as criminals. There are some jurisdictions in which a legal borderland is defined, commonly between the ages of 16 and 18, within which youths may come under the jurisdiction of both juvenile and adult courts, or either, depending upon the gravity of their offenses.

The justification of a special status for youthful offenders rests, again, upon the moral premise that people ought not to feel the full force of the criminal law unless they are "responsible" for their actions. This moral maxim has been bolstered by a practical concern that seeks to *protect* children from harmful influences, *prevent* their waywardness, and *guide* them into acceptable patterns of conduct when they have given indication of deviation that might become chronic.

This mixture of legal purposes has meant that the definition of delinquency in Anglo-American law includes the commission of crime, but it also includes as the object of legal attention some noncriminal conduct and some noxious circumstances. Among the varied jurisdictions of the United States, for example, an "underage" person may be treated as a delinquent for such matters as:

> Being habitually truant
> Being incorrigible
> Growing up in idleness or crime
> Immoral or indecent conduct
> Habitually using vile, obscene, or vulgar language in public
> Attempting to marry without consent in violation of the law
> Being given to sexual irregularities
> Using tobacco or alcoholic beverages or being addicted to drugs
> Habitually wandering about railroad yards or tracks or wandering about
the streets at night (Sussman, 1959, p. 20)

The Juvenile Delinquents Act of Canada, revised in 1972, reads like a blend of definitions. On the one hand, it restricts delinquency to violations of the criminal law, but, on the other hand, it extends the definition to cover "any other act" that might get one into trouble with provincial laws. It defines a juvenile delinquent as "any child who violates any provision of the *Criminal Code* or of any federal or provincial statute, or of any by-law or ordinance of any municipality, or who is guilty of sexual immorality or any similar form of vice, or who is liable by reason of any other act to be committed to an industrial school or juvenile reformatory under any federal or provincial statute" (J. C. Martin et al., 1974).

It is apparent that the extension of the word "delinquency" to cover more than youthful *criminal* activity increases the risk that the law may be vague and that efforts to protect children may violate their civil liberties. It is notable that the laws of Asian, Middle Eastern, and Latin American countries include *only* criminal conduct in their attention to youthful offenders (United Nations, 1953, 1958a, 1958b, 1960, 1965a, 1965b). The legal responsibility of juveniles may be diminished under these statutes, but the status of a "delinquent," if this term is defined at all, implies that the person has broken the criminal law.

The justice of status offenses   Juvenile delinquency legislation is under attack in Anglo-American countries as being unjust. The injustice lies in making a "status," as well as a particular act, an offense. The attack on such status offenses in Canada and the United States is being led by law-reform groups whose objective is to separate child welfare services from attention to juvenile crime.

It is estimated that about one-fourth of the boys and almost three-fourths of the girls held in juvenile institutions are guilty of no crime for which an adult could be prosecuted (McNamara, 1975, p. 1). These status offenders are incarcerated for a variety of noncriminal behaviors such as being "wayward," "unruly," "truant," or "maladjusted," and running away from home. In the United States such children "remain in detention four to five months longer, on the average, than children convicted of criminal offenses" (McNamara, 1975, p. 3).

Helping versus arresting   In Canada and the United States efforts are being made to reform the law and to separate legal attention to juvenile offenders from protection of children's welfare. Such efforts would revise juvenile delinquency acts and bring juvenile crime under a "youth-in-conflict-with-the-law act," as proposed, for example, by the Canadian Law Reform Commission. This kind of reform would eliminate status offenses.

It is here, as in the debate about insanity as a defense, that the legal profession battles with the "helping" professions. Social workers, psychiatrists, and some judges would use the judicial system as part of a welfare system that tries to meet "children's needs." Lawyers, on the other hand, are chary of expanding the power of state agencies to control children under the guise of helping them, unless adequate legal safeguards are built in. The attorneys' caution derives from the fact that many of the juvenile delinquency statutes do not satisfy the legal ideal that *actions* be specified before state control can be applied. "Having done something" is more readily determinable than "being something." Just as we should not want the criminal law to apply to those of us who are "in a state of criminality," lawyers are generally opposed to the idea of charging children with being "in a state of delinquency" (Cousineau and Veevers, 1972, p. 244).

However, many persons associated with the "mental health movement" regard juvenile criminality as but one signal that a child "needs help." They therefore oppose separating the care of juvenile offenders from the care of other "children in need." The attitude of the "child savers," as Platt (1969) calls them, rests on six assumptions:

1   That ". . . the safeguarding of the civil liberties and social rights of a child or young person . . . may be important and helpful to the court but . . . they are of less importance than the provision of legal machinery for meeting their particular needs" (House of Commons of Canada, 1971, p. 2387)
2   That juvenile crime is a symptom of mental disorder
3   That social scientists, and psychiatrists in particular, are better able than other people to judge and predict behavior
4   That expert judgment underlies the decision to treat inappropriate behavior and that such treatment is effective
5   That the requirements of treatment justify indefinite (indeterminate) sentencing until the patient is cured
6   That the indeterminate sentence given within a treatment orientation is *less* punitive than "plain" incarceration

An interpretation   These assumptions are popular among persons in the mental health movement. They are probably incorrect. At the very least, they are questionable (Cousineau and Veevers, 1972). These popular assumptions are not supported by facts, but rather by moral sentiment. We think there is no disputing with morals. Our personal preference, however, is to remove government attention to child welfare from legal concern with juvenile crime.

In summary   All definitions of crime mark off some ages below which people are deemed not to have the capacity for crime. In addition, the literate countries tend to define a borderland, occupied by youths, within which legal liability is acknowledged, but diminished, and in which the stigmatizing effect of the criminal sanction is avoided or attenuated by special treatment.

Insanity as a Defense

A third excuse by which one may reduce or escape the application of the criminal law is the claim that the offender's capacity to control his or her behavior has been damaged. The locus of the damage, the "place" in which one looks for this incapacity, is, again, the mind.

Defects of the mind seem clear in the extremities of senility, idiocy, and the incapacitating psychoses. They are clear, too, as one is able to link abnormal performance to lesions of the central nervous system. However, it is in the gray area between these extremities and more normal behavior that citizens, lawyers, and their psychiatric advisers dispute the capacity of offenders.

It bears repeating that this dispute rests upon moral considerations. The quarrel is stimulated by the belief that only people who "choose" their conduct deserve punishment for their crimes, that "accidents" and "irresistible impulses" do not count, and that other classes of behavior beyond one's control should not be penalized. The philosophical questions opened by this debate range beyond our present concern. These questions include, at a minimum, the ancient issues of free will and determinism, of the justice and the value of praise and blame, and of the proper ends of the criminal law.

These questions intrude upon the law and ensure that attempts to define mental competence are all imperfect. They are less than perfect because moral conceptions of the "causes" of behavior color the assignment of responsibility to actors. They are less than perfect, also, because the boundaries of the defense of insanity move with the justifications of the criminal law. That is, who we believe to be "incompetent" before the law varies with what we want the law to do. These points will be amplified as we consider the tests of incapacity and their relationship to the justifications of the criminal law.

Tests of Insanity   The criminal law attempts to evaluate capacity from signs of sanity. "Sanity" refers to soundness, to wholeness. Being less than whole, being of "unsound mind," is, therefore, a legal defense against accountability to the law.

The definition of insanity is difficult, however, and an embarrassment to a profession which, like the law, depends so heavily upon the precision of its terms. The word "insane" has poor credentials among psychologists and psychiatrists. Nevertheless, the law has looked to these students of the mind for help in assessing the competence of defendants. In the Netherlands, Denmark, Norway, and Sweden, the test of insanity is simply the testimony of such medical experts. In Belgium, France, Italy, and Switzerland, the test is psychiatric judgment concerning the ability of the offender to understand what he was doing at the time of his crime and to control his behavior. Anglo-American law has attempted to guide judges, juries, and psychiatrists in assessing the competence of defendants by formulating more specific tests that have been used alone or in qualified combinations. The most popular of these guidelines are the *M'Naghten rule, the "irresistible impulse" rule, and Durham's rule.* As with all regulations that seek to to implement moral sentiments, none of these principles is perfectly clear. All three contain ambiguities, and all three have been under attack. However, they remain, in various forms, the principal rules by which judges and juries under Anglo-American law attempt to distinguish between sane offenders and insane ones.

The M'Naghten rule   This provides the only definition of insanity in Great Britain and 31 of the United States. The rule promulgated in an English trial in 1843, is

> that every man is to be presumed to be sane, and . . . that to establish a defence on
> the ground of insanity, it must be clearly proved that, at the time of the committing
> of the act, the party accused was labouring under such a defect of reason, from

disease of the mind, as not to know the nature and quality of the act he was doing; or if he did know it, that he did not know he was doing what was wrong [A. S. Goldstein, 1967, p. 45].

Here, as elsewhere, common words become cloudy when one attempts to use them with precision, and each of the key terms in the M'Naghten formula has been debated. "Disease of the mind" is vague. "Wrong" may mean morally so or legally so. The meaning of the phrase "the nature and quality of the act" has been disputed, and the simple verb "to know" is troublesome. Critics of the M'Naghten rule have argued that "knowing" may refer only to intellectual awareness and have wanted to substitute a psychiatric sense of "knowing" that would include emotional appreciation as well as cognitive understanding. As employed in Canada, the "knowledge test" with M'Naghten's rule has been broadened so that "the act must necessarily involve more than mere knowledge that the act is being committed; there must be an appreciation of the factors involved in the act and a mental capacity to measure and foresee the consequences of the violent conduct" (Royal Commission, 1955, pp. 12–13).

As the professions of psychology and psychiatry developed and grew in authority, they attacked M'Naghten's rule for the ambiguities in its language and added to this attack the claim that under M'Naghten's tests psychotic persons could be and had been declared sane. An American judge, J. Biggs (1955), has documented cases of this sort. For example, in *The People v. Willard*, 1907, Willard was formally declared insane by a California court, became enraged at the commitment proceedings, and killed a sheriff who tried to block his escape. Under M'Naghten's rule, then applicable, Willard was judged to have known the nature and quality of his act and to have known that it was wrong, and he was hanged as a legally sane person despite a diagnosis of "alcoholic paranoia."

With the popularizing of psychiatry and, in particular, of the ideas of psychoanalysis, legislators have taken account of the possibility that "knowledge of right and wrong" is only one test of capacity. It is now recognized that some psychotic individuals may be moved by beliefs which we regard as false, but which they believe true and over which they seem to have no control. When such a delusion can be shown to have caused a crime, some jurisdictions excuse the agent as incompetent. Canada, for example, adds the defense of *delusive incapacity* to the M'Naghten rule in defining insanity (Duhamel, 1962, sec. 16), but it qualifies this excuse by saying that "a person . . . shall not be acquitted on the ground of insanity *unless* the delusions caused him to believe in the existence of a state of things that, if it existed, would have justified or excused his act or omission" (italics added).

The "irresistible impulse" or "control" test   This test represents a similar qualification of M'Naghten's rule that is applied in 18 of the United States and in the American federal courts. A defense against criminal conviction on the grounds of insanity is made first by using the M'Naghten rule and then by applying a control test. Such a test acknowledges that there are "mental diseases" in which cognition is relatively unimpaired but volition is damaged.

Some people who know the difference between right and wrong seem, nevertheless, to be unable to control their actions.

The trouble with this principle is, of course, that its application requires a wisdom beyond the skills of psychiatrists. It requires finer psychological tools than are presently available to be able to distinguish reliably between behavior that is *uncontrollable* and behavior that is *uncontrolled*. On this issue, as with other situations in which psychiatric experts are called on to determine "mental disease," the battles between experts testifying for the prosecution and those testifying for the defense do not promote confidence in their science (Hakeem, 1958).

Durham's rule   This rule represents a further extension of psychiatric influence on the definition of insanity. Durham's rule enunciates a principle which had been recommended in 1953 in a report by the British Royal Commission on Capital Punishment and which has been amplified in a series of American trials. The principle holds that the mind which controls human beings is a functional unit in which emotion and reason are blended, and that the separation of knowing from feeling and willing, apparently required by M'Naghten's rule, is false to our knowledge of human nature. Durham's rule would hold people responsible for their conduct only when their emotions, their "will power," and their thoughts appeared to be normal. In *Durham v. United States*, a trial held in the District of Columbia in 1954, Judge Bazelon wrote the opinion that "an accused is not criminally responsible if his unlawful act was the product of mental disease or mental defect."

On its face, Durham's rule appears more humane and more modern than the M'Naghten principle. In practice, however, it turns out to be vague. The difficulties in applying its test of sanity account for the fact that only the District of Columbia, Maine, and the Virgin Islands have adopted it.

The rule is vague because it does *not* equate a "mental disease" with a psychosis, as the latter is understood by psychiatrists. It provides no standard, therefore, by which to judge the capacity of a defendant to control his behavior. Judges and juries are left dependent upon the unreliable estimates of psychiatric experts (Arthur, 1969; Ash, 1949: Eron, 1966; Goldberg and Werts, 1966; Mehlman, 1952; Schmidt and Fonda, 1956; Zigler and Phillips, 1965). The poorly articulated notion of a mental disorder allows such fuzzy categories of character as "psychopathy," "sociopathy," "character defect," and "emotionally unstable personality" to be certified as evidence of a person's lack of responsibility for his crimes. As part of the mental health movement, the Durham principle encourages the tendency to regard disapproved deviations, like homosexuality or addiction to narcotics, as constituting in themselves signs of "mental disease" (A. S. Goldstein, 1967, p. 246). Finally, the criminal act itself can be, and has been, used as evidence of the "mental sickness" which is alleged to have caused it and which, it is argued, should excuse the offender. This is particularly so with bizarre crimes. Here, for example, is a verbatim exchange between a defense counsel and the prosecution's psychiatrist, debating the sanity of a 17-year-old boy who had murdered and dismembered a young woman previously unknown to him (Nettler, 1970, p. 71):

Defense Counsel: "Whether one calls him insane or psychotic, he's a sick man. That's obvious.

Psychiatrist: "I should think that's largely a matter of terminology."

Defense Counsel: "Do you mean to suggest that a man could do what that boy has done and not be sick?"

Other tests   The kind of thinking that calls criminal conduct "insane" if the crime is sufficiently bizarre has been attacked in the Model Penal Code drawn up by The American Law Institute (1953). The Institute's proposed redefinition of "responsibility," adopted in a revised form by Vermont, holds that a person shall not be held accountable for a crime "if at the time of such conduct as a result of mental disease or defect he lacks substantial capacity either to appreciate the criminality of his conduct or to conform his conduct to the requirements of law." This proposal adds, however, that "the terms 'mental disease or defect' do *not* include an abnormality manifested *only* by repeated criminal or otherwise anti-social conduct" (ALI, 1953, sec. 4.01; italics added).

The debate continues as to which people should be held responsible for their actions. It is a debate that moves with the moral tides. The subjective character of definitions of insanity and the intrusion of moral preconceptions upon legal categories are demonstrated by the fact that, while in England one-third to one-half of homicide offenders are classified as legally insane, in the United States only 2 to 4 percent of these offenders are so classified (Wolfgang and Ferracuti, 1967, pp. 201–202).

Psychiatrists versus lawyers   Attempts to expand the defense of insanity to include all those defects of the mind that discomfort us have run into opposition from lawyers, courts, and the psychological professions themselves. R. J. Simon and Shackelford (1965) surveyed opinions of the defense of insanity among a national sample of American lawyers and psychiatrists. While 77 percent of the psychiatrists expressed confidence in their expert testimony in criminal trials, only 44.5 percent of the lawyers expressed confidence in psychiatric expertise. A large majority of the attorneys (72 percent) approved of the system of using experts to challenge experts, but only a minority of psychiatrists (31 percent) agreed. As might be expected, the two professions disagreed also on the relationship between "serious criminal activity and mental illness." Table 3-1 shows that *half* of the psychiatrists believed that "anyone who commits a serious crime is mentally ill" or "most people who commit serious crimes are mentally ill." Only a *third* of the lawyers agreed. Only 15 percent of the physicians, but over a third of the lawyers, believed that there was *no relationship* between mental illness and serious crime.

The continuing resistance of the law to psychiatric intrusion has been documented by Krash (1961) who studied cases in the District of Columbia in which the Durham rule was pleaded but rejected. His research adds to the catalogue of judicial skepticism about the scientific status of psychiatry and of judicial reluctance to view most crime as a symptom of sickness. Judges and juries continue to believe in "free will," in holding people accountable for their wrongs, and in the efficacy of punishment as a deterrent.

At the same time that courts have been hesitant to absolve "mentally

Table 3-1   Psychiatrists' and Lawyers' Opinions on the Relationship between Criminal Activity and Mental Illness

Which best states the relationship between serious criminal activity and mental illness?	Percent of	
	Psychiatrists	Lawyers
a. Anyone who commits a serious crime is mentally ill.	8.0	3.7
b. Most people who commit serious crimes are mentally ill.	41.8	29.2
c. Most people who commit serious crimes are *not* mentally ill.	25.1	20.3
d. There is no relationship between mental illness and serious crime.	15.1	34.2
e. No answer.	10.0	12.6

Source: Reprinted, with permission, from R. J. Simon and Shackelford, 1965, p. 417.

diseased" offenders of responsibility for their crimes, there have been voices within the psychiatric profession claiming that the very idea of "mental illness" is a myth (Szasz, 1961). It has also been argued that allowing psychiatrists to judge which people are and which people are not accountable for their unlawful conduct usurps the role of juries and runs the risk of violating the civil liberties of defendants. Both the Soviet Union and the United States have been accused of using "mental hospitals" as substitutes for prisons for persons distasteful to the regime (Asher, 1974; Bukovsky, 1972; Gorbanevskaya, 1972; Medvedev, 1971; Szasz, 1957, 1958, 1963). Some novelists, and other observers of the social scene, have been alert to the manner in which punishment may be disguised as "treatment." The English philosopher C. S. Lewis phrased the possibility this way: "If crime and disease are to be regarded as the same thing, it follows that any state of mind which our masters choose to call 'disease' can be treated as crime, and compulsorily cured" (1953, p. 224).

In summary   The various tests of sanity are fallible and can never be made perfect. They reflect our changing conceptions of human nature and of morality. The current vogue, sponsored by the social sciences, has been to shift the burden of responsibility from individuals to their environments, to place the blame for offensive acts not on the criminal but on the social forces by which he or she was presumably shaped (Nettler, 1972b). The Durham rule expresses this train of thought, the logical conclusion of which is to regard all undesirable conduct as "sick" and subject to "treatment" by physicians of the body social. However, until a "brave new world" is reached in which all deviance is engineered out of us (cf. Huxley, 1960), it may be expected that states will continue to hold citizens responsible for broad ranges of their behavior and that the defense of insanity will not be available to most of us.

Significance of the Insanity Defense   As presently employed, the insanity defense is of little consequence. In England, for example, there were only *two* successful insanity pleas in 1974. It is expected that Canada and the United States may be subject to the same trend toward disuse of this excuse. The increasing unimportance of the insanity defense has been attributed to "the virtual abolition of capital punishment, the decreasing severity of sentences, and the introduction of parole and probation" (Law Reform Commission of Canada, 1975, p. 31).

Increasingly, tests of mental competence are used to determine "fitness to stand trial," rather than insanity. The effect of this trend is to channel persons conceived to be mentally disabled away from the criminal justice system and into allegedly therapeutic environments. Whether this is good for offenders and their societies is debatable.

On the Tyranny of Treatment   It is now clear that power can be disguised as a form of therapy (Nisbet, 1975b, p. 225) and that there can be a "tyranny of treatment" (Outerbridge, 1968). It is doubtful whether being "treated" by the state for one's crimes is better for one than merely being restrained. The stigma of being officially "crazy" is at least as great as, or greater than, that of being officially criminal. Furthermore, there is evidence that judges and probation officers who are oriented toward treatment perceive more facets of deviance, lawful or not, as ominous. Practitioners of psychic rehabilitation are sensitized to the supposed symptomatic meaning of abnormalities and regard more of them as premonitory of graver offenses to come. There is also reason to believe that those who prefer to treat offenders rather than to punish or restrain them may favor *longer* incarceration (Cousineau and Veevers, 1972, pp. 257–258; McNamara, 1975).

To examine the possibly punitive nature of the orientation toward treatment, S. Wheeler and his colleagues (1968) interviewed "police chiefs, police juvenile bureau officers, juvenile probation officers, juvenile court judges, and psychiatrists who work in juvenile court settings" in 28 court jurisdictions within the Boston Metropolitan Area (p. 34). The interviews were supplemented by structured attitudinal measures designed to assess the respondent's orientation to delinquency and its control. Contrary to expectation, it was found that

> the judges who take the more severe actions are those who read more about delinquents, who read from professional journals, who do not wear their robes in court, and who are more permissive in outlook. They are also the younger judges (who characteristically express more liberal attitudes on these and other issues) and the judges who rank their own experience with delinquents as of relatively less importance than other factors in influencing their views.
>
> Severity of the sanctions, therefore, appears to be positively related to the degree to which a judge uses a professional, humanistic, social welfare ideology in making his decisions. . . . Judges who are most favorably disposed toward the mental health movement and least committed to more traditional doctrines of

punishment and deterrence tend to take what is commonly regarded as the most severe actions regarding delinquents [S. Wheeler, et al., 1968, pp. 55–56].

A similar finding is reported by J. Q. Wilson (1968), who compared two large American police departments to find out whether "professionalization" made any difference in the handling of juvenile offenders. Wilson's conclusion is that "a 'professionalized' police department tends to expose a *higher* proportion of juveniles to the possibility of court action, despite the more 'therapeutic' and sophisticated verbal formulas of its officers . . ." (p. 19; italics added).

CAPACITY AND JUSTIFICATIONS OF THE CRIMINAL LAW

The guidelines for judging the capacity of offenders are imperfect. They continue to be debated because our moral beliefs find the causes of human behavior in different locations. These beliefs move responsibility between the actor and his or her environment so that "who is to blame" and who deserves punishment are points endlessly disputed. Dispute is fostered, too, by the fact that *justifications* of the criminal law are supported by assumptions about the conditions under which human beings can control their own behavior. What we want the law to do and what we believe it does have bearing upon whom we are willing to excuse from criminal liability.

The criminal law is justified by what it supposedly does. If the law is to be respected for what it does, it must be applied in ways that achieve specific ends—or, more accurately, it must be applied in ways that are *believed* to achieve these ends.

The law serves a changing mixture of objectives, however, and this instability of its objectives encourages the continuing quarrel about which people should and which people should not be held responsible for their conduct.

The criminal law is commonly considered to be useful in achieving six ends, some of which are in conflict. These objectives have been described in various ways, but we can classify them as efforts to (1) restrain offenders, (2) deter criminals and others, (3) reform offenders, (4) revive communion symbolically, (5) achieve justice through retribution, and (6) achieve justice through restitution. All these functions are relevant to the issue of who should and who should not be excused for "incompetence."

1   Restraint

The word "arrest" is derived from the Latin word meaning "to stop." A principal function of the criminal law is to stop a person from injuring others. An arrest may involve restraining the miscreant for some time.

The need to restrain a bad actor does not rest upon a desire to punish or correct. Restraint attends only to controlling an offender. Whether the law should also punish or treat the person being restrained is another issue.

Definitions of capacity enter into the problem of achieving restraint principally in terms of determining *how* the lawbreaker is to be repressed. In recent years it has been our practice to restrain sane criminals in prisons and insane ones in mental hospitals. The growing emphasis upon the rehabilitative function of "correctional institutions" has meant, however, that some prisons now have as many psychotherapeutic facilities as mental hospitals (A. S. Goldstein, 1967). It is an open question whether incarceration in prison is more or less painful than incarceration in hospital (A. S. Goldstein, 1967; Kesey, 1964).

2 Deterrence

The criminal law is commonly justified as having a deterrent effect. The notion of deterrence is not a simple one, however, and it is possible to discern many meanings in the concept (Cousineau, 1976). Most criminologists, but not all of them (Zimring and Hawkins, 1973, pp. 224ff.), distinguish between *specific deterrence* and *general deterrence.*

The idea behind specific (or individual) deterrence is that the arrested person is less likely to commit a similar offense in the future as a result of the legal penalty suffered. This concept is similar to that of reforming the offender, although, as we shall see, some people who wish to reform convicts think that their criminal ways ought to be changed by some means other than the threat of punishment.

The assumption underlying the idea of general deterrence is that application of the criminal law to others will reduce the probability that you and I will commit the crimes for which they have been punished. This justification assumes that we are sufficiently normal to get the message. It is further assumed, with some good evidence, that the more closely you and I identify with the miscreant, the more clearly we will get the message. It is believed that the more we resemble the punished person, the more forcefully his or her penalty threatens us and deters us. It is assumed that, if we have felt the same desires as the punished person and have come close to committing similar crimes, the punishment provides us with a deterrent example. If, however, we healthy people observe "sick minds" being punished, then, presumably, the law's lesson is lost on us; in such cases the deterrent example is diluted because we perceive the offender as different from ourselves.

The determination of capacity is considered to be important, therefore, as a means of increasing the efficacy of the law as a deterrent. It is not *known* how effective this determination is in increasing deterrence, but some jurists *believe* it to be very important.

Morals seem more important here than *consequences*. Our moral beliefs find it cruel and unjust to punish persons who are "not responsible for their actions," regardless of the societal ends that such punishment might serve. The test of capacity tries, in a fumbling manner, to define persons who are sufficiently different from us that they may be excused from accountability under the criminal law.

3 Rehabilitation

It is popularly assumed that the criminal law is applied, or ought to be applied, to correct the offender. If the law is employed to improve the criminal's conduct, then it is believed that the candidate for rehabilitation must be capable of recovery with the attention the law provides. This means, to the conventional way of thinking, that the offender must have a mind capable of guiding behavior and amenable to education. The idea implicit in this justification of the law is that just as one does not pummel hydrocephalic idiots for failing at mathematics, so one does not penalize criminals who "can't help themselves."

Does Rehabilitation Work?   It may be humane to refrain from punishing people who seem mentally defective. It may also be humane to refrain from punishing people—period. The ethics of this issue aside, however, some facts ought to inform conceptions of rehabilitation.

A first fact is that arrest "reforms" some offenders, in the sense that their behavior is "corrected." The offensive behavior stops. This change in conduct is seen most notably among some more intelligent criminals, such as embezzlers, and some impassioned offenders, such as murderous spouses (see, for example, Koestler's famous case of "the mace bearer," 1956, chap. 5).

Despite this fact, many observers do not regard a change of conduct after arrest and upon the threat of additional penalty as "rehabilitation." What they seek is not just a change in behavior, but a change of heart that leads to the change in behavior.

Whether or not one requires that a change of character accompany a change in conduct before a person can be deemed to have been "rehabilitated," a second fact deserves reporting: *Efforts to rehabilitate offenders do not work well.*

There is no science of personality change which has yet been verified or which, in its experimental phases, has proved successful. There is counseling, of course, and some people are helped by advice. In particular, *self-selected* groups—those that people join voluntarily, like Alcoholics Anonymous and Synanon—have a better record of successful counseling. *But there is no science of corrections.*

The demonstration of this fact can be found in many places. Martinson (1974) and Lipton et al. (1975) have summarized the evidence on this point.

4 Symbolism

A neglected, but important, function of the criminal law is symbolic. Exercise of the criminal law reaffirms what we are for and what we are against. Thus the courtroom becomes one of the various educational theaters every society uses.

Capacity is part of this legal drama because, again, the drama depends upon identification. One must be able to identify with the roles portrayed if the dramatic lesson is to be learned. The symbolic and the deterrent functions of the law use capacity in the same way: it is, presumably, the "normal mind," not the defective one, that can appreciate the threats and the symbolism of the law.

5 Retribution

"Retribution" means "to give in return." It may refer to recompense for merit or for evil, although in criminology only the returning of harm to the evildoer is implied.

Retribution is the oldest conception of justice. It is the moral demand that evil not go unpunished, that the harm a person does be returned to him or to her in equal degree, if not in kind. Retribution assumes that justice requires a *balance* between the wrong that was done and the penalty the wrongdoer is made to suffer.

Today retribution is not popular as a stated objective of the criminal law, partly because it has become confused with the idea of revenge.

Retribution Is Not Revenge   Revenge is the emotional impulse to wreak havoc on a person who has injured us. Revenge knows no balance.

It may seem difficult to disentangle revenge and retribution in any particular demand that a wrong be punished. However, the balancing principle of retribution distinguishes it from revenge (Atkinson, 1974; Gerstein, 1974). Retribution sets limits to punishment. It seeks a punishment *proportional* to the wrong done. Its standard of punishment is the law of talion (*lex talionis*), the law of "like for like" (Kant, 1965, p. 101). This principle is to be found in the laws of many cultures, notably in Mosaic and Roman law. It is expressed in the code of the Babylonian King Hammurabi (1760 B.C.), which recommended "an eye for an eye, a tooth for a tooth."

Justice and Retribution   Although the idea of retribution runs counter to some facets of the Christian ethic and is opposed by "enlightened" opinion (Long, 1973), the demand for a balancing of wrongs remains a major component of our sense of justice. This conception of justice has been defended on practical grounds (Gerstein, 1974; Kant, 1965; J. G. Murphy, 1971). However, whether or not one agrees with these appeals to the concrete effects of retribution, satisfaction of this motive remains a justice-dealing function of the criminal law.

For example, the moral requirement that evil not go unpunished is well put by the philosopher Hannah Arendt in her study of the trial of the Nazi Eichmann by the Israelis. Arendt justifies the trial and the hanging of Eichmann by saying, "To the question most commonly asked about the Eichmann trial: What good does it do?, there is but one possible answer: It will do justice" (1964, p. 254).

It bears repeating that the criminal law is not merely practical; it is also symbolic. *It expresses morals as well as it intends results.*

Competence and Retribution   It is part of the morality being expressed by the law that people should be held accountable only for what they have "chosen" to do. If Eichmann had been defined as an idiot or a lunatic, justice would not have required his execution. The same sense of justice that calls for retribution also demands some quality of capacity in the offender.

6   Restitution

Restitution is restoration—righting a wrong by returning things to their original state. The idea of restitution is more readily understandable in connection with property offenses, where we can calculate the cost of the damage. However, even in the case of attacks against persons, we often arrive at a price to be paid that may compensate for the injury. In fact, the anthropologist Lowie reports a case in the last century of a North American Indian woman who asked that the murderer of her son be "given" to her as a substitute for her lost boy.

Restitution is recognized in the criminal law of some lands as a proper penalty against the offender and also as a possible means of rehabilitation. The Canadian Criminal Code, for example, recognizes restitution as a form of sentence, but it is a sentence that has rarely been applied. The Law Reform Commission of Canada (1974) found that in 4,294 criminal convictions handed down between 1967 and 1972, the sentence of restitution was given in only six cases.

It is now being urged that restitution be more frequently used as a sentence and that property offenders in particular be given the option of working out their debt to their victims instead of going to prison. This has been recommended in Britain by K. J. Smith (1965), in the United States by Laura Nader (1975), and in Canada by A. J. Katz et al. (1976), directors of the Alberta Restitution Project.

Relevance   The idea of justice through restitution is related to conceptions of competence in several ways. First, it is assumed that only offenders who can understand the restitutive contract and who are able to fulfill it are properly eligible for this sentence. Second, it is assumed that a contract between a thief and his or her victim will restore some sense of the humanity of both. This objective depends, too, on the emotional and intellectual capacities of the contracting parties.

The restitutive contract is an interesting experiment in the uses of the criminal law—one that may save citizens the expense of imprisonment, help in the rehabilitation of wrongdoers, and, at the same time, satisfy a sense of justice. The results are yet to be tallied.

IN SUMMARY

We have seen a relation between the objectives of the criminal law and the kinds of excuses it allows. Citizens in general have some interest in these legal qualifications of the definition of crime. They have more interest, however, in protecting themselves against serious violations of their persons and property. As part of this concern, we seek explanations of changes in the amount of predatory crime. The explanation of these kinds of crime requires that we know something about the conditions under which their rates of commission vary. This kind of knowledge requires the reliable and valid counting of criminal conduct. As the following chapters will show, counting crime is not easy.

Chapter 4

Counting Crime—Officially

Explanations that would aspire to the term "scientific" are created with facts and some assumptions to account for variations in other facts. One trouble with theories of crime causation is that they are built upon shaky facts to explain imperfectly known events. To the extent that we are uncertain about *what* we are explaining, we lose confidence in our ability to distinguish a good explanation from a poor one.

It is a rule of thumb that any measure of human action becomes less representative of all the events it might have gauged as it is filtered through social sieves. To put it another way, the more the records used as measures of crime are "socially processed," the less accurate they are as indicators of all criminal acts. This source of distortion affects in various degrees all attempts to count crime and leads to another criminological "axiom": Every measure of crime for an aggregate[1] of individuals probably *underestimates* its actual amount. This would not be an obstacle to understanding crime causation if the underreporting were random or systematically biased in some known manner. However, if the difference between crimes committed and crimes recorded is biased in some *unknown* way, then many competing explanations can claim to

[1]This qualification has to be added because some measures of an *individual's* criminal activity may *overestimate* the actual amount of his or her offensive conduct (see page 114).

be plausible. As will be seen, there is competition among explanations, and what kind of criminogenic theory one is apt to find most satisfactory is only in part a function of the facts one believes. How satisfactory an explanation seems is also affected by one's philosophy of social life and what one wants to see accomplished.

Six Counts of Crime   Six kinds of tallies have been used in counting crime: official statistics and five types of unofficial measures. The unofficial tallies, to be discussed in Chapters 5 and 6, include counts made through direct observation, private policing, testing, surveys of victims, and self-report measures.

As might be expected of attempts to count complex activities in varied settings, none of these measures is without error. Each has its distinctive set of disadvantages. Each is insensitive to some segment of the range of all possible wrongs. It will be our conclusion, nonetheless, that these different measures point toward similar zones of crime causation, and that this result allows a reasoned choice to be made among explanations of crime.

THE NATURE OF OFFICIAL STATISTICS

The most popular measure of crime is official statistics of offenses "known to the police." This is a different measure, of course, from arrests made, prosecutions begun, and convictions obtained. There is a large loss in numbers as one moves down each of these steps in response to crime. The social processing of crime reduces the amount of crime being assessed.

Crimes known to the police are themselves a result of social processing. The preponderance of crimes to which police departments attend is *reported to* them, rather than *discovered by* them. Complaints to the police are subject to errors that result from mistakes and from lies. With an awareness of such errors, every modern criminal justice system has developed counting rules to be applied by the police in an effort to count only the "actual amount" of crime after discounting for mistakenly and maliciously reported injuries. Crimes known to the police are corrected by subtracting from all complaints those which, upon investigation, are judged to be "unfounded." For example, the *Uniform Crime Reporting Manual* of Statistics Canada (1974c) includes this set of prescriptions:

> Unfounded means that the police investigation has established a crime did not happen or was not attempted, e.g., an automobile is reported stolen. Later the complainant calls the police and advises he has made a mistake and his wife had taken the car. Count . . . an offence "reported or known to police" and "unfounded."
>
> Do not "unfound" an offence because the stolen property is not located, the property is of little value, or the victim refuses to prosecute.
>
> Complaints should not always be scored in the offence classification reported by citizens as they are not generally qualified to define the type of crime

committed. For instance, assaults or domestic quarrels are sometimes reported to police as murders or attempted murders. The police investigate and establish the crime reported did not happen, was not attempted, or things have returned to normal and no one will prosecute. Such complaints should not be scored in the classification reported and then "unfounded" [p. 2.1.3]

It is obvious that discretion is involved in the application of such counting rules. Thus far no one has measured the consistency with which police departments in different locations in Canada or the United States apply their federal rules for classifying crimes.[2]

While we do not know how reliably police accounts are maintained in different jurisdictions, we do know that the proportion of crimes "unfounded" varies with the kind of crime. For example, the figures for the United States discount on the average about 4 percent of the allegations of "serious offenses," according to the FBI's Crime Index. Such discounting ranges from about 2 percent of larceny complaints to around 15 percent of forcible-rape complaints (FBI, 1974, p. 1; 1975, p. 22).

Difficulties in Counting Rape

Difficulties in counting social events are illustrated by the recording of forcible rape. Rape remains, in the words of Lord Hale, "an accusation easily made, hard to be proved, and still harder to be defended by one ever so innocent."

The difficulty is compounded when the rapist and his victim have had an intimate relationship before the alleged attack. In such cases the question of the use of force or its threat becomes problematic. Thus, although *reports* of forcible rape in Canada and the United States have increased steadily during recent years, the proportion of persons *arrested* for this crime, and *charged and convicted*, has not changed correspondingly. In the United States, for example, complaints of forcible rape per 100,000 women increased by 42 percent between 1969 and 1974. The 1974 complaint rate was up 7 percent over the 1973 rate, but the proportion of these complaints "cleared by arrest" remained the same.

Furthermore, of all adults *arrested* for forcible rape in 1974, only 60 percent were *prosecuted* for that crime. And of those prosecuted, almost half were acquitted or had their cases dismissed for lack of evidence. Among the remainder of persons prosecuted for forcible rape—that is, among the 60 percent of those arrested for this crime—35 percent were found guilty as charged, while 16 percent were convicted of lesser offenses (FBI, 1975, pp. 22–24).

As a result of the women's liberation movement and sociological studies of

[2]Although the reliability of crime classification across the country has yet to be assessed, there have been some local studies of police definitions of offense. For example, M. W. Klein and his colleagues (1974) tested the consistency with which 45 record clerks in southern California police departments defined a "juvenile arrest." Eighty percent of these clerks used the same criterion, "brought to the station." Of course, this means that 20 percent of these departments were using some other definition of a "juvenile arrest."

discretion exercised by police officers when making arrests, the high proportion of forcible-rape complaints that are presently "unfounded" is being challenged (*National Observer*, 1971). This challenge, combined with the development of "rape crisis centers," will probably make more forcible rapes "known to the police" and further complicate the counting of trends in this crime.

WHAT DO OFFICIAL STATISTICS MEASURE?

Statistics on crime, like every other public measure, are constantly disputed. They should be. The critical citizen's doubts about the validity of public figures have never been better summarized than by an English economist who was long accustomed to their use. Sir Josiah Stamp (1880–1941) advised us that "the government are very keen on amassing statistics. They collect them, raise them to the nth power, take the cube root and prepare wonderful diagrams. But you must never forget that every one of these figures comes in the first instance from the village watchman, who just puts down what he damn pleases."

Stamp's warning applies today. *There are errors in every tally of social events.* Just counting the *number* of people in a country is difficult enough, as is illustrated by cross-checks suggesting that the latest United States census probably missed 2 to 3 percent of the population (Skogan, 1974, p. 32). If recording mere numbers of people is open to errors, counting *how they are* and *what they do* is even more difficult.

All social statistics are suspect. Modern governments and large interest groups such as labor unions and manufacturers' associations all have "research departments" that count people, conditions, and events. Their tallies are used as arguments for their preferred policies. Yet we are aware that all these enumerations have deficiencies.

Morgenstern (1963) showed this for an assortment of economic observations that were inaccurate. His early warning is now being heeded by economists who recognize that their "indicators" are full of funny figures. It is intelligent to question the meaning of unemployment statistics, retail sales figures, the consumer price index, inventory levels, and measures of economic productivity and gross national product (Schellhardt, 1975). The question every serious student asks is, "Who counted what, and how?"

When this question is raised about the statistics we take for granted, the consequence is an illuminating shock. How, for example, is "race" or "ethnicity" counted? By asking people about their racial background, by guessing from their appearance, or by making judgments on the basis of surnames—with the consequence that tallies of "races" in a multi-ethnic society can be moved about whimsically, as the demographer William Petersen (1969a) has shown with Hawaiian data.

How are "suicide" and other "causes of death" counted? Not by "seeing" these causes, but by attributing them in a social process of definition and negotiation (Douglas, 1967; I. Ross, 1975).

How are "illegitimate" births counted? In some of the United States, not at all. In other states, "children of all married women—including separated women regardless of whether the father of the child is their husband—are considered legitimate" (Berkov and Sklar, 1975, p. 365).

How is "unemployment" counted in industrialized countries? Chiefly by means of a survey that asks a representative sample whether the "head of the house" had been working "last week" and, if not, whether he or she was looking for a job. As many victims of deceit have learned, counting conditions and behaviors by asking questions is risky. The hazards are spelled out on pages 107–115.

Tempered Criticism

A critical attitude toward tallies of social events does not mean that one dispenses with statistics; it only makes one careful about using them. In criminology, those who take such an attitude must admit that the "real" amount of crime is never known.

Differences in police activity, for example, make a difference in the swelling and receding of crime rates. Thus, upon the death of the antipornography laws in Denmark in the 1960s, some "sex crimes" were reported to have declined. It would be more accurate, however, to say that while human sexual behavior probably did not change much in Denmark, the law did, and with it police activity.

A difference in vigilance on the part of the police is apparent, too, in the English experience with changes in laws concerning homosexual offenses. The Wolfenden Committee on Homosexual Offenses and Prostitution was initiated in 1954. Within a year or two, it was common knowledge that this committee would recommend not using the criminal law to interfere with the private sexual behavior of consenting adults. Walker (1971, p. 27) notes that by 1966 the number of recorded homosexual offenses had dropped to *half* the number recorded in 1955, even though no change in the law had occurred. Behavior had undoubtedly not changed all that much, but police activity had.

CRITICISM OF OFFICIAL STATISTICS

Official tallies of criminal activity are questioned, therefore, as to (1) what counts; (2) who does the counting, and how; and (3) how the official numbers are manipulated.

1 What Counts?

An occurrence called a "crime" may involve one offender, or many; one victim, or many; and one breach of the criminal law, or more. A political assassin may kill the President and wound two bystanders. An embezzler may steal $1,000 a month for eight years before being caught and may forge some documents in the process. A father may have intercourse with his daughter several times before he is apprehended. One robber can hold up ten men in a tavern, take their money, shoot and kill the bartender, and make a getaway in a stolen car.

In each of these examples a decision will be involved as to how many crimes to count. The rule in England and Wales for attacks on a person is "one victim, one crime." Canada and the United States follow a similar practice. For offenses against property, the English have as yet no clear rule for counting; the Americans and Canadians try to call "one operation, one crime." In North America, when more than one crime occurs in an "operation," as in our example of the holdup in the tavern, the most serious of the offenses is counted, the gravity of an offense being determined by the maximum legal penalty it carries.

Definitions and decisions intrude upon all these principles, and they do so in a way that makes official statistics inadequate measures of who is doing what to whom. For example, Silverman and Teevan (1975) point out that under the counting rules of Canada and the United States, robbery may be variously tallied depending upon where it occurs, even though the losses are identical. "If," they note, "four people live in four different apartments in the same building and each [is robbed], then four offences are counted in official statistics. However, if those four people happen to be gathered in the lobby of that apartment building and are robbed . . . then only one offence is counted" (p. 72).

In this example, the robber may be *charged* with more than one offense whether or not the tally of offenses shows one crime or four. This possibility suggests yet another difficulty with official counts of crime. From present statistics, there is no way of knowing how many offenders commit how many crimes, of which variety, and with how many victims.

An Interpretation   All social statistics are imperfect measures of whatever they are supposed to indicate. The concerned citizen does well to attend to *what* has been counted when interpreting *all* official figures. Such attention sometimes provides a new view of social reality. It is a healthy exercise, for example, to find out what is counted by the official recorders in one's community as they compute such "social indicators" as unemployment, suicide, per capita income, mental health, and educational opportunity.

The utility of imperfect social measures depends on what one is trying to do with them. It is my thesis that neither official nor unofficial statistics are sensitive measures of all the criminal damage we do to one another. However, if these imperfect indicators are used to gauge approximate quantities of the serious crimes by their social locations and if different measures tend to draw similar maps, then we have increased confidence in our picture of reality.

It should be remembered, however, that different measures of criminal activity can attend to different matters. *Official statistics* record crimes as though they were single events, even though there may have been a series of offenses during one "incident." *Private police reports* yield estimates of amounts stolen, number of victims, and number of offenders apprehended, whether or not they are charged. *Surveys of victims* of crime count each victim separately, transfer the count to a "household," and try also to count criminal incidents. Tallies of crime by means of *direct observation, testing,* and *self-report* attempt to record each breach of the law for each person. Some of the self-report measures assign a "crime score" to each person by weighting the gravity and frequency of admitted offenses.

The S-W Index   Any measure of criminal activity would be more valuable if it could count the *frequency* with which people commit offenses and the relative *gravity* of their crimes. A score, representing frequency multiplied by the judged gravity of each offense, could then be assigned to each person for particular periods of time.

However, weighting the gravity of crimes requires a standard scale. It has been suggested that such a scale might be developed from public conceptions of the relative seriousness of different violations of the criminal law. *If* citizens of a community or a country agreed on the relative gravity of a wide range of crimes, weights could be assigned to those crimes, and scores could be constructed for persons and events.

The American criminologists Sellin and Wolfgang (1964) tried to do this by describing 141 crimes to police officers, juvenile court judges, and university students in Philadelphia and having them rank these crimes according to seriousness. Sellin and Wolfgang were concerned with the relative *order* and *weight* assigned to their described crimes, and they concluded that their evaluators did agree on the gravity of a sample of crimes. Their subjects agreed on the ordering of offenses and on the difference in gravity between offenses (the "ratio" of seriousness).

Sellin and Wolfgang's measure, known as the "S-W index," assigns a score to each criminal occurrence; that score is based on a weighting of *all* the offenses that occurred during an "index event." The score is the sum of the gravity of these offenses, judged according to the standards prevalent in the community subject to the criminal law. In contrast to present recording procedures used by the police, the S-W index considers "each violation of the law occurring during an event [as] a component thereof, and in the evaluation of an event account [is] taken of all its components and not merely of the most serious one" (Sellin and Wolfgang, 1964, p. 297). Table 4-1 shows the scores given to a sample of crimes, ranging from 1 (trivial) to 26 (serious).

The S-W index is currently being tested, and its application compared with official statistics. In one such test, the greater sensitivity of the S-W measure to the injury inflicted in a criminal event revealed some differences between it and official results.

Normandeau's Test   Normandeau (1969) compared robberies known to the police in Philadelphia in the seven years from 1960 through 1966 as diagramed by the Uniform Crime Reports (UCR) and by the S-W index. The differences between the two profiles are shown in Figure 4-1. According to the S-W index, the robbery rate, when assessed for the seriousness of the harm inflicted, *decreased* from 1960 to 1962; the UCR figures, on the other hand, show an *increase*. After that, the S-W measure describes an *increase* year by year, whereas the UCR diagram shows *decreases* in 1963 and 1966. Overall, the S-W index reports that the robbery rate for 1966 increased 16 percent over

Table 4-1   Offense Scores, S-W Index

Offense item	Score
Larceny $1[a]	1
Larceny $5	1
Larceny $20	2
Larceny $50	2
Larceny $1,000	3
Larceny $5,000	4
Burglary $5[b]	2
Robbery $5 (no weapon)[c]	3
Robbery $5 (weapon)[d]	5
Assault (death)	26
Assault (hospitalized)	7
Assault (minor)	1
Rape (forcible)[e]	11
Automobile theft (no damage)	2
Forcible entry[f]	1
Intimidation (verbal)[g]	2
Intimidation (weapon)[h]	4

[a] Derived from analysis of money values.

[b] Burglary $5 has a score of 2, which includes a score of 1 for the money value and a score of 1 for the forcible entry.

[c] Robbery $5 (no weapon) has a score of 3, which includes a score of 1 for the money value and a score of 2 for verbal intimidation.

[d] Robbery $5 (weapon) has a score of 5, which includes a score of 1 for the money value and a score of 4 for intimidation with a weapon.

[e] Rape (forcible) has a minimal score of 11, which includes a basic score of 8 for the forced sex act, a score of 2 for the minimal intimidation (verbal), and a score of 1 for the minimal physical injury (minor).

[f] The score for forcible entry (18.53) may be seen as the result of larceny $5 (22.09) subtracted from burglary $5 (40.62) divided by 16.93.

[g] The score for intimidation (verbal) (30.15) may be seen as the result of larceny $5 (22.09) subtracted from robbery $5 (no weapon) (52.25) divided by 16.93.

[h] The score for intimidation (weapon) (86.33) may be seen as the result of larceny $5 (22.09) subtracted from robbery $5 (weapon) (86.33) divided by 16.93.

Source: Adapted from Sellin and Wolfgang, 1964, table 69. Reproduced by permission.

1960, while the UCR figures report an increase of 22 percent. The disparity in the measures is due to the fact that the S-W index pays greater attention to the *injury* component of a robbery than the UCR figures, which attend only to the *theft* element.

An interesting sidelight of Normandeau's study derives from a separate test of the popular hypothesis that robberies committed by juveniles may be "nasty, but not serious." As measured by the S-W index, this hypothesis was contradicted by the finding that "seriousness per juvenile event or juvenile offender is consistently greater (although not significantly so) than for all robbery events taken together" (Sellin and Wolfgang, 1964, p. 154).

Other Tests   Applications of the S-W index in Canada (Akman and Normandeau, 1968) and Puerto Rico (Velez-Diaz and Megargee, 1970) have demonstrated agreement with the assigned crime weights given in the United

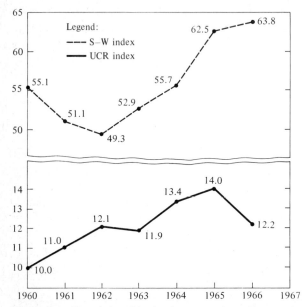

Figure 4-1   Trends in robberies known to the police, as shown by the S-W and UCR indexes, 1960–1966, Philadelphia. Rates are per 10,000 population according to census adjustments. (*Reprinted with permission from Normandeau, 1969: fig. 1 in T. Sellin and M. E. Wolfgang, eds.*, Delinquency: Selected Studies, *copyright John Wiley & Sons, Inc.*)

States. However, questions remain concerning the conditions under which the S-W index is valid and useful. The question of validity asks whether, and when, people actually do agree in their judgment of the relative gravity of crimes. The question of utility asks whether application of the S-W index provides better information than official tallies of crime. To date, the answers to both questions limit the general applicability of this measure.

Validity   Whether citizens agree on the judged gravity of crimes depends on (1) the crimes being judged, (2) whether offenders and their victims are identified, (3) whether the social setting of the crime is described, and (4) who is doing the judging, which can involve the possibility of cultural and sexual differences in judgment. For example, Hsu (1973) observed that most of the follow-up studies of the original S-W project had used male judges and that none of these investigations had gone culturally far afield. Hsu therefore translated the S-W index into Chinese and asked male and female raters in Taiwan to assess the gravity of these index offenses.

Hsu found that, while Chinese males agree with one another concerning the relative gravity of crimes, their judgments differ from those of Chinese women. Chinese women attribute more seriousness to rape than males do, while Chinese men assign a higher gravity to murder than their female counterparts do.

Furthermore, while there is some correlation in the rank order of crimes assigned by Oriental and Occidental raters, the size of the steps between crimes differs. In short, Hsu found some cultural and sexual differences in the application of the S-W index between Chinese and North American subjects, with the sexual difference between Chinese male and female judges being most notable.

Consideration of the many variables that influence such judgments about crime has led some investigators to doubt whether seriousness of crime is a *unidimensional* attribute—that is, whether gravity is "one kind of thing" that can be ordered along a scale as by a ruler (Lesieur and Lehman, 1975). A measure that is not a scale in this sense cannot be used to weigh reliably the seriousness of offenses as defined by a variety of people.

Utility   Even though the objective of constructing a weighted crime score is reasonable, its application may not be worth the effort. Both crude and refined measures may point to the same trends or to the same social locations of crime. This is likely if the activities gauged by an index are highly correlated among themselves. For example, Blumstein (1974) has shown that the various kinds of crime measured officially and by a weighting device such as the S-W index "go together." The "mix" of crimes tends to remain stable, and between 1960 and 1972 the picture of criminal activity drawn by the FBI's figures and that indicated by the S-W index were similar. In short, Blumstein argues, the attempt to weight crimes by their gravity adds little information to that given by a simple, unweighted index. Furthermore, when one is measuring a range of activities such as that included in "crime indexes," more information will be provided if there are separate measures for each kind of activity.

What to count when counting crime remains in contention. The issue is part of the question of who does the counting, and how.

2   Who Does the Counting, and How?

Official statistics on crime are imperfect not only because of what is and is not included but also because of imperfections in those who do the counting. Those who criticize official records on this last count reaffirm Sir Josiah Stamp's skepticism. If human beings are doing the counting, they themselves are a variable and a source of unreliability in the tallies. The question, then, concerns the biases of the recorders and the procedures by which they come to record a crime.

Official statistics on crime are generated by the police in two ways—in response to complaints made to them and through their own surveillance. In both cases, a decision is involved as to whether a crime has been committed and whether it is worth acting upon.

The vigilance with which a police department responds to complaints and records them is a variable with unknown, but estimated, movers. Vigilance varies, for example, with the organization of the police department, with the discipline of its personnel, and with the political pressures upon it. In New York City, for instance, the involvement of the police in the federal government's Uniform Crime Reporting program in 1933 was followed by a year-by-year decline in the number of crimes recorded. There was evidence that some complaints to the police were being "referred to Detective Can"—that is, filed in the wastebasket. Civic bodies took action, and with a change in departmental administration in 1950, some kinds of crime immediately received a higher score on the police blotter, obviously as a result of tightened record keeping (Institute of Public Administration, 1952).

Reactive Measures   One trouble with statistics on crime as recorded by the police is that such measures may be *reactive*; that is, they may respond to considerations other than the events being counted. Statistics on crime as set down by the police are to some unknown extent manipulable for political purposes. Since these figures are used as a measure of police performance, police departments can improve their "paper performance" be misclassifying or downgrading offenses or even by failing to record citizens' complaints (Seidman and Couzens, 1974; Valentine, 1971).

Coding Variations   Political pressures and biases are not the only possible sources of unreliability in official records. Coding practices may differ too.

When a complaint is made to the police and logged as "known to the police," a clerk must classify the crime. What shall it be called? Although modern countries have rules of classification under which local departments are supposed to sort offenses, there is leeway in definition. It is conceivable, then, that even the best-intentioned, "unbiased" police departments may record crimes known to them under different headings. (This is, incidentally, a possible defect in *all* social reporting.)

As an illustration, Silverman (1975) may have found such a coding variation in the crime rates reported for two large Canadian cities, Edmonton and Calgary, between 1966 and 1973. These Alberta municipalities are so similar in size, population composition, and socioeconomic condition that one would expect their crime rates to run in tandem. For many crimes this is so, and yet Silverman notes that during these eight years Edmonton consistently recorded twice as many robberies and rapes as Calgary did and 1 1/2 to 2 times as many assaults. These discrepancies seem more likely to have been the result of coding differences than of differences in criminal activity.

A suggested remedy   A possible remedy is to reduce the role of police in counting crime. For example, Biderman et al. (1972) have recommended the use of trained "crime coders" who would work in police stations recording complaints as they are received by police dispatchers.

This might provide a partial corrective to the adulteration of official statistics. However, the police officer on patrol and the investigating officer remain original sources of data. Their observing and recording functions continue to be basic and to be subject to question.

Studies of Police Discretion   The fact that criminal conduct must be socially perceived and socially processed before it becomes part of the official record has stimulated studies of the differential selection of offenders, particularly juveniles, for arrest and referral to court. These studies do not give evidence of any striking extralegal bias in the treatment of the more serious offenders.

Goldman's research   Goldman (1963) examined arrest records for 1,083 juveniles from four communities in Allegheny County, Pennsylvania, to ascertain whether there were any extralegal factors operating in the referral of these youthful offenders to court by the police. Goldman found what other studies have confirmed: that the majority of police contacts with juveniles are handled informally without referral to court. Sixty-four percent of the apprehended youths were treated without being sent to court. The response of the police varies, of course, with the offense, so that while only about 5 percent of the arrests for "mischief" were placed before the court, 91 percent of the arrests for automobile theft were placed before the court. *The gravity of the crime is a principal factor in determining a decision by the police to proceed with judicial action.*

Interestingly, Goldman discovered a higher arrest rate in the wealthiest of his four towns, but there the arrests were mostly for minor offenses that were settled out of court. In the poorer communities, arrests were for the more serious offenses and resulted in a higher proportion of court referrals.

In Goldman's data, the decision of the police to refer juveniles to court was not influenced by the sex of the offender, but it did vary with age. The older the offender, the more probable a court referral was. Unfortunately, Goldman did not control in his analysis for the relation between age of offender and the number of previous offenses, and it may be suspected that this variable accounts for the differential disposition of cases involving older youths.

A similar situation is found in Goldman's analysis of ethnicity as a factor in court referral. He reports that "there appears to be little difference in the disposition of cases of white and black children who were arrested for serious offenses. However, there does appear to be a statistically significant difference in the disposition of minor offenses. A black child arrested for a *minor* offense has a greater chance of being taken to juvenile court than does a white child" (p. 44; italics are Goldman's). Again, it is impossible to interpret this finding as evidence of extralegal discrimination because there is no control for the number of previous arrests.

McEachern and Bauzer's study   These investigators studied a random sample of 1,010 records drawn from the juvenile index of the Los Angeles County Sheriff's Department and 7,964 police contacts with juveniles contained in the Santa Monica records from 1940 to 1960. As in Goldman's study, these data were analyzed to ascertain what factors affect the disposition of juvenile offenders by the police. The answer of these investigators is that, with samples of this size,

> almost everything is significantly related to whether or not a [court] petition was requested. Sex, age, number of the offense in the youngster's delinquent history, whether or not he comes from an intact family, whether or not he is on probation, and the year in which he was born all apparently have some influence on the police disposition. To balance these findings, the nature of the offense, the police department, and the year in which the incident occurrred are also all very significantly related to whether or not a petition is requested [McEachern and Bauzer, 1967, pp. 150–151].

The one exception to these factors, and a surprising exception in the light of some public charges, is the lack of importance of the child's ethnicity. After apprehension by the police, there was no systematic or consistent difference in the proportions of blacks, Chicanos, or "Anglos" referred to juvenile court.

Police officers on patrol: Piliavin and Briar's study   A deficiency of much of the research on the generation of official statistics is that the research starts *after* a police contact has been made and the first step taken on the judicial escalator. It would be of interest to observe how arrests are made, as well as to count what happens after the arrest. To this end, some sociologists have gone along on police patrols to ascertain how the police use their discretion.

One such investigation was carried out by Piliavin and Briar (1964). They observed the behavior of some 30 policemen in the juvenile bureau of the police department of an American industrial city. A large number of encounters between police and boys were observed, and systematic data were collected on 66 of these cases. The issue to which Piliavin and Briar addressed themselves was whether police discretion in arrest was influenced by the characteristics of the youth or whether it was solely a function of what the youth had done. In the minority of encounters (about 10 percent of the encounters) in which the offense was a *serious* one such as robbery, homicide, aggravated assault, grand larceny, automobile theft, rape, or arson, police discretion was minimally affected by the personal or social characteristics of the offender. However, the majority of the encounters involved *minor* offenses, and in these cases the policeman's assessment of the youth's character affected the decision to arrest or dismiss. In brief, boys whose "group affiliation, age, race, grooming, dress, and demeanor" signified that they were "tough guys" and disrespectful toward the police were more likely to be arrested than boys whose bearing in similar situations was judged less "delinquent." Piliavin and Briar conclude that, for juveniles, and for the large range of minor offenses, police patrolling may be "discriminatory" and may result in legal decisions based more on the "juvenile's character and life-situation than [on] his actual offending behavior" (1964, p. 213).

One qualification should be made here. Piliavin and Briar's study ought not to be generalized into the conclusion that prejudice on the part of the police significantly affects official crime rates. This research was based on detailed observation of 66 encounters in the atmosphere of a "delinquency prevention" program. The policemen assigned to the juvenile bureau were selected partly on the basis of their "commitment to delinquency prevention" and they performed "essentially as patrol officers [cruising] assigned beats" (Piliavin and Briar, 1964, p. 207). However, in the industrialized democracies, most major crimes come to the attention of the police as a result of citizens' complaints rather than as a result of police patrols. "Modern police departments employ primarily a *reactive* strategy," say Black and Reiss, and "the majority of the cases handled . . . originate with mobilizations by citizens" (1967, pp. 2–3; italics added).

Black and Reiss's study   As part of a recent survey by the United States government of crime and law enforcement in American cities, D. J. Black and Reiss (1967) directed a research in selected precincts of Boston, Chicago, and Washington, D.C., during the summer of 1966. Thirty-six trained observers were assigned to record detailed descriptions of the behavior of policemen and citizens. Incidents requiring attention by the police were divided into (1) "calls for service" or "dispatches"; (2) "on-view mobilizations," in which officers initiated contacts in response to events that occurred in their presence; and (3) requests for action by the police from "citizens in the field." More than 5,000 situations involving over 11,000 individuals were observed. The "types of mobilization" of the police were then tabulated by the race and social status of the citizens involved and by the gravity of the offense.

Eighty-one percent of all the occasions for police action were "calls for service"; 14 percent were "on-view" situations; and only 5 percent were initiated by "citizens in the field." In sum, the alerting of the police to crime comes principally from victims and witnesses of crimes. The decision as to the appropriateness of a response by the police is, then, more frequently the citizen's than it is the policeman's.

The persistent allegation—made more strongly in Canada and the United States than in Europe—that the police respond to offenses and offenders in a prejudiced manner was *not* borne out by the investigation made by Black and Reiss. With one qualification, there was no evidence of racial or class discrimination in attending to crime throughout these many observations of interaction between citizens and the police. Unprofessional conduct on the part of police officers did not vary significantly with the race or social status of the citizen. "If anything," Black and Reiss write, "police officers appear less hostile and brusque toward Negroes and to ridicule them less often than whites" (1967, p. 32).

To this finding, as has been noted, there is one major qualification. In response to the serious offenses (felonies), the American police were observed to be *more* vigilant when the complaints were made by "white-collar" citizens than when they were made by "blue-collar" citizens. This was *not* found to be the case for the misdemeanors. The police were particularly attentive when a white-collar complainant reported himself the victim of a felony by a blue-collar offender, and they "discriminated against blue-collar citizens who feloniously offended white-collar citizens by being comparatively lenient in the investigation of felonies committed by one blue-collar citizen against another" (D. J. Black, 1970, p. 746). What this bias entails, of course, is a lowering of the blue-collar arrest rate.

These findings refer to juvenile and adult offenders combined. In a special analysis, Black and Reiss (1970) examined police encounters with juveniles only; 281 contacts with suspects under 18 years of age were examined for type of police mobilization and for signs of discrimination by the police. The findings for juveniles parallel those for adults. The preponderance of police encounters with juveniles was initiated by complaints from citizens (78 percent of nontraffic violations). There was no difference between these types of mobilization as regards the race of the suspect. There was, however, a difference in arrest rate when a complainant was present. "In not one instance did the police arrest a juvenile when the complainant lobbied for leniency," say Black and Reiss (1970, p. 71). "When a complainant explicitly expresses a preference for an arrest, however, the tendency of the police to comply is also quite strong." A portion of the higher juvenile arrest rate among blacks is a result of the fact that more serious crimes were charged against them than against whites, and of the fact that blacks were more frequently involved in encounters where there were complainants, themselves predominantly black.

Terry's research   A similar finding of fairness in the official tallies is reported by Terry (1967), who analyzed over 9,000 juvenile offenses committed in a midwestern American city over a five-year period. Terry was concerned with the possibility of discriminatory treatment by each of three agencies of social control: the police, the probation department, and the juvenile court.

As in the investigation by Black and Reiss, the overwhelming majority of the offenses noted were *not* a result of police surveillance. Over 83 percent of Terry's cases were reported by persons other than the police. Furthermore, the severity of the treatment of juvenile offenders did not vary with their sex, race, or socioeconomic status *when the gravity of their offenses and their records of previous offenses are considered.* Holding constant the seriousness of the crime and the juvenile's record of previous violations, Terry found no indication that the court, the police, or the probation department treated boys differently from girls, poorer adolescents differently from richer ones, or Anglos differently from Chicanos or blacks. Again, there is one qualification: When girls were "processed" beyond the police and probation departments and arrived before the court, they were more frequently sent to institutions than boys were.

Hohenstein's data   Hohenstein (1969) analyzed a 10 percent sample of all serious delinquencies committed in Philadelphia in 1960. His data consisted of 504 such "delinquent events" that were examined to ascertain what had influenced police discretion.

Hohenstein's analysis revealed three major factors determining police decisions: (1) the victim's attitude, (2) the juvenile's record, and (3) the gravity of the reported offense. Of these, the *victim's attitude* was the most important. Even when the instant crime was serious and the accused had a previous record, if the victim did not want to prosecute, the police responded with the least serious disposal available. Hohenstein found that neither the race nor the age of the accused made a difference when the gravity of the offense, the youth's record, and the attitude of the victim were considered.

Parallel studies   With some variation, other studies on a smaller scale have yielded results that counter the charge of prejudice in Western judicial systems. For example, Weiner and Willie (1971) examined the decisions of juvenile officers in Washington, D.C., and Syracuse, New York, in search of racial or class bias. The found no such effect.

Shannon (1963) analyzed reactions of the police to juvenile offenses in three areas of Madison, Wisconsin. One area was predominantly lower-class, one was middle-class with some working-class sections, and one was a mixture of middle- and high-class neighborhoods. More serious offenses were reported in the lower-class areas, and more referrals from those zones were made to juvenile court. When the gravity of offense was taken into consideration, no relationship was found between police action and socioeconomic status. Shannon concludes that "juveniles engaging in comparable types of delinquent behavior receive pretty much the same treatment from the Madison police" (1963, p. 33).

Arnold (1971) studied the operation of one court in a medium-sized American city and found no ethnic discrimination in the actions of probation officers. Once juveniles were referred to court, however, the two judges in this jurisdiction sent fewer Anglos than blacks and Chicanos to a correctional facility. Arnold interprets this more as "letting Anglos get off easy" than as "uncalled-for treatment of the minorities." He recognizes that, given the protective function of the juvenile court, judges must consider the probability of continuing delinquent behavior as suggested by the offender's home and neighborhood. The impact of these variables upon a judge's decisions requires further study and may lead to suggestions for better ways of responding to criminality among young people.

Contrary evidence One significant recent study challenges the general finding of previous research that legal, rather than extralegal, factors are principal determinants of judicial response. Thornberry (1973) used data collected in Philadelphia on all males born in 1945 who had lived in that city from ages 10 through 17 years (Wolfgang, Figlio, and Sellin, 1972). This sample consisted of 9,945 boys, of whom 3,475 were reported to the police for having committed at least one delinquent act.

Thornberry tested the proposition that, when legal variables are held constant, boys' race and socioeconomic status will continue to make a difference in their treatment. His analysis of treatment concerned three stages in response to offenses committed by juveniles:

1   At the police level. Here the decision is whether to refer the case to juvenile court or to make a "remedial arrest." A remedial arrest involves detention in the station house for a few hours while parents or guardians are called. Such cases are often referred to the city's welfare department, but no further legal action is taken.

2   During "intake." At this hearing the decision is whether to "adjust" the case or refer it to juvenile court for a formal disposition.

3   Before the juvenile court. At this stage the judge's decision is whether to use probation or incarceration.

Thornberry controlled for two legal variables in analyzing these data: the gravity of the immediate offense and the number of previous offenses. When such controls were imposed, and when the relationships between race and treatment and social class and treatment were examined, Thornberry found that

the racial and SES [socioeconomic] differences did not disappear. Blacks and low SES subjects were more likely than whites and high SES subjects to receive severe dispositions. Although these differences were more noticeable at the levels of the police and the juvenile court than at the level of the intake hearing, they are generally observable at all three levels [1973, p. 97].

Thornberry acknowledges that there is interaction among all these factors, legal and extralegal, and that he has not controlled for other variables that might have legal relevance in cases involving juveniles. These are such considerations as "demeanor of the youth, the 'quality' of the juvenile's home, and the attitude of the victim" (1973, p. 98). Recalling, again, that the "philosophy" of official response to juveniles is protective and reformative, rather than punitive, official decisions are constrained by viable options, including whether there is a responsible home to which to remand an offending youth.

In summary Getting arrested is an interactional process. The police force, the police officer, the victim, *and* the offender do make a difference—up to some limit—in determining what is recorded as crime. The question is whether this interaction systematically biases the official statistics of a particular jurisdiction for a particular period. The best answer seems to be that official records in democracies reflect the operation of a judicial sieve.

What is counted, finally, as crimes are those offenses that are more obvious and more serious and that have complaining victims or dead ones. In short, what counts is those crimes for which the public puts pressure on the police to make arrests. A recent survey of research on the uses of police discretion in Canada and the United States concludes that "police powers seem to reside, for better or worse, in the hands of the people" (Hagan, 1972, p. 11).

For those localities in which the matter has been studied, official tallies of arrests do not seem to be strongly biased by extralegal considerations. These studies confirm common sense. They indicate that if you are apprehended committing a minor offense, being respectful to the police officer may get you off. If, on the other hand, you are apprehended for a minor violation and you talk tough to the "cop," the encounter will probably escalate into arrest. However, if you are caught in a more serious crime—if, for example, you are found robbing a bank—being respectful to the police is not likely to keep you from being arrested.

Reporting Artifacts   Official statistics of crime are reactive indicators, it has been said. They respond to something *other* than the amount of crime. It has been noted that they may be responsive to changes in police activity—changes either in the use of police discretion with respect to arrest or in police coding of crimes. However, there is an additional source of a reactive effect in statistics on crime, and that is changes in the willingness of victims to complain to the police.

It has been pointed out that police work is largely responsive to citizen's complaints. It is reactive rather than surveillant. This means that the amount of crime "known to the police" will fluctuate with changes in a citizenry's habits of reporting crimes. It is possible, then, that crimes known to the police may increase, not because more crime is being committed, but because more crime is being reported.

Schneider (1975) found this reactive effect in her study of victims of crime in the Portland, Oregon, metropolitan area. For a variety of reasons, victims of burglary were more likely to complain to the police in 1973 and 1974 than in 1971 and 1972. Seventy-one percent of burglaries were allegedly reported during the later period, compared with only half of burglaries in the earlier period. This change in reporting practice would mean an *increase* in burglary according to official statistics. It is conceivable, however, that an increase in citizens' complaints (crimes "known to the police") might occur while the actual rate of victimization was declining, and Schneider found this to be so. Thus, according to the victims, 151 out of every 1,000 households had experienced a burglary in 1971 and 1972, compared with 130 households in 1973 and 1974. Here the victimization rate had declined, while the official rate had climbed.

No one knows, of course, how often this happens or for which crimes. As surveys of victimization become more popular (see Chapter 6), we may have more complete checks on our interpretation of official counts of crime.

3   How Are the Official Numbers Manipulated?

Counting behaviors of social concern is difficult; interpreting the tallies compounds the difficulties; and transforming simple tallies into rates compounds the difficulties further.

Statistics, like any other information, become more or less adequate *in terms of one's purposes*. Much depends upon what we want to do with what we know. Thus, for some purposes, absolute numbers—straight counts—are good enough. Learning that so many thousands of people died of lung cancer last year or that motoring fatalities on a holiday reached a certain number may be sufficient for our concern. To use the demographer Petersen's illustration, "the datum that the Chinese are increasing by 15 million a year . . . could hardly be put more forcibly" (1969b, p. 79). The number stands on its own.

However, when we want to make comparisons for a population over a period of time or comparisons between groups or between treatments, then absolute numbers become less satisfactory. This is so because we are seeking a choice among hypotheses in an attempt to increase our predictive ability. We therefore prefer to think in terms of ratios, proportions, or rates, rather than absolute numbers.[3] This preference leads to questions about the bases upon which rates are computed.

---

[3]Students of populations distinguish between ratios, proportions, and rates.

A *ratio* compares one segment of a population with another where both numbers come from the same tally. The relation is usually reduced by some convenient constant. For example, $a/b\,k$ expresses a ratio in which a is one portion of a population, say, males; b is another sector of that population, females; and k is a constant—in a sex ratio, usually 100.

A *proportion* describes the relation between a part of a population and the whole. It looks like this: $a/(a+b)\,k$ where, again, a = males; b = females; k = a constant.

A *rate* compares events during a specified time against some population base. It takes the form $m/P\,k$, where m is a measure of some occurrence, P is a population count, and k is a constant. An important feature of a rate is that m and P do *not* come from the same records. This is an additional source of error in official accounting.

Bases of the Rates   One criticism of official crime rates, such as those plotted in Figures 2-1 to 2-3 and Table 2-1, is that the population base is known with some certainty only for a decennial year. For each succeeding year within a decade, the national population can only be estimated. If the estimate is low, the reported rate is inflated, so that the crime rates for, say, 1969 are given a spuriously high number in comparison with rates for the census year, 1960.

The question of the appropriate population base to be used in statistics does not end, however, with the problems of counting people. Since not all persons are equally vulnerable to the events that interest us, the *composition of a population* becomes important. Under conditions of *unequal vulnerability*, it is possible that changes in the composition of a population, rather than changes in behavior, may account for variations in the incidence of events. For example, if adolescents are more frequently involved in automobile theft than people of other ages, then a difference in the number of such crimes committed in two populations may reflect a difference in their age composition rather than a real difference in behavior. Just by looking at the age composition, we should expect less automobile theft in a retirement community than in a neighborhood with a large population of young people. Similarly, since males commit murder more frequently than do females, then again a comparison of the homicides in two populations requires some control for differences in the proportion of males in the two populations.

The rationale for the computation of rates is a predictive one. Its ideal is to express the relationship between "the actual and the potential," as Petersen puts it (1969b, p. 79). To increase the accuracy of forecasts, a rate should be "refined" so that it includes in its denominator *all those persons and only those persons who are at risk* of whatever kind of event is being tallied in the numerator.

To refine a rate in this manner means that one must know something about these relative risks. Sometimes the population at risk is obvious; sometimes it is not. For example, the chance of being killed while traveling by automobile requires that one be *in* such a vehicle. (The hazard of being killed *by* an automobile is still another matter.) Official figures of traffic mortality are not computed on this basis, however. In Canada and the United States the number of traffic fatalities per year is compared with the midyear population of a region or of the country. Sometimes this is refined by guessing from gasoline consumption the number of passenger miles traveled. Nevertheless, no one knows how many people travel how many miles by automobile in specific zones. This means that a jurisdiction with a small residential population but a large transient population, like the state of Nevada, will have an artificially inflated rate of deaths in automobile accidents. Traffic mortality rates are, in this sense, "crude."

Crime rates are similarly crude approximations of the calculated risk that individuals, groups, or localities will experience different rates of offense. At a minimum, we should expect crime rates to be refined by controlling for age, sex, and density of population. Infants and the aged are not likely to be offenders. Males and females *do* differ in their conduct. Much crime is a function of things to be stolen and of people meeting people. Comparisons between populations become more accurate, then, when the rates employed are age-specific, sex-specific, and density-specific.

Having said this, however, one runs into dispute. Should the statistician refine his crime rates further—for example, by making them race- and class-specific? The answer depends on the assumptions with which one approaches his data. If it is assumed that, for a given society, people of different ethnic groups and different social status run equal risks of being arrested, then there is no need to refine rates in acknowledgement of the various population sectors. If, however, the "potential" for apprehended crime varies with income or ethnic group, then comparisons become more accurate as rates are made class- or ethnic-specific. For example, a definition of "embezzlement" calls it a criminal violation of financial trust. Obviously, a condition of being able to embezzle is being *in* a trusted, financial position. The embezzlement experience of two populations—say, that of Switzerland and that of the Soviet Union—may be expected to vary with the proportion of their people who are entrusted with others' money and property. The comparative crime rates should thus be occupation-specific.

IN SUMMARY

The major charge against the use of official statistics as data for criminological theory is that they are biased, and biased principally against poor people and against visible minorities. This accusation is more common in Canada and the United States, with their numerous minority groups, than it is on the European continent. However, the belief that rich people can get away with crimes for which poor people are hanged is universal. It is a belief substantiated by the fact that money buys legal defense and by the fact that the kinds of theft available to trusted business and government officers are less public than strong-arm robbery. The act of fraud is more clever, less readily apparent, and more difficult to discover than a burglary or a rape. Apart from the discovery of the *crime*, however, there is also the matter of the discovery of the *criminal*. Here the burglar may have an advantage over the embezzler. It is more difficult to catch an external thief than an internal one.

The question of bias in official records can be raised, but it cannot be definitively answered. It is a charge that could be verified only if there were accurate tallies by segments of societies of the *proportions* of people committing *various offenses* of ranked *seriousness* and known *frequency*.

The *gravity* of the prevalent offenses is one element in evaluating judicial bias. The *number of offenses* and the *proportion of a population* committing them are two additional, and different, measures of criminality. No presently employed measure of criminal activity, official or unofficial, is sensitive to the full range of crime and, at the same time, sensitive to variations in the judged gravity of these crimes while it counts how many persons in each stratum of society commit how many crimes. This fact allows political preference to affect the choice of measures of crime and their interpretation.

The confidence one has in public records increases as other modes of measurement yield similar results. If each method of counting crime gave widely different results, no theories of crime causation could be well supported. As will be seen, however, the various imperfect measures of the serious crimes point in the same general direction for their social location.[4] For answers to the *sociological* questions about crime, this is all that is required.

[4]An interesting test of the convergence of public and private measures in mapping the social location of crime has been conducted by Price (1966). This investigator assumed that the premium rates of insurance against loss of property ought to bear some relation to official statistics. He found such validation and concluded that police figures on offenses against property "are highly correlated with premium rates on the most appropriate insurance coverages" (p. 220).

Chapter 5

Counting Crime—Unofficially
Part One: Tests and Observations

The imperfect nature of official statistics on crime has led sociologists to invent other ways of counting violations of the law. Some of these procedures are helpful in filling out the picture of crime and its causes. They give us a better sense of the variety of crime and criminals and an appreciation of the persistent inventiveness of human beings in devising ways of cheating, stealing, and attacking.

It cannot be said that these optional study methods drastically revise official tallies, however. Some of these observations open our eyes to new forms of criminal enterprise, but they do not change markedly the maps of criminal conduct drawn from official statistics.

A fair conclusion to be drawn from a comparison of different measures of crime is that, where the unofficial tallies of crime disagree with official statistics, no one knows which is the more valid. On the other hand, where the official and unofficial tabulations agree, one is more confident of the facts on which explanations of criminality are built. Fortunately for theories of criminogenesis, official and unofficial counts of crime are in general agreement in mapping the social locations of serious offenses.

Unofficial procedures for counting crime include (1) direct and indirect observations of criminal activity, (2) private-policing reports, (3) test situations, (4) surveys of victims, and (5) studies of confessions of crime. This chapter discusses some of the results of watching people, privately policing them, and testing them. Chapter 6 will describe studies of victims and confessions of criminality.

1 OBSERVATIONS OF CRIMINAL ACTIVITY

An interesting way of counting crime is to live with a group of people and to keep a log on their criminal conduct. But such direct observation is expensive, restricted in its application, and subject to variations traceable to differences in attention and recording on the part of the observer.

Direct observation has been supplemented by indirect assessment of criminal activity, as when sociologists and psychologists interview criminals and their intimates, including their pursuers, the police. The objectives of such indirect evaluations of lives in crime are to ascertain the processes by which individuals become attracted to crime and the satisfactions and dissatisfactions associated with such careers, as compared with the rewards of other lines of work. The library of criminal biography is large, and we shall sample from it particularly in Chapter 9.

Both direct and indirect observations are liable to a selective bias, that is, to a tendency to study offenders who have been caught rather than those who have been more successful and to study groups with a reputation for crime. However, attempts to balance this possible research bias have been made. These attempts broaden the picture of crime, as we shall see, without altering significant features. The major findings of direct and indirect observations mesh with the results of official tallies and surveys of victims.

The Cambridge-Somerville Youth Study

An example of observational research is the Cambridge-Somerville Youth Study, based on a delinquency-prevention project started in 1937 in two crowded industrial cities near Boston, Massachusetts. The project was curtailed in 1941 by the entry of the United States into World War II, but the research persisted with some changes until 1945. In 1955 Joan and William McCord (1959) brought the information up to date and reexamined the findings. Over these years a tremendous dossier was developed for each of the 650 boys originally in the project. The McCords comment that

> seldom has so large a group of children been so carefully studied over such a long period of time. Social workers investigated the neighborhoods and recorded the school progress of each boy. Perceptive investigators visited their homes, talked with their parents, and observed their families. Psychologists and psychiatrists measured intelligence and analyzed the personalities of the children. The social and psychological observations . . . told about their boyhood homes, their families, their neighborhoods, and their personalities [pp. 13–14].

As a part of getting to know the boys, caseworkers maintained records of observed and admitted crimes, whether officially recorded or not. What is of importance for our purposes is, again, the enormous amount of "hidden

Table 5-1   Offenses Committed by Official and Unofficial Delinquents

Type of offense	Unofficial delinquents (N = 61)	Official delinquents (N = 40)	Both groups (N = 101)
City-ordinance offense	739	655	1,394
Minor offense	1,913	2,493	4,406
Serious offense	174	442	616
Total	2,826	3,590	6,416

Source: Reprinted with permission from Murphy et al., 1946, p. 688, table 1.

delinquency" and the *relation between the persistence and gravity of offenses committed and action by the police.* In a special study of 101 of these youths, F. J. Murphy and his colleagues (1946) noted that 61 of the boys had committed a variety of delinquencies without being sent to court. Another 40 boys did appear in juvenile court. Table 5-1 shows the relation between the number and kinds of offenses observed and official response.

It is apparent that boys who commit the more serious crimes, and more of them, run a higher risk of appearing in official statistics. What is not revealed in the chart, but appears in Murphy's report, is that of the more than 6,416 offenses observed, only 95 (about 1.5 percent) resulted in court action. The boys who became "officially delinquent" had committed from 5 to 323 violations each, with a median of 79 crimes. By contrast, the "unofficial delinquents" had committed an average of 30 offenses each.

We may all have broken some criminal laws, but some of us have done so more frequently and more seriously than others. Frequency and gravity of offense are among the strong determinants of official notice.

Thieving Gangs

Under the direction of Walter B. Miller (1967), field workers have become intimate with American urban gangs of males and females and have counted three classes of their larcenous conduct: "behaviors in some way oriented to theft, arrestable acts of theft, and appearance in court" on charges of theft. As happens in all comparisons between official statistics and hidden crime, Miller's workers observed that a large amount of criminal activity was going unrecorded:

> There were three and one-half theft-oriented behaviors for every "hard" act of arrestable theft, and about ten theft involvements for every court appearance on theft charges. This is a rather surprisingly high ratio of court appearances to acts, but it still means that during the study period well over 300 incidents of theft were observed for which no official action was recorded [p. 33].

The significant results of this research show that

> theft [is] a culturally patterned form of behavior. It was mostly place theft [as opposed to theft from persons] with peak frequencies occurring during the

fourteen to seventeen age period; it had a strong utilitarian component; it was far more frequent than any other form of crime; it was predominantly a male activity; its frequency bore little relation to being White or Negro; [and] its patterning was so decisively related to social status that status differences as small as those between lower class 2 and 3 had marked influence on its frequency [p. 37].

Able Criminals

An interesting example of research conducted by means of indirect observations is that of John Mack (1972) and his associates in Europe. By gaining the confidence of the police and some successful thieves, Mack (Mack and Kerner, 1975a, 1975b) was able to draw a portrait of practitioners of "rational-economic" crime, who differ from "textbook crooks" in their success and in certain psychological attributes. These differences are described in Chapter 9. However, it is sufficient for our purposes here to note that while these able criminals differ *psychologically* from less successful thieves—in a manner, incidentally, similar to the ways in which successful dentists or accountants differ from their less able colleagues—they do *not* differ from them in terms of social background (Mack, 1972, p. 45). The map of criminogenesis is not greatly changed by information about this kind of adept thief. There are, of course, other avenues into rational-economic theft that qualify this picture without invalidating it (see Chapter 9).

In summary   Observations of people obeying and breaking criminal laws reinforce the common-sense impression that violations are frequent, that they vary by kind and amount with different social locations, and that the policing process operates like a coarse net that is more likely to catch the repetitive, serious offender than the now-and-then, minor offender. It is also more likely to catch the impulsive and stupid thief than the more deliberate and intelligent one.

2 PRIVATE POLICING

Large retail stores and many other big businesses police themselves. This private policing is done by investigators who may be full-time "store detectives," and sometimes by auditors and management consultants whose major roles may not be the detection of theft. While internal police are employed to apprehend thieves, the less formal detectives, such as accountants and consultants, more often stumble upon stealing. Both kinds of private-policing reports expand our conception of crime, reduce our confidence in public honesty, and confirm other measures of recent increases in larceny.

The Five-Finger Discount

One aspect of private policing is reported by Cameron (1964), who studied that largely unreported crime, shoplifting. Shoplifting is "theft from a retail store by people who pose as legitimate customers of the store" (p. 61).

Thieves who shoplift can be categorized as "honest crooks" and dishonest ones. The honest thieves are a minority among shoplifters. They are the "boosters," the pros who know that they are thieves and who purposively practice their art. By contrast, the overwhelming majority of shoplifters are dishonest thieves. They are "snitches," amateurs who do not acknowledge themselves to be thieves. Both kinds of thief *intend* to steal from the stores they enter, but the booster is more honest than the snitch in recognizing the intention for what it is.

Studies of shoplifting contribute to the social mapping of crime in two ways. First, they confirm the enormous total loss attributable to the five-finger discount (see pages 27–30), even though the amount stolen by each shoplifter on each foray is small. Second, such studies lead us to acknowledge, once again, that not all thieves are the "textbook crooks" from deprived environments. Shoplifters, at least those who are snitches rather than boosters, are "mainly 'respectable' employed persons or equally 'respectable' housewives," says Cameron (p. 147). Of those officially charged with theft, the great majority have no prior criminal record. They are not predominantly denizens of slums. When Cameron diagramed where they lived, she found that "their residential distribution in Chicago was approximately that of the Lost and Found claimants of Lakeside County, a measure presumed to be representative of typical shoppers in that store" (p. 147).

Internal Theft

Shoplifters are thieves external to the business. Their thefts are probably exceeded in dollar value by "internal stealing," that done by employees.

For example, Norman Jaspan (1960), the head of an engineering consulting firm, found that "in more than 50 percent of assignments involving engineering projects with no hint of dishonesty, white collar crime was uncovered. In addition [in 1959 alone] our staff has unearthed more than $60 million worth of dishonesty with more than 60 percent attributable to supervisory and executive personnel" (p. 10). When he was interviewed more recently, Jaspan (1970) said he believed that firms in Canada and the United States suffer a "better than 50 percent chance" of being victims of "sizable dishonesty."

Jaspan's opinion is seconded by surveys within the construction industry. Such studies lead to the belief that on-the-job larcenies have been increasing in recent years and that some 1 to 6 percent of the net worth of a contractor's equipment is stolen each year. No successful method of combating such crime has been worked out, and contractors are reported to be alarmed at indications that organized crime may be becoming involved (Mayer, 1972).

Other Studies

There are numerous other unofficial counts of crime that repeatedly confirm the vast amount of cheating and stealing that goes unrecorded. For example, the American Bankers' Association has compiled one of the longest continuous records of a specific crime, bank robbery. Its tallies, which were begun in 1931, show that bank-robbery rates, calculated either by population or by the number of banks, rose during the 1960s, although the rate has not exceeded that of the worst years of the Depression (Mudge, 1967).

There are also officially unrecorded observations suggesting that a considerable number of murders and suicides may go uncounted because they are concealed as "accidents." The economist Oskar Morgenstern (1965) has examined the work of detectives in one of North America's largest insurance companies. He concludes: "Accidents are another case where often great doubts prevail as to cause and effect. Probably most murders go undetected. For example, a very large proportion of hunting accidents are apparently murders; an investigation showing this was suppressed, however" (1963, p. 23, fn. 15).

These unofficial records indicate again that official statistics underestimate the true amount of crime. Unfortunately, much private policing describes the amount of such unrecorded crime without telling us much about the characteristics of the criminal. In this regard, test situations do better—at least for the minor offenses.

3 TEST SITUATIONS

A fascinating way of studying which kinds of people are more and less honest and violent is to test tendencies to lie, cheat, steal, and attack under conditions that allow the investigator to control the circumstances and count the conduct. Social psychologists have done this in a variety of experiments involving a variety of people—from schoolchildren to adults. Some of these test situations have merely provided opportunities to deceive or attack, but other research has actually tempted people and even ordered them to be offensive. By necessity, most, but not all, of the research on resistance to temptation has involved minor offenses, such as lying and cheating, rather than actual crimes, such as stealing and wounding. However, even these minor experimental temptations are being challenged today as "entrapping" innocent subjects and leading them into unethical behavior. Nevertheless, a large library of experimental work has been accumulated that tells us whom to trust most. Here we can only sample this research for its illumination of the social locations of crime and of the many circumstances under which people wound and deceive each other.

Feldman's Studies

Roy Feldman (1968) and his coworkers tested the relative honesty of French citizens, Greeks, and Americans in a variety of situations in which there was an opportunity to cheat fellow citizens and foreigners. For example, the investigators asked people in Paris, Athens, and Boston for directions. They did this in fluent French, Greek, and Boston-accented English, but they also conducted their tests as foreigners who could not speak the language of the country. The researchers also overpaid cashiers in stores and observed who kept the overcharge, and they counted tendencies of taxi drivers to cheat native and foreign customers. Another kind of test noted which individuals made false claims for money from a stranger.

As common travel experience would suggest, Parisian taxi drivers cheated American tourists significantly more often than their fellow citizens in an ingenious variety of ways. Similarly, cashiers who were overpaid "kept the change" in 54 percent of the Parisian stores, 51 percent of the Athenian shops, and 33 percent of the Boston stores. On the other hand, false claims for money were made by only 6 percent of Parisians, as compared with 13 percent of the Athenians and 17 percent of the Bostonians sampled. A significant finding for mapping the social location of these kinds of larceny was the tendency of cheating to be more common among persons of lower social status.

Hartshorne and May's Research

The correlation of social status with honesty found by Feldman is also reported in a series of studies conducted among American schoolchildren by the psychologists Hartshorne and May (1928–1930) and their associates. These investigators used a variety of opportunities to lie, cheat, and steal in their measurement of honesty. They gave children the chance to cheat on tests of reading, spelling, arithmetic, information, and grammar; on puzzles; and in parlor games. They also devised ways of tempting children to steal coins without being observed, but in a manner that allowed the theft to be recorded. Last, children were given opportunities to make false statements on question-naires where there were two kinds of motive for lying: to win approval and to escape disapproval.[1]

All these measures of deceit run together, but with varying degrees of closeness. There is, for example, a higher association between one kind of cheating and another, and between lying and cheating, than there is between cheating or lying and stealing. The more similar the style of deceit, the greater the consistency of conduct.

Furthermore, Hartshorne and May found what seems obvious—that the amount of cheating, for example, increased as it became easier to cheat, with less risk of being caught, and as a little cheating produced success.

Hartshorne and May thought that while the correlations between the various tests of honesty were positive, they were too low to allow one to speak of a general trait of honesty. However, Burton (1963) recalculated Hartshorne and May's data, omitting from his analysis those tests which were unreliable. Among the reliable measures of behavior, Burton found a *general tendency* for children to be more or less honest. "There is," he concludes, "an underlying trait of honesty which a person brings with him to a resistance to temptation situation" (p. 492).

This general disposition was found to be significantly associated with the social status of the child's family. Furthermore, on Hartshorne and May's tests, honest persons tended to be more consistently honest, while dishonest persons were less consistently dishonest. In addition, these children showed more *consistency* in their behavior as they grew older. This meant that higher-status

---

[1] The "false-statement" tests are not direct measures of lying since the notion of telling a lie includes *intent* to deceive, something the psychologists could not measure.

children became more honest, and lower-status children more dishonest, with age (Burton, 1963). Furthermore, the brighter the child, the more likely he or she was to be honest and to exhibit consistent behavior.

A Caution   These findings are based on moderate correlations. Exceptions are therefore to be expected. The proper interpretation is that these results indicate tendencies rather than absolute determination. People cannot be divided into clear categories of honest and dishonest persons. There is a continuum of deceit that approximates the bell-shaped distribution of other psychological traits (McCurdy, 1961, table 31). Few people are completely honest or dishonest in all situations, and most people are of mixed tendency.

Birds of a Feather   An additional finding from Hartshorne and May's study has significance for both the social location of crime and our understanding of its causes. Birds of a feather do flock together. Children who were friends were found to have more closely related scores on measures of honesty than children paired at random. Additionally, putting friends together in a classroom increased their tendencies toward honesty or dishonesty.

Cheating the Customer

Another way of testing people for honesty in situations where they do not think they are being observed is illustrated by *The Reader's Digest* survey taken among a sample of small businesses in the early 1940s (Riis, 1941a, 1941b, 1941c). A man and a woman were employed by this magazine to tour garages and radio and watch repair shops in the United States. The automobiles, radios, and watches that they submitted for repairs had been deliberately "jimmied" to make them appear out of order. The test of honesty consisted in noting how many shops made charges for false repairs. According to this survey:

Of 347 garages visited, 63 percent were dishonest.
Of 304 radio repair shops visited, 64 percent were dishonest.
Of 462 watch repair shops visited, 49 percent were dishonest.

This seems like an inordinate amount of dishonesty among people we often need to trust. Critics of *The Reader's Digest* study have suggested two explanations in mitigation of its terrible statistics. One is that much of the fraud that Riis and his teams unearthed was induced by the poor business climate of the end of Depression years. This might explain the fact of much cheating without erasing it. Another suggestion is that what appeared to be fraud may actually have been incompetence, as when a television repairman installs a new picture tube because he does not know what is really wrong with the set.

The possibility that incompetence sometimes looks like fraud is a real one. However, the suggestion that it was "only the Depression" that moved repairmen to cheat their customers is challenged by a recent study of garage work in New York City. *The New York Times* recently tested the honesty of automobile repair shops in a manner similar to that used in *The Reader's Digest* study. Thirteen out of twenty-four garages visited either wrongly diagnosed the test car's "defect," lending substance to the idea of incompetence, or recommended expensive and unnecessary repairs (D. C. Bacon, 1976).

Testing Violence

Psychologists have tempted people not only to cheat and steal but also to aggress. Again, there is a large amount of literature on this subject that can only be sampled here to illustrate procedures for counting offensive behavior under controlled circumstances.

One thing we know about evil is that it is banal (Arendt, 1964). Injuring others, even innocent others, is commonplace. We quarrel, however, about how common violence is, about what causes it, and about whether some people "really are" more dangerous than others (Carr-Hill, 1970; Walker et al., 1967).

Milgram's Experiments   Stanley Milgram (1963) tested one aspect of these questions in a now famous experiment that has been adopted, with modifications, by other investigators. Milgram advertised for people to help him in a "learning experiment" in which the volunteers acted as "teachers" who were to train stooges, the "learners," in a paired-associates learning task. The learner was strapped in an "electric chair," and the teacher was to improve the learner's performance by administering an electric shock every time the learner gave a wrong response. Moreover, the teacher was told to increase the shock each time the learner made a mistake.

The teaching machine was a shock generator that bore a large label to this effect, plus the information that it was "Type ZLB, Dyson Instrument Company, Waltham, Mass., Output 15 Volts–450 Volts." An elaborate instrument panel, controlled by 30 switches, was marked off in 15-volt increments from 15 to 450 volts. Each group of four switches carried labels, from left to right, reading: "Slight Shock; Moderate Shock; Strong Shock; Very Strong Shock; Intense Shock; Extreme Intensity Shock; Danger: Severe Shock." The last two switches were marked simply XXX.

Each teacher himself took a shock of 45 volts as part of his learning to use the machine. The experiment then consisted in observing how much pain the teacher would administer to the learner under a sequence of suggestions from the experimenter. No real shocks were administered in the experiment, of course, but the teachers believed that the electric chair was actually working.

Milgram's results   Just as official statistics underestimate the true amount of crime, official students of human behavior underestimate the violent propensity of the creature they study. A first finding from Milgram's work was how wrong psychiatrists and psychologists were when asked, in advance of the study, how others would act. There was considerable agreement among Milgram's colleagues and among other researchers that most people would refuse to do violence against an innocent person. Milgram tells us:

All respondents predicted that only an insignificant minority would go through to the end of the shock series (the estimates ranged from 0 to 3%; i.e., the most "pessimistic" member . . . predicted that of 100 persons, 3 would continue through to the most potent shock available on the shock generator—450 volts). The . . . mean was 1.2%.

Upon command of the experimenter, each of the 40 subjects went beyond the expected breakoff point. . . . Of the 40 subjects, 26 obeyed the orders of the experimenter to the end . . . [1963, pp. 375–377].

Milgram's results have been replicated by other investigators (Kaufmann, 1968). Given the proper authority for violence, human beings are more aggressive than some scholars think they are.

Individual differences   Milgram's research does not adequately describe which individuals are more and less prone to violence under command. His principal finding (1974, app. II) is that individuals who resist such violent authority attribute more responsibility for their actions to themselves. By contrast, people who accede to suggestions to injure another put the responsibility on the official who gave the orders. This finding conforms to a common justification of "normal brutality": "I was only following orders."

Other investigators have used adaptations of Milgram's shocking technique as well as observations of offensive behavior under controlled conditions to ascertain which kinds of people, if any, are more likely to injure others. Such research can be summarized for the light it sheds on the kinds of people and the kinds of circumstance that are more and less violent.

Aggressive People; Aggressive Occasions

1   Males are more violent than females. This fact pertains to children as well as adults, and it is universally true. Males are more aggressive in a variety of cultures and under a variety of conditions.

The fact that males are more violent than females has been substantiated both by direct observation and in test situations. A sex difference in propensity to attack appears early in life, is as observable in our primate cousins as it is in human beings, and is related to sex-hormonal balance (Hutt, 1972; S. Levine, 1971; Maccoby and Jacklin, 1974, pp. 242–243).

The fact that males and females differ in their tendencies toward violence does not mean that females may not be aggressive in other ways—as with the vitriolic tongue, in business, or through the law. Moreover, the fact of a biological sex difference does not mean that aggression cannot be learned or that cultures cannot channel the occasions on which the sexes are more and less aggressive. Chapter 7 will show us that ratios of aggressive crimes committed by males and females do vary with cultures. The biological fact means only that males are more "prepared" to do violence than females. This is in keeping with what official statistics tell us about crimes against the person.

2   Aggression is contagious. Watching violence stimulates it. We are not able to specify how long the stimulation lasts or how far it spreads, but seeing others do violence encourages us to attack (Berkowitz and Macaulay, 1971; Comstock, 1975; Geen and Stonner, 1974; J. H. Goldstein and Arms, 1971;

Hartmann, 1969; Lovaas, 1961; McCarthy et al., 1975; Mussen and Rutherford, 1961; Walters et al., 1962; L. Wheeler and Caggiula, 1966; J. L. Wilkins et al., 1974).

3 Expressing aggression—"blowing off steam"—does not reduce it. Fantasies of violence may have a cathartic effect on some individuals (Feshbach, 1961), but in general this is not the case. Thinking about violence, imagining it, and acting upon it—like watching it in others—are more likely to instigate aggression than to diminish it (Berkowitz, 1965, 1967, 1970, 1973; Berkowitz and Rawlings, 1963; Geen, 1975; Geen et al., 1975; Goranson, 1969; Mallick and McCandless, 1966).

4 Frustration sometimes stimulates attack (Dollard et al., 1939). "Frustration" is a fuzzy word, however, and we must handle it with care. To frustrate someone is to prevent that person from getting what he or she has set out to get. To be frustrated is to be blocked. This usage of "frustration" (goal blocking) should not be confused with the inaccurate, popular usage of "being frustrated" to mean feeling angry or deprived.

To be thwarted in an endeavor does not always make people angry, and attack is not a uniform response to failure to get what one wants (Morlan, 1949). Some people, on some occasions, respond to frustration with resignation; others respond with renewed effort. Some people become apathetic when frustrated; others revert to childlike behavior (Whiting, 1944). And, of course, some people attack the frustrating agent or a substitute.

How we respond to being frustrated may be learned, and it varies also with how much we wanted what we are prevented from getting. It varies, too, with whether the frustrated actor takes the blame for a failure to get over the hurdle or puts the blame on others. Personality differences are important, therefore, and they affect how people define their frustrations and how they handle them (de Charms, 1968; Feather, 1967; Rotter, 1966).

A personal characteristic that *reduces* the likelihood of a violent response is the general trait of *willingness to defer gratification* (Lessing, 1969). However this trait may be produced, it has been found repeatedly to distinguish gang-running delinquents from their less delinquent peers and certain kinds of violent adults from less aggressive persons (Bixenstine and Buterbaugh, 1967; DuCette and Wolk, 1972; F. H. Farley and Farley, 1972; Ganzer and Sarason, 1973; Hindelang, 1973; Lowe, 1966; Quay et al., 1960).

5 Parents who dislike their children produce violent ones. Children who are rejected by their parents are unable to identify with them. Parental rejection and a child's lack of identification with his or her parents are associated, too, with squabbling between the parents.

To compound the matter, the success of attempts by parents to control aggression through punishment depends on whether the child has been nurtured by the parents and identifies with them. Parents who neglect and reject their children are ineffective teachers. Their punishment does not reduce aggression in their children, but actually stimulates it (Eron et al., 1971).

Chapter 16 illustrates in greater detail the relation between parental care and children's tendencies to steal and attack. The social location of such parents coincides with other maps of crime and delinquency.

6 Violence that is approved by others will be more frequently employed. "Approval" here includes tacit approval, that is, being *permitted* to do violence as well as *encouraged* to do it (Berkowitz, 1968; Sears, 1961; Siegel and L. G. Kohn, 1959).

Not all aggression is violent, of course, and different styles of aggression are recommended in different social locations. Intellectual aggression and economic aggression, for example, are middle-class values. Physical attack is a lower-class value. Moreover, the physical attack that is deemed unfair by middle-class standards—"ganging up," for example—is a lower-class prescription: "Hit 'im first, before he's ready, and hit 'im hard" (W. B. Miller, 1958; H. S. Thompson, 1966).

These different recommendations for aggression and injury agree, again, with the social map of kinds of offender drawn by other indicators, including official measures.

7 Violent people like violence. This seemingly circular statement says that people who act violently in one arena adopt the violent style in other places. Thus physically aggressive boys like to *watch* violence as well as practice it (Bandura, 1973; Lefkowitz et al., 1972; McCarthy et al., 1975).

8 Aggression that succeeds escalates. Violence is an instrument as well as an expression, and violence that gets the desired result tends to be repeated (Buss, 1961; Berkowitz, 1974). Furthermore, observing the successful violence of others encourages its imitation (Bandura, 1973; Berkowitz, 1962, chap. 9).

In Summary Points 1 through 8 describe violent people and their circumstances in ways similar to official tallies of attack. In addition, points 2 through 8 say that violence tends to reinforce violence. This reinforcement is provided differently in different social locations. Our knowledge of these differences comes from observations in "real" life and in test situations. It is a knowledge seconded by studies of perpetrators and their victims. These studies can be summarized as locating more assault among low-income families, families receiving public assistance ("welfare"), black or Spanish-speaking families, one-parent families, families in which the mother is poorly educated, and families in which there is more reported conflict between parents and children, more delinquency, more addiction to television, and lower school achievement (Comstock, 1975; Greenberg and Dervin, 1970; Lyle and Hoffman, 1972; McCarthy et al., 1975; McLeod et al., 1972).

Violence is only one face of crime, of course, It remains to be seen whether surveys of victims and collections of confessions provide similar results concerning offenses against property as well as attacks on persons. This is the task of the next chapter.

Chapter 6

Counting
Crime—Unofficially
Part Two: Victims and
Confessions

Unofficial counts of crime help clarify the meaning of official statistics. Of these unofficial tallies, criminologists most frequently use surveys of victims and measures of confessions (self-reports).

4 SURVEYS OF VICTIMS

Questions have been asked of citizens in Canada, the United States, and some European countries concerning their experiences as victims of various crimes. The intention behind such surveys has been to illuminate the "dark figure" of crime, the amount of crime unreported to the police. As these surveys were undertaken, it was also expected that their illumination of hidden crime might change the map of crime, that it might show us social locations of crimes different from those described by official statistics.

The summaries of studies of victimization which follow demonstrate that this research has, not surprisingly, fulfilled the first objective but not the second. The summaries can themselves be summarized as saying that (1) more crime is committed than is known to the police, (2) the amount of unreported crime varies with the kind of crime, and (3) the rank order of crimes in a society appears quite similar whether we use official statistics or victims' statements.

American Studies

American research on victimization was initiated as part of the work of the President's Commission on Law Enforcement and Administration of Justice. This Commission sponsored a pilot study of victimization conducted in the District of Columbia by the Bureau of Social Science Research under the direction of Biderman and others (1967) and a nationwide survey by the National Opinion Research Center, reported by Ennis (1967). Since the findings of these early studies have been generally replicated by later surveys, they will be summarized here. These findings have been of sufficient interest to encourage the U.S. Department of Justice to establish a National Crime Panel to provide a continuous survey of victimization for selected crimes. In addition to this periodic national survey, a number of local studies are now under way, one of which will be reported here.

The Bureau of Social Science Research Study   Trained interviewers sampled selected police precincts of Washington, D.C., in 1966. For each respondent, they ascertained:

1 Whether he personally had been a victim of specific crimes since January 1965
2 Whether any member of his household had been victimized
3 The "very worst crime" that had ever happened to him
4 The "very worst crime" that had ever happened to anyone currently living with him

Five major findings resulted from this poll:

1 Respondents believed that the crime problem in their city was serious, that it had been growing worse, and that it was of immediate personal concern to them (Biderman et al., 1967, p. 119).

2 Official statistics ("crimes known to the police") greatly *underestimate* the total amount of crime to which people say they have been subjected. As Table 6-1 shows, over 9,000 criminal incidents were said to have been experienced; but only some 400 such incidents were "known" to the police—a difference of the order of 23 to 1.

3 The discrepancy between police statistics and reports by victims varies with the type of offense. Again, from Table 6-1 it appears that about 11 times as much rape occurs as is known to the police, 20 times as much burglary, and more than 30 times as much robbery and criminal homicide. (The discrepancy in the enumeration of murders is difficult to believe. If the people accurately perceive so much more murder than is known to the police, Washington is an even more dangerous city than has been thought.)

4 According to this survey, the discrepancy between official figures and

Table 6-1 Offense Classes in Survey and Police Data, Precincts 6, 10, and 14

Class of offense	Incidents mentioned by survey respondents		Actual offenses known	
	N	%	N	%
Part I:				
Criminal homicide	31	*	1	*
Rape	46	*	4	1
Robbery	1,082	11	35	8
Aggravated assault	457	5	20	4
Burglary	2,174	22	110	25
Larceny	1,832	18	116	26
Auto theft	1,381	14	21	5
Part II:				
Other assaults	675	7	30	7
Arson, vandalism	112	1	47	10
Fraud, forgery, embezzlement	143	1	8	2
Other sex offenses	48	*	12	3
Offense against family	3	*	-	-
All other offenses	2,009	20	39	9
Total	9,993	100	443	100

*Less than 1%

Source: Reprinted with permission from Biderman et al., 1967, p. 34.

victims' claims is not due to the failure of citizens to report their injuries as much as it is due to variations in attention by the police. Biderman notes, "If we accept what our respondents say, the discrepancy presumably involves the police not reporting what people report to them in much greater degree than the nonreporting of offenses to the police by the public" (p. 118).

5 Despite the discrepancies between the *amount of crime* gauged by police statistics and by this survey of victims, the *rank order* of the frequency of the crimes reported is quite similar for the two measures.

If one looks only at the FBI's "index crimes," the ordering of the frequency of these offenses by both measures is identical. However, a kind of crime not included in the "index offenses" was found by this survey of victims to be the third most frequently mentioned violation: malicious destruction of property (p. 33).

The National Opinion Research Center Study This polling organization asked a representative sample of Americans about their experiences as victims of crime and about their opinions of the police and of their own personal security. The survey was concerned principally with *crimes against individuals and their property*. It did not intend to inquire about citizens' experiences with gambling and violations of game laws, with abortion, or with violations of liquor and drug laws. This inquiry was not used as a confessional instrument, as self-report measures are. Furthermore, it is clear that a study of *individual victims* omits from its tally crimes against corporations and other institutions.

The findings of interest in the present context are these:

1   As appears from all unofficial measurements of deviant behavior, much more crime is committed than is recorded. Again, the discrepancy between the number of people who say they have been victims of crime and the number of crimes known to the police varies with the type of offense. Forcible rape, robbery, aggravated assault, burglary, and larceny over $50 are all experienced far more frequently than they are reported to the police. Depending on the city and the kind of crime, individual victims say they have suffered from 3 to 10 times the number of offenses that are recorded by the FBI's Uniform Crime Reports. Only automobile theft and homicide appear to be more frequently reported to the police than to survey interviewers. (The finding that citizens are *less* aware of murder than the police are confirms the doubts about the validity of the District of Columbia finding mentioned on page 88). Overall, about twice as much crime, major and minor, was recorded through this survey of victims than appeared on official logs. Table 6-2 compares the estimated rates of the "index crimes" with their official rates as calculated by the FBI.

Table 6-2   Estimated Rates of Part I Crimes (see Table 6-1); 1965–1966

Crime	NORC sample Estimated rate per 100,000 population	Uniform Crime[a] Reports: 1965 total per 100,000 population	Uniform Crime[b] Reports: 1965 (individual or residential rates) per 100,000 population
Homicide	3.0	5.1	5.1
Forcible rape	42.5	11.6	11.6
Robbery	94.0	61.4	61.4
Aggravated assault	218.3	106.6	106.6
Burglary	949.1	605.3	296.6
Larceny ($50+)	606.5	393.3	267.4
Vehicle theft	206.2	251.0	226.0[c]
Total	2,119.6	1,434.3	974.7
		N . . (32,966)	

[a]*Crime in the United States, 1965 Uniform Crime Reports,* Table 1, p. 51.

[b]Crime in the United States, 1965 Uniform Crime Reports, Table 14, Page 105, shows for burglary and larcenies the number of residential and individual crimes. The overall rate per 100,000 population is therefore reduced by the proportion of these crimes that occurred to individuals. Since all robberies to individuals were included in the NORC sample regardless of whether the victim was acting as an individual or as part of an organization, the total UCR figures were used as comparison.

[c]The reduction of the UCR auto theft rate by 10 per cent is based on the figures of the Automobile Manufacturers Association (*Automobile Facts & Figures,* 1966), showing 10 per cent of all cars owned by leasing-rental agencies and private and governmental fleets. The Chicago Police Department's auto theft personnel confirmed that about 7–10 per cent of stolen cars recovered were from fleet and rental sources and other non-individually owned sources.

Source: Reprinted, with permission, from Ennis, 1967, p. 8.

2   A second finding, in agreement with that of the study by the Bureau of Social Science Research, is that, despite the underreporting characteristic of official counts of crime, *the rank order of the frequency of these serious offenses* reported by their victims is, with the exception of vehicle theft, identical to that of the Uniform Crime Reports.

3   The crimes most frequently experienced, according to these victims, are theft of property worth less than $50 and malicious mischief.

4   The probability that one will be a victim of a crime varies with the kind of crime and where one lives.

The centers of American cities are the more probable sites of violent crimes. Forgery, fraud, and other cheats do not vary with type of community. "Petty theft and malicious destruction of property are reported most often in the suburbs" (Ennis, 1967, p. 23). "As one moves from the central city to the suburbs out into smaller towns and rural areas, the crime rates decline, but much more drastically for crimes against the person than for property crimes. The metropolitan center . . . has a violent crime rate about *five times* as high as the smaller city and rural area but a property crime rate only *twice* as high" (pp. 29–30).

Contrary to some professional and popular opinion, the southern United States do not report the highest rates of violent crimes. When community size is controlled for, the West is the most violent area, according to victims there (p. 29).

5   "At all levels of income, Negroes have higher rates of victimization for serious crimes against the person compared to whites. Property crimes show a more complex relationship to both race and income. For whites, there is a general decline of burglaries as income rises, but an *increase* of larcenies and car thefts with income. Among Negroes, the trends are less clear, but they mirror the patterns for whites with an important exception. Burglaries rise with income" (p. 30).

6   The serious offenses of aggravated assault, forcible rape, vehicle theft, grand larceny, and robbery are most likely to occur "close to home and secondarily on the public streets" (p. 40).

7   The NORC investigation found, in disagreement with the pilot study reported for Washington, D.C., that the major reason for a discrepancy between surveys and official statistics on crime is *the failure of citizens to report offenses*. About half the instances of victimization were not reported to the police.

Willingness to report a crime varies with the seriousness of the offense and with the victim's estimate that reporting will have some result. The high proportion of automobile thefts reported is a consequence of the necessity of filing a complaint with the police as a prerequisite to making an insurance claim.

Other serious crimes tend not to be referred to the police principally because the victim believes the police cannot be effective. Secondary reasons given for failure to complain about a crime are the feeling that the affair was "a private matter" and the wish to protect the offender (Ennis, 1967, chap. 5).

National Crime Panel Studies Findings of the National Crime Panel generally confirm the results of earlier studies. These surveys repeatedly tell us what we already believed: that much more crime occurs than is recorded on police logs. In addition, these polls tally the relative risks of suffering from particular crimes, and, if they are maintained, they will provide another indicator of trends in criminal activity. As will be seen, however, the picture of crime drawn by surveys is incomplete, as is any single measure of offensive behavior.

The latest report of the National Crime Panel (1975) describes patterns of victimization in 13 American cities among the population 12 years of age and over during 1973. The findings are based on interviews conducted early in 1974 to ascertain who had been victims of selected crimes during the preceding year.

It should be noted that victimization surveys such as this do not count all crimes. Some offenses are difficult to uncover by asking questions of the possible victims. Thus the Panel's interrogation does not touch on murder or kidnapping. Murder victims obviously cannot answer questions, and it is felt to be inappropriate to quiz children who have been victims of kidnapping. Parallel difficulties cause surveys to omit crimes against governmental agencies and to exclude the so-called "victimless" crimes of drunkenness, impaired driving ability, drug abuse, and prostitution. Furthermore, crimes committed against victims who may not have been aware that they were being "taken" are also excluded from these polls. This means that some domestic fights are not reported to interviewers because the participants do not consider them to be crimes. It means, too, that an unknown quantity of larceny is unreported by its victims—crimes such as internal theft by employees, shoplifting, income tax evasion, the buying of stolen property, and an assortment of frauds. Last, no attempt is made in victimization surveys to study crimes in which the victim "willingly" participates. This again excludes a variety of con games and swindles, blackmail, and illegal gambling.

Among the crimes it studies, the National Crime Panel classifies victims as individuals, households, and commercial establishments and tallies their victimization separately. For individuals, the crimes counted are rape, robbery, assault, and personal larceny. For households, crimes are categorized as burglary, household larceny (stealing by someone who has a right to be in the house), and motor-vehicle theft. Crimes against businesses are classified as burglary and robbery.

Deficiencies of surveys Comparison of the results of victimization surveys with official statistics and other counts of crime requires attention to some of the deficiencies of surveys. For example, a victim's report is subject to defects of memory, particularly when we ask about events over a year's span. Then, too, respondents differ in their interpretations of a question. Furthermore, a victim's report does not adequately locate the crime in terms of the offender's characteristics, and it may not even locate the crime in terms of the victim's residence. A victim may report offenses suffered outside the city in which he or she resides. Thus some portion of the crimes that the Panel lists by cities did not occur within those localities. Estimates of victimization suffered outside the city of the victim's residence run from a low of 4 percent for New Orleans to a high of 20 percent for San Diego (National Crime Panel, 1975, p. 3). This fact should be taken into account when interpreting citizens' vulnerability to crime in different areas, and it also affects the meaning of the population characteristics examined as correlates of victimization.

A last caution is in order before summarizing some findings of the National Crime Panel: Studies of *victims* tell us nothing about the characteristics of *offenders*. Although an early report of the Panel (1974, p. iii) promised to describe "characteristics of the offender as perceived by the victim," this has not been done. The closest approximation to this datum is the recording, for some kinds of crime, of whether the offender was a stranger to the victim.

Summary of findings

1   As might be expected, the single most prevalent crime reported by victims is some kind of theft from individuals. Of all victimization suffered by persons, households, and businesses, about 40 percent involved stealing from individuals. Crimes against individuals that were violent or involved the threat of violence constituted about 15 percent of all victimization. Overall, individuals report about 57 percent of the criminal incidents picked up by this survey, households account for 39 percent, and businesses account for about 4 percent (National Crime Panel, 1974, p. 1).

2   Most of the reported crimes are committed by strangers. Robbery, purse snatching, and pocket picking are almost always performed by strangers. Strangers also account for about three-fourths of the rapes, attempted and completed, and for about two-thirds of all physical attacks. It is only when we get into fights and are injured that we are likely to be victims of people we know—on about half the reported occasions.

3   As other counts of crime have indicated, poor people are more likely to be victims of violence, and rich people are more apt to be victims of theft (National Crime Panel, 1974, p. 5)

4   Males rather than females, blacks rather than whites, and young people rather than older ones suffer most from crimes against individuals. These kinds of people suffer disproportionately from violent attacks, but less clearly from the many varieties of personal larcenies.

Victims in Portland, Oregon   Surveys conducted by Schneider and others (1975) in the Portland metropolitan area amplify some of the National Crime Panel findings. In particular, the Portland studies indicate that victims vary in their tendencies to report crimes to the police. They vary from one neighborhood to another and from one time period to another.

Willingness to report crimes is, of course, affected by the gravity of the injury—the more serious the offense against the person or against property, the more likely it is to be reported. However, the seriousness of the offense does not explain everything about citizens' reporting practices. The Portland studies show that attitudes toward the police and the community have a strong effect upon the likelihood of one's filing a complaint. Schneider and her colleagues conclude:

> 1   Persons are more apt to report crimes . . . if they are more integrated into the community, if they believe the police will be able to catch the offender, if they are more trusting of the police, and if they have been involved in neighborhood-based crime prevention activities such as those sponsored by the Portland Crime Prevention Bureau.
> 2   Serious property crimes are more apt to be reported if the victim believes the police will be able to catch the offender, if the victim has lived in the same place for a longer period of time, if the victim has insurance, and if the crime was committed by a stranger.

Canadian Studies

Canadian surveys have been conducted in local areas. No national poll has been conducted, although one has been proposed. However, to date, Canadian research confirms both the dark figure of crime and the rank ordering of crimes found in other countries.

Victims in Toronto   Courtis (1970) interviewed citizens in Toronto concerning a restricted range of crime and found the usual phenomena: Victims said they had suffered about five times as many crimes as were reported to the police. Failure to call the police is explained by the same kinds of attitudes revealed by surveys elsewhere: fear of being embarrassed by the facts of the victimization and the belief that the police could not do much about the crime.

Again, it was found that young males are more likely to have been victimized. There are exceptions, of course, by kind of crime. Thus women more frequently report having been molested or propositioned. However, of citizens who said they had been thus offended, 42 percent were men.

Victims in British Columbia   Koenig (1974) polled citizens by questionnaire rather than by interview. His questionnaire, which was mailed to a representative sample of voters in British Columbia, inquired about their experience during the preceding year with four categories of crime: theft (burglary and larceny), vandalism, assault, and robbery.

The rank order of crimes allegedly suffered parallels the order of crimes known to the police. Citizens say that they more frequently were victims of theft (about one-fourth of the sample) and of vandalism (about one-fifth of the sample). Assault (4.3 percent) and robbery (1.1 percent) are much rarer experiences.

Moreover, the risks of being the victim of a crime in different social locations appear similar whether one uses official data or victims' reports.

Koenig found that "for all four generic crimes, perceived victimization was disproportionately high among males, ethnic Canadians, and the non-married—results extremely similar to the American pattern" (1974, p. 9).

Scandinavian Studies

Scandinavians have conducted a few surveys of citizens concerning a small range of crimes—in particular, sex offenses and crimes of violence. As in other such research, the dark figure of unreported crime is illuminated without drastically changing the social maps of criminality drawn from official statistics.

Sex Crimes in Denmark As part of an American inquiry into the effects of pornography, Kutschinsky (1970) and his associates interviewed a representative sample of residents of Copenhagen concerning their sexual victimization. This survey was greatly restricted as regards the number of victims studied (about 44), the locale, and the kinds of violations under scrutiny. However, within its limited and often ambiguous area of "sex crimes," this research is of interest for its similarities to the findings of other investigations:

1 Crimes reported to the police are but a small portion of crimes experienced.
2 The *rank orders* of the frequency with which various kinds of sex offenses are experienced and the frequency with which they are reported to the police are highly correlated (Kutschinsky, 1970, p. 116).
3 The *less* serious sex offenses are the most common.

For males in Copenhagen, the most frequently mentioned offense was "minor homosexual interference or attempts." The second most frequently mentioned offense was exhibitionism (Kutschinsky, 1970, p. 115).

Danish women were most frequently victims of exhibitionism and second most frequently victims of "indecent approaches" by other females. The rarest crimes reported by these women were rape and incest.

Violence in Scandinavia Although some people may think otherwise, Scandinavia is not a homogeneous group of countries. Norway and Denmark, for example, have long been held to have more cultural affinity with each other than either has with Sweden or Finland. These cultural differences are both defined by, and reflected in, these countries' crime rates. A question raised by Scandinavian studies of victims is, again, whether citizens' reports of their experiences with crime would confirm or disconfirm official statistics and stereotypes.

Polls have been conducted in the four Scandinavian countries asking representative national samples of adults about their experiences as victims of violence. The data from Sweden have yet to be analyzed; but reports from Denmark, Norway, and Finland confirm police data, with, of course, the qualification of the dark figure. Hauge and Wolf (1974) summarize these polls as follows:

1   For a number of years, the rates of murders known to the police in Finland per 100,000 population have been three to five times the rates given by official statistics in Denmark and Norway. The number of major and minor assaults known to the police in Finland has also been two to three times as great as the number in Denmark and Norway.

2   Interviews with citizens in these countries indicate that the same rank ordering of violent offenses is experienced among these nations as is reported by their police. Only the dark figure differs. The amount of unrecorded violence is greater in Finland than in Denmark or Norway, which means that official statistics in the latter countries more closely parallel citizens' experience than those in Finland. "The dark number for non-fatal violent crimes in Denmark is at least 15," say Hauge and Wolf, "[but] in Finland at least 30" (1974, p. 27).

3   It has been remarked in a different context that violence begets violence (see pages 84–86). Here, too, it is noted that the higher rate of violent offense in Finland results not merely from the fact that more persons are victimized, but also from the fact that more violence is experienced per person.

In Summary

Every measure of a social behavior has its critics, and all the criticism has some substance. If official counts of crime, held up against some criterion of perfect information, may be accused of invalidity, so too may tallies of victims and, as will be seen, measures of confessions.

Surveys of victims suffer from all the handicaps of any public opinion poll—doubts about how representative the sample is, refusals of some potential respondents to participate, bias and cheating by interviewers, and the perennial difficulty of assuring that the same question means the same thing to respondents in widely varying social positions.

In addition, asking people about the crimes they have suffered runs into the problem of how good their memories are and whether people of diverse status have equally good memories for events of possibly different importance to them. Then, too, there is the question of honesty or, if you will, of "openness." Individuals do differ in their willingness to talk about themselves—whether on paper to an anonymous questionnaire or in person to a strange interviewer. The reluctance to disclose various things about oneself is aggravated when confessions of crime are asked for, as in self-report measures, but it is also a possible source of distortion when people are being asked about their victimization.

All these criticisms would be important if surveys of victims revealed striking differences in the social location of major crimes from what is shown on the map drawn by official statistics and other unofficial tallies. One would not know, then, what to believe about crime, and any explanation of crime would be as good as any other. An observer who cannot use the statistics of aggregates of individuals to locate the sites of different kinds of crime cannot speak reasonably of what causes crime. (It must be remarked that difficulties in finding the facts about who commits which crimes, and where, do not prevent politicians, journalists, or even criminologists from advancing hypotheses about the causes and cures of crime.)

Fortunately, despite the repeatedly discovered fact that more crime is committed than is recorded, *when crimes are ranked by the frequency of their occurrence*, the ordering is very much the same no matter which measure is used. Furthermore, the social conditions associated with high rates of serious crimes known to the police are also, with some qualification, associated with high rates of reported victimization. Both measures of criminality show higher rates of some kinds of larceny and of robbery and serious assaults "in areas characterized by low income, physical deterioration, dependency, racial and ethnic concentrations, broken homes, working mothers, low levels of education and vocational skill, high unemployment, high proportions of single males, overcrowded and substandard housing, high rates of tuberculosis and infant mortality, low rates of home ownership and single family dwellings, mixed land use, and high population density" (President's Commission, 1967a, p. 35).

It must be pointed out, again, that these conditions are *correlates* of high crime rates, not necessarily their *causes*. Nevertheless, it is among such factors that criminologists have searched for the roots of crime; and it is of significance here that for most serious crimes, the *pattern* of their incidence as expressed by complaints made to the police is similar to that expressed by reports of victimization to interviewers.

5 SELF-REPORT MEASURES OF CRIMINALITY

The fact that surveys of victims and official crime statistics in general produce parallel findings has only slightly reduced skepticism about the validity of the official tabulations. Doubt remains, and it has moved criminologists to attempt to find out who has committed how much of which crimes by asking people to confess. Measures based on such "self-reports" have been devised in a number of ways:

   1 By asking people to complete anonymous questionnaires (Akers, 1964; Christie et al., 1965; J. P. Clark and Wenninger, 1962; Dentler and Monroe, 1961; Elmhorn, 1965; McDonald, 1969b; Nettler, 1959a, 1959b; Nye and Short, 1957; Porterfield, 1943, 1946; Wallerstein and Wyle, 1947)
   2 By asking people to complete anonymous questionnaires identified in a circuitous fashion and validated against later interviews or police records (Forssman and Gentz, 1962; Voss, 1963)
   3 By asking people to confess to criminal acts on signed questionnaires validated against police records (Hirschi, 1969; McCandless et al., 1972)
   4 By having people complete anonymous questionnaires identified by number and validated against follow-up interviews and the threat of polygraph ("lie-detector") tests (J. P. Clark and Tifft, 1966)
   5 By interviewing respondents (Belson et al., 1970; Gold, 1966; Reiss and Rhodes, 1961; Waldo and Chiricos, 1972)
   6 By interviewing respondents and validating their responses against official records (Erickson, 1971; Erickson and Empey, 1963)

All these procedures provide imperfect measures of what people have done. Whether they are better or worse indicators of criminal activity than official records and victimization surveys is an open question. The findings of the many studies that have used confessional techniques run from consensus to complete disagreement.

Consensus among the Confessions of Criminality

The numerous international studies that have employed self-report scales agree on these rather obvious findings: (1) that almost everyone, by his or her own admission, has broken some criminal law; (2) that the amount of "hidden crime" is enormous; and (3) that people who commit crimes are better described as representing a continuum, as having committed more or less crime, rather than simply being "delinquent" or "nondelinquent." As with most behaviors controlled by social norms, the graph of criminal conduct is a unimodal (one-humped) curve that looks like a "J" or an "L," depending upon how it is drawn.

For example, Figure 6-1 is a graph of "delinquency scores" for schoolchildren in Stockholm, 9 to 14 years of age, who responded to an anonymous questionnaire (Elmhorn, 1965). The delinquency score represents a weighting for each child of the *frequency* and the *seriousness* of the confessed criminal conduct. This chart is similar in form to others drawn from a variety of studies of antisocial behavior, all of which tell us that most people commit some minor infractions of the criminal code and that a few individuals commit many offenses and more serious offenses. For example, on Elmhorn's delinquency index, the highest possible score is 375 points. The average score is about 20; the median is approximately 8.

The number of individuals who exceed these central tendencies decreases as one moves toward the extremity of committing many crimes and more serious crimes. While some criminality is normal, persistent and grave violations of the law are the experience of a minority. *This holds true whether the measure is confession or official statistics.*

Furthermore, there is a relationship in both measures of criminality between being *persistent* as an offender and being a *serious* offender. These data indicate that the more frequently a person breaks the law, the more likely he or she is to commit more grave offenses. The finding of a skewed continuum of admitted delinquencies is in agreement with the distribution of criminal activity indicated by court records. This finding of a small minority of repetitive, serious violators justifies the picture of the incorrigible tough guy, the "hard-core" delinquent.[1]

---

[1]The image of the "hard-core" juvenile delinquent is also substantiated by research on the background factors that, in some degree, differentiate more and less delinquent boys. For example, Eleanor and Sheldon Glueck (1970), who have been studying this subject for years, describe what they call "core delinquents" from poor scores on measures of maternal supervision, maternal discipline, and family cohesiveness. The Gluecks report that such delinquents, when grown to young adulthood, show a somewhat greater tendency than other types of youthful offender toward residential mobility, poor work habits, low occupational status, the use of social service agencies, and failure to be self-supporting.

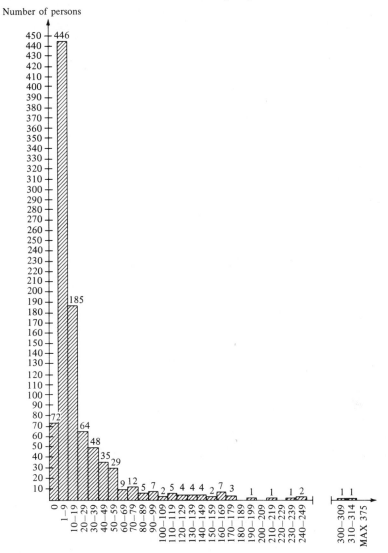

Figure 6-1 Self-reported delinquency among schoolchildren. (*Reprinted with permission from Elmhorn, 1965, p. 129.*)

Disagreement among the Confessions of Criminality

Research with confessional data provides mixed results when one inspects scores of criminal conduct for their relationship with the correlates of criminal behavior usually given by official statistics. (These correlates are summarized in Chapter 7). The presumed value of asking people about their offensive behavior is that it gives a clearer picture of the social location of crime, a picture undistorted by the alleged biases of a judicial system. However, it is not at all certain that self-report measures provide a more accurate description (see pages 107–117); and—what is equally disturbing—the pictures drawn from admissions of criminality vary with who is drawing them.

In the United States, at least seven "social locators" have been correlated with scores from confessional instruments. Sociologists have explored the association between self-report measures and sex, age, socioeconomic status, ethnic group, religion, rural or urban residence, and family relationships. A consistently reported relationship is found between admissions of delinquencies and differences in age, sex, family relations, and rural or urban residence. Disagreement occurs, however, when this extensive research looks at the association between self-report scales and socioeconomic status and ethnicity, including religion. Some American studies find class and ethnic differences in admitted offenses; some do not. Hardt and Bodine provide a summary of these investigations as of 1965 (table 1, pp. *vii–ix*), a summary that has not been seriously emended by later research.

From the point of view of an outsider, this mixture of findings could be attributed to an "experimenter effect," the possibility that investigators find what they believe they will find. The impulse to employ self-report scales has been "democratic," in the sense that official crime statistics and the judicial system out of which they flow have been charged with bias against poor people and ethnic minorities. The search has been, therefore, for a more accurate measure of misbehavior, one which might challenge the assumption that criminality varies with class and nationality. It is notable here that European scholars are *less* reluctant to believe the official records when these records link crime rates to class and ethnicity. "From the American studies," McDonald writes ". . . evidence . . . both supports and denigrates the theory that the working class is more delinquent than the middle class . . . [whereas] almost all of the literature on delinquency in Britain is in favour of the view that the working class is more delinquent" (1969b, p. 19).

Given these disagreements, it is instructive to examine the findings of two of the bigger and better investigations of the class and ethnic correlates of admitted delinquency, one conducted in the United States, the other in England.

Hirschi's Research   Hirschi (1969) used the facilities of the Survey Research Center on the Berkeley campus of the University of California to question a sample of some 4,000 junior and senior high school students in the San Francisco Bay area. A three-part questionnaire was employed to ascertain attitudes toward school, teachers, neighborhood, friends, parents, and human relations. Questions were also asked about work and money, aspirations and expectations, the use of leisure, and participation in school activities. Six items in the questionnaire were used as an index of admitted violations (Hirschi, 1969, p. 54):

1   Have you ever taken little things (worth less than $2) that did not belong to you?
2   Have you ever taken things of some value (between $2 and $50) that did not belong to you?

3   Have you ever taken things of large value (worth over $50) that did not belong to you?

4   Have you ever taken a car for a ride without the owner's permission?

5   Have you ever banged up something that did not belong to you on purpose?

6   Not counting fights you may have had with a brother or sister, have you ever beaten up on anyone or hurt anyone on purpose?

In addition to these data, school records, including grade point averages and academic achievement scores, were collected for each respondent. Police records were also examined, but only for the boys in the sample.

To each of the six questions in the delinquency index, respondents were able to reply that they had "never" committed the offense; that they had committed the offense "more than a year ago"; that they had committed the offense "during the last year"; or that they had committed the offense "during the last year *and* more than a year ago" (p. 56). Replies structured in this manner reflect more than one dimension of behavior. They assess the *recency* of a delinquency, the *persistence* with which one has broken the law, and, in an indirect fashion, the *frequency* of delinquent acts. Among the various indices that might be constructed by weighting recency, persistence, and frequency, Hirschi chose an index based on the "number of acts committed during the previous year" (p. 62). In interpreting Hirschi's data, it should be noted that this index is *not* the same as the so-called "standard index," used by most investigators of confessed crime, which totals all delinquencies ever committed and admitted. Hirschi believes his choice of index to be justified, although the standard index bears a slightly higher relation to other indicators of juvenile misbehavior. Table 6-3 shows the coefficients of correlation between the "recency," "persistence," and "standard" indices and admissions of truancy, suspension from school, apprehension by the police, and police records for part

Table 6-3   Correlations among Alternate Self-Report Indexes and Selected Outside Variables, White Boys Only[a]

	Recency	Persistence	Standard
Recency	1.00	.90	.76
Persistence		1.00	.92
Standard			1.00
Truancy[b]	.39	.42	.42
Suspension[c]	.33	.35	.35
Police contact[d]	.42	.47	.50
Official record[e]	.27	.29	.30

[a]The number of cases upon which these correlations are based is not less than 1,300.

[b]"During the last year, did you ever stay away from school just because you had other things to do?"

[c]"Have you ever been suspended from school?"

[d]"Have you ever been picked up by the police?"

[e]Scored as total number of delinquent acts recorded by police.

Source: Reprinted with permission from Hirschi, 1969, p. 63.

of Hirschi's sample. The standard index has a slightly higher association with these "outside variables" than the other measures.

Summarizing Hirschi's findings provides the following map of the social location of delinquency:

1 "Forty-two per cent of the Negro and 18 per cent of the white boys in the analyzed sample had police records in the two years prior to administration of the questionnaire. When other measures of 'delinquency' are used, the difference between Negroes and whites is sharply reduced. For example, 42 per cent of the Negro and 35 per cent of the white boys report having been picked up by the police; 49 per cent of the Negro and 44 per cent of the white boys report having committed one or more delinquent acts during the preceding year" (pp. 75–76). Table 6-4 plots the relation between race, official offenses, self-reports of apprehension by the police, and self-reports of delinquencies.

2 "Negroes are more likely to report 'non-delinquent' offenses involving interaction with and requiring definition by officials other than the police . . . They are, for example, more likely to report having been sent out of a classroom and having been suspended from school" (p. 79).

3 Hirschi used the father's occupation as his principal measure of socioeconomic status. When the connection between self-reported delinquency and father's occupation is examined (Table 6-5), only "a very small relation [is found] that could easily be upset by random disturbances of sampling or definition" (p. 69).

Table 6-5 shows the socioeconomic pattern of admitted delinquency for white boys only. Hirschi explains his decision to base his analysis on the information from white males on the grounds that the data for blacks were less reliable and that "most independent variables had the same relation to official and self-reported delinquency among Negroes as among whites. . . . The major difference was that the relations among Negroes were consistently smaller, an

Table 6-4 Number of Official Offenses, Number of Times Picked up by Police, and Number of Self-reported Delinquent Acts, by Race (Percent)

Number of acts (or reported contacts with police)	(A) Official offenses		(B) Self-reported police pickup		(C) Self-reported delinquent acts	
	White	Negro	White	Negro	White	Negro
None	81	57	65	57	56	51
One	10	19	18	20	25	25
Two or more	8	23	17	22	19	24
Totals	99	99	100	99	100	100
	(1335)	(888)	(1302)	(833)	(1303)	(828)

Source: Reprinted with permission from Hirschi. 1969. p. 76.

Table 6-5   Self-reported Delinquency by Father's Occupation—White Boys Only (Percent)

Self-reported acts	Father's occupation[a]				
	Low 1	2	3	4	High 5
None	62	53	56	49	61
One	16	26	25	28	25
Two or more	23	21	19	23	14
Totals	101	100	100	100	100
	(151)	(156)	(390)	(142)	(282)

[a] 1 = Unskilled labor; 2 = Semi-skilled labor; 3 = Skilled labor, foreman, merchant; 4 = White collar; 5 = Professional and executive.

Source: Reprinted with permission from Hirschi, 1969, p. 69.

attenuation apparently due to greater unreliability of response" (p. 79, fn. 23).

This kind of exclusion of data points up one of the criticisms of the self-report technique, which will be amplified on pages 107–117. Interpretation of some facets of Hirschi's study becomes difficult, then, because the omission of information from females and from blacks weakens the impact upon delinquency of some of the factors presumed to be associated with misconduct.

4   "Boys whose fathers have been unemployed and/or whose families are on welfare are more likely than children from fully employed, self-sufficient families to commit delinquent acts" (p. 72).

5   "The educational and occupational expectations of delinquents tend to be low" (p. 185). "The less a boy cares about what teachers think of him, the more likely he is to have committed delinquent acts" (p. 123). "The greater the value the student places on grades, the less likely he is to be delinquent" (p. 223). "Academic ability and school performance influence many, if not most, of the variables that turn out to be important predictors of delinquency. The causal chain runs from academic incompetence to poor school performance to disliking of school to rejection of the school's authority to the commission of delinquent acts" (pp. 132, 134).

6   Respect for and attachment to one's parents is a strong correlate of immunity to delinquency. According to Hirschi, "the fact that delinquents are less likely than nondelinquents to be closely tied to their parents is one of the best documented findings of delinquency research" (p. 85). Hirschi's data support this finding and show that "the child attached to a low-status parent is no more likely to be delinquent than the child attached to a high-status parent" (p. 108).

Many of these conclusions are repeatedly found in other studies *whether they employ official records of criminality or confessions of delinquency.* The principal question at issue among investigators who use self-report tools has to do with the class and ethnic distribution of criminal misconduct. Hirschi's research strongly reduces the significance of socioeconomic status for young boys' behavior. Except for the sons of professionals and executives, who were disproportionately free of both admitted and official criminality, Hirschi found little association between confessed delinquencies and the remaining strata of income, education, and occupation. Hirschi locates the causes of lawful conduct in attachment to the prevalent order (parents and schools), positive attitudes toward personal achievement, and belief in the validity of conventional legal and moral rules. Conversely, delinquency is associated with a lack of these characteristics.

This causal attribution need *not* be denied if other studies, using other instruments on different populations, find different patterns for the connection between *class* and illegitimate conduct. As will be argued (pages 129–130, 138–140, and 249–250), there is no necessity for "social class" to have a uniform significance regardless of the milieu in which it is experienced. McDonald's English study, for example, finds a different class distribution of admitted delinquency from that which Hirschi reports. However, other correlates of delinquency, particularly the school correlates, hold true in England as they do in Canada and the United States.

McDonald's Research   McDonald (1969b) distributed anonymous questionnaires to almost 1,000 schoolboys in and about London in middle- and working-class areas and in secondary modern schools and the more traditional grammar schools.

McDonald, like Hirschi, inquired about boys' aspirations and attitudes toward aspects of their lives, although she did not probe as extensively as Hirschi in this area. However, McDonald's questionnaire included about eight times as many delinquency items as Hirschi's.

Responses were analyzed by *frequency* of admitted offense and were correlated separately and in clusters of crimes for their association with four social-class categories: "upper middle, lower middle, upper working, and lower working." The clusters of delinquencies included seven questions about serious theft, twelve questions about petty theft, four questions about vehicle theft, twelve questions about "misconduct" such as truancy and running away from home, seven questions on vandalism, and five questions about violent behavior.

McDonald's findings agree with most of the pictures of delinquency drawn by American self-report studies, with the exception that there is a clearer association in England between measures of socioeconomic status and confessions of crime. McDonald's data may be summarized as follows:

1   When the *proportions* of boys in the four social classes are compared with respect to the *frequencies* with which they admit to the various delinquencies, there are consistently higher rates for working-class boys. This association varies by cluster of offenses. The correlation is particularly strong between

Table 6-6 Admissions of Violence by Social Class

Offence	UM	LM	LW	LW	P
			(Percent admitting)		
Violence	60	64	71	78	< .005
Fist fight	72	75	81	83	< .05
Fight start	44	42	50	57	< .05
Assault	24	22	32	33	< .05
Gang fights	33	39	49	51	< .001
Weapons	16	30	22	24	< .02

Source: Reprinted with permission from McDonald, 1969b, p. 88.

socioeconomic status and admissions of vandalism and violence. For example, Table 6-6 shows the distribution by social class of admissions to five items of violent behavior: being in a fist fight, starting a fist fight, beating someone up without provocation, possessing a weapon, and participating in gang fights. An overall "violence" score is also assigned, and the probability of this distribution's occurring "by chance" is listed under "P" in the table.

The petty-theft and misconduct measures are less clearly distributed by social class. Again, as in other surveys of such peccadilloes, everyone has done so many of these things so often that class makes little difference. In England the majority of these schoolboys say they have stolen things from their schools and done some small shoplifting. Middle-class boys apparently steal more frequently from their parents than working-class boys do, while working-class boys more frequently admit to having pinched fruit and accepted stolen articles.

Of all the clusters of crimes examined by McDonald, the category of admitted "serious theft" showed the weakest relation with social class. Since the number of boys admitting these more grave offenses was small, it becomes difficult to interpret this finding. Among the various kinds of "serious theft" assayed, only larceny and a composite score of "vehicle theft" showed significant differences in the expected direction among the social classes (Table 6-7).

Table 6-7 Admissions of Theft by Social Class

Offence	UM	LM	UW	LW	P
Serious theft					
(percent admitting)	33	34	35	37	> .80
Shoplifting	8	9	10	12	> .10
Larceny	6	9	13	17	< .005
Breaking & entering	22	22	23	22	> .50
Taking car	4	6	7	5	> .70
Car possession	6	8	10	11	> .20
Taking cycle	3	7	8	9	> .05
Taking scooter	4	7	6	11	> .05
Vehicle theft	12	15	16	22	< .05

Source: Reprinted with permission from McDonald, 1969b, p. 83.

Overall, McDonald reports differences in the *proportions* of the social classes admitting to delinquencies and differences in the *frequencies* of their confessed crimes.

2   The type of school attended was associated with differences in admitted delinquencies. Grammar school children reported fewer offenses than boys in the secondary modern schools, and this difference persisted when their social class was held constant. "Amongst middle-class children those attending grammar schools admitted to less delinquency than those attending modern schools. And the same occurred with respect to working-class children" (p. 164).

3   As in Hirschi's American study, self-reported delinquency and school achievement were also correlated in England. When school achievement is judged by the "stream" in which a boy has been placed, "children of lower streams . . . have higher rates of delinquency than children of higher streams, holding class and school type constant" (p. 164).

4   McDonald examined official records of court appearances to ascertain whether the same distribution of offenses by classes obtained. This was done on a school-by-school basis, rather than by checking on the court appearances of the individual respondents. Such an area, or ecological, analysis, does not provide strong validation of self-report measures. However, McDonald was interested in ascertaining whether, among the schools surveyed, the pattern of confessed crime resembled the pattern of officially noticed crime. It did:

> The correlation of numbers of working-class boys per school and numbers of court appearances per school was extremely high . . . As in the admitted delinquency survey the simple social-class variable, father's occupation, was the variable most associated with rates of delinquency [p. 165].

Type of school was also associated with official delinquency, as it was with admitted offenses. While not so important a variable as social class itself, "the rates of court appearances . . . produced a very high and significant correlation" with type of school (p. 166).

In Summary

Self-report measures seem to confirm or disconfirm official records of criminality depending upon where one looks and the kinds of observational instruments one uses. The hope that asking people about their crimes would provide criminologists with better data than official figures cannot be said to have been fulfilled. Where self-report measures *confirm* official statistics, observational studies, and surveys of victims, one can have some confidence in them. Where confessions of criminal conduct *disagree* with these other tallies of delinquencies, it will be political preference or "social philosophy," rather than good reasons, that determines which statistics one chooses. This is so because *asking people questions about their behavior is a poor way of observing it.*

CRITICISM OF SELF-REPORT MEASURES

Sociologists, this one included, continue to ask people questions. It is one thing, however, to ask people their *opinions* about a matter. It is quite another task to ask people to recall *what they have done*, and it is particularly ticklish to ask people to recall their "bad" behavior.

Confessional data are at least as weak as the official statistics they were supposed to improve upon. Self-report studies have been criticized on three grounds: (1) that their tools are poor and varied, (2) that the research designs have often been deficient and conducive to the drawing of false inferences, and (3) that the social settings in which the studies have been undertaken are so varied as to provide inconclusive tests of hypotheses that challenge other ways of counting crime.

1 Weak Instruments

"Measurement is the assignment of numbers to outcomes according to certain rules," Bohrnstedt tells us (1970, p. 81). This suggests that when we measure something, we can do so more or less well. The distinguishing characteristic of "good" measurement is principally, but not entirely, that the measuring instrument assigns numbers *reliably* and *validly*.

Reliability Reliability refers to the *consistency* with which a measuring device—a ruler, for example—yields the same numbers upon repeated applications. A ruler that reports a different size each time it is used to measure the same object is unreliable—assuming, of course, that the object itself has not grown or shrunk.

Psychometricians, those who specialize in constructing measures of human action, check the reliability of their instruments in two ways. One procedure notes the *stability* of results over some period of time, as in a test-retest performance. Assuming, again, that the thing being measured has not changed, a reliable gauge is one that gives similar results today and two weeks from now. Reliability, then, is a matter of degree, not an all-or-none phenomenon.

A second set of checks on reliability is a weaker test than a count of stability. These checks estimate the *internal consistency* of a measuring device. One way of doing this is to see whether different parts of a measuring instrument give the same results, where it is assumed that the entire instrument is measuring one thing. A reliable (internally consistent) measure of spelling ability, for example, would give a person similar scores on odd-numbered and even-numbered items in the spelling test.

Another check on internal consistency measures a quality called "scalability." A measure is consistent in the sense that it "scales" when people who are measured as "tall" are all taller than those who are measured as "short." A measure also scales when, for example, those who solve difficult mathematical problems more frequently solve the easier problems or when those who confess to serious crimes also confess to more trivial offenses.

Yet another form of reliability test applies presumably *equivalent forms* of the same measure to see whether the two gauges of "the same thing" yield similar results.

Neither the equivalent forms nor the internal-consistency tests of reliability give the satisfaction of a stability test. In criminology, however, convenience has made the internal-consistency check the most popular test of reliability.

Validity   Validity refers to the *accuracy* with which a measure gauges the concept being studied. Accuracy requires reliability. The requirement that a measuring instrument be reliable rests on the reasoning that one cannot tell *what* is being measured if scores are produced haphazardly by different parts of the measuring tool or in repeated applications of it. This means that the validity of a measure depends on its reliability.

Accurate counting can be done only with a reliable tool. If a ruler were to expand or contract wildly each time it was used, it could not measure with accuracy the relatively constant reality to which it is applied.

While a valid instrument must be a reliable one, a reliable tool need not be a valid measure. A gauge that measures consistently may still not be measuring what it is supposed to count. Measuring devices, like people, can consistently deceive.

Validity checks   The validity of a measuring instrument, like its reliability, has to be assessed. Psychometricians again do this in several ways, but the procedure of importance in criminology is that which checks the validity of a tally of crime against some *criterion*. The criterion (standard) against which counts of crime are evaluated is criminal acts. A crime measure is more or less valid as it more or less accurately counts what people have actually done.

As we have seen, however, no one knows the real range of others' criminal activity. A true criterion is lacking. We function, then, with more and less accurate estimates—as when we count crime on the basis of complaints logged by the police, what people say has happened to them, or what people say they themselves have done.

The quarrel among criminologists concerns which of these many measures of crime, if any, gives the most valid tally of crime where no tally is "really true." Examination of the reliability and validity of measures of crime based on confessions of it does *not* encourage substitution of self-reports for official statistics.

Reliability of Self-Reports   Of the many possible checks on the reliability of confessions of crime, the one most frequently used is a test of the internal consistency of self-report measures. A few studies have checked the retest reliability of confessions. For both types of reliability check, however, results are mixed.

Table 6-8 Correlations among Self-Report Items, White Boys Only

	1	2	3	4	5	6
1. Theft ($2)	1.00	.45	.26	.27	.28	.27
2. Theft ($2–$50)		1.00	.48	.30	.26	.27
3. Theft ($50 or more)			1.00	.32	.21	.20
4. Auto theft				1.00	.23	.22
5. Vandalism					1.00	.28
6. Battery						1.00

Source: Reprinted with permission from Hirschi, 1969, p. 56.

Hirschi, for example, reports modest correlations among the admissions to the six kinds of crime he measured. According to Table 6-8, these correlations range from a low of .20 between having stolen $50 or more and having deliberately beaten someone and a high of .48 between having stolen $2 to $50 and having stolen $50 or more. These associations are low for several reasons, including the fact that the time span covering these delinquencies was not necessarily the same for all respondents.

Some investigators report higher reliability for *retests* of admissions of criminality. J. P. Clark and Tifft (1966) found that 18.5 percent of the confessions originally given on a questionnaire were changed when the respondents were threatened with a lie-detector check on their veracity. Under such duress, the consistency of response, 81.5 percent, is probably quite adequate.

Dentler and Monroe (1961) report a very high reliability of response (.955) on a retest of their questionnaires, and a similar finding (.98) has been published by Kulik and his colleagues (1968). Kulik's study is of additional interest because it demonstrates that anonymous questionnaires are not necessarily more reliable than signed ones. Although *more* antisocial behavior was disclosed anonymously, the differences between anonymous and signed confessions were slight. The differences were more pronounced for the *minor* infractions than for the serious offenses, and they did not change the rank order of individuals on a measure of their delinquency.

These findings of reliability in confession are qualified by Farrington's study carried out in England.

Farrington's research David Farrington (1973) used a card-sort procedure for assessing delinquent behavior among lower-class, urban English boys. The names of 38 kinds of crime were printed on cards, which were stacked by each youth into "have done it" and "have not done it" piles.

This sample of boys was tested at ages 14 and 15 and again two years later, at ages 16 and 17. Scores were recorded for both *variety* of confessed delinquent act and the *total number* of such acts. Reliability was assessed by the consistency between self-reports at the different ages. Farrington found that *one-fourth* of early confessions turned into later denials.

Denial, in turn, varied with the gravity of the crime. Boys more frequently denied earlier admissions of the "heavier" crimes such as more serious theft and injurious assault. *Half* of all such grave offenses admitted at ages 14 and 15 were repudiated two years later.

With reliability of confessions of crime so uncertain, validity remains questionable.

Validity of Self-Reports The validity of self-report measures is crucial if these indicators are to be used in place of police statistics or surveys of victims. However, results of validation studies are not reassuring.

Validation of criminal confessions has been attempted in three ways: (1) by checking admissions of crime against self-reports of other antisocial behavior, (2) by comparing the self-reports of "known groups," and (3) by comparing confessions with official records. None of these procedures is satisfactory, and some of them assume what was questioned by the use of self-reports, namely, that official records are true ones.

1 Self-reports validated by self-reports Confessions of delinquency have been checked against admissions of other misconduct such as truancy or behavior resulting in school suspension or "contacts" with the police. This is, of course, a redundant form of validation—self-report against self-report. One would expect a high degree of association among such measures. The reported correlations are, however, modest.

Hirschi (1969) found that individual items in his self-report index correlated between .24 and .33 with truancy, between .18 and .28 with admitted school suspensions, and between .28 and .39 with admitted "contacts" with the police (p. 57).

Martin Gold (1966) attempted to check the accuracy of self-reports of delinquency by asking associates of his subjects whether they had observed the subjects in delinquent acts or whether the subjects had told the "validators" of such acts. This is, of course, a dubious mode of validation—checking one set of verbal responses against another. However, Gold concludes that 72 percent of his sample was probably telling the truth, while 17 percent seemed to be "outright concealers." The remaining 11 percent gave replies of questionable validity. In total, there was a 28 percent doubt.

2 Known-group validation "Known-group" validation looks at the patterns of scores from confessions of criminality that are made by segments of the population "known" to have behaved differently. For example, the self-report scores of "official" delinquents, like boys in "training schools," are compared with the scores of a sample of "nondelinquents." When this has been done, significant differences are reported on the confessional instruments between "known delinquents" and less offensive populations (Nye and Short, 1957; Voss, 1963).

This form of validation assumes, of course, what the self-report technique was to have tested, namely, that official delinquents really do behave differently. Such convergent validation gives some assurance that both official statistics and unofficial confessions are measuring the same thing. This convergence does not permit a conclusion about the greater validity of one measure over another, however. This can be said, too, about the third procedure for validating self-report instruments: checking admissions of crime against police or court records.

3 **Self-reports and official records**   It is paradoxical that critics of official records of criminal activity should revert to them as validators of data
from questionnaires and interviews. It is difficult to know what kind of finding
would constitute a validation and yet justify the preferred use of confessions.
Without an informed hypothesis, framed in advance, as to the expected relation between what people say they have done and what they get arrested for, investigators have no way of deciding how strong a correlation is
required to validate the confessions they collect. If the association between
admitted crime and official records approaches zero, presumably the self-
reports are invalid. If the association approaches unity, then one measure may
be substituted for the other. Between these poles, however, one cannot tell
whether a modest correlation signifies the validity, or invalidity, or either
instrument.

Checks against Official Data   Despite these difficulties, investigators
who have used confessions of criminality have sometimes checked the replies
they have received against official data. Results, again, have been mixed. Five
of the better investigations of this matter, in descending order of the validities
discovered, are those of Erickson and Empey, Voss, Farrington, Hirschi, and
McCandless and associates.

Erickson and Empey's study   Erickson and Empey (1963) interviewed
boys between the ages of 15 and 17 in Utah. They had a sample of 50 randomly
selected high school boys who had never been to court, a sample of 30 boys
who had been to court once, a sample of 50 randomly selected repeat offenders
who were on probation, and a sample of 50 randomly selected incarcerated
offenders. After the interviews, the names of all respondents were checked
against court records. "None of those who had been to court failed to say so in
the interview, nor did anyone fail to describe the offense(s) for which he was
charged" (p. 459).

The high coincidence of appearance in court and confession lends
confidence to, but does not prove, the validity of the admissions that may *not*
have resulted in arrest. However, a finding significant for our understanding of
the meaning of official statistics is Erickson and Empey's demonstration that
the *frequency* with which laws are broken is a significant factor in determining
arrest and appearance in court. The distinction between *frequency* of violations
and the *proportions* of persons who have committed an offense is important,
say Erickson and Empey, in helping "to avoid the pitfall of concluding that,
because large *proportions* of two different samples—i.e., students and institutionalized delinquents—have committed various offenses, the samples are
equally delinquent in terms of total volume" (p. 462).

It appears, again, that the law operates like a coarse net; only the biggest
fish are caught.

Voss's research   Voss (1963) was interested in testing whether official
statistics distorted the representation of ethnic groups in delinquent activities.
His locale was Honolulu, a multiethnic city, in which official records show a
disproportionate number of Hawaiians, male and female, charged with delin-

quencies and committed to institutions and an underrepresentation of Orientals so categorized.

Voss selected a 15.5 percent sample of seventh-graders to whom a reliable delinquency scale was administered and its scores compared by ethnicity with both delinquent charges laid against these diverse groups and with their differential institutionalization.

Of the 620 respondents, 52 were known to the police and had been apprehended for 83 offenses. Of these 83 violations, only four were denied on Voss's questionnaire, a remarkable degree of validity. Given this kind of validity, it is not surprising that Voss found a strong convergence between charges laid, juveniles incarcerated, and confessions of delinquency. All three measures pointed to the same social locations of youthful crime.

Farrington's study   Farrington's work with English boys (1973) yields results similar to Voss's. Confessions do correlate with crimes known to the police, according to this research, and both indicators point to the same social locations of crime production.

In Farrington's sample, official delinquents admitted to having committed many crimes (12 or more) about three times as frequently as "nondelinquents." Discounting for the unreliability of these self-reports (see page 108), something is being truly confessed. However, the forecasting value of such confessions is slight. Farrington notes from these data that "to correctly identify 24 future delinquents, it would be necessary to misidentify 53 future nondelinquents" (p. 108).

Not only do confessions add little to predictive power, but they also provide no new information. Farrington analyzed seven socioeconomic factors for their correlation with admitted delinquency: family income, family size, parental supervision, parental criminality, separation from parents, boy's educational attainment, and boy's nonverbal intelligence. All these factors bore some relation, in the expected direction, with admitted criminality. What is important for our purposes here is that confessions of crime draw a picture of offenders similar to that drawn by official statistics. "The self-reported deviants," says Farrington, "appeared to be quite similar to the official delinquents in family background and in personal characteristics" (p. 105).

Hirschi's study   Hirschi's work (1969) yields a more modest convergence of self-reports with official records than the preceding studies. Hirschi found that 15 percent of the white boys in his sample who said that they had *never* stolen anything of "medium value" actually had police records (p. 57). Hirschi does not tell us what this 15 percent had done to get on the police blotter, and so it is difficult to assess the degree of invalidity this figure may represent. Similarly, Hirschi found that 46 percent of the boys in his sample who admitted having stolen something of medium value had police records. Again, it is not clear whether this represents high or low validity.

A better test of validity in Hirschi's data is provided by answers to his question, "Have you ever been picked up by the police?" Fifty-five percent of the white boys who said they had been apprehended by the police did *not* have police records. Sixteen percent of the boys who said they had *never* been picked up by the police actually had records (p. 77). The figures are quite different for the black boys in Hirschi's sample. Among black respondents, 24 percent who said that they had been picked up by the police had no official records, while 36 percent of those who said that they had never been arrested actually had police records. Hirschi attributes some portion of this discrepancy between confession and official records to failure of memory and to arrests that occurred after administration of his questionnaire.

   The research of McCandless and his associates   An even less optimistic validation of self-report measures appears in the investigation by McCandless and others (1972). These psychologists studied institutionalized black and white boys, 15 to 17 years of age, who had been reared in impoverished environments in the southern United States. A self-report instrument was composed of 15 questions taken from scales developed by Nye and Short (1957) and Siegman (1966b). Answers given to the questionnaire were compared with official records, from which an index of "committed delinquency" was calculated that weighted the frequency and the seriousness of offenses known to have been committed by these boys. *The rank-order correlation between these overall measures of admitted and committed delinquency was a low .12.*

   The investigators checked specific answers to particular items in the self-report measure against each boy's intake sheet. In the authors' words,

> Forty of the 51 summary sheets contained information sufficient to check one or more of the Ss' responses to the admitted delinquency questionnaire. Of the total of 69 clear-cut items that could be checked, 48 or 70 per cent were accurate, while 21 or 30 per cent were inaccurate. The large percentage of inaccurate responses is particularly surprising when one considers that the items selected for inspection concerned those offenses that the boys had either been apprehended for or had previously admitted to. Nineteen (almost 50 percent) of the 40 Ss included in this subanalysis were found to have answered at least one item inaccurately [p. 285].

   Conclusion   These results range from high to low agreement between confessions of crime and official records. Where these measures disagree, choice of the more correct map of social reality becomes a function of one's confidence in the cartographer and the instruments used to draw the map. Instruments built out of people's answers to our questions are always tricky. There are good reasons for listening skeptically to what people tell us they have done.

Sources of Unreliability and Invalidity in Questionnaires and Interviews

Social scientists suffer from the bad habit of asking people questions and treating their answers as indicators of their deeds. By one recent count, 90 percent or more of the research reported in principal sociological journals was based on questions asked by means of interview or questionnaire (J. Brown and Gilmartin, 1969). The trouble with this practice is that a host of factors affect the reliability and validity of answers people give.

   Meaning   We give inconsistent and incorrect answers, in the first place, because words and phrases mean different things to us. The form of the question, the choice of words, and the position of the question in a series of items all affect what we think the question means (Durbin and Micklin, 1973; McCourt and D. G. Taylor, 1976; Nuckols, 1949–1950, 1953; Rugg and Cantril, 1942; Stember and Hyman, 1949–1950). In interviews, even vocal intonation affects the comprehension of meaning (Micklin and Durbin, 1969).

Memory   We also give incorrect answers because our memories are faulty. The validity of memory varies with time and with the way in which the memory is evoked (recall versus recognition, for example). Memory also varies with our interest in remembering and, of course, with personality traits (Alper, 1946; Haber, 1970; Waldfogel, 1948).

Memory fluctuates, too, with the emotionality of the subject matter; we tend to forget the unpleasant (Gilbert, 1938; Meltzer, 1930; Waldfogel, 1948; Zeigarnik, 1927). The tendency to forget the unpleasant becomes stronger when we are asked to confess our bad acts. Furthermore, how *wrong* our bad acts seem varies with the culture in which we have been reared (A. L. Edwards, 1957; Sudman and Bradburn, 1974).

Bias on the part of the interrogator   In addition to these many sources of error in answering questions about criminal conduct, there are sources of error in the interrogator. Bias on the part of the interviewer in following instructions and in recording responses, and even cheating by the interviewer, is a recognized distorting factor (Cahalan et al., 1947; Gales and Kendall, 1957; Hanson and Marks, 1958; H. L. Smith and Hyman, 1950).

Lying   Finally, a difficulty in using confessions to measure criminality is the sad fact that people do not always tell the truth. We do not tell the truth for a variety of reasons. The "prestige" of a question, the "social desirability" of its content, has a well-documented impact upon the kind of answer given to it (A. L. Edwards, 1957).

People sometimes lie to conceal their faults, even from themselves, and they sometimes lie when they think that a confession of criminality will make them seem glamorous. Other motivations for practicing deception include carelessness in attending to what is asked and the delinquent's joy in "jiving" his "square" interrogator.

The record of lying to interviewers is well documented. Parry and Crossley (1950), for example, asked citizens of Denver a number of questions in situations where the accuracy of their answers could be checked. The proportion of honest answers ran from a high of 98 percent about having a telephone and 96 percent about homeownership to lows of about 50 percent for voting behavior.

H. McCord (1951) showed that we can get people to lie by asking them about things that do not exist. Thus one-third of his sample remembered having voted in a "special election" that was never held, and 53 percent said that they had heard of the nonexistent "Taft-Johnson-Pepper bill on veterans' housing."

Between 33 and 45 percent of citizens lie when asked the highest school grade they have completed (Haberman and Sheinberg, 1966; Schreiber, 1976); about half lie when asked about having received welfare assistance (Weiss and

R. V. Davis, 1960); and there is considerable deceit about purchases (Neter, 1970) and such sensitive matters as income and occupation (E. Hardin and Hershey, 1960; Schreiber, 1976; C. N. Weaver and Swanson, 1974; Withery, 1954). And, of course, people often lie about their age. The phenomenon of "age heaping," of choosing a "round number," has been repeatedly observed, and its variations have been noted cross-culturally (Stockwell, 1966; Van de Walle, 1966; Wicks and Stockwell, 1975; Zelnik, 1964). In the United States, for example, ages ending in 0 are reported twice as often as ages ending in 5, the next most preferred number.

Interaction There is, in short, an interaction between the interviewer and the respondent, as there is in all communication, and the amount of threat felt in connection with confessing one's crimes to a stranger varies with the status of the respondent and the interrogator. People differ in their "openness" to questions, but in general we are more willing to tell the truth to people of our own race, sex, and class than to "foreigners." This effect has been well documented (Benney et al., 1956; Cosper, 1972; Freeman and Butler, 1976; Hyman, 1954; D. Katz, 1942; Kirsch et al., 1965; Lenski and Leggett, 1960; McClelland, 1974; J. A. Williams, 1964).

The many influences that make questions and answers doubtful measures of behavior should encourage caution in asking for confessions of crime. We shall continue to ask questions, but we should do so with better controls on their validity and without leaping to a conclusion about behavior on the basis of a verbal response.

Correction An attempt to reduce defects in counting crime from confessions has been described by the English psychologist Belson and his colleagues (1970, 1975). These investigators have taken care to develop more sensitive methods for finding out who has stolen how much. Their procedures involve interviews in a depersonalized atmosphere in which threat is removed and anonymity is assured. A list of offenses is used after it has been tested for understanding by the boys studied. Interviewers are trained and strictly regulated, and their note taking is reduced to a minimum. The interview schedule also contains "trap questions" that serve as validators of replies. Belson's findings are reported in Chapters 7 and 9. In general, they confirm the information provided by official statistics.

Research Design and Fair Inference

The defects of self-report measures of criminal conduct do not end with flaws in the instruments. Research design has also been poor and has encouraged improper inferences from ambiguous data.

The trouble derives from the difficulties suggested earlier in comparing official records with measures that are supposed to correct them. Without an external criterion against which to validate statistics—a criterion *independent* of either measure—we can quarrel about the relative accuracy of competing measures, but we cannot test their correctness.

Suppose that researchers interested in the fruitfulness (criminality) of different regions (social classes, ethnic groups) doubt whether counting oranges (crimes known to the police) provides a fair measure of a region's productivity. The skeptics propose that counting apples (confessions) may yield a more accurate estimate of fruitfulness. To prove their case, they compare the distribution of apples and oranges in regions that produce both. Assume, now, that the different regions are found to contribute different proportions of apples and oranges. What has the exercise demonstrated?

A comparison of a new measure of uncertain validity (self-reports) with an old measure of moderate validity (official records) tells us nothing about their relative accuracy *unless there is assurance that both instruments are designed to measure the same thing.* However, questionnaires about delinquency have been heavily weighted with *trivial* offenses, the very kind that most of us have committed and that are least likely to result in arrest. These instruments have even included large numbers of noncriminal acts like "doing things my parents told me not to do" and "being out at night just fooling around after I was supposed to be home" (J. P. Clark and Wenninger, 1962).

Shifting the Cutting Point   From such incomparable measures false inferences can be drawn, and have been drawn, about the true distribution of delinquency among classes or races. The wrong conclusions are stimulated by the artifice of the *shifting cutting point.* The investigator decides that scores above and below x of his or her self-report scale constitute, respectively, being "delinquent" and being "nondelinquent." In one study, for example, it was decided that scores above the median constituted "delinquency" (Chambliss and Nagasawa, 1969). The researcher then compares the proportions of these so-called "delinquents" and "nondelinquents" among social classes or ethnic groups with the proportions given by their official records. *Since it is not known what score on the questionnaire, if any, represents activities equivalent to those for which the same people were arrested, the cutting points are arbitrary.* By moving the cutting points from, say, the 50th percentile to the 70th percentile, different proportions of classes of people may be categorized as "delinquent."

Such arbitrary assignment encourages false inference. False inference results from a semantic trick, the trick of implying that when the word "delinquent" is applied on the basis of arbitrarily grouped scores from a questionnaire, it refers to the same behaviors as those counted in police records.

By contrast with this poor procedure, a fair comparison between two such different measures of criminality requires that the frequency and gravity of admitted offenses be correlated, *individual by individual* among different classes or races, with the crimes for which these persons have been charged.

Varied Social Settings

It has been pointed out that the relation between confessions of criminality and some of the "social locators" of crime, like income and ethnicity, varies with the instruments used and the places studied. This is to be expected. Interpretation of the results of research with self-report tools must consider the social settings in which they have been employed. These settings have varied greatly.

For example, Dentler and Monroe (1961) studied seventh- and eighth-grade students in three small Kansas towns, Voss (1966) asked for confessions of delinquency in a highly Oriental city (Honolulu), and J. P. Clark and Wenninger (1962) quizzed schoolchildren in four Illinois locations that varied from a rural farm setting to a black section of Chicago to one rich suburb and one industrial suburb.

Such variation of types of communities is an important qualifier of the impact of any variable, like money, upon the behaviors to be explained. A researcher who is trying to ascertain the effect of "social class" upon criminality, as is required by many theories of crime causation, must consider that the *ways of life* of people categorized by their income, occupation, or education differ widely depending upon the social setting in which they live as rich or poor, learned or ignorant members of society. Being relatively poor in rural Scandinavia or rural Mexico has an altogether different meaning for one's style of life from being relatively poor in New York City. Being "working-class" in an English town that is ethnically homogeneous, highly religious, and family-centered is a markedly different experience from being "working-class" in a heterogeneous American metropolis. The community setting, then, makes a difference to the expected impact of possibly causal factors, like social status, upon misbehavior. This qualification affects the interpretation of *all* criminal statistics, of course, not just the self-report measures.

IN SUMMARY

Considerable attention has been paid to the utility of self-report measures of criminality because they have been devised and employed as correctives of the apparent deficiencies in official statistics. An evaluation of these unofficial ways of counting crime does *not* fulfill the promise that they would provide a better enumeration of offensive activity.

We know best where certain kinds of crime are generated when the major measures of criminality converge. Fortunately for those who would assess the competing explanations of crime, confessions of delinquency, surveys of victims, test situations, direct and indirect observations, and official records point to similar social sites in both developing countries and industrialized states as producing more murderers, muggers, rapists, robbers, burglars, and heavy thieves than others. We also know something—although with less certainty—about the social locations of less visible crimes like shoplifting and embezzlement.

These social locations constitute the major correlates of crime to be explained by theories of crime causation. The next chapter will describe these correlates in greater detail. However, in thinking about these correlates of crime, we should bear in mind that our defined scope concerns principally the more serious predatory crimes, the crimes *mala in se* that are the objects of most citizens' concern. It bears repeating, too, that these correlates are not necessarily the causes of offenses, but simply the material with which the sociological explicator works.

Social Location of Serious Crime

Explaining crime requires that one be able to describe criminal acts and actors and the social settings of different crimes. The search is for "things that make a difference." This search is an attempt to find the *causes* of crime. It proceeds, however, by counting the *correlates* of crime. Correlates are conditions or events that "go with" the criminal activity. When these conditions or events are of an interpersonal nature, they constitute crime's social location.

On Correlation   For those who have not yet studied statistics, a comment on correlation is necessary.

There are many measures of association. Most of them express the *degree* of association between two variables (things that vary in measured quality or quantity) as decimals between zero (no association) and 1 (perfect correlation). *The direction, degree, and shape of an association can vary.*

It is customary to call the variable considered to be causal, or "independent," x and to call the variable considered to be its effect, or "dependent," y. When measures of x and y are plotted on a graph, called a "scattergram" or "scatterplot," it is again a convention to draw the x variable along the horizontal axis (abscissa), with small amounts on the left and larger amounts toward the right. The y variable is plotted on the vertical axis (ordinate), with small amounts at the bottom and larger quantities toward the top. Thus a graph describing measures of IQ and income might be drawn like Figure 7-1. This would indicate a perfect, rectilinear (straight-line), *positive* association between IQ and income, and it would be read as saying that as x increases or decreases, so does y. The association could run in the opposite direction, of course, and describe a perfect, rectilinear, *negative* (inverse) association between IQ and income, as in Figure 7-2.

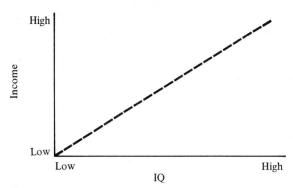

Figure 7-1

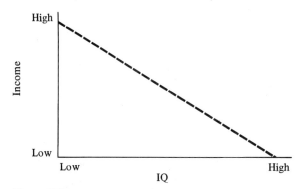

Figure 7-2

Discussions in the social studies speak constantly of positive and negative correlations. Graphically, this is their meaning. However, it must be remembered that *direction* is only one quality of an association. Variables are also correlated by *degree*, that is, by the "closeness" of their association. Furthermore, there is no reason in nature why the things we are measuring must be associated in a straight line, as they have been drawn above in Figures 7-1 and 7-2. Associations may have different *shapes*; they may curve in many ways. This means that there may be "threshold effects," that associations may not be observed for *x* and *y* between values of this and that, but are observed, to such-and-such a degree, after a certain threshold (value) has been passed.

These points, which are elaborated on in courses in statistics, should be remembered when thinking about those correlates of crime that are examined by criminologists in their search for the social location of different kinds of crimes.

Correlations and causes   Locating the social sites of different crimes helps *describe* these activities, but some thinkers leap to the conclusion that the correlated conditions are causes. Such a logical leap is often unjustified. It is more accurate to interpret correlations as *candidates* nominated to be causes.

It becomes the job of explanations, then, to give good reasons for accepting one set of candidates rather than another. In brief, candidates for causes have to be validated. This is to say that not everything that "goes with" the event to be explained is deemed to have produced it. Correlation is a necessary sign of causation, but it is not a sufficient sign. It is not even a clear sign, for we do not know from the correlations that social scientists compute "how much *power* is demonstrated by the finding of a significant association" (Nettler, 1977).

Causal power refers to a prediction, a bet, that if we change x this much, we shall affect z that much. The trouble with social scientists' "causes" is that one cannot infer causal efficacy from correlational significance. Closeness of association is not a measure of productive power.

Causation is, nevertheless, a common idea and an indispensable one. It is not, however, a clear concept. In fact, there is probably more than one idea embedded in the notion of causation (Collingwood, 1940; Hertzberg, 1975). Without becoming entangled in philosophical questions about the meaning of "causation" and the ways in which causes are known, it is sufficient for our purposes here to note that criminologists study the social locations of various offenses as part of their effort to explain differences in conduct. The social locations of the serious crimes constitute facts with which explanations of crime are built. They are also the facts that such explanations must make comprehensible.

It is important, then, to look at the major correlates of the more damaging offenses. But, in reviewing these associations, it should be remembered that these correlations do not in themselves describe causes and that the *strength* and *shape* of these relationships vary with what surrounds them. The connections to be described are not absolutes; they do not operate in a vacuum. They are themselves variables whose meaning for behavior changes with the social setting in which the association occurs.

AGE AND SEX

Two of the most striking and persistent "conditions" associated with the risk of committing serious crimes are being young and being male. If one groups people by age and sex and then looks at their proportional contribution to arrest or conviction rates, the worldwide experience is that young men make higher contributions to crime than old persons and women.

In England and Wales, for example, convictions for indictable offenses tend to peak among boys 14 to 16 years of age. This sex and age differential obtains despite the liberal use of cautioning by the police instead of arrest, particularly at the earlier ages. McClintock and Avison (1968) provide a picture of indictable offenses that dramatically indicates the higher crime rates of teenagers and males (Figure 7-3). A similar pyramid of criminality appears in all European and North American countries (Clinard and Abbott, 1973; Sveri, 1960).

Compared with their proportions in the population, young people are arrested far more frequently than middle-aged or elderly citizens. Table 7-1 shows that, in 1974, American children 10 to 12 years old, and some younger ones, accounted for twice the number of arrests for theft as would be expected

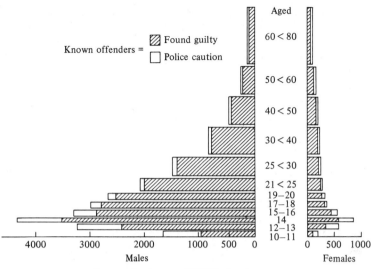

Figure 7-3 The proportion of known male and female offenders in each age group, indictable offenses only, England and Wales, 1965. (*Reprinted with permission from McClintock and Avison,* Crime in England and Wales, *1968, diagram 7.*)

from their representation in the population. Teenagers, who constituted 35 percent of the population, accounted for 56.1 percent of arrests for major offenses against property and for 33.4 percent of arrests for violent crimes.

The most violent years are the twenties. Persons in this age bracket constituted 30.5 percent of the American population in 1974, but they account-

Table 7-1 Selected Serious Crimes (Arrests) by Age Group, United States, 1974

Age group	Percent of population	Percent of arrests for violent crimes*	Percent of arrests for offenses against property+
10 and under	1.2	0.5	2.5
11–12	2.2	1.3	5.3
13–19	35.0	33.4	56.1
20–24	19.4	24.4	16.7
25–29	11.1	14.8	7.6
30–34	7.3	8.7	3.9
35–39	5.7	5.6	2.4
40–44	5.1	4.0	1.7
45–49	4.5	2.8	1.3
50–54	3.6	1.9	1.0
55–59	2.2	1.0	0.6
60 and over	2.6	1.4	0.9

* Violent crimes are murder, forcible rape, robbery, and aggravated assault. Because of rounding, percentages do not add up to 100.
+ Crimes against property are burglary, larceny, and automobile theft.
Source: FBI, 1975, table 34.

ed for almost 40 percent of the arrests for murder, forcible rape, robbery, and aggravated assault. Table 7-1 indicates that one of the best "cures" for crime is age.

The association of age with criminal conduct varies, of course, with the kind of crime. In industrialized countries, burglary, automobile theft, and the "ordinary larcenies" tend to be crimes of the teens and earlier years. The more "intelligent" larcenies like forgery, counterfeiting, fraud, and embezzlement peak during the prime of life, ages 25 to 34.

Age, Sex, and Repetition

There are some interesting interactions between the age at which one begins criminal activity, gender, and repetition of crime. For example, women tend to be arrested for the "chemical offenses"—drunkenness, possession or sale of dangerous drugs, violation of liquor laws, and driving while intoxicated—at earlier ages than men (FBI, 1975, table 32). There is also evidence that, in Western cultures at least, females who become addicted to the "comforting" chemicals do so at earlier ages than males, with graver consequences, and with less probability of reform (Blane, 1968; Block, 1965; Curlee, 1970; Karpman, 1948; Lisansky, 1958; Schuckit, 1972; Sclare, 1970).

Regardless of this possible sex difference, the younger a person of either sex is when first arrested, the greater likelihood of a second arrest and, in general, the shorter the time span between offenses (Mannheim and L. T. Wilkins, 1955; Sellin, 1958).

Sex and Kinds of Crime

The types of crime that men and women tend to commit have also differed. Until recently only men have been charged with forcible rape, and it has been principally, but not entirely, women who have been arrested for prostitution and infanticide. However, this pattern is open to change. For example, in a recent Canadian trial, a woman was convicted of being an accessory to forcible rape, having aided a man in an attack upon another woman. Furthermore, men do rape men, particularly in prisons (Carroll, 1974; A. J. Davis, n.d.), but the charge in such cases is usually something else—like buggery, sodomy, or assault. Because of the difficulties in proving heterosexual rape (see pages 56–57), it is being suggested that such attacks by men on women also be charged as something other than rape—that is, assault.

Cultures and Sex Differences in Crime

Although males have consistently higher arrest and conviction rates than females and although they have exhibited this proclivity over the years in a variety of cultures, *the disparity between the sexes fluctuates with the kind of crime, with time, and with the social setting.* For example, the rate for males of *crimes against the person* exceeds the rate for females in Canada and the United States by more than 8 to 1, but the rate for males of *crimes against property* exceeds the rate for females by about half that, something on the order of 4 to 1 in recent years.

The influence of culture is strong here and affects the sex ratio of crimes exhibited at different times and in different places. For instance, it must not be concluded that any men, anywhere, are always more murderous than any women. As an illustration, Wolfgang's detailed study of homicide in Philadelphia (1958) reports that white males were convicted of criminal homicide eight times as frequently as white females. By contrast, the sex ratio for this offense among blacks was half that, 4:1. However, the disparity in cultures is such that black females in Philadelphia had a recorded homicide rate three times that of white males (Wolfgang, 1958, p. 55).

It is true that men generally produce higher crime rates than women. However, the sex ratios for criminal activity are not constants. The styles of crime differentially practiced by men and women are in flux. The changes are themselves conditioned by the cultures in which they are embedded. For example, in an early study of the criminality of women, Pollak (1951) observes that where poisoning has been recorded as a specific homicidal method, as in Italy, it has appeared as a specialty of women. During the late nineteenth century, 123 women were convicted of the "Borgia practice" for every 100 men. What is of more importance is the conclusion Pollack draws from data obtained in Canada and the United States and in Europe: that if one looks at all the serious crimes for which men and women are convicted, homicide constitutes a larger proportion of all crimes committed by females then of all crimes committed by males.

Equality and Changing Sex Ratios in Crime

The most interesting hypothesis advanced to explain cultural differences in the sex ratios of criminal activities, and changes in these ratios over time, is the suggestion that as women become the equals of men in terms of rights and privileges, they also become their equals in terms of crime.

Cross-culturally, the more distinct and different the roles of the sexes, the wider the reported disparity between their crime rates. As cultures approximate unisexuality, the disparity between the crime rates for the two sexes narrows. For example, Houchon (1967) calculated sex ratios in crime for nine regions of Africa and found that the crime rates for men exceeded the rates for women by differences ranging from 900 to 1 to more than 20,000 to 1. The cultures he studies draw distinct lines between male and female work and privileges. Findings of the same order are reported for Ceylon (1957), where almost all (98 percent) juvenile probationers are male, and for prewar Algiers and Tunis, where the number of men convicted of crime exceeded the number of women by almost 3,000 to 1 (Hacker, 1941).

Such disparities contrast with the figures for North America and Western Europe, where women more closely approach equality with men. For example, P. Wolf (1965) studied a representative sample of Danes and found that 18.8 percent of the men and 2.3 percent of the women had criminal records, a ratio of about 8:1. Similarly, British criminal statistics report that for England and Wales in 1970, the ratio of convictions of males to convictions of females for all indictable offenses was 6.1:1 (Command paper #4708, 1970).

Changes over time, as well as cross-cultural comparisons, support the forecast that as women achieve equality in other spheres, they will also close the gap between their crime rates and those of men. This phenomenon is apparent in Western countries, particularly among people under 18 years of age, as Tables 7-2 through 7-5 show. Such data have been given a cultural explanation called the "convergence hypothesis."

The Convergence Hypothesis   The convergence hypothesis is the assumption that as the social roles of the sexes are equalized, the difference between the sexes in terms of crime rates is diminished. Fox and Hartnagel (1976) provide an interesting test of the hypothesis by analyzing fluctuations in Canadian crime rates from 1931 through 1968 for their association with three measures of changing sex roles.

A "total fertility rate" was used as a measure of women's adherence to the familial role, and it was hypothesized that this would be *negatively* correlated with crime rates among women. Women's participation in the labor force and the proportion of postsecondary educational degrees awarded women were used as measures of more equal sex roles, and it was hypothesized that these signs would be *positively* associated with crime rates among women. Criminal activity was gauged from *conviction* rates for indictable (serious) offenses.

In general, the convergence hypothesis was confirmed by these data. In the aggregate, the familial role is negatively associated with criminality among women, while the work-education factor is positively associated with women's involvement in crime. These effects are particularly striking in connection with convictions for theft.

It bears noting that this conclusion refers to correlated changes *in a population*. It should not be interpreted as having individual significance, that is, as meaning that particular women who work outside the home or receive more education are necessarily more prone to commit a crime.

Toward Sexual Equality   Some of the trends observed during the 1960s are continuing in the 1970s. In some countries, for some crimes, women are closing the gap in criminality between themselves and men.

Patterns of this change are mixed, of course. In Canada, for example, crime rates, which increased slowly during the 1960s, seem to have leveled off in the 1970s, and the pattern of criminality among men and women had not changed as of 1972–1973 (Statistics Canada, 1974a).

In Japan, by contrast, criminality among women increased 22 percent in the first five years of this decade, while overall crime rates were declining (*U.S. News & World Report*, 1975b).

Britain reveals yet another pattern—a pattern of increased criminality among women qualified by age and type of crime. Between 1968 and 1974 the number of women *convicted* of serious offenses rose by 54 percent, more than twice the rate of increase in convictions of men, which was 25 percent (*U.S. News & World Report*, 1975b).

The march toward equal crime rates is most striking among juveniles. Convictions of young girls in Britain rose three times as fast as convictions of boys, and the tendency toward crime among young people is dramatically illustrated in convictions for violent crimes. Table 7-2 indicates that women's

Table 7-2 Number of Men and Women and the Percentage of Females Found Guilty of Violence against the Person, by Age and Sex, in England and Wales, 1950, 1960–71[a]

Year	Under 17		17–20		21–29		30 and over		All ages	
	N	% female	N	% female	N	% female	N	% female	N	% female
1950	315	1.3	468	4.5	1577	6.8	1479	12.4	3,839	8.0
1960	1583	2.7	2762	1.8	3421	3.8	2493	9.7	10,259	4.5
1961	1717	2.4	3006	2.2	3909	5.0	2887	8.5	11,519	4.3
1962	1787	2.4	3293	2.9	3993	4.8	2913	9.2	11,986	5.0
1963	1896	3.0	3463	2.8	4361	4.6	3112	8.7	12,832	4.8
1964	1978	3.6	3985	2.1	4729	4.7	3449	9.4	14,141	5.0
1965	2004	5.8	4495	2.4	5238	5.1	3764	8.8	15,501	5.3
1966	1793	7.1	4616	2.6	5530	5.5	4097	8.1	16,036	5.5
1967	1840	6.6	4849	2.5	5681	5.1	4706	7.9	17,076	5.3
1968	1882	7.7	5051	2.4	6330	5.4	5075	8.3	18,338	5.6
1969	2249	10.8	5742	2.6	7157	4.8	5707	7.7	20,855	5.4
1970	2827	12.6	6298	3.7	7963	5.0	6355	7.4	22,443	5.8
1971	3574	13.6	6927	4.0	8698	5.0	7067	7.0	26,266	5.8

[a] The number includes men and women.
Source: Reprinted with permission from R. J. Simon, 1975, table 8–2. Adapted from Criminal Statistics, England and Wales. Presented to Parliament by the Secretary of State for the Home Department by Command of Her Majesty, July, 1961, 1964, 1969, 1970, 1971. London: Her Majesty's Stationery Office.

overall conviction rates for assault and murder in England and Wales remained fairly constant through the 1960s and was even lower than in 1950. However, convictions of girls *under 17 years of age* jumped from around 1 percent of all persons found guilty of violence in 1950 to about 14 percent in 1971.

While American women have not achieved equality with men in the commission of the major crimes, they have been closing the gap. This is particularly notable among women under 18 years of age during the years from 1960 through 1975 (see Tables 7-3 to 7-5).

When compared with older women and with juvenile and adult males, young American women dramatically increased their commission of negligent manslaughter and assault. They have also been increasingly involved in drug violations and arrests for drunken driving.

American women in general, when compared with men, have increased their arrest rate for illegal possession of weapons, disorderly conduct, burglary, larceny, automobile theft, possession of stolen property, forgery, counterfeiting, fraud, and embezzlement.

These *rates of increase* do not mean equality between the sexes in the commission of crimes. However, from such trends, one sociologist forecasts equality between women and men in arrests for larceny, fraud, and embezzlement by 1990 (R. J. Simon, 1975, p. 42).

Although women have been increasingly charged with murder and nonnegligent manslaughter as well as other violent crimes (Table 7-3), they still contribute far less frequently than men to physical attacks. In Canada in recent years, less than 9 percent of all charges for crimes of violence have been laid against women. In the United States this proportion runs around 12 percent, and closer to 15 percent if forcible-rape arrests are omitted (FBI, 1976, table 31; Statistics Canada, 1974a, p. xiii).

Some sociologists, such as Freda Adler (1975, p. 16), find it "curious" that there should be a continuing disparity in violence between the sexes. Adler

Table 7-3. Changes in American Arrest Rates for Selected Violent Crimes, 1960 Compared with 1975, by Sex and Age (Percent) *

Offense	Males	Males under 18 years	Females	Females under 18 years
Murder and nonnegligent manslaughter	138.2	205.7	105.7	275.0
Manslaughter by negligence	-20.2	30.2	-4.8	333.3
Robbery	214.3	361.3	380.5	646.8
Aggravated assault	130.6	217.1	118.8	438.0
Other assaults	58.3	209.9	137.6	413.0
Weapons: carrying, possessing	154.3	105.3	291.1	410.6
Disorderly conduct	-20.6	31.1	51.0	64.0

* All percentages are *increases* unless otherwise noted.
Source: FBI, 1976, table 31.

Table 7-4 Changes in American Arrest Rates for Selected Property Crimes, 1960 Compared with 1975, by Sex and Age (Percent) *

Offense	Males	Males under 18 years	Females	Females under 18 years
Burglary: breaking and entering	116.9	132.0	288.8	327.5
Larceny: theft	129.6	117.7	464.6	457.3
Motor-vehicle theft	35.6	19.5	163.2	140.3
Forgery and counterfeiting	30.8	129.8	192.3	234.3
Fraud and embezzlement	91.1	224.1	488.5	421.6
Stolen property: buying, receiving, possessing	515.1	622.2	727.2	824.3

* All percentages are *increases.*
Source: FBI, 1976, table 31.

considers the disparity curious because she assumes, as do some other observers (D. Klein, 1974; R. J. Simon, 1975), that committing crime is only, or largely, a matter of opportunity, and certainly not a function of biology. Thus opportunity seems to explain the increased commission of fraud, forgery, and embezzlement by females. And it seems to account for women's involvement in such crimes in both capitalist and communist countries (*U.S. News & World Report*, 1975b). The hypothesis is that changes in occupational structure now allow these kinds of crime to be committed by women.

It is not apparent, however, what greater opportunities women require if they are to achieve equality in violence. It will be argued later (Chapter 12) that "opportunity" is not a clear concept and that not all circumstances called "opportunities" are similarly conceived or equally used.

Nevertheless, there are rumblings of change in violence among women, and Adler notes that they are becoming leaders in "violent, revolutionary" crimes such as "ravaging banks, robbing commercial establishments, and assassinating victims with cyanide-tipped bullets" (1975, pp. 20–21). The criminal status of women in the United States has also been elevated by Ruth Eisenmann-Schier's having become the first female on the FBI's list of "Ten

Table 7-5 Changes in American Arrest Rates for Selected Drug- and Alcohol-related Offenses, 1960 Compared with 1975, by Sex and Age (Percent) *

Offense	Males	Males under 18 years	Females	Females under 18 years
Narcotic-drug violations	1,028.0	4,269.1	1,011.9	5,377.9
Violations of liquor laws	41.9	166.2	46.2	355.8
Drunkenness	−45.9	62.9	−52.9	119.3
Driving under the influence	164.0	490.0	284.7	846.0

* All percentages are *increases* unless otherwise noted.
Source: FBI, 1976, table 31.

Most Wanted Fugitives" (FBI, 1968). Women are no longer a novelty on the
FBI's list, and in recent years as many as 3 of the 10 most-sought fugitives have
been females. These women have been wanted for "murder, bank robbery,
kidnapping, and a variety of violent, revolutionary acts" (Adler, 1975, p. 20).

In Summary

Interpretation of these mixed patterns of sex ratios in crime by age and style of
crime does not require forecasts of absolute equality between the sexes in
criminality. For our present purposes it is sufficient to say that men generally
are more criminally offensive than women, particularly when it comes to
serious physical attack.[1] Furthermore, sex ratios in criminality vary with
culturally assigned differences and similarities in sex roles. As women approach equality with men in work and play, they approach equality in crime.

OCCUPATION, INCOME, AND OTHER INDICATORS OF SOCIAL STATUS

Of all the factors that condition our lives, money has become the most popular
symbol. It is the sign of what ails us and what cures us. Sophie Tucker used to
say, "I've been rich and I've been poor. Rich is better." One of America's most
honored bank robbers, Willie "The Actor" Sutton, would have agreed. "Why
do you rob banks?" an official helper once asked him. "Because that's where
the money is," Sutton replied. The most persistent explanation of stealing, and
of the violence connected with it, is that some people want what others have.

Given the allure of money and our desire for the things it buys, it is no
surprise to find that in all countries for which we have records, a *negative*
association appears between measures of social position, like income and
occupational prestige, and official measures of criminality, whether they be
measures of arrest, conviction, or imprisonment. Within each state, people with
less money, less schooling, lower occupational status, and less measured
intelligence are disproportionately represented in the statistics on the serious
crimes (Cooper, 1960; Mack, 1964; T. P. Morris, 1957; C. F. Schmid, 1960;
P. Wolf, 1962; Wolfgang, Figlio, and Sellin, 1972).

By Which Measure?

The association between socioeconomic status and crime varies, of course,
with the kind of crime. It varies, too, with the measure of crime that is used.
The negative correlation between status and overall offense rates is most
clearly present when official records are used to locate criminality, and it is
secondarily indicated in test situations.

It has been argued, however, that official statistics themselves reflect a
judicial bias against the poor. They more strongly measure the immunity that
money gives, it is alleged, than differences in behavior. Motivated by this

---

[1]There are other forms of aggression, of course, besides physical attack. One can be hostile
and aggressive through the law, for example, and with words. Sex ratios in these forms of attack
have yet to be measured.

suspicion, some sociologists have challenged the usual association of crime and poverty by using self-report measures. Thus an often-cited study by Nye and others (1958) found little relationship between the social-class position of American high school children and admitted delinquencies. But, as we have seen (page 116), confessional measures, including those employed by Nye and his colleagues, neglect the serious crimes in favor of trivial offenses— peccadilloes such as "driving without a license, openly defying parents' authority, petty larceny, taking automobiles without permission, drinking alcoholic beverages, and having heterosexual relations."

Furthermore, as we have noted, confessional surveys do not yield consistent results concerning the relation between socioeconomic status and crime. Much depends on the sample studied, on how the confessions are extracted, and on which delinquencies are investigated.

Thus, in contrast with earlier work in the United States, the study of Belson and others (1975) showed that although *all* of the 1,425 boys in their London sample had stolen something, the kind of stealing varied with the occupational status of their fathers. Belson's interviewers questioned boys about their involvement in 44 kinds of theft, from "getting out of paying one's fare" and "stealing from work" to "breaking and entering." These 44 varieties of theft are interrelated; however, they are interrelated in such a way that ". . . the more serious the level of stealing of a given kind . . . the more frequently [a boy] commits that type of theft" (p. 87). When "theft scores" are assigned for the *variety* of stealing that boys admit to and for the *amount* (money value) stolen, both measures of thieving show a tendency for sons of unskilled and semiskilled workers to admit more frequently to more criminal activity than children of higher-status families. Table 7-6 plots the distribution by variety and amount of stealing and shows other interesting relations, namely, that Jewish boys say they have stolen less than other boys and that boys in "public" (i.e., private) schools say they have stolen less than those in more vocational schools. In addition, boys who say they seek "fun and excitement" more frequently say they steal. Most of these self-reported associations are the kind confirmed by official statistics.

The studies done by Elmhorn in Sweden (1965) and by McDonald in England (1969b) reveal the usual negative association of status and admitted delinquencies, and Hirschi's research (1969) carried out in the United States points in the same direction. Furthermore, those investigations of self-reported crime which have attended to the *frequency* and *gravity* of admitted offenses, rather than merely to the distribution of all offenses among social classes, more frequently indicate a negative correlation between social position and criminality.

Parenthetical Caution

The research reporting this type of correlation shows that it is not fixed and that its shape and its strength vary by region, by type of offense, and over time. There are styles of being rich, poor, and middling, and the social setting in which ascribed status is experienced makes a difference to behavior. In short,

Table 7-6 Quartile Distribution of Variety and Amount of Stealing by Boys' Characteristics (Theft at Level 2 or Over) *

Characteristics of boys	Index of variety of stealing				Index of amount of stealing			
	Low score quartile			High score quartile	Low score quartile			High score quartile
	Q.1 (%)	Q.2 (%)	Q.3 (%)	Q.4 (%)	Q.1 (%)	Q.2 (%)	Q.3 (%)	Q.4 (%)
Social class								
Professional, semi-professional	33	33	19	15	28	35	23	15
Skilled, non-manual	20	27	29	24	20	27	27	26
Skilled, manual	24	20	29	27	24	24	26	26
Partly skilled	22	24	27	27	23	28	23	26
Unskilled	19	20	29	32	19	27	29	26
Born in UK or not								
Yes	24	25	26	24	23	28	25	23
No	31	21	27	21	31	24	22	23
Religion								
Protestant	23	25	28	24	23	28	22	27
Catholic	21	27	25	27	23	22	29	26
Christian	25	13	27	35	21	22	34	23
Jewish	44	33	16	7	33	35	29	3
None	20	26	26	28	22	27	26	25
Type of school last attended								
Secondary modern	19	20	31	30	20	25	27	28
Comprehensive	24	25	24	27	23	26	26	25
Grammar	32	33	20	15	30	30	23	17
Public	39	29	24	8	28	43	15	14
Does he go out "just looking for fun and excitement"?								
Yes	15	21	32	32	15	28	28	29
No	31	27	22	19	31	27	23	19
All	25	25	26	24	24	28	25	23

* Theft Level 2 or over = value of 1 shilling sixpence or more. Because of percentage rounding, totals do not always equal 100.
Source: Reprinted with permission from Belson, 1975, table 2.10.

we must be careful, once more, not to interpret the tendencies described by the reported correlations as uniformities or as causal connections. Locating crime socially is a step toward explaining it, *but the location is not the explanation.* Particularly, we should avoid confusing the *location* with the *cause.*

For example, we note that in modern countries hospitals are the principal sites of deaths without concluding that hospitals *cause* dying. Similarly, we may observe areas of greater or lesser criminality without concluding that the area, or its defining characteristics, causes the differences in crime rates. Van den Haag (1968, p. 283) puts it this way:

> The crime rate in slums is indeed higher than elsewhere; but so is the death rate in hospitals. Slums are no more "causes" of crime than hospitals are of death; they are locations of crime, as hospitals are of death. Slums and hospitals attract people selectively; neither is the "cause" of the condition (disease in hospitals, poverty in slums) that leads to the selective attraction.

With this caution in mind, a sample of the international research may be summarized. Research on the relation between social status and criminality has most often used an area approach, comparing the characteristics of zones of greater and lesser reported crime. However, some studies have directly compared individuals. Results of these two procedures will be discussed separately.

Ecological Studies of Status and Criminality

Studies of "crime zones" have been termed "ecological." "Ecology" is a term borrowed by sociologists from biologists.

In biology, an ecological study relates the differential survival of organisms and their spatial distribution to features of their environments. In sociology, "ecological" studies usually do less than this. They are most frequently descriptions of the geographic clustering of different kinds of people and behaviors. In the social sciences such ecological research is also called "area study" or "social geography."

Criminologists have employed the ecological method to investigate the association of social position and criminal activity by comparing areas of a country or zones within a city. Such area studies have been widely conducted since the nineteenth century and have repeatedly found an association between low status and rates of crime and delinquency. As early as 1861, Mayhew reported a connection between "low neighbourhoods" and the presence of many juvenile thieves.

American Studies With their proclivity for studying themselves and counting things, Americans have elaborated on such early ecological research. For example, Shaw and McKay (1942) constructed indices of the economic status of residential zones in 20 cities and correlated these measures with official crime rates. The usual correlation of poverty and criminality was found, an association that held true for delinquency among males and females and for crime committed by young people and adults. Other accompaniments of poverty, such as families dependent upon state aid and high rates of infant mortality, tuberculosis, and mental disorder, went along with the higher crime rates.

A similar conclusion about the location of crime derives from an intensive investigation of the significance of social status in one American city. Warner

Table 7-7 Arrest Rates by Social Class in "Yankee City"

Class	Percent of Population	Percent of Arrests
Upper	1.45	0.43
Lower-upper	1.57	0.28
Upper-middle	10.30	1.84
Lower-middle	28.36	7.80
Upper-lower	32.88	24.96
Lower-lower	25.44	64.69

Source: Adapted with permission from Warner and Lunt, 1941, table 35.

and Lunt (1941) report for the city they called "Yankee City" a strong negative relation between social position and criminality, as shown in Table 7-7. "The two upper classes," according to Warner and Lunt, "accounted for less than three-fourths of one per cent of those arrested; the two middle classes, for about ten per cent; and the two lower classes for approximately 90 per cent of the crime in Yankee City" (pp. 375–376).

Such a topography of crime appears repeatedly among the cities of North America. Schuessler (1962) examined the clustering of types of crimes with selected "social locators" for 105 American cities and found a strong relation between murder, assault, low income, crowded dwellings, and the nonwhite proportion of the population. Chilton (1964) compared data from Indianapolis, Baltimore, and Detroit to ascertain the relative importance of a host of variables in accounting for delinquency rates. Despite the differences in the size, location, physical plan, population composition, and historical traditions of these cities, Chilton reports a remarkable congruence in the maps of delinquency for them all. Delinquency resides disproportionately in zones characterized by low income, low occupational skills, poor housing, overcrowding, and transience.

Similar findings derive from Bloom's detailed analysis (1966) of the distribution of "socially deviant behaviors" in an American Middle Western city. He found the usual association of delinquency with certain "disruptive conditions," such as:

1 "Familial disruption," the proportion of adolescents not living with both parents
2 "Marital disruption," the number of divorced and separated males per 1,000 married nonseparated males
3 "Economic disruption," the percent of the male civilian labor force unemployed
4 "Environmental disruption," measured by the first-response fire runs of the city fire department as a proportion of total housing units
5 "Educational disruption," the number of public shool dropouts per 10,000 population age 18 and under

Shifting the focus from all juvenile delinquency to gang-affiliated behaviors in particular, Cartwright and Howard (1966) studied the characteristics of

Chicago neighborhoods in which 16 delinquent gangs resided. They found these areas to have more youthful populations than less delinquent neighborhoods and to be characterized by a higher proportion of deteriorated, renter-occupied dwellings. The gang zones had a higher proportion of households headed by women, a higher proportion of separated women, and a lower "family net disposable income" than other neighborhoods. Contrary to the findings of some other investigations, however, the Chicago "ganglands" were *not* differentiated by higher rates of unemployment or by lower educational levels.

These kinds of observations are supported, with some qualifications, by Boggs's research (1965) in St. Louis. Census tracts within this city were rated for social rank, urbanization, and racial segregation. "Social rank" is an index of educational and occupational status. "Urbanization" is a measure based on the fertility ratio, the proportion of single-family dwelling units, and the proportion of women in the labor force, where it is assumed that childless or small families living in apartments and with the women working are more "urban" than their opposites. Racial segregation is measured by a "segregation index," which is the proportion of blacks in each census tract.

An interesting facet of Boggs's study is the distinction she draws between the kinds of crime committed where the offender lives and the kinds of crime that attract offenders from other areas. Businesses that are *crime targets* are those located in high-status neighborhoods close to neighborhoods in which high proportions of offenders live. The neighborhoods in which high proportions of offenders *live*, however, tend to be characterized differently. These are areas of higher rates of homicide, assault, residential (as opposed to business) burglary, "highway robbery" (as opposed to business robbery), high proportions of blacks, more urbanization, and lower social rank.

S. Turner's study (1969) of Philadelphia supports many of Boggs's findings for St. Louis. Turner, too, suggests that a particular type of crime area be distinguished—one in which few criminals reside, but in which a considerable proportion of thefts occur. These "target" areas have a high "effective population"—"effective," that is, for thieves. Many transients move through these target zones which lie close to neighborhoods with high proportions of offenders in the population. When Turner describes the areas high in *resident* offenders, he also finds them characterized by low income and low occupational status, high density, high proportions of blacks, and high proportions of unrelated individuals living in the household and contributing to its income.

Ecological continuity   These many ecological studies tend to confirm each other, with, of course, some variations between cities. What is striking about this kind of research is not merely the parallels in the observations, but also the continuity—the persistence—of the correlations reported. The "things that go together" in the neighborhoods tend to cluster in like fashion over the years. Tryon (1967), for example, measured the characteristics of "social areas" in the San Francisco Bay region and found that the dimensions of his homogeneous neighborhoods held up—persisted—over a decade and a half. The neighborhoods may change, but the *clusters* of social indicators remain fairly constant.

Similarly, Schmid and Schmid, reporting in 1972, found strong similarities in the distribution of the serious offenses recorded since 1945 in the state of Washington and within its major city, Seattle. In like manner, Galle and others (1972) confirm for Chicago what Shaw and McKay discovered decades before: a *negative* relation between social status and such "social pathologies" as the public-assistance rate, mortality and fertility rates, rate of admission to mental hospitals, and officially recorded juvenile delinquency.

Canadian Research   The ecological correlates of crime in Canadian cities appear similar to those reported in the United States. In a preliminary study in London, Ontario, Jarvis (1972) found delinquency rates to be higher in areas characterized by low socioeconomic status, high mobility and heterogeneity of population, and poor housing.

Jarvis and Messinger (1974) conducted a more elaborate study of the same city, using both court appearances and unofficial delinquencies known to the police to compute delinquency rates by census tracts. The clustering of delinquency rates with 38 other variables was examined by the statistical technique of factor analysis. The principal factor (cluster of variables) associated with offensiveness among juveniles was a measure of "social status," which in turn was a compound of poverty, little schooling, and old dwellings.

In this predominantly white, Protestant, English-speaking city, ethnicity also made a difference. Being Protestant and of British ancestry was correlated with high status and low delinquency. By contrast, being of Italian, French, or Greek Orthodox ancestry was part of the factor associated with lower social status and greater risk of delinquency.

British Studies   Cross-cultural comparisons tend to confirm the findings for Canada and the United States. British area studies, for example, reveal the usual inverse association between social class and crime rates. Burt found this pattern in London as early as 1925, and Wallis and Maliphant (1967) note that even after 40 years the social-class characteristics of high-delinquency areas persist in that city.

Similar reports are given by Bagot (1941) for Liverpool, T. P. Morris (1957) for Croydon, Baldwin and others for Sheffield (1976), and Giggs (1970) for Barry in Wales. Giggs's research is the first British study to employ a correlational technique, "principal-components analysis," which, like Tryon's "cluster analysis" and "factor analysis," looks for groupings of correlated variables associated with low and high criminality.

Giggs tested the relation between 43 "intraurban" characteristics, including physical features of areas, plus 13 other measures indicative of what Giggs calls "social defects." Again, social troubles tend to go together; thus in Wales, as elsewhere, zones characterized by higher crime and delinquency rates also have higher shares of divorce, tuberculosis, and people with financial problems.

A later study by M. J. Brown and others (1972) also employed a cluster analysis plotted for electoral wards in a northern English industrial town. These investigators found areas with higher proportions of rented council (subsidized) houses, and with more unemployment and poverty, to be the more violent zones. Offenses against property were negatively associated with owner-occupied houses, but they were positively correlated with government housing, unemployment, poverty, and high proportions of Irish immigrants.

Edwards's research   Anne Edwards (1973) contributed some novel features to area studies in her research on the distribution of delinquency in Newcastle, an industrial city in northeastern England. Her study is one of the few to analyze delinquency rates for females as well as males. It also calculates *prevalence* as well as *incidence* statistics. Prevalence and incidence deserve comment before Edwards's findings are summarized.

Incidence and prevalence   An *incidence* rate tallies the number of people who fall into a category—such as being sick, arrested, or convicted—during a relatively limited time span. It is like counting an *arrival* rate, and it is the figure given by most criminological studies. Incidence refers to the number of "new cases" during a brief period.

Statistics on incidence say nothing, of course, about whether the "arrivals" in a social category have been there before. Furthermore, they do not usually count "departures," such as sick people who get well or offenders who do not repeat their crimes. However, it is possible, although not usual, for an incidence rate to be subdivided into (1) those new cases which occur during the observation period and are still active (or being treated) at the close of observations and (2) those new cases which are no longer active at the close of the time span.

A *prevalence* rate, by contrast, counts all the people "who ever have . . ." during a longer span of time. A prevalence rate *includes* the incidence rate for particular years but goes beyond it. A prevalence rate becomes a more meaningful measure of the amount of crime—or other social events—when it is tied to a *cohort analysis*. A cohort analysis follows a group of people in a particular area as they move in and out of "ages at risk." The risk can be that of committing kinds of crime for which, of course, some years are more hazardous than others, or the "risk" can be that of any other activity, such as childbearing, for which only certain people of certain ages are eligible.

A prevalence rate for a cohort tells us what proportion of that group has ever been arrested or convicted. It constitutes, then, an approximate measure of the *amount* of criminality. A prevalence rate may be made more useful if, *for each individual* in a cohort, it tallies the *number* of offenses during the period at risk and weights them for *gravity*. This refinement has yet to be employed.

Edwards's findings   Edwards calculated incidence rates of court convictions in 1967 among young people 12 to 18 years of age inclusive. She also computed prevalence rates for a cohort born in 1949 and followed through its nineteenth year. Her results can be outlined as follows:

1   The usual negative relation between socioeconomic status and officially recorded delinquency is confirmed. Newcastle wards vary markedly in delinquency rates, and the wards with higher proportions of manual workers have disproportionately higher delinquency rates.

2   As other studies have indicated, boys get into trouble with the law more frequently than girls. This disproportion is on the order of 7 to 1.

A sizable minority of males in Newcastle end up before the courts. About 20 percent of all boys appear in court. In the highest delinquency area, a slim majority of all boys (51 percent) are charged during their ages at risk.

By contrast, the overall rate for girls in the cohort is 3.5 percent, and in the highest ward it is 9 percent.

3 The more urban the area, the higher the rate of delinquency among females. Moreover, areas having the highest rates of delinquency among females are *not* identical with areas having the highest rates of delinquency among males.

In summary   Studies conducted in Europe and in Canada and the United States show certain conditions to be correlated so that goods and evils appear in bunches. A pattern appears in ecological research that associates high rates of crime and delinquency with indicators of physical illness and disability, mental disorder, low standards of hygiene, parental disharmony, and inconsistent, brutal, or lax discipline of children.

Ecological Studies around the World   A similar map of the social location of crime is drawn, with some variation, by ecological studies around the world. For example, Hayner (1946) plotted such criminogenic zones for Mexico City; Grillo (1970), for Caracas, Venezuela; Mangin (1967), for Lima, Peru; and Ferracuti, Dinitz, and Acosta (1975), for Puerto Rico. In San Juan, Puerto Rico, certain districts have a long-standing criminal repute, but high crime rates are also reported for new areas of housing projects for the resettled poor (Caplow et al., 1964; Kupperstein and Toro-Calder, 1969; O. Lewis, 1966). Clinard and Abbott (1973) found parallel concentrations of crime in particular urban zones in Uganda, and they cite research yielding similar results in other African and Asian countries.

In one of the rare reports from a communist country, Todorovich (1970) describes behavioral differences among "housing communities" in Belgrade, Yugoslavia. This investigator found striking variations in delinquency and crime by neighborhood, even among "communities" that were physically adjacent. The more criminal zones had more illegally constructed housing, more unregistered tenants, more occupational and ethnic mixture, and more immigrants, typically with large families.

In Bombay, Sheth (1961) found no juvenile offenders within the wealthy wards, whereas the highest rates of juvenile offenses were recorded among the immigrant squatter settlements. El-Saaty (1946) also discovered a negative association between status and delinquency in Egypt, although the peculiarities of Cairo required him to distinguish, as Boggs and Turner did in the United States, between the slums that produce disproportionate numbers of delinquents and the "attracting areas," the shopping centers, where they commit most of their thefts.

What Area Studies Do and Do Not Tell   Social geography is valuable as one means of finding out what goes with what. Social maps of correlated events describe life patterns and hence may give us an "appreciation," in Matza's sense (1969), of the way others live.

Insofar as the findings of such studies overlap, as they do, we have confidence that something causal is at work. However, what is causal and what is only correlative has to be tested, not assumed. For this test, area studies are not enough.

As we shall see, competing explanations of crime quarrel about facts, accepting some and denying others. They also provide different interpretations of the same facts. The soundness of both fact and interpretation is bolstered as we locate criminality by additional procedures. This is particularly required before drawing inferences from social maps.

The Ecological Fallacy A risk of using area studies as a foundation for conclusions about causes is that of committing what W. S. Robinson (1950) has called the "ecological fallacy" and what other statisticians have called the "aggregative fallacy" (Riley, 1963). The ecological fallacy is the error of assuming that associations found among events when one has studied aggregates will also be found when one studies individuals. It is the mistake of believing that what goes with what when we compare areas will necessarily be found when we compare individuals.

This assumption is sometimes true, sometimes false, and at all times to be resisted. A test of the significance of area research requires study of individuals.

An Individual-Case Study: Reiss and Rhodes Studies of individuals of varied social status tend to confirm the associations revealed by ecological research. In one such extensive investigation, Reiss and Rhodes (1961) examined the official records of delinquency for 9,238 white boys in Tennessee for the period 1950 to 1958. They also collected self-reports of delinquency from a subsample of these boys. Both measures were analyzed for their relation with two indices of social status: the occupation of the head of the household and the class status of the residential neighborhood. The major findings of this study may be summarized as follows:

1 There is more frequent and serious delinquency in the lower strata.
2 The persistent delinquent, the "career-oriented" offender, is found only among lower-class boys.
3 The relation between social status and delinquency is not straightforward. It varies with the status structure of the residential community and the extent to which delinquency is part of a cultural tradition in these residential areas. "The largest proportion of delinquents for any status group comes from the more homogeneous status areas for that group, while the delinquency life-chances of boys in any status group tend to be greatest in the lower status areas and in high delinquency rate areas" (p. 720).
4 There is an interaction between delinquency rate, social status, and intelligence. Holding IQ constant, "the probability of being classified a serious, petty or truancy offender is greater for the blue-collar than white-collar boys" (p. 723). Turning the relation around and holding social status constant, there is

also a substantial association between higher IQ and nondelinquency. Table 7-8 shows the interaction between a boy's social status, his IQ, and levels of delinquency.

Interpretation

If one accepts, with appropriate caution, the correlations repeatedly found between socioeconomic status and the varieties of criminality, there remains the matter of how to interpret these associations. This is, of course, the job of the explanations of crime to be discussed. However, since there is a tendency to jump to conclusions about causes from the associations described, the meanings of money and social class deserve comment here.

An easy interpretation of the relation between wealth and kinds of crime is that "social class" does *not* refer to differences in behavior but that it does make a difference in one's chances of being arrested and convicted. According to this interpretation, money makes possible a better legal defense; thus while rich and poor people may be equally criminal, they are not equally liable to conviction. This idea has recently been expressed by Hirschi, who says, "It is of the essence of social class that it can create differences in reward where none exists in talent, that it can impose differences in punishment where none exists in obedience to rules" (1969, p. 82).

Money does make possible a better legal defense, but this fact does not disprove the existence of differences in conduct that are linked to income and culture. It can be true, and probably is true, that both ideas are correct. Within any society, types of conduct do vary with wealth, albeit unsteadily. Poorer people kill one another at a greater rate than people in middle- and upper-income brackets. They also engage more frequently in robbery, burglary, extortion, kidnapping, and forcible rape. On the other hand, people of middle and high status are more frequently arrested for fraud and treason (R. West, 1964).

Contrary to the allegation that the differential crime rates of "social classes" represent *nothing but* prejudice in the justice system, experimental and ethnographic studies confirm the story told by official statistics. We have noted such trends in test situations. Ethnographic research based on observation by participants gives similar reports. There *are* differences in styles of life and criminal conduct between persons of high and low social status (O. Lewis, 1959, 1961; W. B. Miller, 1958). These differences are not washed away by charges of injustice traceable to differences in income and ability to pay for defense (Chiricos and Waldo, 1975). There are, however, differences in modes of living among people with similar incomes.

Meaning of Money   Money means more than one thing. There are many ways of being rich, poor, or middling. The effects of income upon behavior vary with *how* one becomes more or less wealthy and with the *social context* in which any level of income is embedded.

"Social class" that matters—that makes a difference in behavior—depends on more than money. A sum of money *earned* does not have the same effect as

Table 7-8 Rate of Delinquency per 100 White Schoolboys by IQ and Occupational Status of Father

	IQ							
	Low		Middle		High		Total[b]	
Occupational status of father and type of delinquent offense	Number	Rate per 100	Number	Rate per 100	Number	Rate per 100	Number	Rate per 100
White-collar								
J.C.[a] serious	280	(8.2)	1,263	(6.8)	1,115	(4.6)	3,302	(6.2)
	10	3.6	15	1.2	5	0.4	42	1.3
J.C. petty	8	2.8	25	2.0	15	1.4	67	2.0
Subtotal	(18)	(6.4)	(40)	(3.2)	(20)	(1.8)	(109)	(3.3)
J.C. truant	1	0.4	1	0.1	...	0.0	4	0.1
J.C. traffic	4	1.4	44	3.5	31	2.8	93	2.8
No J.C. record	257	0.0	1,178	0.0	1,064	0.0	3,096	0.0
Blue-collar								
J.C. serious	926	(10.9)	2,091	(9.4)	672	(5.2)	4,661	(8.8)
	42	4.5	47	2.2	11	1.7	124	2.7
J.C. petty	48	5.2	85	4.1	15	2.2	174	3.7
Subtotal	(90)	(9.7)	(132)	(6.3)	(26)	(3.9)	(298)	(6.4)
J.C. truant	10	1.2	11	0.6	2	0.3	33	0.7
J.C. traffic	..	...	53	2.5	7	1.0	81	1.7
No J.C. record	826	0.0	1,895	0.0	637	0.0	4,249	0.0

[a]J.C. = Juvenile court.

[b]Includes all cases for which IQ information was not obtained.

Source: Adapted with permission from Reiss and Rhodes, 1961, table 1.

the same sum *given*. Reward divorced from effort produces syndromes of "learned laziness"—the "spoiled brat" phenomenon—and it does so in laboratories as well as in "real" life (Seligman, 1975). What one *does* makes a difference to what one *is*, regardless of the wealth one *has*.

A "rock" star who makes it big does not have the same tastes as the equally rich corporation executive. A middle-income numbers runner does not behave like a middle-income schoolteacher. A poor peasant does not act like an urban parent on welfare.

In short, the effects of some indicators of "class," such as money, are less strong and less direct than popular theorizing assumes. It is questionable to what extent being of a certain economic status alone *causes* any particular kind of behavior (S. R. Brown, 1970–1971).

There are, to be sure, *accompaniments* of wealth and poverty that are part of the definition of being rich or poor. These correlates of income are the kinds of things money allows one to do, like taking holidays abroad or owning expensive cars, but such things are not the *causes* of any particular patterns of behavior such as being criminal or lawful, disciplined or dissipated. The common-sense proof of this lies in the long-standing recognition that, just as there are the honest poor and the depraved poor, there are also the productive rich and the filthy rich.

When criminologists examine carefully the relation between measures of delinquency and "social class" *in different kinds of communities*, they tend to agree with the authors of one such study that "class membership *per se* . . . is a poor predictor of a variety of different and specific kinds of adolescent behavior" (Empey and Lubeck, 1971, p. 33). These authors add that one should not *expect* class "to have much predictive efficiency when class is treated as an all-inclusive and global concept, without regard to familial, ethnic, sub-cultural, and other differences within it" (p. 34).

As will be seen, there are other influences, more important than money alone, that affect one's lawful or criminal behavior.

Rich Nations, Poor Nations; Good Times and Bad

Money means more than one thing; wealth has more than one consequence. This says that the effects of wealth and poverty vary with the social context—with where one is, as opposed to where one has been, and with how wealth is gained. Given this lack of uniform relation between the money one has and the life one leads, we should expect no single relation between the economic status of a society as a whole and its crime level. Furthermore, the link between prosperous times, or poor ones, and criminal behavior should also be loose. This is, in fact, what we find when we study the connections between wealth and criminality *comparatively*, among many countries, and *historically*, over time.

It is apparent by now that affluence in itself provides no cure for crime. In fact, for industrialized countries in recent times, crime rates and prosperity seem to have moved together. Some criminologists believe this to be true because prosperity means that there are more things to steal and more opportunities for theft. Prosperity also elevates crime statistics, it is said, because affluence is associated with better recording of offenses and because property insurance encourages the reporting of crime. Furthermore, it is maintained that as long as some people have more than others, there is both motivation and justification for theft. The justification of offenses against property is allegedly strengthened by the "close affinity between many of the methods, aims, and ethics employed in legitimate business and criminal business" (K. J. Smith, 1965, p. 7).

Whether or not one agrees with these explanations and justifications of affluent crime, attempts to link criminality to the business cycle or to unemployment figures have not produced any clear conclusion *except* that the relationship between material "need" and criminal behavior is *not* direct.

Ascertaining the relation between national wealth and criminality is itself complicated. Studies of the effects of business cycles are always tangled with quesitons about the validity of economic statistics (Morgenstern, 1963), with questions about the time lag to be allowed between changing economic conditions and their presumed effects on behavior, and with questions about the possible impact of different welfare programs in easing the hardships of depressions.

Similarly, when one tries to study the criminogenic effects of unemployment, the meaning of official statistics is again open to question. "Unemployment" is a difficult term to define because in modern countries the "unemployed" category includes persons with various degrees of motivation to work, various dispositions to accept certain kinds of job, and various states of need. In recognition of these facts, a recent conference has called for changes in the definition, measurement, and interpretation of "unemployment" (Levitan, 1975; O'Neill, 1975; Wetzel, 1975).

Given these uncertainties, the more than 140 years of research on the impact of business cycles upon crime rates have produced the unsatisfactory "finding" that crime may increase with *both* good times and bad. It therefore seems logical to conclude that *neither* the poverty nor the wealth of nations is a major determinant of the level of criminal conduct. The best that can be said is that the serious crimes are associated *ecologically* (in social and physical space *within* a society) with relative economic deprivation. However, such crimes are not associated *historically* (in time) or *comparatively* (across cultures) with relative impoverishment.

ETHNICITY

The distinctive assumption of a *social* science, and particularly of those studies called "sociology" and "anthropology," is that the interesting aspects of human behavior are learned. When what is learned has some discernible pattern for a number of people and when such a pattern is distinguishable from that of other groups, the scholar speaks of the style of life as a *culture*. Although the boundaries of a culture are never mapped exactly, it is assumed that they are roughly discriminable and that cultures are both *products* of human interaction and *generators* of it. Cultures are conceived of as both the causes and the effects of human beings teaching one another how to behave.[2]

Whether one studies cultures professionally or observes them as a peripatetic citizen, it is apparent that *human beings group themselves by categories of learned preferences*. Not only do we group ourselves, but our cultural identity is, in turn, recognized by others. Such "consciousness of kind," acknowledged by insiders and outsiders alike, has been conveniently considered a hallmark of *ethnicity*. The word "ethnic" (from the Greek *ethnos*, "the nations") designates aggregates of individuals who share a sense of being alike, who regard themselves as "a people" with a relatively distinct pattern of "doing things." The term "ethnic" points to a subjective reality—to how people think and feel about their affiliations. These feelings of identification are correlated with objective indicators of ethnic difference such as language, race, religion, citizenship, costume, and dietary and artistic preferences. These correlations are not perfect, however. Not all who are of the same race or who share a citizenship, a language, or a religion regard themselves as being "the same people." Language, particularly *dialect*, is probably the strongest external indicator of ethnic identity. Dialect strengthens an identification, particularly when it is combined with distinctive dress.

Ethnicity is associated, of course, with behaviors other than those that indicate awareness of identity. It is in this association of ethnic identity with a *differing content of lesson learned* that one finds a reason for examining the relation between ethnicity and criminality.

The possible impact of ethnicity upon criminality is usually studied in the context of cultures meeting under the laws of one state. That is, interest in the vulnerability of ethnic groups to arrest is normally a result of there being more than one such group subject to the sovereignty of a government. Where a state is also a nation, homogeneous in its culture, there is little reason to study ethnic differences in criminality. It is where states attempt to govern many "peoples" that ethnicity becomes a significant variable. This is the circumstance that pertains, in differing degree, in the United States, Canada, Israel, Great Britain, India, Spain, the Soviet Union, the Republic of South Africa, and many other states that attempt to govern several nations.

A Sample of Ethnic Differentials in Crime Rates

Ethnic differences are studied as part of the attempt to understand behavior. Although this motive is admirable, the procedure of comparing groups is distasteful. Comparisons are particularly unpleasant when the "good" and "bad" behaviors of "our people" and "their people" are being contrasted, as when one examines ethnic differences in crime rates. Nevertheless, the scholar

[2]It is popular in sociology to add that what we teach each other occurs through "symbolic interaction." For example, Hoult's dictionary of sociological terms (1969) defines culture as "acquired by means of symbolic interaction." Unless one stretches the meaning of the word "symbol" beyond definition, this view of how human beings teach each other is needlessly restrictive and false to much of what is known about learning. Some nonsymbolic ways in which patterned social behaviors are learned are described on pages 315–321.

who would know how things are cannot avoid comparison. The study of differences is part of the procedure of finding out what makes things as they are.

However much we may disapprove of the fact, ethnicity makes a difference. The word, indeed, refers to difference. Of course, after we have described ethnic variations in behavior, we are left with the question of how the differences came to be. But the first task is to ascertain what the differences are.

The variety in amount and kind of crime committed by people of diverse cultural heritage in their states of residence is most apparent in heterogeneous countries like Canada and the United States, but the same point can be illustrated in the records of less varied societies.

Israel, for example, in its short history not only has experienced a steady rise in juvenile delinquency, but also has noted differences in crime and delinquency rates among Jews from different lands. For 1957, Shoham reports rates of serious offenses committed by immigrants to Israel as 13 per 1,000 among immigrants from Africa, 10 per 1,000 among those from Asia, and 5 per 1,000 among those from Europe and the Americas (1966, pp. 80–83).

Studies of patterns of crime among Italian migrants also indicate ethnic differences. Franchini and Introna (1961) and Introna (1963) found that the migration of rural workers from southern Italy to the "industrial triangle" of northern Italy has been associated with increases in their rates of juvenile delinquency and adult crime. At the same time, the Italian workers who migrated to Switzerland exhibited lower crime rates in the period 1949 to 1960 than the Swiss nationals (Neumann, 1963). These rates have been increasing, however, and they differ from rates of crime committed by Swiss nationals in that there is a higher proportion of violent offenses among Italian migrants (Ferracuti, 1968).

Swedish studies of the differential crime rates of resident ethnic groups also indicate cultural differences in criminal activity. According to Sveri's data (1960), corrected for sex and age distributions, conviction rates for Hungarians and Yugoslavs in Sweden are almost twice those of the host population, and this differential seems particularly associated with a greater propensity among the migrant people to crimes against the person. A different style of offense is reported for the Finns in Sweden, who are susceptible to arrests for violations having to do with drinking (Kaironen, 1966).

Ethnicity in England   Drinking is also associated with the high crime rates reported for Irish migrants to England. The Irish settler tends to be a single young man cut off from an Irish community. According to Gibbens and Ahrenfeldt, such a person "has two main occupations: work and drink" (1966, p. 141). For years Irishmen resident in England have had a rate of criminal conviction and recidivism higher than that of the majority population (Bottoms, 1967). While their offenses have covered a broad spectrum of serious crimes, robbery and terrorist murder have recently been increasing among them. Toward the end of the 1950s, some 20 percent of convicted robbers in London were Irishmen, although Irishmen constituted only about 12 percent of the single male population between the ages of 15 and 40 (McClintock and Gibson, 1961). Lambert's later study (1970) of crime in Birmingham shows a continuing propensity of Irish immigrants to receive the attention of the police, and this is so with occupation and age held constant.

England has also experienced increases in the rates of violent crimes committed by immigrants from Commonwealth countries in Asia and the West Indies. Such immigrants, while relatively immune to committing offenses against property, have conviction rates for personal attacks that range from two to three times the rate of the host population (McClintock, 1963; Wallis and Maliphant, 1967).

Ethnicity in North America Canada and the United States have a long record of ethnic differentials among the nations that have met in the New World. The "native"[3] peoples of Canada, for example, are convicted of indictable offenses at rates disproportionate to their representation in the population. Throughout Canada, but in western Canada in particular, Indian, Eskimo, and Metis adults are in jails and prisons in numbers far in excess of their proportions in the general population. In a recent year, in Canada's four western provinces, the Yukon, and the Northwest Territories, the percentages of these groups who were incarcerated ranged from a *low* of 10 percent of the inmates in one jail on Vancouver Island to *highs* of 100 percent of the inmates of the jails for women at Oakalla (British Columbia) and The Pas (Manitoba). The *median* representation of Indians, Metis, and Eskimos in western Canadian correctional institutions runs around 66 percent (Canadian Corrections Association, 1967). A high proportion of the offenses for which these people are convicted are alcohol-related. No one knows why some ethnic groups have difficulty with alcohol, although assumptions come easily, and no one has a cure for the trouble (Lloyd and Salzberg, 1975; Snyder, 1958; Verden and Shatterly, 1971).

The United States also records wide differences in the amount and the style of crime committed by its numerous ethnic residents. At the extremes, it is immediately notable that the Oriental and Jewish populations have low rates of arrest and conviction for the serious predatory crimes, while blacks and Mexican-Americans have high rates. This type of differential persists even where the Orientals constitute a plurality of the population, as in Hawaii. Voss (1963) reports that Hawaiians, who make up about one-fourth of Honolulu's population, account for 40 percent of the delinquency among males and half of the arrests of females. The Japanese and Chinese, who make up about 40 percent of the population, account for less than one-fifth of male delinquency and about 6 percent of violations by females.

Other deviations from the criminal norm are apparent among Dutch,

---

[3]"Native" is another popular, vague word. It comes from the Latin word meaning "to be born of." Calling North American Indians, Metis, and Eskimos "native" just means that more generations of them have been born in the land of their residence. In no other sense are such people more "native" than a first-generation American, Canadian, or Mexican.

German, and Scandinavian migrants to America, and their children, who have experienced low degrees of contact with the police. The lawful behavior of these people is equaled or bettered by that of ethnic religious enclaves such as the Mennonites and the Amish (Reckless, 1967, pp. 472–475).

Listing these facts is enough to make us question the easy explanation of differences in criminality as due only to racial prejudice and economic disadvantage. On the contrary, *low* crime rates are found among some minorities which are physically visible—"racially" distinguishable, if you will—and which have suffered discrimination and persecution. The Jews have one of the longest histories of any people as objects of hatred and oppression. The Chinese have been victims of lynchings and riots in Western American cities. The Japanese are the only Canadian-American ethnic group to have been selected for exclusion and containment in military camps, euphemistically called "relocation centers."

In addition to the hardships of discrimination, all these groups have also suffered great economic disadvantages. Like most migrants to America, the original settlers tended to be poor people seeking a better way of life, rather than rich wanderers seeking more wealth. As ethnic units, their economic careers have varied, of course. The Jews in particular represent a North American success story.

The experience of black people in the New World has been sadly different from that of groups who migrated voluntarily, and it may be expected that their struggle from slavery toward autonomy may have consequences different from those of voluntary migration.

Rates of arrest and conviction of black people for serious offenses in the United States differ markedly from those of other ethnic groups. Although blacks[4] now represent about 12 percent of the American population, they constitute nearly one-third of all persons arrested. This discrepancy has persisted for some years (Wolfgang, 1966, p. 46). At any one time, about one-third of all prisoners in the United States are blacks. Compared with white offenders, *smaller* proportions of black criminals are *first* offenders (Forslund, 1970). In other words, blacks have a higher recidivism rate than whites. They are charged with, and convicted of, more serious crimes, and the population of black offenders is, crime for crime, younger than the population of white offenders (G. B. Johnson, 1970).

Over the past two decades, blacks in the United States have accounted for about 60 percent of all arrests for murder (FBI, 1975, table 38, 1976, table 39; Graham, 1970). Wolfgang's study (1958) of criminal homicide in Philadelphia reported that nonwhite men aged 20 to 24 had a conviction rate more than 25 times that of white men of the same age. Ethnic differences in homicide are of such an order that murder rates among black *women* are two to four times as great as those among white *men* (Wolfgang and Ferracuti, 1967, p. 154).

According to recent FBI figures (1975, table 38, 1976, table 39), blacks

[4]In North America, "black" and "Negro" are sociological terms. These words are associated with racial features, but they are not identical to the anthropometric idea of race. The designation "black" refers more accurately to ethnicity, as we have defined it, than to biological factors.

account for more than half of the arrests for robbery, prostitution, commercial-
ized vice, and murder, and for almost half of the arrests for illegal possession of
weapons and forcible rape. The ethnic differentials are so great that some
criminologists have suggested that the castelike position of the black in
American society calls for "constructing a theory of Negro delinquency and
criminality which would be quite different from a possible model of criminal
behavior among whites" (Savitz, 1967, p. 61).

These reported differences in crime rates do not disappear when comparisons are made holding constant the socioeconomic, sex, and age distributions
of white and black groups (Blue, 1948; Forslund, 1970; Moses, 1970; Stephenson and Scarpitti, 1968). Neither can the differences in *arrest*[5] be attributed
principally to prejudice in law enforcement (D. J. Black and Reiss, 1967, 1970;
Green, 1970; Kephart, 1957; Terry, 1967). As we have seen, studies of
victimization yield the same differentials as official statistics.

A Cohort Analysis

The role of ethnic, as well as socioeconomic, factors in the development
of delinquency is illustrated by a study of the careers of almost 10,000 young
men in the United States. Wolfgang, Figlio, and Sellin gathered information
on "*all* boys born in 1945 who lived in Philadelphia at least between their
tenth and eighteenth birthdays" (1972, p. 244). This is a "cohort analysis."
The term means that the group of subjects to be studied was defined by characteristics *other than those* of interest to the investigators. In this case,
the cohort was defined by date of birth and place of residence rather than by
criminal conduct.

This study differs in still other ways from much criminological research.
The measure of "delinquency" used was not arrest or conviction, but "police
contact." The data are the "officially recorded delinquencies" among 9,945
boys regardless of the disposition of the case by the police. The police can, of
course, make a "remedial disposition" of a case rather than an arrest, and they
did so, in this study, for some two-thirds of the complaints they received. The
authors recognize that using such contacts with the police as the sign of a
violation, instead of arrests or convictions, might mean that some innocent
boys were included as offenders. They present data (pp. 17–22) to show that
this is not likely, however.

This research differs, too, from such previous work in that it made use of
the Sellin-Wolfgang (S-W) "delinquency index" to weigh the seriousness of
reported offenses. Considering these refinements, the findings of this large-
scale study increase in importance. Results reported by Wolfgang and his

---

[5]Differentials in arrest rates should not be confused with differentials in treatment after
arrest. It is commonly alleged that after arrest has taken place, the justice systems in Canada and
the United States discriminate against some, but not all, ethnic groups. As will be detailed in
Chapter 15, much of the research on this question has been poorly done, with inadequate attention
given to the gravity of the instant offense, the number of charges, the number and gravity of
previous offenses, and available correctional resources. More careful studies of sentencing in
Canada and the United States can be interpreted as leaving open the question of possible unfair
treatment, but they do not clearly support the charge of injustice (Chiricos and Waldo, 1975).

colleagues have been modified by a statistical analysis prepared by G. F. Jensen (1974, 1976). The corrected, major findings may be outlined as follows:

About one-third of all the boys in the cohort experienced at least one "police contact."

28.6 percent of the white boys and 50.2 percent of the nonwhite boys were classified as "offenders" by the investigators.

26.5 percent of the group characterized as being of "higher" socioeconomic status (SES) were delinquent, compared with 44.8 percent of the boys of "lower" SES.

The most significant correlate of delinquency was poor schoolwork, and this relationship holds true regardless of race. The second and third strongest correlates of delinquency were race and SES.

School achievement remains correlated with delinquency with race held constant, and race remains correlated with delinquency with achievement level held constant (G. F. Jensen, 1974, 1976). The shape of the relationship between schoolwork and delinquency is not linear, however. It is not until boys become average or better in their schoolwork that their immunity to delinquency becomes apparent (G. F. Jensen, 1976, p. 385).

Repetitive offenders were more likely to be nonwhite boys of low SES. They also have the highest scores for the gravity of their offenses as gauged by the S-W index.

Nonwhite offenders received more severe dispositions from their police contacts than white boys, even when the seriousness of their offense was held constant. The authors acknowledge that they have not studied all the factors that enter into decisions made by the police, but their data suggest bias in the disposition of black delinquents (pp. 220–221).

In summary, this Philadelphia study reports differences in the delinquency rates of black and white boys and suggests that a network of disadvantaging conditions is important to our understanding of the discrepancy. "The nonwhite delinquent boy," these researchers say, "is likely to belong to the lower socioeconomic group, experience a greater number of school and residential moves (that is, be subject to the disrupting forces of intracity mobility more than the nondelinquent) and have the lowest average grade completed, the lowest achievement level, and the lowest I.Q. score" (p. 246). The suggestion in this study of racial discrimination in the *disposition* of boys after a police contact calls for additional investigation of the factors that affect decisions by the police.

Meanwhile, caution is required in the interpretation of differentials in crime rates between whites and nonwhites. In light of the history of ethnic relations, it is difficult today to compare the relative importance of the alleged causes of any differences in observed behaviors. Subjective factors, of an unmeasurable sort, may intrude where objective measures reveal no differences of condition or treatment. Enforced segregation is only now ending, and the marks of oppression may make trivial the scientist's attempts to hold socioeconomic status or schooling constant while examining crime and delinquency differentials between races. The possible operation of such subjective factors can be acknowledged, although it cannot be assessed.

None of this denies, however, that *ethnic differences are real differences.* They have a bearing upon crime rates, and the explanation of this impact is one of the tasks of theories of criminogenesis.

In Summary

The research on the differential criminality of ethnic groups can be summarized cross-culturally by saying that:

Ethnic groups *do* exhibit different patterns of criminal behavior within the states in which they reside.

These patterns differ both in the kinds of crime committed and in the relative amounts of specific crimes.

These patterns cannot be explained away as due only to the length of residence of a minority in a country, its age and sex distribution, or its socioeconomic position, or to prejudice in the judicial system.

Migrants tend to exhibit in their adopted lands the kinds of crime familiar to their homelands.

These ethnic patterns of criminality are, like all else, subject to change with time.

CULTURE CONTACT AND CRIME

The impact of time upon a culture includes the possibility that a way of life may disintegrate as well as the happier possibility that a new culture may grow out of the mixture of old ones. The metaphor of the "melting pot" is just that—a figure of speech. It more often expresses hope rather than fact (Glazer and Moynihan, 1963; Novak, 1972).

In the meantime, while old cultures are dying and new ones are evolving, there is little surprise in finding that the *process* of "assimilation" may mean the substitution of new styles of crime for old. After a generation or two in the United States, for example, southern Europeans abandon their traditionally prescribed code of vendetta for the more American property offenses.

It is also not surprising to find that, as an ethnic enclave breaks down, its crime rates, particularly its juvenile-delinquency rates, go up. So-called "ghettoes," areas of ethnic concentration, may be sites of remarkably *low*, as well as high, crime rates. The popular notion of a "ghetto" as necessarily a slum and necessarily crime-ridden is false.

On Ghettoes and Slums

The popular use, and abuse, of the word "ghetto" should not seduce students of sociology into confusing a ghetto with a slum.

Originally a ghetto was an area inside or outside the walls of early medieval European cities, where Jews lived. *The Random House Dictionary*

(1966) believes the word may have derived from the Italian *borghetto*, a diminutive of *borgo*, a hamlet outside the town walls.

The first ghettoes were *voluntary* congregations of Jews and only later became areas of legally enforced isolation (Wirth, 1929). Such enacted ghettoes first appeared in Spain and Portugal toward the end of the fourteenth century and were justified as a protection of the "true faith." These compulsory ghettoes were usually closed off by gates, and their residents were subject to curfew restrictions. Within the ghettoes, autonomous institutions operated, such as schools, churches, welfare associations, and courts.

Today the term "ghetto" has been expanded from its original meaning to refer to any area of ethnic concentration. In the cities of Western countries, ghettoes are now less independent of the greater societies in which they are situated. They are, at the same time, more voluntary.[6] With the exception of laws concerning the status of reserve Indians in Canada and the United States, the *legally enforced segregation* of cultural groups is now nonexistent in Western Europe and in Canada and the United States. It is debatable, of course, to what extent the law of such states is used to protect or to break down modern ghettoes.

By contrast with a ghetto, a slum need not be a zone of ethnic concentration. The defining characteristics of a slum are vice, dirt, density, and poverty. Fairchild's *Dictionary of Sociology* (1944) calls it "an area of physical and social decadence," while the *Oxford English Dictionary* speaks of "a crowded district . . . inhabited by people of a low class or by the very poor . . . where the houses and the conditions of life are of a squalid and wretched character." "Squalid," in turn, means "foul through neglect or want of cleanliness; repulsively mean and filthy."

It follows that slums and ghettoes are two different things. Some ghettoes may be slums, but some are not. Conversely, some slums may be ghettoes; others are not. It is conceivable that, with time, all slums become ghettoes, while not all ghettoes become slums. What is of interest to sociologists, and to other students who would understand freedom, is the extent to which, in any

---

[6]Some American readers have objected to this statement. American sociologists, in contrast to their European colleagues, are more apt to resist the possibility that ethnic separation results from preference, and they are more willing to attribute ethnic congregation to involuntary or irrational forces, including those wrong attitudes called "prejudices."

Whatever the "deeper sources" of ethnic preferences may be, it remains a fact that "like attracts like" and that ethnic groups congregate differentially, apparently by choice. They do so in varying degrees, of course, but the tendencies are visible residentially and socially—in such varied activities as choosing marriage mates, school friends, vacation resorts, and prison buddies. A sample of the extensive evidence from several countries is found in studies by Barron (1951), Berkowitz and Goranson (1964), Byrne and Griffitt (1966), Cavalli-Sforza and Bodmer (1971, p. 791), Darroch and Marston (1971), K. M. Evans (1962, chap. 4), R. Farley and Taeuber (1968), Guest and Weed (1976), Guest and Zuiches (1971), Hill and Feeley (1968), Hunt and Coller (1957), Kantrowitz (1969), Krovetz (1972), R. A. Levine (1971–1972), G. A. Lundberg and Dickson (1952), Ramsey (1976), Roof (1972), Rossman (1962), Sanders (1966), and Talmon (1956).

We have here another instance of ethics warring with facts. Facts are subject to change, of course, but for recent decades at least, it remains a fact that Western ghettoes are both less independent of the societies in which they occur and more voluntary than those of past centuries.

particular cultural setting and epoch, ghettoes or slums are voluntary. This is meat for debate. In this debate, clarity requires that slums and ghettoes be regarded as distinct.

Ghettoes and Crime

Holding this distinction, it is possible to ask whether ghettoes are more or less criminogenic than "melting pots." Are ghettoes the distinctive locations of high crime rates? Do rates of offenses in ghettoes change with a weakening of their boundaries?

American studies are particularly rich in reporting the effects of the meeting of cultures upon crime rates. These investigations indicate that migrants, and more specifically their children, are relatively immune to the configurations of crime about them as long as a ghetto is intact.

This phenomenon has been well documented, for example, among Oriental residents in the United States and their children (Crook, 1934; Kitano, 1967; Lind, 1930a, 1930b; McGill, 1938; Petersen, 1967). A similar pattern of ethnic protection is reported by Beynon (1935) for Hungarian immigrants to America and by Vislick-Young (1930) for Russian immigrants.

The low delinquency rates among descendants of Chinese and Japanese immigrants to North America have already been noted. These rates tend to remain low, however, as long as ethnic identity is maintained, but to rise with assimilation to the host culture. For example, Kitano (1967) found some interesting signs of this "contamination" when he compared Japanese-American delinquents and their parents with Japanese-American nondelinquents. The delinquents and their families were considerably *less* "Japanese" than the nondelinquents. Moreover, the delinquent children exhibited their greater identification with the American culture in their speech, dress, hair styles, and patterns of friendship.

Similar observations have been made of the Chinese ghettoes that have defended their children against delinquency in the United States. Sollenberger (1968) lived among the residents of the New York City enclave and, with the help of a Chinese interpreter-interviewer, observed family life and behavior of children in this densely populated ghetto. In this area of near-zero delinquency, Sollenberger found children to be remarkably well behaved—to be able, for example, to go on an all-day outing with "no crying, no scolding, no scuffling or quarreling of any kind" (p. 17). He considered that the sources of this were to be found in family solidarity. There were no divorced or separated parents in this community. Mothers held their husbands in high regard, and authority was shared. The Chinese children spent much time in the company of their parents. Sollenberger reports that, as compared with a sample of Caucasian mothers, the Chinese women were *more strict* in their control of children's aggression, but *more permissive* in regard to weaning, toilet training, and bedtime routines.

This kind of community is, of course, subject to disruption. It is now reported that Chinese ghettoes are feeling the winds of change and that, under the impact of new immigrants, mostly young men, the delinquent warfare reminiscent of other enclaves is being reenacted in some Chinatowns where youths have organized themselves as "Red Guard" and "Wah Ching" gangs (Harvey, 1970; J. Peterson, 1972).

The experience of blacks in the Americas has been made different by the fact of their involuntary migration to, and enslavement in, the New World. The lively question, however, is whether, today, their "ghettoization" proceeds differently from that of any other ethnic group and whether, therefore, the consequences may differ.

There is no definitive answer to this question, but informed opinion about it has changed. During the 1940s and 1950s the popular liberal attitude toward this subject was assimilationist. Its ideal was the melting pot. This ideal tended to minimize or to deny cultural differences between blacks and whites and to reduce such alleged differences to class distinctions. The contrary suggestion, that behavior of blacks and whites might differ culturally and not merely as a function of socioeconomic status, was resisted. An illustration of this resistance was the professional response to an anthropologist's study (Herskovits, 1941) demonstrating that it was "a myth of the Negro's past" to believe that *no* cultural elements had been borne by the slaves from West Africa to the Americas. The reviews of this book in professional journals have been characterized as "a furor."

Times change. With the black demand for identity, it now becomes more comfortable for white students to agree that blacks, like other migrants, brought a culture with them (J. Jones, 1972; Metzger, 1971).[7] To the extent to which a black culture has been maintained, and to the extent to which it is being revived, it should be expected that the ghetto experience would have the same relationship to delinquency rates among blacks that it has had to delinquency rates among other minorities. The evidence is not at all clear, however. A few attempts have been made to study the effects of ethnic congregation upon crime rates among blacks by examining the variations in known violations as the races live apart or together. The findings vary with the time and place of the investigation.

An early study conducted by the research bureau of the Houston Council of Social Agencies (Hooker, 1945) found that for Houston "the higher the proportion of Negro population, the lower is the rate of Negro delinquency . . . conversely, the higher the proportion of white population, the higher is the rate of Negro delinquency" (p. 23).

A later study in Baltimore reported similar results (Lander, 1954). More recently, Willie and Gershenovitz (1964) tested for this distribution of crime among mixed and separated tracts in Washington, D.C. They too found that ethnic concentration had the effect of reducing crime, with one qualification:

---

[7]Although cultural patterns can be measured (Cattell, 1950; Inkeles and Levinson, 1969), social scientists continue to debate the distinctiveness of a black culture in the Americas. The debate leads to inconsistent testimony when social scientists offer "evidence" in court (E. P. Wolf, 1976). It seems easier for sociologists to acknowledge differences in "life-style" rather than in "culture," since the former sounds less permanent.

1   In higher socio-economic areas, there are no differences in juvenile delinquency rates between neighborhoods of homogeneous and heterogeneous racial composition.

2   In lower socio-economic areas, juvenile delinquency rates tend to be higher in racially heterogeneous than in racially homogeneous neighborhoods [p. 743].

When the effects of the ghetto upon crime rates among blacks have been tested outside Southern or Border states, however, no such immunization against criminality has been apparent. Chilton (1964) tested for such a "parabolic" association between delinquency and the proportion of nonwhites in Indianapolis census tracts. He reported that the relation is unclear because of the large number of census tracts in Indianapolis that are almost completely white, and he recommends that the curvilinear findings for Houston, Baltimore, and Washington be tested against large bodies of data from other cities. In one such study Bordua (1958–1959) also could find no evidence that delinquency rates in Detroit varied with the proportions of white and nonwhite residents.

The conflicts among these findings have been attributed to differences in police activity and to regional differences in the willingness of victims to call the police. The question remains open whether residential segregation of the races is more or less criminogenic than residential mixing.

An interesting interpretation of the varied findings on this issue holds that the peculiarities of black history in North America do not allow an easy equation of residential segregation with ghetto life, in the classic sense, any more than residential mixing signifies ethnic integration. For example, Molotch (1969) concludes from a study of a changing community that "biracial propinquity," the physical closeness of the races residentially, does not mean "racial integration." In short, when peoples meet, they do not necessarily become one. Ethnic identity is frequently stimulated by ethnic contact, so that the claims of difference and the pleas for a separate life become stronger *after* one has tested assimilation than they were before such an experience. Borhek (1970) found this to be true of ethnic groups in Canada, and a similar pattern of ethnic cohesion is being demonstrated by the more militant blacks in the United States (W. J. Harris, 1972). Research on attitudes of black students, for instance, finds that black students in white colleges are *more militant* and *more separatist* than black students in black colleges (Kilson, 1971).

When peoples meeet, they may assimilate or separate. "Group boundaries can become wider or narrower" (Horowitz, 1975, p. 115). There are contexts in which diverse peoples meet, and these contexts make a difference in the meaning of the meeting (Patterson, 1975). We need not spell out these contexts; our purposes here require only the recognition that residential and educational mixing may not betoken or produce integration. Conversely, the simple fact of segregation may not be a strong sign of "ghettoization." Some "ghetto effects" may become *stronger* as ethnic groups meet one another. Research on this issue awaits the development of better measures of ethnic identification and cultural difference than mere patterns of propinquity.

URBANISM

The city has long been considered more productive of crime than the countryside, and there is a popular explanation for this: that the crowding, impersonality, and anonymity of urban relations generate crime.

Like most popular theories, this one contains some truth, but it also deserves some qualification. The truth resides in the fact that the official statistics for Canada and the United States and for Europe report a tendency for serious crimes to increase with the size of the city (Clinard, 1942, 1960; Harries, 1976; Lottier, 1938; Ogburn, 1935; P. Wolf, 1965; Wolfgang, 1968). In this light, the President's Commission on Law Enforcement (1967a) estimated that 7 or 8 percent of the increase in crime reported between 1960 and 1965 may be attributed to increased urbanization.

The relation between metropolitan size and crime rates according to FBI data has been summarized by Harries (1974). Table 7-9 shows that attacks against both property and the person increase uniformly with increases in the numbers of people in concentrated areas.

Harries refined these figures by calculating correlations between four kinds of violent crime and numbers of people for 189 Standard Metropolitan Statistical Areas (SMSAs)[8] in the United States for the years 1965 through 1969. Table 7-10 indicates that the relations between the different kinds of personal attack and between each offense and numbers of people are positive. However, the relations vary in significance. The association between urbanism and assault is low (.19), which means that rural residents fight too. The correlation of numbers of people with murder is also modest (.26), a reflection, in part, of the tendency of rural Southerners to kill one another (Harries, 1974, Fig. 2.1). Rape shows a more significant connection to urban size (.44), and robbery has the highest correlation (.68).

Urban Crime Correlates

To ascertain which features of urban life are associated with higher and lower crime rates, Harries analyzed the correlations between 32 "social indicators" for 134 SMSAs that had more than 200,000 inhabitants in 1970. Factor analysis was employed to test for clustering among the 32 variables. Nine factors were identified. Table 7-11 shows how the social indicators are correlated among themselves. The plus and minus signs indicate whether the particular variable is positively or negatively associated with the factor of which it is part. For

[8]Standard Metropolitan Statistical Areas are counties or combinations of counties in the United States.This measure has been developed in an attempt to distinguish urban ways of life from rural conditions and, given the limits of city boundaries, is considered to be a more accurate unit of study than cities. However, SMSAs differ widely in density of population, and hence they are crude measures of urbanism (Bogue, 1969, p. 531).

Table 7-9   Crime Rates, 1971, by Population Groups, per 100,000 Inhabitants

Population group	Crime index total	Violent index crime*	Property index crime†
I 57 cities over 250,000; population 42.7 million Rate	5,413.5	1,047.5	4,366.0
6 cities over 1 million; population 18.8 million Rate	5,778.5	1,314.1	4,464.4
21 cities 500,000 to 1 million; population 13.5 million Rate	5,406.4	953.9	4,452.5
30 cities 250,000 to 500,000; population 10.4 million Rate	4,758.9	684.6	4,074.3
II 98 cities 100,000 to 250,000; population 14.1 million Rate	4,382.5	503.3	3,879.2
III 260 cities 50,000 to 100,000; population 18.2 million Rate	3,222.7	299.8	2,922.9
IV 509 cities 25,000 to 50,000; population 17.7 million Rate	2,798.4	242.8	2,555.6
V 1,224 cities 10,000 to 25,000; population 19.4 million Rate	2,243.5	187.6	2,055.9
VI 2,810 cities under 10,000; population 13.1 millino Rate	1,829.1	170.8	1,658.2
Suburban areas 2,795 agencies; population 62.6 million Rate	2,410.8	205.7	2,205.1
Rural areas 1,667 agencies; population 25.2 million Rate	1,099.8	115.7	984.0

* Murder, rape, robbery, assault.
† Burglary, larceny $50 and over, auto theft.
Source: Harries, 1974. Adapted from FBI, *Uniform Crime Reports — 1971,* Government Printing Office, Washington, 1972, table 9, pp. 100–101.

Table 7-10   Simple Correlations between Violent Crime and Population (189 SMSA's, 1965–1969)

Variable	Murder	Rape	Robbery	Assault	Population
1. Murder	1.00	.53	.48	.71	.26
2. Rape		1.00	.67	.61	.44
3. Robbery			1.00	.50	.68
4. Assault				1.00	.19
5. Population					1.00

Source: Reprinted with permission from Harries, 1974. Adapted from Harries, "Spatial aspects of violence and metropolitan population," *Professional Geographer,* **25:** 2, 1973.

example, birthrates are positively correlated with factor 4 (youth), while death rates are negatively correlated with this factor.

Factor analysis also showed that the FBI's index crimes clustered in two groups. One factor is composed of burglary, automobile theft, larceny, robbery, and rape. This cluster Harries calls "general crime." A second factor, which Harries calls "violent crime," is made up of assault and murder.

Harries then used a statistical technique (regression analysis) to find out how the nine factors of social indicators were associated with the two clusters of crimes. His findings can be summarized as follows:

1   The single largest contribution to general crime is made by the size of the SMSA. This is like saying that as more people congregate, the opportunities for theft increase.

2   The second most important factor accounting for variations in general crime is the proportion of people employed in manufacturing. The *higher* the proportion of people so employed, the *lower* the general crime rate. This finding confirms results reported by Schuessler (1962) and Schuessler and Slatin (1964) in earlier studies of differences in urban crime rates.

3   Five other factors are positively correlated with metropolitan rates of general crime, but their associations are weak. These factors are per capita personal income (the *higher* the income, the *more* general crime there is), "social disorganization" (high divorce and marriage rates and high population movement are associated with higher general crime rates), population change (the more movement of black and white people in and out of central cities, the higher the general crime rate), unemployment, and proportion of blacks in the population.

4   All seven factors combined account for 54 percent of the variation in general crime among the SMSAs. This means, of course, that something not measured in Harries's study is also generating differences in metropolitan criminality.

Table 7-11 Structure of Social Factors

Variable (Data refer to SMSA's unless otherwise indicated)	Direction of relationship	Name of factor
Total population, 1970	+	
Pop. density per square mile, central cities, 1970	+	SMSA
Total antipoverty funds allocated, 1969	+	size
Community Action Program funds allocated, 1969	+	
Net population change (%) 1960–70	+	
Net population change, central cities (%) 1960–70	+	Pop.
White population change, central cities (%) 1960–70	+	change
Black population change, central cities (%) 1960–70	+	
Black population (%) 1970	+	
Black population, central cities (%) 1970	+	Black
Local expenditures for health (%) 1967	+	pop.
Southerness Index	+	
Median age in central cities, 1970	−	
Median age outside central cities, 1970	−	
Birth rate per 1,000. 1968	+	Youth
Death rate per 1,000. 1968	−	
Dwellings with >1.01 persons per room (%) 1970	+	
Unemployed (%) 1969	+	Unemploy-
Local expenditures for welfare (%) 1967	+	ment
Pop. density per sq. mi. outside central cities, 1970	+	
Population in one-unit structures (%) 1970	−	Suburban
Population in one-unit structures outside central cities (5) 1970	−	pop. density
Net population change, outside central cities (%) 1970	+	Social
Marriage rate per 1,000. 1968	+	disorgan-
Divorce rate per 1,000. 1968	+	ization
Manufacturing employment (%) 1970	+	Manu-
Local expenditures for education (%) 1967	+	facturing
Physicians per 100,000 people, 1970	−	Employ.
Ave. hourly earnings of prod. workers in manufacturing, 1970	+	
Per capita personal income as % of national ave., 1970	+	
Substandard black occupied dwellings (%) 1970	−	Income
Monthly average AFDC payments, 1971	+	

Source: Reprinted with permission from Harries, 1974. Adapted from U.S. Bureau of the Census, *Metropolitan Area Statistics,* and from Gastil, 1971.

5   Rates of violent crime (homicide and assault) vary significantly among urban areas with six of the social-indicator factors. The proportion of the population that is black is the major factor. The second most significant factor is income—the poorer the population, the more violent it is. A third correlate is the density of the suburban population in the metropolitan area—the more people in the suburbs, the less violence there is. Contrary to expectation,

unemployment was found to be *negatively* associated with murder and assault. Violent crimes increase, however, with the size of the SMSA and with the amount of population change. These six factors together account for about 63 percent of the variation among metropolises in violent crime.

Density and Crime

Harries's research and earlier ecological studies point to several factors in urbanization that may be crime-productive. One of these is density—the number of people packed into an area.

Although the words "density" and "crowding" are used interchangeably, they should be distinguished. *Density* refers to the number of persons per unit of space. *Crowding* refers to the experience of being uncomfortably congregated (Eoyang, 1974; Gillis, 1975; Lawrence, 1974; Stokols, 1972).

The distinction is important because there is no one-to-one relation between density and crowding. Many factors mediate between variations in interpersonal distance and feelings of being crowded—factors such as the physical features of the spacing, temperature, whether one is packed in with strangers or intimates, cultural preferences, and psychological traits such as being temperamentally "sensation-seeking" or "sensation-reducing."

It may be crowding, then, rather than density that is more criminogenic. However, for practical reasons density has been studied where crowding might have been more relevant. This fact limits research findings and should be kept in mind when interpreting studies of density and crime.

Galle and His Associates on Density   Galle and others (1972) studied the impact of population density upon the usual "social pathologies," including juvenile delinquency, by using a group of measures of people-packing. These investigators examined the connection between delinquency and other disapproved conditions with four dimensions of density in Chicago:

> Number of persons per room
> Number of rooms per housing unit
> Number of housing units per structure
> Number of residential structures per acre

Their findings, given in Table 7-12, show a strong correlation between juvenile delinquency and density and also between juvenile offensiveness and social class and ethnicity. The correlation of the combined four density measures with official delinquency approaches .50 when ethnicity and socio-economic status are held constant. The correlation of delinquency with ethnicity and social status is slightly higher (.57) when density is held constant. This means that ethnicity and economic status are somewhat more closely associated with official delinquency than the density index is, but all these factors are important correlates of lawless conduct among young people, at least in Chicago.

Table 7-12 Social Pathology, Density, Ethnicity, and Social Class

	Social pathologies				
Parameter	Standard mortality ratio	General fertility rate	Public-assistance rate	Juvenile-delinquency rate	Admissions to mental hospitals
	Population densities and social pathology				
Multiple correlation coefficients of the four components of density[a] on each of the social pathologies	.867	.856	.887	.917	.689
Multiple-partial correlation coefficients of each pathology with the four components of density, controlling for ethnicity and social class	.476	.371	.584	.498	.508
	Social class, ethnicity, and social pathology				
Multiple correlation coefficient of each pathology with social class and ethnicity	.828	.853	.885	.927	.546
Multiple-partial correlation coefficient of each pathology with ethnicity and social class, controlling for the four components of population density[a]	143[b]	.351	.574	.574	.086[b]

[a]All measures of density are transformed into natural logarithms.
[b]Not significantly different from zero at $P = .05$.
Source: Reprinted with permission from Galle et al., 1972, table 3.

Other Studies Galle and his colleagues (1973) extended their investigation to a comparison of rates of violent crime in American cities graded by their four measures of density. Homicide and aggravated assault, as officially recorded, were positively related to the density index.

Booth and his associates (1976) analyzed data for 656 cities in the United

States with 25,000 or more people. On the assumption that there is a critical size beyond which density begins to produce a criminogenic effect, these researchers compared large cities (population 100,000 and over) with smaller ones using two measures of density: (1) density within the household—the proportion of households with more than one person per room—and (2) dwelling units per square mile, a measure of areal density.

Booth and his coworkers recognized that their two measures of density were differently associated with social status and therefore had to be applied with appropriate controls. For example, people per room is negatively correlated with income $(-.43)$ and with education $(-.55)$, but it is positively correlated with percent of a population that is nonwhite $(+.56)$. By contrast, areal density is associated with city size and with region rather than with the socioeconomic status of the population. Calculations were performed, therefore, holding constant region, city size, and the education, age, race, nativity, and income characteristics of urban populations.

With such controls, some density effect is found for kinds of crime and city size by kinds of density:

1 Automobile theft, robbery, and rape are associated with *areal density* in large cities.
2 In large cities *household density* bears almost no relationship to rates of serious offenses against property and the person.
3 None of the correlations between the two measures of density and crime rates are high. Some of the correlations approach "significance" in large cities, but these associations evaporate in smaller aggregations. This finding may confirm the researchers' assumption of a "critical mass" necessary to produce a density effect.

The Urbanizing Process

Studies such as these tell us about the correlates of crime within metropolitan areas. The connection between urbanization and crime is additionally illuminated by a study of the urbanizing *process*—the conditions under which people move from countrysides to cities.

We should expect that the effects of urbanization will vary with the rapidity of the process and with the ability of cities to absorb migrants economically and culturally. In this regard, urbanization in the twentieth century differs from that in the nineteenth century. If differs in its rapidity, in its volume, and in the economic assimilability of migrants. The rich countries of North America were urbanized during the nineteenth century at a much slower rate than that which the poor countries of Africa, Asia, and Latin America have experienced in the twentieth century since the end of World War II. The movement from rural areas to cities in some of these Third World states is novel and disturbing. One observer compares the urban rush in these countries to the swarming of lemmings (Culliton, 1975).

This movement is seen, of course, against a backdrop of increasing world population, an increase presently at a rate that ensures a *doubling* of our numbers every 35 years (G. Hardin, 1972, pp. 169–172). This proliferation of people is most sorely felt in poor countries. It has been accompanied by the migration of landless peasants into cities, where most of them become squatters in shanty towns. Among all the so-called "developing" countries 15 years ago, there were only 16 cities with 1 million people or more. Fifteen years from now there may be 200 such cities. In Latin America, there were only nine cities with populations over 1 million in 1960. It is estimated that by 1980 there will be 27 such congregations. By the end of this century two-thirds of all people may be living an urban life (Culliton, 1975).

The urbanizing process is now marked by some signs of technological change and increasing affluence for some portion of the population, but it is also characterized by increasing demands on governments to provide a wide variety of services, ranging from the provision of food, shelter, and energy to the removal of garbage and the control of crime. A picture of these correlated troubles is provided by a case study of change in one African country, Uganda. Uganda is one of the least urban African states, and yet its major city, Kampala, with about 3.5 percent of the country's population, accounts for one-fourth of its crime, according to Clinard and Abbott (1973, p. 91). Clinard and Abbott not only noted these changes in crime with changes in settlement, but they also described the criminogenic process in the breakdown of tribal life with movement of people from countrysides to cities.

As Figure 7-4 demonstrates, crime in Uganda increased for the country as a whole during the 1960s as its population increased and became more urban and more wealthy.

Qualifications

A description of the transformation of rural societies into urban ones provides material with which to explain changes in crime rates. The interpretation of this material is disputed, however. There are two important qualifications of the general finding that serious crime increases with density of population: one qualification concerns counting errors, and the other notes exceptions.

First, no one knows whether the underreporting characteristic of all crime is more prevalent in rural areas than urban ones. Some observers of the rural scene argue that many backwoods brawls and even murders ("hunting accidents") are unreported criminal events. This failure to report criminal events may be explained, in part, by the lack of policing in remote areas and in part by the "normality" of some kinds of violent offenses. At present there is no resolution of this question. It is not known whether the underreporting of crime is greater, less, or the same for human aggregations of different sizes.

A second qualification of the assumption that serious crime increases with urbanization is the finding that *some* rural areas and small towns have higher crime rates than larger cities and that cities of the same size within a political territory may have widely varying rates. Radzinowicz (1946) reports this for Poland; and Christie (1960) found some signs of a similar phenomenon in Norway. Wiers (1939) observed that, while urban areas in Michigan had high delinquency rates, there were yet significant differences in rural rates between the logging counties of the north and the agricultural counties of the south, with

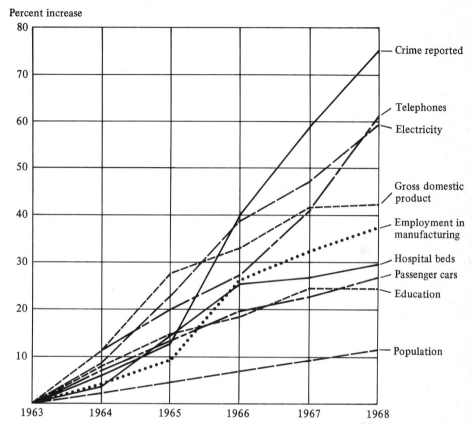

Percent increase

Figure 7-4 Cumulative percent increase of development indicators and total reported crime, Uganda, 1963–1968. (*From M. B. Clinard and D. J. Abbott,* Crime in Developing Countries: A Comparative Perspective. *Copyright © by John Wiley & Sons. Reprinted by permission.*)

the northern woodsmen being the more delinquent. French and Swedish rural crime rates are increasingly reported to approximate urban rates (E. H. Sutherland and Cressey, 1970, p. 179); and in Israel "the highest rate of delinquency in the whole country was recorded in the rural region of the Jerusalem area, whose population is composed entirely of 'new' immigrants" (Shoham, 1966, p. 82).

This mix of statistics may be interpreted as saying that the effect of population density upon crime rates is not direct. Again, as with the impact of the economy or of occupation upon criminality, those ways of life called "cultural" seem to intercede between the environment, including its human density and its wealth, and the behaviors to be explained.

CULTURE AND CRIME

The explanations of criminality in the following chapters are unanimous in attributing criminogenesis to something in the ordering of relations among people. When these arrangements have some regularity and persistence, they define a "culture." Cultural accounts of criminality are alike in discounting any important contribution to crime rates by such *unlearned* variables as the natural environment or biological differences. This is not to say that these variables have no impact. Some theories of criminogenesis allow for the "triggering effects" of noncultural factors such as the weather and some take into consideration the facts of biological difference. However, today the only persuasive theories of crime causation are theories that look toward some aspects of the social environment as more or less criminogenic. These explanations differ among themselves as to the facets of culture emphasized. They therefore differ in their predictions and in their recommendations.

Chapter 8

Questions and Answers

Explanations of crime, or of any other kind of conduct, are considered to be adequate or inadequate depending on the questions we have asked and on what we want to do with the answers. The explanations of crime described in the following chapters will be evaluated in terms of the questions they purport to answer and in terms of those they leave unanswered. It is advisable, therefore, to clarify the connection between questions, answers, and explanations before criticizing theories of crime production.

Three major points will be made:

1 That there are styles of questions and that these styles differ as to the answers that are acceptable.

2 That, in the social studies particularly and in everyday life generally, answers that are considered to be explanations suggest *causes*—implicitly or explicitly. Therefore, the following chapters classify theories of criminogenesis by their choice of *causal location*.

3 That locating causes has political and moral consequences.

Each of these points deserves comment.

1 To explain something is to make it clear, to make it plain. *How* we clarify an event depends, then, on *what* is to be explained. An answer is considered satisfactory or not in terms of the question we have asked and in terms of what we want to do with the answer. Satisfaction depends also on what we *can do* with the answer.

(a) Levels of explanation. What is to be explained about human behavior can be conceived as referring to different "levels" of action. "Level" refers to the unit of analysis. Units of analysis commonly employed in discussions of human conduct are *individual* and *aggregate*, and the kinds of questions asked on these different levels are recognized as *psychological* and *sociological*, respectively.

Thus, in talking about criminal activity, a frequent question is the psychological one: "Why did he (or she) do it?" By contrast, the sociological question asks about the behavior of aggregates: "Why does this society have more crime of type X than that one?" or "Why have crime rates for our society risen?"

We ordinarily expect answers to these two levels of question to be consistent, and we often explain the behavior of groups by referring to the motives or intentions of their members. In short, many sociological explanations may refer to the psychology of individuals taken collectively.

This need not be the case, however. It is possible to explain the actions of aggregates *without* reference to the actions of their individual components. One can explain and foretell the movement of a cloud, for example, without accounting for the behavior of the droplets of water within it. So too with human action. It is possible to explain group behavior without describing the motives of individuals within the group. There may be an implicit psychology underlying the sociological explanation, of course, but the behavior of aggregates can be studied without making statements about individuals within the collectivity.

It is an open question whether the behavior of human populations is better explained on the sociological or the psychological level. Sociological explanations that omit reference to individuals do not always satisfy. Intellectual satisfaction depends, again, upon the question that is asked and upon what one wants to do with the explanation.

(b) Empirical questions, and other kinds. All "sane" people, by definition, can tell the difference between a silly question and an answerable one. We can tell the difference at some extreme, as when someone asks, "What color is justice?" or "Why are you growing your father's hair?"

There is nothing to be experienced—there are no observables—that can tell us whether answers to such questions are correct or not. These questions are not empirical.

The frontier between empirical questions and silly ones is vague, however. Within this borderland we acknowledge that some questions are not foolish, although they do not require empirical answers. Such utterances sound like questions. They are phrased as questions, and we may respond to them as if they were inquiries. But when we think about these "meaningful, nonempirical" questions, we recognize that they are not questions but, rather, shouts or cries, lamentations, expressions which do not require empirical answers and which will not be satisfied by empirical replies.

"Why did she have to do that?" cries the wounded lover. "Why my child?" asks the anguished parent.

Those who ask such questions will not be satisfied with an empirical answer, although they may be comforted with appropriate words. Words can relieve pain without giving information.

There are times, then, when we express emotion in the form of questions. These questions do not require empirical answers. At other times, however, we want to be rational. We want to know what course of action will economically get us what we want. On such occasions, we ask empirical questions. An empirical question is one whose answer can be tested by facts, by something observable.

By contrast, if an answer can be maintained as "true" regardless of what occurs, then the question to which the answer is addressed is not empirical. If nothing that happens, or everything that happens, makes the answer correct, then the question is beyond experience. Whether such questions and answers are foolish depends upon whether the interrogator is being expressive or rational.

A piece of advice follows: *Know your question.* To know one's question is to know what experience, what fact, could conceivably answer it, negatively as well as affirmatively.

(c) To ask how, or whether, need not be to ask why. It is possible to ask *how* things work, or *whether* something has happened or is likely to happen, without requiring an explanation of *why* things occur as they do. In other words, it is possible to describe events and to forecast them without being able to specify their causes. Our experience may have taught us, for example, that when the sky is filled with dark, low clouds and the wind is shifting to the west, rain is likely. We can know this without being able to state why it is so. The same possibility exists when it comes to estimating human behavior.

2 Statements that only describe events or only state continuities between events usually do not qualify as explanations. When we ask for an explanation of something, particularly of social action, we want to know what causes it.

The idea of causation is a tangled one, as we have seen (pages 119–120). It is so complex a notion that some observers have urged that we mend our social affairs without thinking of their causes (Horton, 1973; L. T. Wilkins, 1968). It is possible to do this. When we respond to our environment as individuals, we adjust quite well to a variety of conditions without first having to analyze their causes. Thus we can sidestep abusive people without having to know what "made" them that way.

However, when we wish to do more than "merely adjust"—when we wish to explain occurrences and, more important, to shape events according to plan—we argue for a preferred policy by referring to the alleged causes of the happenings that concern us. Even criminologists who explicitly advise us to avoid thinking about causes and trying to explain them (Hartjen, 1974; Quinney, 1974a) are nonetheless constrained to think in terms of causes (Nettler, 1975, 1977; Scriven, 1968a). What is explicitly denied is implicitly assumed.

Explanations of crime thus emphasize different causes of conduct. The differing emphases arise from more than our imperfect knowledge of the causes of social events. These competing theories are also stimulated by the different questions we ask and by the fact that the very concept of causation is vague.

"To cause" means more than one thing, and there are varied criteria by which we identify causes. Furthermore, the events nominated as the "causes" of crime come in assorted packages (dense and sparse), in assorted shapes (rectilinear, curvilinear, and interacting), and with differing content. These variations need not be discussed here; their description can be read elsewhere (Beauchamp, 1974; Gorovitz, 1965; Nettler, 1977; Scriven, 1968b, 1971, 1974; H. A. Simon, 1972; R. Taylor, 1967; Weinberg, 1968). For our purposes, it is sufficient to be reminded of two facts (see pages 119–120) and to be informed by an interesting hypothesis.

The first fact is that, despite the variety of causal models available, social scientists always think causally with correlations. The second fact is that neither high nor low correlations between things nominated as causes and their supposed effects tell us what *generating power* these causes may have. Our estimates are based on judgments, and our judgments are amalgams of facts and preferences.

Balancing causes with preferences. The mixing of preference with fact in the judgment of causation has suggested a hypothesis to explain the differential attribution of causation and responsibility (Nettler, 1970, p. 35). This hypothesis has recently received experimental support and deserves description in preparation for our evaluation of explanations of crime. The hypothesis says that we move the location of causation according to our approval or disapproval of actors and their acts.

When people we prefer do things we approve of or when people we dislike do things we disapprove of, we locate the causes of their conduct *within* them, and we speak of their dispositions or purposes as sources of their action.

For example, "Why is Millicent Innocent [whom we like] marrying John Goodbody [whom we also like]?" Our answer refers to their dispositions ("They are in love") or their purposes ("They want to share a life and have a family").

However, when our preferences are thrown out of balance, as when "good guys" do bad deeds or when bad actors perform good deeds, then we tend to move causation *outside* the actors, and we refer to circumstance, pressure, accident, or luck.

The balancing of preferences with causal locations is diagramed in Table

Table 8-1   Evaluating Actors and Acts and Locating Their Causes

	Location of the cause of behavior	
Approval/disapproval of person/behavior	In person (character; intention)	In circumstance (luck; accident; "pressure")
Good person, good deed	+	
Bad person, bad act	+	
Good person, bad act		+
Bad person, good act		+

Source: Reprinted with permission from Nettler, 1976, table 13–1.

8-1. Evidence of this tendency is provided in research by J. L. Evans (1968), Regan et al. (1974), and Schiffman and Wynne (1963).[1]

3   Preferences that move the location of causes are embedded in our morals and our politics. The things we want to see done become elevated from values in themselves to general cures for a variety of miseries. If poverty offends us, while affluence does not, and if we consider relieving poverty an end in itself, it becomes tempting to justify our political preference by expanding its suggested causal power. Our prescribed program for alleviating poverty then becomes a program with a promise to reduce crime, alienation, and unhappiness.

Conversely, our assessment of explanations of crime is influenced by more than the factual soundness of the explanations. There is a tendency to be influenced also by what an explanation suggests we can and cannot do about crime. If the explanation points to evil sources of wrong acts—sources that we would just as soon liquidate anyway—it becomes easier for us to accept it. On the other hand, if the explanation does not point to what can readily be changed or if it does not point to things we are prepared to change, it tends to be devalued, and this devaluation is produced more by our morals than by the state of our science.

All this is more true when a science is thin. However, the tendency has been illustrated even in more firmly grounded sciences than the behavioral studies. The tug of ethicopolitical preference upon knowledge occurs in many scientific arenas. Historians of science have been particularly energetic in showing how frequently scientific hypotheses are accepted or rejected, not just because of the evidence available, but also because of a moral pressure to interpret the evidence in a congenial way. A recent example is provided by

[1]One of my students, Neil Warner, has suggested that moving causes from inside actors to outside them may be a function of the frequency with which we experience morally balanced and imbalanced acts-actors. Warner proposes that we more commonly experience events in "moral balance"—as when good deeds are produced by approved people and bad deeds by disapproved people. It would make an interesting, but difficult, project to test whether moral imbalance continues to move causes when the relative frequency of morally congruent and incongruent acts-actors is held constant.

Provine (1973), who studied the inferences drawn by biologists from their research on the genetics of racial mixture. In Provine's demonstration, the *morals* of scientists changed their *beliefs* without there having been any change in their *knowledge*.

IN SUMMARY

If our three points about questions and answers are accepted, what shall we conclude?

A first conclusion is that an answer to one person's question may not be an answer to another's. The adequacy of an explanation depends upon the question it attempts to answer.

A second inference is that some questions and their answers may be so vaguely phrased that one can never tell whether an answer is correct or not. The advice is to be clear about one's concepts.

A third lesson is that all explanations of complex social events may have some truth in them. Since ethicopolitical preferences look in different places for the causes of our troubles, it is likely that they will attend to some true things while ignoring others.

A fourth conclusion is that explanations are to be tested by what they *distinctively predict*. Both italicized words are important.

Causes and Predictions

To be of value, an explanation should be distinctive in the sense that it improves our ability to forecast events, or to predict them, more accurately than we could if we employed just common sense. Explanations which are vague or which do not suggest distinctive courses of action with warranted results are not scientific explanations. They do not increase knowledge, although they may provide other comforts such as being congenial to our morals.

Improving *predictive power* means something different from increasing *forecasting ability*. It has been argued earlier (page 165) that forecasts can be made without knowledge of causes. A forecast is a statement of the probable course of events, made on the basis of public evidence,[2] where the forecaster has no control over those events. The forecaster may adapt to them, naturally, but cannot alter their course. This is why we say that we forecast the weather, not that we predict it.

By contrast, to be able to predict means to be able to say, on the basis of public evidence again, that if one does x and y, so much of z will result.

We look for the causes of conduct when we want to increase our predictive power. We remain content with statements about the correlates of

---

[2]Public evidence is a required foundation of forecast and prediction. The difference between a seer, prophet, or clairvoyant and a scientist is that the scientist's forecasts and predictions are based on evidence that is public. The seer's visions are private.

conduct, and with descriptions of continuities among situations and behaviors, when we are satisfied to forecast events.

Some of the explanations of crime to be discussed contribute to forecasting ability; few contribute to predictive power. Nevertheless, the explanations of crime emphasize different causal locations, and it is both useful and convenient to classify them by the causes they nominate.

EXPLANATIONS OF CRIME CLASSIFIED BY CAUSES

Causes of conduct, individual and collective, have been held to be (1) the situations people are in, (2) their mode of interpreting their situations, and (3) the way in which they learned their interpretations. The first group of causes attributes our behavior to *where we are*. The second set locates causation in *attitudes* we have acquired. The third set of explanations goes beyond what we have learned to describe *how we learned* it.

When causal locations are identified in this manner, it becomes apparent to most observers that our conduct is caused by all these nominated determinants. It is apparent, too, that these suggested causes have different powers, which vary with the situation and the behavior to be explained.

In brief, *where we are*, *what we are* (which includes *how we think*), and *how we became that way* are intertwined. In the determination of any particular action, these alleged causes interact. What is disputed is how they interact and how much causal power each of the interacting agents possesses. This dispute is settled, we have argued, not so much by evidence as by what a conclusion tells us we can and cannot do.

It is our task to examine each set of causes in the explanatory modes provided by criminologists. One way of classifying these explanations by nominated causes is to regard theories of criminogenesis as differentially emphasizing:

1 Social structures that make it more and less *rational* to commit crime
2 Social structures that give some people the *power* to call others' actions "criminal"
3 Social structures that provide differential *opportunities* for lawful and criminal conduct
4 *Subcultures* that are more and less criminogenic
5 *Ideas* that are more and less criminogenic
6 *Training*, or its lack, that is more and less criminogenic

The first three sets of hypotheses share a common causal base in the *social structure*. They overlap, therefore, but they differ in terms of what it is in the social structure that most effectively produces crime.

The fourth and fifth sets of hypotheses share a common causal location in the *learned interpretations* of our worlds. They differ in the size of the causal network to which they attend. Subcultural explanations, the fourth group of

Table 8-2 Explanations of Crime Classified by Their Emphasized Causes

Locus of causation	Emphasis	Theme	Chapter location	Sample of advocates
Social structure	Choice	Rationality	9–10	C. Beccaria, J. Mack, E. H. Sutherland in his description of "white-collar crime," and economists W. E. Cobb, I. Ehrlich, B. Fleisher, J. P. Gunning, L. R. McPheters, M. Sesnowitz, R. Shinnar, S. Shinnar, M. Silver, and G. Tullock
	Power	Injustice in the production and administration of criminal law	11	W. J. Chambliss, A. A. Platt, R. Quinney, H. Schwendinger, J. Schwendinger, I. Taylor, A. T. Turk, P. Walton, and J. Young
	Opportunity	Inequality in life chances	12	R. A. Cloward, A. K. Cohen, P. Goodman, S. Kobrin, L. McDonald, R. K. Merton, K. Polk, W. E. Schafer, and A. L. Stinchcombe
Interpretations of the world	Cultures as learned patterns of thinking, valuing, doing	Subcultures as distinctive ways of appreciating and responding to the world	13	E. H. Banfield, D. Downes, F. Ferracuti, O. Lewis, W. B. Miller, B. M. Spinley, P. P. Willmott, and M. E. Wolfgang
	Actors' ideas	Differential definitions of situations	14	D. R. Cressey and E. H. Sutherland
	Reactors' ideas	Labeling; stigmatizing	15	H. S. Becker, J. Kitsuse, E. M. Lemert, E. M. Schur, and F. Tannenbaum
Socialization; nurturing	Training regimes	Method of training and content of lesson taught	16	A. Bandura, S. Dinitz, H. J. Eysenck, T. W. Hirschi, W. B. Reckless, G. Trasler, and R. Walters

theories, emphasize the *totality* of a way of life in which learned interpretations are acquired and operate. By contrast, the fifth group focuses on *ideas* as causes. This explanatory mode derives from a particular sociopsychological formulation called "symbolic interactionism," which stresses the importance of a people's definition of their situation as the source of their behavior. As applied in criminology, symbolic interactionism means that the ideas that are deemed causal are sometimes described as the beliefs held by offenders and sometimes as the beliefs held by those who react to offenders and label them.

The sixth location of causation does not deny the importance of situations and their interpretations, but it emphasizes the role of *training* in producing the interpretation and making it operational in particular situations. Because the sixth set of causes attends to practices that develop personal and social control, this kind of explanation has been called—unfortunately, some think—"control theory."

Each of these explanatory styles will be described and criticized in the chapters to follow. Our attention will be given principally to the adequacy of these explanations as answers to the sociological, rather than the psychological, questions. Their particular emphases are outlined in Table 8-2.

Chapter 9

Rational Crime

Many of the wrongs we do each other serve our purposes. They get us what we want.

There are other causes of the damage we produce, of course—accidents and impulses, for example. Yet some ill-defined but important amount of crime is intentional. It is decided upon; it is chosen in satisfaction of some objective. This is true of both offenses against persons and offenses against property. When a criminal act achieves one's purpose economically, it is rational.

Being Rational versus Being Moral

At first blush, it sounds paradoxical to call crime "rational." "Rational" is a good word with favorable connotations. Most of us claim to be rational, and we generally consider it better to be rational than to be nonrational or irrational.

However good it may be to be rational, being rational is not the same thing as being good or doing good. One can be rational without being moral, and the terms should be disentangled.

To be rational is to employ one's "reason" to select the most appropriate means for the attainment of one's empirical ends (Cousineau, 1967). All the terms in this definition are important.

This definition states, first, that a rational act is a purposive act. It is done consciously to obtain an objective. A purposive act may be contrasted with an expressive one. Purely expressive behavior, behavior that is its own end, is not rational in this sense. Dancing for joy is an expressive act, for example. It may be fun and it may be "good," but it is something other than rational.

Second, our definition limits the objectives of a rational act to those that are empirical, to those that can be experienced. The ends of rational actions must be ascertainable. Good goals whose attainment can never be experienced, like getting to heaven or achieving "the greatest good for the greatest number,"[1] are not rational goals.

Finally, a rational act is one based upon a reasoned—that is, informed—choice of the most economical means for the actor. "Economical means" are not only those which are efficient in obtaining a particular objective but also those which do not carry a cost in the reduction of other goals that the actor values.

This definition of rationality, it should be noted, says nothing about the goodness of the ends toward which the agent is using his or her reason efficiently. Neither does it say anything about the goodness of the actor's means. The idea of *moral* behavior is quite another matter. It has its own difficulties, which need not concern us here. The point being made is simply that many categories of crime, however they may be judged morally, are nonetheless rational.

An Implication   An immediate implication of the conception of some crime as rational is a challenge to the popular psychiatric assumption, readily adopted by many schools of social work, that crime is a "symptom" of social and personal sickness. In this medical model of criminogenesis, criminals are considered to be sick people, but never rational ones.

"Symptom" is, of course, another emotionalized term that special-pleads. Its use signifies that the behavior called a "symptom" is regarded as an effect that is itself not to be controlled. Calling a behavior a "symptom" recommends, and sometimes demands, that something other than the behavior that concerns us be treated. In the social studies "symptom" becomes "a *transfer term*. . . . [It] *shifts the burden of blame* from the actor to his social setting" (Nettler, 1976, p. 3).

The medical image of crime causation rests on a common belief expressed by a former Attorney General of the United States who told us that ". . . healthy, rational people will not injure others. . . . Rehabilitated, an individual will not have the capacity . . . to injure another or to take or destroy property" (R. Clark, 1970, p. 220).

Such a statement is either a tautology or an unsupported hope. Carried to

---

[1]An attempt to achieve "the greatest good for the greatest number" is not rational because it is impossible to maximize two or more values simultaneously. The mathematical proof is provided by von Neumann and Morgenstern (1947), who comment: "A particularly striking expression of the popular misunderstanding about this pseudo-maximum problem is the famous statement according to which the purpose of social effort is 'the greatest possible good for the greatest number.' A guiding principle cannot be formulated by the requirement of maximizing two (or more) functions at once. Such a principle, taken literally, is self-contradictory. (In general one function will have no maximum where the other function has one)" (p. 11).

its logical extremity, this therapeutic recommendation leads to such futilities as doing social work among the Mafia.[2]

CRIME AND ECONOMICS

Economists differ from social workers, and from some psychologists and sociologists, in assuming that most human beings are rational—even when they are criminal. They do *not* assume that bad actors are necessarily sick ones.

Economists assume that human behavior—particularly that called "action" or "conduct"—is chosen. Human action is voluntary action, and voluntary action is understood as behavior directed toward goals selected by individuals (L. von Mises, 1966, p. 11).

Economists agree with one breed of psychologist, that called "behaviorist" (Skinner, 1938, 1953, 1974), that a major cause of conduct is its consequence. It is assumed that people have something called "self-interest," that they know what it is, and that they change their actions to maximize their interests (Stigler, 1975, chap. 3).

Economics becomes, then, the study of how people *choose* to employ scarce resources to satisfy their desires (R. L. Miller, 1973, p. 23; Samuelson, 1973, p. 3). Economists believe that people try to get what they want at a price they can afford. Conduct is deemed to be rational.

Classical Roots

In criminology, this assumption was once considered radical and liberating. In the eighteenth century the idea that criminals were rational and responsible actors was proposed as part of a larger program of humane treatment of offenders. The recommended societal response to crime, a response deemed to be just, would mete out penalties proportioned to the crime. It would refrain from using the law to "make an example of offenders" or to reform them. The ideas of this orientation in criminology were best expressed in the writing of Cesare Beccaria (1738–1794), whose famous *Essay on Crimes and Punishments* was first published in Italy in 1764. It is notable that Beccaria was an economist as well as a jurist.

Advocates of ideas such as Beccaria's considered themselves to be liberals who wished to limit the punitive action of the state and protect the rights of individuals against arbitrary exercise of state power. Their attitudes influenced legislation throughout Europe in the nineteenth century and are identified today as being of the "classical school."

The classical assumption has recently been invigorated by economists interested in applying their expertise to the study of crime. However, their notion that criminals may be as rational as other people contrasts with the

---

[2]On the "cure" of the Mafia in Sicily, Barzini writes, "Obviously most remedies tried were once again only partial. Some turned out to be no remedies at all, but incentives. Obviously the Mafia can exist even without poverty, illiteracy, social injustice, feudalism, *latifundia*, and foreign rulers. Like all other activities, it prospered, in fact, when backward social and economic conditions were removed" (1971, p. 368).

working premises of many other students of social behavior. It runs against the grain of deterministic interpretations of conduct that view actors as victims of circumstance rather than as agents. In particular, the economist's assumption is at war with the Freudian interpretation of human action, which until recently dominated schools of social work and psychiatry in Canada and the United States (Sargant, 1964).

Of course, some non-Freudian psychological theory and some sociological theory also assume a deterministic conception of conduct. As a result of the popularity of such theories, many students of social events vacillate: they sometimes regard behavior as rational, and sometimes as impelled. The assumption that behavior is impelled, strongly caused, is encouraged by several other, congenial assumptions: that people sometimes do not know what they want, that they want conflicting things, that they are pushed into action against their wishes or against their own "best interests," or, finally, that appetites are *drives* rather than *preferences*. Without judging who is correct or incorrect at this point, we can see that psychologists and sociologists are less consistent than economists in adopting an assumption to underwrite their studies.

Bounded Rationality

The economists's assumption of human rationality admits that there are crazy people and irrational ones. It recognizes, too, that we operate with imperfect knowledge and that, even when we try to act rationally, we may be less than efficient because we are ignorant of the full range of consequences of our acts. Our ignorance, in turn, is a function not only of lack of information but also of our difficulties in handling much information and in processing it. H. A. Simon (1958, chap. 4) has termed rational action under such limitations "bounded rationality."

With the qualification that our efforts to be rational are thus constrained, economic analysis starts with the premise that most of us, most of the time, know what we are doing. The idea of knowing what we are doing assumes that we have preferences—however they were caused[3]—and that we select means of achieving these values in terms of their estimated costs and rewards.

Moving Causes, Again

The assumption that criminal activity is rational is considered a form of structural explanation because economists regard situations as determining how one achieves one's purposes. Situations are viewed as constraints, or opportunities, that affect how a person's objectives can be achieved. Circumstances impose costs upon the satisfaction of desires, and the economist is

---

[3]Economists begin their reasoning with differences in preferences as givens. They do not ask how preferences are themselves produced. It is this omission that annoys some sociologists, reduces the ability of economists to predict action, and is answered, partially, by control theorists (discussed in Chapter 16).

This omission underlies the criticism of economic explanations of crime noted on pages 202–204.

interested in how people weigh costs against satisfactions (McKenzie and Tullock, 1975, pp. 9–13).

It should be noted here, however, that the same action can be differently interpreted. It is possible to move the cause of conduct from what the situation allows and the costs it imposes to the *preferences* that are to be satisfied, to the *ideas* one has about expected costs and benefits, or to the *learning process* by which one has acquired both preferences and ideas. Emphasis on differential preferences ("values") is part of the *subcultural* explanatory style. Emphasis on ideas is the preferred explanatory mode of *symbolic interactionists*. And attention to learning-training processes is the explanatory task of *control* theory.

Crime-producing Situations

The possibility of various explanations of the same action tells us, again, that we may shift the location of causes in accordance with our preferences for the acts and actors being explained and for the policies suggested by the explanations.

However, if we regard the economist's interpretation of crime as a form of structural explanation, there are at least four kinds of overlapping situations that are seen to produce crime:

1 Circumstances in which criminal action yields high reward at low cost. This may be viewed as the general condition that underlies (explains) crime in such particular situations as those listed below.
2 Circumstances in which ordinary work "requires" crime.
3 Circumstances in which a market exists, or is generated, for crime.
4 Circumstances in which crime may be chosen as a preferred career.

1 **Rewarding Crime** The most obvious way in which a social structure produces crime is by providing chances to take property illegally. The idea of a "chance" is the notion that rewards may be high, and costs low. This notion agrees with the common-sense assumption that most people will take money if they can do so without penalty. It is an assumption that led the cynical journalist Ambrose Bierce (1842–1914?) to define honesty as "a deficiency of reach." It is an idea that was well phrased over two hundred years ago by the Scottish philosopher David Hume, who wrote: "A man who at noon leaves his purse full of gold on the pavement at Charing Cross may as well expect that it will fly away like a feather as that he will find it untouched an hour after" (1758, p. 101).

Obviously, there are differences in personality that raise or lower resistance to temptation. These differences are the concern of those sociopsycholog-ical explanations which emphasize the "controlling" functions of character. However, without attending to these personal variables, it is notable that the common human proclivity to improve and maintain status will produce offenses against property when these tendencies meet the "appropriate situation." "Appropriate situations" abound in rich countries. They include the many circumstances in which supplies, services, and money are available for theft. They range from taking what is not nailed down in public settings to stealing factory tools and store inventories, cheating on expense accounts, embezzling funds, and perpetrating a wonderful assortment of frauds.

Some studies of public honesty were reported in Chapters 2 and 5. These investigations, and others, lead to a common conclusion—that "getting something for nothing" is a popular frailty. For example, Merritt and Fowler (1948) measured "the pecuniary honesty of the public at large" by dropping, on the streets of a number of American cities, stamped, addressed postcards, envelopes containing letters, and envelopes containing letters as well as a lead coin that felt like a 50-cent piece. While 72 percent of the postcards and 85 percent of the envelopes containing just letters were placed in mailboxes, only 54 percent of the letters containing the "coins" were mailed.

In other studies "lie-detector" (polygraph) tests were conducted among employees of chain stores and banks. McEvoy (1941) reports that about three-fourths of the workers had taken money or merchandise from his sample of chain stores. About one-fifth of the employees of the banks surveyed were reported to have "increased their salaries" by stealing money or property.

Thefts from libraries are now so great that institutions ranging from Harvard University to San Quentin are employing costly "sensing" devices to detect culprits (*Time*, 1964), and from Mexico to Canada things left unguarded on public streets—"roller skates, bicycles, baby carriages, appliances, garbage cans, tools, lawn mowers, and the like—disappear as if by magic" (F. Lundberg, 1954). *The Wall Street Journal* verified this picture from its own experience when Dow Jones and Company, which publishes the paper, moved into new offices while the building was still under construction. A spokesman for Dow Jones reports:

> "They stole us blind. As much as $10,000 worth of office equipment and furnishing was taken, despite the presence of uniformed guards on each floor."
>
> Among the items taken:
>
> —A 15-by-20 foot piece of carpet ("It was glued to the floor and they peeled it right up," the spokesman says).
>
> —A 20-foot long walnut counter-top ("I don't know what anyone wanted with the Payroll Department's counter—maybe someone needed a bar").
>
> —At least 30 chairs, worth about $200 each ("We had the guards sitting in them").
>
> In addition, so many telephones were stolen, the spokesman says, that "the phone company threatened to stop installing them. Not because they're so expensive but because they were running out of phones" [1972, p. 12].

This sample of measures of public honesty could be expanded, of course. It is sufficient, however, to illustrate the point that much theft occurs when the stealing carries a low risk of penalty.

Honest crooks, crooked crooks, and others   Governments and their laws change. Technologies change too, and with these variations in laws and technologies go changes in chances to steal. For example, credit cards are a new form of money, and they provide new opportunities for theft. Similarly, doing business by computer provides "computer jockeys" with chances to steal by doctoring tapes, which they do (Farr, 1975). Similarly, automated telephone instrumentation challenges "phone freaks" ("phreaks") to develop devices for stealing telephone services. They now manufacture a simple gadget called a "blue box" that allows one to make long-distance calls toll-free. Amateur radio magazines carry articles on how to make a blue box at home, and the cheating devices themselves go through transformations into "black, red, and cheese boxes" that have specialized telephone-theft functions (Jacobs, 1976).

The fluctuating opportunities to steal draw into crime varying proportions of people who are deemed to be "otherwise law-abiding." It is as though there were a gray area—a foggy no-man's land—bctween that minority of honest thieves devoted to a career in crime and that minority of honest citizens dedicated to obeying the law. Into this obscure frontier, varying proportions of "dishonest crooks" are tempted. "Crooked crooks" are people who do not admit that they steal, who may not "think" their theft is theft, and who seem ordinarily engaged in lawful work. Examples are plentiful. They include entertainers and business people who travel much and need to talk at long-distance and who therefore see the rationality of the blue box (Jacobs, 1976). Additional examples are people "pressured" into crime by personal troubles, business, or politics, as described on pages 180–184. And other examples include the apparently growing number of persons drawn into "business-type crime."

The crime industry   Business-type crime, as John Mack (1975a) describes it, involves "the criminal exploitation of business opportunities" (p. 13). This is a different dimension of thievery from that of the classical criminal predator such as the robber, burglar, or con man, whose basic style of operation has not changed much. It is also a different dimension of criminality from that of the "organized criminal," like Al Capone, who thinks of himself as "doing business" in meeting a market for illegal goods and services (see page 184).

These styles of thief differ not only in their mode of operation but also in their honesty. That is, they differ in the objectivity with which they face what they are doing. Traditional thieves are usually honest about their larcenous work. They know what they are doing, and they call it by the correct name. The "organized" gangster, by contrast, seems less clear—he sometimes identifies himself as a thief, and sometimes as a "legit" businessman. In justifying himself, for example, "the Godfather" says that his killing is as legitimate as his nation's warring.

As we move away from these vocational thieves toward the more lawful side of the spectrum of honesty, we run into that gray area in which resides a vast mass of "dishonest crooks" who steal only when it is convenient, when the victim is distant and dispersed, and when the risk is slight. Such watered-down, part-time theft permits these thieves to regard themselves as honest.

As we have seen, opportunities abound for thievery that is less than a full-time career. In particular, being in business in a changing climate of law and technology means that opportunities are opening and closing to survive and to succeed by breaking the law. These changing chances generate business-type crime, a kind of crime that differs from the older conception of white-collar crime as developed by E. H. Sutherland (1949).

Sutherland's idea of white-collar crime included many activities which were *not* technically criminal but which violated civil laws or "rules of the game." Sutherland raised the question of whether the damage done by such technically noncriminal acts, committed by business people of good repute, ought to be considered criminal. The distinguishing mark of white-collar criminals, as Sutherland pictured them, was that their principal work was lawful, while their criminal activity was partial.

Mack and his colleagues have enlarged and clarified this conception by showing that there is a flexible frontier between honest theft and the varieties of dishonest deceit. The styles of partial and complete honesty can be classified by the legality of actors' original intentions and by their current objectives and modes of doing business. Borrowing from Zirpins and Terstegen (1963), Mack's associate, Kerner (1975), produced a classification that appears in Table 9-1.

Table 9-1 Styles of Business-Type Crime

Type of company	Origin	Objective and mode of activity	Description
1 Dishonest, but not criminal (i.e., not liable to imprisonment)	Non-criminal	Non-criminal	Firms with borderline morals which deceive others and trap them in an unfair, but legal, manner; premeditated violation of civil law; offenses against tax laws, etc., which just reach border of criminal liability
2 Dishonest, and on occasion, criminal	Non-criminal	Non-criminal and criminal	Operates on both sides of the law
3 "Evasive" firms, prepared to adopt criminal means to survive as legitimate firms	Criminal	Criminal and non-criminal	Includes embezzlement in emergency; fraudulent conceal-ment or transfer of capital, including bankruptcy; tax frauds — with the object of reverting to legitimacy after the emergency
4 Camouflage firms	Non-criminal	Criminal	These firms are usually created for purposes of espionage, usually political espionage; their objective and mode of activity is criminal but not fraudulent. In this, they differ from #5 below.
5 Swindling firms	Criminal	Criminal	Criminal *and* fraudulent

Source: Adapted with permission from Kerner, 1975.

An example   A complicated and exciting way of making money legally is through the business of *arbitrage*. Arbitrage involves the simultaneous purchase and sale of securities or moneys of different countries in order to profit from quickly changing differences in exchange rates. This perfectly legal work has expanded in its variety and possibility with increased governmental efforts to control production and prices through taxes and subsidies. In short, governments that redistribute wealth by taxation and subvention create opportunities to steal. A gradient evolves, a slope that runs downhill from doing what is lawful, to doing what is legal but shady, to practicing outright fraud. Mack and Kerner (1975a, p. 17) give this example, which was made possible by subsidies provided by the European Economic Community:

> Salesmen from France, Germany, Yugoslavia, and Rumania sent a large consign-
> ment of butter on a European tour, by ship and train. While the butter was being
> transformed, whether in the course of nature or by a fiscal fiction, to butter-fat, the
> butter-fat to mayonnaise, the mayonnaise to fat for industrial use, e.g., soap, the
> industrial fat to seasoning sauce, a series of export or import subsidies was paid for
> each transformation until 10 million DM (Deutschmarks) compensation money was
> accumulated on this one consignment.

This legal, but nonproductive, mode of making money suggests to the enterprising dealer that, if governments pay for such "trade," it may be possible to apply for the state's funds by filing the proper papers without troubling oneself with the actual shipments. Thus, say Mack and Kerner:

> The pure form of this type of crime is reached when firms are established which
> have no capital or personnel (i.e., of which the only personnel are the swindlers)
> and which operate large export and import transactions entirely on paper for the
> purpose of obtaining subventions, refunds of customs duty, etc. One fraudster got
> away with over 11 million DM entirely on the basis of fictitious transactions [1975a,
> p. 17].

2   Crime-producing Pressures of Lawful Work   Opportunities to make money out of crime are only one of the conditions that make thievery seem rational. A second set of circumstances that makes crime appear practical is usually referred to as "pressures," the troubles associated with lawful work in business and in politics that make the criminal shortcut seem sound.

Crime in the board room   Ordinary work carries the risk of difficulties in getting the job done. There are the difficulties of competing in an uncertain market and the difficulties of meeting standards of quality and quantity in production. These troubles generate the temptation to violate the law, particularly if the law is an administrative rule or government regulation, a crime *malum prohibitum*, rather than a traditional predatory crime that is "wrong in itself" *(malum in se)*. In other words, troubles in lawful work provide temptations to break laws, administrative and criminal, that appear meddlesome rather than "really criminal."

An outstanding example is the "incredible electrical conspiracy," a price-fixing fraud among some of the world's largest manufacturers of electrical equipment. In this case, 45 executives of 29 corporations were indicted for conspiracy to violate the Sherman Antitrust Act by preestablishing prices, "rigging" bids, and thus dividing more securely a market valued at close to $2 *billion* a year. This crime, or series of crimes, was rational, and the testimony of the defendants indicates their confusion of what seemed efficient with what was lawful. As R. A. Smith (1961), who reported the trial, points out, "There was . . . a failure to connect ordinary morals and business morals; the men involved apparently figured there was a difference."

Crime in the factory   There are other work-inspired pressures to break the criminal laws in ways which are less larcenous than misrepresentation, theft, and fraud, but which can have dangerous consequences. These are the many circumstances in industry where the demands of production quotas and quality-control standards encourage faking. Such cheats occur in both communist and capitalist economies (Bensman and Gerver, 1963; Berliner, 1961; Connor, 1972; Moore, 1954; Vandivier, 1972). These crimes in the factory, like frauds in sales and service, result from the plurality of objectives existing in any large organization and from the ever-present conflict between efficient means, moral codes, and empirical ends.

The urgency to get the job done makes such criminal activity rational in the short run. Its long-run rationality (how much does one "get away with" and for how long?) is not always known. Its morality, we have seen, is another matter.

Crime in politics   Being political is another form of legitimate work that generates its own pressures for fraud. To be political is to be entangled by the need to attain and maintain power, through the appeasement of conflicting interests, within the limitations of a real world. This entanglement stimulates lying—to oneself and to others.

Lying is the vocational hazard of the politician. It is the politician's risk of the trade because he or she promises, and sometimes desires, to make things other than what they are. It is the politician's risk of the trade because in the real world truth and utility are not always friends. They are often at war. To say that truth and utility are in conflict is to say that there are inconvenient truths. It does not matter which ideals a political person espouses. As long as the promises are ideal, they deviate from the real, and the path to power then requires some denial.

It is thus that the philosopher Hannah Arendt (1967) could argue that "it may be in the nature of the political realm to be at war with truth in all its forms, and hence . . . a commitment . . . to factual truth is felt to be an anti-political attitude" (p. 52).

The prominent German sociologist Max Weber (1864–1920) said much the same thing in his famous essay "Politics as a Vocation" (Gerth and Mills, 1946). In Weber's words, "He who lets himself in for politics, that is, for power and force as means, contracts with diabolical powers and for his action it is *not* true that good can follow only from good and evil only from evil, but that often the opposite is true. Anyone who fails to see this is, indeed, a political infant" (p. 123).

Scholars—truth seekers and truth tellers—cannot be political. Those who choose the political calling over the scholarly vocation commit what Julien Benda (1928) called the "treason of the intellectuals."

Testing the treason of the clerks. Tests of arguments such as those advanced by Arendt, Benda, and Weber are plentiful. They can be found in histories and in modern journalism, and they have even been subjected to social science methods. For example, H. Hart (1947) performed a content analysis of articles in sociological journals to ascertain whether there was a relation between "passionate advocacy" and the avoidance of facts. Avoiding facts is not the same thing as telling lies, of course, but neither is it telling truths. Hart found a significant, positive association between the tendency of sociologists to make "unsupported value judgments" and their proclivity to make "unsupported sweeping non-evaluative generalizations." Conversely, sociologists whose papers were more factual were also sociologists who refrained from "unsupported value judgments."

More recently, Winter (1970) purposely tested Weber's hypothesis by examining the morals of American clergymen who were more and less devoted to politics. Winter found that the more a clergyman is involved in politics, "the less he objects to the use of a strategy for social change which employs deceit, threats, bluffs, and hostility, [and] the less he disapproves of the use of power and conflict in general" (p. 36).

This general thesis about the corrupting pull of politics is as old as social thought. The concern of criminologists, however, is with current innovations in fraud, particularly those concocted by governments. The Watergate scandal and the military lying about Vietnam are but two compounds of deceit in a long history of political chicanery. What is more interesting as a variation on a corrupt theme is the involvement of many modern states in one of the oldest con games, named for one of its more successful perpetrators the "Ponzi."

Playing Ponzi in government. A repeatedly successful swindle involves robbing Peter to pay Paul. The "con" works by the thief's inventing a get-rich-quick scheme that promises high return on one's investment.

Ponzi devised a form of arbitrage with international money orders and postal certificates (Dunn, 1975). In such a scheme the con artist convinces people that, since the margin of profit is small, it takes large amounts of money to make money. A few investors try their luck, and, sure enough, they are paid back as promised—90 days later, say, with 15 percent interest on their money for the quarter. The investors, like once-rewarded gamblers, become believers. They put more money into the scheme and tell their friends. As long as the flow of investment exceeds the payoffs, the Ponzi scheme works. The con artist's trick, of course, is to quit while still ahead and to flee the country. The con man's weakness is that, when the scheme gets working, he cannot bring himself to abandon it. The swindler waits for just a little larger "score," and this is when accidents happen. Or the demand for repayment suddenly exceeds the cash flow, and the lucrative game is over.

Modern governments play at Ponzi through their deficit financing. This involves spending more than they have and financing the deficit by borrowing. Once on this escalator, they must borrow more to pay back what has been loaned. The initial borrowing and the additional borrowing are accomplished, of course, by promising to pay investors a return on their money. The cheat occurs when governments print more money and devalue their currency, with the result that inflation consumes the gain promised the investor. In brief, a government sells a bond worth $1,000 today with the promise to return the money plus, say, 6 percent interest per annum. With inflation running between 12 and 30 percent in recent years, depending on the country, the government is returning to investors less than it borrowed from them.

Like all Ponzi schemes, this one works in the short run. Days of reckoning arrive, however, when people see through the game, lose confidence in the government's ability to repay their money, and refuse to invest further. The German debacle of the 1920s is a major example of the destruction of an economy by government-induced inflation. Italy and Great Britain are more recent cases.

Up to this point, the chronicle of governments playing Ponzi may be legal without being honest. However, the Ponzi game puts one on the slippery slope toward fraud. As the situation gets desperate, as the sources of loans dry up, politicians in charge are pushed toward misrepresenting their finances and juggling their accounts. They are now committing fraud. New York City provides a prime illustration.

"Cooking the books" in New York City. It is probable that government officers and bankers in New York participated in what the investigative reporter Ken Auletta (1975a) has called "the biggest securities swindle in history," bringing America's largest city to the brink of bankruptcy.

The motive for this series of official deceits was not the ordinary one of getting something for nothing. It is not alleged that the officials responsible for New York's financial disaster stole money. The major motive was political—to get into office and to stay there. A minor motive may have been "to do good." The impulse toward bankruptcy was well expressed by one of New York's mayors, Robert Wagner, who declared in his budget speech of 1965 that "I do not propose to permit our fiscal problems to set the limits of our commitments to meet the essential needs of the people of this city" (Auletta, 1975b, p. 29).

Ten years later New York City owed investors in its bonds $54 *billion.* Some 160,000 people who had bought city securities stood to lose their money, and the interest costs on the city's debt alone were running at almost one-fourth of its expense budget (Auletta, 1975a, p. 38).

This financial fiasco was lubricated with fraud. In simplest terms, urban officials misrepresented the financial status of their city when they went to borrow money. They claimed collateral they did not have. In July and August of 1975, State Comptroller Arthur Levitt noted that city officers listed as collateral "$324 *million* in fictitious state and federal aid [and] overstated by a staggering $408.3 *million* the real-estate taxes it could expect to collect" (Auletta, 1975a, p. 38; italics added).

A state auditor of the city's finances commented: "All of the city's fiscal tricks over the years are variations on a single theme: to make the budget appear balanced when it wasn't" (Auletta, 1975a, p. 38).

We have here a costly example of the "pressure" of legitimate work producing crime. Since the intention that generated these frauds was not the desire to steal, but rather the urge to maintain power, some of the offenders distinguish themselves from outright thieves. As one official put it, "Our crime was cowardice, not dishonesty" (Auletta, 1975a, p. 40).

Such a corrupt use of language compounds the felony and reminds us that we are not far from George Orwell's *1984*, a state in which "Newspeak" takes the place of plain English, so that one can "doublethink." With doublethink (Orwell, 1961, pp. 218–219), "slavery becomes freedom," "war, peace," and, as in the words of our official, deceit is no longer dishonesty.

Calling wrongs by different names is our way of condemning acts or justifying them. Circumstances that make crime rational make them seem justified, as we shall see (pages 185–188). Those who accept a justification readily convert justification into explanation. Whether or not one subscribes to this illicit translation, justifying fraud does not alleviate its pain.

The cheats we have described in commerce, industry, and politics damage people against their will. In this respect such deceits differ from crimes that are produced in the marketplace, where people meet voluntarily to exchange goods and services.

3 Markets for Crime   Some criminal activity involving offenses against both person and property is an enterprise engaged to fulfil the demands of a market. There are always people ready to make their living supplying any public "needs" that are made. illegal. Whenever a relatively inelastic demand, like that for gambling, sex, and the habituating chemicals, meets a short supply, the price of the service goés up and, with it, the opportunity to make money illegally. Some of the largest incomes ever gained have been made by criminal merchants supplying the public with illegal merchandise. Thus the gangster Al Capone is reported to have earned the highest gross income ever achieved by a private citizen in a single year, something in the order of $105 million for 1927 (McWhirter and McWhirter, 1966, p. 230). This money came principally from the illegal manufacture and marketing of liquor, but also from gambling, prostitution, extortion, and some legitimate businesses. In his time, Capone had some popularity. If he and his henchmen killed their rivals, it was only assassin murdering assassin, and good riddance. Meanwhile, a public "need" was being met. As Capone himself said, "Public service is my motto. I've always regarded it as a public benefaction if people were given decent liquor and square games" (Kobler, 1972, p. 210).

There is a criminal gradient, again, from organized crime serving an illicit market to people "doing the best they can" when government regulations promote black markets. Working the black market, although punished as a crime, is not regarded by its traders as criminal. In the Soviet Union, for example, there are "expediters" who "get things done" by finagling goods and services. Bribes and unofficial barter become ways of sidestepping laws that interfere with markets. Interestingly enough, Soviet traders in the black market are said to be "working on the left" (Kaiser, 1976; H. Smith, 1976).

Repeated examples of the criminal service of a market occur whenever a commodity in relatively inelastic demand is differentially taxed by neighboring states. Smuggling then becomes profitable. For example, New York City taxes cigarettes at 26 cents a pack. It is now estimated by the *United States Tobacco Journal* that half the cigarettes smoked in New York City are smuggled. "The smugglers load 40-foot trailers with 60,000 cartons purchased legally [in adjoining states] at $2.40 each and peddle them in the city via the organized-crime network for $3.75, which is $1.25 or more below legitimate retail" (*Wall Street Journal*, 1976).

Governments are forever torn between attempting to control people through police power and allowing them to do what they want. The justification of control is that a people's unbridled economic activity is harmful or that their appetites are vices. Making people better than they are is a continuing motive for making the satisfaction of some desires criminal. The idea was clearly expressed by Vladimir Ilyich Ulyanov (Lenin), who told us that "the people themselves do not know what is good or bad for them."

Laws that prohibit constant impulses—to trade, to think and speak freely, and to satisfy hungers for sex, food, and the comforting chemicals—create markets for crime. Such laws are usually justified by calling the activities they forbid "vices." However, vice is durable. With the exception of cases in which heavy majorities control slim minorities through the application of severe and probable sanctions, attempts to suppress vice will create black markets and their criminal suppliers (Schelling, 1967).

4   Crime as a Preferred Career

Thievery   Regarding some kinds of crime as rational responses to "structures" indicates that the seeds of many crimes lie in the struggle to stay alive and in the desire to improve one's material condition. Some robbery, but more burglary; some "snitching," but more "boosting" (Cameron, 1964); some automobile theft by juveniles, but more automobile "transfers" by adults, represent a consciously adopted way of making a living. All "organized crime" represents such a preference. The organization of large-scale theft adopts new technologies and new modes of operation to keep pace with increases in the wealth of Western nations and changes in security measures. Such businesslike crime has been changing from "craft crime" to "project crime" (McIntosh, 1971) involving bigger risks, bigger takes, and more criminal ingenuity.

Conversations with successful criminals, those who use intelligence to plan lucrative thefts, indicate considerable satisfaction with their work. There is pride in one's craft and pride in one's nerve. There is enjoyment of leisure between jobs. There is expressed delight in being one's own boss, free of any compelling routine. The carefree life, the irresponsible life, is appreciated and contrasted with the drab existence of more lawful citizens.

When John Mack (1972) studied such "able criminals" in Scotland, he found, as we have seen (page 78), that these successful thieves came from the same social background as less adept thieves, the "textbook criminals." They differ from these inept offenders, however, in their greater freedom from emotional disturbance, in their higher IQs, and, of course, in their greater ability to stay out of jail. Mack's able criminals had spent, on the average, only about one-fifth as much time in jail as the "textbook crooks." Mack describes these successful criminals as making much more money than they would in such law-abiding occupations as are open to them, and he reports that their expenditures and style of life are "very high by ordinary standards."

Given the low risk of penalty and the high probability of reward, given the absence of pangs of guilt and the presence of hedonistic preferences, crime is a rational occupational choice for such individuals.

On a level of lesser skill, many inhabitants of metropolitan slums are in situations that make criminal activity a rational enterprise. Young men in particular who show little interest in school, but great distaste for the authority of a boss and the imprisonment of a menial job, are likely candidates for the rackets. Compared with "work," the rackets combine more freedom, more money, and higher status at a relatively low cost. In some organized crimes, like running the numbers, the risk of arrest is low. The rationality of the choice of these rackets is therefore that much higher for youths with the requisite tastes.

Even for those who get caught, the rationality of crime may still seem clear to the actor himself. For example, Hassan (1972), a several-time loser, tells us:

> Wrong was my only salvation. . . . Don't be telling me what is right. . . . There ain't no such thing as right or wrong in my world. Can you dig? Right or wrong is what a chump chooses to tell himself. And I chose to tell myself that stealing is right. I had a choice: to be a poor-ass, raggedy-ass mathafukker all my life or to go out into the streets and steal me some money. . . . I ain't ashamed of what I did or who I am [pp. 21–22].

Hassan's language is important. It is relevant to the argument about how to explain crime and where to locate its causes. Hassan speaks repeatedly of his *choosing*. He does not view himself as a pawn, something manipulated, but as a rational actor. He conceives of himself as a person, and without knowing it, he agrees with Aristotle that "a man is the origin of his actions."

Hassan was a hustler. "Hustling," as the word is used by its practitioners, is a general term for doing wrong and living better for it. It is a career chosen by some people as a sensible mode of life. Chosen occupations, legal or criminal, are justified, and hustlers can rationalize their vocational choice by claiming that "everyone has his racket; everyone is on the take."

It does not require a dispute about the validity of this justification to comprehend that, for some rational people, becoming a thief may be as reasoned a choice as becoming an accountant. This possibility raises the ancient question about whether crime pays, to be addressed in the next chapter.

Rationality of terror   We have been speaking of thievery as a type of rational activity. There are other rational criminal careers, however, that specialize in killing, with thievery as an adjunct.

The terrorist is a rational careerist who threatens to kill, and kills, as a chosen means of achieving political ends. This style of killer differs from another rational murderer, the hired gun or "enforcer," in that the terrorist kills for ideals, while the mercenary, by definition, kills for money. These homicidal types differ in another respect: *The terrorist consciously kills innocent people,* including official symbols of the hated society, as part of his or her program of intimidation. The hired gun, by contrast, kills only "professional" targets and those innocents who happen to get in the way (Joey, 1974). In this, the mercenary is less dangerous than the idealist. Both killers are criminal— although the terrorist often denies this—in that they violate the criminal law of the country in which they do their killing.

Terrorists are to be distinguished by their more consistent rationality from another type of political killer, those who are only sometimes rational and who are more often psychotic—assassins. Assassins run a range of sanity from the cold-blooded, rational killer, like the murderer of Leon Trotsky (I. E. Levine, 1960), to the deluded assailant (Donovan, 1955; Hastings, 1965).

Terrorists are as rational, or irrational, as any of us who seek broad, mixed objectives. In such cases, rationality becomes difficult to assess because political objectives always run the risk of a shift from the real toward the ideal, from what is possible and observable toward what may be impossible but desired. With this "risky shift," rationality becomes difficult to measure because it becomes a matter of degree, a matter of weighing costs of action against benefits, where many of the values on both sides of the ledger are psychological. What will satisfy psychologically is not known in advance of political action, and hence a cost-benefit analysis—an evaluation of rationality—is not possible in any exact, measured sense. However, this difficulty confronts every assessment of human action—from going to college, to getting married, to using terror in politics. This difficulty means that rationality is better conceived as achieved by degree than in all-or-none categories.

Terrorists are considered to be rational because they intend to gain an empirical objective, power, through the intimidation of governments. They are rational in that they consciously employ violence and its threat as a means. Their rationality, like everyone's, is *bounded* by the efficacy of their chosen means. Choice of efficient means is limited, in turn, by ignorance, morality, and hope.

Since terrorism is fueled by ideals, it is seldom answered by compromise. It is as efficient as governments allow. Totalitarian regimes have no difficulties with terrorists. More open societies do. Walter Laqueur (1976) writes:

An "advanced authoritarian" regime has never had the slightest difficulty in suppressing terrorism. There was no terror in Nazi Germany nor in Fascist Italy other than that sponsored by the government, and there is none now in the Soviet Union or in China. Even in such non-advanced dictatorships as Algeria, Uganda or

Afghanistan one looks in vain for a terrorist danger. Almost without exception it is the democratic regimes and those that have to make concessions to democratic practices which have to cope with this problem [p. 362].

Free societies are ambivalent in their response to terrorism for two reasons: first, because repression of terror often requires short-cutting the due process that protects civil liberties and, second, because such societies are themselves divided between condemning the terrorist "of the other side" and commending the killers "on our side" (Rapoport, 1971). It is this division which has prevented the United Nations from taking a stand against terrorists and which confirms the judgment of some wit who long ago described the UN as "an association admirably designed to prevent all wars except those likely to occur."

Terrorism, like theft, is more often adopted as it succeeds. "Success," however, is itself variously defined. Its measure depends on what actors want. Here it becomes easier to estimate the rationality of thieves than that of terrorists. It is easier to judge whether crime pays in the case of thieves because material ends are more prominent in their work than ideal ones, whereas, in the case of terrorists, ideals often make killing its own satisfaction, whether or not material ends are thus gained. Murder committed by terrorists is often called "symbolic." It *says* something as much as it attempts to *achieve* something.

Judgment of rationality, our own or others', is complicated, therefore, by the mixture of purpose and expression in action, even that action which seems consciously taken in the name of an empirical end. Terrorists kill to achieve something, but there is also pleasure in the process. The means are exciting, just as the goals are inviting.

We can acknowledge, then, that "psychic satisfactions" make it difficult to assess whether crime pays. We wish, nonetheless, to weigh the material benefits of careers in crime, particularly those in theft. This is the task of the following chapter.

Chapter 10

Does Crime Pay?
Testing Rationality

The fact that most people enjoy getting something for nothing and the possibility that theft is encouraged when it promises high reward with little risk give point to the old question about whether crime pays. Asking whether crime pays includes another ancient question: whether punishment works. This additional question is raised because assessing the rewards of crime requires counting its costs. And punishment, as van den Haag reminds us (1975b, p. 17), is society's means of increasing the cost of crime to the offender. Studies of deterrent effects therefore become part of the answer to the question of whether crime pays.

Answering this general question is a way of testing competing hypotheses about offenders against property, in particular. If crime against property does not pay, then thieves may be sick persons rather than rational ones. On the other hand, if such crime does pay, the thesis that thieves are rational gains support (Cobb, 1973). An immediate difficulty in testing these competing hypotheses is that of measuring costs and benefits to actors.

COSTS AND BENEFITS

Price and profit are of several kinds, of course. There are "material" costs such as the work and expense involved in any enterprise, legal or illegal, compared with the financial gain. But there are also "psychic" costs. There is the question of how interested a person is in one kind of work rather than another, for example, and the matter of the value placed on one's time. There are also psychic costs and benefits in the value placed on one's reputation, lawful or criminal, and it should be remembered that one may gain repute in either line of work.

An inventory of the possible costs and benefits of engaging in theft is set out in Table 10-1. This inventory does not assign weights to the advantages and disadvantages of living by theft. Our inability to assign values to these costs and benefits makes economists' models of crime causation suggestive rather than definitive. Tests of the rationality of larceny must therefore be interpreted as estimates rather than as certainties. This becomes more clear as we note that economists who attempt to measure the profit-loss balance from theft must disregard the psychic costs and benefits and concentrate on the more material values of crime (see page 202). If these qualifications are allowed, the results of some provisional studies indicate that crime does pay.

In a material sense, theft seems to pay *in general*. However, the economist's scales do not weigh the variability that must exist among thieves in their success. Just as there is a great difference in the rewards of successful and unsuccessful lawyers, accountants, and teachers, so too there must be a great

Table 10-1   Cost-Benefit Schedule for Theft*

Costs	Benefits
Probability of being caught: probability of being punished if caught *times* dollar value of punishment: fine or time; lost earnings	Market value of stolen property when fenced plus money stolen
	Use value of stolen property retained by thief
Loss of legal income: time out from lawful occupation	Tax freedom
Loss of peripheral benefits of lawful occupation: paid vacation, medical insurance	Leisure: e.g., a burglar's workweek versus workweek of legal job available to thief
Job costs: learning skills and acquiring tools; payoffs to inside men and others; fencing	Job satisfaction: pleasure in one's work, self-employment satisfaction, excitement, pleasure in being skillful thief
Job risks: accident, being wounded or killed	Security: freedom from risk of unemployment
Work involved in theft: casing and doing	Security: free room and board, free health care, aid to dependents, wages earned *if* imprisoned
Subjective cost: anxiety about getting caught and punished	Repute: as successful thief
Subjective costs of punishment: shame, guilt. How much does a specific fine hurt? How much does imprisonment hurt? How much are time and freedom worth, subjectively?	
Damaged repute: as thief, or as unsuccessful thief if caught	

*Costs and benefits are *possible* ones. They need not all pertain to a particular actor, and they may, of course, differ in actuality from an actor's *judgment* of them.

difference in the net payoff of skillful thieves when compared with that of bungling burglars. The study of careers in crime, like the study of lawful occupations, tells us something about the conditions of success and failure in different vocations (see page 203).

Cobb's Estimate

Cobb (1973) tested some of the material advantages gained in the commission of grand larceny and burglary by using FBI statistics for Norfolk, Virginia, for 1964 and 1966.

Cobb's analysis estimates the value of property stolen during these years and corrects this estimate for the amount of unreported crime indicated by victimization surveys. Cobb counted money stolen at face value, but he discounted property stolen at the guessed fenced value of different kinds of things taken—jewelry and furs, for example, were judged to be worth 20 percent of their value to the thief who must dispose of them.

Costs were estimated from arrest and conviction statistics and from fines levied and prison sentences served. Cobb then looked at the occupational background of the arrested thieves and calculated their potential lawful earnings on the varied assumptions of these persons' having worked 30, 40 or 50 weeks a year. Income lost through imprisonment was added to the cost of crime, although Cobb did not deduct income tax from such lost lawful earnings. This means that his figures *over*estimate the costs of the crimes he was measuring.

On the basis of this rough cost-benefit analysis, one that omits psychic rewards and penalties, Cobb concludes that thieves in general produce a net benefit for themselves. On "the most likely assumption that the convicted criminals would have worked thirty weeks per year," he writes, "the benefits from theft are more than double the costs" (pp. 29–30). Cobb adds that for individuals who served sentences, the average value of their lost freedom would have to be placed at more than $3,225 per year "before one could say that theft is not profitable" (p. 30). He then cites one study (Gunning, 1970) that claims that prisoners would pay an average of only $1,500 per year in return for their freedom.

Krohm's Research

Krohm (1973) made a similar estimate of the net return to the "average" burglar in Chicago in 1969. From police and court data, Krohm figured that "the chance of an 'adult' (seventeen or older) burglar being sent to prison for any single offense is .0024. For juveniles . . . the risk was much lower, .0015. An adult who was actually sent to the penitentiary spent an average of 26.8 months (1964 data). Convicted juveniles, on the other hand, could expect to be institutionalized for about nine months" (p. 33). From these provisional data, Krohm concludes:

    1 Burglary is a highly superior source of income as opposed to legitimate employment if an individual has little aversion to risk or, alternatively, a low rate of time discount.

2   After we adjust the average earnings to reflect the time spent unemployed, the comparative income advantage of burglary vanishes for adults, unless one includes income in kind.

3   The income incentives to commit burglary are especially large for juveniles. These findings are consistent with the fact that most burglaries are committed by youths who have little to lose from seeking their fortunes in crime [p. 34].

Gunning's Calculation

Gunning (1973) computed a similar cost-benefit balance from official data for Delaware for the year 1967. Benefits of burglary were estimated as the sale price of the loot sold and the use value of the property kept. The cost of crime was reduced to "the amount of money which could have been earned by the average burglar during the time that he spent in jail . . . times the number of burglars" (p. 36).

Using these crude measures of material cost and benefit, and consciously omitting psychic prices such as the value of freedom, Gunning calculated two rates between the profits from burglary and the possible earnings from lawful work available to the convicted thieves. The first rate uses figures for all burglars, large and small, and yields a reward-to-legal–earnings balance of 1.28. This means that the average burglar would have to earn about 30 percent more than his or her probable legal wage to make staying out of jail worthwhile. Of course, no one knows the value placed on freedom by the "average" burglar in contrast with the pain of holding a legal job. All that Gunning's balance shows is that burglary carries some *economic* advantage over lawful work, omitting from calculation the price of freedom.

Gunning's second estimate of the benefits of burglary was limited to eight thieves who·were among the more successful ones—at least they had stolen larger amounts than the average burglar. When a balance is drawn for burglars known to have stolen more than $1,000 in the crime for which they were apprehended, Gunning figures that such "successful" criminals would have to earn twice their probable lawful income before they could match their profit from burglary. We are reminded, again, that the value of freedom is omitted from this reckoning. Gunning assumes, however, that "bigger thieves" may place a higher value on their freedom than lesser ones and that, if this could be calculated, it might reduce the benefits of burglary for them.

A Negative Result: Sesnowitz's Study

These rather uniform findings that crime pays are contradicted by Sesnowitz's research (1972) on the rewards of burglary in Pennsylvania in 1967. Sesnowitz tried to evaluate the returns to burglary by estimating the probability of an adult thief's being caught and convicted, the value of the loot, and the dollar equivalent of the penalty imposed on those who were convicted.

Sesnowitz omits from his calculation the rewards of theft among juveniles since young people are treated differently in terms of both prosecution and punishment and their cost-benefit balance may therefore differ from that of adults. With this omission, Sesnowitz reckons the probability of a burglar's being convicted in Pennsylvania at about six chances for every 100 burglaries, and he assumes the average value of property stolen to have been $137 when fenced. Upon conviction in 1967, 58 percent of Pennsylvania's burglars were sent to prison, where they served an average of 40 months. However, Sesnowitz estimates that these inmates represent a small proportion of burglars, and he judges that only about 3 percent of all burglars during a year end up incarcerated.

Despite these low odds of getting caught, convicted, and imprisoned, Sesnowitz concludes that burglary did not pay Pennsylvania's adult thieves, principally as a result of the low yield of their work. He figures that burglars lost an average of $197 a year when their rewards are compared with the expected returns of their lawful occupations.

In evaluating Sesnowitz's research, and that of other economists, it must be remembered that cost-benefit analysis is no better than the assumptions—the guessed probabilities of arrest and values of time—that are put into the computations.

McPheters on Robbery

The studies reported thus far have been concerned principally with the rewards of burglary. McPheters (1976) used FBI data to estimate the benefits of robbery. His economic assumption was that the "supply of offenses" is a function of actors' estimates of the value of the payoff from crime, the probability of arrest, and the probability of conviction if arrested (p. 140).

McPheters used annual robbery rates in the United States from 1959 through 1971 as his measure of the "supply of crime." These rates were translated into a measure of "annual average real gains from robbery" by omitting all bank robberies, since these thefts are relatively rare, though lucrative, and by adjusting average robbery losses (gains to the thief) to the consumer price index. McPheters then calculated the relationships between "real average gain" from robbery, the robbery rate, the proportion of all robberies "cleared by arrest," and the proportion of all arrested persons convicted of robbery. Table 10-2 and calculations based on it show some interesting associations:

   1   That while robbery rates in the United States were increasing during these 13 years, the average real gain from nonbank robbery declined.
   2   That the probability of arrest and the probability of conviction upon arrest fell during this period.
   3   That robbery rates declined as clearance and conviction rates rose and, conversely, that robberies increased as clearance and conviction rates decreased.
   4   That the strongest association among these data is that between probability of arrest and robbery rate. The more probable the arrest, the lower the rate.

Table 10-2   Data on Robbery for McPheters's Analysis (1959–1971)

Year	Real average gain from robbery[a]	Robbery Rate[b]	Robbery clearance rate[c]	Robbery conviction rate[d]
1959	255	40.3	42.5	64.8
1960	278	49.6	38.5	58.7
1961	287	50.1	40.5	45.4
1962	234	51.3	40.5	54.4
1963	275	53.1	41.0	51.8
1964	274	58.4	38.5	51.3
1965	243	61.4	38.4	46.7
1966	246	78.3	30.1	44.2
1967	237	102.1	28.5	38.0
1968	237	131.0	27.3	41.1
1969	247	147.4	25.8	35.0
1970	187	171.5	27.7	36.3
1971	170	187.1	24.6	31.5

[a]Total non-bank losses divided by non-bank robberies, adjusted by Consumer Price Index, 1967 = 100.
[b]Rate per 100,000 persons.
[c]Percent of all reported robberies cleared by arrest.
[d]Percent of persons arrested for robbery who were convicted of robbery.
Source: Reprinted with permission from McPheters, 1976.

McPheters explains the apparently unusual association of declining real gains with higher robbery rates by the possibility that robbers, like other rational persons, may be "satisficers" rather than maximizers. A satisficer is one who recognizes that accurately estimating *maximum* gains from different enterprises is costly. It is costly because the variables determining maximum gain are complex and because actors cannot know all these variables. Therefore, people attempt to achieve some satisfying level of gain. They are satisficers, rather than maximizers.

From this assumption, it is conceivable that a decline in the probability of arrest and conviction may draw marginal robbers into crime. These amateurs, some of whom may be "moonlighters," may lack thieving skills or be less discriminating in their choice of victim. Thus McPheters explains the anomaly of increasing crime with decreasing payoff. Robbery remains rational, then, even though its "wage rate" may have declined during a particular period.

ECONOMETRIC MODELS

Attempts to estimate the costs and benefits of crime, and of other work, have been aided by the development of computers that allow us to examine connections between a host of measures simultaneously. This increase in calculating power contributes somewhat to knowledge, but it is limited, again, by the uncertain reliability and validity of the measurements fed the calculating machines. In addition, many of the concepts we use in thinking about crime causation have not been measured and may be impossible to measure. Among these impossible measurements, for example, is the true rate of criminal activity.

Despite these difficulties, economists have developed models of crime causation that provide rough assessments of the rationality of theft.

Ehrlich's Research

Isaac Ehrlich (1973) has provided a prominent example of econometric assessment of the rationality of crime. He examined the relationship between a host of presumed determinants of crime and officially recorded rates of the FBI's "index offenses" for 1940, 1950, and 1960, state by state. Measures of association were calculated both simultaneously and with a one-year lag between crime rates and such nominated "causes" as:

1 Probability of arrest and imprisonment, estimated as the number of offenders imprisoned per offenses known to the police
2 Average time served by offenders in state prisons
3 Median income of families by state
4 Percentage of families below one-half of the state median income
5 Percentage of nonwhites in the population
6 Percentage of males in the age group 14 to 24
7 Unemployment rate of civilian urban males in the age groups 14 to 24 and 25 to 39
8 Labor-force participation rate among civilian urban males 14 to 24 years of age
9 Mean number of years of schooling among the population 25 years of age and older
10 Percentage of the population in Standard Metropolitan Statistical Areas
11 Per capita expenditure on police
12 Sex ratio: males per 100 females
13 Dummy variable isolating Northern and Southern states

Ehrlich's calculations allowed him to test for the separate impact of some *costs of crime*—probability of arrest and imprisonment and length of time served—and some of the possible *causes of crime*. He found that some of the nominated causes were significantly associated with variations in offense rates. Thus states with higher proportions of poor people—poor relative to the state's average—tend to have more crime against property. However, the finding of interest for the economist's hypothesis is that, in Ehrlich's words: "The rate of specific crime categories, with virtually no exception, varies inversely with estimates of the probability of apprehension and punishment by imprisonment and with the average length of time served in state prisons" (p. 545).

The Shinnars' Model

Shlomo and Reuel Shinnar (1975) constructed a model of crime generation in New York City and New York State that parallels Ehrlich's. They were stimulated to think of this model by two facts—facts, at least, as reported by official statistics. The first fact was that the probability of being a victim of a violent crime had changed dramatically in New York State and in most of the boroughs of New York City over the 30 years between 1940 and 1970. For example, the Shinnars figure that the lifetime probability of being a victim in Manhattan of what they call "safety crimes"[1] increased from 14 percent in 1940 to 59 percent in 1960 to 99 percent in 1970 (p. 582).

The second fact that appeared striking to the Shinnars was that the risk in committing crime had declined during this period. Risk was calculated as the average time a convicted person was incarcerated. This risk had been reduced by a factor of 6 between 1960 and 1970 and by a factor of 10 between 1940 and 1970 (p. 584). This reduced cost of crime to the criminal is a function of both shorter prison terms and the greater use of probation in place of incarceration.

From these interesting facts, the Shinnars constructed a mathematical model to test whether reducing the cost of crime to the offender increased offense rates. Their model works with the following figures:

1   Crime rates as reported by the FBI
2   The fraction of reported crime that results in a conviction
3   The number of offenders committed to prison (or other institutions) for each type of crime
4   The total number of criminals in prison
5   The average length of prisoners' incarceration
6   The proportion of convicts who are first-time offenders

The relations between these measures are such that the Shinnars conclude that "there is a strong correlation between increased crime rates and recent changes in the criminal justice system which sharply reduced the chances of a criminal going to prison as well as the length of his stay there. It was also shown that any factor that decreases the chance of a criminal to get convicted has a direct effect on increasing crime rates in an almost proportional way" (p. 607).

This conclusion, like that drawn from any mathematical model, is as good as the data that go into the calculations and the assumptions with which the data are manipulated. The Shinnars recognize these limitations. Nevertheless, their findings are important and are generally supported by additional research.

Avio and Clark's Test

With some variation, the economists Avio and Clark (1976) confirm these results with data from Canada. These investigators tested the rationality of theft by analyzing four kinds of crimes against property in Canada over the three years from 1970 through 1972. The four categories of theft were robbery, burglary (breaking and entering), fraud, and a miscellaneous category which

---

[1]"Safety crime" is a concept introduced by Avi-Itzhak (1973) to denote offenses affecting physical security. It includes violent crimes such as homicide, forcible rape, felonious assault, robbery, and, in addition, burglary. Burglary is included since a forced entry may escalate into physical attack if the resident confronts an intruder.

includes both summary and indictable offenses (misdemeanors and felonies) and which ranges from "taking a motor vehicle without consent" ("joy-riding") through professional automobile theft and a variety of larcenies.

Both police and judicial data for these crimes were gathered from eight Canadian provinces. Alberta, Quebec, the Yukon, and the Northwest Territories were excluded because of deficiencies in data.

The *possible costs* of committing these crimes were estimated in terms of:

1   The probability of being caught. This is judged from a "clearance rate," the number of charges laid by the police divided by the number of offenses known to the police.

2   The probability of conviction when caught. This is calculated as the ratio between the number of offenses resulting in conviction and the number of charges laid.

3   The average length of sentence corrected for earned remissions and parole.

4   "Opportunity cost." This cost refers to the income that would have been received from legal work. This cost was estimated, and inadequately so, from three imperfect indicators: a tally of unemployment in each province, a count of labor-force participation, and the distribution of income in the province relative to the distribution of income in Canada as a whole. "Opportunity cost" did *not* include the "average real wage rate" because this measure was found, contrary to prediction, to be *negatively* associated with theft rates.

The *possible rewards* from stealing were measured by estimating the amount of wealth available for theft in each province. This is, of course, an inadequate indicator of the gains from theft, real or expected. This inadequacy is compounded by the use of *one* measure of provincial wealth open to theft: "the number of households with record-playing equipment" (p. 27).

With these estimates of the possible costs and benefits of theft, Avio and Clark's principal findings are that:

1   The probability of getting caught is *negatively* correlated with burglary and robbery rates. A *negative* correlation is also found for fraud rates when the proportion of the male population 15 to 24 years of age is included in the equation.

2   The probability of being convicted is *negatively* related to robbery rates and miscellaneous larceny rates. The probability of being convicted has no association, however, with fraud and burglary rates.

3   Average length of sentence for these crimes does not appear to be associated with the amount of such crime.

4   The associations of "labor-force variables" with these kinds of crime are "weak and mixed" (p. 41). In other words, the "opportunity costs" of crime, as measured, contribute little to the explanation of these crime rates.

Avio and Clark conclude that their results "generally support the economical model of crime" (p. 43). They draw this conclusion despite their "surprise" at finding the two risk variables, arrest and conviction, to have such relative strength (p. 41). Not surprisingly, these results are also reported by other econometric studies.

Silver's Summary

Silver (1974) analyzed 19 econometric studies, including Ehrlich's but excluding the Shinnars', as a step toward showing what mathematical models can do and where their limitations lie. These economic models assume, in varying degree, that crime against property is produced by the following variables, not all of which are measured:

SPAC: The subjective probability of punishment, that is, the actor's judgment of the likelihood of being arrested and punished.

SLS: The subjective estimate of severity of punishment, that is, the actor's estimate of how severe the punishment may be, if he or she is caught. Since a population's conceptions of *SPAC* and *SLS* are not known, economists substitute recorded rates of arrest and conviction and length of sentence served for the prospective thief's judgment of these probabilities.

% Pun.: The proportion of the population physiologically capable of having been punished by imprisonment.

% Inc.: The number of currently incarcerated persons as a proportion of all physiologically capable persons ever convicted of a particular crime. Again, the two variables *% Pun.* and *% Inc.* are conceived, but not measured. Economists take note of them but have not included them in their calculations.

E: Expected legal earnings minus expected earnings from criminal activity. Since direct measures of the balance between criminal payoffs and alternative lawful earnings are not available, various proxy measures are substituted such as median family income and poverty indexes.

V: Availability of victims. It is assumed that more densely populated areas mean more victims available with less expenditure of the thief's energy.

T: "Tastes." This indicator refers to a variety of attempted measurements of preferences for work and citizens' willingness to commit crimes.

CJF and *PLC:* Measures of the "criminal justice function" and "police labor and capital." Some studies have attempted to include expenditures for courts and police and measures of court-police manpower as additional indicators of the risks of criminal activity.

In sum, although economists' models assume a possible impact of such variables, they have not measured all of them. Current studies reduce to models that estimate the effects of probability of punishment, severity of punishment, population density, community size, ethnicity, and poverty upon recorded crime rates classified as larceny, burglary, and robbery. With these qualifications, Silver concludes the following from his survey:

1 *Probability of punishment affects crime rates.* "Taken as a whole," he writes (p. i), "the evidence convincingly demonstrates that crime rates are reduced by higher probabilities of punishment."

2 *Severity of punishment also seems to reduce crime rates,* but the evidence for this effect is not so convincing as that for probability of punishment.

3   *When crime pays, it is produced.* "Larger illegal payoffs and smaller alternative legal incomes induce individuals to commit crimes," Silver notes (p. 32).

These conclusions are, of course, only as sound as the data from which they are drawn. They are strongly suggestive, however, of the rationality of some crime against property. Future research would benefit if we knew:

1   Actual offenses and offenders, rather than recorded ones
2   Actors' estimates of the probability of arrest and severity of likely punishment
3   The criminal histories of individuals
4   Measures of police and court activity in different "crime zones"
5   The financial rewards of crime compared with actors' options to earn money lawfully where this balance is computed from direct evidence

Judging Rewards and Costs

Actors' *judgments* of the likelihood of rewards of, and punishments for, crime have been omitted from most econometric models. However, Belson's research among English boys, referred to earlier (page 129), assessed some of these subjective factors. In addition, this inquiry into youthful confessions of theft tested the economic assumption that *actual* costs, as well as conceived costs, reduce crime.

Belson and his associates found several major "causes" of stealing and some minor ones. The major correlates of juvenile theft can be summarized in these propositions:

1   That lack of conscience, lack of specific training about the immorality of theft, and lack of remorse make stealing more probable.
2   That truancy is associated with thieving.
3   That contact with thieves is associated with theft.
4   That stealing is part of the search for fun and excitement.
5   That "boys take up stealing or continue to steal partly because they think no one will catch them" (p. 105). A corollary to this finding is the fact that "boys reduce their stealing if they get caught by the police" and if they fear the consequences of being caught (p. 105).

ON DETERRENCE

All the studies mentioned above say something about deterrence, that is, about the effects of punishment, actual and imagined, upon (1) those who are punished and (2) those who know that others have been punished.

The assumption that punishment controls the behavior of those who receive it is known as the hypothesis of *specific*, or *individual, deterrence.* The assumption that punishment of bad actors controls the behavior of those who might be tempted into similar offenses is the hypothesis of *general deterrence*. The research issues raised by the hypotheses of specific and general deterrence are not the same, and they should be kept distinct (Cousineau, 1976). For example, many students confuse specific and general deterrence and conclude from studies of the failure of individual deterrence—as when an offender repeats a crime—that there is no generally deterrent effect. Such a conclusion is unwarranted.

It is also important to be clear about whether deterrence, individual or general, is regarded as *absolute* or *relative*. Some authors argue as if a deterrent effect does or does not occur; others suggest that it is wiser to think of deterrent effects as matters of degree, as varying by "more or less" among differing sanctions (A. R. Jensen, 1969; Zimring and Hawkins, 1973).

In addition to these dimensions of the deterrence question, there are many subsidiary questions that arise when we ask whether punishment works. These additional questions need only be outlined here, along with their suggested answers, to indicate that *no simple relation should be assumed between something called "punishment" and the course of conduct.* At least these questions deserve consideration:

1   What is punishment?
Cousineau (1976) has shown that many social scientists who write about sanctions and their effects fail to define punishment. This lack of definition obscures a striking possibility raised by a second question.

2   Is one person's pain another person's pleasure, and vice versa?
The answer is obvious: "Yes, quite often." Examples are public schools, cigarettes, and "rock concerts."

This question asks whether differences in personality make for differences in response to what appear to be equally painful stimuli. Again, the answer is affirmative. The "same injury" inflicts differing amounts of pain on different persons (Gendin, 1967; Kennedy and Willcutt, 1964; B. Martin, 1963; Petrie, 1967; Sandler, 1964). There *are* sadists and masochists.

3   Are there types of punishment?
Yes. Shaming is not whipping; ostracism is not exile; a fine is not imprisonment. Other styles of pain are described by Church (1963), Gibbs (1966), and LaVoie (1974).

4   Do the timing of punishment and its severity make a difference?
Of course. For examples, see Aronfreed and Reber (1965), Walters et al. (1965), and pages 317–318. Intense punishment administered just prior to a forbidden act tends to inhibit it; intense pain administered long after a forbidden act loses its deterrent effect.

5   Do differences in the probability of punishment influence its deterrent effect?

This question is often phrased, inexactly, as a question about the "certainty" of punishment. Most of the consequences of our actions are probable, of course, rather than certain, and the probability of punishment does make a difference in our conduct. The probability of pain makes a difference in both ways—as it is estimated by the actor and as it is objectively calculated by some "outside observer." Evidence has been reported in our econometric studies; additional evidence is provided by Salem and Bowers (1970), Teevan (1972), Tittle (1969), and Tittle and Logan (1973).

Some studies, such as that by Chiricos and Waldo (1970), contradict these findings. The discrepancies are partly explained by the kinds of crime studied and by differences in measures of "certainty."

6   Does the schedule of punishment influence its effects?

This asks whether the frequency, consistency, and patterning of punishment alter its consequences. The answer is, again, affirmative, but the effects are not produced in linear fashion. The relations are complex (Appel and Peterson, 1965; Leff, 1969).

7   Does the relationship between the punisher and the punished—the history of their association—make a difference?

Yes. Punishment administered by someone who has been rewarding is more painful than punishment administered by someone who has long been punitive (Church, 1963). This fact is related to the next question and its answer.

8   Does one's previous experience with punishment make a difference in response to present pain?

This question is related to the preceding one, obviously, and also to the question about personality differences in response to punishment. The various ways of asking the question result in similarly affirmative answers. Punishment becomes more effective as a "contrast effect," that is, as it is different from the usual course of one's experience (Abel and Walters, 1972; Estes, 1944, 1969a, 1969b; Powers, 1974).

9   Does the social support given the punisher and the punished affect the consequences of pain?

Of course. Actions that are morally reinforced by one's tribe are not likely to give way to penalties imposed by foreigners. This is why gypsies persist as mobile thieves (Maas, 1975) and why the punishment of "war criminals" will not deter future warriors (Taft, 1946).

10   Does it make a difference whether the behavior to be controlled through punishment is instrumental (purposeful, planned) or expressive (passionate)?

Probably. For example, H. L. Ross and others (1970) report that such relatively instrumental action as drunken driving may be reduced by punishment. By contrast, B. Schwartz (1968) could find no evidence that a more impulsive behavior, such as rape, was deterred by the possibility of punishment.

11   Are there side effects, unintended consequences, and other costs of punishment?

Of course. This fact calls caution to glib prescriptions for punishment (Skinner, 1953). However, there are prices we pay for every action, or inaction, and being cautious about being punitive ought not to be translated, as it often is, into the foolish notion that "punishment does not work."

In Summary: Deterrence

A brief review of questions concerning deterrence demonstrates that the economist's conception of conduct, with its assumption that punishment is a way of increasing the cost of crime, deserves qualification. It is true, but it is only partly true. The economist's explanation is tangled, rather than clear.

Deficiencies in Economics   There are two difficulties with the economic attitude toward human action:

1   The economist's explanation does not tell us where we get our *wants*, when these are more than our *needs*.[2]

2   The economist's explanation does not describe how we come to accept some means, but not others, as appropriate instruments for satisfying our wants. To say that we accept the least costly means, as the economist does, begs the question because, again, one person's price is not another's. Thus prices that involve costs to the conscience are considered, but not measured, in the economist's calculations.

Other explanations of conduct, particularly of criminal conduct, attempt to answer these questions. They are discussed in following chapters, especially Chapter 16. For the present, we can recognize deficiencies in regarding action as nothing but rational and yet attempt to draw some lessons from economists' assumptions and research.

SOME CONCLUSIONS

1   The question, "Does theft pay?" has the same form as the question, "Does legitimate business or lawful work pay?" The answer, obviously, is "It depends. . . ." It depends on how one works, on where and when one works, and, also, on one's morals and on what one wants out of life.

Given these many unmeasured contingencies in judging the "success" or

---

[2]Everyone recognizes the difference between a desire and a necessity of life. However, the saturation of language with morality means that the lexical boundaries between words are moved in accord with our preferences. Thus some sympathizers with bad actors transform "what they want" into "what they need." This is a moral translation, of course, and one we need not accept.

"failure" of our careers, it seems best to answer the question about the rewards of thievery with double negatives, like this: "In general, it cannot be said that theft does not pay." In particular, crimes against property seem to pay if one steals large amounts, by plan, and without conscience or partners (Lipman, 1973). Playful, impulsive, and unskillful[3] theft seems not to pay.

2 Punishment has a deterrent effect. It deters both the individuals punished and others who are liable to receive the same punishment. However, we are not able to assign quantities to units of pain and to units of resistance to temptation. This inability invites continuing quarrel and suggests, again, that the conclusion be phrased in double negatives: "It cannot be said that punishment does not deter."

Pain changes us, but it does so uncertainly, in accord with all the contingencies described on pages 199–202. Pain is not a foolproof deterrent. Its effects are more pronounced as punishment becomes more probable and immediate. Its effects vary with the severity of pain, too, but not so much as with its timing, its probability, and its social setting (Antunes and Hunt, 1972; Bean and Cushing, 1971; Erickson and Gibbs, 1973; L. N. Gray and J. D. Martin, 1969; Kobrin et al., 1972; Tittle and Logan, 1973; Tittle and Rowe, 1974; Votey and Phillips, 1972, 1974).

3 Attitudes toward punishment and its use in the control of crime are more moral than pragmatic. That is, such attitudes are based more on what one wants to *do* than on what one wants to *achieve.*

For example, the distinguished psychoanalyst Karl Menninger (1968) believes that punishment itself is a crime. He tells us: "Being against punishment is not a sentimental conviction. It is a logical conclusion drawn from scientific experience." This is, of course, another misuse of the abused word "science."

The quarrel, again, is about the rationality of crime. It is a question of whether we drift into careers (Matza, 1964), choose them, or are pushed into them. The correct answer is probably a mixture of all three possibilities—depending on the person, the circumstance, and the career.

However, sociologists have exhibited a tendency to regard wrong actions as caused, and right ones as chosen. Or they convert all of us into nonrational creatures who act out "an unconsciously developed way of life," as Horton and Leslie put it (1965, p. 168). These authors argue, therefore, that it is "unrealistic" to assume "that people consciously *decide* whether to be criminal" (p. 167). "Since a rational choice between criminal and noncriminal careers is rare," they continue, "deterrence is unnecessary for the law-abiding and ineffective for the criminal" (p. 168).

This logic angers economists, two of whom have replied that some juvenile delinquents seem "far better qualified to advise our government on matters of

---

[3]Saying that "unskillful theft" may not pay is not a tautology. Work skills can be measured independently of their use in "real life."

crime prevention than most professors of criminology" (McKenzie and Tullock, 1975, p. 156). These economists believe that "much of the advice given to governments by sociologists over the past 50 years is clearly wrong. Indeed," they say, "such advice might well be one of the major reasons for the rising crime rate" (p. 149). This debate has been aptly summarized by Duesenberry, who comments, "Economics is all about how people make choices. Sociology is all about why they don't have any choices to make" (1960, p. 233).

A mediation. It is doubtful that any of us can behave as consistent determinists. Free will may be an illusion, and choice too, but most of us regard these illusions as necessary. At least we seem more willing to believe that *we decide*, while *others may be determined.*

Causation, however, is not a train of events that one can board and leave at convenient moral stations. There is no reason to assume that causes determine bad acts, but not good ones. If there are causes that produce bad actors, there must be causes that produce good ones. Similarly, if there is choice, it must be possible to choose to do evil as well as to do good—as Christians and Hassan (see page 186) have told us.

The economist is probably more correct here than the sociological determinist. But to say that some crime is rational is not to say that all crime is.

The same point can be made about any other facet of our lives. We do not always know what we are doing. There are degrees of rationality in all our plans and varieties of rationality at different steps in our careers. Consequences—costs and rewards—do shape our conduct, but the consequences of our acts that channel our behaviors are assigned different values by different actors. Rationality *is* bounded.

4   The many studies of the real and judged rewards and costs of crime listed in this chapter and the preceding one confirm Hume's suspicion that "a quantity of gold left unguarded" will disappear. It is not at all clear, however, what public policy should be recommended from such a conclusion—other than to guard one's wealth.

The difficulty is this: Research by economists and sociologists on the rationality of crime is all based on correlations. Correlations, we are reminded, suggest causes, but they do not demonstrate them. They do not demonstrate the *power* of the nominated causes, and they do not tell us unequivocally in which *direction* to draw the causal arrow.

It is conceivable, for example, that penalties for crime have decreased because crime rates have increased, not that crime rates have increased because penalties have decreased. In short, Blumstein (1975) suggests that "it may be that those States suffering high crime rates simply have had to adapt to their crime by becoming more lenient in the imposition of sanctions" (p. 7).

It is possible, of course, that causation runs both ways. Reducing the costs of crime to criminals increases their activity. An increase in their activity results in lowered penalties because imposing penalties also costs citizens something. It costs us financially, and it costs us morally. What is sought, but never achieved, is an *optimal* enforcement of law (Stigler, 1970). The calculation of an optimum is difficult, and perhaps impossible, because consumers of laws are not in agreement as to how much each of us should be taxed to enforce which laws. The variability with which we enforce laws allows for flexibility in accommodating to conflict, much as hypocrisy lubricates moral friction (Warriner, 1958).

Another Attitude

If crime is made rational by a social structure that creates needs for theft and provides chances to steal, the defender of that social structure calls for reformation or punishment of those who feel those needs and take advantage of such chances.

If, on the other hand, the social structure itself is deemed unworthy, corrupt and corrupting, then the recommendation is for overthrow of the entire structure in the hope of a new start. This remedy is the preferred course of sociologists who identify themselves by many names—as "new," "Marxian," "radical," "critical," or "conflict" criminologists. Their explanation of crime is the subject of the next chapter.

Chapter 11

Crime and Conflict

Every explanation of crime production rests on a notion of conflict. The conflict is moral and material. It is a dispute over what is right and wrong and whose ethics should be codified in criminal law, but it is also a dispute over who should have the "right" to which freedom, which privilege, and which wealth.

Economists who look at theft as rational are conflict theorists in the sense that they observe some people wanting, and taking, what others have. Subcultural theorists who look at crime as produced by people of different tastes living together under one law are also resting their explanation on conflict. Similarly, from their different points of emphasis, social psychologists who stress the causal importance of opportunities, interpretations of situations, or training regimes all rest their explanations of crime on some sort of conflict. For these theorists, conflict resides in differences—whether the differences be in opportunities, in ideas, or in nurturing.

The distinctive feature of the criminology that has appropriated the title of the "conflict" school is its emphasis on "conflicts of interest" as origins of the criminal law and its differential application.

The point of this emphasis is to stress that crimes are defined by the interests they threaten. "Interest groups" are conceived as struggling to impose their definitions of wrong upon others who live within the same jurisdiction. It is assumed, then, that criminal laws more frequently represent the interests of particular groups within a society than agreed-upon social norms (Turk, 1966). The emphasis upon *conflict* contrasts with the emphasis upon *consensus*. The research question asks which criminal laws have evolved in defense of particular moral and economic interests and which have evolved in defense of a more general "public interest."

On Naming a School   Criminologists who stress conflict as criminogenic are not of one mind, and they quarrel among themselves. They therefore use a variety of titles, in addition to "conflict," with which to identify their theses. They use such titles as "radical deviancy theory" (I. Taylor et al., 1975, p. 2), "new criminology" (I. Taylor et al., 1975), "radical human rights criminology" (Schwendinger and Schwendinger, 1975), "radical criminology" (Platt, 1974), and "critical Marxism" (Quinney, 1974a, p. v).

The appropriation of the Marxian title has been contested (Hirst, 1972) since, of course, there is more than one Marx, a result of the difficulties of reading all the work of Marx and Engels and interpreting their voluminous writing. Thus an early participant in this school concluded that "[we are] more agreed on what we are against than what we are for" (S. Cohen, 1971, p. 16).

It seems useful to consider a minority of conflict criminologists as non-Marxist and a majority as adhering to some version of Marxist thesis. The unifying Marxian theme is the kind of conflict emphasized. In the Marxian version of the conflict perspective, it is *class conflict* that produces the criminal law. This school believes that crime is *defined* by a ruling class as part of its program of exploitation and repression of powerless people, the "working class." The criminal law and the state that enforces it are conceived to be instruments by which one social class oppresses another and maintains its privileges against the demands of the oppressed.

With the acknowledgement, then, that conflict criminologists differ among themselves on some issues, their major theses can be described and assessed. Since a central theme holds that "capitalist"[1] societies are criminogenic, this school may be regarded as offering a structural explanation of crime.

RADICAL PROPOSITIONS

The following assumptions characterize conflict criminologists.

1   Situated Ideas

Ideas, including explanations of crime, are socially situated. They reflect our times, and, in particular, they justify our economic interests.

---

[1]"Capitalist" is placed in quotation marks to indicate its vagueness. There is no society today, nor has there ever been one, that is purely capitalist in the sense of allowing market forces to generate the private accumulation of capital and its uses free of state regulation. Capitalism, like the varieties of fascism, socialism, and communism, is better understood as an ideal than as a real social system. There are, of course, *approximations by degree* toward these idealized economies.

2 Critical Philosophy

There is a better way to think than to assume that objective knowledge is possible and that a reality exists independent of the thinker.

The critical criminologist borrows from a philosophy called "phenomenology" the reasonable assumptions that it is a person who is doing the thinking, that persons are time-and-place–situated, and that there is therefore more than one way in which to think. It is then argued that the possibility of different styles of thought indicates that, as Richard Quinney puts it (1970, p. 4), "'We cannot be certain of an objective reality beyond man's conception of it. Thus, we have no reason to believe in the objective existence of anything."

However, despite the possibility of many ways of comprehending our experiences, a particular mode of thinking *is* recommended. Recommending a particular cognitive style is congenial to being radically political because the claim that one has a different and better way of thinking supports the assumption that one has valid credentials for *judging* this world and *promising* a better one.

The assumption of an improved style of thought strengthens one's political claims. This premise justifies our "understanding"[2] of the situation as correct and as guaranteeing achievement of our moral objectives. Thus a radical criminology that would be "relevant" recommends a particular style of thought, one called "critical philosophy." This is a philosophy that allegedly does the following things:

   a ". . . Goes to the roots of our lives, to the foundations and the fundamentals, to the essentials of consciousness" (Quinney, 1974a, p. 11).
   b Roots out presuppositions, "demystifies." Critical thinking removes "the myths—the false consciousness—created by the official reality." It reveals "conventional experience . . . for what it is—a reification of an oppressive social order. The liberating force of radical criticism is the movement from relevation [sic] to the development of a new consciousness and an active life in which we transcend the established existence. A critical philosophy is a form of life" (Quinney, 1974a, p. 11).
   c Enables us "to think negatively. This dialectical form of thought allows us to question current experience. By being able to entertain an alternative, we can better understand what exists. Rather than merely looking for an objective reality, we are concerned with the negation of the established order. Through

---

[2]"Understanding" is another of those appealing words that are useful precisely because they are obscure. Scholars who urge that we attempt to understand human action or social conditions are not speaking of the same kind of understanding that one has of a language, that is, the ability to translate it. Understanding action refers to "grasping the *point* or *meaning* of what is being done" (Winch, 1958, p. 115).

The process prescribed for developing "human understanding" is something called "empathy," a putting of oneself in the other's situation (Nettler, 1970, pp. 36–43). The defect in appealing *solely* to understanding as a guarantee of knowledge is that there is no way to validate one person's understanding when it differs from another's. We are left alone, each of us claiming to possess "real" understanding, as opposed to the other's "false consciousness."

this negation we are better able to understand what we experience. Possibly only by means of this dialectic can the present be comprehended" (Quinney, 1974a, p. 13).

d Allows us to think of new possibilities. Thinking negatively "will move us to a radical reconstruction of our lives—indeed, to revolution itself. In order to reject something, we must have some idea of what things could be like. It is at this point that a critical philosophy must ultimately develop a Marxist perspective. In the Marxian notion of the authentic human being, we are provided with a concrete image of the possible" (Quinney, 1974a, p. 13).

e Develops "an understanding of the true meaning of the legal order [that enables us] to transcend the present and create an alternative existence. Liberation is the ultimate objective of a critical philosophy of legal order" (Quinney, 1974a, p. 15).

3 Contrapositivism

An additional theme of conflict criminology expresses dissatisfaction with the causal thinking of conventional criminology. It is alleged that conservative and liberal criminologists subscribe to a philosophy called "positivism" and that this philosophy is defective. Its defects are said to be both philosophical and political.

Philosophically, it is argued that positivists make the mistake of applying a "mechanical conception" of causation to human affairs (Quinney, 1970, pp. 5–7, 1975, pp. 9–10). The conflict criminologist argues, quite rightly, that we need not always think in terms of causes and that there are styles of causation (see Chapters 7 and 8). The radical criminologist recommends, then, that *if* a causal explanation is formulated, it be founded on "the social reality created by man" (Quinney, 1970, p. 6). A "social reality" is a world of assigned meanings, of interpretations of situations. It follows that causal importance, if it is to be assumed at all, must include the influence of ideas. This is a notion, we shall see, common also to symbolic interactionism (see Chapters 14 and 15).

Positivism is said to be defective not only in its philosophy, however, but also in its correlative (caused?) politics. The politics of positivism, it is claimed, "accepts the status quo. Positivists do not question the established order, just as they do not examine scientific assumptions. The official reality is the one within which the positivist operates and which he accepts and supports" (Quinney, 1975, p. 9).

4 Crime Defined

Conflict criminology emphasizes that crime is defined, not discovered. This means that there is no "essence" of criminality that is "merely perceived" by everyone; rather, calling an action "criminal" imposes a definition. This imposition is deemed to be a political act, that is, an act reflecting the differential distribution of power.

It is further argued that, in capitalist societies, people do *not* agree on what is right and wrong and on what should be considered criminal (Chambliss and Ryther, 1975, p. 349). On the contrary, it is held that it is a minority with economic privilege that has the power to enact laws defining as crimes those acts which threaten its economic interests.

"Criminal law," says Quinney (1975, p. 291), "is an instrument that the state and dominant ruling class use to maintain and perpetuate the social and economic order." And Chambliss (1974, p. 37) adds, "In any complex, modern society there is no value-consensus that is relevant to the law."

5 Unjust Justice

It is then argued that criminal justice systems in capitalist countries apply these *class-determined* definitions of crime. It is claimed, therefore, that these systems of justice are unjust. They are unjust because they "discriminate."[3] They are said to be applied against classes of people rather than against classes of behavior. Decisions concerning guilt, innocence, and sentencing are alleged to depend more on *who one is* than on *what one has done.*

This allegation is used to explain the differential arrest records of people who are young, poor, male, black, Chicano, and native Indian. The charge of discrimination implies that *extralegal* factors, such as the social status of the accused, determine one's fate before the bar much more than the offensiveness of one's behavior.

6 Human Rights Denied

In addition, it is claimed that capitalist societies commit crimes against "human rights" (Schwendinger and Schwendinger, 1975).

It is argued that if crime is defined rather than discovered and that if it is defined by a powerful minority in its exploitation of a weak majority, then a task of a humane criminology is to redefine crime. Much of radical criminology is thus directed toward issues in the sociology of law, that is, toward questions of who should have the right to legislate which deviance into criminality and what, therefore, deserves the coercive attention of a state.

From these assumptions, new definitions of crime are called for. These new definitions are to rest on some conception of "human rights." This conception, in turn, calls *inequality* of treatment or condition the fundamental crime. The communist advocate Angela Davis expresses the idea this way:

> I think that if we look around us we see that somehow or another a very small minority of people in this country have all of the wealth in their hands and to top that, we don't even see them out working. We do not see them in the factories. We don't see them in the fields. . . . That tells me that something is *wrong* and it tells me that maybe *the real criminals* in this society are not all of the people who populate the prisons across the state, but those people *who have stolen the wealth*

---

[3]It is well to recall an earlier comment (page 11, footnote 10) about the many meanings of "discrimination." The term has greater emotional utility than descriptive clarity.

of the world from the people. Those are the criminals. And that means the Rockefellers and the Kennedys, you know, that whole Kennedy family, and that means the state that is designed to protect their property, because that's what Nixon's doing, that's what Reagan's doing, that's what they're all doing. And so every time a black child in this city dies, we should indict them for murder, because they're the ones who killed that black child [1970, p. 27; italics added].

If one advances human rights as a standard of justice and the violation of these rights as crimes, then new categories of conduct and condition are nominated for criminalization. Thus the Schwendingers (1975) advocate that "imperialistic war, racism, sexism and poverty" be made criminal (p. 136). This recommendation would call *individuals* criminal who deny equal rights to others, but, more to the point, it would call *social systems* criminal "which cause the systematic abrogation of basic rights" (p. 137). "What is important," say the Schwendingers, "is that":

> hundreds of thousands of Indo-Chinese persons are being denied the right to live; millions of black people are subjected to inhuman conditions which, on the average, deny them ten years of life; the majority of the human beings of this planet are subjected because of their sex; and an even greater number throughout the world are deprived of the commodities and services which are theirs by right. And no social system which systematically abrogates these rights is justifiable [p. 137].

7 Liberation Promised

Last, conflict criminologists promise a new and better world. They hold that once basic human rights are secured through socialist or communist revolution, there will be no reason for a coercive state to exist. The radical program calls for creating "a society in which the facts of human diversity, whether personal, organic or social, are not subject to the power to criminalize" (I. Taylor et al., 1973, p. 282).

The "end product" of this revolution, Quinney assures us (1974b), "will be a life released from the repressions of today," for, "ultimately it is not law that makes man good. Man is basically good. It is the institutions which oppress him that make for any shortcomings in man. Let man be free. Let him control his own institutions rather than be controlled by them. And he will be the good man that he is by the nature of his being" (p. 485).

ADVANTAGES OF RADICAL CRIMINOLOGY

Radical criminology has several advantages. Simply being radical, in the sense of being challenging, is refreshing. It suggests new ways of thinking about our lives.

Among these suggestions are questions raised about the uses of the criminal law. Conflict criminology suggests studies in the sociology of law as tests of its functional explanation[4] of the evolution of legal conceptions of crime. The radical thesis that laws are created in capitalist countries by the powerful to dominate the powerless and that criminal justice systems function to maintain that dominance has been alleged, but not proved (see pages 214–219 and 291–298).

The new criminology can also be interpreted as supporting the more general structural theme—economic or opportunistic—that says that where one is in the social structure opens or closes opportunities to lawful and unlawful ways of getting what one wants. In this way the conflict thesis emphasizes the parallel roots of the different kinds of theft committed by white-collar criminals and lower-class offenders. The different styles of stealing are seen as generated by a common structure of pressures and opportunities. Given the injustice it sees in bourgeois countries, radical criminology makes some crime rational, and at the same time it justifies those "political" crimes it considers to have been caused by unjust social relations.

The greatest advantage of conflict criminology, however, lies in its popular appeal. It is popular because it criticizes and promises.

Criticism, we are reminded, is one of the vocational characteristics of intellectuals, the "professionally thoughtful people" (Furst, 1952; Shils, 1972; L. von Mises, 1960). "The intellectual group cannot help nibbling," Joseph Schumpeter (1947) wrote, "because it lives on criticism and its whole position depends on criticism that stings; and criticism of persons and of current events will, in a situation in which nothing is sacrosanct, fatally issue in criticism of classes and institutions" (p. 151).

Criticism is pleasurable. It is part of our making discriminations in the world, part of our preferring this to that. Criticism becomes popular, however, when it is inspirational, when it promises a better world upon acceptance of its assumptions. Political movements, like religious ones, promise, at the minimum, improvement. At the maximum, they promise salvation, the end of human misery.

---

[4]Radical criminologists do not like to think of their explanatory schema as "functional," but it is. It is, at least, in the not too clear sense in which sociologists and anthropologists have come to use the idea of a "functional explanation." This is a sense, incidentally, that differs from the idea of "function" in biology, physiology, and classics (Munch, 1976).

As anthropologists and sociologists employ the notion, a functional explanation is one that tries to account for actions by showing that they have consequences that maintain a system. The consequences may be intended, as when they serve the actor's purposes, or they may be unintended results appreciated by some external observer. Intended effects are called "manifest" functions; unintended consequences are referred to as "latent" functions (Merton, 1949).

An explanation of criminal law in terms of the interests it serves is, then, a form of functional explanation. However, radical criminologists resist the functionalist label because they believe it has been associated with the defense of Western social systems rather than with their criticism. Nevertheless, the logic of "functional explanation," as it is employed by social scientists, does not require that it have only conservative uses. This kind of "functionalism" may also serve radical ends, as Gans (1972) has shown.

Political attitudes toward "functional explanation" say nothing about the scientific utility of such an idea for the social studies. The concept is sufficiently vague, however, that Peter Munch (1976) calls functional analysis a "jungle of semantic confusion," while Kingsley Davis long ago (1959) termed this "method" a "myth."

Promise is comforting, of course. For people who live in impoverished circumstances—and this does *not* include most Western intellectuals—and for those whose lives are hollow—and this may include many intellectuals—promise gives one "something to live for." It becomes unpleasant, then, to say nay to the needy person's faith. It is part of the scholar's job, nevertheless, to be critical, and there is much to be critical about in radical criminology.

DEFICIENCIES OF RADICAL CRIMINOLOGY

The deficiencies of radical criminology are epistemological, factual, sociological, moral, and promissory.

1 Quarrels about Knowledge

Epistemological quarrels are debates about what it means to have knowledge, whether knowledge is possible, and, if it is possible, how it can be acquired and verified. Attempts to answer these questions occupy volumes. Our purposes require only the demonstration that people who deny the existence of a reality independent of the knower do not believe what they say.

"To believe" refers to some "appropriate" meeting of what one thinks and says with what one does. This definition reminds us that people do not believe all that they say, nor do they say all that they believe. This fact underlies the common challenge we give each other: "Put your money where your mouth is."

A belief in what one says is shown in two ways: by *consistency* of what one says and, more important, by *action* that accords with what is said. To put it negatively, we conclude that people do *not* believe what they say when they contradict themselves in other things that they say and by their deeds. When their utterances concern moral issues, contradiction between words and deeds is called "hypocrisy."

A contradiction in words is apparent when scholars tell us that "we have no reason to believe in the objective existence of anything." The contradiction is apparent when students tell us that social realities are only constructed and never perceived. If this were so, if there were no external world against which our conceptions bumped, there would be no point in discussing racism, sexism, exploitation, or poverty. These are concepts, true enough, but their utility for *responsible* action depends on their being reducible to something that can be experienced objectively—that is, that can be experienced with some degree of intersubjective reliability and not just as a private hallucination.

If, however, there is no possibility of objective knowledge, of agreement on what is, then there is nothing to "demystify." Each person's myth becomes as valid as any other's, and truth itself becomes a pretentious claim for what we wish. The philosopher C. I. Lewis (1946) argues against this notion:

> Without something determined independently of the decision to verify, there would be nothing for the verifying experience to disclose—except itself; it would verify nothing because there would be no independent fact to be evidenced. Whoever believes in independent reality, believes in such real connections which

may be disclosed in experience; and whoever believes in such connections, verifiable in experience, believes in knowable but independent reality. And whoever *dis*believes in such real connections—if he is not merely confused and inconsistent—not only disbelieves the possibility of empirical knowledge; he disbelieves that there is anything to be so known which it is possible to state [p. 227].

Conflict criminologists' verbal contradictions consist, then, in speaking on some pages of reality as though it were only constructed, while speaking on other pages of "being authentic," "truly human," and "aware of oneself" (Gouldner, 1970, p. 493). On yet other pages, radicals refer to "inaccurate descriptions of the world" (Hartjen, 1974, p. 194) and to the necessity of working "with concepts that are adequate to reality from the beginning" (Myrdal, 1970, p. 15). However, to be "authentic," accurate, and "adequate to reality" requires that there be a *real* world, an objectively knowable world, that serves as a standard of authenticity, accuracy, and adequacy.

A more damaging contradiction than the merely verbal ones is the contradiction between the promissory words and the actual consequences of believing them (see pages 221–222). It is a contradiction that can be tested, and known, because the promise of a better world is a promise of a real world, not an imagined one. Bread in the belly is really to be there, not merely conceptualized. So too, if we are serious, are equality and liberation.

Motives That Divorce Conceptions of the World from Perceptions of It   Students often ask how such inconsistency could develop in the ideas of learned people. The motive that energizes these contradictions is a common political one: *the desire to make the world other than it is* (see Chapter 9).

This is the motive which Hannah Arendt (1967) told us makes lying a tool of the political trade. It is the same motive that has guaranteed the success of inspirational religion ("Disease is an error of thought") and the popularity of a recent novel about a silly seagull (Bach, 1970) that transcends its "gullyness" through the power of positive thinking ("If reality is ugly, and if it is only constructed, redefine it and fly through the barriers").

Imagining a different world, wanting it, and believing it are graduated steps toward the denial of reality and, hence, toward the denial of any observable regularities in human behavior that would allow an explanation of it.

2 Factual Deficiencies

Conflict criminology suffers from factual deficiencies as well as epistemological ones. All attempts to explain human behavior scientifically claim to rest upon facts and to make sense of those facts. Thus the central theme of radical criminology is useful only if it is both factual and clarifying. The central theme says that criminal laws in bourgeois societies define crimes as interested minorities want them defined and not as a majority agree they should be defined.

This hypothesis is empirical; it refers to facts. However, those who have advanced this assumption have not tested it adequately. The only tests of this allegation advanced by conflict criminologists have been anecdotal. That is, a few criminal laws have been studied in an attempt to show how interested minorities, rather than consensual majorities, have pushed for their passage. Laws studied in this way have been largely those regarding administrative offenses and crimes *mala prohibita* rather than the more universal crimes *mala in se*. Thus Chambliss (1964, 1973) studied the evolution of the laws of vagrancy in England to demonstrate that these laws changed to serve the needs of landowners for a supply of cheap labor. Such a demonstration requires, of course, an accurate reading of the laws and an accurate representation of public support for their passage and enforcement. Both the reading of these English laws and their alleged causal link with particular economic interests have been challenged by the Canadian attorney T. Allan Edwards (1976). However, the debate about the history of vagrancy laws need not be resolved for our purposes here. *The significant deficiency of conflict criminology is its lack of evidence for its central allegation*: that criminal law in capitalist countries is entirely, or mostly, produced by elites to defend their economic interests.

The burden of proof rests on the affirmative side. Those who advance a hypothesis have the responsibility for proving it. Conflict criminologists, however, have *not* submitted their major thesis to empirical test. They are not even clear as to how much of the criminal law, and which laws, do and do not serve particular economic interests. Thus Chambliss (1973, p. 442) concludes his study with a vague summary:

> What is true of the vagrancy laws is also true of the criminal law in general. To be sure, not all criminal laws so clearly follow the economic interests of the ruling classes. Some laws are irrelevant or tangential to economic interests. Other laws serve the interests of some elite groups and not others.

The Issue and Its Test   The issue is not whether any laws, regulatory or criminal, have ever been legislated to serve the interests of minorities. There is no doubt that such minority-supported legislation occurs. What is crucial to the conflict explanation is whether crimes *mala in se* are defined as such by majorities or only by elites. Are treason, murder, manslaughter, kidnapping, wounding, forcible rape, robbery, burglary, and fraud considered criminal by the majority of citizens in bourgeois societies, or are definitions of these wrongs only imposed upon the majority by powerful minorities? It is a significant defect of conflict criminology that its advocates have not tried to answer this crucial question.

An approximate answer to this question is found in studies of the judged *gravity* of crimes. These investigations compare the seriousness of kinds of crime as rated by a sample of citizens and as ranked by the penalties allowable under their criminal laws (Boydell and Grindstaff, 1972, 1974a, 1974b; Gardiner, 1967; Gibbons, 1969; Mäkelä, 1976; Rooney and Gibbons, 1966; Rose and Prell, 1955).

Such studies show both agreement and discrepancy between the popularly judged gravity of some offenses and the legal definition of their seriousness. They show, however, that the people and their laws in capitalist countries tend to rank gravity of offense in parallel fashion. Thus attacks on persons are judged as more serious than attacks on property, and both these wrongs are felt to be more serious than some kinds of "victimless" crime. Nevertheless, this demonstration does not answer the central question about how much agreement there is among the citizenry and their laws in the *definition* of acts as crimes.

Answering such a question with the tools of social science is relatively simple.[5] The failure of conflict criminologists to perform an empirical test of their major assumption makes their schema suspect. The failure allows C. W. Thomas (1976, p. 15) to say that the assumptions of both consensus and conflict "lie more in the realm of self-evident truths than empirically validated facts."

However, when Thomas and his associates tested the conflict hypothesis in a limited way, they found no support for its central assumption. On the contrary, they found considerable support for a consensual model.

Consensus about Crime: Thomas's Study   C. W. Thomas (1976) and his coworkers received questionnaires in 1973 from 3,334 households in the Norfolk, Virginia, Standard Metropolitan Statistical Area. These questionnaires asked citizens what would be a "fair sentence" for each of 17 offenses committed by a hypothetical person who was guilty, adult, and a first offender.

Respondents were divided into 12 classes by their distribution on six indicators of their relative position in the social structure: age, sex, race, education, income, and occupational prestige. It was hypothesized that, if the conflict perspective were correct, there would be considerable *disagreement* between people of low and high status in their evaluation of the 17 sample crimes.

Contrary to this hypothesis, the rankings of the gravity of crimes was close to perfect among persons in different social positions.

> The average correlation was .977 for the six social background variables and .989 for the twelve comparisons involving the social background characteristics and the total sample ranking. The lowest correlation we obtained . . . was the .917 coefficient yielded by a comparison of the rankings of our black and white respondents [1976, p. 10].

Like other studies of judged *gravity* of offense, the study by Thomas is not a direct test of a citizenry's agreement in its *definition* of acts as criminal. However, a later study by Newman does directly assess the amount of agreement among people in their definition of crime.

[5]Scholars who attempt research on public and legal definitions of acts and conditions as deserving state attention as criminal should be encouraged to use more than one method of inquiry. Direct questioning, by interview and "opinionnaire," ought to be supplemented with tools such as the semantic-differential and semiprojective techniques. We are more confident of the meaning of our findings when the results of multiple methods converge.

Consensus about Crime: Newman's Research Graeme Newman (1976), with the cooperation of students in six countries, tested the degree to which nine acts were considered to be more or less serious and worthy of control by the state or other agency.

Samples of residents in urban and rural districts were questioned in India, Indonesia, Iran, Italy (Sardinia), Yugoslavia, and the United States (New York). These individuals of diverse culture were asked to consider nine acts that range from crimes *mala in se* and crimes *mala prohibita* to those which are morally ambiguous. The nine acts are described briefly below:[6]

> *Robbery:* A person forcefully takes $50 from another who, as a result, is injured and has to be hospitalized.
>
> *Incest:* A person has sexual relations with his adult daughter.
>
> *Not helping:* A person sees someone in a dangerous situation and does nothing.
>
> *Abortion:* A woman who is two months pregnant seeks and obtains an abortion.
>
> *Factory pollution:* A factory director continues to permit his factory to release poisonous gases into the air.
>
> *Homosexuality:* A person has homosexual relations in private with the consent of the partner.
>
> *Protest:* A person participates in a protest meeting against government policy in a public place. No violence occurs.
>
> *Appropriation:* A person puts government funds to his own use.
>
> *Taking drugs:* A person takes drugs (specified "heroin" in U.S., "soft" in Sardinia, "opium" in Iran, "gange" in India and Indonesia).

About each of these six acts respondents were asked six questions:

1 Do you think this act should be prohibited by law?
2 *Is* this act prohibited by the law?
3 How active do you think the government is in trying to stop acts of this kind?
4 To whom (if anyone) would you report this act?
5 How serious do you think this act is?
6 What do you think should be done with a person who performs an act of this kind?

Newman's findings contradict the radical criminologist's allegation that "crime" is only "political," a definition imposed by the powerful upon the powerless. To the contrary, Newman's data demonstrate that

> there is a universal (i.e., cross-cultural) consensus concerning the disapproval of a number of crimes and deviances [*sic*]. This applies especially at the general level of opinion and intensity of reaction. A generally deep, probably emotional reaction, as measured by choice of sanctions, was also found cross-culturally [p. 153].

[6]Reprinted with permission from Graeme Newman, *Comparative Deviance: Perception and Law in Six Cultures.* © 1976 by Elsevier Scientific Publishing Company.

Furthermore:

> Respondents in all cultures tended to classify the acts into similar groupings. . . .
> For traditional crimes, a high degree of consensus was found for their disapproval.
> . . . One might argue that these crimes have *always* been disapproved of. They are
> therefore not relative to particular periods or places, but are standards; one
> hesitates to say it, but they are, functionally speaking, *absolute* standards [pp.
> 285–286].

Agreement among individuals in their conceptions of "traditional crimes"
means, of course, that "class position" in a society does *not* affect the
definition of criminality, as it is supposed to do, according to conflict criminology. Attitudes toward robbery, incest, drug use, and embezzlement are not class
attitudes, but definitions of a more universal character. So, too, is disapproval
of the new version of the old crime of poisoning the environment. It is only as
one inquires about acts that have not always been considered wrongs in
themselves—acts such as abortion, homosexuality, protest, and not helping—
that wide differences are found in opinions.

The fact of widespread disapproval of acts long considered to be inherently wrong means that other "background variables," in addition to social class,
are also of minor significance in response to the "traditional crimes." Newman
found low correlations between age, sex, schooling, literacy, occupation,
rural-urban residence, and conceptions of crime. Among such variables,
however, the one most highly correlated with reaction to wrongs was *religiosity*. This finding confirms a frequently reported tendency of conventionally
religious persons—quite apart from their particular faith—to favor more
punitive responses to crime and deviance (Kaupen, 1973; Newman et al., 1974;
Weil, 1952).

General disapproval of "traditional crimes" in disparate cultures does
not signify unanimity, of course, and the proportion of people who wish to
control deviant acts varies somewhat by country and crime. So, too, the
kind of recommended control varies. Where informal controls, such as
the family, remain active, they may be preferred to more formal control by
law.

The major point holds, however. Contrary to the allegation of radical
criminologists, the classic crimes against the person and against property are
widely condemned by people of diverse culture and social position. A notable
aberration in Newman's data is that only 71 percent of his New Yorkers felt
that incest, as defined by his example, should be prohibited by law. This
contrasts with proportions in the high 90 percents for citizens of other
countries. On this and other issues, Newman reminds us that New Yorkers are
not to be confused with the rest of Americans (p. 100).

Difference between crime and deviance   Findings from Thomas's study
and Newman's research suggest a difference between crime and deviance,
along lines proposed by Aubert (1970). The frontier between crime and
deviance may be defined by the *degree of agreement* among a people about acts
deserving social condemnation and control. In terms of Aubert's schema and

current information, there *are* wrongs generally conceived as crimes that stand in contrast to a range of morally ambiguous acts about which we disagree.

These data seem to indicate that the central assumption of the conflict school is less well grounded in fact than that of consensus theorists. There are, however, additional factual deficiencies in the radical perspective.

Additional Factual Deficiencies Conflict criminology has failed to demonstrate the truth of other of its allegations. In outline, these failures include lack of proof that:

a Unnamed persons called "positivists" do not "question the established order" and do not "examine scientific assumptions."

There is more than one brand of "positivism," as every philosopher knows (Abbagnano, 1967; Ayer, 1959; H. L. A. Hart, 1967; Passmore, 1967; R. von Mises, 1956). To say that this variety of positivist philosopher does not question social relations and does not examine scientific assumptions is, to put it mildly, absurd.

b Criminal justice systems in bourgeois societies are instruments of class oppression that apprehend people less for their crimes than for the powerless position they occupy.

The charge of such discriminatory application of the law has been investigated principally in capitalist societies and rarely in socialist states. Comparison of the justice of legal systems is therefore tentative. Such data as we have, however, do not support the allegation that criminal justice in bourgeois countries is nothing but class justice (see pages 291–298). To the contrary, it is in capitalist lands that due-process protection of defendants is most strong (Gastil, 1976). Freedoms *are* correlated.

c Capitalist societies are peculiarly guilty of "crimes against humanity."

Racism, sexism, and poverty are "crimes" allegedly more characteristic of market economies than of planned ones. War, too, is alleged to be a distinctive product of capitalism when it is conceived as a certain kind of war called "imperialist" (Schwendinger and Schwendinger, 1971, p. 136).

None of these conditions is defined with that *specificity* required of the criminal law in Western countries. Vagueness of the nominated crimes against "human rights" permits emotional charges to be made without proof, and it makes comparison of the protection of these rights in different societies difficult. It is apparent, however, that deprivation of these rights is *relative.* Violation is more readily seen where these privileges are most protected. Thus Hollander (1973) notes:

> Paradoxically poverty is seen as a social problem in the United States, but not in the Soviet Union. It is an American social problem to a large extent *because* the standard of living is high and consequently expectations are also higher. In the Soviet Union, against the background of generally low living standards, poverty is not a social problem, but rather a normal state of affairs [p. 334].

The burden of proof rests, again, on those who lay a charge. Proof of the greater violation of "human rights" in market economies than in planned economies has thus far not been given, and, in fact, such evidence as we have runs counter to the radical allegation (Gastil, 1976).

3 Sociological Weakness

Sociological deficiencies flow from factual deficiencies, and factual debility reinforces sociological weakness. Errors of fact and thinness of theory are both results of the difficulties of conceiving of a "society" as a whole and of finding out whether our image of how things are and how things work is more or less true.

No image of social relations developed by thoughtful persons is entirely true or false, although many such models are sufficiently vague as to be beyond test. A theme of this book is that all the explanations of crime causation point to something causal. My criticism is based, however, on the *clarity* of the nominated causes, the *factual evidence* for each nomination, and the *predictive accuracy* of the many theories of criminogenesis.

With this qualification, a major sociological deficiency of conflict criminology becomes apparent. It is the assumption that only property divides us. It is the assumption that if private property in the instruments of production were eliminated, there would be, by definition, no "social classes" and therefore no elite with the power to criminalize the deviance of anyone. Crime, then, would wither away, as would the state, which is said to be required only as an instrument of class oppression.

In contradiction of this image of social relations, studies in anthropology, psychology, and sociology demonstrate repeatedly that struggles over material things are only one source of division among people. Deviation is a normal feature of our living together, and even moral communities find it necessary to define boundaries of acceptable behavior as a means of ensuring moral continuity. This thesis has been well expressed by one of the founders of sociology, Emile Durkheim (1858–1917), who urged us to:

> Imagine a society of saints, a perfect cloister of exemplary individuals. Crimes, properly so called, will there be unknown; but faults which appear venial to the layman will create there the same scandal that the ordinary offense does in ordinary consciousness. If, then, this society has the power to judge and punish, it will define these acts as criminal and will treat them as such [1958, pp. 68–69].

Durkheim's thesis has been tested in studies of tribes and sects (Erikson, 1966; W. I. Thomas, 1937, chaps. 7, 14, 15). The results of such tests confirm Durkheim's conception of crime as an offense against moral sentiment, against the "collective conscience." In a famous passage, Durkheim argued:

> We must not say that an action shocks the common conscience because it is criminal, but rather that it is criminal because it shocks the common conscience. We do not reprove it because it is a crime, but it is a crime because we reprove it. As for the intrinsic nature of these sentiments, it is impossible to specify them.

They have the most diverse objects and cannot be encompassed in a single formula. We can say that they relate neither to vital interests of society nor to a minimum of justice [1949, p. 81].

In short, private property and differences in wealth may define wrongs and, hence, crimes for some groups, but these conditions, condemned by conflict criminologists, do *not* exhaust the repertory of morals that define crimes. It is no surprise, then, to find modern socialist states punishing old and new categories of crime and criminals even after they have been "freed" of private ownership of the means of production (Berliner, 1961; J. A. Cohen, 1968; Gsovski, 1961).

4 Moral Debility

Moral deficiencies in conflict criminology are related to its factual and theoretical weaknesses. It is always uncomfortable to point to the moral inadequacy of others' images of society because morals are emotionally loaded and immune to facts.[7]

Nevertheless, the ethical soundness of radical criminology is at issue because this school bases its perspective and its prescriptions so strongly on its presumed moral superiority. Two questions may be asked of any moral code: "How consistently is it applied?" and "What consequences follow from believing it?"

a "Foolish consistency [may be] the hobgoblin of little minds," as Emerson (1841) claimed, but we do not regard it as foolish to expect moral commandments to be consistent within themselves. We expect them to be just, and this means uniformly applied so that the wrongs we condemn remain wrong when committed by our friends and when committed by our enemies.

No one has counted the relative consistency of competing moralities, but without such a tally it is apparent that conflict criminologists attribute their newly nominated "crimes against humanity" principally, if not entirely, to bourgeois countries and seldom, if ever, to socialist states. Thus brutality, poverty, and the persecution of dissidence are consistently charged against the United States and consistently overlooked in the Soviet Union. Thus radical criminology is vocal about state violence in North America and Western Europe and silent about such violence in approved African and Asian countries and in Eastern Europe.

These charges reverse the true order of affairs, as best we know them. They locate "crimes against humanity" where they least occur and ignore them where they are most frequent (Beichman, 1972; Conquest, 1968; Gastil, 1976; Kaiser, 1976; Salisbury, 1974; Shub, 1969; H. Smith, 1976; Solzhenitsyn, 1973). The moral credentials of the conflict school would be worth more if its moral code were consistently applied.

---

[7] While moral codes are *justified* by reference to some facts, they are also *superior* to them, that is, beyond refutation by facts (J. Ladd, 1957). There is a continuing debate, however, as to whether morality is rational or can be made so. A personal opinion is expressed more fully elsewhere (Nettler, 1972a, 1973).

b A consequence of inconsistency in applying moral prescriptions, and of broadening the definition of crime to include such undefined wrongs as "racism, sexism, poverty, and imperialist war," is the production of radical criminology's own brand of injustice. This brand of injustice includes laying charges for nonspecific acts and conditions, applying these vague definitions of crime selectively, and allocating responsibility for imprecisely defined acts and conditions to groups as opposed to individuals, as per the communist notion of "collective responsibility" (Ammende, 1936; Conquest, 1968; Frank, 1950; Pepinsky, 1976; Petersen, 1963).

5 Promissory Defects

A theory of the human condition which is based on a defective way of knowing it, on fact-free assumptions about it, and which is, in addition, morally inconsistent is a theory that will be both sociologically unsound and predictively inaccurate. It is a theory that will default on its promises.

The new criminology promises a utopia in which "the facts of human diversity, whether personal, organic or social, are not subject to the power to criminalize" (I. Taylor et al., 1973, p. 282). In this new world there will be no need for criminal law or for a state to enforce it.

Unfortunately, radical criminologists do not *know* how to achieve what they promise, and the real world casts doubt on their vision. The liberation promised through socialist and communist revolutions has not been achieved. Its opposite, tyranny, has been the most common consequence of the destruction of freedom in the marketplace. Under socialism and communism the state has grown, not withered away, and fewer people have more power over more aspects of the lives of their subjects.

The radical rebuttal to this sad fact is to claim that "not all the evidence is in" and that "it takes time to build socialism." The evidence is *never* all in, of course, and how long one is willing to wait for political promises to come true depends on judgment. Judgment, in turn, depends on one's need to hope, on the information one has, on where one is, and on the options available.

It is easier to condemn the liberties one has while in a free society than to criticize those freedoms while in a totalitarian state. The ultimate test of the liberties allowed in capitalist and socialist countries is to note how people vote with their feet when they can. By this democratic test, most people vote for capitalist reality and against socialist promise (Nettler, 1976, pp. 269–270).

OTHER CAUSES OF CRIME

The new criminology has been assessed as one version of a structural story about crime causation. The exciting element in conflict criminology is its condemnation of the total structure of contemporary Western societies and its abandonment of reform in favor of a revolution that will eliminate the power of one group over another.

Against the enthusiasm of such promise, competing theories of criminogenesis seem pallid. For many scholars they are boring because they suggest tedious reforms and little hope. This lack of promise does not make such explanations of crime untrue, of course, but it does make them less interesting. Nevertheless, scholars who would expand their experience will examine other ideas about crime production.

The next chapter describes a peculiarly North American version of structural explanation of crime—the notion that crime is generated by the balance of lawful and criminal opportunities.

Chapter 12

Structures of Opportunity

Structural explanations of crime consider the ways in which social systems generate and satisfy human wants. Such explanations consider, also, the ways in which rewards and punishments are handed out.

Economists emphasize human striving as rational, as mediated by costs and benefits that are judged, imperfectly of course, by actors in particular situations. Conflict criminology moves attention from the rationality of criminality—which it does not deny—to differentials in power that allow minorities to exploit majorities and to define threats to their power as crimes.

Another form of structural explanation parallels the views of economic and conflict theorists in that it conceives of actors as struggling in webs of circumstance to achieve their ends. However, to emphasize the criminogenic features of a structure of *opportunities* is to emphasize choice less and "pressure" more than economists do. And, in comparison with the conflict school, those who speak of opportunities as determining criminality emphasize power less and economic chances more.

To speak of opportunities as moving individuals toward more and less lawful activity is to assume that "people everywhere are pretty much the same" and that there are no significant differences in abilities or desires that might account for lawful and criminal careers. Attention is paid to the organization of social relations that affects the differential exercise of talents and interests which are assumed to be roughly equal for all persons.

Theory Boundaries   It is emphasis upon *equality* that marks boundaries between an "opportunity-structure" thesis of crime and delinquency and other hypotheses such as those advanced by subcultural theorists (see Chapter 13) or control theorists (see Chapter 16). The boundaries are drawn by the *causes* nominated as sources of crime.

This point is important because some authors who stress opportunities also write about subcultures. For example, A. K. Cohen (1955), whose work is discussed on pages 235–236, gave his book *Delinquent Boys* the subtitle "The Culture of the Gang," and the famous study by Cloward and Ohlin, *Delinquency and Opportunity* (1960), also speaks of "delinquent subcultures."

Present assessment of varying ideas about criminogenesis is based on *what is emphasized as causing criminal conduct.* It is apparent, and will be more obvious, that there is overlap among the attempted explanations of crime. However, we can distinguish these explanations by what they stress as causal, rather than by the incidental language they use. And what is stressed as causal is best recognized by the policy prescriptions, if any, that these many authors offer.

The classification presented here of explanations as structural, rather than subcultural, is based on the political advocacy provided by the respective themes. Thus some authors who speak of delinquent subcultures do *not* recommend change of individuals or cultures, but change in "the social setting that," in the words of Cloward and Ohlin, "gives rise to delinquency" (1960, p. 211).

Opportunity-structure theories, then, are those which see all members of a society as wanting much the same things. Such explanations do not emphasize difference, as subcultural or control hypotheses do. Rather, people are conceived to be "pressured" into different courses of action by the structure of life chances available to them. This is a thesis that has appropriately been named "strain theory" (Hirschi, 1969).

DURKHEIM'S ANOMIE

The conception of social relations as opportunities that push and pull people into different courses of action borrows heavily from the ideas of the French sociologist Emile Durkheim. Durkheim viewed human beings as social animals as well as physical organisms. To say that we are *social* animals means more than the obvious fact that we live for a long time as helpless children, depending on others for our survival. More is implied, too, than that *Homo sapiens* is a *herding* animal who tends to live in colonies. For Durkheim, the significantly social aspect of human nature is that human physical survival also depends upon *moral* connections. Moral connections are, of course, social. They represent a bond with, and hence a bondage to, others. "It is not true," Durkheim writes, "that human activity can be released from all restraint" (1951, p. 252). The restraint that is required if social life is to ensue is a restraint necessary also for the psychic health of the human individual.

The notion of *pressure* is implied by Durkheim and his followers. Human beings are depicted as requiring a social environment to keep them sound. The pressure of that environment must be neither too little nor too great. Just as one can be crushed by the excessive demands of others upon his life, so, too, he "falls apart" when he lives without restraint. The metaphor is that of a denizen of the deep sea that requires just so much pressure to survive and explodes when brought to the surface.

Absolute freedom, the escape from all moral bonds, would, for Durkheim, be a precursor of suicide. The suicide might be the act of a moment—"taking one's own life"—or it might be the piecemeal and prolonged suicide of those bored with life who kill themselves with vice.

Social conditions may strengthen or weaken the moral ties that Durkheim saw as a condition of happiness and healthy survival. Rapid changes in one's possibilities, swings from riches to rags and, just as disturbing, from rags to riches, may constitute, in Durkheim's words, "an impulse to voluntary death" (1951, p. 246). Excessive hopes and unlimited desires are avenues to misery.

Durkheim's conception of the human being is similar to that found among the ancient Greeks: the idea that men and women require a balance, a proportion, between their appetites and their satisfactions, between their wants and their abilities. "No living being," Durkheim tells us, "can be happy or even exist unless his needs are sufficiently proportioned to his means" (1951, p. 246).

Social conditions that allow a "deregulation" of social life Durkheim called states of *anomie*. The French word *anomie* derives from Greek roots meaning "lacking in rule or law." As used by contemporary sociologists, the word *anomie* and its English equivalent, "anomy," are applied ambiguously, sometimes to the social conditions of relative normlessness and sometimes to the individuals who experience a lack of rule and purpose in their lives. It is recommended that the term be restricted to societal conditions of relative rulelessness (Nettler, 1957, p. 671).

When the concept of *anomie* is employed by structuralists to explain behavior, attention is directed toward the "strains" produced in the individual by the conflicting, confusing, or impossible demands of his social environment. Writers have described *anomie* in our "schizoid culture," a culture that is said to present conflicting prescriptions for conduct (Bain, 1958; Henry, 1963). They have also perceived *anomie* in the tension between recommended goals and available means.

It is this tension between ends and means to which many "social problems" are attributed, including the undesirable conditions of hatred of oneself and hatred of one's social connections. There is truth in Durkheim's vision, and many writers have incorporated it into their political attitudes. The rub comes, however, in deciding whether the gap between desires and abilities is to be narrowed by modifying the desires or changing the world that frustrates their fulfillment. Eastern philosophies and conservative thinkers emphasize the first path; Western philosophies and radical thinkers, the second.

MERTON'S APPLICATION OF THE CONCEPT OF *ANOMIE*

The American sociologist R. K. Merton (1957) has applied Durkheim's ideas to the explanation of deviant behavior with particular reference to modern Western societies. His hypothesis is that a state of *anomie* is produced whenever there is a discrepancy between the goals of human action and the societally structured legitimate means of achieving them. The hypothesis is, simply, that crime breeds in the gaps between aspirations and possibilities. The emphasis given to this idea by the structuralists is that both the goals and the means are given by the pattern of social arrangements. It is "the structure" of a society, which includes some elements of its culture, that builds desires and assigns opportunities for their satisfaction. This structural explanation sees illegal behavior as resulting from goals, particularly materialistic goals, held to be desirable and possible for all, that motivate behavior in a societal context that provides only limited legal channels of achievement.

OPPORTUNITY-STRUCTURE THEORY: CLOWARD AND OHLIN'S *DELINQUENCY AND OPPORTUNITY*

The most prominent application of Merton's ideas has been to the explanation of juvenile delinquency and, in particular, to that of urban gangs. One formulation is given by Cloward and Ohlin's work, aptly titled *Delinquency and Opportunity* (1960). The central hypothesis is this:

> The disparity between what lower-class youth are led to want and what is actually available to them is the source of a major problem of adjustment. Adolescents who form delinquent subcultures . . . have internalized an emphasis upon conventional goals. Faced with limitations of legitimate avenues of access to these goals, and unable to revise their aspirations downward, they experience intense frustrations; the exploration of nonconformist alternatives may be the result [p. 86].

This type of explanation sees delinquency as *adaptive*, as instrumental in the achievement of "the same kinds of things" everyone wants. It sees crime, also, as partly *reactive*—generated by a sense of injustice on the part of delinquents at having been deprived of the good life they had been led to expect would be theirs. Finally, this hypothesis, which may with accuracy be described as the social worker's favorite, looks to the satisfaction of desires, rather than the lowering of expectations, as the cure for crime. To be sure, it approaches the satisfaction of desires not directly but indirectly, through the provision of "expanded opportunities" for legitimate achievement.

Since this explanatory schema has been so popular, and since it has provided the theoretical justification of government programs for the reduction of delinquency, its key ideas deserve special note.

It is apparent, first, that, in common with other sociological explanations, this hypothesis is *socially deterministic*. Cloward and Ohlin's statement does not talk about "what lower-class youths want." It talks about "what lower-class youths *are led* to want." The causal agent is "in the society" that does things to a youth, rather in the youth himself.

Second, it is assumed that the gap between the desires of lowerclass people and their legitimate opportunities is *greater* than the discrepancy between the aspirations of middle-class persons and their legitimate opportunities. This can be believed, but it is not known.

It is argued, third, that gang-running delinquents have "internalized conventional goals," and, fourth, that legitimate avenues to these goals are structurally limited.

Fifth, the hypothesis holds that lower-class youths do not (and cannot) "revise their aspirations downward." Finally, it is said that the breach between promise and fulfillment generates intense frustration and that the frustration *may* lead to criminal conduct.

While the opportunity-structure thesis as a whole sounds plausible, closer attention to its assumptions lessens confidence in its explanatory power.

Criticism of the Opportunity-Structure Hypothesis

There are four principal charges brought against the opportunity-structure hypothesis. Each criticism has numerous points to it, but the various doubts can be brought together under four questions: (1) "Are the key concepts of the theory clear?" (2) "Is the theory correct about the way gang-running delinquents are?" (3) "Is the theory correct about how they got that way?" (4) "Are the recommendations of the opportunity-structure theory feasible and effective?" The answers to all four questions seem more negative than affirmative.

1   Are the Key Concepts Clear?   Two words are central in thinking about crime in terms of the opportunity-structure hypothesis: "aspiration" and "opportunity." Neither concept is clear. Both words are borrowed from lay language, where the denotations of many useful concepts are embedded in emotionalized connotations so that common words, the principal currency of communication, become slippery. Such ambiguity is comforting in politics and journalism where points can be proved by sliding from one respectable meaning of a term to its less reputable meanings. Ambiguity may be a social lubricant in this sense, but it is a defect in a social science that would guide rational social policy.

Like many other explanations of human behavior, the opportunity-structure theory starts with what people want. The engine of action is desire. It is assumed that the desires called "aspirations" have been quite similar for all North Americans, if not for all Westerners, at some time in their careers. However, opportunity-structure theory is silent about the life histories of delinquents and hence takes for granted what needs to be known—the extent to which lawful careers and all they entail *are* preferred or derided.

Saying is not wanting   This neglect is both cause and effect of the structuralist's ready assumption that what people *say* they want out of life is an adequate measure of their "aspiration." Such an easy equation of words with motives leaves out of the definition of "aspiration" that which most dictionaries and common usage include: ambition, drive, yearning. To accept words at face value as indicators of aspiration strips the concept of its motivating power and permits students to confuse daydreaming with the desire that fuels intent. In response to the interviewer with his clipboard and questionnaire, it is easy for any of us to tell "what we'd like"—usually "money and repute." It is another matter, however, to equate this ready verbalization with *aspiration*—with intention, direction, plan.

Values are words and deeds   The likelihood that there is a difference between verbal aspiration and effective motivation is increased by evidence that the values of the more persistent delinquents *are* different from those of lesser offenders. "Values" here refers to what people want as noted in *both* their words and their deeds. The values that energize "aspiration," and give it its proper meaning, *do* differ between committed violators and more lawful people. On this issue, the advocate of the subcultural theory seems to be on firmer ground than the structuralist.

The evidence of such difference is found in a host of studies that draw us a portrait of the more serious offender as a hasty hedonist and jungle cat. The "philosophy" of persistent miscreants is cynical, hostile, and distrustful. Their morality denies the rules of the game. It avoids responsibility for fulfilling obligations to others except under fear of reprisal. It downgrades the victims of their crimes and categorizes them as "punks, chumps, pigeons, or fags" (Schwendinger and Schwendinger, 1967, p. 98). The delinquent's "jungle philosophy" sees friends as fickle and "everybody as just out for himself" (Nettler, 1961). According to the criminal ethic, you should "do unto others as they would do unto you . . . only do it first"; and, "If I don't cop [steal] it . . . somebody else will" (Schwendinger and Schwendinger, 1967, p. 98).

It does not matter whether we agree or disagree with these offensive values. The point is that the difference in attitude is real. It is not just a difference in words; it is a difference that is acted out. The opportunity-structure hypothesis neglects this difference, apparently as a result of its weak conception of aspiration.

Vague opportunities   The other term central to this explanation of crime, "opportunity," is equally vague. As dictionaries define the word and as most people use it, it refers to a time or situation favorable to the attainment of a goal; it refers to a "chance." Now, the perception of a chance is always a function of the perceiver and where he or she stands. Its assessment involves some notion, usually tacit, of what a person could have done if he or she had had the chance or had seen it.

There is, then, a possible difference between *perceived* opportunities and *real* ones—between what was there and what we thought was there, between what we might actually have done and what we, or other observers, believe we might have done if we had thought differently or acted differently.

Opportunities are by their nature much easier to see after they have passed than before they are grasped.

These many intangibles in the idea of an opportunity mean that sociologists who employ the term "opportunity" come to judge differences in opportunity from differences in result. If people do not end up equally happy, healthy, lawful, or rich, these differences are attributed to differences in "opportunity." This attribution does two questionable things: (1) it assumes that all or most of the causes of a career are encompassed in something called "the chances" or "the breaks," and (2) it performs a semantic cheat by substituting *how one is* for *the chances one had*. This is illegitimate because it first poses a cause of conduct called "opportunity" and then it uses the alleged effects of that "opportunity" as a measure of it. It is as if one were to argue that

C causes E, and then prove the causal connection by using E as the measure of C.

For most of us, the proper attribution of a causal relationship requires that whatever is called a "cause" must be a *different set of circumstances* from that which is called its effect. Otherwise we are trapped in a logical circle, an entrapment that may be comfortable for purposes of moral or political debate but that is a hindrance to effective action. The scientific requirement of any hypothesis which proposes that opportunities may be the causes of careers is that the indicators of "opportunity" be defined *before* the signs of outcome are decided upon. The two sets of indicators must then be kept separate if any inference is to be derived as to the causal relation between them.

This research requirement applies with particular force to the opportunity theorists, because going to school has been defined by scholars and laymen alike as one legitimate opportunity. As with any other "chance," some people grasp it while others reject it. Persistent delinquents, we shall see, prefer the latter course when faced with schooling. The difference in career, then, lies less in the *presence* of the opportunity than in its *use*. Both the subcultural and the sociopsychological explanations of crime pay more attention to the determinants of differential use of opportunities.

2   Does the Opportunity-Structure Thesis Accurately Describe Gang-affiliated Delinquents?   The fundamental assumption of opportunity-structure theory is equality. Not equality of "opportunity," of course, but equality of aspiration, interest, motivation, application, and ability.

Cloward and Ohlin, for example, attribute juvenile delinquency to the offender's sense of injustice. These authors argue that delinquents see unfairness in "the system," with people of the same ability as themselves, or less ability, getting a bigger slice of the pie. Furthermore, Cloward and Ohlin contend that the delinquents' perception is correct.

The first part of this allegation is hardly news. It has long been common for criminals to argue that "the system" is more crooked than they, that "straight people" are just as dishonest as thieves, and that "it's not what you do, but who you know" that determines one's fate. What is surprising is that social scientists accept this rationalization and, in so doing, confuse a justification of delinquency with the causes of delinquency.

Cloward and Ohlin say:

> It is our impression that a sense of being unjustly deprived of access to opportunities to which one is entitled is common among those who become participants in delinquent subcultures. Delinquents tend to be persons who have been led to expect opportunities *because of their potential ability* to meet the formal, institutionally established criteria of evaluation [1960, p. 117; italics added].

They then support this allegation of equal ability with a footnote stating:

> There is no evidence . . . that members of delinquent subcultures are objectively less capable of meeting formal standards of eligibility than are nondelinquent lower

class youngsters. In fact, the available data support the contention that the basic endowments of delinquents, such as intelligence, physical strength, and agility, are the equal of or greater than those of their nondelinquent peers [p. 117, fn. 10].

Unless one is to earn one's keep as a professional athlete, the "basic endowments" of physical strength and agility are of slight relevance to occupational achievement. Intelligence, persistence, diligence, reliability, interest, emotional control—these traits are of greater relevance to climbing the class ladder. Contrary to the belief of opportunity-structure theorists, gang-running delinquents do *not* exhibit these abilities in the same proportions as more legitimately successful youths.

Such evidence as we have of how people legitimately climb upward in society indicates that those who successfully use lawful means exhibit differences in interests, motivation, and ability. These differences are apparent early in adolescence and sometimes even before puberty. Furthermore, achievers, when compared with their less successful counterparts, differ in these attributes even when social-class origins are held constant (Jayasuriya, 1960; Straus, 1962). The pattern of difference is found consistently in industrial countries of otherwise varied cultures.

Quality of difference People who are legitimately successful tend to be more interested in schoolwork, to score higher on tests of mental ability, and to be more emotionally stable and diligent than those who are less successful. They move toward their vocational objectives with greater persistence and defer other gratifications in favor of these longer-range goals. They demonstrate greater self-confidence and a greater need to achieve. They function more independently of their parents while yet respecting their parents more. They are described as being possessed of greater self-control, responsibility, and intellectual efficiency. The evidence of these differences is widespread and may be sampled in the reports of Beilin (1956), Burt (1961), Crockett (1962), Douvan (1956), Douvan and Edelson (1958), Haan (1964), Sewell et al. (1969), Sorokin (1959), Srole et al. (1962), Stacey (1965), Terman and Oden (1947, 1955), P. G. Thompson (1971), Warner (1953), and Warner and Abegglen (1955).

Opportunity in school Until recently, at least,[1] going to school has been the major legitimate ladder by which people have climbed upward in society. A multiplicity of studies tells us that juvenile offenders, and particularly the more serious offenders, differ from their less delinquent counterparts in their greater resistance to schooling. They hate schoolwork and they hate their teachers. They more frequently "ditch" school and destroy school buildings and equipment. They do poorly in academic work, are more frequently retarded in grade, and score low on tests of mental performance. They are perceived by

---

[1]This qualification is required because the higher the proportion of a population that achieves educational certification, the lower the probable value of that accomplishment as an instrument of socioeconomic improvement. Subject, of course, to the unknown effects of future changes in technologies and economies, it may be suggested that there is some limit beyond which it will be the case that the more people climb the educational ladder, the shorter that ladder will become as a means of moving upward in class. For discussions of the oversupply of educated manpower, see Berg (1971), Ginzberg (1972), and Grubb (1971).

both their teachers and their classmates as troublemakers, and they are, in general, disliked by both. This dislike is, of course, reciprocated. A partial roster of the evidence of these differences includes studies by Cooper (1960), Glueck (1964), Hathaway and Monachesi (1957), Healy and Bronner (1936), Hewitt and R. L. Jenkins (1946), Mannheim (1965), Paranjape (1970), D. R. Peterson et al. (1959), Porteus (1961), Quay et al. (1960), Rivera and Short, (1967), Shulman (1929), Stinchcombe (1964), Stott (1966), Teele et al. (1966), D. J. West (1969), and H. D. Williams (1933).

Descriptive failure   The central hypothesis fails. The notion that juvenile delinquents and adult criminals are persons who in adolescence are the same in ability and motivation as less offensive persons and that they differ only in their lack of "legitimate opportunities"—this assumption is unfounded. This untenable assumption is but part of a more general descriptive weakness inherent in the opportunity-structure theory. The theory does *not* accurately portray the talents, preferences, desires, and views of the world that reliably distinguish serious, career offenders from their more lawful counterparts.

This descriptive failure has been attributed to the possibility that the inventors of the opportunity-structure hypothesis are middle-class persons who are imposing their conceptions upon others, who, in fact, reject them. However this may be, the hypothesis does slight the fact that tastes differ and that lower-class ways of life may have a rationale and a definition of "how things ought to be" that have their own validity. This structural explanation is blind, therefore, to the *fun* that is involved in being delinquent—fun like skipping school, rolling drunks, snatching purses, being chased by the police, staying out till all hours, going where one wants, and doing what one wants without adult supervision.

3   Does the Opportunity-Structure Hypothesis Accurately Describe How Delinquents Are Produced?   If there is something deficient in a description of how people are, it is likely that there is something wrong with the related explanation of how they got that way.

The opportunity-structure story holds that the delinquent's response is *adaptive*, a necessary consequence of a "social structure." The theory is therefore sympathetic to the motives it attributes to a wide category of offenders. It accords "frustration" to the gang-running delinquent and sees the frustration as produced by the correct perception of unjust deprivation.

What is frustration?   "Frustration" is another fuzzy word. Sometimes it refers to a blocking, a thwarting, to not getting what one wants. At other times it refers to emotions, to feelings of despair and anger, to a free-floating discontent. The first meaning is *objective*. Observers can watch animals strive for goals and can agree about their success or failure: whether the monkey gets the banana or the runner wins the race. The second meaning is *subjective*. It refers to feelings attributed to the striver who fails.

The objective failure that is sometimes called "frustration" is not the same set of events as the angry feelings also called "frustration." The relationship between the two meanings of "frustration" is far from perfect, and it is presumptive to infer one from the other. No one has yet mapped the coordinates of frustration. No one knows which persons under which circumstances feel more or less frustrated by which failure. In fact, the very ideas of "success" and "failure" have not been adequately diagramed for people of diverse ways of life.

These uncertainties about the meaning of "frustration" and its location leave the opportunity-structure hypothesis untested and perhaps untestable. In the absence of such testing, critics of the hypothesis will rely on more plausible depictions of the process by which serious offenders are produced. They will, for example, continue to stress "structures" as affecting the realization of talent *without* the assumption of equal interests and abilities. They will continue, with the social psychologists, to stress the importance of early family socialization and, with the subcultural theorists, to emphasize the authenticity of ethnic values that may be more or less criminogenic within a given "social structure."

4   Are the Recommendations of Opportunity-Structure Theory Feasible and Effective?   A fair test of a hypothesis is whether it works. The work of a hypothesis is to prescribe a distinctive course of action that will reliably get one more of what he wants at known and lower costs.

The opportunity-structure explanation of criminogenesis has been interpreted as saying that if young people had more legitimate opportunities to satisfy their aspirations, they would resort less frequently to crime. In the United States several large-scale projects have attempted to expand opportunities and thereby reduce juvenile delinquency. Their record has been one of uniform failure (Hackler, 1966; Hackler and Hagan, 1972; Moynihan, 1969; Weissman, 1969).

Failure itself has many explanations and, when it follows upon kind efforts, many apologists. The failure of programs designed to prevent criminality and to reform offenders can always be attributed to insufficient funding or to unforeseen resistance by evil others, rather than to errors in the theories underlying the programs.

Failure may also be attributed to selective attention to what the theory recommends. In fairness to Cloward and Ohlin, they have *not* said in their major work that the cure for crime is simply the expansion of legitimate opportunities. Their emphasis has given this impression, of course. However, Cloward and Ohlin argue that "extending services to delinquent individuals or groups cannot prevent the rise of delinquency among others" (1960, p. 211). They hold that "the major effort . . . should be directed to the reorganization of slum communities" because "the old structures, which provided *social control* and avenues of social ascent, are breaking down" (p. 211, italics added).

"Social control" has been emphasized in this quotation because the opportunity hypothesis finally reverts to an assumption that is common to all sociological and sociopsychological explanations of criminality *mala in se*. All these explanations see serious crime as the result of a weakening of social controls. The explanations differ only in how they believe this deregulation of social life has come about, in what they emphasize as the crucial regulator, and hence in where they specify effort ought to be applied to reduce the harm we do each other.

In Summary

The proposal that differences in the availability of legitimate opportunities affect crime rates is but one version of the structural style of explanation. The weaknesses of this particular hypothesis do not deny the validity of the structural notion in general. There *are* features of the "structure" of a society that seem clearly and directly antecedent to varying crime rates.

Divisions within a society, "culture conflict," are one such general aspect of a society's structure that seems to promote criminality. Durkheim's *anomie*, the deregulation of social life, may be another such feature, as yet inadequately applied to the explanation of crime. Merton's application of the idea of *anomie* to the production of criminality seems plausible in general, particularly if one avoids translating *anomie* into "opportunity." This more general use of the notion of *anomie* predicts that serious crime rates will be higher in societies whose public codes and mass media simultaneously stimulate consumership and egalitarianism while denying differences and delegitimizing them.

More concretely, the age distributions and sex ratios of societies or of localities can be interpreted as structural features and related to differences in crime rates. Thus it comes as little surprise to learn that situations in which the sex ratio is greatly distorted result in different patterns of sexual offense. Homosexuality, including forcible homosexual rape, increases where men and women are kept apart from the opposite sex, as in prisons. Prostitution flourishes where numbers of men live without women but with the freedom to "get out" on occasion, as from mining camps or military bases.

These more concrete features of the "social structure" seem at once more obvious and less interesting, however, than the "class structure" of a society—the way in which its wealth and prestige are differentially achieved and awarded. It is among these differentials that sociologists and many laymen continue to look for the generators of crime.

The opportunity-structure hypothesis is one way of attending to class differences and attempting to show how they breed crime. It views criminality as *adaptive*, as utilitarian, as the way deprived people can get what we all want and have been told we should have.

There is yet another type of explanation that looks upon the pattern of rewards in a society as causing crime. This theory differs from the opportunity-structure theory in its emphasis. It interprets crime as more *reactive* than adaptive to social stratification.

REACTIVE HYPOTHESES

Reactive hypotheses are related to other structural schema in emphasizing the role of the status system of a society in producing crime and delinquency. As one kind of sociological explanation, these formulations also partake of some of the subcultural ideas. The reactive hypotheses, however, describe criminal subcultures as formed in response to status deprivation. They see criminality as less traditional, less ethnic, and more psychodynamically generated. They interpret delinquency as a status-seeking solution to "straight" society's denial of respect. The reactive hypotheses are, then, a type of structural theory that carries a heavy burden of psychological implication.

Crime and Compensation

The "pure" reactive hypothesis claims that the social structure produces a "reaction formation" in those whom its rules disqualify for status. *Reaction formation*, or reversal formation, is a psychoanalytic idea: that we may defend ourselves against forbidden desires by repressing them while expressing their opposites. In such circumstances, the behaviors of which the ego is conscious are psychoanalytically interpreted as an armor against admitting the unconscious urges that have been frustrated. An excessively neat person really wants to be messy but can't. In the case of a painfully polite person, the psychoanalyst perceives hostility ranging beneath the good manners. It is the phenomenon of the sour grapes: "If I can't have it, it must be no good." Thus, it is held, someone who can't play the middle-class game, or won't be let into it, responds by breaking up the play. The denial is proof of the desire. For example, Kobrin (1951, p. 660) says of the young vandal, "The vigor of the rejection of the value system is the measure of its hold upon the person."

Where the subcultural theorists see delinquent behavior as "real" in its own right, as learned and valued by the actor, and where the social psychologists agree but emphasize the training processes that bring this about, the proponents of reactive hypotheses interpret the defiant and contemptuous behavior of many delinquents as a compensation that defends them against the ego-wounding they have received from the status system. Kobrin writes: "The aggressively hostile response of the young male in the delinquency area to his devaluation by representatives of the conventional culture arises entirely from the fact that the criteria of status in the conventional culture have validity for him" (1951, p. 660).

Cohen and Others on Compensatory Crime   There are many other students of offensive behavior who believe that hating a social system and doing injury to it are encouraged by status differences. The reactive hypotheses are in agreement with the differential-opportunity theory in regarding denial of status as frustrating and motivating. However, the motivation that results from an invidious lack of status is differently conceived by these two types of structural explanation. The opportunity theorist describes crime as more utilitarian, more rational, and hence as an alternative way of achieving common goals. The reactive hypotheses, by contrast, perceive much crime as nonutilitarian, as expressive rather than instrumental, and as an attack upon the values by which the criminal is himself disqualified.

The reactive hypotheses differ further from the opportunity structure story in accepting the fact that people may *not* be equally equipped to use the legitimate means of achievement. One of the chief spokesmen for this point of view, A. K. Cohen, writes:

> The delinquent subculture, we suggest, is a way of dealing with the problems of adjustment we have described. These problems are chiefly status problems: certain children are denied status in the respectable society *because they cannot meet the criteria of the respectable status system*. The delinquent subculture deals with these problems by providing criteria of status which these children *can* meet [1955, p. 121; italics added in the second sentence].

One can accommodate these differing views by holding that they explain different types of crime or criminals. Certainly the reactive theories are more alert to the gratuitous hostility, the vandalism, and the joy in destruction that characterize some youthful gangs. This explanation recognizes, too, the existence of "uneconomic theft," theft accomplished for the fun of it, with the loot afterward thrown away. The reactive hypotheses are sensitive to the delights of hatred and to the pleasures gained by being shockingly outcast. H. S. Thompson, for example, describes the motorcycle gang with whom he ran for a year as "losers—dropouts, failures and malcontents. [The Hell's Angels] are rejects looking for a way to get even with a world in which they are only a problem" (1966, p. 260). "Their lack of education has not only rendered them completely useless in a highly technical economy, but it has also given them the leisure to cultivate a powerful resentment" (p. 258).

The resentment Thompson describes is expressed by "outraging the public decency" (p. 117). The provocation of public outrage becomes for the gang member a measure of his status with his fellow outcasts. "When you walk into a place where people can see you, you want to look as repulsive and repugnant as possible," reports one Angel. "Anything good, we laugh at. We're bastards to the world and they're bastards to us. I think this is what really keeps us going. We fight society and society fights us. It doesn't bother me" (p. 118).

Other students besides Cohen, Kobrin, and Thompson have proposed that some kinds of criminality should be viewed as reactions to status frustration. H. Schwendinger (1963) has collected one of the world's largest inventories of recorded interviews and moral game-playing with adolescents of varying delinquency. Although he titled his work *The Instrumental Theory of Delinquency*, the motives he attributes to his youthful offenders have to do with status seeking, and the function of much hostile crime is for him what it is for Cohen, Kobrin, and Thompson—an expression of resentment over deprivation of status.

Questions about the Reactive Thesis

The disadvantage of the reactive hypothesis lies in its plausibility. Given the phenomenon of angry young men and women who reject what others accept, it "makes sense" to explain their hostility as a reaction against what has allegedly been denied them. There is also a certain humanity to this interpretation, for it sees bad actors as just like everyone else, wanting to be like others but frustrated in their aspirations, kicking back at those who have frustrated them, and destroying what they want but can't have.

The trouble with this plausible idea is that it may not be correct. The Italians have a phrase for such convincing but unproved ideas. "It may not be true," they say, "but it's a good story." So here. The assumption that extremely hostile behavior represents a reaction formation cannot be verified. Worse, for scientific purposes, the assumption cannot be falsified. How, for example, could one prove or disprove Kobrin's statement that vandals' "defiance and contempt can be understood as an effort on the part of the delinquents to counteract their own impulses to accept and accede to the superior status of such representatives of the conventional order as school principals" (1951, p. 660)?

Alternatives to Reactive Hypotheses

In scientific work there is a criterion, not rigidly adhered to, which says that the simple explanation is preferable to the complex, that the hypothesis with few assumptions is preferable to the one with many. There are simpler explanations of criminal hostility than the reactive hypotheses. One such theory holds that violence comes naturally and that it will be expressed unless we are trained to control it. Another theory calls envy a universal and independent motive.

Expressing Violence and Learning It Some social psychologists believe that children will grow up violent if they are not adequately nurtured (Eron et al., 1971). Adequate nurturing includes both *appreciating* children and *training* them to acknowledge the rights of others. From this theoretical stance, the savagery of the urban gangster represents merely the natural outcome of a failure in child rearing.

Similarly, on a simple level of explanation, many sociologists and anthropologists believe that hostile behavior can be learned as easily as pacific behavior. Once learned, the codes of violence and impatient egoism are their own "positive values." Fighting and hating then become both duties and pleasures, the more so where enemies are defined. For advocates of this sociopsychological point of view, it is not necessary to regard the barbarian whose words and deeds "laugh at goodness" as having the same motives as more lawful persons.

The Autonomy of Envy Another interpretation of the reactive hypothesis lends it support, but places a different construction upon the resentment described by Cohen, Schwendinger, and Kobrin. This interpretation sees *envy* as a persistent, universal emotion that every society has attempted to control (Schoeck, 1966). According to this view, envy of the superior and hatred of the different are drives lying "at the core of man's life as a social being [which occur] as soon as two individuals become capable of mutual comparison" (Schoeck, 1966, p. 1). Envy is "the consuming desire that no one should have anything [that I do not have]. [It is] the destruction of pleasure in and for others, without deriving any sort of advantage from this" (p. 115).

   Although the Freudians believe that envy represents a conflict between the desire to emulate the superior and the desire to reject his difference, as we have seen in Kobrin's construction, there is no need to assume that an individual's resentment is born of his desire to be *like* those whom he resents. One can envy what others *have* without wishing to be as they *are*. One can envy others' status—their success, fame, wealth, and happiness—without wanting to *do* the things that have secured these advantages or to *be* the kind of person who has won them. Superiority is its own affront, and the more so as its legitimacy is attacked.

   Those theorists who acknowledge the normality of envy place less emphasis on the structure of a society as generating resentment and more emphasis upon the cultural themes that justify the expression of it. For these theorists, envy represents a persistent emotion to be controlled through institutionalized beliefs that legitimize differences. They are one with Merton on this point at least—that they accord a determining power to the culture-wide myths and values that raise appetites or control them. For example, the philosopher Ortega (1932) believed that the criminal expression of envy was encouraged by the belief that everyone is as good as anyone and that the fruits of a civilization—the results of discipline, work, effort—are "natural rights" rather than social gains. For Ortega, this ideology, which he called that of the "massman," confuses nature with the social order and denies the legitimacy of difference, particularly that of superiority. The result of this confusion and this denial is violence. Shoeck concurs: "Envious crime—a concept which embraces most juvenile crime and vandalism—will occur chiefly in those societies whose official credo, constantly recited in school, on the political platform and in the pulpit, is universal equality" (p. 114).

SCHOOLS, VOCATIONS, AND DELINQUENCY

The structural theories that have been described thus far all contain some truth. If they are criticized, it is because they sometimes go beyond their cores of veracity and assume too much. The kernel of truth in the structural views of criminogenesis described so far is that young people need apprenticeship to maturity. Human beings who are moving from protected childhood toward independent adulthood need to practice the activities that will be their acceptable ways of life as adults. The best that can be hoped is that adults' lives will include vocations which meet their interests and which, therefore, are satisfying. There can be no guarantee of this, of course, and aspirations that are constantly raised are bound to be disappointed. However, structuralists have called attention to some of the grosser deficiencies in the ways in which present social arrangements use youth and produce crime.

Useless Youth

Rich societies pay prices for their affluence. One price is the uselessness of many young people. Multitudes of young people in their teens are presumably not needed by the more successful Western industrial societies. They are, as a consequence, kept in an ambiguous state, half child and half adult. Since these industrialized countries have gained their wealth by employing products of education, sicence, and technology, it is concluded that more of the same education for everyone will increase the benefits. If academic schooling is good for some, up to some age, it is believed that such academic work is good for everyone for as long as a quarter or even a third of their lives. Under compulsory attendance laws, the schools then become a giant holding operation. They are an "opportunity," of course, for those with academic interests, but they are a jail for those without such interests. For the numerous remainder, who reside somewhere between a modest academic interest and a boredom relieved by social life and sports, the schools are a huge repository.

If this picture of teenage life in industrial societies seems accurate, no involved psychological assumptions are required to propose that youthful inutility and protracted semichildhood will generate disturbance, some of it criminal. We need only assume, with Marx and Veblen as with many contemporary psychologists, that human beings are curious animals, makers and doers, who "do best" when they have a vocation that others appreciate and that is rewarding in itself.

Rich societies are hard put to provide such meaningful work for everyone. Many jobs are dull but necessary; and not everyone has the talent for the exciting work of a criminal lawyer or a neurosurgeon. For the sake of domestic peace and psychic health, the societal requirement is to employ the great middle ranges of aptitude and ineptitude (Goode, 1967).

Irrelevant Schools

Given such assumptions, several writers have suggested that secondary schools in the Western world are excessively committed to college preparation and insufficiently adjusted to the interests of future workers in trade, industry, and the paraprofessions. It is argued that the pressure to succeed academically and the built-in probability of failure assured by lack of interest and ability produce hostility (McDonald, 1969b; Polk and Schafer, 1972). If to this cauldron of discontent one adds poor teaching, resentment is brought to a boil.

The hostility is further stimulated by the meaninglessness of academic work for what many young people want to do, and see themselves doing, as adults. Such a way of life for juveniles is a way of "growing up absurd," Paul Goodman says (1956). Similarly, the sociologists Polk and Schafer (1972) and Stinchcombe (1964) see a source of rebellion in the disjunction between school life and the adult life toward which many young people, the boys in particular, are moving. The thesis advanced by many critics of Western education is that compulsory schooling is itself criminogenic for those youngsters who find no immediate gratification in academic work and who can see, correctly, no future reward from their present training.

Such critics claim that schools in many rich countries threaten the self-respect of those who don't achieve academically and that the reaction to such wounding is violent. Polk and Schafer (1972) quote one such student who reacted to his downgrading in school as follows:

> You know, all of a sudden the guys you used to hang out with won't hang out with you no more. They hang out with a new class of people. Like they're classifying themselves as middle class and you're low brow and, you know, you start feeling bad and I said I can prove that I'm middle class and I don't have to go to school to prove it. And so I did. I got out of school. All those kids' mothers buying them nice things in ninth and tenth grades. I said, baby, you ain't talking about nothing—and what your mother has to buy you I can get everyday. I used to sport around. Yeah—I used to show them $125—*every* day. I used to say—you have to go to school for 12 years and I only went for 9. (How did you get this money?) I'd take it. (How did you take it?) I broke into things. I used to have a little racket set up. I used to have a protection fee—anybody who wants to cross the street, anybody who wants to come into my territory, they has to pay me 25 cents. I gave boys certain areas where they couldn't cross. A cat used to live up there. I say, "Okay, that's your deadline right there. If you want to go through this way, you give me 25 cents. If I ever catch you coming down through this way, you got a fight on your hands." And they gave me 25 cents (p. 200).

Stinchcombe and other sociologists hold that the violent reaction to failure in school is accompanied by the substitution of "ascriptive symbols" of personal worth for the achieved marks of academic success. These ascriptive symbols are signs of adulthood and a denial of the adolescent and submissive role in which schools place young people. Things like smoking, drinking, owning a car, freer dating, and financial independence are status symbols that take the place of the school symbols. By their very adoption, they challenge the legitimacy and authority of the school. They are more than mere challenges, however; they are also indicators of an alienation from the honors that schools value and can give.

Growing Up Absurd

Goodman's description of "growing up absurd" is in accord with the pictures provided by sociologists, but his interpretation proposes a more radical rejection of industrialized Western societies. Goodman believes that there is not enough "man's work" in North America and that our absurd societies are "lacking in the opportunity [for young men] to be useful," that they "thwart aptitude and create stupidity," that they "corrupt the fine arts . . . shackle science . . . and dampen animal ardor" (1956, p. 12). Goodman believes that delinquent behavior "speaks clearly enough. It asks for manly opportunities to work, make a little money, and have self-esteem; to have some space to bang around in, that is not always somebody's property; to have better schools to open for them horizons of interest; to have more and better sex without fear or shame; to share somehow in the symbolic goods (like the cars) that are made so much of; to have a community and a country to be loyal to; to claim attention and to have a voice" (pp. 50–51).

The extremity of Goodman's position is likely to obscure the validity of what he and other authors have pointed out—that Western schooling does *not* provide an adequate apprenticeship in adulthood for a sufficient number of young people and that this inadequacy may be criminogenic. The schools are changing, however, and some educators are experimenting with broader avenues on which adolescents may move as they grow up. There is criticism of compulsory schooling of the same kind for every youth. There is experimentation with "electronic self-teaching." There is awareness among educators that, beyond establishing some minimum of literacy and calculating competence, schools may *not* be the best providers of vocational initiation.

Against Utopia   Such experimentation is not assisted, however, by the stimulating comments Goodman offers. Goodman is essentially an anarchist. His vision is utopian and, consequently, disillusioning. The high ideals are in accord with neither present reality nor future possibility, and they do not generate useful recommendations. As always, it is one thing to decry the world we live in; it is quite another matter to know how to change it without making it worse.

It is, for example, debatable whether there is "not enough manly work" in our societies. Much depends upon who is defining "manly." It is even more debatable whether the pastoral life Goodman proposes is an adequate substitute for the jobs, the organization, the "system" which Goodman despises but which, nevertheless, produce the wealth that makes possible his disaffection. Goodman's recommendation is for something no one can give and no group can create. No one can produce the "symbolic goods (like the cars)" without *organizing* the work. Some of that work will be dirty work, and calling it "unmanly" will not help us appreciate it. Similarly, in a world growing more crowded, space will always be allocated, whether it be "somebody's property" or the state's. As for the "more and better sex" that Goodman recommends "without fear or shame," delinquents are certainly less deprived in this regard than more conventional young people (Kinsey et al., 1948), and it is difficult to see how this remedy might be implemented or how it might reduce the rates of serious crimes, with the exception, perhaps, of forcible rape.

A Gloomy Conclusion

No radical vision is necessary to agree with Goodman and other critics that the school systems of Western societies presently provide poor apprenticeship in adulthood for many adolescents. A poor apprenticeship in growing up *is* criminogenic.

In this way the structures of modern countries encourage crime and delinquency. They lack institutional procedures for moving people smoothly from protected childhood to autonomous adulthood. During adolescence, many youths in affluent societies are neither well guided by their parents nor happily engaged by their teachers. They are adults in body, but children in responsibility. Placed in such a no-man's-land between irresponsible dependence and accountable independence, they are compelled to attend schools which do not thoroughly stimulate the interests of all of them and which, in too many cases, provide the uninterested child with the experience of failure and the mirror of denigration.

Conflicting Objectives   Educators wrestle with remedies. However, in democratic societies, they are torn between conflicting prescriptions. On the one hand, the democratic ethic is interpreted as demanding that everyone be given the *same* education with at least some minimum of *equal result*—such as an "adequate" competence in reading, writing, and arithmetic. On the other hand, beyond this undefined minimum level of literacy and basic skills, the reformer acknowledges that different schools or different curricula must be provided for children of varied talents and interests. Thus Schafer and Polk (1972) recommend "creating diversity within student bodies" through government-enforced racial and class mixing (pp. 254–255) while at the same time recommending "divergent, not uniform, teaching styles for different populations" (pp. 191–192).

Such openness in apprenticing institutions would *not* produce uniform results in academic skills, in knowledge, in know-how, or—what hurts most—in status. This is the dilemma of democratic educators. They want equality *and* individuality, objectives that thus far in history have eluded societal engineers. Meanwhile, the metropolitan schools of industrialized countries make a probable, but unmeasurable, contribution to criminality.

IN SUMMARY

Structuralist emphasis of the criminogenic features of a stratified society is popular, persuasive, and partly correct. Employment of this type of explanation in the reduction of crime becomes political.

If the *anomie* that generates crime lies in the gap between desires and their gratification, criminologists can urge that desires be modified, that gratifications be increased, or that some compromise be reached between what people expect and what they are likely to get. Our differing political positions prescribe different remedies for our social difficulties. Radical thinkers use the schema of *anomie* to strengthen their argument for a classless or, at least, a less stratified society. Conservative thinkers use this schema to demonstrate the dangers of an egalitarian philosophy. At one political pole, the recommendation is to change the structure of power and opportunity so as to reduce the pressure toward criminality. At the other pole, the prescription is to change the public's conception of what is possible.

Between Structure and Conduct: Thought

All of us are caught up in this debate. However, a major tradition in anthropology, sociology, and, in particular, social psychology emphasizes that structures have to be *interpreted* before they become causes of conduct. Between structure and action, this scholarly tradition places ideas. Significant numbers of students of behavior rest their explanations of conduct on what has been called "a belief in belief."

Chapter 13

Subcultures and Crime

A fundamental observation upon which behavioral sciences rest, and a fact which they attempt to explain, is that people do *not* behave the same way in what appear to be similar situations. If people did behave identically in identical circumstances, a social science would be simplified. If this were so—and assuming, of course, that similarity and difference of action and condition can be measured—one could construct laws of behavior specifying that whenever people are in situation X, they tend with such-and-such probability to do Y.

The Idea of Culture There is some such regularity between circumstance and conduct. But there is also sufficient variation among individuals, and among groups of individuals, that students of human action have been led to propose *mediators* between situation and action. When these mediators have some generality and continuity among a people that regards itself as distinct—among a people that has, in Gidding's phrase, a "consciousness of kind"—anthropologists and sociologists speak of these "intervening variables" as a *culture*. Culture refers to

> a way of life of a people who have a sense of common history, a sense of being a "we" as opposed to a "them," and who, usually, live within a bounded territory.
> In Eliot's phrase (1948, p. 57), "Culture is a peculiar way of thinking, feeling, and behaving." Culture describes the pattern of our lives together, a pattern that is

Between how things are, then, "the structure of chances," and how one responds to this world, many scholars place "attitude," "value," or "definition of the situation." The crucial question becomes one of assessing how much of any action is simply a response to a structure of the social world and how much is moved by differing interpretations of that reality.

In answering this question, a subcultural explanation of crime production emphasizes *group-connected values* as more and less criminogenic. The subcultural theme is the topic of the next chapter.

discernible in our art; in our diet, dress, and customs; in our religion and values; in our obligations to each other; and in our language. Dialect, a distinctive way of using a language, is one of the most sensitive indicators of cultural membership [Nettler, 1976, p. 91].

The concept of a culture includes standards of behavior, observable in both words and deeds, that are learned, transmitted from generation to generation, and hence somewhat durable. To call such behavior "cultural" does not necessarily mean that it is "refined," but rather that it is "cultured"—that is, acquired, cultivated, and persistent.

The Idea of a Subculture When people of diverse nationalities live together under the laws of one state, they come to share some aspects of a common culture; this has been particularly true since the spread of electronic communication. However, modern states that govern many nations do not become "melting pots," as early sociologists thought they would. On the contrary, ethnic differences persist. In addition, societies may be characterized by generation gaps and by sex and class differences in commitment to however much common culture there is.[1]

The possibility, then, that groups will share some elements of a common culture while retaining different cultural tastes has led to the idea of *subcultures*.

Again, it is part of the definition of a subculture, as of a culture, that it is relatively enduring. Its norms are termed a "style," rather than a "fashion," on the grounds that the former has some persistence, while the latter is evanescent. The quarrel comes, of course, when we try to estimate how "real" a cultural pattern is and how enduring it may be.

CONFLICT OF CONDUCT NORMS

Standards by which behavior is guided vary among us and change with time. It is in this change and variety that norms of conduct may conflict, and it is out of this conflict that crime is defined.

An early application of this principle to criminology was given by Sellin (1938), who found the roots of crime in the fact that groups have developed different standards of appropriate behavior and that, in "complex cultures," each individual is subject to competing prescriptions for action. "A conflict of norms is said to exist," Sellin wrote, "when more or less divergent rules of conduct govern the specific life situation in which a person may find himself" (p. 29).

---

[1]The fact that modern states have distinctive names, flags, laws, and territories over which they claim sovereignty does not in itself mean that the citizens of such states share a common culture. There are degrees of such community within countries, and these degrees of common culture can be measured, as Cattell (1950) has shown. This fact means that many modern states are not nations. They do not have a distinctive common culture, and their search for "national identity" is but one sign of the lack. A nation knows its identity; it does not have to seek it.

Sellin's description of how crime is caused differs from other explanations of the sociological variety in that it is broader. Sellin is interested in the conflict of *all* norms of conduct, not merely in those that are codified in the criminal law. However, he sees the concern with crime as flowing from the conflict of standards about how we should behave.

In criminology, two kinds of conflict have received particular attention: that between social classes and that between ethnic groups.

CLASS CULTURES

One version of subcultural explanation of crime derives from the fact that, as we have seen, "social classes" experience different rates of arrest and conviction for serious offenses. When strata within a society are marked off by categories of income, education, and occupational prestige, differences are discovered among them in the amount and style of crime. In addition, differences are usually found between these strata in their tastes, interests, and morals. It is easy, then, to describe these class-linked patterns as cultures. Thus the anthropologist Oscar Lewis (1959, 1961) speaks of the "culture of poverty," and the sociologist Walter B. Miller (1958) writes about "lower-class culture."

A Thesis

This "class" version of the subcultural explanation of crime holds that the very fact of learning the lessons of the subculture means that people acquire interests and preferences that place them in greater or lesser risk of breaking the law. Miller, for example, argues that being reared in the lower class means learning a different culture from that which creates the criminal laws. The lower-class subculture is said to have its own values, many of which run counter to the majority interests that support the laws against the serious predatory crimes.

Miller's "Focal Concerns"

Miller (1958) describes these lower-class values as "focal concerns" with "trouble, toughness, smartness, excitement, fate, and autonomy." He claims that the lower class differs from the strata called "middle" and "upper" class in its greater subscription to these focal concerns.

The lower-class person believes, with Zorba, that "life *is* trouble," that much in one's career is fated regardless of what one does, and that the proper response to "the way the world works" is to be tough, cunning, and independent. It is considered smart to be "hastily hedonistic," to enjoy what one can when one can and let tomorrow take care of itself.

According to Miller, some 40 to 60 percent of the citizens of Canada and the United States may be "directly influenced" by these values, but about 15 percent of the populations of these countries are said to be "hard-core lower-class"—that is, people for whom the focal concerns constitute a style of life. These hard-core lower-class people are also described as being produced by households headed by women, in which "serial monogamy" is practiced—in which, that is, the mother has one "spouse" at a time but more than one in a lifetime. Sheehan (1975, 1976) draws a powerful picture of this "syndrome" in her study of a welfare mother.

By contrast with lower-class values, those of the middle class are usually described as emphasizing ambition, cultivation of talent, the ability to postpone gratification and to plan for the future, and the acceptance of individual responsibility and social duties (A. Davis and Havighurst, 1947; Hyman, 1953; Kohn, 1959; Kohn and Schooler, 1969; LeShan, 1952; Pearlin and Kohn, 1966; Rosen, 1956). A number of studies report a class-linked clustering of attitudes toward time with ability to work for long-term rewards, with "achievement motivation," and with success in lawful occupations and immunity to criminality. These attributes, in turn, are often found in association with feelings of "internal control," that is, the belief that one is master of his or her own fate (Barndt and Johnson, 1955; Heckhausen, 1967; Jessor et al., 1968; Lefcourt, 1972; Lessing, 1968, 1971; Mischel, 1973; Teahan, 1958).

It is also reported that the middle class emphasizes being rational and reasonable, having good manners, and using leisure healthfully (*to dissipate*, we recall, means "to waste"). The middle class stresses respect for property and the control of violence.

Miller's thesis is that middle-class values are themselves lawful; whereas acquiring lower-class preferences automatically involves one in a greater risk of breaking the laws against the more serious crimes.

Banfield's "Propensity and Incentive"

A similar class-oriented thesis is advanced by the political scientist Banfield (1968). He holds that

> crime, like poverty, depends upon two sets of variables. One set relates mainly to class culture and personality (but also to sex and age) and determines an individual's *propensity* to crime. The other relates to situational factors (such as the number of policemen on the scene and the size of the payroll) and determines his *incentive*. The probability that he will commit crimes—his *proneness* to crime—depends upon propensity *and* incentive [p. 159].

Banfield's description of the lower-class "propensity" to crime parallels Miller's description of its focal concerns. Banfield contends that lower-class culture develops a different type of morality, one that he calls "preconventional," in which conduct is guided by what succeeds and what can be gotten away with, and in which the only authority is power.

The propensity to crime is also encouraged, according to Banfield, by the shorter "time horizon" and lesser "ego strength," or ability to control impulses, of the lower class. The lower class is seen as placing a low value on the avoidance of risk. It is less prudent than the middle class and hence more prone to criminality. Furthermore, Banfield, like other reporters, describes the lower class as being encouraged to violence by its training, so that part of its greater propensity to crime lies in its greater willingness to inflict injury.

The "Deprived" and the "Privileged" in England

Similar portraits of subcultural differences have been drawn for English samples by Downes (1966), T. P. Morris (1957), Spinley (1964), and Willmott (1966).

Downes's and Willmott's studies, in particular, challenge the ideas of American structuralists. The English investigators do not find that young people of the working class engage in thievery out of lack of legitimate opportunity or that they resort to vandalism out of resentment of their low social position. The findings of the English investigators agree with those of Miller, Banfield, and others that lower-class criminality is more a function of subcultural differences in taste than of compensatory reaction against failure. Working-class young people in urban England are described as reconciled to careers in unskilled labor. Contrary to the American structural picture, these English young people are said *not* to aspire to be middle-class and are *not* motivated to achieve fame or fortune. Their focal concerns are doing what they want, avoiding responsibility, and having fun.

These differences in value are culturally acquired, rather than rationally derived, responses to circumstance. Downes writes:

> The encouragement of spontaneity and autonomy from an early age leads the working-class boy to resist the assertion of middle-class authority he is bound to encounter via school and the law. Working-class culture is at once rigorously defined and sufficiently at odds with the controlling middle-class culture to make a head-on clash almost inevitable [1966, p. 111].

This description of subcultural differences is supplemented by the research of Morris and Spinley, who were interested in patterns of child rearing and in the nature of the values found among families of different occupational status.

Again, the findings of the English investigators agree with the description of delinquent subcultures provided by Miller and Banfield for Americans. Among the families of unskilled English workingmen, discipline of children is much more haphazard and inconsistently punitive than among middle-class families. Children tend to be ignored or rejected. Punishment is more a function of how the parents feel than of what the child does. Abstract moral lessons are not taught, and life is lived in the present rather than for any future. As a result of such rearing, pangs of guilt and anxiety about shame are noticeably absent.

Time and Class in West Germany

Subcultural studies of criminality and other behaviors refer repeatedly to differences among people in their sense of time. They do so for good reason. As the psychologist Mari Riess Jones (1976) demonstrates in a review of research, "Time is one of the defining properties of our world and so of ourselves" (p. 353). Perception of time and the uses of time are correlated, and both are important markers of differences in character.

The hypothesis of Miller and Banfield and its English equivalents propose class-linked orientations to time, and, as we have seen, research in Canada, the

United States, and England lends support to this thesis. Additional support comes from West Germany, where Lamm and others (1976) in the University of Mannheim found parallel class-correlated conceptions of time. These investigators asked youngsters of high school age about their hopes and fears for the future. They then analyzed these sentiments as pertaining to private or public matters, as optimistic or pessimistic, and as being dependent principally on themselves or on luck and circumstance. Hopes and fears were also examined for their "extension," that is, for how far into the future they were projected.

As previous research suggested, middle-class youngsters have a longer time perspective than lower-class youngsters, and this holds true in their attitudes toward both public and private affairs. This finding is made doubly interesting by the fact that, although middle-class adolescents expressed more concern about *public* affairs than lower-class adolescents, they still had a longer time orientation than lower-class adolescents about matters of *private* concern.

A Caution: On the Shifting Boundaries of Class Cultures

In reading these descriptions of class cultures, one should not assume that such ways of life are fixed. A "culture" has some stability, but stability is not permanence. Cultures move and mix. The quality of their markers changes and, with that, class boundaries change too. For example, given some social mobility and shifts in income distribution, Bohlke (1961) has suggested that what has been called "middle-class delinquency" may more accurately represent "middle-income" crime rather than "middle-class-culture" crime. Bohlke means by this that the values taught and exhibited by some portion of the middle-*income* stratum are no longer the traditional middle-*class* values of prudence, personal responsibility, restraint, and achievement through disciplined effort.

It need not be expected, then, that merely increasing income will increase whatever *used to be* associated with income. Everything depends on the values that are cultivated as one's standard of living is elevated. An economic determinism is misleading if it assumes that the style of life *presently* associated with different income levels will automatically be generated by changes in income *however* such a change is effected. Being *given* money does not require, or produce, the same culture as *earning* it does. The subcultural theorist reads with skepticism propositions about "the economics of delinquency" such as Fleisher (1966) advances—namely, that "the combined effects of a $500 increase in income would probably be a reduction of about 5.2 arrests per 1,000 population. In areas of high tendencies toward crime, a 10 per cent rise in incomes might well result in a 20 per cent decline in delinquency" (p. 117). The subcultural theorist would say that Fleisher's proposal confuses culture with one of its fluctuating correlates.

Indicators of Class Are Not Descriptions of Class

Proponents of subcultural explanations of crime do not define a class *culture* by any assortment of the objective indicators of rank, such as annual income or years of schooling. The subcultural theorist is interested in *patterned ways of life* which may have evolved with a division of labor and which, then, are called "class" cultures. The pattern, however, is not described by reference to income alone, or by reference to years of schooling or level of occupational skill. The pattern includes these indicators, but it is not defined by them. The subcultural theorist is more intent upon the *varieties of human value*, as C. W. Morris (1956) has depicted and measured them. These are preferred ways of living that are acted upon. In the economist's language, they are "tastes."

The thesis that is intimated, but not often explicated, by a subcultural description of behaviors is that single or multiple signs of social position, such as occupation or education, will have a different significance for status, and for cultures, with changes in their distribution. Money and education do not mean the same things socially as they are more or less equally distributed. The change in meaning is not merely a change in the prestige value of these indices, but also betokens changes in the boundaries between class cultures.

Devaluation of Status Signs

An unpopular version of this thesis might be termed "the devaluation of status signs." It proposes a kind of "Gresham's law of cultures." Just as "bad money drives out good money," according to Gresham's law, so it may be that "low culture" corrupts "high culture."

This allegation is made particularly with respect to the influence of the mass media upon aesthetic taste, the uses of the intellect, and even crime rates. Studies of the uses of leisure in the Western world indicate, for example, that the optimistic promise that rising affluence would mean "the maintenance of high standards of diversified excellence among the keepers of high culture combined with gradual improvement of mass tastes" has been largely unfulfilled (Wilensky, 1964, p. 173).

Wilensky conducted a study of the tastes for leisure activities of a sample of American men who ranged from denizens of Skid Row through the "middle mass" and self-employed merchants to prominent professionals. His research reveals the fragility of exacting standards of *aesthetic* preference, at least. In industrialized countries the mass media, and television in particular, are part of everyone's life—with exceptions so rare as to be almost bizarre. Being schooled or unschooled, monied or not, seems now to make little difference in preferences for the uses of leisure. Wilensky writes:

> High culture has always been precarious, but what *is* new to our time is a thorough interpenetration of cultural levels: the good, the mediocre, and the trashy are becoming fused in one massive middlemush. There is little doubt, from my data as well as others', that educated strata . . . are becoming full participants in mass culture; they spend a reduced fraction of time in exposure to quality print and film. . . . The chief culprit, again, is TV [p. 190].

A similar finding is reported by Mark Abrams (1958) for England. Abrams studied the media habits of a random sample of 13,620 adults over 24 years of age. He found that "the upper one per cent in educational and occupational status reported media habits so similar to those of the mass public, that one is reluctant to use the label 'cultural elite.'"

Whether one believes such tendencies to be good or bad, the point of this lengthy aside is simply that the criteria of "social class" that have been generally employed—criteria like income and schooling—may change meaning with changes in the distribution of these advantages in a population and with the heavy impact of the electronic media. "Class cultures," like national cultures, may break down.

ETHNIC PREDISPOSITION

A more general subcultural explanation of crime, not necessarily in disagreement with the notion of class cultures, attributes differences in crime rates to differences in ethnic patterns to be found within a society. Explanations of this sort do not necessarily bear the title "ethnic," although they are so designated here because they partake of the general assumption that there are group differences in learned preferences—in what is rewarded and punished—and that these group differences have a persistence often called a "tradition."

Such explanations are of a piece whether they are advanced as descriptions of regional cultures, generational differences, or national characteristics. Their common theme is the differences in ways of life out of which differences in crime rates seem to flow. Ethnic explanations are proposed under an assortment of labels, but they have in common the fact that they do *not* limit the notion of "subculture" to "class culture." They seem particularly justified where differences in social status are *not* so highly correlated with differences in conduct as are other indicators of cultural difference.

Thus Gastil (1971) argues that in the United States "economic and status positions in the community cannot be shown to account for differences [in homicide rates] between whites and Negroes or between Southerners and Northerners" (p. 414). Gastil then constructs an "index of Southernness" which he finds to be highly correlated with homicide rates in the United States. He claims, therefore, that there is a measurable regional culture that promotes murder.

The Subculture of Violence

In a similar vein, but examining the world as a whole, Wolfgang and Ferracuti (1967) have tried to explain variations in the amounts and kinds of violent behavior by describing the lessons that are transmitted from generation to generation within ethnic groups. Their study brings together an enormous bibliography on the psychology of killing, on the characteristics of aggressors, and on the cultures that facilitate violence. Wolfgang and Ferracuti's thesis, as phrased by one of their reviewers, is this:

> Granting all the difficulties of counting behaviors, suppose one observes that persons affiliated with an intimate group, "The Baddies," when compared with

their hosts, "The Goodones," more often carry weapons, take umbrage to a wide range of stimuli, and more frequently fight. Suppose, too, that measures of the Baddies' attitudes and values reveal a consensual perception of resort-to-violence as (a) the way life is, (b) the way one had better act in order to maintain a proper identity, get along, survive, and fulfill his ethic, and (c) the way things ought to be.

Assume, last, that these two broad classes of events, *being* violent and *valuing* violence, are causally related, the latter impelling the former [Nettler, 1968].

The Politics of Explanation

The beauty of a subcultural explanation of group differences in conduct is that it is descriptive and it is true. Furthermore, it seems more true as it becomes more descriptive. Adding detail adds truth value.

Discomfort with a subcultural explanation arises because such an explanation gives no handle for reasoned remedy. If there are violent others and we wish to pacify them, how do we do it?

The notion that their violence is compact—that it is generated and supported not just by circumstance but also by a valued way of being and doing—rules out the easy ideas of social work. If there are cultures and subcultures, we know that they may break down, but we also are told that they may persist, and that they may persist beyond some facile cures such as a guaranteed income and improved housing.

It is political preference, again, that fuels debate about the validity and utility of subcultural explanation.

CRITICISM OF SUBCULTURAL EXPLANATION

Criticism of this style of explanation runs on two tracks. It asks whether subcultural explanation may not be circular, and it questions the degree to which subcultures are persistent or responsive to changed circumstances.

1   Is Subcultural Explanation Circular?

A circular explanation is one in which whatever is supposed to do the explaining (the explanans) is part of the event to be explained (the explanandum). A circular explanation is a *tautology*, a sentence whose predicate is contained within its subject. For example:

"You won't get bald if you don't lose your hair."—an American mother
"When many men are out of work, you have unemployment."—a President of the United States
"You can observe an awful lot just by watching."—a baseball philosopher

Subcultural explanation is accused of being tautological. It is said to explain one kind of behavior by reference to attitudes and other behaviors that are of the substance of what is to be accounted for. It is as though one were to say, "People are murderous because they live violently" or "People like to fight because they are hostile."

Such redundant statements are true, of course, but they seem not to satisfy. There are, however, at least three ways to reduce the circularity: (*a*) to *describe* the subculture more completely, (*b*) to tell *how* it is learned, and (*c*) to *mix* subcultural explanation with other explanatory devices.

a Detailed Description A first way out of circularity is to describe the culture that generates the behavior of interest in such breadth that "the whole way of life" is seen as making a particular kind of conduct more probable. This description usually includes a history of how the people "got that way." And it becomes more plausible as an explanation when details of the differences between one group and another are added. These details can be *directly* associated with the behavior to be explained—as when Gastil describes the tradition of carrying weapons as "Southern" and relates such "Southernness" to higher homicide rates. Or the differences may be only *remotely* associated with the behavior in question, but nevertheless useful as marks of ethnic difference, as religion and language are.

When given such a larger picture of a culture, consumers of explanations are frequently satisfied. Their curiosity rests. Whether curiosity ought to rest here—whether this explanation, or any other, is adequate—depends, again, on what one wishes to do with explanations.

If a student wishes only to "understand" variations in violence, his or her curiosity will be satisfied to the degree to which the "subculture of violence" has been thoroughly described so that its end product, assault and homicide, seems logically related to the description of everything else that is going on within the subculture.

Similarly, if one wants to know whether, and how, to protect oneself, a subcultural description will suffice. It provides a basis for forecast, and its prophetic utility does not require further knowledge of what *makes* violent people as they are.

The rub comes, however, if one wishes to "cure" a subculture of its violence.

Questionable cure A subcultural explanation, by itself, provides no informed instruction for remedy of the criminal conduct it explains. This does not make it untrue, of course; it just makes it unsatisfactory for some purposes. And this is, again, a political reason for rejecting a subcultural thesis.

Insofar as a subculture of violence is a *patterned* way of life, there is no particular lever for reformers to use. One might as well attack one facet of the offending culture as another—child-rearing practices or religious beliefs; leisure pursuits or job satisfaction.

A hazard of accepting a subcultural explanation and, *at the same time*, wishing to be a doctor to the body politic is that the remedies advocated may as easily spread the disease as cure it. For example, among Wolfgang and Ferracuti's recommendations for reducing our killing of one another is "social action" to *disperse* the representatives of the subculture of violence. This alleged remedy is now quite commonly advocated for a variety of social concerns from crime and delinquency to poor schooling and poverty (Polk and Schafer, 1972).

Quite apart from the political and moral questions involved in such a *coerced* dispersion of people, the proposal assumes more knowledge than we have. We do not *know*, for example, what proportion of the violent persons would have to be mixed with what proportion of pacific people in order to break down the culture of violence. What is more important, we do not know to what extent the dispersed people may act as "culture carriers" and contaminate their hosts.

In sum, reducing the circularity of subcultural explanation by adding descriptive detail will satisfy some purposes but not others.

b   Adding Social Psychology   A second way in which subcultural explanation can be made less circular is by adding a sociopsychological explanation to it. Sociopsychological explanations, particularly those of the "control" variety (see Chapter 16), tell *how* cultural prescriptions and preferences "get inside" actors. They therefore answer questions about the transmission and durability of subcultures.

c   Mixing Subcultures and Structures   A third way out of the tautology of subcultural explanation is to combine it with another presumed determinant of criminality: the situation. The situation that is most frequently nominated as a cause of conduct is the web of economic circumstance. One's economic situation, in turn, has been analyzed as the income one receives, the wealth one has, the income one expects or needs, the kind of work one does, and the "opportunity" available for improvement. These signs of economic circumstance are not the same, of course, and their interchangeable use contributes to confusion in isolating the sources of behavior.

Despite this confusion, students of human action continue to "blame circumstances" for conduct. A persistent debate, then, is whether ethnic differences *reduce* to class differences or whether ethnicity has an *independent role* in the determination of crime rates.

The first position is defended by sociologists who emphasize the causal importance of economic power and the "structure of opportunities." When this position is placed in an ecological context, as Shaw and McKay (1942) have done, it contends that "diverse racial, nativity, and national groups possess relatively similar rates of delinquents in similar social areas" (p. 162).

Some critics of such propositions have been cited (pages 141–148). One of the strongest of these critics, Jonassen (1949), has charged advocates of Shaw and McKay's thesis with espousing "ecological determinism"—that is, with assuming that areas *cause* behaviors. To this accusation, Jonassen added the charge that there is a "professional ideology of social pathologists" which confuses democracy with uniformity and which refuses, therefore, to recognize differences in cultures.

A reconciliation   Toby (1950) has provided a resolution of this debate, along with an interesting proposal that incorporates both *ethnic values* and *economic structures* as sources of criminality. Toby's proposal shows how ethnicity and opportunity structures meet to determine risks of illegal conduct.

"Ethnic tradition," Toby argues, "is an intermediate structure between class position and the personality of the individual." Ethnic traditions that foster the particular attitudes and skills required by legitimate careers within a society reduce culture conflict and crime. On the other hand, those ethnic traditions which are less congruent with the requirements of a "system" are likely to be associated with higher crime rates.

Toby's reconciliation of the cultural-structural debate holds that ethnic traditions, opportunity structures, and personality traits are intertwined determinants of lawful and criminal careers.

We are back on the general ground of culture conflict. However, a blending of variables, such as Toby proposes, makes the subcultural explanation of crime less tautological.

2   Does Culture Cause?

It seems reasonable to explain group differences in behavior by mixing the facts of cultural difference with sociopsychological data on how we learn the lessons of our tribe, along with a description of the situations we are in. However, this reasonable mixture does not satisfy many students of human conduct because it does not specify the relative powers of the ingredients. We are not told *how much* of *which behavior* is caused by *how* we were trained, *what* we learned (our culture), and *the chances* we really had or thought we had.

Social scientists continue to quarrel, therefore, about differences between people. Perhaps no questions are more uncomfortable for modern intellectuals than questions of difference:

How different are individuals and groups?
What *causes* the difference, if there is any?
How changeable are these differences, and *by what techniques*?

The quarrel becomes heated as the debate moves from a description of the different conditions under which people live to differences in their conduct that are sometimes alleged to be *effects* of their circumstances and sometimes alleged to be their *causes*.

Denying Difference   Among scholars, as opposed to the people they study, equality is an ideal (Bereiter, 1973; Coleman, 1974; Della Fave, 1974; Herrnstein, 1973; Jencks et al., 1972; Keyfitz, 1973; Nisbet, 1974a, 1974b, 1975b). This ideal requires equality of condition as well as equality of opportunity. The ideal is therefore challenged by the possibility that people differ in talent or taste. The moral movement in favor of equality has made it unpopular today to recognize differences in conduct among groups, and subcultural explanations of crime have not escaped this condemnation. Thus common responses to the description of criminogenic subcultures include (1) denying the difference, (2) denying the durability of the difference, and finally, whether or not these denials seem plausible, (3) calling the difference "rational," "responsive," or in some other way "understandable," if not actually preferable.

An example of this type of criticism, combining all three charges against a subcultural explanation of crime, is given by one critic (among many) of Banfield's thesis. Peter Rossi (1971) writes:

> There is no "lower class" in Banfield's sense. Indeed, there is little firm evidence that there are many people, black or white, who are permanently hedonistically present-oriented. The existing evidence is just as supportive of a theory that there are poor people, black and white, whose position in society is such that they might as well be hedonistically present-oriented since acting otherwise does little to improve their position [p. 820].

In one paragraph, this critic of a subcultural hypothesis contends that (1) subcultures are not *that* different, (2) they are certainly not *permanently* that different, and (3) in any event, poor people *ought* to be hasty hedonists.

A SUMMARY OPINION

In defense of the significance of culture for conduct and in refutation of the structural argument that behavior is nothing but a response to circumstance, several questions can be posed, and their answers suggested.

1   A first question is whether people do behave differently in similar circumstances.

The answer is obviously "yes," and the evidence is written in the library of ethnography. As individuals and as inbreeding groups, we do things differently in what seem to be parallel circumstances. This fact, we have said (page 244), is the justification of those special studies called "psychology" and "sociology." These studies are supposed to explain the differences.

The differences have been counted in many ways, in many times and places, and among many categories of activity—sexual, recreational, economic. Particular attention has been paid to economics, the "material bases" of life, about which two broad questions are asked: "Do different ways of organizing the uses of labor and capital produce different quantities of wealth and qualities of life?" and "To what extent do economic circumstances, variously defined, cause conduct?"

Quarrels continue about the fine points in answers to these questions, but, for present purposes, the answers can be summarized as follows: First, there *are* better and worse ways of responding to material conditions in the production of wealth, and groups do *not* behave with equal efficiency.

Second, there is abundant evidence that, while our economic situation *sets limits* to what we can do, it does not *determine* what we must do. Thus, under apparently similar economic circumstances, some ethnic groups have much higher murder rates than others (see Chapter 7). In similar economic conditions some ethnic groups have difficulty handling alcohol and dope, while others do not (Snyder, 1958).[2]

Some poor people use their schools; others abuse them. Some poor people throw garbage out their windows, urinate in their streets, and defecate in their halls; others do not (Sheehan, 1975, 1976). At the other end of the financial spectrum, some rich people are idle and bored. Other rich people are productive and happy.

There is no "necessity" in these circumstances that *requires* one kind of behavior rather than another. Even at the subsistence level, when we are reduced to trying to survive, it cannot be said that any one mode of response is necessitated (Turnbull, 1972).

How we *are* determines what we *do* when faced with difficulty or opportunity. And how we are is a result of a distinctive genetic constitution upon which particular experiences have impressed different lessons (see Chapter 16). When these experiences have been roughly similar and when their lessons have a pattern, we speak of the process and the product as *cultural*.

To become human, says the anthropologist Geertz (1973), is to become individual, "and we become individual under the guidance of cultural patterns, historically created systems of meaning in terms of which we give form, order, point, and direction to our lives" (p. 52). Culture makes a difference.

2   A second set of questions follows. It asks how durable these "historically created systems" may be and under what circumstances they change and how much.

There is no easy answer to this set of questions. We do not know the determinants of cultural change except roughly, and we therefore cannot predict the effects of particular altered circumstances.

No culture is permanent, of course, but would-be societal engineers are repeatedly surprised by the durability of cultural ways. Cultural persistence has been noted for a wide variety of groups (Alpert, 1972; Armor, 1972; Glazer and Moynihan, 1963, 1975; Glenn, 1974–1975; Herskovits, 1941; Howe, 1976; Isaacs, 1975; J. Jones, 1972; Maas, 1975; Metzger, 1971; Novak, 1972; Reed, 1975; A. Sutherland, 1975).

The mysteries of cultural persistence are well summarized by a student of Jewish culture who concludes: "Almost every planned change has brought about results different from those anticipated. The student of culture is therefore highly skeptical of too optimistic plans for controlled culture change" (Anonymous, 1942, p. 260).

---

[2]Indians in Canada and the United States have long had difficulty using alcohol moderately. They are not alone in this difficulty, of course, but they suffer it disproportionately and historically. It is thus saddening to hear the leader of an Alberta band of Indians recently plead with government and academia to provide a cure for the alcoholism which, he said, is destroying his people. It is sad because no one has a cure. The costly, and only partly effective, proposal to keep alcohol away from Indians is now disallowed as "racially discriminatory."

3   A third question concerns the relative rationality of differing codes of conduct.

As we have seen (page 256), scholars who deny the efficacy of cultural differences at the same time justify difference as rational. They tell us that one might as well be a hasty hedonist, which includes being a prolific parent (Rainwater, 1960; Sheehan, 1975, 1976), since, it is said, acting differently does not help. The paradox in this argument is clear: People are not really that different, but, if they are, they are rational to be so.

Cultural relativity and comparative rationality. Professional students of behavior—anthropologists, psychologists, and sociologists—are themselves not clear about whether collective ways of acting (cultures) are equally rational. They are not even clear about the applicability of the concept of rationality in the evaluation of patterned ways of living. Social scientists *use* the idea of rationality while they remain critical of it.

Confusion has been promoted by the doctrine of *cultural relativism*, a doctrine built into the ideas of modern social studies. This attitude flows from and reinforces an egalitarianism which is, says Jarvie (1967), "the fundamental metaphysical framework within which the tradition of social anthropology has arisen" (p. 76). Cultural relativists "see no rational justification for ranking societies morally, cognitively, or culturally. This key argument . . . makes any relativism into a combined relativism regarding truth, morality, justice, and everything else" (Jarvie, 1975, p. 344).

From this relativistic assumption, it follows that "people do the best they can." All are equally rational, given their circumstances.

This is a difficult position to maintain, for it is impossible to be a cultural relativist and, at the same time, to argue that knowledge is better than ignorance and that professional expertise is expert. It is logically inconsistent to be a cultural relativist and, at the same time, to declare that happiness is better than misery and that kindness is an improvement over brutality.

Such logical inconsistency is apparent, for example, in the *Statement of Human Rights* submitted by the American Anthropological Association (1947) to the United Nations Commission on Human Rights. Since the very notion of "human rights" is culturally embedded, a logical cultural relativist can make no universal prescription for its defense. Logic often bends to desire, however, and logic did not prevent American anthropologists from "saying something" about the moral concept of "rights." Their three principles are stated as follows:

   1   The individual realizes his personality through his culture, hence respect for individual differences entails a respect for cultural differences.
   2   Respect for differences between cultures is validated by the scientific fact that no technique of qualitatively evaluating cultures has been discovered.
   3   Standards and values are relative to the culture from which they derive so that any attempt to formulate postulates that grow out of the beliefs or moral codes of one culture must to that extent detract from the applicability of any Declaration of Human Rights to mankind as a whole.

The third statement contradicts the first two. "Respect" is a moral prescription. It too must be culture-bound. If there is no universal standard justifying "respect," then there is no reason for "respecting" others' cultural differences—including such different preferences as have promoted cannibalism and built concentration camps.

One way out. Arguments for the greater or lesser rationality of different ways of living involve matters of taste and morals, as the cultural relativist maintains. These preferences stand in some relation to the ways of life being evaluated. They may be part of the cultures being studied, in opposition to them, or indifferent to them, but in all cases the professional student of behavior has no special competence for choosing among these *preferences*.

However, arguments about the comparative rationality of cultures also involve matters of truth and consequences. And truth and consequences, if they are to be talked about sensibly, do not wander idly between cultural camps. The boundary of cultural relativism is drawn by some public test of truth, as the statistician Kendall (1949) notes:

> A friend of mine once remarked . . . that if some people asserted that the earth rotated from East to West and others that it rotated from West to East, there would always be a few well-meaning citizens to suggest that perhaps there was something to be said for both sides and that maybe it did a little of one and a little of the other; or that the truth probably lay between the extremes and perhaps it did not rotate at all [p. 115].

In brief, we may admit the cultural relativism of morals and tastes while denying the cultural relativism of truth and consequences.

It becomes possible to test the relative rationality of different styles of life as actors themselves agree about what they want. There is some such agreement, by degree of course, in the matter of "social concerns" (Nettler, 1976, chap. 1). In particular, there is agreement about those material concerns which characterize the object of medicine (the protection of health), the object of economics (the production of wealth), and the object of criminology (the defense of persons and property).

In these studies it is assumed that there are more and less efficient responses to circumstances. We assume this while acknowledging the constraints placed on rationality by ignorance, morality, hope, and the conflict of our desires. Rationality *is* bounded.

The trap. The fact that rationality is bounded narrows the circumstances under which the idea of "being rational" applies. The very requirements of rationality put us in a trap. The trap is that rationality assumes that people know what they want and that their desires are not in conflict. The "catch" is in the assumption that the satisfaction of one desire does not exact "too much" of a price in the frustration of other desires. If these assumptions fail, as they probably do, the idea of rationality cannot be applied in the evaluation of different ways of life.

To be rational, we are reminded (see Chapter 9), is to use means known to be efficient toward the attainment of empirical ends. The difficulty is that we are not always clear about what we want and that we often want many things "all together." We never want just one thing. "No one ever acts from a single motive," Dostoyevsky assures us. Motives are always mixed, and sometimes they are in conflict.

If people want tangled, and differentially weighted, mixtures of results, the comparative rationality of a way of life cannot be assessed without assigning values to each of the objectives in the mixture. These values must be "theirs," of course, not ours.[3]

This means, among other things, that people must know what they want—in a rather precisely graded hierarchy of desires. But, of course, we do not always know what we want. And what we think we want changes as we get some of what we thought we wanted. This is why Oscar Wilde could have a character in one of his plays say: "In this world there are only two tragedies. One is not getting what one wants, and the other is getting it" (1893, act I).

Given the complexities of measuring the objectives of action and the tangled demands of a people's desires, no one has yet devised a calculus for computing the relative rationality of cultures. It is only for *bounded* questions—those which assume no objectives other than those contained within the question—that experts can extract answers for policy from knowledge. In a democracy, knowledge is usable in the direction of social policy only if a people knows what it wants and agrees on the gradient of its desires. The hazards of this assumption make it easier, and safer, for persons with knowledge to specify what will *not* work and what people can *not* have than to prescribe what will work and what people can have with planned social action (Popper, 1959, chap. 1, 1962, chap. 16).

Conclusion

"Outside observers," such as anthropologists and sociologists, have no moral authority for imposing cultural objectives, but they can count their consequences. Among the consequences of subcultural differences are differences in crime rates.

Culture makes a difference, but the question remains, "How?"

Social psychologists attempt to answer this question in two broadly different ways: by emphasizing how we *think* and by emphasizing *what* we were trained to be and *how* we were trained.

Social psychologists of the symbolic-interactionist persuasion stress the importance of thought. They work to build a bridge between *structures* of social relations and our *interpretations* of them, and in this manner they try to describe how crime is produced. Their ideas are the subject of the following chapter.

---

[3]Revolutionaries and reformers characteristically evade this difficulty by assuming that what other people *want* is not what they *need*. Such "false" desires are given bad names—like "candyfloss" in England. It becomes a typical task of reformers to change what others value.

Chapter 14

Definitions of Situations and Crime: Differential Association

Social psychology is the study of human behavior based on the assumption that significant portions of conduct are the result, directly or indirectly, of what other human beings have done to us and for us. Social psychology is concerned with the alterations in behavior that seem to be influenced by both enduring and short-term relations with others. The influential others may be physically present or only symbolically so. Social psychology is interested in the behavioral effects of "immediately present" others, but it also includes as a "social effect" the influence of past human interactions such as may be represented by a printed page, a work of art, or a folktale.

With so wide a definition of its interest, social psychology becomes coterminous with the study of conduct. Its distinctive perspective, however, is *interactional*. It accepts the possibility that it may be difficult, if not impossible, to divide the sources of behavior between those "inside" the organism and those external to it. It assumes that human behavior, particularly the "significant" behaviors to which moral approval is attached or denied, is the result of some reciprocal connection between an organism and its environment. According to a popular sociopsychological saying, in the production of human behavior "there is no environment without a heredity, and no heredity without an environment."

The interactionist perspective is carried beyond the study of heredities and environments and is applied also to the study of the effects of different styles of relationship between individuals. The assumption, again, is that John's behavior toward Mary is influenced by Mary's conduct toward John and by John's memory of previous experiences with other Marys.

This assumption perceives *less continuity* in the behavior of individuals or groups than a cultural or a statistical explanation of behavior does. In contrast with these ways of describing action, the sociopsychological premise is more optimistic as regards the possibility of "engineering" behavioral changes. It looks for the ways in which behavior is conditioned by the social environment, and it is hopeful, then, that knowledge of the "laws" of such influence will permit the beneficent control of behavior.

VARIETIES OF SOCIOPSYCHOLOGICAL ATTENTION

The interactionist assumption on which social psychology is based does not, and could not, function as an explanation without specifying particular variables to be attended to. It is easy to agree with the general idea that people somehow influence one another. The question is, "How?" In attempting to answer this question, social psychologists have looked at different portions of reality. For example, many scholars have attended to the patterns of rewards and punishments by which behaviors seem to be shaped. Others have studied the kinds of models and associates with whom the developing human is reared. Such investigators tend to emphasize the necessity of "control" if crime is to be reduced; their ideas are discussed in Chapter 16.

There are other social psychologists, however, who are less concerned with training in self-control as one kind of interpersonal relationship. These scholars pay more attention to what they regard as a distinctively human product of interpersonal influence: *thought.*

The kind of thought that is assumed to be important in the guidance of conduct is thought that assigns meanings to actions. It is assumed that, before we act in social settings, we interpret our situation. Our interpretation includes an assessment of the physical world around us, but it also includes an assessment of what significant others intend and of how they are likely to respond to our actions.

Conduct, then, is generated in interaction with others, but the important aspect of interaction is the exchange of meanings. Since such interpretation requires thought and since thinking is believed to depend heavily on the manipulation of symbols,[1] the sociopsychological school that emphasizes the

---

[1]The fact that thinking depends heavily on manipulation of symbols does not mean that thinking is *nothing but* symbolic activity. Psychologists distinguish between *thinking,* which is "any activity . . . which demonstrates . . . intelligence" (Furth, 1966, p. 23); a *symbol,* which is a conventionalized sign of some object or event; and *language,* which is a system of symbols. Symbolic activity is one indicator of thinking, but thinking is more than just symbolic activity. Thinking is neither restricted to human beings nor "neatly separated from other human activities" (Furth, 1966, p. 23). What is more, human beings are *not* the only animals that can symbolize. The great apes also can use symbols, but, of course, to a lesser degree than Homo sapiens. On this, see Langer (1967), Mason (1976), Premack (1971), and Premack and Premack (1972).

guiding function of thought has become known as "symbolic interactionism."

THE SYMBOLIC-INTERACTIONIST PERSPECTIVE

The fact that human beings symbolize their worlds means that we regard some parts of our environment as stable, as being "out there," and as capable of being known. As a corollary of this assumption, the recognition of a world "out there" is associated with awareness of a "self" which can be distinguished from other objects and which, however vaguely, may become the object of its own thought.

It is assumed that awareness of "self" is developed in a process that is characterized, largely but not entirely, by the development of symbols and their interpersonal exchange. It is believed also that this process teaches each individual to take the role of the other person, that is, to imagine one's "self" in the other person's situation. This empathy, this ability to generalize from one's self-awareness to that of others, is both a social bond and a means by which we continue to instruct each other. The descriptions and the explanations that are given by art, drama, poetry, and even psychology and sociology gain much of their plausibility through their appeal to empathy (Nettler, 1970, chap. 3).

The interactionist's attention to symbolic activity has meant that this kind of social psychology is cognitive psychology. It looks for the explanations of social behavior in *learned dispositions identified through their expression in symbols*. These dispositions are variously called "attitudes," "beliefs," "meanings," "perceptions," "expectations," "values," and "definitions of the situation."[2] Such concepts refer to assumed "internal states of the organism," located largely in the frontal lobes of the cerebral cortex.[3] These internal states are defined as "symbol-containing." The symbols are conceived of as "images" that represent our worlds and that are subject to such manipulations as *reasoning* (internal symbolic exchange), *translation* (transfer from one system of vocabulary to another), and *communication* (interpersonal symbolic exchange). It is assumed that the presence of these symbol-containing states can be reliably inferred from certain classes of behavior like speech, gesture, and perception.

The distinctive professional task of social psychologists of the interactionist school has been to describe and measure these cognitive conditions, to assess how they vary with circumstance, and to determine how they affect

---

[2]These concepts are often used as synonyms. They should not be. Rose (1962, p. 5), for example, distinguished between the *meaning* of a symbol and the *value* associated with that meaning. The best recent clarification of parts of this conceptual tangle is that offered by Fishbein and Ajzen (1972).

[3]"Attitudes," "meanings," "beliefs," and "definitions of the situation" have been held to be "internal states of the organism." The neural characteristics of these internal states are not specified by the symbolic-interactionist theory. It is assumed, however, that changes in neural switching are associated with the learning of these dispositions.

feeling and action. The last point is crucial. Symbolic interactionism locates the *causes* of our behaviors in our *interpretations* of reality.

APPLICATIONS OF SYMBOLIC-INTERACTIONIST THEORY TO CRIMINOLOGY

There have been two major applications of symbolic-interactionist assumptions to the explanation of crime. The earlier representation is that advanced by the late E. H. Sutherland and his students under the title "differential-association theory." A more recent version of symbolic interactionism in criminology is known as the "labeling" hypothesis, to be discussed in Chapter 15. Both types of explanations are more North American than European or Asian.

In evaluating these explanations of criminality, it is worth remembering that they need not contradict other hypotheses. There is overlap among various accounts of crime; the difference is often one of emphasis. However, differences in what is emphasized as *causal* remain important as the emphases are translated into policies.

The Differential-Association Hypothesis

Differential association was, until recently, a popular explanatory style among Western criminologists. Like many other sociological theories, it is poorly titled. The title, "differential association," sounds as though it refers to *people* in association. The hypothesis, however, does *not* refer to who associates with whom. What is differentially associated, according to this school, is definitions of situations. As E. H. Sutherland and Cressey (1970) have put it, a person commits a crime "because of an excess of definitions favorable to violation of law over definitions unfavorable to violation of law" (p. 75). Note the emphasis on *definition*, that is, on *interpretation*.

The differential-association hypothesis proposes that most members of complex societies are subject to a continuing balance, a competition, among definitions of situations which justify breaking a particular law and definitions which legitimize that law in the actor's mind and thereby provide immunization against the propensity to break it. This is what is meant by "differential association." Contrary to what the term suggests, this hypothesis is not just a statement about *the kind of people* with whom one associates, or even a statement about *the kind of behaviors* with which one is familiar. The "differential association" refers to a differing balance, a changing balance, within each actor among *the definitions* he or she has learned to associate with categories of conduct defined by law as legal or criminal. These "definitions" are attitudes. They are evaluations. As such, they are presumed to be motivating.

The central idea of the differential-association hypothesis is that of all symbolic-interactionist explanation: that *cognition causes conduct*. This key idea is then embedded in other assumptions. It is assumed that criminal behavior is learned behavior (rather than the release of some inherited predisposition). It is further assumed that learning such behavior includes acquiring both the techniques of committing certain kinds of crime and the motives for committing them. In turn, "the specific direction of motives and drives is learned from definitions of the legal codes as favorable or unfavorable" (E. H. Sutherland and Cressey, 1970, p. 75). In short, this hypothesis reduces to the common-sense idea that people are apt to behave criminally when they do not respect the law.

Learning Contingencies Proponents of this schema acknowledge that definitions of situations as justifying crime vary in the *intensity* with which they have been learned, in the *time* at which they have been acquired, in the *frequency* with which the definition is repeated for the learner, and in the *span of time* over which the lesson is reinforced or challenged. It is assumed, without detailed specification, that some lessons are taught more authoritatively and have a greater emotional charge attached to them and that, therefore, lessons may vary in the intensity with which they are impressed upon one. It is also assumed, without elaboration, that lessons learned early in life and repeated often and over a long span of one's life have a greater impact than those acquired later and "associated" less frequently and more briefly with one's actions.

Roots in Culture Conflict While the differential-association schema does not emphasize culture conflict, the assumption of conflict underlies it. The existence of changing ratios between the criminogenic and lawful definitions of situations requires, at bottom, culture conflict. Competing attitudes toward the law constitute a principal indicator of the conflict of norms of conduct. The differential-association hypothesis is thus similar to other interpretations of criminality in considering criminality a consequence of breaches in the moral bond. *Despite their different foci of attention, all explanations of crime that locate its source in the social web reduce to a description of conditions that weaken moral community.* In this, such theories accord with the moral beliefs of the great religions. They thus say little that is new *except* as they specify processes characteristic of alienation among men. It is the *description* of these processes that lends substance and authority to theories of criminogenesis. It is *what* such theories specify as eroding moral unity that makes them interesting and of political importance. It is on this point that the differential-association theory has been called "both true and trivial," for it does not describe in detail the learning process it assumes to be central to the manufacture of criminality.[4] This deficiency has led critics to regard the differential-association theory as plausible, probable, and logical (DeFleur and Quinney, 1966), but at the same time irrefutable and uninformative (Gibbons, 1968, p. 204; Jeffery, 1959).

---

[4]Although the originators of differential-association theory have not described the process by which differential definitions are acquired, other investigators may do so. Burgess and Akers (1966), for example, have strengthened the differential-association notion by adding "reinforcement theory" to it.

Specific criticisms are that differential-association theory (1) neglects individual differences, (2) neglects variations in opportunity, and (3) neglects passionate or impulsive crime. A more serious criticism is that the theory (4) is so general and so loosely phrased as to be impossible to disprove. A further consequence of this generality is that the formulation (5) provides no sure guide for action. Each of these criticisms deserves attention.

Criticism of the Differential-Association Hypothesis

1   The Differential-Association Hypothesis Neglects Individual Differences The neglect of individual differences is common to all sociological explanations of criminality. Such neglect may not be a disadvantage if one is interested only in comparing crime rates among aggregates of people or in changes in crime rates within a population over time. However, the neglect of differences in individual interests and abilities makes it difficult for the differential-association schema to explain some things that concern us. For example, it is unable to explain adequately the nondelinquent child who lives in a highly criminal neighborhood or the "bad actor" reared in a "good" environment. Sociopsychological explanations of the control variety attempt to explain these interesting anomalies.

2   The Differential-Association Hypothesis Regards Opportunity as a Constant   Common-sense ideas about crime assume that the opportunity to commit an offense has something to do with the probability that it will be committed. Temptations are strong or weak, close or distant. Although it is agreed that grasping an opportunity may be a function of the actor's definition of his or her chances, structuralists and others assume also that degrees of opportunity exist. The gold at Charing Cross was, or was not, left unguarded. The gangster did, or did not, offer the police officer a bribe. The emphasis in differential-association theory upon beliefs and attitudes obscures the role of situations in the production of crime. This means, in turn, that impulsive crimes are less well explained.

3   The Differential-Association Hypothesis Does Not Explain Crimes of Passion   Criminal law agrees with most observers of the social scene in distinguishing between premeditation and impulse and between plan and accident. The distinctions sometimes become blurred and open to debate. For example, psychoanalysts see "unconscious motivation," and even plan, where others see only accident. Nevertheless, the proposals of the differential-association theory seem to fit better those behaviors which are routine, characteristic, and patterned. It is more comfortable to think of definitions as affecting *decisions* than it is to think of interpretations as causing *accidents*. Furthermore, it is easier for us to attribute *choice* to an actor when there is some consistency between utterances of intention and actual deeds. By contrast, it becomes more difficult to attribute action to "definitions of the situation" when the behavior is unusual, out of character, or impulsive. In such cases, the action is less easily linked to a "choice," and, as action is divorced from decision, it seems less readily explained as produced by an idea.

Many homicides, for example, are impulsive crimes. The killing occurs in the heat of an argument between spouses, lovers, friends, or acquaintances. There is often a record of squabbling, and the arguments are frequently assisted toward their fatal end by alcohol in both the killer and the victim (Pokorny, 1965; Wolfgang, 1958). A sociopsychological observer might wish to explain such passionate outbursts as produced by a change in "definition of the situation," but it is not clear what this adds to our understanding of such crime, much less our ability to predict it. Saying that such crimes occur because of a changing balance of attitudes in the actor does *less* to help us comprehend the acts, or predict them, than a detailed description of the actors' histories.

4   The Differential-Association Hypothesis Is Impossible to Falsify   An explanatory account that holds true no matter what happens is ordinarily considered unsatisfactory by scientists, although it may satisfy other consumers of explanations. The proposals of differential-association theory, like many other explanations of human behavior, locate the causes of conduct in dispositions inside the actor which are to be inferred by observers. Such inference is not necessarily false. It is built upon empathy, upon a projection of our own thoughts and feelings in similar situations, and it is therefore useful in developing an understanding of the other person, particularly when this person is similar to us. The difficulty with explaining behavior by inferring dispositions is that an inference can always be constructed after the fact to fit every act. Dispositions, like instincts, can be multiplied endlessly. "The ratio of definitions of the situation favorable and unfavorable to the law" can be moved about at will by the explicator to suit every crime. The risk of using dispositions as an explanation, then, is that one may construct a circular explanation in which the acts are said to be caused by the dispositions (beliefs, attitudes) and the dispositions are known from the acts. Such circularities may be comfortable and may allay curiosity. They may not, however, point the way to defenses against crime.

5   The Differential-Association Hypothesis Gives Poor Advice   An important test of the adequacy of an explanation is the efficacy of the distinctive prescription it proposes. A valuable explanation, as opposed to a merely congenial account, is one that organizes information in such a way that predictive accuracy is increased. The term "predictive accuracy"[5] refers to an ability, provided by public evidence, to say that if one does *X*, *Y* is likely to result.

---

[5]We are reminded that prophecy, forecast, and prediction are different ways of "seeing" the future. A *prophecy* is a statement about future events made on the basis of private cues. A *forecast* is a statement about future events made on the basis of public signs, but in situations in which the forecaster cannot manipulate the causes and the course of events being foreseen. We can, of course, adjust to forecast events; we can prepare for them.

A *prediction* is a statement of the likely course of future events made on the basis of public evidence in situations in which it is possible to manipulate the causes of these events.

We predict well when we can manipulate the particular causes specified by a theory so that we more often get the desired effect. The differential-association hypothesis does not give us this power. What is worse, believing the differential-association hypothesis probably leads to poorer prediction than accepting some common-sense assumptions about conduct.

An illustration: prevention of embezzlement   A definitive test of the relative predictive power of differential-association explanation is difficult to conceive because its proposed distinctive cause, *balance of definitions of the situation*, is vague. However, a tentative test is provided by listening to what practitioners of symbolic interactionism tell us to do in response to certain kinds of crime. We have such a test in recommendations for the control of embezzlement made by a prominent exponent of the differential-association hypothesis. Donald Cressey (1953, 1971) has studied hundreds of embezzlers and has interpreted their careers in the light of symbolic-interactionist theory. He has, in addition, prescribed procedures for reducing embezzlement that follow from his explanation of this crime.

Embezzlement, as criminologists use the term, is a peculiar crime. It is peculiar in that, while it is more planned than impulsive, it is "out of character." An embezzler is a person who accepts a position of financial trust *without* the intention of abusing that trust. By contrast, a person who takes such a position with the intention of stealing is a con man rather than an embezzler.

People who are given positions of financial responsibility are usually "noncriminal" types. They have ordinarily not been delinquent as young people, and they usually have no record of theft. They tend to be better educated than the "textbook thief," and they are often respected members of their community prior to arrest.

These facts make explanation of the embezzler intriguing. How does such "out-of-character" theft develop?

Cressey proposes a few steps in this career. These few steps, however, are alleged to occur *without exception* as a lawful person is caused to steal. This exceptionless course, as described by Cressey, includes the following elements:

1   The person is in a position of financial trust. The position was initially accepted without the intention to steal.
2   The trusted person develops what Cressey calls a "nonsharable problem." This is vaguely defined, and its illustrations run the gamut of difficulties in living. However, whatever the "problem" is considered to be, it is soluble with money, and, most important for Cressey, it is not shared. It is not discussed with others. A "shared problem," it is said, will not lead to crime.
3   The honest person being converted to a thief has technical skills for stealing. This is a minor step in the causal chain since any person in a position of financial responsibility learns how to violate it.
4   Last, and most important in the symbolic-interactionist formulation of this career, the embezzler acquires a rationalization that justifies stealing. For symbolic interactionists, it is this justification that indicates the actor's "construction of reality" and constitutes the criminal motive.

The justification is a verbalization; it is recognized as words uttered by the actor to himself or herself and repeated, later, to others. "The process of verbalization," Cressey claims, "is the crux of the individual embezzlement problem. This means that the *words* that the potential embezzler used in his conversation with himself actually are the most important elements in the process which gets him into trouble, or keeps him out of trouble. The rationalization is his *motive*" (Cressey, 1964, pp. 19, 22). In a later publication, Cressey emphasizes that "rationalization is a motive *preceding* an act" (1971, p. iv).

From this set of assumptions about the career of the embezzler, particular recommendations follow. Cressey's prescription is twofold:

1   That companies start programs designed to reduce those "unshared problems" that Cressey believes create breaches of the employer's trust.
2   That companies institute "education programs emphasizing the nature of the verbalizations commonly used by trust violators." We must, advises Cressey, "make it increasingly difficult for trusted employees . . . to think of themselves as 'borrowers' rather than as 'thieves' when they take the boss's money" (1964, pp. 25–26).

The soundness of this explanation of a crime and of the preventive measures it proposes rests on the clarity and power of the causes it nominates. The causes selected by the symbolic-interactionist explanation are *not* without exception, as stated, and they are neither clear nor powerful.

In a test of Cressey's hypothesis carried out in Canada among a sample of six large-scale embezzlers, only *one* instance was found that conformed with the symbolic-interactionist interpretation of this kind of theft (Nettler, 1974). The confirming case was that of "an attorney whose charm, confidence, and enterprise involved friends in a wide stream of under-capitalized investments. Out of concern for his own name and his friends' fortunes, money left in trust was 'borrowed' until it was beyond recovery and the theft was discovered" (Nettler, 1974, p. 74).

However:

The five other embezzlers . . . did not steal out of any similar set of circumstances. With one possible exception, none of the remaining offenders initiated his series of thefts because he was "in a crack," to use Cressey's phrase. The possible exception that might be described as a person "in a bind" was a man who had been renting a farm and its buildings and improving the property. When the farm was to be sold and our subject to be evicted, he converted funds left in his trust so that he could purchase the estate. In this case, however, the "problem," how to keep the beloved land, was *not* unshared. It was fully and repetitively discussed with the embezzler's wife [Nettler, 1974, pp. 74–75].

Two traditional ways of explaining embezzlement compete with the symbolic-interactionist version. They are the *detective's theory* and the *auditor's hypothesis*.

Detectives called to investigate embezzlement look for the "Three B's—babes, booze, and bets." They assume that what turns a straight man, or woman, crooked is some variable combination of sex, the alcoholic "sweet life," and gambling. Their advice to employers and partners is always to be alert to signs of vice and to indications that a trusted person is living beyond his or her means. Detectives are not interested in rationalizations.

Auditors agree with detectives, but they go further. Auditors assume that theft is generated by some meeting of *desire* and *opportunity*. Vice is only one generator of desire, and the temptation to take money that is readily available is deemed to be a timeless possibility for all of us.

Intensity of desire and the perception of opportunity are personality variables, variables that "control" hypotheses take into account (see Chapter 16). "These criminal seeds," it has been argued, "are variously germinated" (Nettler, 1974, p. 75):

> In addition, the balance between desire and opportunity moves. In two [of the Canadian cases] the opportunities were so open for so long that it would have required strong defenses or weak desires to resist enjoying other people's money. For example, a social worker in charge of a welfare agency resisted for seven years stealing the inadequately guarded funds entrusted him. Only after these years of handling easy money did he succumb to the pleasures of acquiring some $25,000 annually in "welfare payments" made to non-existent clients. These benefits accrued for eight years before his arrest. The thefts were *not* engaged to meet a secret financial difficulty. They did, of course, *produce* an unshareable financial embarrassment. In this case, money was stolen because it was, like Everest, there [Nettler, 1974, p. 75].

One of the largest one-person embezzlements in North American history confirms the auditor's hypothesis. This "proper theft" of at least $4.7 *million* by a small-town banker is better explained by the conjunction of desire and opportunity than by the stress of an "unshared problem" (Maxwell, 1972). However, what remains at issue in evaluating the symbolic-interactionist explanation of crime is the power of words as motors of action.

The power of words   Ideas—those images which are put into words, numbers, and other symbols—are important. The crucial question, which can only be touched on here, is, "How important are ideas, and when are they important?"

Symbolic interactionists put thought, recognized by words, in the engine room of the causal train. Psychologists, particularly those of a behaviorist persuasion, put some thoughts in the motor of action, but they regard much thinking—or, to be more exact, much verbalization—as an *accompaniment* of action and its *consequence*. By this account, some thoughts identified in the words of actors are but part of the total complex of conduct that is otherwise caused. At other times, the words that justify come *after* the action that is being rationalized. Ideas can be in the caboose as well as in the locomotive of the causal train.

Indeed, when one studies criminal careers, or other patterns of lives, one sees that much rationalization of these careers appears to develop rather late in the causal process. There are, of course, offenders who do not rationalize their crimes at all except as the official helper asks them, "Why did you do it?"

Reasons versus motives When we ask people "Why did you . . . ?" and listen to their answers, we are collecting their reasons. These reasons can be given honestly or dishonestly, but the point is that reasons are not necessarily motives. A motive is that which *impels* action. Motives are sometimes intentions, in which case they may be verbalizable, but motives are often conceived as causes, in which case the actor may not be aware of them.

It is apparent that it is more difficult to know motives—our own or others'—than it is to gather reasons. This difficulty tempts us to confuse reasons with causes, but this is a temptation to be resisted. There may be instances of behavior in which reasons and motives unite, but the person who confuses the two and who accepts reasons as the causes of action is apt to be a poor predictor of conduct.

This is so because words are only loosely linked to deeds; attempts to predict what people will do from what they say have been disappointing (Acock and DeFleur, 1972; Coopersmith, 1969; Gross and Niman, 1975; Pace, 1949; Phillips, 1971; Rose, 1961; H. L. Smith, 1958; Wicker, 1969, 1971; Zunich, 1962).

Words correlate with deeds only when the deeds are highly specific, nonprestigious, near in time, and characteristic of the actor-talker (Crespi, 1971). Words tend to agree with deeds when the behaviors are institutionalized, routinized, specific, and devoid of moral significance.

The lesson to be learned The lesson to be learned from this, and from other research on forecasting behavior, is the one taught us long ago by Henry Adams (1907), who wrote: "No one means all he says, and yet very few say all they mean, for words are slippery and thought is viscous."

In explaining action, and in foretelling it, it is wiser to count continuities in conduct than to assign motor power to reasons. The evidence for this is extensive (Fancher, 1966, 1967; Goldberg, 1968, 1970; Kleinmuntz, 1967; Meehl, 1954, 1959; Owens, 1968, 1971; Sawyer, 1966; Wiggins and Kohen, 1971).

SUMMARY: THE FRAILTY OF THOUGHT, EXPRESSED IN WORDS, AS A CAUSE OF CONDUCT

The differential-association hypothesis attributes crime to a balance of ideas called "definitions of the situation." It has been argued that acting upon this assumption leads to poor prediction and poor protection. Since the symbolic-interactionist persuasion is so strong among social psychologists in Canada and the United States and since it enters the labeling school's explanation of crime as well (see Chapter 15), the difficulties in employing thoughts expressed in words as causes of conduct deserve outlining and some repetition:

1 A major difficulty is that the thought that is supposed to explain behavior is not known *independently* of the action that is to be explained.

Symbolic interactionists cite the dictum of the great sociologist W. I. Thomas, who wrote: "If men define situations as real, they are real in their consequences" (W. I. Thomas and Thomas, 1928, p. 572). This means that ideas are important—that if you believe the shadow is a ghost, you will respond to it as if it were one.

This sounds informative, but it is not. When we try to use the proposition, its explanatory power vanishes, and Thomas's famous statement reduces to one of the grandest tautologies in social science. It is a tautology because we know whether a person "defines a circumstance as real" only when he or she *acts* as if it were. The predicate is part of the subject. The "definition" that was to have explained the action is known only by the action that was to have been explained.

In short, it is difficult to ascertain how others "define" their situations. It is difficult to know what others—and even what we ourselves—*believe*.

Belief is usually evidenced by what people say *and* do. When belief is thus demonstrated, the doing that is part of the believing is also the doing that was to have been explained by the thinking part of the believing. I know that you "really believe" *X* when you *act* as though *X* were true. However, acting *that* way is what we set out to explain. One is trapped in a circle by this kind of explanation.

In trying to get out of this trap, symbolic interactionists turn their attention from acting to saying as a measure of "definition of the situation." As Lindesmith and Strauss put it, "In order to explain why people do what they do we must know how they think. The chief source of information about how people think is what they say" (1956, p. 9).

Such reliance upon talk as the best measure of thought entangles the inquirer in the deficiencies of words as indicators of motives. These deficiencies result from the fact that we do not *do* all that we *think*, nor do we *say* all that we *think*, nor do we always *act* as we *say* we want to, or should, or intend.

2   A second source of the poverty of thought as an explanation of action is that we do not know *how much* people think before they act. Everything depends, of course, on which kinds of act we are trying to explain. In our daily lives, fortunately, much social interaction is the result of habit rather than thought. This is fortunate because, as Thorngate (1976) reminds us, thinking is costly. It is costly in time and in energy. As a consequence, many skillful performances, including interpersonal ones, occur with little thought. In Thorngate's words, "[we] attempt to keep the costs of thought below some threshold set by [our] information processing capacities" (p. 32).

3   A third defect in assigning causal priority to ideas is that, for considerable segments of our conduct, our thoughts may not be *independent* sources of activity.

The philosopher Ludwig Wittgenstein (1889–1951) came to the same conclusion through a different route. He said: "There is a kind of general disease of thinking which always looks for (and finds) what would be called a mental state from which all our acts spring as from a reservoir" (1958, p. 143).

In opposition to this "disease," there is an alternative possibility. It is that thought, particularly as it is recognized in verbalized ideas, is acquired *along with* the varied doing that the thinking is supposed to explain.

Social psychologists who study the development and socialization of human beings consider ideas and other actions to be learned together. They consider *how we think, the ideas we have,* and *what we do* to be acquired in harness. These aspects of being persist in dynamic tension. They are sometimes in conflict, but, in the case of healthy persons, they are more often in harmony. Our acts and our ideas reinforce one another.

When one conceives of human action in this developmental manner, it is not assumed that thinking and, in particular, verbalization are causally prior to other kinds of doing. It is not assumed that *believing* comes before *being.*

Social psychologists of a behaviorist inclination view human action more as a closely woven fabric out of which the thread of "what we think" can be pulled for inspection. However, the color and texture of the whole cloth will be only imperfectly known from an examination of this thread. Application of this sociopsychological attitude to criminology is described in Chapter 16. However, for our purposes here, the weakness of attributing *independent* causal power to words and ideas can be illustrated by an extreme example.

Verbal Impotence Illustrated

The frailty of words and ideas as self-starting motors of action can be illustrated in an extreme condition. Consider a man who exhibits a syndrome called, for communicative convenience, "paranoia." Our subject differs in degree from the rest of us by:

Being more nervous, tense, and excitable.

Being exquisitely sensitive and alert to interpersonal cues.

Acting and talking *self-referentially*, by which we mean that more acts of others are seen by our subject as directed toward him than you and I can perceive.

Being suspicious and jealous.

Demanding much of loved ones at the same time that he is critical of them for their obvious lack of appreciation of him.

Talking with hate and behaving aggressively.

Saying that he is rejected unfairly.

Believing that people and the fates are against him.

Talking more dirty sex than is "normal" and seeing more perversion in others.

Being unreasonable.

And, of course, talking and acting as though the social world were a jungle. (There is much of the jungle in our social lives, but the world is not *just* that.)

Now, in looking at this package of actions—and we must bear in mind that talk is a form of action—we may, if we wish, isolate those actions to be called "attitudes" or "ideas." We can even measure those characteristic behaviors of our subject which we might wish to call his "definitions of the situation." Having done this, two questions remain. First, "Are the subject's peculiar ideas causal or only correlative?" "Did thinking that way make him that way, or is thinking that way part of his being that way?"

The answer to this first question lies in a test proposed by a second question: "If our subject's physician works on his paranoid notions, will he change the subject's behavior?" The best answer to this question is, "Not much." The curative record of the talking therapies is poor (Bergin and Garfield, 1971; Cross, 1964; Eysenck, 1966a; Levitt, 1957).

After the fact of such evidence, we can ask why working on people's ideas is so weak an instrument for changing their conduct. The answer has already been given. It is that our ideas are not all that is "in our minds." Our "minds" include sensing, feeling, willing, conceiving, and consciously doing (Langer, 1967; Ryle, 1949). And all "this" that is "in" our minds was acquired together.

What is more, this acquisition is primarily a result of developmental processes and of training and only secondarily of teaching (see pages 314–325). We do learn by being taught, but more that is "in our minds" results from being trained. *It becomes difficult, then, to change by teaching what has been acquired by training.*

It makes as much sense, therefore, to say that actions cause ideas as to say what is more conventional—that ideas cause actions. On the record, it seems easier to change thoughts by changing actions than it is to change actions by changing thoughts (Boardman, 1962; Clement, 1970; Lang and Lazovik, 1963; Lang and Melamed, 1969; V. Meyer and Levy, 1970; Romanczyk and Goren, 1975; Stolz et al., 1975; Youell and McCullough, 1975).

Conclusion

Our conclusion is that we do not say much when we say that "definitions of the situation" are causal. Explaining conduct by reference to such a symbol-laden cause is conventional and comforting, but it is not productive, and it does not answer public questions about crime. After citizens hear explanations from balanced definitions of situations, they still ask, "Yes, but where do these differing definitions come from?" and "Why do some people accept some definitions but not others?"

A brief answer to such questions is given in Chapter 16. On our way to this answer, it is important to consider a popular variation on the symbolic-interactionist theme—one that attributes the production of crime to modes of societal response.

Chapter 15

Definitions of Situations and Crime: Societal Reaction

There are fashions in ideas as there are in costume, and scholars are not immune to changing fads in the explanation of crime. Over the past 10 years the two most visible, and perhaps most popular, views of crime among its Western students have been the ideas of radical criminologists and those of "labeling" theorists. Neither of these conceptions is supported by citizens in general, and both are currently under challenge (Banks et al., 1975; Gove, 1975; Hoo, 1972; *Newsweek*, 1971; E. O. Wilson, 1975).

As with all explanations of behavior, there are variations within each style, and the labeling orientation is also called by other names, such as the "societal-reaction" or "social-definition" hypothesis (Schur, 1975, p. 288) and the "interactionist theory of deviance" (Becker, 1974, p. 6). The set of assumptions common to these variations emphasizes the *causal power of response*—verbal and nonverbal—to classes of people and classes of acts. The so-called "labels" with which this school is concerned are not merely titles; they also include differential responses to categories of persons and conduct. With this understanding, we can use the names for this set of ideas interchangeably for variety's sake.

Origins   The central assumption of the labeling perspective is an old one. It is the notion that the poet Johann Wolfgang von Goethe (1749–1832) expressed when he wrote:

When we treat a man as he is, we make him worse than he is;
When we treat him as he could be, we make him better.

Criminals, then, are "made" by the way they are treated. Tannenbaum (1938) called the process the "dramatization of evil." He believed:

> The process of making the criminal is a process of tagging, defining, identifying, segregating, describing, emphasizing, making conscious and self-conscious; it becomes a way of stimulating, suggesting, emphasizing, and evoking the very traits that are complained of.
>
> The person becomes the thing he is described as being. . . . The way out is through a refusal to dramatize the evil. The less said about it the better [pp. 19–20].

Shifting the Blame The assumptions that *dramatized* evil is a major source of evil and that evildoers reform when other cheeks are turned are rehabilitative notions and hopeful ones. They contain some truth, but not all the truth. These assumptions are in the vein of the symbolic-interactionist idea that what counts as a cause of our behavior is the *exchange of interpretations* of ourselves and others.

Emphasis on interaction does not stand still, however. It is difficult to place the cause of conduct in something as ill defined and fluid as an *exchange* of interpretations. Given this difficulty, it is not surprising that, despite obeisance to interaction, proponents of the labeling hypothesis come to stress one side of the exchange of meanings. They stress the causal efficacy of significant others' *response* to the way we are. This shifts attention from what we did to how others reacted to it. It also moves causation from *what we do* to *who we are* as sources of others' response. In criminology, such an emphasis transfers responsibility for conduct from bad actors to powerful reactors.

This reversal of the commonly assumed causal chain makes the societal-reaction school interesting. It gives the school distinction by its challenge of "conventional wisdom," a phrase that is, of course, pejorative. Indeed, the philosopher Murray Davis (1971) contends that social theories are "considered great, not because [they] are true, but because they are *interesting*" and that "all *interesting* . . . social theories . . . constitute an attack on the taken-for-granted world of their audience" (pp. 309, 311).

The societal-reaction school is certainly interesting because it suggests that things may not be as they appear to be and that attempts to explain crime by its conventional causes and attempts to control crime by conventional means may be uneconomic. The assumptions of this school therefore deserve description and evaluation.

THE LABELING THEME

The interactionist approach to criminology repeats the idea that right and wrong are socially defined and that "crime" is a word, not an act. It questions, then, the validity and the utility of particular definitions of crime.

Sympathy for Deviation

Questioning the legitimacy of conventional definitions of crime is associated with sympathy for those accused of socially constructed, and *maligned*, categories of difference. The sympathy is expressed in the labeling theorist's preference for speaking of "deviance" rather than criminality.

"Deviance" is a sociological neologism, to be found only in the most recent editions of English dictionaries. It is a term invented from the notion of deviation, a wandering from the way (*via*). The concept connotes sin or offense, a departure from a desirable course (*Webster's New Collegiate Dictionary*, 1976).

As we have seen (pages 1–16), such ideas of wrong are less exact than the idea of crime, but adoption of the term allows sociologists to consider the general theme of "disvalued people and behavior" (Sagarin, 1975). What concerns students of deviance, then, is not just crime, as legally defined, but difference that is depreciated.

This shift in terminology directs attention to the fact that, in the "crime game," majorities are reacting to minorities. Or it is sometimes held that it is powerful elites that decide what is to be penalized as crime. In either case, the translation of "crime" as "deviance" suggests the possibility that it may not be what one does that occasions arrest, censure, and punishment, but, rather, that what counts is being different in the sense of being powerless because of small numbers or other "social disadvantage."

Such a viewpoint is obviously sympathetic to those who have been despised for their difference. The labeling school has consequently been termed an "underdog philosophy." Its proponents ask, "Whose side are we on?" (Becker, 1967).

The side chosen by advocates of the "interactionist theory of deviance" favors only certain of those minorities that get labeled by the law. Thus, societal reaction is not deemed to be important in explaining the careers of corporation executives who break antitrust laws or government officials who take bribes or produce Watergates. Money presumably immunizes such offenders against the effects of bad names. At any rate, the student of "deviance" is not interested in the stigmatization of once-rich or once-powerful people, but only in the stigmatization of offenders thought to have been less fortunate.

The philosophy of the underdog turns the tables on conventional thought. Instead of assuming that it is the deviant's difference that needs explanation, it asks why the majority responds to *this* difference as it does. Shifting the question reverses the normal conception of causation. It suggests that another's peculiarity has not caused us to regard this person as different so much as our labeling has caused the peculiarity.

Noting a difference, and naming it, may then confirm it. Thus proponents of the labeling school distinguish between "primary deviance," that is, some offensive characteristic or act, and "secondary deviance" (Lemert, 1951). Secondary deviance is the process by which the reaction of others to an initial difference may confirm the deviant in the stigmatized behavior. Being cast out means being an outcast and makes it comfortable for stigmatized persons to band together in defense of their egos and in justification of their "peculiar" interests.

Transcendence of Roles over Behaviors

According to symbolic interactionists, the exchange of meanings that occurs when we meet and the differences in mutual treatment that result from this exchange push us toward the attribution and acceptance of *roles*. Roles, we note, are "parts that we play." They may not originally "have been us," but they may become us as we act them.

Emphasis upon role construction calls attention, then, to the way behavior may be shaped by the expectations of those with whom we interact. It suggests a process—what has sometimes been called a "career"—in which our conceptions of one another are reinforced by the early assignment of labels to samples of our acts.

Once roles are defined and acted upon, clusters of attributes are inferred. Such inference stimulates a selective attribution of traits to the actor and permits a linking together of diverse acts under some meaningful label (R. H. Turner, 1972, p. 310).

Stressing role formation means that less attention is paid to how people behave, and more to how we categorize one another on the basis of small segments of behavior. The tendency of the labeling theorist is therefore to deny or ignore differences in the ways in which we act and to emphasize the consequences of having power to categorize. Throughout the literature on labeling, the prevailing sentiment denies original difference, at least, and casts doubt on the validity and justice of popular images of deviants.

Implications for Methodology

Given this orientation, a preferred method of study follows. The research method advocated by labeling theorists is intensive observation of labelers and their victims. Field work is preferred to the collection of statistics. The result of such study is a description of how the labeler comes to recognize and define the deviant and of how the deviant reacts to and interprets his own world. The test of the adequacy of such a description is understanding and insight rather than prediction and control.

As compared with statistical and experimental studies, the reportorial field work recommended by the labeling theorist is more fun for students. It is good sport to engage in "participant observation," particularly among people who are "different." To this element of pleasure, labeling theory has added the advocacy of the "rights" of minorities. Its appreciative methodology and its political stance have combined to make it a fashionable way of thinking about undesirable behaviors and "social problems." The fashion has spread from its application to crime and has been extended, with variations, to attempts to understand blindness (R. A. Scott, 1969), stuttering (Lemert, 1967), illness (Lorber, 1967), civil disturbances (R. H. Turner, 1969), "welfarism" (Beck, 1967), paranoia (Lemert, 1962), death and dying (Sudnow, 1966), mental retardation (Mercer, 1965), and neurosis and psychosis (Braginsky et al., 1969; Plog and Edgerton, 1969; Scheff, 1966). An evaluation of this popular mode of explanation must recognize both its advantages and its liabilities.

EVALUATING LABELING HYPOTHESES

Assessing explanations of crime, or any other kind of conduct, requires a standard. In studies of social behavior, evaluative standards move about. They are sometimes aesthetic, more often moral, and only infrequently practical. We *do* evaluate from "the side we're on."

Against this tendency, we struggle to be objective, and the attitude underlying our evaluation of explanations of crime is skeptical. Skepticism asks of each explanation three questions (see the Preface, page x):

1 How clear are its concepts and hypotheses?
2 What factual evidence tests these hypotheses and with what result?
3 When one acts upon the distinctive prescriptions of an explanation, do the predicted consequences follow?

The subject matter of criminology makes it easier to answer the first two questions than the third one. Without the power to experiment with human beings, the third question can be only tentatively tested, and the burden of assessment falls on issues of clarity and evidence.

Even here, however, labeling theorists have not been helpful. They have been reluctant to phrase clear propositions, and they have defended their reluctance by saying that they are more concerned with producing "sensitizing observations" (Schur, 1971, p. 27) than with promoting empirical tests. In company with radical criminologists, labeling proponents prefer to "jostle the imagination, to create a crisis of consciousness which will lead to new visions of reality" (Scheff, 1974, p. 445).

Given its intention to be more provocative than empirical, the societal-reaction school evades the confines of fact, and its propositions become elusive. Indeed, one of the fathers of this perspective, Howard Becker (1974), has recently said:

> Labelling theory . . . is neither a theory, with all the achievements and obligations that go with the title, nor focused so exclusively on the act of labelling as some have thought. It is, rather, a way of looking at a general area of human activity; a perspective whose value will appear, if at all, in increased understanding of things formerly obscure [p. 6].

Such a statement relieves the societal-reaction school of the burden of being scientific, for it is one of the "obligations" of a scientific stance to be propositional and empirical. Relieved of this responsibility, labeling advocates can lay claim to "increased understanding." To this claim, the skeptic replies with two questions:

1 As used here, what does "understanding" mean?
2 Without a specified empirical test, how will we know when we have it?

Although proponents of the labeling orientation shift their ground as we try to comprehend them, two major propositions, with some auxiliary assumptions, can be extracted from their writing. The major hypotheses are:

1 That it is the *definition* of the deviant, rather than what he or she has done, that determines societal response
2 That a 'negative" societal reaction, one that is hostile and demeaning, *produces* more of the stigmatized conduct.

The first proposition examines societal response as a *dependent* variable. It asks what causes the application of a denigrating title and the punitive response. In the administration of justice, this proposition raises the possibility that arrest and sentence depend less on what the person did than on his or her legally irrelevant social characteristics.

The second hypothesis examines labeling as an *independent* variable. It suggests that stigma, degraded difference, increases offensive behavior among the stigmatized.

Both hypotheses are *causal*. The first says that it is disadvantage on the part of a minority and incorrect conception (stereotyping) on the part of a majority or its powerful elite that nominate people differentially for the title of "criminal" when all other facts and acts are equal.

The second hypothesis says that the criminal justice system *creates* crime by branding with the criminal label those whom it treats.

The first proposition calls Western justice systems "unjust"; the second calls them "uneconomical." It is important, then, to test these hypotheses, but evidence is difficult to develop. The difficulty is compounded by the tacit assumptions and imprecise ideas that are interwoven with the societal-reaction school's major premises. We can disentangle these ideas by addressing four questions to the labeling mode of explanation:

1 Are the names we call one another correct?
2 Is "stigma" one thing—or, whose label counts?
3 Is societal response to crime produced more by the fact of the act or by the legally irrelevant social characteristics of the accused?
4 Does a "bad name" cause bad action?

1 Are the Definitions We Apply to One Another Correct?

The political appeal of the societal-reaction school lies in its assumption that, "at the outset," we are equal. We are particularly equal in goodness and badness, in obeying criminal laws or breaking them. A first lesson in the labeling shcool is that everyone has offended, sometime, and that the "dark figure" of crime is so impressive as to challenge a glib division of people into lawful and criminal. "The seeds of every crime are in each of us."

There are degrees of criminal conduct, of course, as there are degrees of all other behavior, but the advocate of the labeling hypothesis is less interested in measuring these degrees of action than in rightly criticizing neat dichotomies—honest and crooked, pacific and violent, good and bad. However, the attack on such absolute partitions is used in the societal-reaction school to foster an equally untenable notion: that, when it comes to committing crimes, we are probably initially equal.

What matters, according to this, is getting caught—and, more than getting caught, getting officially handled. Arrest, conviction, and sentence are assumed *causes* of careers. They are turning points that change our identity.

Certainly such official response affects the course of lives, and there is no news in this idea. What is more interestingly implied by the labeling perspective is that these career-turning events depend more on *definitions* of categories of people than on *what they have done.*

These deviant-defining labels are supposedly imposed by majorities upon minorities, and since they are presumably based on conceptions of others rather than on observations of them, these labels are held to be mostly incorrect. An assumption, then, that is coiled through the interactionist theory of deviance is the assumption of misunderstanding of others (Icheiser, 1949). This premise is embedded in the social psychologist's concept of the "stereotype."

Images of Others   The word "stereotype" has been borrowed by social scientists from journalists. Walter Lippmann suggested the notion in his book *Public Opinion* (1922). Lippmann did not define the concept, but he wrote about it at length (five chapters), and the idea he conveyed was that while perceiving the world is difficult enough, conceiving it is even more difficult.

Lippmann believed that we often respond to others with "pictures in our heads" that are caricatures rather than portraits. These pictures are alleged to be partly true, partly false, and always exaggerated. "The perfect stereotype," according to Lippmann, "precedes the use of reason. . . . [It stamps] the data of our senses before the data reach the intelligence" (p. 98).

It is true that we sample only a small slice of life and that we have to make judgments on the basis of such few experiences. The questions are whether our samples are biased—that is, untrue—and whether the inferences we draw from these samples are correct.

These questions are as old as philosophy, and thoughtful people continue to wrestle with them. Neither Lippmann nor later scholars have shown us how to answer these questions with surety. We are only cautioned to recognize these possibilities and to be careful in judging others.

Unfortunately, social psychologists have used the notion of stereotyped images of others uncritically. The problem is not just that the concept is itself unclear—how "stereotyped" must a public image of others be before it is sufficiently consensual to be a "stereotype"? What is worse is that it has been assumed, without adequate evidence, that ordinary citizens' conceptions of "different" kinds of people are mostly wrong. However, this sociopsychological assumption is itself more false than true. The few studies that have attempted to test the accuracy of popular images have shown that "stereo-types" are more accurate than inaccurate. This has been found true of popular conceptions of occupations (Rice, 1928) and of ethnic groups (Mackie, 1971, 1973).

Stereotypy is a concept that has been neither well defined nor well tested (Mackie, 1971; Nettler, 1970, pp. 29–30). The notion of a stereotype is itself a label most frequently employed to disqualify other persons' images of their social worlds.

Relevance to Criminology   Despite the poor conceptual status of the idea of stereotypy, the notion is pertinent to the attitude taken by the interactional explanation of criminogenesis. The labeling advocate assumes that stereotypes of offenders influence use of the law. It is assumed, furthermore, that these stereotypes are false and that the criminal law is therefore applied less against classes of acts and more against classes of people. It is contended that this unfair application will be stronger where there is more judicial discretion, as there is in response to misdeeds committed by juveniles. Thus the labeling proponent Schur (1973) tells us:

> We are likely to have specific ideas of what "criminals" and "delinquents" are like, even if we have never had any direct encounters with known law-violators. Reactions based on these stereotypes may significantly affect how individuals are treated throughout the various stages in the administration of juvenile justice. Indeed, the considerable discretion vested in officials at all levels of the juvenile justice system makes them vulnerable to the influence of stereotypical thinking. . . . the philosophy of the juvenile court . . . virtually ensures that stereotypes will influence judicial dispositions [pp. 120–121].

These allegations stimulate two critical responses. The first is that labeling theorists *only assume* that there are stereotypes of offenders and that these images are incorrect. They advance no evidence in support of this assumption. There have been no studies of public conceptions of classes of offender—much less of the validity of such images—although one such research project has been proposed (Solhaug, 1972).

A second criticism, and a more important one, is that, again, it is *only assumed* that stereotypes influence judicial practice more than actual criminali-ty does. This allegation is easily made but seldom proved (see pages 214–220, 284–298).

Our discussion of stereotypy has been necessitated, then, by the uncritical adoption of the concept by the societal-reaction school. If the assumptions of this school were correct—*if* stereotypes were mostly false and *if* such erroneous images actually did influence arrest or trial—then, of course, injustice would be done. Against this possibility, doubt cast on the assumed inaccuracy of popular judgmental categories, and on the alleged function of these incorrect images in judicial systems, weakens the charge of the labeling proponent. It does not answer the charge completely, and additional questions remain.

2 Whose Label Counts?

A major assumption of the societal-reaction school is that the labels that matter in the creation of criminals are those which hurt. Hurting, in fact, is part of the definition of "deviance." So Ericson (1975, p. 134) writes: "The labelling analyst sees all imputations of deviance as punitive."

If such a statement is to be more than a definition—if, that is, it is to be converted into a proposition—it will be necessary to separate the stigmatizing act from the experience of its intended pain. Such a proposition asks more than what "societal reactors" intend when they "label." It also raises the question of what hurts whom.

It is true that legal labels applied to rule breakers are intended to set them apart and to condemn them and their acts. The theater of the court is designed to produce this effect, and, as we have seen, one function of the criminal law is symbolic (see pages 50–51). The trial dramatizes the morality threatened by crime and defended by law. The procedures of a justice system constitute, then, a form of "degradation ceremony," as Garfinkel (1956) has so aptly titled it. The question raised by Garfinkel and others, but never answered in the context of the manufacture of deviant careers, is, "When do degradation ceremonies work?"

Children sing a classic taunt:

Sticks and stones
May break my bones;
Your dirty names
Can't hurt me.

Not all labels stick, and not all labels hurt. Some attempts to condemn are futile. As with punishment, so with stigma—what hurts varies with a host of contingencies.

Stigma is not one thing, one denigrating act with one effect (Shoham, 1970). What stigmatizes varies with who applies which label to whom at what stage in a career. It varies also with the support given by "significant others" to the accused person. Social disapproval, even official disapproval, does not count with some categories of actor. Their reference groups are not made up of police officers and judges. There is a mass of evidence that rule breakers who are supported by "their own kind" ignore some attempted degradation ceremonies and are honored by others. Samples of this evidence can be found in such studies as those by Hobsbawm (1969), Keiser (1965), Maas (1975), Polsky (1967), Schwendinger and Schwendinger (1967), A. Sutherland (1975), Taft (1946), and H. S. Thompson (1966).

The *unanswered* question, crucial to the labeling perspective is, "When is a 'personal identity' changed, and how much, by whose stigmatizing effort?"

3 Are We Reacting More to What People Do or to Who They Are?

Labeling theory says that it is "disadvantage" that determines against whom the law is applied. Proponents of this view are never definite about what constitutes disadvantage, and they seem to arrive at their conception *after the fact* of differential arrest. Thus, males, young people, and the members of some poor ethnic groups but not others *are* differentially arrested and convicted of serious crimes. After this fact, it is alleged that it was not so much what such categories of people did as who they were that determined their being legally handled. Moreover, as we have seen in connection with the notion of stereotypy, who people "are" is also held to be problematic and *incorrectly defined* by official judges of deviants.

The central allegation—that response to offenders depends on their social status rather than their deeds—is itself not clear. As Tittle (1975) points out, labeling advocates do not tell us whether "being disadvantaged" is supposed to have *some* effect on societal response or, what is more important, whether the effect of disadvantage is supposed to be *greater* than the effect of actual rule breaking.

The first suggestion is neither novel nor precise. Justice is not totally blind, and some effect may occur, but we are not told how much would have to occur to validate the labeling hypothesis.

The challenging question, and one that would add importance to the societal-reaction explanation if it were answered in its favor, is whether Western systems of justice are responding *more* to the legally irrelevant social characteristics of the accused than to the quality of their acts. Tittle (1975, p. 164) shows that a rigorous answer to this question would require data that allowed us:

a To hold constant actual rule breaking while observing the relation between societal reaction and selected disadvantages
b To *compare* the size of that relation with the association between actual rule breaking and societal reaction when disadvantages are held constant

In other words, confirmation of the labeling hypothesis requires not merely the demonstration of a positive correlation between disadvantage and societal reaction but also a demonstration that such a correlation is *stronger* than the correlation between rule breaking and legal treatment.

A Test Only a few investigations approximate such a requirement. Hindelang (1974), for example, studied how retail stores handled shoplifters. He wanted to find out whether the decision to refer culprits to the police depended more on who the offenders were or on what they had done. He found that the correlation between societal response and the value of goods stolen, holding constant the age, sex, and race of the accused, was *greater* than the correlation between these social characteristics and societal reaction, holding constant the value of the stolen property. In short, what was stolen, how it was stolen, and how much was stolen affected societal reaction more strongly than the social status of the offenders did.

A weakness of Hindelang's study is that it did not include socioeconomic position as a mark of an offender's disadvantage and it did not examine the effects of combinations of rule-breaking circumstances and social characteristics. Nevertheless, this research provides evidence of the comparative strength of doing versus being as a cause of legal reaction. This evidence is *contrary* to the assumption of the labeling school.

Other Tests Many other studies of the determinants of societal reaction provide data that have been used in evaluating the labeling school's charge of injustice in Western legal systems. For methodological reasons noted below (pages 286–291), most of these investigations are inadequate as crucial tests of the labeling hypothesis. Given their methodological weaknesses, it is no surprise that the findings of many of these studies are inconsistent. They are particularly inconsistent as studies of the treatment of juvenile delinquents, where laws allow more discretion in response to offenses and where "delinquencies" include a range of misbehavior from "status offenses" to misdemeanors and felonies. Inconsistency is encouraged also by the fact that investigations have been conducted in different jurisdictions and at different times.

Factors usually nominated as extralegal, and hence biasing, are age, sex, race, and socioeconomic status. Such factors are, however, intertwined with legal considerations, and it cannot be assumed, offhand, that their correlation with judicial action, if any, necessarily indicates injustice. What is required for a fair test is analysis of the interplay of such variables with legally relevant grounds. For example, if race is correlated, as it is, with proportions of intact homes, then looking at race alone as a possible determinant of judicial treatment of juveniles will itself bias our interpretation of the results. In short, the social-status markers that have been used as possible indicators of "discrimination" may be either directly relevant to legal considerations or correlated with legal allowances.

With these qualifications in mind, the most reasonable conclusion we can draw from a mass of imperfect data is that the interactional hypothesis is provocative, but unconfirmed. The force of possible nonlegal factors in determining societal response appears to be minimal. There is some effect of such variables in the administration of Western justice, but it cannot be said that these "labeling" effects are strong effects or, more to the point, that they *outweigh* legally relevant factors in response to lawbreakers. It is this charge which makes the societal-reaction school interesting and which, if verified, would make its perspective valuable. However, with some qualification, the bulk of the data point the other way. It is not so much who we are, or who officials think we are, that determines legal response to our acts. On the contrary, it is principally what we have done that dictates our treatment by the criminal law.

This conclusion derives from studies of police-citizen interaction (see pages 64–70), decisions to prosecute, plea bargaining, conviction and sentencing, and granting of probation and parole. The number of investigations testing the influence of extralegal factors in the administration of criminal law is enormous. Fortunately for our purposes here, much of this research has recently been evaluated. Hirschi (1975) has done this for juvenile delinquency, Tittle (1975) for adult criminality, and Hagan (1974b) for sentencing practices.

Hirschi's assessment of the evidence pertaining to treatment of juvenile delinquents in the United States addresses both sides of the labeling hypothesis: (1) Is it label or deed that provokes societal reaction, and (2) are there "amplification effects"—that is, do labels cause delinquency? His answers to both questions are *negative*. Concerning the first question at issue here, Hirschi writes:

> Research on the processing of juveniles by official agencies shows that, on the whole, the major determinant of the severity of the social reaction is the seriousness and frequency of the child's delinquent behavior. It shows, further, that the system is inclined to err in the direction of labelling the guilty innocent . . . [1975, p. 191].

Tittle's analysis of studies of reaction to adult offenders reaches a similar conclusion, although Tittle suggests that there might be a "kernel of truth" in the labeling hypothesis if one can overlook the poor reasearch methods characteristic of most tests of interactional assumptions. Tittle summarizes:

> Not a single good test of either of the major propositions of labelling theory currently exists in the criminological literature. Moreover, most of the research does not even attend to the most fundamental requirements of scientific methodology. The truth is, we simply cannot judge the empirical adequacy of the labelling theory with any confidence at the present time. Hence it would be foolish to conclude that it is unfounded. But by the same token, it is even more foolish to accept it as if it were tried and proven.
>
> The most that can be concluded is that social disadvantages may have some effect on labelling and that labelling may have some influence in producing criminal behavior [1975, p. 175].

Research Deficiencies Illuminated Hagan's evaluation of studies of sentencing is important because his assessment points clearly to shortcomings of much of this research. Officials and concerned citizens are well-advised to note these deficiencies before they leap to a verdict of guilty against Western judicial practice.

Correlations and Causes Again The deficiencies of many studies of human behavior derive from the fact that social scientists, like all the rest of us, try to find causes by looking at associations (see Chapter 8). When we set out to ascertain whether it is *what one does* or *who one is* that causes societal response, we do so by collecting correlations.

Looking for causes in this way tempts us into a trap. The trap is probably the most common error made in thinking about our lives: that of inferring causation from correlation. This error awaits us because correlation is necessary as a sign of causation, but it is not sufficient as an indicator of it.

Confusing *one* of the elements in causal inference—the necessary criterion—with *all* the elements required to substantiate a causal relation is a constant temptation. It leads both to silly conclusions about causes and to some inferences that seem plausible even though the causal connection remains undemonstrated. For example, most observers would resist seeing causation in the factual association of numbers of storks in European neighborhoods and numbers of babies born there or in the relationship between the number of fire engines present at fires and the damage done (Lazarsfeld, 1955).

The trouble is that it may be true, as *I Ching* tells us, that everything is related to everything (Gardner, 1974). If we look diligently, we can find correlations everywhere, and statisticians show us how to do this by calculating seemingly silly associations. For example, George Marshall computed the correlation between the death rate in Hyderabad, India, from 1911 to 1919 and membership in the International (really only American) Association of Machinists from 1912 to 1920. Marshall found a coefficient of correlation of $+.86$, meaning that as death rates rose or fell in Hyderabad, membership in the American trade union followed suit one year later (cited by M. R. Cohen, 1931, p. 92).

A more recent illustration of peculiar correlation has been composed by Lyster (1974). His data show a remarkable negative relation between the rates at which Americans killed one another from 1900 to 1973 and the rates at which they reproduced. As annual homicide rates increased, fertility rates declined, and vice versa. Lyster does not know what this means, but he does not believe it is just another "nonsense correlation." However, no student has yet interpreted this correlation as signifying that murders *cause* a reduction in birthrates or, conversely, that increasing birthrates *cause* a decline in murder rates.

Spurious Interpretation   Social scientists are alert to the possibility of mistakenly concluding that things that go together cause each other. Sometimes things that go together have a common cause; they are joint effects. Sometimes events that are associated are linked by intervening variables; the causal bond is indirect.

When a correlation is mistakenly read as evidence of causation, this interpretation is called "spurious," that is, false. It should be noted that it is not the correlation that is false, but rather its *interpretation* as indicating causation that is incorrect.

Students of behavior consider the possibility of a correlation's being incorrectly interpreted as demonstrating causation by examining relations between events nominated as cause and effect, while *holding constant* other events or conditions that might have preceded both the alleged cause and its presumed effect. If the original correlation "holds up" when such controls are introduced, it may point toward causation. If, on the other hand, the original correlation reduces toward zero, it is believed that an interpretation of causation from that correlation is spurious.

Controlling for other variables is itself problematic, since we can, and do, quarrel about what should be considered. Theory is supposed to tell us what to "control for," but theory provides no insurance of correct inference. What is needed to test an inference of causation, once some correlations seem correctly interpreted, is an experiment. It is, of course, our limited ability to experiment with proposed causes in the social arena that restricts the science in social studies and allows us to continue disputing causes of crime.

Test adequacy   From this discussion, it should be clear that if we are to test the hypothesis that labels, more than deeds, cause societal response, we shall have to examine the relation between being categorized and being differentially handled by the criminal justice system, while *holding constant* all legally relevant considerations.

For logical reasons,[1] this test should be complemented by its converse: an examination of the relation between kinds of crime and societal response, holding labels constant. The relation between labels and arrests or sentences, while holding constant all legally relevant considerations, is then to be compared with the relation between deeds and arrests or sentences, while holding labels constant. The point of the comparison is to test which association is stronger.

Such a comparison requires use of multiple correlation techniques. These are operations that allow us to assess the *relative degree* of association between an effect, such as a sentence, and a number of possible causes considered together.

Many studies of the influence of extralegal factors have not done this, but have looked at a relationship between, say, race and sentence, holding constant one or two variables at a time—usually seriousness of offense and prior record. A court's judgment, however, is more like a gestalt—a patterned decision that is not based on bits of information received and processed one at a time. For this reason, multiple regression models of the judicial process should be used. They are unfortunately rare.

Furthermore, the measure of association used in testing the hypothesis of unjust treatment should be just that—a measure of correlation, *not* a measure of "statistical significance." This point has to be made because many investigations have tested the "statistical significance" of differences in the treatment of groups.

"Statistical significance" refers to a finding of a relation between events that seems greater than would occur as a result of "chance." Such a finding requires only that some association between the things being measured be more than zero, and more than zero by an amount not to be expected if everything occurred at random (Labovitz, 1969). But again, according to *I Ching*, most

---

[1]The logical reasons for comparing a hypothesis concerning causes with its converse are described by Blalock (1961, pp. 35–38).

measurable things have some relationship, and the more things we measure, the more likely we are to find some association between them. Assuming some connection between the things being counted "in the world out there," we increase the probability of finding a statistically significant relation between our samples of events by increasing our sample size (Blalock, 1960, p. 225). The statistician William Hays (1963) calls this device "testmanship," and he comments: "*Virtually any study can be made to show significant results if one uses enough subjects, regardless of how nonsensical the content may be*" (p. 326).

Finding some statistically "significant difference" in the treatment of offenders is not the same as finding a substantive difference. A test of statistical significance is more like a test of the reliability of findings from sampling. "Significance" tells us that we are apt to find the same kind of difference with repeated samples of such people and behavior. However, this does not tell us *how strong* the relation is between the nominated cause and the effect in which we are interested. We are not informed *how much* difference in the effect is produced by the "significantly different" things being measured, such as labels.

Weak measures Hagan's survey (1974b) makes this point forcibly in evaluating research on sentencing in the United States. Hagan selected 20 frequently cited investigations of the effects of offenders' social characteristics on their sentences. The selected studies are those repeatedly quoted by criminologists, and some of them have been cited as evidence before United States congressional committees and courts (Wolfgang, 1974).

Hagan notes, first, that such studies characteristically use large samples; thus we should expect to find "statistical significance" for even small degrees of association. He then observes that, of these 20 prominent investigations, eight employed *only* tests of significance as possible signs of causal connection. Such tests, I repeat, are *not* measures of power of association.

Another eight of these important studies applied no test of association. Only four of these research efforts computed measures of correlation.

Controlling for legally relevant factors Deficiencies in tests of the labeling school's charge of judicial discrimination do not end here. Weak measures are but one defect of such research. Another defect is poor control for legally relevant factors in the interpretation of correlations. This defect marks much research concerning the treatment of juveniles and the differential arrest and sentencing of members of ethnic groups.

A fair test of the allegation that the law responds to people on the basis of their social categories rather than their deeds requires that outcomes—arrest, conviction, sentence—be assessed against *all* legally relevant considerations. This is seldom done. This requirement is neglected because of the inadequacy of the information with which researchers work, because of the methodological innocence of some investigators, and because of the expense involved in conducting an adequate *longitudinal* study of offenders' behavior. In addition to these sources of neglect in research, the underdog philosophy of the interactional school motivates researchers to look at law, rather than at actors, as a cause of crime. There is a tendency, then, to ignore the many factors in offenders' histories—other than the crime itself—designed by law to affect societal response.

Judicial response in Western countries is ideally to be individualized, to be tailored to the individual offender. Such tailoring can occur only if there is judicial discretion. Discretion, in turn, is to be guided by legal objectives. The charge of labeling theorists is that discretion, rather than being so guided, is more strongly influenced by legally irrelevant stereotypes of rule breakers.

An illustration from journalism   The flavor of this charge is illustrated in the journalistic treatment recently given George Jackson, a black convict made famous as one of the "Soledad Seven," whose imprisonment was alleged to be "political."

Journalists seek sensation, and they repeat one another. What goes out "on the wires" often goes unchecked once a reporter has put a story in print or on the air (Altheide, 1976; E. J. Epstein, 1973, 1976; Roshco, 1976). Thus a uniform tale about Jackson's sentence was presented to readers and viewers. *Time, Newsweek*, the *New York Review of Books*, and other influential journals repeated the part-truth that Jackson was sentenced to prison for "marginal participation" in the armed robbery of a Los Angeles gas station that yielded $70 (Carney, 1974). The implication was that of injustice—heavy sentence for minor crime.

However, what was omitted from journalists' accounts was Jackson's history of crime. The particular sentence referred to as an injustice was *not* meted out "merely" for a $70 robbery. Jackson's sentence was based on a criminal record—repeated, intensive, and serious—that went back to his fourteenth year, when he unsuccessfully burgled a motorcycle shop.

What Is Required   Such partial reporting is unfortunately not limited to journalists. Social scientists also suffer the liability of ignoring all the legal considerations affecting decisions. This neglect arises from the difficulties of doing research on large numbers of offenders while yet attending to the host of legally relevant variables which may affect decisions and which are *intended* to influence discretion.

For example, in studying the possible impact of race upon the exercise of judicial discretion in sentencing for the crime of forcible rape, Wolfgang and Riedel (1973) considered this roster of variables of varying legal relevance:

1 Offender characteristics
    a Age
    b Marital status
    c Prior criminal record
    d Previous imprisonment
    e Employment status
2 Victim characteristics
    a Age
    b Marital status
    c Dependent children

      d Prior criminal record
      e Reputation for chastity
  3 Nature of relations between victim and offender
      a Offender known to victim
      b Prior sexual relations
  4 Circumstances of offense
      a Contemporaneous offense
      b Type of entry—authorized or unauthorized
      c Location of offense—indoors or outdoors
      d Display of a weapon
      e Carrying a weapon
      f Amount of injury to victim
      g Threatened victim
      h Degree of force employed
      i Victim made pregnant by offense
      j One or more offenders
      k Date of offense
  5 Circumstances of the trial
      a Plea
      b Defense of insanity
      c Appointed or retained counsel
      d Length of trial
      e Defense of consent
      f Whether defendant testified

Controls in Practice   Controls are the burdens of adequate research. It is clear that offenders' histories, the number of charges laid along with the instant offense, and the characteristics of the crime of notice must be among the factors controlled in examining relations between the social status of accused persons and their treatment under the law. However, even these important legal considerations are slighted in much research on the effect of social characteristics upon societal response to crime. Hagan's study (1974b) of American research on sentencing is instructive on this issue also.

Four of the 20 major studies of sentencing that Hagan assessed applied no controls for legally relevant variables. Nine of these investigations considered only type of offense in measuring the association between social status and outcome. Seven of these studies controlled for type of offense and prior record, while four of these seven also included counts of number of charges associated with the instant offense.

Even those studies that instituted some controls for legally relevant variables did so in a less than comprehensive manner. Information was lost in handling the data. For example, "prior record" is treated in some of the studies as "some or none." Such a dichotomy loses the tally of *number* of prior convictions and the *weighted gravity* of each (Hagan, 1974b, p. 368).

Findings on Sentencing in the United States   Despite the weak measures of association employed by much research on sentencing differentials, and bearing in mind the loose control of the many legally relevant variables that may have affected decisions, Hagan (1974b) summarizes the more prominent studies as showing the following relations between sentence and race, socio-economic status, age, and sex:

    a   *Race*: Evidence of differential sentencing was found in inter-racial *capital cases* in the southern United States. In samples of *non-capital cases*, however, when offense type was held constant among offenders with *no* prior record, the relationship between race and disposition was diminished below statistical significance. Holding offense type constant, among offenders with "some" previous convictions, a modest, statistically significant relationship between race and disposition was sustained in two of three studies. The need for stricter control over the *number* of previous convictions was indicated.

    b   *Socio-economic status*: With social class as the relevant variable, some evidence of differential sentencing was again found in *capital cases* in a non-southern state. . . . In a sample of *non-capital cases*, however, the relationship between class and disposition was . . . reduced below statistical significance, by holding constant the effects of offense type and prior record.

    c   *Age and sex*: In *capital and non-capital* cases alike, initial relationships between both age and sex, and judicial disposition, were reduced below statistical significance by the introduction of controls for legally relevant factors [p. 378].

These conclusions are qualified by the facts that (1) capital cases constitute a small proportion of all criminal cases, (2) some of the studies include cases going back to the turn of the century, and (3) the studies under review included both cases tried before juries and cases tried before judges alone.

    With all the deficiencies of such important research at hand, Hagan (1974b) concludes:

While there may be evidence of differential sentencing, knowledge of extra-legal offender characteristics contributes relatively little to our ability to predict judicial dispositions. Only in rare instances did knowledge of extra-legal attributes of the offender increase our accuracy in predicting judicial disposition by more than five percent [p. 379].

The labeling hypothesis, in its strong version, again is not confirmed.

Testing Justice for Juveniles   Since it is in the treatment of juveniles that due process may be least protected, Meade's test (1973) for status bias in judicial disposition of young people is important. Meade analyzed factors affecting juvenile-court decisions in 500 cases heard in a metropolitan district in the Southeastern United States during the three years from 1968 through 1970. He found no evidence of extralegal bias on the part of court personnel. Neither race nor socioeconomic status played a role, independent of offense, in determining decisions.

    When Meade looked at the correlates of *seriousness of first offense*, he found sex, race, and family structure to be consistently related to the gravity of juvenile crime. Males, blacks, and young people from "disrupted" families were disproportionately among those charged with serious first offenses. These factors remained predictive of the gravity of first charge when other variables, such as socioeconomic status, were held constant.

This study illustrates a point to be repeated (page 298), namely, that status and deeds may be correlated, as race and serious offenses are associated in Meade's data. With such a correlation, it is easy, but illogical, to jump to the conclusion that it is the label rather than the deed that determines judicial response.

A California Test Additional findings on the determinants of sentencing come from research in California. Investigators there used what they call "offender-based transaction statistics" (OBTS), a record of how each person, originally charged with a felony, proceeds through the criminal justice system. Persons arrested for indictable offenses in 12 counties from 1969 through 1971—32,694 people—constituted the sample (C. E. Pope, 1975b).

Seven possible determinants of sentence were examined, some of legal significance and some of possibly extralegal importance: sex, age, race, prior record, criminal status, original charge, and rural or urban venue.

Prior record is an index that attempts to weigh the *number* of previous crimes with their *gravity*. It constitutes a "crude seriousness index measuring the extent and nature of an offender's exposure to the criminal justice system" (C. E. Pope, 1975c, p. 12).

Criminal status refers to whether, at the time of arrest, a person was under some type of legal supervision, like probation or parole. Prior record and criminal status are closely related, of course; persons under supervision must have had a previous conviction, although the converse is not true. The felony for which a person was arrested was classified as "violent, property, drug, and 'other' offenses" (p. 13).

Offenders were then followed through criminal justice channels. A large proportion of those arrested for felonies had their charges reduced and were prosecuted for misdemeanors in lower courts. Sentence outcome there was classified as "probation, jail, and other." Where combinations of such sentences were imposed, the more severe disposition was recorded.

Arrested persons prosecuted for felonies were tried in higher courts, where sentence could include the three categories noted for lower courts plus the possibility of a prison sentence. Length of sentence, whether in jail or on probation, was also counted.

Relationships between judicial reaction and such possibly extralegal factors as age, sex, race, and rural or urban venue were examined, controlling, when possible, for three legal factors simultaneously: prior record, criminal status, and original charge. These controls could not always be applied because of the reduction in the number of cases such controls imposed. When only one legal factor could be controlled, it was *prior record* because ". . . this variable was consistently found to be most determinant of outcome. That is, those individuals with serious prior records were likely to receive the most severe dispositions, irrespective of criminal status and charge at arrest" (C. E. Pope, 1975c, p. 16).

Qualifications   Relations between these many variables were examined by tabular analysis, a procedure in which much information is lost. In such analysis, many of the variables are "collapsed," that is, grouped into broader categories. Thus a special study of judicial processing of assault and burglary offenders collapsed prior record into "yes" and "no" bunches and age into "under 30" and "30 and over" (C. E. Pope, 1975a, p. 16).

Looking at offender characteristics in such gross categories can be justified if this test of the labeling hypothesis is regarded as exploratory. It can be used, then, to ascertain whether injustice is sufficiently apparent to warrant more refined analysis.

Another qualification of this test is that it does not include the possible impact of socioeconomic status, one of the extralegal conditions claimed by interactional theorists to bias justice.

With these qualifications in mind, major results can be summarized:

   1   In both lower and higher courts, females were likely to receive milder sentences than males.
   This tendency is stronger in urban than in rural areas. However, the sex differential is *not* found in higher courts when defendants' criminal histories are considered.
   2   Age made a difference in sentencing in higher courts, but not in lower ones. In superior courts, younger offenders received lighter sentences and, in particular, were spared prison.
   3   Blacks received heavier penalties than whites in rural courts, but not in urban ones. This rural-urban racial difference was found in both lower and higher courts.
   4   When sentences were analyzed for specific categories of crime, assault and burglary, it was found that males received more severe sentences than females and, in particular, that they were more frequently incarcerated.
   5   Sentences for assault and burglary were associated most strongly with legal considerations: prior record and criminal status at time of charge. Racial differences in sentence for assault and burglary proved negligible in both rural and urban areas at both court levels. An exception is the greater likelihood of black persons in comparison with white persons to be incarcerated by lower courts in urban areas when the offender was under criminal commitment at the time of arrest for assault [C. E. Pope, 1975a, pp. 28–29].

These provisional results demonstrate the greater impact of legal considerations than of possible extralegal biases in determining sentence. They thus cast doubt on the strong charge that labels determine judicial response more than deeds do.

Sexism in Justice   The most notable fact that might lend support to the labeling hypothesis is sexual differentials in sentencing. However, even this fact, qualified as it is, requires interpretation. The interpretation will vary depending on which sex one thinks is the underdog in the judicial arena and on whether the more lenient treatment of women is regarded as favoritism or condescension.

The leniency in sentencing of women noted in this California study should not be confused with lenience in response to juvenile offenders, particularly those "treated" for so-called "status offenses."[2] Although research on this matter has not controlled well for all relevant factors, there is reason to believe that juvenile courts may assume a more "protective" role in response to wayward women. As we now know (see pages 47–48), "protection" is often against the wishes of the protected and regularly results in *longer* detention than "mere" restraint (Kratcoski, 1974; Velimesis, 1975).

Feminist writers regard "chivalry," of course, as a "sexist" bias (Anderson, 1976). This is to say that any differential response to persons before the bar by reason of their sex in unjust. As with all debates about the determination of wrongs, crimes, and justice, this is more a matter of moral definition than of facts of life.

A Midwestern Test   Burke and Turk (1975) applied a more sensitive test of determinants of judicial disposition. These investigators are well aware of the difficulties of disentangling the many variables that affect judicial decision. They are particularly aware that the factors usually measured as determinants of judicial decision are probably interacting. There is, as it were, a "resonance" among such variables as age, sex, race, socioeconomic status, prior record, and instant offense.

With this recognition, Burke and Turk employed a procedure, a "log-linear analysis," which allows an estimate of the *net* effect of each variable upon disposition and which permits construction of several models of possible interactions between the test factors. They applied this procedure to a 20 percent sample of males arrested in Indianapolis in 1964 and tested for interactions between age, race, occupational status, prior incarceration (which, incidentally, is not the same as prior record), and the most serious charge in the current arrest.

For present purposes, the most interesting finding of this study is confirmation of the *complex interactions* between the many factors correlated with judicial decision. A straight-line description, calling one factor "cause" and another "effect," is not accurate. The sentencing process is like other important decisions we make in everyday life; these decisions are better conceived as produced in a causal web than in a single-linked causal chain.

When specific allegations of the labeling hypothesis are tested by these data, they again fail to gain strong support. Summary conclusions are the following:

[2]I have put the term "status offenses" in quotation marks because there is evidence that status offenders are *also* violators of the criminal law (C. W. Thomas, n.d.). In other words, the category of "status offender" may not be a pure one.

1   The lower the offender's social status, the more severe the disposition. However, this relationship disappears when offense is considered. It is behavior, rather than status, that accounts for judicial decision.

2   The relationship between occupational status and judicial decision is complicated by the fact that there is also an association between social position and the probability of prior imprisonment. And prior incarceration is itself a factor affecting judicial decision, even when the present offense is held constant. This complication is compounded, in turn, by the relationship between race and occupation.

3   "When type of offense is controlled . . . race has no independent effect upon case disposition" (Burke and Turk, 1975, p. 328). Interpretation of the null effect of race upon sentence is complicated by interactions between race, occupational status, age, and prior incarceration. The interactions are difficult to interpret, but they provide no confirmation of the labeling hypothesis. Burke and Turk conclude:

> Our . . . analysis has done little more than to point up the difficulties of determining, much less explaining, the extent and nature of discrimination against the socially disadvantaged in postarrest proceedings. Nonetheless, even this limited exploration demonstrates that assertions of such bias in the legal system require better evidence than has so far been offered in their support [1975, pp. 328–329].

A Western Test   Possible confirmation of labeling theorists' charge of ethnic discrimination in sentencing is provided by Hall and Simkus (1975). These investigators attempted to ascertain determinants of judicial decisions in Montana, where native Indians constitute about one-fourth of the state's prison population but only about 3 percent of the total population. This disproportion is even more startling when one considers that breaches of state criminal laws committed on six of the seven reservations do not come under the jurisdiction of state courts.[3] All reservations are subject to federal criminal laws, however.

Hall and Simkus examined the correlates of dispositions of all offenders under probationary types of sentence from July 1966 to March 1972. Controls were instituted for type of offense, number of prior felonies, juvenile record, and the usual demographic variables. With such controls, ethnicity continued to make a difference, although a slight one, in the kind of sentence imposed, with Indians, in general, receiving more severe dispositions. However, "the proportion of variance explained" by ethnicity of offender is small (p. 215). "The probability of a native American offender [receiving] a deferred sentence was .08 less than the probability of a similar white offender [receiving] this type of sentence" (p. 214).

---

[3]Indian reservations in the United States can elect to have concurrent jurisdiction of criminal law with the state in which they are located. If a reservation does not elect for concurrent jurisdiction, it remains sovereign within treaty limitations but subject to federal criminal law. In Montana, one of the seven reservations chose concurrent jurisdiction.

Hall and Simkus acknowledge the difficulties of interpreting this remaining ethnic differential. It is an interpretation set against such background facts as these:

1   "Native American offenders were more likely to have been adjudicated delinquent . . . more likely to have been committed to a juvenile institution . . . and more likely to have had a record of prior felony convictions. In addition, the native American minority were lower in regard to . . . education, occupation, and employment status. Finally, more of the native American offenders were women" (pp. 208–209).

2   Among the most serious offenders, the ethnic differential in sentencing is reversed. White persons who had been adjudicated delinquent and committed to a juvenile institution, who had two or more prior felony convictions, and who were between 30 and 39 years old were more likely to be severely sentenced than their counterparts in the Indian sample.

From these data, it is impossible to isolate a prejudicial factor operating independently of legal considerations in sentencing. A more detailed analysis of judicial process is provided by research done in Canada.

A Canadian Test   John Hagan (1974a) conducted his own investigation of the exercise of criminal justice in a Canadian province recently, and wrongly, alleged to be among the most punitive jurisdictions in the Western world (Matthews, 1972; Swanton, 1973).

Hagan counted outcomes of the administration of the criminal law at three stages of the judicial process: (1) charging in the Crown Prosecutor's Office in Edmonton, Alberta; (2) presentence report preparation in offices of the Adult Probation Department; and (3) sentencing. His tallies were in test of the allegation of labeling theorists that people of lower socioeconomic status, native Indians, and Métis (those of mixed blood) receive differential treatment not justified by the nature of their offenses.

The findings of this research again run contrary to the hypothesis of the societal-reaction school. "When legal variables are held constant," Hagan reports, "differences in sentences are minimal. Legal variables—prior convictions and the number and types of charges—are found to be salient at all three stages of the sentencing process" (p. v).

The only discrepancies found in legal treatment of offenders by their ethnicity were (1) a greater tendency of rural than urban probation officers to treat Indians severely and (2) a greater tendency of Métis and Indians to serve jail sentences instead of paying a fine.

Furthermore, this ethnic differential in serving jail sentences is stronger for minor violations—the summary offenses—than for the major, indictable crimes. Interpretation of this difference notes that Indians and Métis are disproportionately arrested for alcohol-related infractions of the law. When Indian and Métis offenders are compared with white inmates on a prison classification as "temperate" or "intemperate" users of alcoholic beverages, two times as many Indians and Métis as whites are diagnosed as having drinking difficulties—an unfortunate confirmation of a stereotype.

In looking at the amount of fine decreed in lieu of incarceration, and controlling for race and gravity of offense, Hagan found no difference in this levy among ethnic groups.

Interpretation of the greater tendency of Indians and Métis to be jailed instead of paying fines rests on the fact that payment of a fine is an *option*. It is not known, however, whether native persons choose jail rather than payment of a fine or whether they are less able to pay.

Correlated labels and deeds   The case of societal response to Canadian Indians and Métis illustrates another difficulty in assessing justice. The difficulty occurs when labels and deeds are themselves associated, as they are in public stereotypes and official records of drinking among Indians. In such cases, researchers are hard put to disentangle the causes of differential sentencing.

To complicate matters, the way in which drunkenness is exhibited may differ among ethnic groups and hence make them differentially liable to arrest. Hagan (1977a) puts it this way:

> Indians more frequently than whites drink and recover in public. There are differences in access to, and preferences for, privacy in drinking. Given the resulting group-linked differences in behavior, equal treatment of those who violate public drinking norms cannot produce an equality of legal outcomes [p. 609].

A remedy for this particular differential in legal effects is to use detoxification centers rather than jails in response to alcohol-abusers.

In summary, the general conclusion to be drawn from this extensive Canadian study, as from American research, contradicts the interactionist's allegation that "labels" determine societal response more than crimes do.

4   Does a "Bad Name" Cause Bad Action?

The labeling hypothesis has called attention to the possibility that official reactions to some kinds of disapproved behavior may confirm actors in their deviant ways. This is probably the most valuable contribution of the perspective.

It is suggested that some "sick behaviors" improve more rapidly when they are untreated and that some cures are worse than the diseases they treat. The interactionist school emphasizes how minor events in the stream of life may become major events as a result of official reaction. The careers of some different kinds of people are made even more different by the fact that some portion of their lives must be spent dodging the consequences of official response to their deviation. The model here is that of the marijuana user,[4] whose life may be changed by the criminalization of this preference.

---

[4] The labeling theorist's point can be made by substituting for the criminalization of marijuana the criminalization of tobacco or alcohol, for example, which many people habitually use.

Labeling theory gains credence as it develops biographies showing that being "officially handled" increases the chances of future official attention. There is reason to assume that this risk is increased by the stigma associated with a criminal label and the consequent reduction in lawful opportunities (R. D. Schwartz and Skolnick, 1962). *We do not know, however, how much of repeated offense is so caused.*

What Is Required   The answer to the question about the causal power of stigma depends on how the question is phrased. There is not much point in asking whether official handling has *some* effect on crime because such a question is vague, and its answer conceded.

A more interesting way of putting the question is to ask, as labeling theorists do, whether stigma may not be one link in a causal chain that proceeds from some initial offense through labeling to discriminatory reaction to changed self-concept to differential association with other stigmatized persons to more crime than the actor would have exhibited if he or she had not been so handled.

There has been no test of this alleged linkage. In particular, there has been no study that would allow assignment of a *relative causal force* to official handling as crime-producing. We are left with anecdotes—selective biographies—and with the assumption that stigma is criminogenic. Lacking again a crucial test of the interactionist hypothesis, we revert to studies that are suggestive, but not conclusive.

Provisional Tests   Attempts have been made to ascertain whether similar classes of offenders behave differently if they are treated differently. As is true of studies of the impact of nonlegal variables on societal reaction, everything depends on the quality of controls employed to assure us that classes of offender are actually homogeneous and that it is only difference in societal response that affects their careers.

This shaky assumption underlies studies that have compared differences in later criminality among allegedly similar offenders granted probation, placed on parole, and released from prison after full time had been served. Follow-up studies of these differences disagree—some find probationers doing better than those sentenced to prison, and some find no differences (Babst and Mannering, 1965; Beattie and Bridges, 1970; Levin, 1971; L. T. Wilkins, 1969). Such studies do not answer our question, however, since probationers are *selected* because they are considered to be better risks. The groups being compared are not similar in all relevant respects.

Tittle (1975) tried to estimate the criminogenic effects of stigma through a survey of 16 longitudinal studies reporting "failure rates" among released inmates. "Failure rates" are themselves a mixed bag since they include technical violations of parole as well as convictions for new crimes. However, Tittle makes the point that, if the labeling hypothesis is correct in saying that societal reaction creates crime, then the recidivism rate of stigmatized offenders ought to be considerably greater than chance, assumed to be 50-50. His summary shows failure rates ranging "from 24 percent to 68 percent with the average being 44 percent, a figure that is inflated because a large percentage were returned for technical parole violations in several of the studies" (p. 174).

The imperfect data on recidivism rates do *not* support the interactionist hypothesis.

SUMMARY

The major proposals of the interactionist school are not well grounded in fact. This does not mean that the labeling orientation is without value. The value is, as promised, more political than scientific and, like everything of worth, carries a price.

Value of the Labeling Perspective

The advantage of assuming the labeling perspective lies where most recent' advocates place it—in alerting us to the possibility that official reaction may do more harm than good.

Acceptance of this possibility is entirely within the nineteenth-century liberal tradition of getting governments out of our lives (see pages 8–10). We would rather have the state do less *to* us, although we are unclear about what it should do *for* us. The challenge of the societal-reaction school intends to be liberating, and, given our politics, it is valuable on this score.

Advocates of interactionist theory recommend particular policies, and they assume that their policies follow directly from their assumptions. However, it is possible to agree with many of this school's prescriptions without basing policy on its dubious assumptions.

For example, proponents of labeling theory want to decriminalize many offenses, particularly those "without victims." They would have more legal provision for erasing criminal stigmata—for expunging a criminal record—and for protecting the privacy of personal files. They favor experiments with diversionary programs, particularly for young people, and "radical nonintervention." "Leave the kids alone wherever possible," Schur (1973) advocates.

There is a strong concern with safeguards in protection of individual liberty against arbitrary power. As a consequence, there is opposition to the substitution of indeterminate "treatment" programs for legally circumscribed punishment. There is also a strong tendency to remove the "protective" functions of delinquency laws—those which define "status offenses"—and to return young people to full rights under law, to legal defenses against discretionary "treatment." In short, defense of due process, even for young people, moves advocates of the interactionist theory away from the idea that offenders must be ignorant or "sick" and toward the idea that they are rational persons. "This means that labelling analysts prefer to opt for a conservative 'crime-responsibility-punishment' framework, because it is less likely to infringe on individual liberties and more likely to maintain a sense of justice" (Ericson, 1975, p. 133).

It has been noted earlier (pages 9–13) that it is easier to speak generally of decriminalizing different tastes than it is to be consistent about our advocacy. It is also easier to recommend leaving people alone "wherever possible" than it is to agree on the boundaries of "wherever possible." Nevertheless, we can accept the liberating prescriptions of the labeling perspective without subscribing to its unproved assumptions. The reasons for doubting its assumptions, while approving its prescriptions, lie in the disadvantages of this orientation.

Liabilities of the Labeling Perspective

The societal-reaction school has been criticized for (1) ignoring the differences in behavior described by labels. The labeling schema draws attention from deeds to the public definitions of those deeds. Such diversion means that (2) labeling theory does not increase, and may well decrease, our ability to predict individual behavior. Its low predictive power is a result not only of its neglect of individual differences but also of the fact that (3) it contains a defective model of causation. This in turn means that (4) its relevance to social policy is lessened. Each of these points will be amplified.

1   Labeling Theory Does Not Explain the Behaviors That Lead to the Application of Labels   The labeling theorists argue as if popular and legal categories were devoid of content, as if they were never "well earned." The labeling explanation pays little or no attention to the fact that people do *not* behave similarly. It slights the possibility that a label may *correctly* identify consistent differences in conduct, and it pays little attention to the reasons why "society" continues to apply a label once it has been used.

Labeling theory denies, therefore, the causal importance and explanatory value of personality variables. In fact, labeling theorists regard as futile the search for personality differences that might distinguish categories of more or less criminal persons. The labeling hypothesis prefers a political interpretation to such a psychological one. It prefers to believe that deviants are minorities lacking power to challenge the rules by which a majority has labeled them. The theory denies, then, that a label may be properly applied to describe personality differences which may underlie real behavioral differences. This denial has unfortunate consequences for the prediction of individual behavior.

It has unfortunate consequences, too, for the development of public policy. The prescription that follows from the labeling hypothesis is to change the attitudes of majorities toward misbehaving minorities. In reply, majorities tell us that they are not yet convinced that a more compassionate attitude toward robbers or burglars will change these offenders' behavior and reduce the pain they cause.

2   When Applied to the Understanding of Individual Behavior, the Labeling Hypothesis Has Low Predictive Power   The low predictive power of labeling theory results from its denial of personality differences. The interactional bias of the labeling theorist encourages such optimistic but risky beliefs as these:

He will be honest if I trust him.
She will be reasonable if you are.
He will be pacific if we are.

Her psychosis is not "in her," but "in her situation." When the mirrors in which she sees herself are changed, she will change.

On the contrary, there *are* personality differences that are reliably associated with behavioral differences and that are remarkably persistent. These persistent ways of feeling and acting are not readily changeable with changes in the labels attached to them. Regardless of what we have been called, *most of us continue to be what we have been a long time becoming.*

The research literature on this subject is vast. It may be sampled in the works of Honzik (1966), Kelly (1963), Mischel (1969), Robins and O'Neal (1958), Roff (1961), Schaefer and Bayley (1960), A. Thomas et al. (1970), Witkin (1965), and Zax et al. (1968). The point is made in the autobiography of the playwright S. N. Behrman (1972), who, after years of failure and impoverished struggle, wrote a play that was a hit. Behrman comments: "With the production of a successful play . . . you acquire overnight a new identity—a public label. But this label is pasted on you. It doesn't obliterate what you are and have always been—doesn't erase the stigmata of temperament" (p. 37).

The statement that there are persistent temperamental and cognitive differences underlying our behaviors can be qualified by adding that such personality variables have more of an impact upon behavior as circumstances are equalized. Nevertheless, most of us can tell the difference between behavior—our own and others'—that is only situationally reactive and behavior that is characteristic. All of us operate, implicitly or explicitly, with the idea of *character*—the idea that there *are* enduring personal predispositions relevant to moral behavior. This means that, unless there are tremendous changes in environments, people are likely to continue to behave as they have behaved. Against the optimistic recommendations of the interactionist, it seems more sensible to believe that:

Embezzlers may need to be arrested, and stigmatized, before they "turn honest."
Being reasonable with a fanatic is futile.
A soft answer turns away the wrath of some people, but not of others, and there is no point in pleading for your life with a Charles Manson.
The cures of psychoses are exceptional. Most people who are "peculiar" are not disordered in all ways, all the time. Misbehavior may be episodic; but ordinarily, safety lies in the assumption of behavioral continuity.

When calling a name helps   Every way of knowing the world categorizes. There is no escape from classification, although there is dispute about whose categories are more useful.

As professional thinkers we are helped by acknowledging that we shall continue to "define" and that to define means to draw boundaries around events. We are also aware that these boundaries may be incorrectly set for predictive purposes and that they may not be fixed. We are careful, then, with words that establish rigid frontiers. We protect ourselves against "semantic constipation," the obstructive belief that words have some magical and immovable connection to the things they describe. Our defense against this illness includes a skepticism about verbs like "is" that fix people in categories: "He *is* a criminal." "She *is* a lesbian." The defects of such "is-ness" are that (1) it infers what we *are* from what we *do*, which is all that can be observed (Sagarin, 1976), (2) it ignores *degrees* of activity, and (3) it produces an inflexible categorization congenial to dogmatism.

A second defense against becoming a believer in the "magic" of words is to prefer adjectives and verbs to nouns. Nouns are substantial; they drop us into categories which fit us more or less well, but from which it is difficult to escape. Adjectives and verbs, on the other hand, connote degree and possible variations in quality. It is more sensible, then, to say "She tends to steal" than "She is a thief" or to say "He murdered his wife" rather than "He is a murderer."

These cautions against fixed classification do *not* save us, however, from the need to categorize. They only make us chary of predictively misleading categories. Even when we substitute more careful verbs and adjectives for the more lumpish nouns, we are classifying. These verbal classes function as a psychological shorthand. They provide abbreviated descriptions of what a person has been doing, of what goes along with that doing, and of what we can reasonably expect. More accurately, a label may tell us what *not* to expect.

The words with which we describe one another *diagnose*. And each diagnosis carries with it a *prognosis*. The names we call one another may therefore do us good as well as harm. Everything hinges on the validity of the diagnosis, and diagnosis is always less than certain.

The point being made is that, while there are risks in classification, the risks are always taken. They cannot be avoided. The risks are taken by omission or commission, by denying a description or by accepting it. We may appreciate one another with adjectives and verbs rather than with nouns, but the adjectives and verbs are still prophetic categories. They are forecasting tools—some better, some worse. But the fact that they are predictive instruments means that there are times when learning the name that describes what we, or others, have been doing yields an economy, a relief, and a forecasting advantage. The predictions that mark our daily doings rest on "labels."

3 The Model of Causation Implicit in the Labeling Hypothesis Is Questionable Every explanation of human behavior makes assumptions about its causes. The labeling theory locates the causes of adult behavior in an unusual place—in the people who respond to it. It shifts the "responsibility" for my action from me to you. It stresses how much of what I do is a result of what you have done to me, and for me. My "self," it is said, is reflected to me by the social mirrors available to me. My "self" is the presumed agent of my actions, but my "self" is itself largely constructed by the responses of "significant others" to my initial efforts.

This is a shorthand statement of the hypothesis of "socialization." In its general formulation, there is no quarrel with such a hypothesis. All theories that would explain human behavior, including popular theories, assume that our behavior has been shaped by the actions of others. The sociopsychological hypotheses of the "control" variety pay particular attention to the "how" of this socialization process.

It is not denied, then, that how people respond to us when we misbehave may affect our subsequent conduct. The lively questions are, however, at what periods of our development, and to what degree, others mould us. What is at issue is *how much* of the adult behavior to be explained varies with the response of others to it.

It is our ignorance that permits the continuing quarrel, for *no one knows which kinds of behaviors, in which kinds of personalities, at which "stage" of life, are affected how much, by which kinds of response, from which others, in which situations.*

Some generalization about this is part of our popular wisdom, but much of that is truistic. We expect more than truisms from criminological theories.

The valuable contributions of the labeling hypothesis have tended to obscure its deficiencies. It is one thing to study the way in which a defining process affects our response to the behavior of others. It is another matter to study the causes of the events we are defining. Studying how we respond to deviant others may suggest to us a more economical mode of reacting. This suggestion should not be confused, however, with information about the causes of the crimes that concern us.

Such confusion is created when advocates of labeling theory tell us, for example, that "*social groups create deviance by making the rules whose infraction constitutes deviance*, and by applying those rules to particular people and labeling them as outsiders" (Becker, 1963, p. 9).

Some readers translate statements like this as saying that "social groups create crime by making the laws whose infraction constitutes crime." This translation is slippery; it slides between the truth that social groups create the definition of "crime" and the falsehood that the injuries condemned by these definitions would disappear (or would not have been produced) if the definition had not been formulated.

To the lay person, it sounds as though the labeling theorist believed that people would not wish to defend themselves against burglary or murder if they had not learned a rule defining those acts as crimes. It sounds, also, as though the interactionist believed that there would be less "burglary" if we did not use that term. The nonprofessional consumer of criminological explanations recognizes this for the semantic trick that it is—the trick of saying, "If a crime is a breach of a rule, you won't have the crime if you don't have the rule." The ordinary reaction to this semantic sleight of hand is to say, "A mugging by any other name hurts just as much."

Applied to "real life," the labeling hypothesis functions as another of the "power of positive thinking" philosophies: "If disease is an error of thought, positive thinking will cure it." "If crime resides in our definitions of deviance, redefining it will change it."

Our question has to do with the location of causation. When the causation implied by the labeling hypothesis is tested, it fails. The causes specified by this schema do not account for the production of the behaviors that disturb us. "Mental hospitals" do not cause "mental illness" (Gove, 1970), nor do the agencies of social control, or the labels they apply, account for crime (Ward, 1971).

The assumption of labeling theory is that those who become "criminal" are mostly those who, while behaving much like everyone else, just happened to get tagged, or that those labeled "criminals" were more liable to the tagging because they fit some public's prejudiced stereotype of the criminal. Contrary to these assumptions, however, studies of the operation of the system of justice show that it works like a sieve: as we have seen, the people who end up caught in the sieve tend to be the more serious and persistent lawbreakers (D. J. Black and Reiss, 1970; Bordua, 1967; Terry, 1967).

In summary, the labeling theorist does not think about causes and effects, about antecedents and consequents; he prefers to think about interactions. This preference does not eliminate the idea of causation; it only obscures it by shifting the locus of causes from actors to their judges. This shift has some moral and political value in the fight between outsiders and insiders. It justifies a challenge of the police and the courts, or any other mechanism of social control, that would condemn the conduct of minorities. When the labeling hypothesis is applied to the explanation of the serious crimes, however, its model of causation reduces its value for public policy.

4 On the Level of Social Concerns, the Labeling Hypothesis Does Not Answer the Perennial Questions about Crime We are reminded that explanatory theories are only as good as the questions they answer. The answers provided by the labeling theorists are not addressed to the questions about crime that are asked by most people. These questions are, again, "What causes crime?" "What accounts for increases or decreases in crime rates?" "How can crime be reduced?"

To these questions, the labeling theorists give no good reply. The policy recommendation of the labeling hypothesis comes down to "Avoid unnecessary labelling" (Schur, 1971, p. 171). This may be helpful in decriminalizing some activities. It is a recommendation useful in suggesting diversion of some misbehavior from official handling, and it is provocative in suggesting that we let people alone.

These policy prescriptions can be followed, it has been noted, without subscribing to the interactionist school. For beyond these prescriptions lies no explanation of crime that answers the main public questions. These questions are better answered for citizens[5] by social psychologists who give accounts that have received the unfortunate title of "control" theories because they emphasize ways in which behavior is channeled. Changing the label, however, would not change the substance of these formulations, which are taken up in the next chapter.

---

[5]Public opinion polls consistently show that the majority of citizens locate the causes of crime where control theory does (Erskine, 1974a, 1974b, 1975; *Newsweek*, 1971).

Chapter 16

Sociopsychological Explanations: Control Theory

Some crime, we have seen, is rational. There have always been "good reasons" for people to commit some of the serious offenses. It is to one person's advantage to take what the other person has—if this can be done without penalty. There is advantage, too, at times, in seeing the other person dead. The fact that killing and stealing have these rational justifications means that, for some people, some of the time, they *are* justified. It is this fact with which moralists have wrestled for centuries and from which ordinary people and philosophers have developed the tragic sense of life.

For centuries, too, there has been agreement that this tragic fact can be countered, to some degree, only by training the human organism *not* to do "what comes naturally"—*not* to take, grab, kick, bite, and walk over other people if they get in the way. When those who must live together lack this training, the only remaining defense is force. If we will not control ourselves "internally," out of conscience, we shall attempt to control one another "externally," through force. If we are not regulated by our "will," we shall be controlled against our will.

Pacific human association requires this moderation of appetite. This requirement contends constantly with self-interest and with the aspiration for freedom. A major issue in political philosophy is how to reconcile the need for social order with the struggle to be free. The best answers to this question recognize the seeming paradox that freedom requires order, which means that freedom in a social web does *not* include doing whatever one likes at the prompting of an impulse. Civil life is a controlled life. Civilization is bought at the cost of "repression," Sigmund Freud told us (1958). Civilization requires that not every desire be appeased or every feeling expressed. The prohibition of license is a price paid for civility. In exchange, civil life constitutes the condition of freedom and makes it possible for us to be creative and to be different while living among strangers.

The tradition in political thought that has produced this compromise between order and freedom has been carried into social psychology by investigators who acknowledge that "aggression is as original as sin" (Rieff, 1959, p. 274). These students, like the Church before them, see no great difficulty in explaining why people injure each other. Self-interest is "original." It is part of how we are. In response to how we are, law has evolved. Law is one of the many efforts to control "what comes naturally." Some anthropologists and some psychologists assume that the "crimes forbidden by law are crimes which many men have a natural propensity to commit" (Rieff, 1959, p. 225).

THE BASIC ASSUMPTION OF CONTROL THEORY

What needs to be explained, then, is not so much why we behave badly as how we can be induced to behave well. The sociopsychological accounts that try to answer this question are called "control theories." They start from the assumption that the higher organisms require training if they are to behave socially. The psychologists Margaret and Harry Harlow say that "one of the most important functions of social learning in primates—and perhaps in all mammals and many other classes of animals as well—is the development of social patterns that will restrain and check potentially asocial behavior. These positive, learned social patterns must be established *before* negative, unlearned patterns emerge" (1967, p. 47; italics added).

So too with Homo sapiens, a creature that is born only *potentially* human. If the potentiality is to be realized, if the infant is to develop into a recognizable human being, nurturing must take place. Without nurturing, the human animal grows up wild. It behaves violently. It destroys what it has not been trained to appreciate. It does not understand "right and wrong" except as greater and lesser might. As a consequence, what offends the conscience of socialized persons cannot offend the conscience of the unsocialized. There is nothing to offend.

To speak of the "originality" of theft and assault is not to deny that these kinds of behavior may also be learned, channeled by a culture, and justified by its philosophy. To say that the feral person *expresses* violence does not deny that the nurtured person may *learn* it. There *are* patterned urges toward larceny and aggression as well as unlearned sources of such self-interest. The subcultural and structural theories of criminogenesis attend to the patterning of these antisocial behaviors; the control theories attend to their expression in the absence of discipline.

There is general agreement among students of human behavior as to the validity of the basic assumption of control theory: that *social* behavior requires socialization. Ethnological, developmental, and experimental studies repeatedly demonstrate that human egoism is reduced, and balanced with altruism, only as the organism is reared by parents or their substitutes and as it identifies with them and the moral codes they represent (Ainesworth, 1967; Bowlby, 1969; Goldschmidt, 1959; Harlow et al., 1966; Spitz, 1965).

The central assumption of control theory is neither new nor novel. It says, with Alexander Pope (1731–1735), that "just as the twig is bent, the tree's inclined." Disagreement arises only in describing how human beings become socialized and in assigning weights to the various influences that mold us.

Emphases

Like other attempted explanations of crime, "control theory" is not a theory in the rigorous, scientific sense. It is, rather, a point of view with its own preferred locus of causation. Scholars of this school share some assumptions, which, we have noted (page 305, footnote 5), are also shared by the public at large:

1   That the human animal requires nurturing.

2   That differences in nurturing account for variations in attachment to others and commitment to an ordered way of living.

3   That attachment and commitment may be described as "internal controls," commonly called "conscience" and recognized in *guilt*, and "external controls," usually tested by the production of *shame*.[1]

4   That evidence from experimental studies, longitudinal research, comparative studies, and cross-cultural investigation tells us *how* attachment and commitment are developed. Conversely, such evidence describes the situations which loosen the moral bond with others and which, then, are crime-productive.

VARIETIES OF CONTROL THEORY

Sociologists have advanced these assumptions with a medley of propositions. Reckless (1967) and his associates call their ideas "containment theory." Hirschi (1969) speaks directly of "control theory," with emphases which differ somewhat from those of containment hypotheses but which, even so, overlap some of them.

Pyschologists have also contributed to control theory without giving their ideas this title. The British psychologists Eysenck (1964) and Trasler (1962),

---

[1]Psychologists, anthropologists, and some dictionaries distinguish between guilt and shame. Guilt is the anxiety occasioned by our having violated our tribe's codes. Shame is the embarrassment of having been caught in a violation of our tribe's code. The difference is that guilt may be elicited without others' knowing of our crime, while shame requires public identification.

Since guilt is privately generated, it may also be wrongly generated. That is, our offense may be imagined as well as real—a possibility that characterizes some maladjusted people called "neurotic." Shame, too, may be "wrongly" produced, depending on who is attempting the shaming.

Both emotions, guilt and shame, vary by degree, and both may function as powerful guides to conduct.

working independently of each other, have noted how training interacts with individually different constitutions to affect conduct. With less emphasis upon constitutional differences, psychologists in Canada and the United States, such as Bandura (1973) and Bandura and Walters (1959, 1963), have emphasized an aspect of training that they call "social learning" or "modeling."

These three families of ideas will be described as containment theory, Hirschi's propositions about attachment and commitment, and training hypotheses.

Containment Theory

Containment theory recognizes that not everyone in the same environment catches the same disease. There are differences in immunity. So, too, with criminality. Individuals are differentially immunized against the temptation to be criminal. Reckless and his colleagues conceive of immunity to criminality as a matter of control, of one's being "contained," or restrained, against the excitement of some crime and its conceivably rational benefits. The controls that "contain" a person are considered to be of two orders: "outer" and "inner."

Outer Containment, or Social Pressure   This source of restraint consists of social pressures to obey the norms of one's group. The pressures are exerted through training in roles, through affiliation with a community and a tradition, and hence through the development of a sense of "identity and belonging." The exercise of these external pressures may be seen in such relatively crime-free groups as the Hutterites of Alberta and Manitoba and the Mennonites of Pennsylvania and Ohio. The pressures to conform to community expectations constitute a defense against crime as long as the religious community remains segregated from the host society. The point is that there *are* community standards condemning antisocial conduct, and there *is* training in obedience to those standards.

Inner Containment, or Self-Control   No community can depend completely upon the constant control of individuals through social pressure. All socialization aims implicitly, if not explicitly, at the development of self-control. The agent of such control is commonly called "conscience." In Reckless's schema this inner control is the result of a moral training that produces five indicators of its presence: (1) a healthy self-concept, (2) goal-directedness, (3) a realistic level of aspiration, (4) the ability to tolerate frustration, and (5) an identification with lawful norms.

1 Self-concept   Reckless and his associates have conducted a number of studies that demonstrate the generally poorer "self-concept" of young boys who get into trouble with the law. Their measure of feeling about oneself is verbal—answers to questions—and their definitions of "good" and "bad" refer to being conventionally law-abiding. It seems, then, that "self-concept," as measured here, is much like "respect for the law." For this reason, some criminologists have criticized use of such an indicator of self-concept as redundant to the explanation of crime and delinquency (G. F. Jensen, 1973; Tangri and Schwartz, 1967).

Not all the containment theorists' items are so contaminated, however, and their verbal measure does discriminate among more and less delinquent young people. Reckless and Dinitz's questions (1967) are a mixture of items concerning one's associates and one's present and future difficulty with law and authority such as the following:[2]

    2   Will you probably go to jail sometime?

    3   If you found that a friend was leading you into trouble, would you continue to run around with him or her?

    6   Are grown-ups usually against you?

    8   Are you a big shot with your pals?

    13   Have most of your friends been in trouble with the law?

    14   Do you confide in your father?

    15   Do your parents punish you?

    16   Do you think you are quiet __   average __   active __?

The original justification for including items of such varied reference as a measure of one attribute, "self-concept," was the ability of such questions to discriminate between boys considered by their teachers to be "good" boys and those considered to be "bad." However, such items work outside the school as well. At an early age, boys from the *same* neighborhood and economic background show differences in how they feel about themselves, their families, their fate, and persons in positions of authority. The more delinquent boys are more likely to believe that they will break the law and go to jail and that their friends will too. They are more likely to believe that they will not finish school, that their families are "no good," and that teachers, clergymen, judges, and police officers are not worthy of respect (Dinitz et al., 1962; Rothstein, 1961).

These differences are interesting, and some of them are objective. That is, they do not depend on our believing what boys *say*. However, a difficulty with verbal reports as indicators of something "inside" one that causes conduct is, again, that we do not know how much independence, if any, the verbalization (nominated cause) has from its tested effect: more and less criminality.

There is evidence that people who "talk bad" about themselves also admit to more "bad acts" (H. B. Kaplan, 1976). People who "put themselves down" also confess to more delinquency. Now, we do not know whether these are two similar ways of *telling the truth* or two similar ways of *saying* the same thing or whether something *causal* is at work. If something causal is at work, we still do not know in which direction causation runs—from bad acts to bad feelings about oneself or from bad feelings to bad acts. And, of course, an additional possibility is the likely one that being good, doing good, feeling good, and saying good things about oneself are a package with a similar set of causes. Psychologists, such as O. H. Mowrer (1960, 1964), who believe that neurosis and sin are related, would agree that there is such a package.

---

[2]Item numbers indicate placement in the original measure.

In an attempt to clarify Reckless and Dinitz's notion of "self-concept," G. F. Jensen (1973) "purified" their scale and produced three dimensions of "inner containment": feelings of self-esteem, ability to control oneself, and acceptance of conventional morality. These measures, with their narrower focus, were administered to more than 4,000 students in junior and senior high schools in the San Francisco Bay area. Tabulated results from 1,001 black and 1,588 white males indicate that, when race, class, family, and peer-group situations are held constant, all three dimensions of feeling toward oneself make a difference. The association is not a strong one, but it is contributory. This is to say that, when one looks at young men from (1) similar socioeconomic conditions, (2) similar family situations, and (3) "similar categories in terms of number of friends picked up by the police" (G. F. Jensen, 1973, p. 470), there yet remains an element in "attitude toward oneself" that contributes to immunity or vulnerability to delinquency. An exact weight cannot be given this factor, but this variable is a vindicated aspect of the containment thesis.

2 Goal-directedness An element of "inner containment," according to Reckless, is orientation to goals. It is claimed that individuals who commit themselves to long-range, legitimate goals are thereby insulated against criminality. Critics see circularity here since a commitment to a legitimate career is, by definition, a defense against crime and therefore part of what theories of criminogenesis seek to explain. However, Reckless and his colleagues use signs of such commitment as *indicators* of self-control rather than as the causes of it.

3 Realistic objectives A related sign of effective inner control is the "realism" of a person's goals. As Durkheim does in his model of human beings, Reckless and his colleagues judge some goals of young people to be extravagant. Such unrealistic aspiration, such striving beyond one's means, indicates to Reckless the possibility of a "collapse" of inner containment.

4 Tolerance of frustration Living *is* frustrating. We call a grown person who has not yet accommodated to this fact a "baby." An indicator of the self-control that is expected of adults is tolerance of frustration, the ability to avoid the extremes of rage and despair when we do not get what we want when we want it. Some varieties of adult offender and the more committed juvenile delinquent exhibit *less* tolerance of frustration than their more lawful counterparts.

Being tolerant of frustration is, of course, related to having realistic goals and to *being oriented toward a future*. A person whose goals are out of reach is bound to be frustrated, and one who is easily frustrated is not apt to pursue long-range objectives. Conversely, when one has a dedication to some distant and achievable goal, present obstacles are *less* frustrating than they are to the person who lives for nothing but the present.

In support of Reckless's hypothesis on this point, there is evidence that urban delinquents are more hedonistic, impulsive, and impatient than nondelinquents. Time seems *longer* to them. That is, when you ask youngsters to "guess a minute"—to tell you when a minute has passed—the delinquent guesses *sooner*. This impatience is compounded by the delinquent's less rich fantasy life; it is recognized that fantasy is one of our mechanisms (an "inner resource") for "filling up time." Being impatient and being deficient in imaginative self-stimulation mean being easily bored. These attitudes toward time are related, in turn, to less realistic views of the past, present, and future. Differences in temperament and time perspective of this sort have been reported between offenders and their more lawful neighbors, juvenile and adult (Barndt and Johnson, 1955; Bixenstine and Buterbaugh, 1967; W. A. M. Black and Gregson, 1973; Davids et al., 1962; Landau, 1976; Mischel, 1961; Siegman, 1966a; K. B. Stein et al., 1968).

This sociopsychological evidence fits findings from studies of moral development. Research on the moral judgment of children and on the corre-lates of their judgments indicates that *concepts of time and concepts of morality develop together.* The evidence is abundant (Kohlberg, 1964; Kohlberg and Turiel, 1971; Schleifer, 1976; Schleifer and Douglas, 1973; Seltzer and Beller, 1969).

Our attitude toward time is part of our attitude toward ourselves, others, and our situations. Moral judgment develops along with ways in which we estimate time and use it. These attitudes, in turn, are connected to how we act, including how we act when frustrated. The package looks like this: Happy people, productive people, and morally principled people make more long-range commitments, are more punctual and efficient, and tend to *over*estimate the amount of time needed to do their work (Seltzer and Beller, 1969; Wessman and Ricks, 1966). There are good grounds for suggesting, as control theorists do, that frustration tolerance and time orientation build immunity against criminal proclivity.

5 Identification with lawfulness A fifth aspect of the "self" which, according to containment theory, immunizes a person against criminality is attitudinal. It is a set of beliefs in support of the law and its agents. The beliefs acknowledge the legitimacy of the criminal law and "identify" the actor with lawful standards of conduct. Again, there is abundant evidence that this feature of the "self," this attitude toward the law, does distinguish more lawful people from the more serious lawbreakers. The distinction is discernible *before* a criminal career is developed, although, as labeling theory argues, official handling of offenders in response to their crimes may confirm them in their hostility toward the law.

It is no surprise to learn that people who break the law dislike the law. A host of studies report that convicted offenders have more unfavorable concep-tions of the law, the court system, and the police than nonoffenders who live in the same environment. Toro-Calder and others (1968) found this to be true in Puerto Rico, and similar findings have been reported in Ohio, Ontario, Quebec, Rome, Athens, West Pakistan, and South Korea (Cho, 1967; Mylonas and Reckless, 1963; Toro-Calder et al., 1968).

In Summary Containment theory, like other explanations of crime, describes some true things. At the same time, it is quite general. It points to a set of interlocking conditions that move people toward or away from criminal careers.

For some critics, the theory is too broad to inform public policy and its concepts too vague for explanatory precision. For other critics, this generality is "good enough" to illuminate the roots of crime. Hirschi has attempted to clarify some of the propositions of control theory, and to test them, with cleaner measures of its concepts.

Hirschi on Attachment, Commitment, Involvement, and Belief

Hirschi (1969) conceives of the "controls" that allow us to live together pacifically as "attachment, commitment, involvement, and belief." According to Hirschi, these are separable, but interrelated, strands tying us to one another and defining our sense of obligation and duty.

Attachment refers to an individual's sensitivity to the opinion of others. It is measured as a feeling of obligation to others and of consideration of one's relations with others as guides to conduct. The person who lacks such attachment is called psychiatric names like "psychopath." The psychopath appears sane and can mouth a morality for which there is no feeling. The psychopath, we say, lacks conscience, which, in Hirschi's terms, is the same as saying that he or she lacks sympathy and empathy.

Commitment is expressed in the investment of time and energy in a chosen way of living. The commitment may be, of course, to more or less lawful careers, and we judge the strength of our ties, one to the other, through signs of this differential investment.

Commitment, for Hirschi, "is the rational component in conformity" (1969, p. 20). It refers to how one has decided to live as signified by the use of time and the direction of energy.

Involvement is a consequence of commitment. If one chooses a patterned existence, some lines of action are opened, while others are closed. Every distinctive mode of living exposes us to different possibilities. For example, being committed to the life of a scholar involves one in a routine that reduces the opportunity to sample the full range of experience. We cannot do everything. Involvement describes the constriction of our actions demanded by a chosen way of living.

The relevance to crime production is that involvement in many lawful activities reduces exposure to many illegal opportunities. Conversely, the lack of commitment to a conventional life and the lack of involvement in conventional activities unavoidably provide an opportunity for accepting the costs and benefits of rational or expressive crime.

Belief is Hirschi's term for acceptance of the "moral validity" of conventional rules. In opposition to conflict criminologists, the control theorist "assumes the existence of a common value system within the society . . . whose norms are being violated" (1969, p. 23). What varies, then, between more and less lawful people is the degree to which individuals agree with the rightness of legal rules. This element in Hirschi's hypothesis is measured as an idea and is similar to the ordinary conception of "respect for the law."

Hirschi's Findings   Hirschi tested these four elements by using a self report measure of juvenile delinquency with a sample of California youths described earlier on pages 100–104, where some findings were also reported. Remembering that Hirschi's data are largely verbal—responses to a questionnaire—we can say that they support the assumptions of control theory:

1 Attachment to parents is strongly associated with lawful conduct among youths, and this relationship holds regardless of "social class."
2 Attachment to school—liking schoolwork and being concerned about the opinions of one's teachers—is also associated with resistance to delinquency. Academic ability and school performance are among the important predictors of lawful behavior, and these factors operate quite apart from any reported "social disability" such as being shy, less than popular, or unathletic.
3 Attachment to peers is also important, but not in the direct way commonly assumed. Birds of a feather do flock together, but the birds that so congregate acquired their feathers before they flocked. Boys who have been otherwise immunized against delinquency are rarely attracted to juvenile gangs. Young men choose friends who have similar interests, and the corrupting influence of the adventurous gang is limited to boys with little attachment to a conventional career.
4 Involvement in conventional activities such as doing one's homework reduced involvement in self-reported delinquency. Conversely, the more time one spends "riding around" or "rapping with buddies," the more likely delinquency is.
5 Hirschi measured "belief" by asking questions about respect for the police, the rightness of evading the law, the innocence of delinquents, and the harmlessness of delinquency. These and similar questions point in the direction predicted by control theory. That is, more delinquent boys compared with less delinquent youths, agree that:

"Most criminals shouldn't really be blamed for the things they have done."
"I can't seem to stay out of trouble no matter how hard I try."
"Most things that people call 'delinquency' don't really hurt anyone."
"Policemen [do not] try to give all kids an even break."
"It is alright [sic] to get around the law if you can get away with it" [1969, pp. 203–211].

In Summary Thus far, control theorists tell a cogent story and one consistent with the data. The sociological versions of control theory have been accused, however, of employing some vague concepts and of using some descriptions that seem to be part of the activity being explained. Moreover, while all the correlates variously called "belief," "self-control," "frustration tolerance," and "attachment" seem plausible as both cause and accompaniment of criminality, these correlates do not in themselves explain how these attributes are acquired or how they come to characterize us differentially. Psychologists have attempted to answer these questions.

Training and Teaching

The psychological assumption in explanation of crime holds that criminal behavior results from *defective social training* in lawful standards of conduct.

Social training, which the sociologist calls "socialization," is conceived by Eysenck (1964) and Trasler (1962) to involve two distinct, but overlapping, processes: teaching and training.

Teaching is the conscious transmission of techniques that may be used in solving problems. The techniques include using information, mechanical and research skills, and knowledge.

Teaching may be distinguished from another way in which we learn—that called "training." *Training* is the process by which values, purposes, preferences, and moral codes are instilled. It is also the process by which we learn our native tongue.

Training differs from teaching in the way it works and what it is used for. Training is more likely to proceed by manipulations of the environment of which the trained organism is unaware. Teaching, on the other hand, is more "intellectual," more cognitive. Whereas learners in a teaching situation know that the teacher is teaching, learners in a training situation are less apt to know what is happening to them. This is a matter of degree, of course, but of a degree that makes a difference. It is also a matter of timing; thus a learning process that begins with training may end with teaching.

The Training Repertoire   The training of mice and men is accomplished by rewarding desired behaviors, punishing unwanted behaviors, and setting models of behavior for the organisms to imitate. This is the repertoire of techniques by which moral desires are instilled. This is how one learns what is forbidden. It is also how one learns moral preferences.

One result of training is channeled behavior. Another result is conscience—the feelings of duty and responsibility, of shame and guilt, of the *need* to do "the right thing" and anxiety lest one do the wrong thing. It is because the training process is so subtle, and so much less cognitive than teaching, that moral people do not necessarily know "where their morality comes from." This is why we recognize that we have touched the other person's morality when, despite all reasons and against all arguments, the moral man says, with Luther, "I cannot do otherwise."

The training repertoire is not limited to one kind of learning. There is an assortment of training tools available. Each human being has experienced these training techniques to some extent, but for each person the blend, consistency, timing, and content are unique. The inventory of training tools includes at least (1) *classical conditioning*, (2) *operant conditioning*, and (3) *modeling*. A deficiency of Eysenck and Trasler's formulation is that it emphasizes the first of these training methods to the exclusion of the other two processes (V. Hamilton, 1965). The addition of these procedures here is intended to amplify Eysenck and Trasler's theory and to describe more fully how we have come to be as we are.

1   Classical, or respondent, conditioning   In this form of associational learning, a stimulus, previously inadequate to produce a response, becomes adequate through simultaneous or nearly simultaneous association with an adequate stimulus. Pavlov's dogs are a famous example: they were trained to salivate to the sound of a bell rung, repeatedly, just before the hungry animals received their meat. In this sort of training situation, the experimenter looks for stimuli that "unconditionally" produce a response. For example, a strong light directed into the eye will produce a pupillary contraction. Any other stimulus, such as a sound, that is presented about the same time as the flash of light will, with repetition, become adequate to cause a pupillary contraction. Such an associated cue is called the "conditioned" or "conditional" stimulus.

There are humanists who deny that human beings are "conditionable." This is nonsense, as a large research literature demonstrates (Franks, 1961; Greenspoon, 1962; A. W. Staats, 1968). We have all been "classically conditioned," although we cannot easily ascertain for ourselves how much or to what. The important psychological questions concern the conditions under which respondent conditioning occurs, the degree to which a conditional response is similar to an unconditional response, the permanence of the conditional "lesson" learned, and how much of our conditioning has been planned and how much has been accidental or incidental.

Present purposes do not require answers to these questions. It is enough to acknowledge that one way in which we have become as we are is through such associational training. A sign that we have been thus trained is our preference for the familiar (R. C. Johnson et al., 1960). The process by which associational training can occur has been described in numerous studies, both observational and experimental. For example, C. W. Staats and Staats (1957), gave emotional significance to nonsense syllables by presenting these meaningless letters in association with pleasant and unpleasant words. In this manner, what began as nonsense ended with emotional meaning.

2 Operant, or instrumental, conditioning This is one of the most powerful ways of guiding behavior. It differs from classical conditioning in that the organism is changed by the consequences of its acts. Whereas in classical conditioning a new stimulus is "hooked up" to an adequate stimulus *before* the organism responds, in operant conditioning the organism is trained by what *follows* upon its action.

Apart from the varying heredities with which we begin life, probably no discernible influence has a greater effect upon our individual destinies than the immediate consequences of our acts. *What happens when we act determines how we act.*

The consequences of our conduct are usually classified as "rewards" and "punishments," although this classification is not always neat. We may express the hypothesis of operant conditioning, then, by saying that conduct is molded by the pattern of reward and punishment it has elicited. The pattern can be studied in terms of the *styles* of punishment and reward experienced, in terms of their *balance*, and in terms of their *intensity, timing,* and *consistency.* Furthermore, psychologists have studied the varying effects of *giving* a reward as opposed to *withdrawing* it and of *giving* punishment as opposed to *relieving* it (Campbell and Church, 1969).

It is not necessary here to review comprehensively the many investigations of the effects of punishment and reward. The inventory of research is large. It allows generalizations about the shaping of behavior that are sufficient for the purpose of specifying crime-producing conditions. A sample of these research findings will give their flavor and show us how "densely packed" are the many kinds of consequences that flow from our actions.

Reinforcement contingencies: A sample of effects. We know, first, that neither a reward nor a punishment has a uniform effect. A pain, or a pleasure, is "an event in a temporal and spatial flow of stimulation and behavior, and its effects will be produced by its temporal and spatial point of insertion in that flow" (Solomon, 1964, p. 242). Thus, if a dog or cat is given an electric shock *while* it is eating, it will become fearful and avoid the feeding dish even to the point of starvation (Lichtenstein, 1950; Masserman, 1943). On the other hand, if the pain *precedes* the reward, if the animal is first shocked and then fed, the punishment becomes a cue that food is available and the learner feeds without disturbance (Holz and Azrin, 1962).

As a training tool, punishment varies in its effectiveness with its frequency, its intensity, and its timing. It also varies in its effects depending upon who administers the punishment and upon the trainee's personality, his previous experience with punishment, and the "schedule" of pleasures and pains administered to him. "A punishment is not just a punishment," Solomon tells us. "The effects of punishment are partly determined by those events that directly precede it and those that directly follow it" (1964, p. 242).

Punishment is more effective as a training technique when it is administered to the acts that are *premonitory* of forbidden behavior than when it follows the undesirable behavior. Furthermore, the longer the delay in punishment *after* the bad act, the less effective is the pain. Punishment "when Dad gets home" and punishment in prison have little power to change conduct. They are too remote in time from the anticipatory cues that mark the start of a disapproved act. On the other hand, intense pain administered *early* in the series of acts leading to the undesirable behavior readily conditions the organism (Aronfreed and Reber, 1965; Solomon, 1964; Walters and Demkow, 1963). Moderate punishment administered later in the series of acts preceding an unwanted behavior, but given consistently and in a supportive environment, has an enduring effect in shaping behavior (Walters, 1967). If pain is attached to what a person *does* as opposed to *how he or she has been*, its controlling effect is greater (Church, 1963). Under some conditions, even *observing* the punishment of others can inhibit behavior (Walters et al., 1965), just as observing the aggression of others can stimulate it (Bandura et al., 1961; Geen and Berkowitz, 1967; Lovaas, 1961; Walters et al., 1962).

Operant conditioning and criminal careers. This brief summary is sufficient to indicate the variety of circumstances that determine the efficacy of punishment as either a conditional stimulus or an operant. What is of significance in producing more and less lawful persons is the childhood diet of reward and punishment. A balanced diet is, of course, recommended, with the balance inclined toward the child's being nurtured, appreciated, and guided by a rewarding model, rather than toward being only "disciplined." For the appreciated child, the very withdrawal of approval becomes a penalizing consequence and a substitute for the physical pain otherwise used as an operant. By contrast, it is notable that juvenile delinquents and their parents consistently speak of having punished each other, physically and verbally, and observation of their behaviors confirms their memories (Glueck and Glueck, 1962; Shulman, 1959). The point is that punishment by parents who reject their children is likely to be erratic and hostile. Its efficacy as an operant is reduced by its being inappropriately scheduled and imposed in the absence of nurturing—that is, in an environment in which the organism's acts result more frequently in punishment than in reward. A relationship between parent and child that is loaded with penalties and devoid of reward is not an efficient system of guidance toward moral conduct. It tells the child what *not* to do, but it does not tell the child *what to do*. In psychological language, the operants for preferred behavior are lacking.

3 Modeling and "social learning" The terms "modeling" and "social learning" refer to the age-old observation that human beings and a host of other animals learn by imitation. In many languages, the verb "to teach" is synonymous with the verb "to show" (Reichard, 1938). Much of what we have been taught or, better, trained to be is a result of what we have been shown.

In their theory of criminogenesis, Eysenck and Trasler do not stress the role of modeling. However, the impact of social learning should not be neglected. There is a convincing body of research that shows how large segments of behavior are acquired by watching others perform. This is most striking at youthful ages, of course, and it is now well substantiated that even behaviors unusual for a species can be "imprinted" if a deviant model is presented exclusively to the organism at certain critical periods in its development (Cairns, 1966; P. H. Gray, 1958; Hess, 1959, 1972; Sluckin, 1965).

The role of a model in training a child has been most thoroughly documented in the imitation of aggression (Bandura and Walters, 1959). However, there is also experimental evidence that dependent behavior, sexual conduct, and fearful reactions can be transmitted from models to children (Bandura, 1972; Bandura and Walters, 1963).

The training given by models interacts with that acquired by conditioning. The effect of a model varies, so that models who have been rewarding to us are more likely to be imitated. Similarly, those models who are deemed to be competent or prestigious—who, in short, have high status in our eyes—are more likely to be copied. For example, in a simple but effective experiment, Lefkowitz and others (1955) employed a rich-looking person and a poor-looking person to act as models of illegal behavior. They had these models walk against a traffic light and observed how many pedestrian bystanders followed them in their lawbreaking. More people imitated the rich model.

Bandura and Walters (1963, p. 107) point out that what happens to the model also influences imitation. Models who are rewarded for their aggression, for example, are more readily copied. Similarly, aggressive models who are *not* punished, who are seen to "get away with" being violent, are more likely to be imitated by children (Soares and Soares, 1969).

The tendency to imitate varies not only with what happens to the model, but also with certain personality characteristics of the observer. Soares and

Soares present evidence that children who have had a history of failure more readily copy violent models. So, too, children who are comparatively incompetent in social relations and who exhibit low self-regard and dependent behavior are more likely to imitate aggressive models.

Additional factors that affect imitative behavior include the individual's experience in having been rewarded or punished for copying the model; his mood; and his perceived similarity to the model (Rosekrans, 1967). All these bonds between personality traits and imitative tendencies are strengthened in emotionally charged situations (Soares and Soares, 1970).

Given the abundant evidence of modeling effects, it is not surprising to learn that dramatic crimes are contagious. This seems true of the assassination of public figures (Berkowitz and Macaulay, 1971) and also of skyjacking, campus vandalism, and urban guerrilla warfare (Moss, 1972). The "communications revolution" that brings televised images of distant violence into almost every European and American house may in this sense be regarded as criminogenic.

The effects of televised models. In rich nations, generations are now being reared before the television tube. In the United States and urban Canada, and in the metropolises of Europe and Latin America, almost all homes have one or more television sets. In the United States, at least 96 percent of all homes have television, and the sets are running an average of six hours a day. Children in Canada and the United States are now normally television viewers by age 3, and their attention to television remains high until about age 12. The impact of television's violent models upon children's aggressive behavior has been demonstrated in limited circumstances. The issue of how great this impact is, however, continues to be debated (Surgeon General's Committee, 1972).

Most research on the effects of televised violence tests the short-run results of aggressive modeling. For example, Liebert and Baron (1972) exposed boys and girls of two age groups, 5 to 6 years and 8 to 9 years, to portions of actual television programs that were rated "aggressive" and "nonaggressive." The children were then given a chance to act aggressively toward a playmate and were also observed in play situations. Liebert and Baron report:

> Children exposed to the aggressive program engaged in longer attacks against an ostensible child victim than subjects exposed to the nonaggressive program. The aggressive program also elicited a higher level of aggressive play than the nonaggressive one, particularly among the younger boys [p. 469].

Bailyn (1959) also tested the possible effects of exposure to violence on television by gathering data on the social characteristics of children's families, the children's viewing preferences, their "psychological adjustment" as measured by a variety of standard tests, and reports of their aggressive behavior. Bailyn found that there was a correlation in the range of .50 between viewing habits and violent acts, but that this correlation was limited to a small proportion of the child subjects, that proportion (about 3 percent) that had already exhibited signs of emotional disturbance.

R. M. Kaplan and Singer (1972) reviewed a host of experiments assessing the effects of television on aggressive behavior. They conclude that "the majority of the experimental studies showed that witnessing violence can instigate 'aggressive' behavior." These experiments, however, most frequently gained their effectiveness through the intentional arousal of subjects and the use of dependent measures that removed ordinary sanctions against aggression. Instigation effects were rarely found in studies or experimental conditions in which the subjects were not aroused intentionally. When the measure of aggression has been some *naturally occurring* behavior, it has been shown that television violence either has no effect (Feshbach and Singer, 1971; Siegel, 1956) or affects only those children who were initially highly aggressive (A. H. Stein et al., 1971). In the latter case, there is evidence of an "aggravation effect."

Immediate imitation of dramatic modeling might be expected, particularly among those predisposed in the direction of the model. However, the long-range consequences of a taste for televised violence are of more interest, although they are more difficult to establish. Eron and others attempted to isolate such long-range effects by following a group of youngsters over 10 years. They studied 875 children in the third grade and found that, at that age, "children who preferred violent television programs were more aggressive in school as rated by peers than children who preferred less violent programs" (1972, p. 262).

Of these youngsters, 427 were studied again 10 years after the original observations. This group was almost equally divided between boys and girls. *For the boys only*, a continuing correlation was discovered between early television habits and aggressive behavior as teenagers. Since the correlation between teenagers' viewing habits and measures of their "violence" (.31) is slightly higher than the correlation that was obtained when these boys were 8 and 9 years old (.21), the investigators conclude that television viewing had an *enduring, independent causal impact* upon adolescent aggressive behavior. This effect appears both when adolescents are rated for aggression by their peers and when they are scored for "aggression" on a standard psychometric, the MMPI. The television effect was said to "explain a larger portion of the variance than does any single factor which we studied, including IQ, social status, mobility aspirations, religious practice, ethnicity, and parental disharmony" (p. 623).

The conclusion of this longitudinal study—that television viewing has an *independent causal* significance for the development of violent behavior—ought not to be accepted too readily. Such an interpretation may be regarded as suggestive, but not as conclusive, because controls were lacking for possible causal factors *common to both aggressive behavior and taste* in television viewing. Whenever a correlation of this sort is reported for behaviors that may be assumed to be generated in a dense causal web, the scholar must consider whether the correlation is unidirectionally causal or, rather, a common product of many causes that produce the associated behaviors.

It must be concluded, then, that the long-range effects of televised models have yet to be ascertained. In the short run, a modeling influence of a qualified nature has been demonstrated. These research findings may be used to support the modeling thesis. However, no proponent of social learning theory maintains that imitation is the exclusive agent shaping behavior or that it is all-powerful. It is recognized, as we have seen, that situational variables affect the copying of a model. In addition, personality differences influence how we learn.

Individual Differences in Response to Training A German proverb says, "The fire that melts the butter hardens the egg." We do not respond equally to the same stimulation, even as newly born creatures (Clarke, 1975; Freedman, 1971, 1974; Nichols and Broman, 1974; Post, 1962a, 1962b, 1964; Salmon and Blakeslee, 1935; Seligman and Hager, 1972; Vandenberg, 1966).

The effects of conditioning and modeling vary with personality. What pains one person may please another, and what is stress for this individual may be a challenge for that one (Petrie, 1967).

In contrast to other theories of crime production, control assumptions acknowledge individual differences and recognize that some of us need more training than others. It has long been noted that this is true of the "lower" species, but we have been reluctant to admit that it is true of Homo sapiens. Different breeds of dogs, for example, are more or less easy to train (Lorenz, 1952). Sheepdogs condition readily, while Basenjis are relatively difficult to control (Freedman, 1958). Similarly, human beings may be differently "wired" and may require differing balances of support, pleasure, and pain if they are to develop conscience and resistance to temptation.

Eysenck and his colleagues emphasize the introversion-extraversion dimension as affecting the way in which we learn. There are data showing that introverts condition more readily than extraverts. Franks (1956) reports that both the eyeblink and psychogalvanic reflexes can be conditioned to an auditory stimulus "significantly more easily" for introverts than for extraverts. Furthermore, the loss of these conditional responses, their "extinction," is reported to be considerably greater for extraverts than for introverts.

It is assumed, then, that extraverts need more training than introverts. They may also require a different style of training. Praise and blame seem to affect them differently (G. G. Thompson and Hunnicutt, 1944). "While praise motivates introverted children," Eysenck writes, "blame motivates extraverted children" (1966, p. 23). Of interest to this point is Kennedy and Willcutt's report that, while praise *generally improves* the performance of schoolchildren, it *lowers* the performance of "underachievers" (1964).

There are other aspects of personality than introversion-extraversion that seem related to how people learn. One's "need to be nurtured" is another such dimension. R. Epstein (1964) finds that children who need much approval are easier to condition than those who are less oriented to approval. In addition, the child who needs more nurturing is more sensitive to the *hostile* content of stimuli and conditions more readily to it.

It is a well-established fact that individuals respond to sensations differently. Styles of perception vary among us and are enduring features of our personalities (Witkin, 1965; Witkin et al., 1962). In a series of clever experiments, Petrie (1967) and others have demonstrated that people can be ranked along a continuum in the way in which they "handle sensation." While some people are fairly accurate in their perceptions, others markedly "reduce" what they perceive and others "increase" what they perceive. Petrie had subjects estimate the width of blocks of wood felt with the thumb and forefinger of one hand by running the fingers of the other hand along a tapered block until the subject felt he was at a place on the tapered bar that was the same width as the measuring block. She found that some people consistently overestimated the width of the measuring block, in some cases by as much as 50 percent. These persons are "augmenters." Others consistently underestimated the size of the stimulus, and to as great a degree. They are "reducers."

Whatever may have caused these differences in the handling of sensation, they are there, and they affect how we learn. Compared with the augmenter, the reducer needs more stimulation before he "gets the message." Whether male or female, this type of person is less responsive to pain (Ryan and Foster, 1967; Ryan and Kovacic, 1966). Among males, the reducer tends to be more "athletic" (mesomorphic) in body build (Wertheimer, 1955) and to prefer contact sports. He has a quicker reaction time and, like the persistent delinquent, estimates moments of time to be longer than they are (Ryan and Foster, 1967). The reducer cannot stand isolation, silence, or monotony as well as the augmenter can. He needs "to do things" and to have things happen. In the poet Wordsworth's terms, the extreme reducer has "a raging thirst for outrageous stimulation."

It is notable that serious juvenile offenders, male and female, disproportionately perceive their worlds as reducers do (Petrie, 1967, chap. 5). Petrie believes that, as reducers, such delinquents have a greater immunity to pain, which explains, in part, their inability to sympathize with the pain of others. This might underlie the reducer's greater involvement in accidents, his or her noisiness, and even the preference among both male and female reducers for tattooing, an ornamentation rather painful to acquire. Petrie suggests that the often-remarked more frequent bedwetting among delinquents (Michaels, 1955) may result from the reducer's lesser responsiveness to internal cues.

Petrie's findings, along with those of the Gluecks (1950, 1956), Eysenck, Trasler, Sheldon (1949), and others, tell us that some individuals need greater stimulation before they can be trained. These findings fit in with the repeated descriptions of serious offenders as bored with school, conscience-free, adventurous, and difficult to condition (Franks, 1961).

There is evidence that introversion-extraversion and perceptual style have constitutional and, probably, genetic roots (Rosenthal, 1970; Sontag, 1963). Assuming this to be so, the facts that there are personality differences which affect the way individuals respond to reward and punishment and that the more persistent offenders score differently on these traits do *not* mean that criminality is inborn. They mean only that, in learning to conduct ourselves, some of us need more lessons than others.

Consequences of Training An organism that has been trained through some history of classical conditioning, operant conditioning, and modeling is a different organism from an untrained one. What has been learned is not merely stored in some nonphysical space called the "mind." The learning is in the physiology: the trained organism's neurochemical response system has been changed. This is why we commonly say things like, "I know I shouldn't be afraid of the snake. It's harmless, but I can't help myself." In a case like this, involuntary alarms are going off in the "internal environment" of the organism. Such alarms are largely a result of training, and they *literally* affect us in gut and gland and heart (DiCara, 1970; Gaito and Zavala, 1964; N. E. Miller, 1969).

Eysenck and Trasler hold that, in the morally conditioned person, these internal alarms constitute an anxiety triggered by the cues preceding a "bad deed" and that the anxiety is inhibiting. There is evidence that such inhibition of the forbidden act in the well-trained organism results from a different pattern of conditioning from that which produces guilt.

Resisting temptation versus feeling guilty   Punishment that is administered *early* in a response sequence leading to an unwanted act is more likely to produce immunity to temptation; punishment given *late* in the sequence is more likely to generate "self-punitive" behavior (Aronfreed, 1963).

Puppies punished as they approach tempting food learn to resist it with little emotionality. Puppies punished while they are eating the forbidden food show little resistance to temptation, but more "emotional behavior" (A. H. Black et al., 1960).

As with puppies, so with children (Allinsmith, 1960; Burton et al., 1961; Whiting and Child, 1953). Resistance to temptation is learned by a different process from that which teaches guilt. Bandura and Walters (1963, p. 203) believe that resistance to temptation is learned largely by classical conditioning, while the self-punitive habit (guilt) is learned through operant conditioning. However this may be, the important point is that the person who has been trained to resist temptation need feel no guilt; the person trained to feel guilty need have little resistance to temptation. Both resistance and guilt, however, are acquired by human beings who have been *reared*. These activities do not come "naturally"—that is, they do not come without training.

Conscience as a motivator   "Conscience," measurable either as immunity to temptation or as vulnerability to guilt, is built by means of conditioning and modeling. The result of this training is not merely inhibition, as our examples may have suggested. Another result is the *development of new drives*.

An "honest" person is not merely one who *refrains* from stealing under opportunity. The honest person also *does* things that are honest. The story of Abe Lincoln walking many miles to return his customer's forgotten change is a paradigm.

Similarly, the moral aversion to cruelty or to sexual license is *not* inborn, yet the person who has been trained in these values will engage in prolonged behavior to defend them.

Training does not only change physiology. It also builds motivation. Once constructed, the acquired motives operate without memory of their origins. They are autonomous.

Three Determinants of How We Are   How we are today, then, is a result of three classes of causes. These determinants lie in our neurophysiological constitutions, in *how* we were reared, and in *what* we were taught.

In assessing the career of one person or in explaining the varieties of conduct within a group, behavioral scientists do not have measuring instruments that allow a definitive assignment of relative importance to these three determinants. An impact of each of these sets of causes can be separately ascertained, but the interaction of these causes cannot be accurately gauged because the causal web in which they achieve their effects is dense. Each set of determinants has variations within it, and the numerous causes are closely intertwined. These determinants of our lives can be assumed, and they can be observed, but they cannot be accurately weighed.

In considering the first determinant, we acknowledge that there are individual differences in amenability to training, including persistent differences in temperament, tempo, and cognitive capacity. It need not be debated here how much of our different neural "wiring" and chemical construction is genetic, how much is constitutional, and how much has been affected by the environment. The fact of difference in learning ability and ways of becoming conditioned is indisputable. But the question of *how malleable* we are remains open. An inherited constitution is not a fixed one.

The second set of determinants has to do with how we were brought up. *The quality of training* we have received has been studied in terms of at least these dimensions of learning:

1   Respondent (classical) conditioning
2   Operant (instrumental) conditioning
3   Modeling ("social learning")

Each of these dimensions is itself a variable, as we have seen. For example, operant-conditioning theory holds that a principal determinant of how we are is what has happened when we have acted. What happened when we acted may, in turn, be analyzed in terms of "reward" and "punishment," although these nouns are themselves without clear boundaries. However, the effects of "reward" and "punishment" are known to vary with at least their:

Intensity
Frequency
Consistency
Balance
Temporality (their placement in time)
Setting (which includes who gave the reward or punishment and in what "social context")

The third determinant of how we are is what we were taught. The *content of the lessons* we have learned can be assessed as:

Rules, preferences, tastes, values
Skills (which may range from solitary manual performances to interpersonal abilities)
Information and ideas

In considering this third determinant we recognize that the same quality of training can impart different lesson content. "Good" training can teach "bad" lessons. It is possible for wicked lessons to be well taught and for good lessons to be poorly taught. If we can learn to be lawful, we can learn to be criminal. If we can learn how to earn money, we can learn how to take it.

Among these three sets of the causes of our careers, sociologists tend to ignore the first, to slight the second, and to emphasize the third. Subcultural, rational, and symbolic-interactionist explanations of crime attend to *what* has been learned. It is only the control variety of sociopsychological explanation that stresses *how* we were trained. Both sets of determinants are important, however.

CHILD REARING AND THE CORRELATES OF CRIMINALITY

There is a neat fit between the control thesis and the social location of serious crime. This is particularly so as one adds to Eysenck and Trasler's emphasis on classical conditioning the possibilities of other modes of learning such as operant conditioning and modeling.

Both the ethnic and the class correlates of the graver offenses fit with what is known about the training routines, the content of the socializing lessons, and the nature of the models available for children reared in different status and ethnic situations. The sociopsychological attention to individual differences in training susceptibility is a way of allowing for variations in the effects of these social climates upon individual behavior. At the same time, the sociopsychological attention to *patterns* of child rearing brings this schema into harmony with subcultural explanations of criminality. Both modes of explanation have emphasized the impact of human nurturing upon human development.

Modeling Deficiency and Delinquency

The control hypothesis holds that serious juvenile offenders have been defectively reared. In particular, it is claimed that such persons have lacked adequate models of lawful conduct. This fact can be documented in two ways. One procedure is to observe children from different nurturing environments and to record how they grow up. Another procedure is to compare the childhood backgrounds of serious offenders with those of less criminal people from a comparable environment. The two methods of study yield similar conclusions.

Developmental Studies   Observations of children in orphanages, hospitals, foster homes, and intact families uniformly indicate that there is some physical, mental, and social damage to the child who lacks nurturing (Spitz, 1946). The damage to physical functioning is least; that to cognitive functioning is most serious; and that to social conduct is midway between these extremities (Bowlby, 1952). Children who have been reared in institutions or concentration camps tend to be more aggressive and to have difficulties in interpersonal relations, including difficulty in behaving honestly (A. Freud and Dann, 1951; Goldfarb, 1943c; Trasler, 1961).

Longitudinal research confirms these findings. Goldfarb (1943a, 1943b, 1943c, 1944a, 1944b, 1945a, 1945b) reports a series of studies of adolescents who had spent the first three years of their lives in institutions. In addition to the learning deficits frequently associated with such rearing, Goldfarb found the institutionalized children to have trouble controlling their impulses. Either they were overcontrolled, rigid, and submissive, or they were aggressive. Furthermore, the children who were aggressive did not exhibit normal anxiety about, or guilt reactions to, their aggressiveness.

An earlier follow-up study by Theis (1924) yields similar results. Theis studied over 200 adults who had been orphaned in infancy and compared the careers of those who had been institutionalized for at least five years with those who had lived in foster homes. The proportion of institutionalized children with records of persistent criminality was *three times* that of the foster children, and there were corresponding, but smaller, differences in their records of less serious misconduct.

Rohrer, Edmonson, and a team of behavioral scientists (Rohrer and Edmonson, 1960) observed blacks in the Southern United States *20 years after* these same individuals had been described by other investigators (A. Davis and Dollard, 1941). Rohrer and Edmonson's research is a clinically oriented study concerned with the development of individual careers. Although this longitudinal research did not use a control group for comparison, it confirmed the image of the male gang-running criminal as a person who denies the legitimacy of religion, schools, law, and morals, and who considers occupational striving worthless. The descriptions of each career are well drawn and illustrate a central theme of control theory, namely, the harmful impact of fatherless households upon the emotional development of boys. In the authors' words:

> Our data reaffirm, often dramatically, the great importance of significant adults to the shaping of the individual's personality. The presence or absence of such figures and the nature of the model they present are intimately linked to the individual's development of ego ideals: vague or vivid images of what he would like to become [1960, pp. 299–300].

A cross-cultural study   A similar conclusion was reached by M. K. Bacon and others (1963), who brought together ethnographic data from 48 societies and examined them for the correlates of crime. These societies, most of them preliterate, were distributed across Africa, Asia, Oceania, and North and South America. They represent a range of family settings, child-rearing practices, degrees of social stratification, and levels of political integration.

The investigators concluded that "the frequency of both Theft and Personal Crime increases as the opportunity for contact with the father decreases" (p. 294). Crimes against the person, in particular, were found to be significantly associated with a mother-child household in which there was "inadequate opportunity in early life for identification with the father," in which the sleeping arrangements for the mother and child fostered "a strong dependent relationship between the child and the mother," and in which the training for independence was abrupt and punishing (p. 298).

The authors of this study incline toward a psychoanalytic interpretation of their findings. In the present context, however, this cross-cultural analysis corroborates the repeatedly reported relationship between hostility and dishonesty in males and the lack of a loving and lawful father figure with whom to identify.

Comparative Studies   Comparing the early training of criminals and more lawful persons is made difficult by the obstacles to direct observation of familial practices. The usual research procedure involves asking parents how they treated their children and asking parents, peers, and teachers how the children behave. Investigators have a problem in coding these reports, but, in addition, the defects of memory, the inaccuracies in parental observation of themselves and their children, and the defensiveness of parents in responding to interviewers have guaranteed that there can be only a slight relation between how parents *say* they trained their children and what actually went on (Yarrow et al., 1968). Furthermore, training is subtle. It is composed of many lessons taught and learned of which both teacher and learner may be unaware. Parents, even highly schooled ones, are not necessarily accurate recorders of their own behavior toward their children.

Sociologists have tried to compensate for these obstacles to observation by analyzing the effects of broad categories of childhood environment, such as illegitimacy and broken homes. In addition, self-report instruments have been used to compare the ratings of family climates given by delinquents, nondelinquents, and their parents.

Illegitimacy and delinquency   One measure of the quality of model available to youngsters is an indirect gauge of the presence or absence of a parent. Rates of illegitimate births have been used as such an index with which to correlate crime rates.

"Illegitimacy," like the "broken home," is a crude category, however. It is crude because the social meaning of "illegitimacy" varies with the culture. There are societies in which being born out of wedlock carries less stigma and betokens less lack of fathering than it does in the Western industrialized states (Goode, 1960). For example, "consensual unions" in South American countries often constitute stable marriages; thus the illegitimacy rates of 50 percent reported for some of the shantytowns in Latin America (Germani, 1961) and of 65 to 75 percent reported for some of the West Indies (United Nations, 1970) need not indicate the same degree of deficient fatherhood that comparable rates would in European or North American locations.

Among cultures in which illegitimacy is more accepted, accommodations are often made so that a substitute may serve as the model for the child without a father. Such father surrogates are largely lacking, however, in the urban centers of Western nations, many of which have experienced an increase in both the numbers and the rates of illegitimate births since World War II (United Nations, 1970). For the United States, the overall illegitimacy rate is estimated to have risen from about 4 percent in 1940 to nearly 5 percent in 1960 (Goode, 1966, p. 490). During the 1960s both Canada and the United States experienced increases in rates of illegitimate births, while the rate in Mexico declined somewhat. The United Nations reports a steady increase in illegitimate births in the United States from 6.3 percent in 1963 to 9.7 percent in 1968 (1970, p. 415). Canada's illegitimacy rate also rose year by year from 5.3 percent in 1963 to 8.3 percent in 1967.

In cities of the Western nations, illegitimacy now occurs at a disturbing rate. Copenhagen, Denmark, reports a rate of about one illegitimate child for every seven live births. The rate is one in four in Washington, D.C., Dallas, and Houston, and close to one in three in Chicago (U.S. Department of Health, Education, and Welfare, 1963). In central Harlem, New York, the illegitimacy rate among nonwhites for 1963 was reported at 43.4 percent of all live births (Moynihan, 1965, p. 8).

The control theorist argues that, *in these urban settings*, being illegitimate means being functionally fatherless. This lack of a father shows itself in deficits in almost every measurable aspect of socially important behavior (Jenkins, 1958). Functionally fatherless children, according to Goode, "are more likely to die at birth or in the first year, to do poorly in school, to become juvenile delinquents, and to land eventually in unskilled jobs" (1966, p. 491).

For individual children, the damage of illegitimacy in such settings may be lessened by early adoption and the compensatory training given by parental substitutes. However, on the ecological level, the social location of high rates of illegitimacy overlaps the social classes and the ethnic groups that yield higher crime rates. To this extent, the control hypothesis receives support. Similar indirect "proof" of the control hypothesis has been attempted, with dubious results, from the many studies of broken homes and their behavioral effects.

Broken homes and delinquency   The trouble with attempting to test control hypotheses, or any other explanations of criminality, by looking at "broken homes" is that the concept of the broken home is not a clear one. As regards effects on child rearing, there may be as many styles of "broken homes" as there are of "intact" ones. There is, in fact, evidence that some ruptured families may be healthier nurturing environments than some whole ones (Burchinal, 1964; Goode, 1956; Nye, 1957). Much depends on how the home was broken, when in the child's life the break occurred, and what kind of modeling relationship succeeded the disruption of the household. A household broken by divorce after years of wrangling provides a different psychic climate from one disrupted by sudden death; and a family that changes early in an infant's life has a different impact from one that is broken during a child's middle years. There are differences in effect, too, dependent upon the sex, as well as the age, of the child and upon the sex of the parent with whom the child remains. For example, Toby (1957) presents data showing that the "broken home" has a different effect upon girls and preadolescent boys from that which it has upon older boys. The impact is greater (worse) for girls and for the younger boys.

Despite these weaknesses in the notion of the "broken home" as a measure of a child's nurturing, research on delinquency has produced a mass of indigestible data on the comparative incidence of broken families among more and less lawful youth.

An early study by Shaw and McKay (1931) compared 1,675 black and white delinquent males 10 to 17 years of age in Cook County, Illinois, with a sample of 7,278 less delinquent schoolboys of like age. Shaw and McKay reported that 42.5 percent of their offenders came from broken homes, as compared with 36.1 percent of the nonoffenders, and this small spread is interpreted as insignificant.

Other students have quarreled with this finding and, as might be expected, have challenged the kinds of controls employed, the lack of females in the sample, the lumping together of all styles of disrupted households as "broken" ones, and even the interpretation of the statistical spread.

Maller (1932), for example, argued that, given the shape of the distributions of delinquency among broken and intact families, a difference of 6.4 percent between them *is* statistically significant. Hodgkiss (1933) conducted a replication of Shaw and McKay's investigation in Cook County using *female* subjects. Here a wide discrepancy was found between delinquents and lesser offenders in the experience of broken homes. Of the delinquent girls, 67 percent came from broken homes, as compared with just under 45 percent of the nondelinquent sample.

Investigations in England and the United States tend toward findings that juvenile offenders are the products of broken homes from $1^{1}/_{2}$ times to 2 times more frequently than nonoffenders. An illustrative result derives from the Gluecks' research (1950), which compared the familial experiences of 500 delinquent boys with a matched control group of 500 nondelinquents. More than 60 percent of the delinquents were from broken homes as compared with 32.4 percent of the nondelinquents. Merrill (1947) found comparable differences in a study of 300 consecutive arraignments in juvenile courts in the United States in which the offenders were matched by age, sex, and ethnicity with a sample of nondelinquents. Some 50 percent of these delinquents were from disrupted families as compared with 26.7 percent of the control group.

Monahan (1957) studied all delinquency charges brought over a six-year period in Philadelphia. He analyzed the family status of over 44,000 cases, holding constant the sex and race of the offenders. His findings are in essential agreement with those of Merrill and the Gluecks, with the additional observation that the broken home had a more harmful effect upon the girls and the blacks in his sample than upon the boys and the whites. The proportions of delinquent girls and blacks from broken homes exceeded those found for delinquent boys and whites. In addition, Monahan reports that repetitive offenders were disproportionately from broken homes and that the highest recidivism rate was among children who had been reared in institutions.

A more recent replication of this type of research yields parallel conclusions. Chilton and Markle (1972) compared the family situations of 5,376 delinquent children in Florida with the family situations of children in the general United States population. As expected, they observed that children from disrupted families were more likely to be charged with delinquency and that this association was closer for the more serious offenses.

Studies conducted in England produce comparable findings. Burt's early research (1925) contrasted the domestic experience of young delinquents and nondelinquents, holding constant their cultural background, social class, age, and place of residence and school attendance. Burt reports that 61.3 percent of the delinquents came from broken homes, as compared with 25.1 percent of the nondelinquents.

These, and similar investigations, are retrospective studies. They look backward from the age of delinquency to ascertain whether the young person's family was disrupted. As noted, these studies seldom control for *when* the family was broken, for *how much* decay the family experienced before its rupture, or for the *quality of control* exercised after the break. Longitudinal studies that begin *before* the domestic breach or *before* the commission of a crime are rare. In one such investigation, however, Gregory (1965) followed the careers of boys who had lost parents during childhood and found that the children of divorced and separated parents were disproportionately represented among delinquents. Boys who had lost parents through death were slightly more likely to be involved in delinquencies than boys from intact families, but their rates of offense did not approach those of the boys from the homes disrupted by divorce and separation.

A summary conception and a caution   A common summary of this kind of research claims, as D. R. Peterson and Becker do, that "the gross relationship is well established—the families of delinquents have been disrupted by death, desertion, divorce, separation, or prolonged parental absence much more frequently than the families of nondelinquents" (1965, p. 68).

It must be cautioned, however, that the research on the association of "broken homes" with criminality provides a weak test of the control hypothesis. The test is poor for all the reasons mentioned, reasons that can themselves be summarized by saying that a "broken home" is not the only kind of broken family. Families can be divided, and are divided, while they continue to share a legal status and domicile. For a measure of the possible extent of such riven households among prominent Americans, read the report by Cuber and Harroff (1966).

It is the *quality of training* and the *content of the lessons* taught that are the important determinants of lawful behavior, according to control theory. Neither of these dimensions of nurturing is well described by statistics on divorce, although they may be better described by the figures on desertion.

Meanwhile, times change. Divorce is now the expectation of about one-fourth of all people who marry in Canada and the United States, and remarriage is the expectation of about one-fifth of all who marry. With these and other changes in the nature of the family, it is probable that family ties may loosen so that "intact" homes in various social settings may come to have no more modeling effect upon the youngsters involved than some kinds of single-parent households.

These changes may be expected, too, with changes in socioeconomic stratification, with a blurring of differences in child-rearing practices among families of high and low occupational status, with a decline of neighborhoods and neighborhood schools, and with the intrusion of other models of behavior for youngsters as replacements for defaulting parents. The independent role of television viewing has already been mentioned (pages 319–321).

Memories of childhood and portraits of the present Another way of comparing the backgrounds of more and less lawful people is to analyze their memories of their childhoods and their conceptions of their present family relations.

Research on this matter uniformly finds that "bad actors" say their rearing was unpleasant. Persistent lawbreakers disproportionately reject the parental models that are normal for most children in most cultures (Medinnus, 1965).

For example, delinquents tend to deny that "My mother was a good woman" (Hathaway and Monachesi, 1957). Compared with their more lawful counterparts, young criminals believe that "My parents were too strict with me when I was a child" and that "I was often punished unfairly." Offenders also believe that their parents "never really understood them" and that their home lives were miserable (Gough and Peterson, 1952). For these memories, there is independent evidence that the delinquent is probably correct (Barker, 1940; Burt, 1925; Glueck and Glueck, 1950; Healy and Bronner, 1936).

Such findings confirm those reported by the developmental studies. These pictures of the making of the less lawful person have a cross-cultural validity, a validity that lends credence to the control hypothesis.

A recent study of a cross-cultural nature that adds to these findings was conducted by Rosenquist and Megargee (1969). These investigators and their aides compared delinquent and nondelinquent samples from similar socioeconomic levels among three cultures: lower-class "Anglos" in San Antonio, Texas; "Latins" living in the same city; and Mexicans living in Monterrey, Nuevo Leon. There was extensive testing of physical and intellectual abilities, along with an assortment of psychological probes concerning personal values, self-perception, and attitudes toward parents. The major observations of importance for control theory are these:

   1   The delinquents in all three [ethnic groups] expressed significantly more deviant behavior and attitudes and less family cohesiveness. The Latin and Mexican delinquents were much more likely to express disrespect of the father, criticism of the mother, and disrespect of elders [pp. 305–306].
   2   Marital stability was evaluated in a number of ways, and it was found that significantly more of the delinquents in each sample came from unstable or broken homes [p. 457].

3 In every sample the Card Sort responses indicated that more delinquents wanted to leave home, that more delinquents felt rejected, and that fewer delinquents confided in their parents. Moreover, the Card Sort data indicated that within the delinquents' families there was less communication and more quarreling and dissension [p. 457].

4 In all three cultures more delinquents depicted one or both of the parents as using threats of punishment when confronted with undesirable behavior, while more nondelinquents indicated the parents would reason with their sons [p. 459].

5 Delinquents' parents were less likely to be aware of their sons' whereabouts or behavior [p.459].

Rosenquist and Megargee draw a conclusion that is contradictory to the premises of radical criminology and labeling theory and supportive of the control hypothesis:

The same basic factors differentiated the delinquents from the nondelinquents in all [ethnic groups]. This means that delinquency cannot be ascribed to fundamentally different factors in the different cultures sampled. Mexican, Latin, and Southwestern Anglo delinquency are basically the same. It is not valid to ascribe the Latins' delinquency to culture conflict, for example, or the Mexicans' to poverty. . . . the patterns found in one ethnic group are for the most part generalizable to other ethnic groups, which suggests that theoretical explanations derived in one sample could well apply to others [p. 461].

IN SUMMARY

Both developmental and comparative studies yield the same description of what makes us the way we are. If we grow up "naturally," without cultivation, like weeds, we grow up like weeds—rank. If our nurturing is defective—unappreciative, inconsistent, lax, harsh, and careless—we grow up hostile, and the hostility seems as much turned inward as turned outward. The nurturing environments that produce this denigration of self and others are the same ones that breed criminality.

Control theories have an advantage over the more strictly sociological explanations of crime causation in that they allow for individual differences in reaction to an environment. It is not assumed that "culture" or "class" or "the family" is a huge stamping mill producing stereotyped images upon the human material. The material varies. Some is tough alloy; some is more malleable. Furthermore, the production process itself varies. Being taught and being trained are not just one kind of procedure. *The Oxford English Dictionary* tells us that education is "the process of 'bringing up' [young people]." The "bringing up" is not accomplished on only one escalator. We have been brought up, in some part, by parents, if we had them, or by substitutes for parents. We have been trained, too, by everything that happened when we acted, and this means that we have learned from friends and strangers, from lovers and enemies, and even from the jumbled lessons available in books and paintings, in newspapers, and on film. This means, further, that we are still learning, that there are lessons in adulthood as there are in childhood, and that, therefore, even "well-brought-up" children may be moved by their later lessons into rational or impetuous crime.

For a theory of criminogenesis, it is not necessary to give exact weights to the many determinants of our destinies. It is particularly unnecessary if we are interested in the sociological questions. To answer these questions it is enough to know the kinds of causes that make a difference so that the consequences of broad changes in any of them may be estimated.

The Control Story in Brief

Both the subcultural and the control orientations point to the same requirements if we are to reduce the injuries we inflict on one another. A requirement is that young people be nurtured and taken care of so that they grow up as adults whose lives are explicable and purposeful. A requirement is that, as adults, we live in some pattern of accord with others, an accord that allows us individuality bounded by the legally defined rights of those with whom we live and limited by the reasonably probable possibilities open to each of us.

The theme of this theory is that human beings may be domestic animals, but they need domestication. Human creatures may be civic organisms, but they need civilization. And this means steeping in a culture.

The trouble with this theme is that it gives no political handle for planned change.

Dissatisfaction with the Control Thesis   Explanations, particularly correct ones, need not promise cures. Knowing the causes of earthquakes does not prevent them, although such knowledge may promote better defense against them.

A difficulty with control theory is that it gives politicians and others who would "solve social problems" no lever with which to manipulate change according to plan. For people who want promising answers, control theory is unsatisfactory.

No one has polled social scientists on this matter, but it seems likely that the control orientation, despite its empirical grounding, is less popular among sociologists than its more fact-free explanatory competitors. By contrast, it has been noted that the public at large accepts the propositions of control theory and places the "blame" for crime where control hypotheses do—in the nurturing process (see page 305, footnote 5).

The reluctance of some criminologists to accept the control formulation is attributable to politics. No one need be surprised today to learn that the politics of professors of the social studies differs from the politics of most of their students and from that of the citizens they represent. Measures of self-characterization, of voting behavior, and of attitudes toward issues consistently indicate that social scientists, when compared with other academics and people in general, are to be found disproportionately "on the left" (E. C. Ladd and Lipset, 1975; Yankelovich, 1972, 1974).

The favored locations of the causes of crime and the favored remedies may be expected to differ according to political persuasion, and these differences in political belief explain much of the disagreement between criminologists and their audiences. When these differences have a persistent structure, Walter Miller (1973) calls them "ideologies."[3]

There are ideologies of right and left, of course, and there are degrees of belief on each side of the spectrum. The flavor of ideological views of crime can be given by abstracting the extreme (5) and moderate (1) positions outlined by Miller concerning the causes of crime. Intermediate positions and attitudes toward societal response have been omitted, but the reader can find them in Miller's interesting, original article:

I. Sources of crime: Locus of responsibility[4]

Left

5 Behavior designated as "crime" by the ruling classes is an inevitable product of a fundamentally corrupt and unjust society. True crime is the behavior of those who perpetuate, control, and profit from an exploitative and brutalizing system. The behavior of those commonly regarded as "criminals" by establishment circles in fact represents heroic defiance and rebellion against the arbitrary and self-serving rules of an immoral social order. These persons thus bear no responsibility for what the state defines as crime; they are forced into such actions as justifiable responses to deliberate policies of oppression, discrimination, and exploitation.

1 Crime is largely a product of social ills such as poverty, unemployment, poor quality education, and unequal opportunities. While those who commit crimes out of financial need or frustration with

Right

5 Crime and violence are a direct product of a massive conspiracy by highly-organized and well-financed radical forces seeking deliberately to overthrow the society. Their basic method is an intensive and unrelenting attack on the fundamental moral values of the society, and their vehicle is that sector of the populace sufficiently low in intelligence, moral virtue, self-control, and judgment as to serve readily as their puppets by constantly engaging in those violent and predatory crimes best calculated to destroy the social order. Instigators of the conspiracy are most often members of racial or ethnic groups that owe allegiance to and are supported by hostile foreign powers.

1 The behavior of persons who habitually violate the law is caused by defective upbringing in the home, parental neglect, inade-

---

[3]An ideology, as opposed to any other set of ideas, is characterized by immunity to fact and by a promise of a better world upon accession to power of its believers. Ideology is directed toward evaluating the world and correcting it. It is less concerned, then, with knowledge and more concerned with justice. For this reason, ideologies prefer to fuse facts and values, rather than to distinguish them (Bergmann, 1968). The fusion allows an ideology to weigh truth morally. For the ideologist, what is true is what is "socially useful." As Gletkin, the Commissar, told Rubashov, the Revolutionary, "Truth is what is useful to humanity, falsehood what is harmful" (Koestler, 1941, p. 227).

[4]Reprinted with permission from Walter Miller, "Ideology and Criminal Justice Policy: Some Current Issues." © 1973 by *The Journal of Criminal Law and Criminology*.

their life conditions deserve understanding and compassion, those who continue to commit crimes in the absence of adequate justification should in some degree by held accountable for their behavior; very often they are sick or disturbed persons who need help rather than punishment. Officials dealing with crime are often well-meaning, but they sometimes act unjustly or repressively out of an excessively narrow focus on specific objectives of law-enforcement. Such behavior in turn reflects frustration with the failure of society to provide them adequate resources to to perform their tasks for which they are responsible, as it also fails to provide the resources needed to ameliorate the community conditions which breed crime.

quate religious and moral training, poor neighborhood environment, and lack of adequate role-models. These conditions result in a lack of proper respect for the law and insufficient attention to the basic moral principles which deter criminality. The federal government also contributes by failing to provide local agencies of prevention and law-enforcement with sufficient resources to perform adequately the many tasks required to reduce or control crime.

Therefore?   Others may be ideologists, but you and I resist the label. To resist the label requires that we acknowledge that accurate explanations may not be good ones (see Chapter 8). Accurate explanations are not adequate for those who demand more of an explanation than that it describe things truthfully. What is often demanded, beyond truth, is utility—that the explanation show us what to do to get us what we want.

Those who seek such "illumination" will receive it, but insofar as an explanatory promise is less than factual, it will get its believers less than what was promised. The truth sometimes tells us more clearly what we can *not* have and what will *not* work. The truth about the human condition also tells us that there is a price for everything of value. Some of the "trade-offs" that constitute the price of reducing crime are described in the following pages, where we consider what may be generally crime-productive conditions.

Chapter 17

Criminogenic Conditions

A review of the explanations of criminality reminds one of the fable about the blind philosophers confronting for the first time that marvelous beast, the elephant. The blind man who felt the elephant's ear thought the animal resembled the leaf of the banana plant. The philosopher who grasped his tail described the elephant as like a rope. The one who felt the elephant's flank thought the animal was like a mud wall. And the one who felt his leg believed the elephant to be like the trunk of a tree. All the descriptions are partly true—as are the explanations of crime rates.

The structural theories stress *where we are*. The symbolic-interactionist theories emphasize *where we believe we are, what we think we want*, and *how we believe others to be*. The subcultural thesis and, more strongly, the control propositions describe *how we came to be where we are, wanting and believing and behaving as we do*.

For the various consumers of explanations, how satisfactory the different theories are is only in small part a function of how logical and factual they are. The study of criminal conduct, and of society's responses to it, is approached out of concern. This concern has moral roots. The moral conceptions, in turn, affect policies and politics. The morality that determines what we would like to see done politically influences our choice of an explanation of crime.

Causes as Comforts The motivation to believe those explanations which best accord with our moral urges makes it difficult to present a dispassionate statement about criminogenic conditions. One of the comforts of thinking about the "causes" of crime is that the notion of causation carries with it the promise that correcting causes provides cures. This assumption moves us, then, to attend only to those causes which we should wish to change. "Good" causes of crime ought to be left alone; "bad" causes ought to be corrected. Our selection of "*the* causes" of crime is thus biased by our preference for one moral prescription rather than another and for this course of public action rather than that one.

Against this tendency, scholars who would look clearly at criminogenic conditions are constrained to discipline their moral preferences and to do without the comforting delusion that undesirable behaviors must have only evil causes. On the contrary, the behavior of aggregates, like the behavior of individuals, is probably generated in a *dense* system of causes, a system in which the roots of action are numerous, intertwined, and not uniformly entangled. Some roots are more closely bound to each other; some are stronger than others. It may be impossible, however, to disentangle one source of action from all others. In dense causal systems there are ramifications. Touching the system here affects it there, and there, and there. The despair of would-be societal engineers is this fact, that in the social web one cannot "do just one thing." One cannot change a law, enforce it, ignore it, or enact any reforms of our collective enterprise without starting a chain of effects, many of which are bound to be unforeseen and some of which are bound to be undesirable.

Values and Prices This preamble to a statement of criminogenic conditions is required as part of our understanding that the *specification* of a probable crime-making condition does not constitute an *evaluation* of it. Description need be neither commendation nor condemnation.

This qualification recognizes the fact that values have prices. The social arrangements we prefer carry a cost. Crime may be one such cost. It is its own pain. It may be a consequence, nonetheless, of some of the circumstances, and some of the movements, that are otherwise preferred.

This is said as a caution against zealotry. Images of how people ought to be and, more to the point, images of how to get people from where they are to where they ought to be—both these images are encouraged by *denial* of their costs, by the *disclaimer* that such good intentions and good ends might involve pains as discomforting as the social "dis-eases'"they are designed to cure.

In brief, and to repeat, a description of some of the roots of crime does not signify that all these causes ought to be removed. Some kind of crime, under some circumstances, may constitute a price paid for other things we value—like freedom.

The Key to Criminogenesis: Culture The governor of crime, as well as its generator, is culture. Every "factor" that is selected for attention as possibly criminogenic is embedded in a culture and reflects that culture. Every current explanation of crime looks at some facet of culture as central.

"Culture" refers to a way of life of a people with a sense of identity and, usually, with a demarcated territory. Culture is, in Eliot's phrase, "a peculiar way of thinking, feeling, and behaving" (1948, p. 57). It is a patterning of our way of living together. The pattern is discernible in its partial manifestations—in the art of a people; in their diet, dress, and customs; in their religion and values; in the structure of their society; and in their language. These dimensions can be, and have been, measured (Cattell, 1950).

Calling culture the key to crime emphasizes the point that each factor listed as criminogenic makes its impact in terms of the total way of life of which it is a part. That way of life probably *over*determines many behaviors, including some criminal careers. Culture means a *reinforcement* of the way we are, as well as a *rearing* in how we are.

If this conception is correct, it implies that, for some people, lawful or criminal conduct is more than "just caused." It is "overcaused"; thus amelioration of cause 1 leaves alive causes 2, 3, 4, and 5—any one of which may be sufficient to produce the behavior under attention.

To the extent to which this is so, attempts to treat crime by acting upon any singular factor or any small set of factors—like housing, schools, incomes, or families—will be only as successful as the culture allows. This is to say that, just as social reform can seldom "do just one thing," so too does social reform require "doing more than just one thing."

Culture means regulated conduct. This includes the regulation of criminal conduct. A culture includes the training that controls crime. At the same time it defines the occasions on which crime is rational and, even, required. The code of *vendetta* requires murder in defense of honor. The same honor, however, that moves the vengeful man to murder makes it difficult for him to lie or to steal from "his own." Culture limits crime and channels crime where it calls for it. The circumstances that destroy a culture are, therefore, the circumstances that induce crime.

Cultures live and die. Patterns of behavior and belief fluctuate. They receive more and less allegiance. Innovators are ever-present to question customs; barbarians are ever-present to destroy them. Technologies change, and with them the economic arrangements that underlie a culture. Information changes, too, and with it the beliefs that were our morals.

These are some of the forces that change cultures. As they change cultures, they weaken them. The debility is seen in the failure of institutions—schools that become "irrelevant," laws that become unjust, families that become unnecessary. The failure of institutions is a cause, a sign, and an accompaniment of the loss of community, and it is with this loss that the serious crimes are generated. *Whatever destroys community fosters an increase in the predatory crimes.*

There is nothing novel in this proposition. It is an idea embedded in the moral teachings of every major religion. It is an idea reflected in each of the propositions to follow.

A ROSTER OF CRIMINOGENIC CONDITIONS

Outlines of "the causes of crime" are always artificial. They can never do more than point to conditions whose impact is subject to "everything else that is happening." Since "everything else that happens" occurs uniquely in each historical instance, it becomes impossible to assign weights to each of the criminogenic conditions. These conditions can be listed, but they cannot be ranked in importance. This is why each proposition in an inventory of criminogenic conditions requires the deadening qualification "other things being equal."

On "Other Things Being Equal"

Any set of statements about the causes of crime ought to carry the defensive *caeteris paribus* clause, the qualification that the proposition holds true insofar as "other things remain equal." This defense is an admission that the observer is looking at factors one at a time, when, in actuality, they never operate that way. The fact that variables do not function "one at a time" is a justification of speaking of patterned variables, of culture, as central to the understanding of criminogenesis. However, it is part of Western thinking to attend to the kinds of things that make crime more or less probable. As we have seen, this style of thought is congenial to the assumption of reformers that if they know causes, they can treat them and cure "social diseases." To treat causes requires their isolation. It is the desire to isolate causes that has led to the naming of criminal conditions. If we go along with this intellectual custom, it is only with the proviso that each criminogenic condition be considered, *not* as "its own thing" with strongly independent effects, but as one among a shifting complex of causes that affects crime rates.

The nine crime-generating "conditions" listed below are better regarded as hypotheses than as certainties. Evidence in their favor is found in the correlates of differential crime rates noted in Chapter 7 and in the data of those explanatory attempts reported in Chapters 9 through 16.

1 Movement of People Cultures require transmission, indoctrination, and room in which to operate. The flow of carriers of diverse cultures weakens the process by which a culture is nurtured. When people of diverse cultures meet in large numbers and attempt to live together in some accommodating way, each culture is threatened. *The physical relocation of large masses of people is a criminogenic condition.*

a This statement is more true as the meeting of culture carriers occurs under conditions of "freedom," that is, under conditions in which there is no etiquette that governs the relations between them.

b Proposition 1 refers to the *process* of peoples' meeting. It is this process that is criminogenic, and it is during the time of seeking a settlement that crime rates may be expected to increase. Once separate settlements are established, a stable accommodation may develop, accompanied by lower rates of the serious offenses.

c States that attempt to make one nation out of many will have higher crime rates than states of similar development that allow voluntary separation.

d Multination states that regionalize their nationalities, as the Soviet Union and Switzerland have done, will have lower crime rates than states of similar development that do not regionalize.

2 Crowding Beyond some ill-defined threshold, the more crowded an area, the higher will be its crime rate.

a Crowding is difficult to measure, since where one *resides* may not be where one *lives*. People are somewhat mobile, and some denizens of dense cities have periodic chances of "getting away from it all." Furthermore, the psychological dimension of *crowding* is only imperfectly gauged from measures of *density*, like the number of people per square mile. See, again, the studies by Galle, Harries, and others referred to earlier (pages 153–159).

b Cultures of long standing may have developed particular accommodations to density that minimize crowding effects—the houseboat dwellers of Hong Kong are an example. If this were proved true, it would be necessary to qualify proposition 2 as regards *stable* populations and to apply the proposition with even greater force to areas that have recently become crowded.

3 Social Mobility It is to be expected that, when large proportions of a population climb up or fall down class ladders, the effect will be criminogenic. This does not mean that particular individuals who change their status need be more prone to criminality. The proposition refers more strongly to the correlative conditions, the culture-challenging conditions, that seem to go along with high rates of vertical mobility.

4 Relative Deprivation This subjective state is criminogenic. It feeds on the perennial emotion, envy, against which all people have tried to defend themselves. Whatever contributes to such feelings is part of the crime-making process. Such sentiments are stimulated widely today by political ideologies and disseminated by the mass media and schools. This fact says nothing about the "justice" of such stimulation.

It is commonly believed that inequalities in economic condition, in prestige, and in power are jointly, and separately, sufficient to stimulate the resentful sense of unjust deprivation. However, both historical and experimental studies have shown that there is no necessary connection between inequality and grievance. Rather, such studies have shown that it is the *process of equalization* that is productive of feelings of relative deprivation. For example, Runciman (1966) concludes from his historical research and his survey of opinion in Britain that "a heightening of prosperity [brought with it] a heightening of grievance" (p. 4) and that the period between 1918 and 1966 was one "in which relative deprivation of status was rising in both magnitude and frequency as equality of status came closer to being achieved" (p. 233).

5 Child Neglect and Misuse of Youth Any conditions or any teachings that weaken the loving and the training of offspring are part of the crime-causing system.

a Challenges to the family and criticisms of family life, including literature and drama based on its sadness, are contributory. Saying this says nothing about the *truth* of this literature, but only about its probable *effects*.

Such challenges are contributory unless, and until, substitute institutions for the education of generations *evolve*. The term "evolve" is used because the *creation* of institutions in mass societies is difficult, if not impossible. The Israeli *kibbutzim*, of course, represent one created alternative within a relatively homogeneous socioeconomic and cultural setting.

b Schools that shame children, or imprison them, are criminogenic.

c Schools that provide no moral models are criminogenic. Those religious bodies that set up their own separate schools acknowledge that their formal education should include moral modeling as well as the teaching of facts and skills.

d Societies that have little use for adolescents will have higher crime rates. The term "little use" betokens poor apprenticeship for adulthood.

6 Mass Media The mass media make a contribution to crime. These instruments function in Western societies as culture breakers and as generators of feelings of relative deprivation.

The economic motive to gain and maintain large audiences means that the "creative" people of the media must stimulate us, which often means shock us. Consequently, television, cinema, and theater stretch the limits of our morals.

More directly, the media—television and movies in particular—provide heroic models of criminals: of burglars (*The Anderson Tapes*), of whores (*Klute*[1]), of dope peddlers (*Easy Rider*[2]), of bank robbers (*The Getaway; Butch Cassidy and the Sundance Kid*), and of gangsters (*The Godfather*).

Royal commissions and congressional committees have employed social scientists to evaluate the effects of our mass arts. While we debate the meaning of the results of social research and doubt whether social-scientific scales are sensitive enough to weigh the influence of the arts, we note that no moral community doubts their effectiveness. Hence, censorship is a normal feature of such varied attempts to maintain moral difference as can be observed in religious and political movements—among the Hutterites and Amish, for example, and the Nazis and Communists.

[1]"Vivienne, a pretty 22-year-old girl, averages 3,000 to 5,000 tax-free dollars a month hustling in the San Francisco area. She started in 'the life' about seven months ago, inspired by Jane Fonda's performance as a high-priced call girl in 'Klute.' 'I estimate that thousands of girls got turned on to tricking after seeing that movie,' she says" (*Newsweek*, 1973a).

[2]Evaluation of the effects of the visual media is made difficult by the selective attention with which we view the arts. Thus several anonymous criminologists who read these pages in review objected that "Easy Rider" was a dope user, not a dope peddler. He was both, of course. Such selective viewers forget the first sequences in the movie, in which the "heroes" buy in Mexico and sell in the States to get the "bread" for their easy ride.

7   Comforting Chemicals   Human beings have always attempted to alter their experience—if not steadily, at least episodically. Regularity is monotony, and monotony is a bore. The human animal sometimes seeks to elevate sensation above the normal and sometimes seeks to depress feelings toward forgetfulness. We do this through music and drama, through poetry and dancing, and through ceremonies that celebrate the mysteries.

We also do this with the aid of comforting chemicals. The comforts run from such innocent things as chewing gum and betel nut to eating, drinking, sniffing, rubbing, and "shooting" an amazing pharmacopoeia. Once habituated to these chemical aids, we find withdrawing from them painful. When the legal supply of such chemicals is cut off or restricted, an illegal market will come into being. Criminalizing the use of tobacco, alcohol, marijuana, and the more dramatic drugs of oblivion makes criminals by definition.

The public question is whether the criminal law should be employed against any or all of such chemical solace. The question is not solely a matter of the bodily harm that chronic use of these comforts may produce. Here some legal chemicals, like tobacco, have a worse record than some illegal ones like marijuana or heroin. The question is also one of the *moral* effects of habituation to soporifics and of the *practical* effects of public intoxication.

The practical effects—drunken driving, for example—might be penalized without forbidding the use of alcohol or marijuana. Our moral concern intrudes, however, upon our decision to make this separation. We are concerned lest vices that are permitted spread and change the moral tenor of our lives.

The moral question becomes a civic problem in democracies where a libertarian tradition denies that the state has any business protecting individuals from themselves. This tradition would restrict crime to the damage we do others.

The question of when and how the state ought to intervene in our lives might be more readily resolved if we could calculate the costs of ignoring vice, or suppressing it, against the benefits for mass society. This calculation has never been attempted; perhaps it cannot be. Meanwhile, the huge efforts to apply the criminal law against the use of intoxicants, narcotics, and the hallucinogenic chemicals is, of course, criminogenic.

There is no certain advice for us. The advice that psychology might lend to social policy here is difficult to apply. Psychology says, first, that rewards for desirable behavior are less costly (more effective) than penalties for undesirable behavior. Persons whose lives are "good in themselves" do not need the deadening chemicals. However, persons who receive as much pain as pleasure when they look at reality each morning need what comfort they can get. The difficulty is that there is no formula for giving joy to others. There is, moreover, no science of societal engineering that knows how to build more rewarding societies without risking tyranny.

Some schools of psychology provide a second piece of advice. They would license the perennial vices and allow them to seek their own segregated corners. To this school of thought, leaving people alone when they damage only themselves seems less costly than jailing them.

It is doubtful, however, whether any of us can maintain this liberality of attitude consistently. At some point, the damage we do "only to ourselves" is seen to have a societal impact. Vice is contagious. When the medical analogy of "contagion" is adopted, it becomes questionable whether "crimes without victims" are victimless. Furthermore, when one thinks that private vices may become epidemic, he gives a different answer to the question about the "right" of the state to intrude upon the "civil liberties" of its citizens. No one has the "right" to spread smallpox, and no civil libertarian seems offended by the quarantine of Typhoid Mary.

The analogy of contagion and the epidemic has been applied, with good reason, to the spread of the use of opiates. J. Q. Wilson and his colleagues argue that "heroin is so destructive of the human personality that it should not be made generally available" (1972, p. 26). They provide evidence that addiction to opiates fits the model of contagion, since the way addicts get started is by contact, through the instigation of a friend. These investigators also present data that contagion can be contained through vigorous law enforcement, that the *probability and severity* of enforcement reduce the spread of the addiction. In their words, increasing "the 'expected costs' of an arrest to the user [reduces] the number of addicts in the city. By 'expected costs' [is meant] the probability of being arrested multiplied by the probability of being sentenced to prison and the length of the average prison sentence" (p. 19).

Containing the spread of opiates through law enforcement need not be equated, however, with jailing junkies. Quarantine is confining, but its intent is not punitive.

8 Anarchy and Authority The Western world has recently experienced a mood of rebellion. "Authority" in itself sounds "authoritarian," and that adjective is certainly pejorative. "Expression" has increased in value as "respect" has declined. For example, C. W. Morris and Small (1971) compared the preferences for 13 ways of life as rated by American college students in the early 1950s and in the 1970s. "Preserving the best that man has attained" dropped markedly in value during these decades, as did "social restraint" and "self-control." By contrast, in 1970 the students gave greater value to "withdrawal and self-sufficiency," "receptivity and sympathetic concern," and "self-indulgence and sensuous enjoyment."

Dilemma: Does freedom from authority produce freedom from morality? A new "American dilemma" is with us. It is the choice between allowing children to be free and wishing them to behave well.

A recent movement, apparent in home and school, would permit children to "find" themselves, their own etiquette, and their own rules. It is hoped that this individuation will release their "creative" powers and make them happy. As with every value, there is a cost, however. The cost is a decline in respect for elders, fathers in particular, with a compensatory rise in respect for peers and a vulnerability to peer-sponsored misbehavior.

The price tag on freedom from authority is not fixed. Research is tentative and does not tell us the *power* of the alleged causes. The research is, nevertheless, provocative. For example, Bixenstine and others (1976) tested the "readiness [of children] to engage in antisocial behavior" among youngsters in grades 3, 6, 8, and 11 from two different school environments. One school was a university-connected teacher-training institution with a reputation for being "progressive, experimental, and purposefully nonauthoritarian" (p. 235). The other school was a suburban facility that was "more nondescript, less self-consciously philosophic. It appears to be . . . more traditional, with quieter halls and classrooms and more attention to codes and rules" (p. 235). The university-related school had more children from middle- and upper-middle-class homes, while the suburban school had more children from working- and middle-class families.

Readiness for, or resistance to, misbehavior was measured by response to questionnaires, one of which was adapted from Bronfenbrenner's studies (1967, 1970) of differences in the rearing of Soviet and American children. Findings confirm Bronfenbrenner's earlier research, namely that American children resist temptation more as they are "attached" to their parents and resist it less as they conform to their peers. The effect, however, is not that the child "is won away from parents to children," but, rather, that the child is, "at least for a time, lost to adults" (Bixenstine et al., 1976, p. 235).

The conclusion to be drawn from these studies, those cited in the preceding chapter, and a library of corroborating research is that children who become distant from their parents feel that lying, vandalism, and disobedience are less wrong than do children who remain closer to their parents—and, notably, to their fathers. In addition, parents who permit aggression and deceit promote these activities. These correlations have been repeatedly noted in research which is cross-cultural as well as local, which is longitudinal as well as cross-sectional, and which has used observations of conduct as well as verbal measures. Additional evidence of these associations can be found in the works of M. K. Bacon et al. (1963), Bandura and Walters (1959), Decter (1975), W. McCord and McCord (1960), Rosen and D'Andrade (1959), Sears (1961), and Siegel and Kohn (1959).

Prescription: Prudence   Whatever one's pleasure or displeasure in "generation gaps," a price is paid. The question becomes one of limits, or of what the Greeks used to think of as "balance." At one extreme lies anarchy; at the other, uncritical submission to authority. The ancient Greek prescription was for *sophrosyne*, a prudent moderation between self-expression and self-control, between being oneself and respecting others.

This recommendation is relevant to the study of criminogenesis, for people who recognize no external authority will have no internal authority.[3] They will have no reliable self-control that limits their actions vis-à-vis others. What one

[3]This statement may be a tautology. The suggested measure of "internal authority" is self-control, that is, acting in accord with a sense of obligation when no police officer is present to enforce compliance. It seems possible, but difficult, to assess this quality independently of measures of allegiance to "external authority." If these characteristics could be reliably and independently gauged, our plausible sentence would be saved from its seeming circularity.

wants to do will be what one does. The person who asks, "What's wrong with that?" is already infected.

9 Laws and Their Enforcement Laws without force are criminogenic. Despite our reluctance to pay its costs, force *is* effective in containing crime. To say this is not to imply that there are no limits to force. It is as Talleyrand said to Napoleon: "You can do everything with your bayonets, sire, except sit on them."

The fact that there are limits to legal sanctions (Packer, 1968) does not mean that sanctions are without effects. It is true that where there is moral control, there is less need for legal control; and it is true, as Bickel (1972) reminds us, that "law can never make us as secure as we are when we do not need it" (p. 61).

This has been a theme of the theories of criminogenesis we have described—that it is in culture conflict that crime is bred. It is in such conflict between majorities and minorities that the criminal sanction is effective. There *is* a deterrent effect in the enforcement of the criminal law. It has been recorded in a wide context of behaviors—from the reduction of reckless and drunken driving (Cramton, 1969; Shumate, 1958) to the containment of the "index crimes" (Tittle, 1969) to the reduction of ritualized robbery, murder, and gangsterism (Bruce, 1969; Pantaleone, 1966) to the control of political turmoil (Feierabend and Nesvold, 1970). The conditions and the limits of the deterrent effect deserve study, but the *fact* of deterrence needs to be taken seriously (Andenaes, 1966; Gibbs, 1975; Tittle, 1969; Zimring and Hawkins, 1973).

The fact that we are deterred, sometimes, by the threat of punishment has been obscured by three muddles: (*a*) the confusion of specific and general deterrence, (*b*) the confusion of law on the books and law in action, and (*c*) the confusion of crime as sickness and crime as rational conduct.

a Confusion of specific and general deterrence *Specific*, or *individual*, *deterrence* refers to the impact of a penalty, or its threat, upon the person who receives it. Our earlier discussion of punishment contingencies (pages 199–204) made it clear that penalty is not one thing. It is no surprise, then, that some kinds of people, when "punished," are not deflected from committing further crimes. Recidivism is a common phenomenon among those punished under the criminal law.

The failure, at times, of individual deterrence does not mean, however, that enforcement of the law has no general deterrent effect. *General deterrence* is the assumption that the punishment of offenders causes others to abstain from such crimes as might otherwise be tempting. The hypothesis of general deterrence is that punishment raises the threshold of temptation for many individuals.

A general-deterrent effect is difficult to measure, and this is why we quarrel about it. It is difficult to measure for many reasons, as Cousineau (1976) has shown, but a major reason is that general deterrence is something we can *not* observe, namely, the fact that anonymous others do *not* commit some crime. Observing what people do *not* do is impossible in the abstract. In concrete cases, among individuals we "know," including ourselves, we make judgments about temptations resisted because of the ugly consequences of succumbing to them. But, in the aggregate, the assumption of general deterrence is tested only by approximation, and we acknowledge, with Gibbs (1975), that "the term denotes an *inherently unobservable* phenomenon" (p. 3).

The assumption of general deterrence remains an active one, however, and one to be abandoned only at risk. It is possible to maintain the assumption while recognizing that some kinds of people, psychotically alone or fortified by peers and an ideology, are *not* deterred from some kinds of crime by fear of punishment (Ball, 1955; Guze, 1976; Taft, 1946). But it does not follow from all this that there is no general-deterrent effect or, worse, that "social science" has disproved the existence of such an effect. Much depends on the relative sizes of majorities and minorities, on the swiftness of enforcement and its probability, and on the severity of the penalties a society is willing to impose.

b Confusion of law on the books and law in action A second source of obscurity about the efficacy of the criminal law confuses the laws people make with the laws they enforce. It is one thing, for example, to debate whether capital punishment works by comparing jurisdictions that do and do not "have" it. It is another matter to assess the deterrent effects of such a penalty when it is applied. Unfortunately, some research has confounded the two uses of law.

c Confusion of crime as sickness and crime as rational conduct Possible deterrent effects are obscured also by the imposition of a psychiatrically buttressed system of belief upon the definition of crime. According to this way of thinking, crime is called a "symptom." "Symptoms," of course, are to be ignored, suffered, or palliated, while physicians treat their causes. Our study of theories of criminality has shown us, however, that the causes of criminal conduct are imperfectly known. It has taught us that such causes are probably numerous, intertwined, "more than sufficient," and costly to manipulate.

The medical model that defines crime as "symptomatic" regards criminals as sick persons and never as rational ones. There are crazy criminals, of course, just as there are psychotic law-abiders. But, however much it is shown that some crime is rational (see Chapters 9 and 10), the medical model of criminality persists. It persists in the hope that, where there is sickness, therapy can be found. This is proof by "word magic." However, when attempts to "cure" criminals of their "sickness" are evaluated, the results are largely negative (Fishman, 1975; Lipton et al., 1975). No one knows a therapy, economically applicable, that reliably rehabilitates.

Students of the failed efforts to reform offenders have abandoned the medical model of criminality. Abandoning the presumptuous notion that most crime is illness leads Wilks and Martinson (1976) to make two major recommendations:

1   That the legal objective of *restraining* the offender be more effectively implemented. This requires, among other things, "the removal of the criminal justice system from the treatment business" (p. 5).

2 That "the indeterminate sentence and parole boards" be abolished (p. 5).

IN SUMMARY

It bears repeating that values have prices and that calling conditions "crime-productive" says nothing about their possible rewards.

Physical and social mobility may be desirable in themselves. Certainly many people say so and behave as if this were so. Furthermore, some level of density is required if there is to be social activity and excitement; many people feel bored and lonely in sparse settlements.

Similarly, the sense of relative deprivation is justified morally and politically. Criminal actions that are taken in the name of reduction of deprivation are considered by some citizens to be excusable. This excuse is applied to a wide range of crimes, including even rape (Cleaver, 1968).

Mothering may once have been a virtue beyond reproach, but today it is argued that the weakening of the bonds of family and wider kinship, through which children have been acculturated, is justified because it is "liberating." So, too, among the followers of Reich (1942), there are defenders of "free schools" that allow each child to find his or her own morality by bumping into others.

The mass media are also valued despite their prices. They provide pleasure and information. They teach other lessons than criminal ones, and not all their heroic models break laws.

The comforting chemicals have their costs, and sometimes very high ones, but their existence throughout history and across cultures tells us that they are not likely to be abandoned. We can work most effectively for moderation in their use and for control of their public consequences. A similar prudence is recommended in the denigration of authority and in the passage of laws without force.

We are returned to our theme, which claims that the "causes" of crime, like the "causes" of any other set of social behaviors, lie in the social fabric. The fabric is flexible. It stretches as it is altered. It can be torn, patched, and rewoven without being destroyed. What weakens one part of a culture may strengthen another.

There are limits, of course. This we believe we have learned from the histories of dead civilizations. We move uncertainly, however, like the blind philosophers, since we have not been told what these limits are. We do not know how much abrasion of the social fabric leads to its dissolution.

One conclusion is certain: We destroy cultures at our peril. Culture is an acquisition, not an endowment. It is transmitted, not invented. The best hope for containing the damage that our self-interests "naturally" inflict on each other lies in the continuity of a culture.

References

Abbagnano, N. 1967. "Positivism." In P. Edwards (ed.), *The Encyclopedia of Philosophy*. New York: Macmillan.

Abel, E. L., and G. C. Walters. 1972. "Reactions to punishment determined by infant experience with aversive stimulation." *Developmental Psychology*, 7:1–3.

Abrams, M. 1958. "The mass media and social class in Great Britain." Paper read at the Fourth World Congress of Sociology, Stresa, Italy.

Acock, A. A., and M. L. DeFleur. 1972. "A configurational approach to contingent consistency in the attitude-behavior relationship." *American Sociological Review*, 37:714–726.

Adams, H. 1907. *The Education of Henry Adams*. Boston: Houghton Mifflin.

Adler, F. 1976. *Sisters in Crime: The Rise of the New Female Criminal*. New York: McGraw-Hill.

Ainesworth, M. D. S. 1967. *Infancy in Uganda: Infant Care and the Growth of Love*. Baltimore: Johns Hopkins.

Akers, R. L. 1964. "Socio-economic status and delinquent behavior: A retest." *Journal of Research on Crime and Delinquency*, 1:38–46.

Akman, O. O., and A. Normandeau. 1968. "Towards the measurement of criminality in Canada: A replication study." *Acta Criminologica*, 1:135–260.

Allinsmith, W. 1960. "The learning of moral standards." In D. R. Miller and G. E. Swanson (eds.), *Inner Conflict and Defense*. New York: Holt.

Alper, T. B. 1946. "Memory for completed and incompleted tasks as a function of personality: Analysis of group data." *Journal of Abnormal and Social Psychology*, 41:403–420.

Alpert, R. 1972. "A fever of ethnicity." *Commentary*, **53**:68–73.

Altheide, D. 1976. *Creating Reality: How TV News Distorts Events*. Beverly Hills, Calif.: Sage.

American Anthropological Association. 1947. "Statement on human rights." *American Anthropologist,* **49**:539–543.

American Law Institute. 1953. *Model Penal Code*. Philadelphia: The Institute.

Ammende, E. 1936. *Human Life in Russia*. London: Allen and Unwin.

Andenaes, J. 1966. "The general preventive effects of punishment." *University of Pennsylvania Law Review*, **114**:949–983.

Anderson, E. A. 1976. "The 'chivalrous' treatment of the female offender in the arms of the criminal justice system: A review of the literature." *Social Problems*, **23**:350–357.

Annuaire Statistique de la France. 1970–1974. Paris: Institut National de la Statistique et des Etudes Economiques.

Annual Abstract of Statistics. 1974. London: Government Statistical Service.

Annuario Statistico Italiano. 1967–1973. Roma: Institute Centrale di Statistica.

Anonymous. 1942. "An Analysis of Jewish Culture." In I. Graeber and S. H. Britt (eds.), *Jews in a Gentile World: The Problem of Anti-Semitism*. New York: Macmillan.

Antunes, G., and A. L. Hunt. 1972. *The Impact of Certainty and Severity of Punishment on Levels of Crime in American States: An Extended Analysis*. Evanston, Ill.: Northwestern University, Center for Urban Affairs.

Appel, J. H., and N. J. Peterson. 1965. "What's wrong with punishment?" *Journal of Criminal Law, Criminology, and Police Science*, **56**:450–453.

Archer, D., and R. Gartner. 1975. "Some aspects of reliability and validity in comparative crime data." Santa Cruz: University of California. Unpublished paper.

Arendt, H. 1964. *Eichmann in Jerusalem: A Report on the Banality of Evil*. New York: Viking.

Arendt, H. 1967. "Reflections: Truth and politics." *The New Yorker*, **43**:49–88 (February 25).

Armor, D. J. 1972. "The evidence on busing." *The Public Interest*, (28):90–126.

Arnold, W. R. 1971. "Race and ethnicity relative to other factors in juvenile court dispositions." *American Journal of Sociology*, **77**:211–227.

Aronfreed, J. 1963. "The effects of experimental socialization paradigms upon two moral responses to transgression." *Journal of Abnormal and Social Psychology*, **66**:437–448.

Aronfreed, J., and A. Reber. 1965. "Internalized behavioral suppression and the timing of social punishment." *Journal of Personality and Social Psychology*, **1**:3–16.

Arthur, A. Z. 1969. "Diagnostic testing and the new alternatives." *Psychological Bulletin*, **72**:183–192.

Ash, P. 1949. "The reliability of psychiatric diagnoses." *Journal of Abnormal and Social Psychology*, **44**:272–277.

Asher, J. 1974. "Committing dissidents: Is it a problem in U.S.?" *APA Monitor*, **5**:1, 8.

Atkinson, M. 1974. "Interpreting retributive claims." *Ethics*, **85**:80–86.

Aubert, V. (ed.), 1970. *Sociology of Law*. London: Penguin.

Auletta, K. 1975a. "Should these men go to jail?" *New York*, **8**:36–41 (December 1).

Auletta, K. 1975b. "Who's to blame for the fix we're in?" *New York*, **8**:29–41 (October 27).

Avi-Itzhak, B., and R. Shinnar. 1973. "Quantitative models in crime control." *Journal of Criminal Justice*, **1**:185–217.

Avio, K. L., and C. S. Clark. 1976. *Property Crime in Canada: An Econometric Study.* Toronto: University of Toronto Press.

Ayer, A. J. (ed.). 1959. *Logical Positivism.* New York: Free Press.

Babst, D. V., and J. W. Mannering. 1965. "Probation versus imprisonment for similar types of offenders." *Journal of Research in Crime and Delinquency,* **2**:60–71.

Bach, R. 1970. *Jonathan Livingstone Seagull.* New York: Macmillan.

Bacon, D. C. 1976. "Ripoffs: New American way of Life." *U.S. News & World Report,* **80**:29–32 (May 31).

Bacon, M. K., et al. 1963. "A cross-cultural study of correlates of crime." *Journal of Abnormal and Social Psychology,* **66**:291–301.

Bagot, J. H. 1941. *Juvenile Delinquency: A Comparative Study of the Position in Liverpool and England and Wales.* London: Cape.

Bailyn, L. 1959. "Mass media and children: A study of exposure habits and cognitive effects." *Psychological Monographs,* **73** (Whole #471).

Bain, R. 1958. "Our schizoid culture and sociopathy." *Sociology and Social Research,* **42**:263–268.

Baldwin, J., et al. 1976. *The Urban Criminal.* London: Tavistock.

Ball, J. C. 1955. "The deterrence concept in criminology and law." *Journal of Criminal Law, Criminology, and Police Science,* **46**:347–354.

Bandura, A. (ed.) 1972. *Psychological Modeling: Conflicting Theories.* Chicago: Aldine.

Bandura, A. 1973. *Aggression: A Social Learning Analysis.* Englewood Cliffs, N.J.: Prentice-Hall.

Bandura, A., and R. H. Walters. 1959. *Adolescent Aggression.* New York: Ronald.

Bandura, A., and R. H. Walters. 1963. *Social Learning and Personality Development.* New York: Holt.

Bandura, A., et al. 1961. "Transmission of aggression through imitation of aggressive models." *Journal of Abnormal and Social Psychology,* **63**:575–582.

Banfield, E. C. 1968. *The Unheavenly City*; rev. 1974 as *The Unheavenly City Revisited.* Boston: Little, Brown.

Banks, C., et al. 1975. "Public attitudes to crime and the penal system." *British Journal of Criminology,* **15**:288–240.

Barker, G. H. 1940. "Family factors in the ecology of juvenile delinquency." *Journal of Criminal Law and Criminology,* **30**:681–691.

Barndt, R. J., and D. M. Johnson. 1955. "Time orientation in delinquents." *Journal of Abnormal and Social Psychology,* **51**:343–345.

Barnett, A., et al. 1974. *On Urban Homicide: A Statistical Analysis.* Cambridge, Mass.: Massachusetts Institute of Technology, Operations Research Center.

Barron, M. L. 1951. "Research on intermarriage: A survey of accomplishments and prospects." *American Journal of Sociology,* **57**:249–255.

Barzini, L. 1971. *From Caesar to the Mafia.* New York: Library Press.

Bassiouni, M. C. 1974. "A survey of the major criminal justice systems in the world." In D. Glaser (ed.), *Handbook of Criminology.* Chicago: Rand McNally.

Bayley, D. H. 1976. "Learning about crime: The Japanese experience." *The Public Interest,* (44):55–68.

Bean, F. D., and R. G. Cushing. 1971. "Criminal homicide, punishment, and deterrence: Methodological and substantive reconsiderations." *Social Science Quarterly,* **52**:277–289.

Beattie, R. H., and C. K. Bridges. 1970. *Superior Court Probation and/or Jail Sample.* Sacramento, Calif.: Department of Justice, Bureau of Criminal Statistics.

Beauchamp, T. L. (ed.). 1974. *Philosophical Problems of Causation.* Belmont, Calif.: Dickenson.

Beccaria, C. 1764. *Essay on Crimes and Punishments*. Trans. 1963 by H. Paolucci. Indianapolis: Boobs-Merrill.

Beck, B. 1967. "Welfare as a moral category." *Social Problems*, 14:258–277.

Becker, H. S. 1963. *Outsiders: Studies in the Sociology of Deviance*. Glencoe, Ill., Free Press.

Becker, H. S. 1967. "Whose side are we on?" *Social Problems*, 14:239–247.

Becker, H. S. 1974. "Labelling theory reconsidered." In S. Messinger et al. (eds.), *The Aldine Crime and Justice Annual—1973*. Chicago: Aldine.

Behrman, S. N. 1972. "People in a diary: I." *The New Yorker*, 48:36–94 (May 13).

Beichman, A. 1972. *Nine Lies about America*. New York: Library Press.

Beilin, H. 1956. "The pattern of postponability and its relation to social class mobility." *Journal of Social Psychology*, 44:33–48.

Belson, W. A., et al. 1970. *The Development of a Procedure for Eliciting Information from Boys about the Nature and Extent of Their Stealing*. London: London School of Economics and Political Science, Survey Research Centre.

Belson, W. A., et al. 1975. *Juvenile Theft: The Causal Factors*. New York: Harper and Row.

Benda, J. 1928. *The Great Betrayal*. Trans. by R. Aldington. London: Routledge.

Benney, M., et al. 1956. "Age and sex in the interview." *American Journal of Sociology*, 62:143–152.

Bensman, J., and I. Gerver. 1963. "Crime and punishment in the factory: The function of deviancy in maintaining the social system." *American Sociological Review*, 28:588–598.

Bereiter, C. 1973. "Education, socioeconomic status, IQ, and their effects." *Contemporary Psychology*, 18:401–403.

Berg, I. 1971. *Education and Jobs: The Great Training Robbery*. Boston: Beacon Press.

Bergin, A. E., and S. L. Garfield. 1971. *Psychotherapy and Behavior Change*. New York: Wiley.

Bergmann, G. 1968. "Ideology." In M. Brodbeck (ed.), *Readings in the Philosophy of the Social Sciences*. New York: Macmillan.

Berkov, B., and J. Sklar. 1975. "Methodological options in measuring illegitimacy and the difference they make." *Social Biology*, 22:356–371.

Berkowitz, L. 1962. *Aggression: A Social Psychological Analysis*. New York: McGraw-Hill.

Berkowitz, L. 1965. "The concept of aggressive drive: Some additional considerations." In L. Berkowitz (ed.), *Advances in Experimental Social Psychology*. (Vol. 2.) New York: Academic Press.

Berkowitz, L. 1967. "Readiness or necessity." *Contemporary Psychology*. 12:580–582.

Berkowitz, L. 1968. "Impulse, aggression, and the gun." *Psychology Today*, 2:18–22.

Berkowitz, L. 1970. "The contagion of violence: An S-R mediational analysis of some effects of observed aggression." In W. J. Arnold and M. M. Page (eds.), *Nebraska Symposium on Motivation*. Lincoln: University of Nebraska Press.

Berkowitz, L. 1973. "Words and symbols as stimuli to aggressive responses." In J. F. Knutson (ed.), *The Control of Aggression: Implications from Basic Research*. Chicago: Aldine.

Berkowitz, L. 1974. "Some determinants of impulsive aggression: Role of mediated associations with reinforcements for aggression." *Psychological Review*, 81:165–176.

Berkowitz, L., and R. E. Goranson. 1964. "Motivational and judgmental determinants of social perception." *Journal of Abnormal and Social Psychology*, 69:296–302.

Berkowitz, L., and J. Macaulay. 1971. "The contagion of criminal violence." *Sociometry*, **34**:238–260.

Berkowitz, L., and E. Rawlings. 1963. "Effects of film violence on inhibitions against subsequent aggression." *Journal of Abnormal and Social Psychology*, **66**:405–412.

Berliner, J. S. 1961. "The situation of the plant manager." In A. Inkeles and K. Geiger (eds.), *Soviet Society: A Book of Readings*. Boston: Houghton Mifflin.

Beynon, E. D. 1935. "Crimes and customs of the Hungarians in Detroit." *Journal of Criminal Law, Criminology, and Police Science*, **25**:755–774.

Bickel, A. M. 1972. "The 'uninhibited, robust, and wide-open' first amendment: From 'Sullivan' to the Pentagon Papers." *Commentary*, **54**:60–67.

Biderman, A. D., et al. 1967. *Report on a Pilot Study in the District of Columbia on Victimization and Attitudes toward Law Enforcement*. Field Survey I: President's Commission on Law Enforcement and Administration of Justice. Washington, D.C.: GPO.

Biderman, A. D., et al., 1972. *An Inventory of Surveys of the Public on Crime, Justice, and Related Topics*. Washington, D.C.: Law Enforcement Assistance Administration.

Biggs, J., Jr. 1955. *The Guilty Mind: Psychiatry and the Law of Homicide*. Baltimore: Johns Hopkins.

Bixenstine, V. E., and R. L. Buterbaugh. 1967. "Integrative behavior in adolescent boys as a function of delinquency and race." *Journal of Consulting Psychology*, **31**:471–476.

Bixenstine, V. E., et al. 1976. "Conformity to peer-sponsored misconduct at four grade levels." *Developmental Psychology*, **12**:226–236.

Black, A. H., et al. 1960. Cited in O. H. Mowrer, *Learning Theory and the Symbolic Processes*. New York: Wiley.

Black, D. J. 1970. "Production of crime rates." *American Sociological Review*, **35**:733–748.

Black, D. J., and A. J. Reiss, Jr. 1967. "Patterns of behavior in police and citizen transactions." Section I of *Studies of Crime and Law Enforcement in Major Metropolitan Areas*. (Vol. II.) Washington, D.C.: GPO.

Black, D. J., and A. J. Reiss, Jr. 1970. "Police control of juveniles." *American Sociological Review*, **35**:63–77.

Black, W. A. M., and R. A. M. Gregson. 1973. "Time perspective, purpose in life, extraversion and neuroticism in New Zealand prisoners." *British Journal of Social and Clinical Psychology*, **12**:50–60.

Blalock, H. M., Jr. 1960. *Social Statistics*. New York: McGraw-Hill.

Blalock, H. M., Jr. 1961. *Causal Inferences in Nonexperimental Research*. Chapel Hill: University of North Carolina Press.

Blane, H. T. 1968. *The Personality of the Alcoholic*. New York: Harper and Row.

Block, M. A. 1965. *Alcoholism: Its Facets and Phases*. New York: John Day.

Bloom, B. L. 1966. "A census tract analysis of socially deviant behaviors." *Multivariate Behavioral Research*, **1**:307–320.

Blue, J. T., Jr. 1948. "The relationship of juvenile delinquency, race, and economic status." *Journal of Negro Education*, **17**:469–477.

Blum, R. H. 1971. "To wear a Nostradamus hat: Drugs of the future." *The Journal of Social Issues*, **27**:89–106.

Blum, R. H., et al. 1969. *Students and Drugs*. San Francisco: Jossey-Bass.

Blumenthal, M. D. 1972. "Predicting attitudes toward violence." *Science*, **176**:1296–1303 (June 23).

Blumenthal, M. D. et al. 1972. *Justifying Violence: Attitudes of American Men*. Ann Arbor: University of Michigan, Institute for Social Research.

Blumstein, A. 1974. "Seriousness weights in an index of crime." *American Sociological Review*, **39**:854–864.

Blumstein, A. 1975. Testimony before Subcommittee on Domestic and International Scientific Planning and Analysis: Committee on Science and Technology. Washington, D.C.: House of Representatives (July 16).

Boardman, W. K. 1962. "Rusty: A brief behavior disorder." *Journal of Consulting Psychology*, **26**:293–297.

Boggs, S. L. 1965. "Urban crime patterns." *American Sociological Review*, **30**:899–908.

Bogue, D. J. 1969. *Principles of Demography*. New York: Wiley.

Bohlke, T. 1961. "Social mobility, stratification inconsistency and middle-class delinquency." *Social Problems,* **8**:351–363.

Bohrnstedt, G. W. 1970. "Reliability and validity assessment in attitude measurement." In G. F. Summers (ed.), *Attitude Measurement*. Chicago: Rand McNally.

Booth, A., et al. 1976. "Crowding and urban crime rates." *Urban Affairs Quarterly*, **11**:291–307.

Bordua, D. J. 1958–1959. "Juvenile delinquency and 'anomie': An attempt at replication." *Social Problems*, **6**:230–238.

Bordua, D. J. 1967. "Recent trends: Deviant behavior and social control." *The Annals of the American Academy of Political and Social Science*, **369**:149–163.

Borhek, J. T. 1970. "Ethnic-group cohesion." *American Journal of Sociology*, **76**:33–46.

Bottoms, A. E. 1967. "Delinquency amongst immigrants." *Race*, **8**:357–383.

Bowlby, J. 1952. *Maternal Care and Mental Health*. Geneva: World Health Organization.

Bowlby, J. 1969. *Attachment and Loss*. (Vol. I: *Attachment*.) New York: Basic Books.

Boydell, C. L., and C. F. Grindstaff. 1972. "Public opinion and criminal law: An empirical test of public attitudes toward legal sanctions." In C. L. Boydell et al. (eds.), *Deviant Behavior and Societal Reaction*. Toronto: Holt.

Boydell, C. L., and C. F. Grindstaff. 1974a. "Public attitudes and court dispositions: A comparative analysis." *Sociology and Social Research*, **58**:417–426.

Boydell, C. L., and C. F. Grindstaff. 1974b. "Public opinion toward legal sanctions of crimes of violence." *Journal of Criminal Law, Criminology, and Police Science*, **65**:113–116.

Braginsky, B. M., et al. 1969. *Methods of Madness: The Mental Hospital as a Last Resort*. New York: Holt.

Bridge, P., et al. 1974. "Why some Scout leaders padded troop rolls." *The National Observer*, **13**:6 (June 22).

Brock, D. 1960. "The innocent mind: Or, my days as a juvenile delinquent." *Canadian Journal of Corrections*, **2**:25–35.

Bronfenbrenner, U. 1967. "Response to pressure from peers versus adults among Soviet and American school children." *International Journal of Psychology*, **2**:199–207.

Bronfenbrenner, U. 1970. "Reactions to social pressure from adults versus peers among Soviet day school and boarding school pupils in the perspective of an American sample." *Journal of Personality and Social Psychology*, **15**:179–189.

Brown, J., and B. G. Gilmartin. 1969. "Sociology today: Lacunae, emphases, and surfeits." *American Sociologist*, **4**:283–291.

Brown, M. J. et al. 1972. "Criminal offences in an urban area and their associated social variables." *British Journal of Criminology*, **12**:250–268.

Brown, S. R. 1970–1971. Review of M. L. Kohn, "Class and Conformity: A Study in Values." *Public Opinion Quarterly*, **34:**654–655.

Bruce, G. 1969. *The Stranglers: The Cult of Thuggee and Its Overthrow in British India*. New York: Harcourt, Brace.

Bukovsky, V. 1972. "The Bukovsky papers: Notes from Soviet asylums." *National Review*, **24:**633–636 (June 9).

Burchinal, L. G. 1964. "Characteristics of adolescents from unbroken, broken, and reconstituted families." *Journal of Marriage and Family Living*, **26:**44–51.

Burgess, R. L., and R. L. Akers. 1966. "A differential association-reinforcement theory of criminal behavior." *Social Problems*, **14:**128–147.

Burke, P. J., and A. T. Turk. 1975. "Factors affecting post-arrest dispositions: A model for analysis." *Social Problems*, **22:**313–332.

Burt, C. 1925. *The Young Delinquent*. New York: Appleton. 4th ed., 1944. London: University of London Press.

Burt, C. 1961. "Intelligence and social mobility." *British Journal of Statistical Psychology*, **14:**3–24.

Burton, R. V. 1963. "Generality of honesty reconsidered." *Psychological Review*, **70:**481–499.

Burton, R. V., et al. 1961. "Antecedents of resistance to temptation in four-year-old children." *Child Development*, **32:**68–710.

Buss, A. H. 1961. *The Psychology of Aggression*. New York: Wiley.

Byrne, D., and W. Griffitt. 1966. "A developmental investigation of the law of attraction." *Journal of Personality and Social Psychology*, **4:**699–702.

Cahalan, D., et al. 1947. "Interviewer bias involved in certain types of opinion survey questions." *International Journal of Opinion and Attitude Research*, **1:**63–77.

Cairns, R. B. 1966. "Attachment behavior of mammals." *Psychological Review*, **73:**409–426.

Cameron, M. O. 1964. *The Booster and the Snitch: Department Store Shoplifting*. Glencoe, Ill.: Free Press.

Campbell, B. A., and R. M. Church (eds.). 1969. *Punishment and Aversive Behavior*. New York: Appleton-Century-Crofts.

Canadian Corrections Association. 1967. *Indians and the Law*. A survey prepared for the Hon. Arthur Laing, Department of Indian Affairs and Northern Development. Ottawa: The Canadian Welfare Council.

Canadian Press. 1974. "Crime approach hit" (December 28).

Canadian Press. 1975a. "Maloney due in court Dec. 4" (November 7).

Canadian Press. 1975b. "NDP budget figures 'crooked'—B.C. official" (December 24).

Canadian Press. 1975c. "Two charged over pamphlets" (June 30).

Canadian Press. 1975d. "We can police NHL, Morrison says" (November 7).

Caplow, T., et al. 1964. *The Urban Ambiance: A Study of San Juan, Puerto Rico*. Totowa, N.J.: Bedminster Press.

Carney, F. 1974. "George Jackson and his legend." *New York Review of Books*, **21:**17–19 (November 28).

Carr-Hill, R. 1970. *The Violent Offender: Reality or Illusion?* Oxford: Blackwell.

Carroll, L. 1974. "Race and sexual assault in a prison." Kingston: University of Rhode Island, Department of Sociology. Mimeographed.

Cartwright, D. S., and K. I. Howard. 1966. "Multivariate analysis of gang delinquency: I. Ecologic influences." *Multivariate Behavioral Research*, **1:**321–372.

Cattell, R. B. 1950. "The principal culture patterns discoverable in the syntal dimensions of existing nations." *Journal of Social Psychology*, **32:**215–253.

Cavalli-Sforza, L. L., and W. F. Bodmer. 1971. *The Genetics of Human Populations*. San Francisco: Freeman.

Ceylon Department of Census and Statistics. 1957. *Juvenile Probationers in Ceylon*. Ceylon: Government Press.

Chadwick, O. 1976. *The Secularization of the European Mind in the Nineteenth Century*. London: Cambridge.

Chambliss, W. J. 1964. "A sociological analysis of the law of vagrancy." *Social Problems*, **12**:67–77.

Chambliss, W. J. 1973. "Elites and the creation of criminal law." In W. J. Chambliss (ed.), *Sociological Readings in the Conflict Perspective*. Reading, Mass.: Addison-Wesley.

Chambliss, W. J. 1974. "The state, the law, and the definition of behavior as criminal or delinquent." In D. Glaser (ed.), *Handbook of Criminology*. Chicago: Rand McNally.

Chambliss, W. J., and R. H. Nagasawa. 1969. "On the validity of official statistics: A comparative study of white, black, and Japanese high-school boys." *Journal of Research in Crime and Delinquency*, **6**:71–77.

Chambliss, W. J., and T. E. Ryther. 1975. *Sociology: The Discipline and Its Direction*. New York: McGraw-Hill.

Chilton, R. J. 1964. "Delinquency area research in Baltimore, Detroit, and Indianapolis." *American Sociological Review*, **29**:71–83.

Chilton, R. J., and G. E. Markle. 1972. "Family disruption, delinquent conduct, and the effect of subclassification." *American Sociological Review*, **37**:93–99.

Chiricos, T. G., and G. P. Waldo. 1970. "Punishment and crime: An examination of some empirical evidence." *Social Problems*, **18**:200–217.

Chiricos, T. G., and G. P. Waldo. 1975. "Socioeconomic status and criminal sentencing: An empirical assessment of a conflict proposition." *American Sociological Review*, **40**:753–772.

Cho, Sung Tai. 1967. *A Cross-Cultural Analysis of the Criminality Level Index*. Columbus: Ohio State University, Department of Sociology. Ph.D. dissertation.

Christie, N. 1960. *Unge Norske Lovovertredere. (Young Norwegian Lawbreakers.)* Oslo: Universitetsforlaget.

Christie, N., et al. 1965. "A study of self-reported crime." In K. O. Christiansen (ed.), *Scandinavian Studies in Criminology*. (Vol. 1.) London: Tavistock.

Church, R. M. 1963. "The varied effects of punishment on behavior." *Psychological Review*, **70**:369–402.

Clark, J. P., and L. L. Tifft. 1966. "Polygraph and interview validation of self reported deviant behavior." *American Sociological Review*, **31**:516–523.

Clark, J. P., and E. P. Wenninger. 1962. "Socio-economic class and area as correlates of illegal behavior among juveniles." *American Sociological Review*, **27**:826–834.

Clark, R. 1970. *Crime in America*. New York: Simon and Schuster.

Clarke, B. 1975. "The causes of biological diversity." *Scientific American*, **223**:50–60.

Cleaver, E. 1968. *Soul on Ice*. New York: McGraw-Hill.

Clement, P. W. 1970. "Elimination of sleepwalking in a seven-year-old boy." *Journal of Consulting and Clinical Psychology*, **34**:22–26.

Clinard, M. 1942. "The process of urbanization and criminal behavior: A study of culture conflicts." *American Journal of Sociology*, **48**:202–213.

Clinard, M. 1960. "A cross-cultural replication of the relation of urbanism to criminal behavior." *American Sociological Review*, **25**:253–257.

Clinard, M., and D. J. Abbott. 1973. *Crime in Developing Countries: A Comparative Perspective*. New York: Wiley.

Cloward, R. A., and L. E. Ohlin. 1960. *Delinquency and Opportunity: A Theory of Delinquent Gangs*. New York: Free Press.

Cobb, W. E. 1973. "Theft and the two hypotheses." In S. Rottenberg (ed.), *The Economics of Crime and Punishment*. Washington, D.C.: American Enterprise Institute for Public Policy Research.

Cohen, A. K. 1955. *Delinquent Boys: The Culture of the Gang*. Glencoe, Ill.: Free Press.

Cohen, J. A. 1968. *The Criminal Process in the People's Republic of China: 1949–1963*. Cambridge, Mass.: Harvard University Press.

Cohen, M. R. 1931. *Reason and Nature*. New York: Harcourt, Brace.

Cohen, S. (ed.). 1971. *Images of Deviance*. Middlesex, England: Penguin.

Coleman, J. S. 1974. "Review essay: Inequality, sociology, and moral philosophy." *American Journal of Sociology*, **80**:739–764.

Collingwood, R. G. 1940. *An Essay on Metaphysics*. Oxford: Clarendon Press.

Columbia Broadcasting System. 1975. "Poll on presidential election issues." (November 10.) New York: CBS.

Command Paper #4708. 1970. *Criminal Statistics: England and Wales*. London: Her Majesty's Stationery Office.

Comstock, G. 1975. "The effects of television on children and adolescents: The evidence so far." *Journal of Communication*, **25**:25–34.

Connor, W. D. 1972. *Deviance in Soviet Society: Crime, Delinquency, and Alcoholism*. New York: Columbia.

Conquest, R. 1968. *The Great Terror: Stalin's Purge of the Thirties*. New York: Macmillan.

Cooper, C. C. 1960. *A Comparative Study of Delinquents and Non-Delinquents*. Portsmouth, Ohio: Psychological Service Center Press.

Coopersmith, S. 1969. Review of M. R. Yarrow et al., *Child Rearing*. *Contemporary Psychology*, **14**:369–371.

Cosper, R. 1972. "Interviewer effect in a survey of drinking practices." *Sociological Quarterly*, **13**:228–236.

Courtis, M. C. 1970. *Attitudes to Crime and the Police in Toronto: A Report on Some Survey Findings*. Toronto: University of Toronto, Centre of Criminology.

Cousineau, D. F. 1967. *Some Current Conceptions of Rationality and the Policy Sciences*. Edmonton: University of Alberta, Department of Sociology. M.A. dissertation.

Cousineau, D. F. 1976. *General Deterrence of Crime: An Analysis*. Edmonton: University of Alberta, Department of Sociology. Ph.D. dissertation.

Cousineau, D. F. and J. E. Veevers. 1972. "Juvenile justice: An analysis of the Canadian Young Offenders' Act." In C. Boydell et al. (eds.), *Deviant Behavior and Societal Reaction*. Toronto: Holt.

Cramton, R. C. 1969. "Driver behavior and legal sanctions: A study of deterrence." *Michigan Law Review*, **67**:421–454.

Crespi, I. 1971. "What kinds of attitude measures are predictive of behavior?" *Public Opinion Quarterly*, **35**:327–334.

Cressey, D. R. 1964. "Causes of employee dishonesty." Paper presented at the Top Management Business Security Seminar, East Lansing, Mich. (April 16). Mimeographed.

Cressey, D. R. 1953; 2d ed. 1971. *Other People's Money: A Study in the Social Psychology of Embezzlement*. Belmont, Calif.: Wadsworth.

Crockett, H. J. 1962. "The achievement motive and differential occupational mobility in the United States." *American Sociological Review*, 27:191–204.

Crook, E. B. 1934. "Cultural marginality in sexual delinquency." *American Journal of Sociology*, 39:493–500.

Cross, H. J. 1964. "The outcome of psychotherapy: A selected analysis of research findings." *Journal of Consulting Psychology*, 28:413–417.

CTV broadcast. 1974. "Eye-to-eye: On public apathy" (January 28).

Cuber, J., and P. Harroff. 1966. *The Significant Americans*. Garden City, N.Y.: Doubleday.

Culliton, B. J. 1975. "Habitat: U.N. conference to face crises in human settlements." *Science*, 190:1181–1183 (December 19).

Curlee, J. A. 1970. "A comparison of male and female patients at an alcoholism treatment center." *Journal of Psychology*, 74:239–247.

Darroch, A. G., and W. G. Marston. 1971. "The social class basis of ethnic residential segregation: The Canadian case." *American Journal of Sociology*, 77:491–510.

Davids, A., et al. 1962. "Time orientation in male and female juvenile delinquents." *Journal of Abnormal and Social Psychology*, 64:239–240.

Davis, A. 1970. "Her revolutionary voice cries damnation of the system." *Life*, 69:26–27 (September 11).

Davis, A., and J. Dollard. 1941. *Children of Bondage*. Washington, D.C.: American Council on Education.

Davis, A., and R. Havighurst. 1947. *Father of the Man: How Your Child Gets His Personality*. Boston: Houghton Mifflin.

Davis, A. J. n.d. *Report on Sexual Assaults in the Philadelphia Prison System and Sheriff's Vans*. Philadelphia: District Attorney's Office and Police Department.

Davis, K. 1959. "The myth of functional analysis as a special method in sociology and anthropology." *American Sociological Review*, 24:757–772.

Davis, M. S. 1971. "That's interesting!" *Philosophy of the Social Sciences*, 1:309–344.

de Charms, R. 1968. *Personal Causation: The Internal Affective Determinants of Behavior*. New York: Academic Press.

Decter, M. 1975. *Liberal Parents, Radical Children*. New York: Coward-McCann.

DeFleur, M., and R. Quinney. 1966. "A reformulation of Sutherland's differential association theory and a strategy for empirical verification." *Journal of Research in Crime and Delinquency*, 3:1–22.

Della Fave, L. R. 1974. "On the structure of egalitarianism." *Social Problems*, 22:199–213.

Dentler, R. A., and L. J. Monroe. 1961. "Social correlates of early adolescent theft." *American Sociological Review*, 26:733–743.

de Toledano, R. 1975. *Hit and Run: The Rise—and Fall?—of Ralph Nader*. New Rochelle, N.Y.: Arlington.

Devlin, P. 1965. *The Enforcement of Morals*. London: Oxford University Press.

DiCara, L. V. 1970. "Learning in the autonomic nervous system." *Scientific American*, 222:31–39.

Dinitz, S., et al. 1962. "Delinquency vulnerability: A cross group and longitudinal analysis." *American Sociological Review*, 27:515–517.

Dirks, R. L., and L. Gross. 1974. *The Great Wall Street Scandal*. New York: McGraw-Hill.

Dollard, J., et al. 1939. *Frustration and Aggression*. New Haven, Conn.: Yale University Press.

Dominion Bureau of Statistics. 1967. *Crime Statistics*. Ottawa: The Bureau.

Dominion Bureau of Statistics. 1970. *Crime Statistics*. Ottawa: The Bureau.

Dominion Bureau of Statistics. 1971. *Crime Statistics*. Ottawa: The Bureau.

Donovan, R. J. 1955. *The Assassins*. New York: Harper.

dos Santos, A. T. 1959. "Lampeao, king of the bandits." Cited by E. J. Hobsbawm, 1969. *Bandits*. London: Weidenfeld and Nicolson.

Douglas, J. D. 1967. *The Social Meanings of Suicide*. Princeton, N.J.: Princeton University Press.

Douvan, E. 1956. "Social status and success strivings." *Journal of Abnormal and Social Psychology*, **52**:219–223.

Douvan, E., and J. Edelson. 1958. "The psychodynamics of social mobility in adolescent boys." *Journal of Abnormal and Social Psychology*, **56**:31–44.

Downes, D. M. 1966. *The Delinquent Solution*. New York: Free Press.

DuCette, J., and S. Wolk. 1972. "Locus of control and extreme behavior." *Journal of Consulting and Clinical Psychology*, **39**:253–258.

Duesenberry, J. S. 1960. "Comment." In Universities-National Bureau Committee for Economic Research, *Demographic and Economic Change in Developed Countries*. Princeton, N.J.: Princeton University Press.

Duhamel, R. (ed.). 1962. *Office Consolidation of the Criminal Code and Selected Statutes*. Ottawa: Queen's Printer and Controller of Stationery.

Dunn, D. H. 1975. *Ponzi! The Boston Swindler*. New York: McGraw-Hill.

Durbin, M., and M. Micklin. 1973. "Differential effects of syntactic variation in an experimental situation." *Linguistics*, **115**:5–13 (November 1).

Durkheim, E. 1949. *The Division of Labor in Society*. Trans. by G. Simpson. Glencoe, Ill.: Free Press.

Durkheim, E. 1951. *Suicide: A Study in Sociology*. Ed. by G. Simpson. Glencoe, Ill.: Free Press.

Durkheim, E. 1958. *The Rules of Sociological Method*. Trans. by S. A. Solovay and J. H. Mueller. Glencoe, Ill.: Free Press.

Edmonton Journal. 1976. "Police briefed on adult age" (January 27).

Edmonton Report. 1976. "The law: Equality." **3**:11–12 (January 19).

Edwards, A. 1973. "Sex and area variations in delinquency rates in an English city." *British Journal of Criminology*, **13**:121–137.

Edwards, A. L. 1957. *The Social Desirability Variable in Personality Assessment and Research*. New York: Dryden.

Edwards, T. A. 1976. *A Test of Vagrancy Law Research Used by Chambliss in Support of the Conflict Perspective in Criminology*. Edmonton: University of Alberta, Department of Sociology. M.A. dissertation prospectus.

Ehrlich, I. 1973. "Participation in illegitimate activities: A theoretical and empirical investigation." *The Journal of Political Economy*, **81**:521–565.

Eliot, T. S. 1948. *Notes towards a Definition of Culture*. London: Faber.

Elmhorn, K. 1965. "Study in self-reported delinquency among school-children in Stockholm." In K. O. Christiansen (ed.), *Scandinavian Studies in Criminology*. (Vol. 1.) London: Tavistock.

El-Saaty, H. 1946. *Juvenile Delinquency in Egypt*. London: University of London, Faculty of Arts. Ph.D. dissertation.

Emerson, R. W. 1841. *Essays: First Series*. Reprinted 1968. New York: AMS Press.

Empey, L. T., and S. G. Lubeck. 1971. *Explaining Delinquency*. Lexington, Mass.: Heath.

Ennis, P. H. 1967. *Criminal Victimization in the United States: A Report of a National Survey*. The President's Commission on Law Enforcement and Administration of Justice. Washington: GPO.

Eoyang, C. K. 1974. "Effects of group size and privacy in residential crowding." *Journal of Personality and Social Psychology*, **30:**389–392.

Epstein, E. J. 1973. *News from Nowhere: Television and the News*. New York: Random House.

Epstein, E. J. 1976. *Between Fact and Fiction: The Problem of Journalism*. New York: Vintage.

Epstein, R. 1964. "Need for approval and the conditioning of verbal hostility in asthmatic children." *Journal of Abnormal and Social Psychology*, **69:**105–109.

Erickson, M. L. 1971. "The group context of delinquent behavior." *Social Problems*, **19:**114–129.

Erickson, M. L., and L. T. Empey. 1963. "Court records, undetected delinquency and decision-making." *Journal of Criminal Law, Criminology, and Police Science*, **54:**456–469.

Erickson, M. L., and J. P. Gibbs. 1973. "The deterrence question: Some alternative methods of analysis." *Social Science Quarterly*, **53:**534–551.

Ericson, R. V. 1975. *Criminal Reactions: The Labelling Perspective*. Lexington, Mass.: Heath.

Erikson, K. T. 1966. *Wayward Puritans*. New York: Wiley.

Eron, L. D. (ed.). 1966. *The Classification of Behavior Disorders*. Chicago: Aldine.

Eron, L. D., et al. 1971. *Learning of Aggression in Children*. Boston: Little, Brown.

Eron, L. D., et al. 1972. "Does television violence cause aggression?" *American Psychologist*, **27:**253–263.

Erskine, H. 1968–1969. "The polls: Recent opinions of racial problems." *Public Opinion Quarterly*, **32:**696–703.

Erskine, H. 1974a. "The polls: Causes of crime." *Public Opinion Quarterly*, **38:**288–298.

Erskine, H. 1974b. "The polls: Fear of violence and crime." *Public Opinion Quarterly*, **38:**131–145.

Erskine, H. 1975. "The polls: Politics and law and order." *Public Opinion Quarterly*, **38:**623–634.

Esquire. 1974. "The last time we had dinner at Melvin Laird's we thought the silver pattern looked familiar." **81:**90.

Estes, W. K. 1944. "An experimental study of punishment." *Psychological Monographs*, **57** (Whole #263).

Estes, W. K. 1969a. "Outline of a theory of punishment." In B. A. Campbell and R. M. Church (eds.), *Punishment and Aversive Behavior*. New York: Appleton-Century-Crofts.

Estes, W. K. 1969b. "Reinforcement in human learning." In J. Tapp (ed.), *Reinforcement and Behavior*. New York: Academic Press.

Evans, J. L. 1968. *Affect and the Attribution of Causation*. Edmonton: University of Alberta, Department of Sociology. M.A. dissertation.

Evans, K. M. 1962. *Sociometry and Education*. London: Routledge.

Eysenck, H. J. 1964. *Crime and Personality*. Boston: Houghton Mifflin.

Eysenck, H. J. 1966a. *The Effects of Psychotherapy*. New York: International Science Press.

Eysenck, H. J. 1966b. "Personality and experimental psychology." *Bulletin* of the British Psychological Society, **19:**1–28.

Fairchild, H. P. (ed.). 1944. *Dictionary of Sociology*. New York: Philosophical Library.

Fancher, R. E., Jr. 1966. "Explicit personality theories and accuracy in person perception." *Journal of Personality*, **34:**252–261.

Fancher, R. E., Jr. 1967. "Accuracy vs. validity in person perception." *Journal of Consulting Psychology*, **31:**264–269.

Farley, F. H., and S. V. Farley. 1972. "Stimulus-seeking motivation and delinquent behavior among institutionalized delinquent girls." *Journal of Consulting and Clinical Psychology*, **39**:94–97.

Farley, R., and K. E. Taeuber. 1968. "Population trends and residential segregation since 1960." *Science*, **159**:953–956 (March 1).

Farr, R. 1975. *The Electronic Criminals*. New York: McGraw-Hill.

Farrington, D. P. 1973. "Self-reports of deviant behavior: Predictive and stable?" *Journal of Criminal Law and Criminology*. **64**:99–110.

Feather, N. T. 1967. "Some personality correlates of external control." *Australian Journal of Psychology*, **19**:253–260.

Federal Bureau of Investigation. 1968. *Crime in the United States: Uniform Crime Reports—1967*. Washington, D.C.: GPO.

Federal Bureau of Investigation. 1974. *Crime in the United States: Uniform Crime Reports—1973*. Washington, D.C.: GPO.

Federal Bureau of Investigation. 1975. *Crime in the United States: Uniform Crime Reports—1974*. Washington, D.C.: GPO.

Federal Bureau of Investigation. 1976. *Crime in the United States: Uniform Crime Reports—1975*. Washington, D.C.: GPO.

Feierabend, I. K., and B. Nesvold. 1970. "Political coerciveness and turmoil: A cross national inquiry." *Law and Society Review*, **5**:93–118.

Feldman, R. E. 1968. "Response to compatriot and foreigner who seek assistance." *Journal of Personality and Social Psychology*, **10**:202–214.

Ferracuti, F. 1968. "European migration and crime." In M. E. Wolfgang (ed.), *Crime and Culture: Essays in Honor of Thorsten Sellin*. New York: Wiley.

Ferracuti, F., S. Dinitz, and E. Acosta. 1975. *Delinquents and Nondelinquents in the Puerto Rican Slum Culture*. Columbus: Ohio State University Press.

Feshbach, S. 1961. "The stimulating versus cathartic effects of a vicarious aggressive activity." *Journal of Abnormal and Social Psychology*, **63**:381–385.

Feshbach, S., and R. D. Singer. 1971. *Television and Aggression*. San Francisco: Jossey-Bass.

Field, M. D. 1973. "California poll" (March 24). Privately circulated.

Fire Protection Association. 1970. *Fire Protection of Computers and Ancillary Equipment*. London: Aldermary House.

Fishbein, M., and I. Ajzen. 1972. "Attitudes and opinions." In P. H. Mussen and M. R. Rosenzweig (eds.), *Annual Review of Psychology*. Palo Alto, Calif.: Annual Reviews.

Fishman, R. 1975. *An Evaluation of the Effect on Criminal Recidivism of New York City Projects Providing Rehabilitation and Diversion Services*. New York: City University of New York, Research Foundation and Graduate School and University Center.

Fleisher, B. M. 1966. *The Economics of Delinquency*. Chicago: Quadrangle.

Footlick, J. K., et al. 1975. "Children and the law." *Newsweek*, **86**:66–71c (September 8).

Forslund, M. A. 1970. "A comparison of Negro and white crime rates." *Journal of Criminal Law, Criminology, and Police Science*, **61**:214–217.

Forssman, H., and C. F. Gentz. 1962. "Kriminalitetsförekomsten hos presumtivt ostraffade." *Nordisk Tidsskrift for Kriminalvidenskab*, 318–324.

Fox, J., and T. F. Hartnagel. 1976. "Changing social roles and female crime in Canada: A time series analysis." Paper in submission.

Franchini, A., and F. Introna. 1961. *Delinquenze Minorile*. Padova: Cedam.

Frank, L. K. 1950. *Society as the Patient*. New Brunswick, N.J.: Rutgers University Press.

Franks, C. M. 1956. "Conditioning and personality." *Journal of Abnormal and Social Psychology*, **52**:143–150.

Franks, C. M. 1961. "Conditioning and abnormal behavior." In H. J. Eysenck (ed.), *Handbook of Abnormal Psychology*. New York: Basic Books.

Freedman, D. G. 1958. "Constitutional and environmental interactions in rearing of four breeds of dogs." *Science*, **127**:585–586 (March 14).

Freedman, D. G. 1971. "Genetic influences on development of behavior." In G. B. A. Stoelinga and J. J. Van der Werff ten Bosch (eds.), *Normal and Abnormal Development of Behavior*. Leiden: Leiden University Press.

Freedman, D. G. 1974. "Cradleboarding and temperament: Cause and effect." Paper presented at the annual meeting of the American Association for the Advancement of Science, San Francisco (February 28).

Freeman, J., and E. W. Butler, 1976. "Some sources of interviewer variance in surveys." *Public Opinion Quarterly*, **41**:79–91.

Freud, A., and S. Dann. 1951. "An experiment in group upbringing." In R. S. Eissler et al. (eds.), *The Psychoanalytic Study of the Child*. (Vol. 6.) New York: International Universities Press.

Freud, S. 1958. *Civilization and Its Discontents*. Garden City, N.Y.: Doubleday.

Furst, T. M., Jr. 1952. *Unifying Theory and Practice: The Pragmatic Program*. Los Angeles: University of California, Department of Political Science. Mimeographed.

Furth, H. G. 1966. *Thinking without Language: Psychological Implications of Deafness*. New York: Free Press.

Gaito, J., and A. Zavala. 1964. "Neurochemistry and learning." *Psychological Bulletin*, **61**:45–62.

Gales, K., and M. G. Kendall. 1957. "An enquiry concerning interviewer variability." *Journal of the Royal Statistical Society*, **120** (Series A).

Galle, O. R., et al. 1972. "Population density and pathology: What are the relations for man?" *Science*, **176**:23–30 (April 7).

Galle, O. R., et al. 1973. "Population density, social structure, and interpersonal violence: An intermetropolitan test of competing models." Paper read at the annual meeting of the American Psychological Association, Montreal.

Gans, H. 1972. "The positive functions of poverty." *American Journal of Sociology*, **78**:275–289.

Ganzer, V. J., and I. G. Sarason. 1973. "Variables associated with recidivism among juvenile delinquents." *Journal of Consulting and Clinical Psychology*, **40**:1–5.

Gardiner, J. 1967. "Public attitudes toward gambling and corruption." *The Annals of the American Academy of Political and Social Science*, **374**:123–124.

Gardner, M. 1974. "Mathematical games: The combinatorial basis of the *I Ching*." *Scientific American*, **230**:108–113.

Garfinkel, H. 1956. "Conditions of successful degradation ceremonies." *American Journal of Sociology*, **61**:420–424.

Gastil, R. D. 1971. "Homicide and a regional culture of violence." *American Sociological Review*, **36**:412–427.

Gastil, R. D. 1976. "The comparative survey of freedom: VI." *Freedom at Issue*, (34):11–20.

Geen, R. G. 1975. "The meaning of observed violence: Real vs. fictional violence and consequent effects on aggression and emotional arousal." *Journal of Research in Personality*, **9**:270–281.

Geen, R. G., and L. Berkowitz. 1967. "Some conditions facilitating the occurrence of aggression after the observation of violence." *Journal of Personality*, **35**:666–676.

Geen, R. G., and D. Stonner. 1974. "The meaning of observed violence: Effects on arousal and aggressive behavior." *Journal of Research in Personality*, **8**:55–63.

Geen, R. G., et al. 1975. "The facilitation of aggression by aggression: Evidence against the catharsis hypothesis." *Journal of Personality and Social Psychology*, **31**:721–726.

Geertz, C. 1973. *The Interpretation of Cultures*. New York: Basic Books.

Gendin, S. 1967. "The meaning of punishment." *Philosophy and Phenomenological Research*, **28**:235–240.

Germani, G. 1961. "Inquiry into the social effects of urbanization in a working-class sector of Greater Buenos Aires." In P. M. Hauser (ed.), *Urbanization in Latin América*. New York: Columbia University Press.

Gerstein, R. S. 1974. "Capital punishment: 'Cruel and unusual'?: A retributivist response." *Ethics*, **85**:75–79.

Gerth, H., and C. W. Mills (eds.). *From Max Weber: Essays in Sociology*. New York: Oxford University Press.

Gibbens, T. C. N., and R. H. Ahrenfeldt (eds.). 1966. *Cultural Factors in Delinquency*. London: Tavistock.

Gibbons, D. C. 1968. *Society, Crime, and Criminal Careers: An Introduction to Criminology*. Englewood Cliffs, N.J.: Prentice-Hall.

Gibbons, D. C. 1969. "Crime and punishment: A study in social attitudes." *Social Forces*, **47**:391–397.

Gibbs, J. P. 1966. "Sanctions." *Social Problems*, **14**:147–159.

Gibbs, J. P. 1975. *Crime, Punishment, and Deterrence*. New York: Elsevier.

Giggs, J. A. 1970. "The socially disorganised areas of Barry: A multivariate analysis." In M. Carter and W. K. D. Davies (eds.), *Urban Essays: Studies in the Geography of Wales*. London: Longmans.

Gilbert, G. M. 1938. "The new status of experimental studies on the relationship of feeling to memory." *Psychological Bulletin*, **35**:26–35.

Gillis, A. R. 1975. *Density and Crowding*. Edmonton: University of Alberta, Department of Sociology. Ph.D. dissertation.

Ginzberg, E. 1972. "The outlook for educated manpower." *The Public Interest*, (26):100–111.

Glazer, N., and D. P. Moynihan. 1963. *Beyond the Melting Pot*. Cambridge, Mass.: M.I.T. and Harvard University Press.

Glazer, N., and D. P. Moynihan (eds.). 1975. *Ethnicity: Theory and Experience*. Cambridge, Mass.: Harvard University Press.

Glenn, N. D. 1974–1975. "Recent trends in white-nonwhite attitudinal differences." *Public Opinion Quarterly*, **38**:596–604.

Glueck, S. 1964. "The home, the school, and delinquency." In S. Glueck and E. Glueck (eds.), *Ventures in Criminology: Selected Recent Papers*. London: Tavistock.

Glueck, S., and E. Glueck. 1950. *Unraveling Juvenile Delinquency*. Cambridge, Mass.: Harvard University Press.

Glueck, S., and E. Glueck. 1956. *Physique and Delinquency*. New York: Hoeber-Harper.

Glueck, S., and E. Glueck. 1962. *Family Environment and Delinquency*. Boston: Houghton Mifflin.

Glueck, S., and E. Glueck. 1970. *Toward a Typology of Juvenile Offenders: Implications for Therapy and Prevention*. New York: Grune and Stratton.

Gold, M. 1966. "Undetected delinquent behavior." *Journal of Research in Crime and Delinquency*. **13**:27–46.

Goldberg, L. R. 1968. "Simple models or simple processes?: Some research on clinical judgments." *American Psychologist*, **23**:483–496.

Goldberg, L. R. 1970. "Man versus model of man: A rationale, plus some evidence, for a method of improving on clinical inferences." *Psychological Bulletin*, 73:422–432.

Goldberg, L. R. and C. E. Werts. 1966. "The reliability of clinicians' judgments: A multitrait-multimethod approach." *Journal of Consulting Psychology*, 30:199–206.

Goldfarb, W. 1943a. "Effects of early institutional care of adolescent personality." *Child Development*, 14:213–223.

Goldfarb, W. 1943b. "Effects of early institutional care on adolescent personality." *Journal of Experimental Education*, 12:106–129.

Goldfarb, W. 1943c. "Infant rearing and problem behavior." *American Journal of Orthopsychiatry*, 13:249–265.

Goldfarb, W. 1944a. "Effects of early institutional care on adolescent personality: Rorschach data." *American Journal of Orthopsychiatry*, 14:441–447.

Goldfarb, W. 1944b. "Infant rearing as a factor in foster home replacement." *American Journal of Orthopsychiatry*, 14:162–173.

Goldfarb, W. 1945a. "Effects of psychological deprivation in infancy and subsequent stimulation." *American Journal of Psychiatry*, 102:18–33.

Goldfarb, W. 1945b. "Psychological privation in infancy and subsequent adjustment." *American Journal of Orthopsychiatry*, 15:247–255.

Goldman, N. 1963. *The Differential Selection of Juvenile Offenders for Court Appearance*. New York: National Council on Crime and Delinquency.

Goldschmidt, W. 1959. *Man's Way: An Introduction to the Understanding of Human Society*. New York: Holt.

Goldstein, A. S. 1967. *The Insanity Defense*. New Haven, Conn.: Yale University Press.

Goldstein, J. H., and R. L. Arms. 1971. "Effects of observing athletic contests on hostility." *Sociometry*, 34:83–90.

Goode, W. J. 1956. *After Divorce*. Glencoe, Ill.: Free Press.

Goode, W. J. 1960. "Illegitimacy in the Caribbean social structure." *American Sociological Review*, 25:21–30.

Goode, W. J. 1966. "Family disorganization." In R. K. Merton and R. A. Nisbet (eds.), *Contemporary Social Problems*, (2d ed.). New York: Harcourt, Brace.

Goode, W. J. 1967. "The protection of the inept." *American Sociological Review*, 32:5–19.

Goodman, P. 1956. *Growing Up Absurd*. New York: Random House.

Goranson, R. E. 1969. "The catharsis effect: Two opposing views." In R. K. Baker and S. J. Ball (eds.), *Violence and the Media: A Staff Report to the National Commission on the Causes and Prevention of Violence*. Washington, D.C.: GPO.

Gorbanevskaya, N. 1972. *Red Star at Noon*. New York: Holt.

Gorovitz, S. 1965. "Causal judgment and causal explanations." *The Journal of Philosophy*, 62:695–711.

Gough, H., and D. R. Peterson. 1952. "The identification and measurement of predispositional factors in crime and delinquency." *Journal of Consulting Psychology*, 16:207–212.

Gouldner, A. W. 1970. *The Coming Crisis of Western Sociology*. New York: Basic Books.

Gove, W. R. 1970. "Societal reaction as an explanation of mental illness: An evaluation." *American Sociological Review*, 35:873–884.

Gove, W. R. (ed.). 1975. *The Labelling of Deviance: Evaluating a Perspective*. New York: Wiley.

Graham, F. P. 1970. "Black crime: The lawless image." *Harper's Magazine*, 241:64–78.

Gray, L. N., and J. D. Martin. 1969. "Punishment and deterrence: Another analysis of the Gibbs' data." *Social Science Quarterly*, 50:389–395.

Gray, P. H. 1958. "Theory and evidence of imprinting in human infants." *Journal of Psychology*, **46**:155–166.

Green, E. 1970. "Race, social status, and criminal arrest." *American Sociological Review*, **35**:476–490.

Greenberg, B. S., and B. Dervin. 1970. *Uses of the Mass Media by the Urban Poor*. New York: Praeger.

Greenspoon, J. 1962. "Verbal conditioning and clinical psychology." In A. J. Bachrach (ed.), *Experimental Foundations of Clinical Psychology*. New York: Basic Books.

Gregory, I. 1965. "Anterospective data following childhood loss of a parent: Delinquency and high school dropout." *Archives of General Psychiatry*, **13**:99–109.

Grillo, E. G. 1970. *Delincuencia en Caracas*. Caracas: Universidad del Zulia.

Gross, S. J., and C. M. Niman. 1975. "Attitude-behavior consistency: A review." *Public Opinion Quarterly*, **39**:358–368.

Grubb, W. N. 1971. Review of I. Berg, *Education and Jobs*. *Harvard Educational Review*, **41**:580–583.

Gsovski, V. 1961. "Revision of the criminal code." In A. Inkeles and K. Geiger (eds.), *Soviet Society: A Book of Readings*. Boston: Houghton Mifflin.

Guest, A. M., and J. A. Weed. 1976. "Ethnic residential segregation: Patterns of change." *American Journal of Sociology*, **81**:1088–1111.

Guest, A. M., and J. J. Zuiches. 1971. "Another look at residential turnover in urban neighborhoods: A note on 'Racial change in a stable community' by Harvey Molotch." *American Journal of Sociology*, **77**:457–467.

Gunning, J. P., Jr. 1970. *A Report on the Study of the Costs of Incarceration*. Blacksburg, Va.: Virginia Polytechnic Institute and State University. Mimeographed.

Gunning, J. P., Jr. 1973. "How profitable is burglary?" In S. Rottenberg (ed.), *The Economics of Crime and Punishment*. Washington, D.C.: American Enterprise Institute for Public Policy Research.

Guze, S. B. 1976. *Criminality and Psychiatric Disorders*. New York: Oxford University Press.

Haan, N. 1964. "The relationship of ego functioning and intelligence to social status and social mobility." *Journal of Abnormal and Social Psychology*, **69**:594–605.

Haber, R. N. 1970. "How we remember what we see." *Scientific American*, **222**:104–112.

Haberman, P. W., and J. Sheinberg. 1966. "Education reported in interviews: An aspect of survey content error." *Public Opinion Quarterly*, **30**:295–301.

Hacker, E. 1941. *Kriminalstatische und Kriminalaetiologische Berichte*. Miskolc, Hungary: Ludwig.

Hackler, J. C. 1966. "Boys, blisters, and behavior: The impact of a work program in an urban central area." *Journal of Research in Crime and Delinquency*, **3**:155–164.

Hackler, J. C., and J. L. Hagan. 1972. "Work, programs, and teaching machines." Edmonton: University of Alberta, Department of Sociology. Mimeographed.

Hagan, J. L. 1972. "The labelling perspective, the delinquent, and the police: A review of the literature." *Canadian Journal of Criminology and Corrections*, **14**:150–165.

Hagan, J. L. 1974a. *Criminal Justice in a Canadian Province: A Study of the Sentencing Process*. Edmonton: University of Alberta, Department of Sociology. Ph.D. dissertation.

Hagan, J. L. 1974b. "Extra-legal attributes and criminal sentencing: An assessment of a sociological viewpoint." *Law and Society Review*, **8**:357–383.

Hagan, J. L. 1977a. "Criminal justice in rural and urban communities: A study of the bureaucratization of justice." *Social Forces*, **55**:597–612.

Hagan, J. L. 1977b. "Finding 'discrimination': A question of meaning," *Ethnicity*, **4.** In press.

Hakeem, M. 1958. "A critique of the psychiatric approach to crime and correction." *Law and Contemporary Problems*, **23**:650–682.

Hall, E. L., and A. A. Simkus. 1975. "Inequality in the types of sentences received by native Americans and whites." *Criminology*, **13**:199–222.

Hamilton, P. 1973. *Computer Security*. Philadelphia: Auerbach.

Hamilton, V. 1965. Review of H. J. Eysenck, *Crime and Personality. British Journal of Social and Clinical Psychology*, **4**:159–160.

Hanson, R. H., and E. S. Marks. 1958. "Influence of the interviewer on the accuracy of survey results." *Journal of the American Statistical Association*, **53**:635–655.

Hardin, E., and G. L. Hershey. 1960. "Accuracy of employee reports on changes in pay." *Journal of Applied Psychology*, **44**:269–275.

Hardin, G. 1972. *Exploring New Ethics for Survival*. New York: Viking.

Hardt, R. G., and G. E. Bodine. 1965. *Development of Self-Report Instruments in Delinquency Research: A Conference Report*. Syracuse, N.Y.: Syracuse University, Youth Development Center.

Harlow, H. F., and M. Harlow. 1967. "The young monkeys." *Psychology Today*, **1**:40–47.

Harlow, H. F., et al. 1966. "Maternal behavior of rhesus monkeys deprived of mothering and peer associations in infancy." *Proceedings of the American Philosophical Society*, **110**:58–66.

Harries, K. D. 1974. *The Geography of Crime and Justice*. New York: McGraw-Hill.

Harries, K. D. 1976. "A crime based analysis and classification of 729 American cities." *Social Indicators Research*, **2**:467–487.

Harris, L. 1968. *The Public Looks at Crime and Corrections*. Washington, D.C.: Joint Commission on Correctional Manpower and Training.

Harris, W. J. 1972. "The militant separatists in the white academy." *The American Scholar*, **41**:366–376.

Hart, H. 1947. "Factuality and the discussion of values." *Social Forces*, **25**:290–294.

Hart, H. L. A. 1965. *The Morality of the Criminal Law*. London: Oxford University Press.

Hart, H. L. A. 1967. "Legal positivism." In P. Edwards (ed.), *The Encyclopedia of Philosophy*. New York: Macmillan.

Hartjen, C. A. 1974. *Crime and Criminalization*. New York: Praeger.

Hartmann, D. P. 1969. "Influence of symbolically modeled instrumental aggression and pain cues on aggressive behavior." *Journal of Personality and Social Psychology*, **11**:280–288.

Hartshorne, H., and M. A. May. 1928–1930. *Studies in the Nature of Character*. (3 vols.) New York: Macmillan.

Harvey, P. 1970. "Problems in Chinatown." *Human Events*, **30**:21 (May 16).

Hassan, A. 1972. In E. Pell (ed.), *Maximum Security: Letters from Prison*. New York: Dutton.

Hastings, D. W. 1965. "The psychiatry of presidential assassination." *The Journal Lancet*, **84** (March, April, May, July).

Hathaway, S. R., and E. D. Monachesi. 1957. "The personalities of predelinquent boys." *Journal of Criminal Law, Criminology, and Police Science*, **48**:149–163.

Hauge, R., and P. Wolf. 1974. "Criminal violence in three Scandinavian countries." In N. Christie et al. (eds.), *Scandinavian Studies in Criminology*. (Vol. 5.) Oslo: Universitetsforlaget.

Hayner, N. S. 1946. "Criminogenic zones in Mexico City." *American Sociological Review*, **11**:428–438.

Hays, W. L. 1963. *Statistics for Psychologists*. New York: Holt.

Healy, W., and A. F. Bronner. 1936. *New Light on Delinquency and Its Treatment*. New Haven, Conn.: Yale University Press.

Heckhausen, H. 1967. *The Anatomy of Achievement Motivation*. New York: Academic Press.

Henry, J. 1963. *Culture against Man*. New York: Random House.

Herrnstein, R. J. 1973. "Education, socioeconomic status, IQ, and their effects." *Contemporary Psychology*, **18**:403–405.

Herskovits, M. J. 1941. *The Myth of the Negro Past*. Boston: Beacon Press.

Hertzberg, L. 1975. "Blame and causality." *Mind*, **84**:500–515.

Hess, E. H. 1959. "Imprinting." *Science*, **130**:133–141.

Hess, E. H. 1972. " 'Imprinting' in a natural laboratory." *Scientific American*, **227**:24–31.

Hewitt, L. E., and R. L. Jenkins. 1946. *Fundamental Patterns of Maladjustment: The Dynamics of Their Origin*. Springfield: State of Illinois.

Hill, R., and M. Feeley (eds.). 1968. *Affirmative School Integration: Efforts to Overcome De Facto Segregation in Urban Schools*. Beverly Hills, Calif.: Sage.

Himmelfarb, G. 1974. *On Liberty and Liberalism: The Case of John Stuart Mill*. New York: Knopf.

Hindelang, M. J. 1973. "Time perceptions of self-reported delinquents." *British Journal of Criminology*, **13**:178–183.

Hindelang, M. J. 1974. "Decisions of shoplifting victims to invoke the criminal justice process." *Social Problems*, **21**:580–593.

Hirschi, T. 1969. *Causes of Delinquency*. Berkeley and Los Angeles: University of California Press.

Hirschi, T. 1975. "Labelling theory and juvenile delinquency: An assessment of the evidence." In W. R. Gove (ed.), *The Labelling of Deviance: Evaluating a Perspective*. New York: Wiley.

Hirst, P. 1972. "Marx and Engels on law, crime, and morality." *Economy and Society*, **1**:28–56.

Hobsbawm, E. J. 1969. *Bandits*. London: Weidenfeld and Nicolson.

Hodgkiss, M. 1933. "The influence of broken homes and working mothers." *Smith College Studies in Social Work*, **3**:259–274.

Hohenstein, W. H. 1969. "Factors influencing the police disposition of juvenile offenders." In T. Sellin and M. E. Wolfgang (eds.), *Delinquency: Selected Studies*. Toronto: Wiley.

Hollander, P. 1973. *Soviet and American Society: A Comparison*. New York: Oxford University Press.

Holz, W., and N. H. Azrin. 1962. "Interactions between the discriminative and aversive properties of punishment." *Journal of Experimental Animal Behavior*, **5**:229–234.

Honzik, M. P. 1966. "Prediction of behavior from birth to maturity." In J. Rosenblith and W. Allinsmith (eds.), *The Causes of Behavior*. (2d ed.) Boston: Allyn and Bacon.

Hoo, S. 1972. "The rights of the victims: Thoughts on crime and compassion." *Encounter*, **38**:11–15.

Hooker, E. L. 1945. *The Houston Delinquent in His Community Setting*. Houston, Tex.: Council of Social Agencies, Research Bureau.

Horowitz, D. L. 1975. "Ethnic identity." In N. Glazer and D. P. Moynihan (eds.), *Ethnicity: Theory and Experience*. Cambridge, Mass.: Harvard University Press.

Horton, P. B. 1973. "Problems in understanding criminal motives." In S. Rottenberg (ed.), *The Economics of Crime and Punishment*. Washington, D.C.: American Enterprise Institute for Public Policy Research.

Horton, P. B., and G. R. Leslie. 1965. *The Sociology of Social Problems*. (3d ed.) New York: Appleton-Century-Crofts.

Houchon, G. 1967. "Les Mécanismes criminogénes dans une société urbaine africaine." *Revue Internationale Criminologie et de Police Technique*, **21**:271–292.

Hoult, T. F. (ed.). 1969. *Dictionary of Modern Sociology*. Totowa, N.J.: Littlefield, Adams.

House of Commons of Canada. 1971. *House of Commons Debates*. Ottawa: Queen's Printer.

Howe, I. 1976. *World of Our Fathers: The Journey of the East European Jews to America, and the Life They Found and Made*. New York: Harcourt, Brace.

Hsu, M. 1973. "Cultural and sexual differences in the judgment of criminal offenses: A replication study of the measurement of delinquency." *Journal of Criminal Law and Criminology*, **64**:348–353.

Hume, D. 1758. *An Inquiry concerning Human Understanding*. Reprinted 1957. New York: Liberal Arts Press.

Hunt, C. L., and R. W. Coller. 1957. "Intermarriage and cultural change: A study of Philippine-American marriages." *Social Forces*, **35**:223–230.

Hutt, C. 1972. *Males and Females*. Middlesex, England: Penguin.

Huxley, A. 1960. *Brave New World*. New York: Harper and Row.

Hyman, H. H. 1953. "The value systems of different classes." In R. Bendix and S. Lipset (eds.), *Class, Status, and Power*. New York: Free Press.

Hyman, H. H. 1954. *Interviewing in Social Research*. Chicago: University of Chicago Press.

Icheiser, G. 1949. "Misunderstandings in human relations." *American Journal of Sociology*, **55**: Whole Part II.

Inkeles, A., and D. J. Levinson. 1969. "National character: The study of modal personality and sociocultural systems." In G. Lindzey and E. Aronson (eds.), *The Handbook of Social Psychology*. (2d ed.; vol. IV.) Reading, Mass.: Addison-Wesley.

Institute of Public Administration. 1952. *Crime Records in Police Management*. New York: The Institute.

Introna, F. 1963. "Aspetti degenerativi e criminologici delle migrazioni interne." *La Scuola Positiva*, **5**:668–692.

Isaacs, H. R. 1975. *Idols of the Tribe: Group Identity and Political Change*. New York: Harper and Row.

Jacobs, S. L. 1976. "Blue boxes spread from phone freaks to the well-healed." *The Wall Street Journal*, **94**:1, 15 (January 29).

Jarvie, I. C. 1967. *The Revolution in Anthropology*. London: Routledge.

Jarvie, I. C. 1975. "Cultural relativism again." *Philosophy of the Social Sciences*, **5**:343–353.

Jarvis, G. K. 1972. "The ecological analysis of juvenile delinquency in a Canadian city." In C. Boydell et al. (eds.), *Deviant Behaviour and Societal Reaction*. Toronto: Holt.

Jarvis, G. K., and H. B. Messinger. 1974. "Social and economic correlates of juvenile delinquency rates: A Canadian case." *Canadian Journal of Criminology and Corrections*, **16**:361–372.

Jaspan, N. 1960. *The Thief in the White Collar*. Philadelphia: Lippincott.

Jaspan, N. 1970. Interview. *U.S. News & World Report*, **69**:32–33 (October 26).

Jayasuriya, D. L. 1960. *A Study of Adolescent Ambition, Level of Aspiration and Achievement Motivation*. London: University of London. Ph.D. dissertation.

Jeffery, C. R. 1959. "An integrated theory of crime and criminal behavior." *Journal of Criminal Law, Criminology, and Police Science*, **49**:533–552.

Jencks, C., et al. 1972. *Inequality: A Reassessment of the Effect of Family and Schooling in America*. New York: Basic Books.

Jenkins, W. W. 1958. "An experimental study of the relationship of legitimate and illegitimate birth status to school and personal and social adjustment of Negro children." *American Journal of Sociology*, **64**:169–173.

Jensen, A. R. 1969. "Counter response." *Journal of Social Issues*, **25**:219–222.

Jensen, G. F. 1973. "Inner containment and delinquency." *Journal of Criminal Law and Criminology*, **64**:464–470.

Jensen, G. F. 1974. Review of M. E. Wolfgang et al., "Delinquency in a birth cohort." *American Journal of Sociology*, **80**:546–549.

Jensen, G. F. 1976. "Race, achievement, and delinquency: A further look at 'Delinquency in a birth cohort.'" *American Journal of Sociology*, **82**:379–387.

Jessor, R., et al. 1968. *Society, Personality, and Deviant Behavior*. New York: Holt.

Joey, with D. Fisher. 1974. *Killer: Autobiography of a Hit Man for the Mafia*. New York: Simon and Schuster.

Johnson, G. B. 1970. "The Negro and crime." In. M. E. Wolfgang et al. (eds.), *The Sociology of Crime and Delinquency*. (2d ed.) New York: Wiley.

Johnson, R. C., et al. 1960. "Word values, word frequency, and visual duration thresholds." *Psychological Review*, **67**:332–342.

Jonassen, C. T. 1949. "A re-evaluation and critique of the logic and some methods of Shaw and McKay." *American Sociological Review*, **14**:608–617.

Jones, J. 1972. *Prejudice and Racism*. Reading, Mass.: Addison-Wesley.

Jones, M. R. 1976. "Time, our lost dimension: Toward a new theory of perception, attention, and memory." *Psychological Review*, **83**:323–355.

Joseph, R. A. 1975. "Bodyguard business booms as kidnappings and crime rate rise." *The Wall Street Journal*, **93**:1, 33 (November 20).

Kaironen, V. A. 1966. *A Study of the Criminality of Finnish Immigrants in Sweden*. Strasbourg: Council of Europe.

Kaiser, R. G. 1976. *Russia: The People and the Power*. New York: Atheneum.

Kant, I. 1965. *The Metaphysical Elements of Justice*. Trans. by J. Ladd. Indianapolis: Bobbs-Merrill.

Kantrowitz, N. 1969. "Ethnic and racial segregation in the New York metropolis, 1960." *American Journal of Sociology*, **74**:685–695.

Kaplan, H. B. 1976. "Self-attitudes and deviant response." *Social Forces*, **54**:788–801.

Kaplan, R. M., and R. D. Singer. 1972. "Psychological effects of televised fantasy violence: A review of the literature." Riverside, Calif.: University of California, Department of Psychology. Mimeographed.

Karpman, B. 1948. *The Alcoholic Woman: Case Studies in the Psychodynamics of Alcoholism*. Washington, D.C.: Linacre.

Katz, A. J., et al. 1976. *Progress Report: The Pilot Alberta Restitution Centre*. Calgary: The Centre.

Katz, D. 1942. "Do interviewers bias polls?" *Public Opinion Quarterly*, **6**:248–268.

Kaufmann, H. 1968. "The unconcerned bystander." Paper read at the annual meeting of the American Psychological Association, San Francisco, Calif.

Kaupen, W. 1973. "Public opinion of the law in a democratic society." In A. Podgorecki et al. (eds.), *Knowledge and Opinion about Law*. London: Martin Robertson.

Keiser, R. L. (ed.). 1965. *Hustler!: Henry Williamson*. Garden City, N.Y.: Doubleday.

Kelly, E. L. 1963. "Consistency of the adult personality." *American Psychologist*, **10**:659–681.

Kendall, M. G. 1949. "On the reconciliation of theories of probability." *Biometrika*, **36**:101–116.

Kennedy, W. A., and H. C. Willcutt. 1964. "Praise and blame as incentives." *Psychological Bulletin*, **62**:323–332.

Kephart, W. M. 1957. *Racial Factors and Urban Law Enforcement*. Philadelphia: University of Pennsylvania Press.

Kerner, H-J, with J. Mack. 1975. *The Crime Industry*. Lexington, Mass.: Heath.

Kesey, K. 1964. *One Flew over the Cuckoo's Nest*. New York: Compass Books.

Keyfitz, N. 1973. "Can inequality be cured?" *The Public Interest*, (31):91–101.

Kilson, M. 1971. "An American profile: The black student militant." *Encounter*, **37**:83–90.

Kinsey, A. C., et al. 1948. *Sexual Behavior in the Human Male*. Philadelphia: Saunders.

Kirsch, A., et al. 1965. *An Experimental Study of Sensitivity of Survey Techniques in Measuring Drinking Practices*. Washington, D.C.: George Washington University.

Kitano, H. H. L. 1967. "Japanese-American crime and delinquency." *Journal of Psychology*, **66**:253–263.

Klein, D. 1974. "The etiology of female crime: A review of the literature." In S. L. Messinger et al. (eds.), *The Aldine Crime and Justice Annual, 1973*. Chicago: Aldine.

Klein, M. W., et al. 1974. "The ambiguous juvenile arrest." Los Angeles: University of Southern California, Department of Sociology. Mimeographed.

Kleinmuntz, B. 1967. "Sign and seer: Another example." *Journal of Abnormal Psychology*, **72**:163–165.

Kobler, J. 1972. *Capone*. London: Michael Joseph.

Kobrin, S. 1951. "The conflict of values in delinquency areas." *American Sociological Review*, **16**:653–661.

Kobrin, S., et al. 1972. *The Deterrent Effectiveness of Criminal Justice Sanction Strategies*. Los Angeles: University of Southern California, Public Systems Research Institute.

Koenig, D. J. 1974. "Correlates of self-reported victimization and perceptions of neighbourhood safety." Victoria, B.C.: University of Victoria, Department of Sociology. Mimeographed.

Koestler, A. 1941. *Darkness at Noon*. New York: Macmillan.

Koestler, A. 1956. *Reflections on Hanging*. London: Gollancz.

Kohlberg, L. 1964. "Development of moral character and moral ideology." In M. L. Hoffman and L. Hoffman (eds.), *Child Development Research*. (Vol. 1.) New York: Russell Sage.

Kohlberg, L., and E. Turiel. 1971. *Recent Research in Moral Development*. New York: Holt.

Kohn, M. L. 1959. "Social class and parental values." *American Journal of Sociology*, **64**:337–351.

Kohn, M. L., and C. Schooler. 1969. "Class, occupation, and orientation." *American Sociological Review*, **34**:659–678.

Krash, A. 1961. "The Durham rule and judicial administration of the insanity defense in the District of Columbia." *Yale Law Journal*, **70**:905–906.

Kratcoski, P. C. 1974. "Differential treatment of delinquent boys and girls in juvenile court." *Child Welfare*, **53**:16–22.

Krohm, G. 1973. "The pecuniary incentives of property crime." In S. Rottenberg (ed.), *The Economics of Crime and Punishment*. Washington, D.C.: American Enterprise Institute for Public Policy Research.

Krovetz, M. L. 1972. "Effects of desegregation studied." *Newsletter* of the Society for the Psychological Study of Social Issues, (130):10.

Kulik, J. A., et al. 1968. "Disclosure of delinquent behavior under conditions of anonymity and nonanonymity." *Journal of Consulting and Clinical Psychology*, **32**:506–509.

Kupperstein, L. R., and J. Toro-Calder. 1969. *Juvenile Delinquency in Puerto Rico: A Socio-Cultural and Socio-Legal Analysis*. Rio Piedras: Social Science Research Center.

Kutschinsky, B. 1970. *Studies on Pornography and Sex Crimes in Denmark*. Copenhagen: New Social Science Monographs.

Kwitny, M. K. 1975. "Shackled justice: Some solutions." *The Wall Street Journal*, **93**:16 (October 8).

Labovitz, S. 1969. "The nonutility of significance tests: The significance of tests of significance reconsidered." *Pacific Sociological Review*, **13**:141–148.

Lachenmeyer, C. W. 1971. *The Language of Sociology*. New York: Columbia University Press.

Ladd, E. C., Jr., and S. M. Lipset. 1975. *The Divided Academy: Professors and Politics*. New York: McGraw-Hill.

Ladd, J. 1957. *The Structure of a Moral Code*. Cambridge, Mass.: Harvard University Press.

Lambert, J. R. 1970. *Crime, Police, and Race Relations: A Study in Birmingham*. London: Oxford University Press.

Lamm, M. R., et al. 1976. "Sex and social class as determinants of future orientation (time perspective) in adolescents." *Journal of Personality and Social Psychology*, **34**:317–326.

Landau, S. F. 1976. "Delinquency, institutionalization, and time orientation." *Journal of Consulting and Clinical Psychology*, **44**:745–759.

Lander, B. 1954. *Towards an Understanding of Juvenile Delinquency*. New York: Columbia University Press.

Lang, P. G., and A. D. Lazovik. 1963. "Experimental desensitization of a phobia." *Journal of Abnormal and Social Psychology*, **66**:519–525.

Lang, P. G., and B. G. Melamed. 1969. "Case report: Avoidance therapy of an infant with chronic ruminative vomiting." *Journal of Abnormal Psychology*, **74**:1–8.

Langer, S. K. 1967. *Mind: An Essay on Human Feeling*. Baltimore: Johns Hopkins.

Laqueur, W. 1976. "Coming to terms with terror." *Times Literary Supplement*, (3,864):362–363 (April 2).

LaVoie, J. C. 1974. "Type of punishment as a determinant of resistance to deviation." *Developmental Psychology*, **10**:181–189.

Law Reform Commission of Canada. 1974. *Restitution and Compensation*. Working Paper No. 5. Ottawa: Information Canada.

Law Reform Commission of Canada. 1975. *The Criminal Process and Mental Disorder*. Working Paper No. 14. Ottawa: The Commission.

Lawrence, J. E. S. 1974. "Science and sentiment: Overview of research on crowding and human behavior." *Psychological Bulletin*, **81**:712–720.

Lazarsfeld, P. F. 1955. "Interpretations of statistical relations as a research operation." In P. F. Lazarsfeld and M. Rosenberg (eds.), *The Language of Social Research*. Glencoe, Ill.: Free Press.

Lefcourt, H. 1972. "Recent developments in the study of locus of control." In B. A. Maher (ed.), *Progress in Experimental Personality Research*. New York: Academic Press.

Leff, R. 1969. "Effects of punishment intensity and consistency on the internalization of behavioral suppression in children." *Developmental Psychology*, 1:345–356.

Lefkowitz, M. M., et al. 1972. "Environmental variables as predictors of aggressive behavior." Paper read at the annual meeting of the American Association for the Advancement of Science, Washington, D.C.

Lefkowitz, M. M., et al. 1955. "Status factors in pedestrian violation of traffic signals." *Journal of Abnormal and Social Psychology*, 51:704–706.

Leifer, R. 1964. "The psychiatrist and tests of criminal responsibility." *American Psychologist*, 19:825–830.

Lemert, E. M. 1951. *Social Pathology: A Systematic Approach to the Theory of Sociopathic Behavior*. New York: McGraw-Hill.

Lemert, E. M. 1962. "Paranoia and the dynamics of exclusion." *Sociometry*, 25:2–20.

Lemert, E. M. 1967. *Human Deviance, Social Problems and Social Control*. Englewood Cliffs, N.J.: Prentice-Hall.

Lenski, G., and J. Leggett. 1960. "Caste, class, and deference in the research interview." *American Journal of Sociology*, 65:463–467.

LeShan, L. L. 1952. "Time orientation and social class." *Journal of Abnormal and Social Psychology*, 47:589–592.

Lesieur, H. R., and P. M. Lehman. 1975. "Remeasuring delinquency: A replication and critique." *British Journal of Criminology*, 15:69–80.

Lessing, E. E. 1968. "Demographic, developmental, and personality correlates of length of future time perspective." *Journal of Personality*, 36:193–201.

Lessing, E. E. 1969. "Racial differences in indices of ego functioning relevant to academic achievement." *Journal of Genetic Psychology*, 115:153–167.

Lessing, E. E. 1971. "Comparative extension of personal and social-political future time perspectives." *Perceptual and Motor Skills*, 33:415–422.

Levin, M. A. 1971. "Policy evaluation and recidivism." *Law & Society Review*, 6:17–46.

Levine, I. E. 1960. *The Mind of an Assassin*. New York: Signet Books.

Levine, R. A. 1971–1972. "The silent majority: Neither simple nor simple-minded." *Public Opinion Quarterly*, 35:571–578.

Levine, S. 1971. "Sexual differentiation: The development of maleness and femaleness." *California Medicine*, 114:12–17.

Levitan, S. A. 1975. "The case for revising the definition of unemployment." Paper read at the 30th annual meeting of the American Association for Public Opinion Research, Itasca, Ill.

Levitt, E. E. 1957. "The results of psychotherapy with children: An evaluation." *Journal of Consulting Psychology*, 21:189–196.

Lewis, C. I. 1946. *An Analysis of Knowledge and Valuation*. La Salle, Ill.: Open Court.

Lewis, C. S. 1953. "The humanitarian theory of punishment." *Res Judicatae*, 6:224–230.

Lewis, O. 1959. *Five Families: Mexican Case Studies in the Culture of Poverty*. New York: Basic Books.

Lewis, O. 1961. *The Children of Sanchez: Autobiography of a Mexican Family*. New York: Random House.

Lewis, O. 1966. *La Vida: A Puerto Rican Family in the Culture of Poverty*. New York: Random House.

Lichtenstein, F. E. 1950. "Studies of anxiety: I. The production of a feeding inhibition in dogs." *Journal of Comparative and Physiological Psychology*, 43:16–29.

Liebert, R. M., and R. A. Baron. 1972. "Some immediate effects of televised violence on children's behavior." *Developmental Psychology*, 6:469–475.

Life. 1971. "A flood of responses to our crime questionnaire." **71:**3 (December 10).

Life. 1972. "Are you personally afraid of crime?: Readers speak out." **72:**28–30 (January 14).

Lind, A. W. 1930a. "The ghetto and the slum." *Social Forces,* **9:**206–215.

Lind, A. W. 1930b. "Some ecological patterns of community disorganization in Honolulu." *American Journal of Sociology,* **36:**206–220.

Lindesmith, A. R., and A. L. Strauss. 1956. *Social Psychology.* New York: Holt.

Lipman, M. 1973. *Stealing: How America's Employees Are Stealing Their Companies Blind.* New York: Harper's Magazine Press.

Lippmann, W. 1922. *Public Opinion.* New York: Macmillan.

Lipton, D., et al. 1975. *The Effectiveness of Correctional Treatment: A Survey of Treatment Evaluation Studies.* New York: Praeger.

Lisansky, E. S. 1958. "The woman alcoholic." *Annals of the Academy of Political and Social Sciences,* **351:**73–82.

Lloyd, R. W., Jr., and H. C. Salzberg. 1975. "Controlled social drinking: An alternative to abstinence as a treatment goal for some alcohol abusers." *Psychological Bulletin,* **82:**815–842.

Loftus, E. F. 1976. "Federal regulations: Make the punishment fit the crime." *Science,* **191:**670 (February 13).

Long, T. A. 1973. "Capital punishment: 'Cruel and unusual'?" *Ethics,* **83:**214–223.

Lorber, J. 1967. "Deviance as performance: The case of illness." *Social Problems,* **14:**302–310.

Lorenz, K. Z. 1952. *King Solomon's Ring: New Light on Animal Ways.* London: Methuen.

Lottier, S. 1938. "Distribution of criminal offenses in metropolitan regions." *Journal of Criminal Law and Criminology,* **29:**37–50.

Lovaas, O. I. 1961. "Effect of exposure to symbolic aggression on aggressive behavior." *Child Development,* **32:**37–44.

Lowe, G. R. 1966. "Response inhibition and deviant social behavior in children." *British Journal of Psychiatry,* **112:**925–930.

Lundberg, F. 1954. *The Treason of the People.* New York: Harper and Row.

Lundberg, G. A., and L. Dickson. 1952. "Inter-ethnic relations in a high-school population." *American Journal of Sociology,* **58:**1–10.

Lunde, D. T. 1975. "America's murder epidemic: A psychiatrist's report." *The Stanford Observer,* No. 5.

Lyle, J., and H. R. Hoffman. 1972. "Children's use of television and other media." In E. A. Rubinstein et al. (eds.), *Television and Social Behavior.* (Vol. 4: *Television in Day-to-Day Life: Patterns of Use.*) Washington, D.C.: GPO.

Lyster, W. R. 1954. "Homicide and fertility rates in the United States," *Social Biology,* **21:**389–392.

Maas, P. 1975. *King of the Gypsies.* New York: Viking.

Maccoby, E. E., and C. N. Jacklin. 1974. *The Psychology of Sex Differences.* Stanford, Calif.: Stanford University Press.

Mack, J. A. 1964. "Full-time miscreants, delinquent neighbourhoods, and criminal networks." *British Journal of Sociology,* **15:**38–53.

Mack, J. A. 1872. "The able criminal." *British Journal of Criminology,* **12:**44–54.

Mack, J. A., and H-J Kerner. 1974a. *The Crime Industry.* Lexington, Mass.: Heath.

Mack, J. A., and H-J Kerner. 1975b. "Le crime professionel et l'organisation criminelle." Paris: Lecture, University of Paris (May 20).

Mackie, M. M. 1971. *The Accuracy of Folk Knowledge concerning Alberta Indians,*

Hutterites and Ukrainians: An Available Data Stereotype Validation Technique. Edmonton: University of Alberta, Department of Sociology. Ph.D. dissertation.

Mackie, M. M. 1973. "Arriving at 'truth' by definition: The case of stereotype inaccuracy." *Social Problems*, **20**:431–447.

Mäkelä, K. 1967. "Public sense of justice and judicial practice." *Acta Sociologica*, **10**:42–67.

Maller, J. B. 1932. "Are broken homes a causative factor in juvenile delinquency? IV. Discussion." *Social Forces*, **10**:531–533.

Mallick, S. K., and B. R. McCandless. 1966. "A study of catharsis of aggression." *Journal of Personality and Social Psychology*, **4**:591–596.

Malloy, M. T. 1972. "Security means lifting the phone and saying: 'Operator, get me the rent-a-cops.'" *The National Observer*, **11**:1, 18.

Mangin, W. 1967. "Latin American squatter settlements: A problem and a solution." *Latin American Research*, **2**:65–69.

Mannheim, H. 1965. *Comparative Criminology.* (2 vols.) London: Routledge.

Mannheim, H., and L. T. Wilkins. 1955. *Prediction Methods in Relation to Borstal Training.* London: Her Majesty's Stationery Office.

Martin, B. 1963. "Reward and punishment associated with the same goal response: A factor in the learning of motives." *Psychological Bulletin*, **60**:441–451.

Martin, D. 1976. "Spreading fires: An epidemic of arson afflicts many cities." *The Wall Street Journal*, **94**:1, 16 (May 24).

Martin, J. C., et al. 1974. *Martin's Annual Criminal Code.* Agincourt, Ont.: Canada Law Book.

Martinson, R. 1974. "What Works?: Questions and answers about prison reform." *The Public Interest*, (35):22–54.

Mason, W. A. 1976. "Environmental models and mental modes: Representational processes in the great apes and man." *American Psychologist*, **31**:284–294.

Masserman, J. M. 1943. *Behavior and Neurosis.* Chicago: University of Chicago Press.

Matheson, J. 1975. "Baun recalls tough times." *The Edmonton Journal*, 65 (November 7).

Matthews, V. 1972. *Socio-Legal Statistics in Alberta.* Edmonton: Human Resources Research Council.

Matza, D. 1964. *Delinquency and Drift.* New York: Wiley.

Matza, D. 1969. *Becoming Deviant.* Englewood Cliffs, N.J.: Prentice-Hall.

Maxwell, N. 1972. "Passing judgment: How little town reacts when banker is accused of taking $4.7 million." *The Wall Street Journal*, **82**:1, 14 (August 8).

Maxwell, N. 1973. "Voice of experience: Lamar Hill, embezzler, says stealing is easy." *The Wall Street Journal*, **88**:1, 14, (January 26).

Mayer, A. J. 1972. "Men working: Builders seek to end the ancient tradition of on-the-job larcenies." *The Wall Street Journal*, **86**:1, 12 (June 19).

Mayhew, H. 1861–1862. *London Labour and the London Poor.* (2 vols.) London: Griffin.

McCandless, B. R., et al. 1972. "Perceived opportunity, delinquency, race, and body build among delinquent youth." *Journal of Consulting and Clinical Psychology*, **38**:281–287.

McCarthy, E. D., et al. 1975. "The effects of television on children and adolescents: Violence and behavior disorders." *Journal of Communication*, **25**:71–85.

McClelland, L. 1974. "Effects of interviewer-respondent race interactions on household interview measures of motivation and intelligence." *Journal of Personality and Social Psychology*, **29**:392–397.

McClintock, F. H. 1963. *Crimes of Violence*. London: Macmillan.

McClintock, F. H., and N. H. Avison. 1968. *Crime in England and Wales*. London: Heinemann.

McClintock, F. H., and E. Gibson. 1961. *Robbery in London*. London: Macmillan.

McCord, H. 1951. "Discovering the 'confused' respondent: A possible projective method." *Public Opinion Quarterly*, **15**:363–366.

McCord, W., and J. McCord. 1959. *Origins of Crime: A New Evaluation of the Cambridge-Somerville Youth Study*. New York: Columbia University Press.

McCord, W., and J. McCord. 1960. *Origins of Alcoholism*. Stanford, Calif.: Stanford University Press.

McCourt, K., and D. G. Taylor. 1976. "Determining religious affiliation through survey research: A methodological note." *Public Opinion Quarterly*, **40**:124–127.

McCurdy, H. G. 1961. *The Personal World: An Introduction to the Study of Personality*. New York: Harcourt, Brace.

McDonald, L. 1969a. "Crime and punishment in Canada: A statistical test of the 'conventional wisdom.'" *Canadian Review of Sociology and Anthropology*, **6**:212–236.

McDonald, L. 1969b. *Social Class and Delinquency*. London: Faber.

McDowell, E. 1973. "Tokyo, where law means order." *The Wall Street Journal*, **89**:12 (November 29).

McEachern, A. W., and R. Bauzer. 1967. "Factors related to disposition in juvenile police contacts." In M. W. Klein (ed.), *Juvenile Gangs in Context: Theory, Research, and Action*. Englewood Cliffs, N.J.: Prentice-Hall.

McEvoy, F. P. 1941. "The lie-detector goes into business." *The Reader's Digest*, **38**:69–72.

McGill, H. G. 1938. "Oriental delinquents in Vancouver juvenile court." *Sociology and Social Research*, **22**:428–438.

McIntosh, M. 1971. "Changes in the organization of thieving." In S. Cohen (ed.), *Images of Deviance*. Baltimore: Penguin.

McKenzie, R. B., and G. Tullock. 1975. *The New World of Economics: Explorations into the Human Experience*. Homewood, Ill.: Irwin.

McLeod, J. M., et al. 1972. "Adolescents, parents, and television use: Adolescent self-report measures from Maryland and Wisconsin samples." In G. A. Comstock and E. A. Rubinstein (eds.), *Television and Social Behavior*. (Vol. 3: *Television and Adolescent Aggressiveness*.) Washington, D.C.: GPO.

McNamara, H. P. 1975. "News letter." The National Council on Crime and Delinquency. Hackensack, N.J.: The Council.

McPheters, L. R. 1976. "Criminal behavior and the gains from crime." *Criminology*, **14**:137–152.

McWhirter, N., and R. McWhirter (eds.). 1966. *The Guinness Book of Records*. London: Guinness.

Meade, A. 1973. "Seriousness of delinquency, the adjudicative decision and recidivism: A longitudinal configuration analysis." *Journal of Criminal Law and Criminology*, **64**:478–485.

Medinnus, G. R. 1965. "Delinquents' perceptions of their parents." *Journal of Consulting Psychology*, **29**:592–593.

Medvedev, Zh. 1971. *A Question of Madness*. New York: Knopf.

Meehl, P. E. 1954. *Clinical versus Statistical Prediction*. Minneapolis: University of Minneapolis Press.

Meehl, P. E. 1959. "Some ruminations on the validation of clinical procedures." *Canadian Journal of Psychology*, **13**:102–124.

Mehlman, B. 1952. "The reliability of psychiatric diagnosis." *Journal of Abnormal and Social Psychology*, **47**:577–578.

Meltzer, H. 1930. "The present status of experimental studies on the relationship of feeling to memory." *Psychological Review*, **37**:124–193.

Menninger, K. 1968. *The Crime of Punishment*. New York: Viking.

Mercer, J. R. 1965. "Social system perspective and clinical perspective: Frames of reference for understanding career patterns of persons labelled as mentally retarded." *Social Problems*, **13**:18–34.

Merrill, M. A. 1947. *Problems of Child Delinquency*. Boston: Houghton Mifflin.

Merritt, C. B., and E. G. Fowler. 1948. "The pecuniary honesty of the public at large." *Journal of Abnormal and Social Psychology*, **43**:90–93.

Merton, R. K. 1949; rev. 1957. *Social Theory and Social Structure: Toward the Codification of Theory and Research*. Glencoe, Ill.: Free Press.

Metzger, L. P. 1971. "American sociology and black assimilation: Conflicting perspectives." *American Journal of Sociology*, **76**:627–647.

Meyer, H. E. 1975. "How government helped ruin the South Bronx." *Fortune*, **92**:140–146, 150, 154.

Meyer, V., and R. Levy. 1970. "Behavioral treatment of a homosexual with compulsive rituals." *British Journal of Medicine*, **43**:63–67.

Michaels, J. J. 1955. *Disorders of Character*. Springfield, Ill.: Charles C Thomas.

Micklin, M., and M. Durbin. 1969. "Syntactic dimensions of attitude scaling techniques: Sources of variation and bias." *Sociometry*, **32**:194–206.

Milgram, S. 1963. "Behavioral study of obedience." *Journal of Abnormal Psychology*, **67**:371–378.

Milgram, S. 1974. *Obedience to Authority: An Experimental View*. New York: Harper and Row.

Mill, J. S. 1859. *On Liberty*. Reprinted 1964. New York: Dutton.

Miller, N. E. 1969. "Learning of visceral and glandular responses." *Science*, **163**:434–445 (January 31).

Miller, R. L. 1973. *Economics Today*. San Francisco: Canfield.

Miller, W. B. 1958. "Lower class culture as a generating milieu of gang delinquency." *Journal of Social Issues*, **14**:5–19.

Miller, W. B. 1967. "Theft behavior in city gangs." In M. W. Klein (ed.), *Juvenile Gangs in Context: Theory, Research, and Action*. Englewood Cliffs, N.J.: Prentice-Hall.

Miller, W. B. 1973. "Ideology and criminal justice policy: Some current issues." *Journal of Criminal Law and Criminology*, **64**:141–162.

Minear, R. 1972. *Victors' Justice: The Tokyo War Crimes Trial*. Princeton, N.J.: Princeton University Press.

Mischel, W. 1961. "Preference for delayed reinforcement and social responsibility." *Journal of Abnormal and Social Psychology*, **62**:1–7.

Mischel, W. 1969. "Continuity and change in personality." *American Psychologist*, **24**:1012–1018.

Mischel, W. 1973. "Toward a cognitive social learning reconceptualization of personality." *Psychological Review*, **80**:252–283.

Mitchell, G. D. (ed.). 1968. *A Dictionary of Sociology*. London: Routledge.

Molotch, H. 1969. "Racial integration in a transition community." *American Sociological Review*, **34**:878–893.

Monahan, T. 1957. "Family status and the delinquent child: A reappraisal and some new findings." *Social Forces*, **35**:250–258.

Moore, B. 1954. *Terror and Progress in the USSR*. Cambridge, Mass.: Harvard University Press.

Morgenstern, O. 1963. *On the Accuracy of Economic Observations*. (2d ed.) Princeton, N.J.: Princeton University Press.

Morgenstern, O. 1965. Personal communication (November 15).

Morlan, G. K. 1949. "A note on the frustration-aggression theories of Dollard and his associates." *Psychological Review*, **56**:1–8.

Morris, C. W. 1956. *Varieties of Human Value*. Chicago: University of Chicago Press.

Morris, C. W., and L. Small. 1971. "Changes in conceptions of the good life by American college students from 1950 to 1970." *Journal of Personality and Social Psychology*, **20**:254–260.

Morris, T. P. 1957. *The Criminal Area: A Study in Social Ecology*. London: Routledge.

Moses, E. R. 1970. "Negro and white crime rates." In M. E. Wolfgang et al. (eds.), *The Sociology of Crime and Delinquency*. (2d ed.) New York: Wiley.

Moss, R. 1972. *Urban Guerrillas*. London: Temple Smith.

Mowrer, O. H. 1960. " 'Sin,' the lesser of two evils." *American Psychologist*, **15**:301–304.

Mowrer, O. H. 1964. *The New Group Therapy*. New York: Van Nostrand.

Moynihan, D. P. 1965. *The Negro Family: The Case for National Action*. Washington, D.C.: U.S. Department of Labor.

Moynihan, D. P. 1969. *Maximum Feasible Misunderstanding: Community Action in the War on Poverty*. New York: Free Press.

Mudge, E. M. 1967. *Bank Robbery in California: A 35-Year Comparison with the Rest of the United States and an Intensive Study of 1,965 Offenses*. Scaramento, Calif.: Criminal Statistics Bureau.

Munch, P. A. 1976. "The concepts of 'function' and functional analysis in sociology." *Philosophy of the Social Sciences*, **6**:193–213.

Murphy, F. J., et al. 1946. "The incidence of hidden delinquency." *American Journal of Orthopsychiatry*, **16**:686–695.

Murphy, J. G. 1971. "Three mistakes about retributivism." *Analysis*, **31**:166–169.

Mussen, P. H., and E. Rutherford. 1961. "Effects of aggressive cartoons on children's aggressive play." *Journal of Abnormal and Social Psychology*, **62**:461–464.

Mylonas, A. D., and W. C. Reckless. 1963. "Prisoners' attitudes toward law and legal institutions." *Journal of Criminal Law, Criminology, and Police Science*, **54**:479–484.

Myrdal, G. 1970. *The Challenge of World Poverty: A World Anti-Poverty Program in Outline*. New York: Pantheon.

Nader, L. 1975. Address at the First International Symposium on Restitution, Minneapolis (November 10–11).

National Crime Panel. 1974. *Criminal Victimization in the United States, January–June, 1973*. Washington, D.C.: U.S. Department of Justice.

National Crime Panel. 1975. *Criminal Victimization Surveys in 13 American Cities*. Washington, D.C.: U.S. Department of Justice.

National Education Association. 1974. "Teacher opinion poll." *Today's Education*, **63**:105.

National Observer. 1971. "Women attack rape justice." **10**:1, 21 (October 9).

Neter, J. 1970. "Measurement errors in reports of consumer expenditures." *Journal of Marketing Research*, **7**:11–25.

Nettler, G. 1957. "A measure of alienation." *American Sociological Review*, **22**:670–677.

Nettler, G. 1959a. "Antisocial sentiment and criminality." *American Sociological Review*, **24**:202–218.

Nettler, G. 1959b. "Cruelty, dignity, and determinism." *American Sociological Review*, **24**:375–384.

Nettler, G. 1961. "Good men, bad men, and the perception of reality." *Sociometry*, **24**:279–294.

Nettler, G. 1968. Review of M. E. Wolfgang and F. Ferracuti, *The Subculture of Violence. Social Forces*, **46**:427–428.

Nettler, G. 1970. *Explanations*. New York: McGraw-Hill.

Nettler, G. 1972a. "Knowing and doing." *The American Sociologist*, **7**:3–7.

Nettler, G. 1972b. "Shifting the load." *American Behavioral Scientist*, **15**:361–379.

Nettler, G. 1973. "Wanting and knowing." *American Behavioral Scientist*, **17**:5–25.

Nettler, G. 1974. "Embezzlement without problems." *British Journal of Criminology*, **14**:70–77.

Nettler, G. 1975. Review of C. Hartjen, *Crime and Criminalization,* and R. Quinney, *Critique of Legal Order. Contemporary Sociology*, **4**:243–245.

Nettler, G. 1976. *Social Concerns*. New York: McGraw-Hill.

Nettler, G. 1977. "Causes and explanations." In G. Nettler, *Causes of Conduct*. Forthcoming.

Neumann, K. 1963. *Die Kriminalität der italienischen Arbeitskräfte im Kanton Zurich*. Zurich: Juris Verlag.

Newman, G. 1976. *Comparative Deviance: Perception and Law in Six Cultures*. New York: Elsevier.

Newman, G., et al. 1974. "Authoritarianism, religiosity, and reactions to deviance." *Journal of Criminal Justice*, **2**:249–259.

Newsweek. 1971. "The public: A hard line." **77**:39–45 (March 8).

Newsweek. 1973a. "The light-fingered shopper." **82**:23 (November 26).

Newsweek. 1973b. "Sexploitation: Sin's wages." **81**:78–79 (February 12).

Nichols, P. L., and S. H. Broman. 1974. "Familial resemblance in infant mental development." *Developmental Psychology*, **10**:442–446.

Nisbet, R. A. 1974a. "The pursuit of equality: Review essay." *The Public Interest*, (35):103–120.

Nisbet, R. A. 1974b. "Rousseau and equality." *Encounter*, **63**:40–51.

Nisbet, R. A. 1975a. "The new despotism." *Commentary*, **59**:31–43.

Nisbet, R. A. 1975b. *Twilight of Authority*. New York: Oxford University Press.

Normandeau, A. 1969. "Trends in robbery as reflected by different indexes." In T. Sellin and M. E. Wolfgang (eds.), *Delinquency: Selected Studies*. New York: Wiley.

Novak, M. 1972. *The Rise of the Unmeltable Ethnics*. New York: Macmillan.

Nuckols, R. C. 1949–1950. "Verbi!" *International Journal of Opinion and Attitude Research*, **3**:575–586.

Nuckols, R. C., 1953. "A note on pre-testing public opinion questions." *Journal of Applied Psychology*, **37**:119–120.

Nye, F. I. 1957. "Child adjustment in broken and unhappy unbroken homes." *Journal of Marriage and Family Living*, **19**:356–361.

Nye, F. I., and J. F. Short, Jr. 1957. "Scaling delinquent behavior." *American Sociological Review*, **22**:326–331.

Nye, F. I., et al. 1958. "Socioeconomic status and delinquent behavior." *American Journal of Sociology*, **63**:381–389.

Ogburn, W. F. 1935. "Factors in variation of crime among cities." *Journal of the American Statistical Association*, **30**:12–20.

O'Neill, J. 1975. "Interpreting unemployment differentials." Paper read at the 30th annual meeting of the American Association for Public Opinion Research, Itasca, Ill.

Ortega y Gasset, J. 1932. *The Revolt of the Masses*. New York: Norton.

Ortega y Gasset, J. 1946. *Concord and Liberty*. New York: Norton.

Orwell, G. 1961. *1984*. New York: New American Library.

Outerbridge, W. R. 1968. "The tyranny of treatment . . . ?" *Canadian Journal of Corrections*, **10**:378–387.

Owens, W. A. 1968. "Toward one discipline of scientific psychology." *American Psychologist*, **23**:782–785.

Owens, W. A. 1971. "A quasi-actuarial basis for individual assessment." *American Psychologist*, **26**:992–999.

Pace, C. R. 1949. "Opinion and action: A study of the validity of attitude measurement." *American Psychologist*, **4**:242.

Packer, H. L. 1968. *The Limits of the Criminal Sanction*. Stanford, Calif.: Stanford University Press.

Pantaleone, M. 1966. *The Mafia and Politics*. London: Chatto and Windus.

Paranjape, W. 1970. *Some Aspects of Probation: An Exploration of Labelling Theory in Six Urban Junior High Schools*. Edmonton: University of Alberta, Department of Sociology. M.A. dissertation.

Parry, H. J., and H. Crossley, 1950. "Validity of responses to survey questions." *Public Opinion Quarterly*, **14**:61–80.

Passmore, J. 1967. "Logical positivism." In P. Edwards (ed.), *The Encyclopedia of Philosophy*. New York: Macmillan.

Patterson, O. 1975. "Context and choice in ethnic allegiance: A theoretical framework and Caribbean case study." In N. Glazer and D. P. Moynihan (eds.), *Ethnicity: Theory and Experience*. Cambridge, Mass.; Harvard University Press.

Pearlin, L. J., and M. L. Kohn. 1966. "Social class, occupation, and parental values: A cross-national study." *American Sociological Review*, **31**:466–479.

Penn, S. 1973. "Black Watch Farms collapse investigated: Fraud, $3.2 million embezzlement alleged." *The Wall Street Journal*, **88**:4 (June 1).

Pepinsky, H. E. 1976. *Crime and Conflict: A Study of Law and Society*. New York: Academic Press.

Petersen, W. (ed.). 1963. *The Realities of World Communism*. Englewood Cliffs, N.J.: Prentice-Hall.

Petersen, W. 1967. "Family structure and social mobility among Japanese Americans." *Abstracts*, American Sociological Association, 119–120.

Petersen, W. 1969a. "The classification of subnations in Hawaii: An essay in the sociology of knowledge." *American Sociological Review*, **34**:863–877.

Petersen, W. 1969b. *Population*. New York: Macmillan.

Peterson, D. R., and W. C. Becker. 1965. "Family interaction and delinquency." In H. C. Quay (ed.), *Juvenile Delinquency*. Princeton, N.J.: Van Nostrand.

Peterson, D. R., et al. 1959. "Personality and background factors in juvenile delinquency." *Journal of Consulting Psychology*, **24**:555.

Peterson, J. 1972. "Thunder out of Chinatown." *The National Observer, **11**:1, 18 (March 8).

Petrie, A. 1967. *Individuality in Pain and Suffering*. Chicago: University of Chicago Press.

Phillips, D. L. 1971. "Sociologists and their knowledge." *American Behavioral Scientist*, **14**:563–582.

Piliavin, I., and S. Briar. 1964. "Police encounters with juveniles." *American Journal of Sociology*, **70**:206–214.

Plate, T. 1975. *Crime Pays!* New York: Simon and Schuster.

Platt, A. A. 1969. *The Child Savers: The Invention of Delinquency*. Chicago: University of Chicago Press.

Platt, A. A. 1974. "Prospects for a radical criminology in the United States." *Crime and Social Justice*, 1:2–10.

Plog, S. C., and R. B. Edgerton (eds.). 1969. *Changing Perspectives in Mental Illness*. New York: Holt.

Pokorny, A. D. 1965. "A comparison of homicides in two cities." *Journal of Criminal Law, Criminology, and Police Science*, 56:479–487.

Polk, K., and W. E. Schafer (eds.). 1972. *Schools and Delinquency*. Englewood Cliffs, N.J.: Prentice-Hall.

Pollak, O. 1951. *The Criminality of Women*. Philadelphia: University of Pennsylvania Press.

Polsky, N. 1967. *Hustlers, Beats, and Others*. Chicago: Aldine.

Pope, A. 1731–1735. "Moral essays." In H. Davis (ed.), *Poetical Works*, 1966. London: Oxford University Press.

Pope, C. E. 1975a. *The Judicial Processing of Assault and Burglary Offenders in Selected California Counties*. Washington, D.C.: U.S. Department of Justice.

Pope, C. E. 1975b. *Offender-Based Transaction Statistics: New Directions in Data Collection and Reporting*. Washington, D.C.: U.S. Department of Justice.

Pope, C. E. 1975c. *Sentencing of California Felony Offenders*. Washington, D.C.: U.S. Department of Justice.

Popper, K. R. 1959. *The Logic of Scientific Discovery*. Toronto: University of Toronto Press.

Popper, K. R. 1962. *Conjectures and Refutations: The Growth of Scientific Knowledge*. New York: Basic Books.

Porterfield, A. L. 1943. "Delinquency and its outcome in court and college." *American Journal of Sociology*, 49:199–208.

Porterfield, A. L. 1946. *Youth in Trouble*. Austin, Tex.: Leo Potishman Foundation.

Porteus, S. D. 1961. "Ethnic group differences." *Mankind Quarterly*, 1(4).

Post, R. H. 1962a. "Population differences in red and green color vision deficiency: A review, and a query on selection relaxation." *Eugenics Quarterly*, 9:131–146.

Post, R. H. 1962b. "Population differences in vision acuity: A review, with speculative notes on selection relaxation." *Eugenics Quarterly*, 9:189–212.

Post, R. H. 1964. "Hearing acuity variation among Negroes and whites." *Eugenics Quarterly*, 11:65–81.

Power, M. J., et al. 1972. "Neighborhood, school and juveniles before the courts." *British Journal of Criminology*, 12:111–132.

Powers, W. T. 1974. "Behavior reinforcement." *Science*, 186:782 (November 29).

Premack, D. 1971. "On the assessment of language competence in the chimpanzee." In A. M. Schrier and F. Stollnitz (eds.), *Behavior of Nonhuman Primates*. New York: Academic Press.

Premack, D., and A. J. Premack. 1972. "Teaching language to an ape." *Scientific American*, 227:92–99.

President's Commission on Law Enforcement and the Administration of Justice. 1967a. *The Challenge of Crime in a Free Society*. Washington, D.C.: GPO.

President's Commission on Law Enforcement and the Administration of Justice. 1967b. *Crime and Its Impact: An Assessment*. Washington, D.C.: GPO.

Price, J. E. 1966. "A test of the accuracy of criminal statistics." *Social Problems*, 14:214–222.

Provine, W. B. 1973. "Genetics and the biology of race crossing." *Science*, 182:790–796 (November 23).

Quay, H. C., et al. 1960. "The interpretation of three personality factors in juvenile delinquency." *Journal of Consulting Psychology*, **24**:555.

Quinney, R. 1970. *The Social Reality of Crime*. Boston: Little, Brown.

Quinney, R. 1974a. *Critique of Legal Order: Crime Control in Capitalist Society*. Boston: Little, Brown.

Quinney, R. 1974b. "The ideology of law: Notes for a radical alternative to legal oppression." In J. Susman (ed.), *Crime and Justice: 1971–1972*. New York: AMS Press.

Quinney, R. 1975. *Criminology: Analysis and Critique of Crime in America*. Boston: Little, Brown.

Radzinowicz, L. 1946. "Criminality by size of communities." London: University of London. Mimeographed.

Rainwater, L. 1960. *And the Poor Get Children: Sex, Contraception, and Family Planning in the Working Class*. Chicago: Quadrangle.

Ramsey, S. J. 1976. "Prison codes." *Journal of Communication*, **26**:39–45.

Random House Dictionary of the English Language. 1966. (Unabridged ed.) New York: Random House.

Rapoport, D. C. 1971. *Assassination and Terrorism*. Toronto: CBC Learning Systems.

Reckless, W. C. 1967. *The Crime Problem*. (4th ed.) New York: Appleton-Century-Crofts.

Reckless, W. C., and S. Dinitz. 1967. "Pioneering with self-concept as a vulnerability factor in delinquency." *Journal of Criminal Law, Criminology, and Police Science*, **58**:515–523.

Reed, J. S. 1975. *The Enduring South: Subcultural Persistence in Mass Society*. Chapel Hill: University of North Carolina Press.

Regan, D. T., et al. 1974. "Liking and the attribution process." *Journal of Experimental Social Psychology*, **10**:385–397.

Reich, W. 1942. *The Discovery of the Orgone*. New York: Orgone Institute Press.

Reichard, G. A. 1938. "Social life." In F. Boas (ed.), *General Anthropology*. Boston: Heath.

Reiss, A. J., Jr., and A. L. Rhodes. 1961. "The distribution of juvenile delinquency in the social class structure." *American Sociological Review*, **26**:720–732.

Rhees, R. 1947. "Social engineering." *Mind*, **56**:317–331.

Rice, S. A. 1928. *Quantitative Methods in Politics*. New York: Knopf.

Rieff, P. 1959. *Freud: The Mind of the Moralist*. New York: Viking.

Riis, R. W. 1941a. "The radio repair man will gyp you if you don't watch out." *The Reader's Digest*, **39**:6–13.

Riis, R. W. 1941b. "The repair man will gyp you if you don't watch out." *The Reader's Digest*, **39**:1–6.

Riis, R. W. 1941c. "The watch repair man will gyp you if you don't watch out." *The Reader's Digest*, **39**:10–12.

Riley, M. W. 1963. *Sociological Research: I. A Case Approach*. New York: Harcourt, Brace.

Rivera, R. J., and J. F. Short, Jr. 1967. "Occupational goals: A comparative analysis." In M. W. Klein (ed.), *Juvenile Gangs in Context: Theory, Research, and Action*. Englewood Cliffs, N.J.: Prentice-Hall.

Robins, L. N., and P. O'Neal. 1958. "Mortality, mobility, and crime." *American Sociological Review*, **23**:162–171.

Robinson, J. P. 1970. "Public reaction to political protest: Chicago, 1968." *Public Opinion Quarterly*, **34**:1–9.

Robinson, W. S. 1950. "Ecological correlations and behavior of individuals." *American Sociological Review*, **15**:351–357.

Roff, M. 1961. "Childhood social interaction and young adult bad conduct." *Journal of Abnormal and Social Psychology*, **63**:333–337.

Rohrer, J. H., and M. S. Edmonson (eds.). 1960. *Eighth Generation: Cultures and Personalities of New Orleans Negroes*. New York: Harper.

Romanczyk, R. G., and E. R. Goren. 1975. "Severe self-injurious behavior: The problem of clinical control." *Journal of Consulting and Clinical Psychology*, **43**:730–739.

Roof, W. C. 1972. "Residential segregation of blacks and racial inequality in Southern cities: Toward a causal model." *Social Problems*, **19**:393–407.

Rooney, E., and D. Gibbons. 1966. "Social reactions to 'crimes without victims.' " *Social Problems*, **13**:400–410.

Rose, A. 1961. "Inconsistencies in attitudes toward Negro housing." *Social Problems*, **8**:286–292.

Rose, A. 1962. "A systematic summary of symbolic interaction theory." In A. Rose (ed.), *Human Behavior and Social Processes*. Boston: Houghton Mifflin.

Rose, A., and A. Prell. 1955. "Does the punishment fit the crime?" *American Journal of Sociology*, **61**:247–259.

Rosekrans, M. A. 1967. "Imitation in children as a function of perceived similarity to a social model and vicarious reinforcement." *Journal of Personality and Social Psychology*, **7**:307–315.

Rosen, B. C. 1956. "The achievement syndrome: A psychocultural dimension of social stratification." *American Sociological Review*, **21**:203–211.

Rosen, B. C., and R. D'Andrade. 1959. "The psychosocial origins of achievement motivation." *Sociometry*, **22**:185–218.

Rosenquist, C. M., and E. I. Megargee. 1969. *Delinquency in Three Cultures*. Austin: University of Texas Press.

Rosenthal, D. 1970. *Genetic Theory and Abnormal Behavior*. New York: McGraw-Hill.

Roshco, B. 1976. *Newsmaking*. Chicago: University of Chicago Press.

Ross, H. L., et al. 1970. "Determining the social effects of a legal reform: The British 'Breathalyser' crackdown of 1967." *American Behavioral Scientist*, **13**:493–509.

Ross, I. 1975. *The Social Organization of Unnatural Death: The Eclipse of a Coroner System*. Edmonton: University of Alberta, Department of Sociology. Ph.D. dissertation prospectus.

Ross, L. 1975. "Letter from Oslo." *The New Yorker*, **51**:102–128 (October 6).

Rossi, P. H. 1971. "The city as purgatory." *Social Science Quarterly*, **51**:817–820.

Rossman, E. N. 1962. "A fund-raiser comes to Northrup." *Commentary*, **33**:218–225.

Rothstein, E. 1961. *An Analysis of Status Images as Perception Variables between Delinquent and Non-Delinquent Boys*. New York: New York University. Ph.D. dissertation.

Rotter, J. B. 1966. "Generalized expectancies for internal versus external control of reinforcement." *Psychological Monographs: General and Applied*, **80** (Whole No. 609):1–28.

Royal Commission. 1955. *Report of the Royal Commission on Law of Insanity as a Defence in Criminal Cases*. Ottawa: Queen's Printer and Controller of Stationery.

Rugg, D., and H. Cantril. 1942. "The wording of questions in public opinion polls." *Journal of Abnormal and Social Psychology*, **6**:472–476.

Runciman, W. G. 1966. *Relative Deprivation and Social Justice: A Study of Attitudes to Social Inequality in Twentieth Century England*. London: Routledge.

Ryan, E. D., and R. Foster. 1967. "Athletic participation and perceptual augmentation and reduction." *Journal of Personality and Social Psychology*, **6:**472–476.

Ryan, E. D., and C. R. Kovacic. 1966. "Pain tolerance and athletic participation." *Perceptual and Motor Skills*, **22:**383–390.

Ryle, G. 1949. *Concept of Mind*. London: Hutchinson.

Sagarin, E. 1975. *Deviants and Deviance: An Introduction to the Study of Disvalued People and Behavior*. New York: Praeger.

Sagarin, E. 1976. "The high personal cost of wearing a label." *Psychology Today*, **9:**25–29.

Salem, R. G., and W. J. Bowers. 1970. "Severity of formal sanctions as a deterrent to deviant behavior." *Law and Society Review*, **5:**21–40.

Salisbury, C. Y. 1974. *Russian Diary*. New York: Walker.

Salmon, T. N., and A. F. Blakeslee. 1935. "Genetics of sensory thresholds: Variations within single individuals in taste sensitivity for PTC." *Proceedings* of the National Academy of Science, U.S.A., **21:**78–83.

Samuelson, P. A. 1973. *Economics*. (9th ed.) New York: McGraw-Hill.

Sanders, M. K. 1966. "The several worlds of American Jews." *Harper's Magazine*, **232:**53–62.

Sandler, J. 1964. "Masochism: An empirical analysis." *Psychological Bulletin*, **62:**197–204.

Sanford, D. 1976. *Ralph and Me: Is Nader Unsafe for America?* New York: New Republic Books.

Sargant, W. 1964. "Psychiatric treatment: Here and there." *The Atlantic Monthly*, **214:**88–95.

Savitz, L. 1967. *Dilemmas in Criminology*. New York: McGraw-Hill.

Sawyer, J. 1966. "Measurement *and* prediction: Clinical *and* statistical." *Psychological Bulletin*, **66:**178–200.

Scanlan's Monthly. 1972. "The student who burned down the Bank of America." Reprinted in J. Susman (ed.), *Crime and Justice: 1970–1971*. New York: AMS Press.

Schaefer, E. S., and N. Bayley. 1960. "Consistency of maternal behavior from infancy to preadolescence." *Journal of Abnormal and Social Psychology*, **61:**1–6.

Schafer, W. E., and K. Polk. 1972. Cf. reference to Polk and Schafer, 1972.

Scheff, T. J. 1966. *Being Mentally Ill*. Chicago: Aldine.

Scheff, T. J. 1974. "The labelling theory of mental illness." *American Sociological Review*, **39:**444–452.

Schellhardt, T. D. 1975. "Why economists go wrong." *The Wall Street Journal*, **93:**18 (December 17).

Schelling, T. C. 1967 "Economics and criminal enterprise." *The Public Interest*, (7):61–78.

Schiffman, H., and R. Wynne. 1963. "Cause and affect." Princeton, N.J.: Educational Testing Service, RM-63-7 (July).

Schleifer, M. 1976. "Moral education and indoctrination." *Ethics*, **86:**154–163.

Schleifer, M., and V. Douglas. 1973. "Moral judgments, behaviour and cognitive style in young children." *Canadian Journal of Behavioural Science*, **5:**133–144.

Schmid, C. F. 1960. "Urban crime areas: Part II." *American Sociological Review*, **25:**655–678.

Schmid, C. F., and S. E. Schmid. 1972. *Crime in the State of Washington*. Olympia: Washington State Planning and Community Affairs Agency.

Schmidt, H. O., and C. P. Fonda. 1956. "The reliability of psychiatric diagnosis: A new look." *Journal of Abnormal and Social Psychology*, **52:**262–267.

Schneider, A. L. 1975. *Crime and Victimization in Portland: Analysis of Trends, 1971–1974*. Eugene: Oregon Research Institute.

Schneider, A. L., et al. 1975. *The Role of Attitudes in Decision to Report Crime to the Police*. Eugene: Oregon Research Institute.

Schoeck, H. 1966. *Envy: A Theory of Social Behavior*. New York: Harcourt, Brace.

Schreiber, E. M. 1976. "Dirty data in Britain and the USA: The reliability of 'invariant' characteristics reported in surveys." *Public Opinion Quarterly*, **39**:493–506.

Schuckit, M. 1972. "The woman alcoholic: A literature review." *Psychiatry in Medicine*, **3**:37–44.

Schuessler, K. F. 1962. "Components of variations in city crime rates." *Social Problems*, **9**:314–323.

Schuessler, K. F., and G. Slatin, 1964. "Sources of variation in U.S. city crime, 1950 and 1960." *Journal of Research in Crime and Delinquency*, **1**:127–148.

Schultz, H. D. 1972. *Panics and Crashes and How You Can Make Money out of Them*. New Rochelle, N.Y.: Arlington House.

Schumpeter, J. A. 1947. *Capitalism, Socialism, and Democracy*. (2d ed.) New York: Harper and Row.

Schur, E. M. 1965. *Crimes without Victims: Deviant Behavior and Public Policy*. Englewood Cliffs, N.J.: Prentice-Hall.

Schur, E. M. 1971. *Labeling Deviant Behavior: Its Sociological Implications*. New York: Harper.

Schur, E. M. 1973. *Radical Non-Intervention: Rethinking the Delinquency Problem*. Englewood Cliffs, N.J.: Prentice-Hall.

Schur, E. M. 1975. "Comments." In W. R. Gove (ed.), *The Labelling of Deviance: Evaluating a Perspective*. New York: Wiley.

Schwartz, B. 1968. "The effect in Philadelphia of Pennsylvania's increased penalties for rape and attempted rape." *Journal of Criminal Law, Criminology, and Police Science*, **59**:509–515.

Schwartz, R. D., and J. H. Skolnick. 1962. "Two studies of legal stigma." *Social Problems*, **10**:133–142.

Schwendinger, H. 1963. *The Instrumental Theory of Delinquency*. Los Angeles: University of California, Department of Sociology. Ph.D. dissertation.

Schwendinger, H., and J. Schwendinger. 1967. "Delinquent stereotypes of probable victims." In M. W. Klein (ed.), *Juvenile Gangs in Context: Theory, Research, and Action*. Englewood Cliffs, N.J.: Prentice-Hall.

Schwendinger, H., and J. Schwendinger. 1975. "Defenders of order or guardians of human rights?" In I. Taylor et al. (eds.), *Critical Criminology*. London: Routledge.

Sclare, A. B. 1970. "The female alcoholic." *British Journal of Addictions*, **65**:99–107.

Scott, R. A. 1969. *The Making of Blind Men*. New York: Russell Sage.

Scott, W. A., and J. Rohrbaugh. 1975. "Conceptions of harmful groups: Some correlates of group descriptions in three cultures." *Journal of Personality and Social Psychology*, **31**:992–1003.

Scriven, M. 1968a. "In defense of all causes." Berkeley: University of California, Department of Philosophy. Mimeographed.

Scriven, M. 1968b. "Note on the logic of causes." Berkeley: University of California, Department of Philosophy. Mimeographed.

Scriven, M. 1971. "The logic of cause." *Theory and Decision*, **2**:49–66.

Scriven, M. 1974. "Causation as explanation." Berkeley: University of California, Department of Philosophy. Mimeographed.

Sears, R. R. 1961. "Relation of early socialization experiences to aggression in middle childhood." *Journal of Abnormal and Social Psychology*, **63**:466–492.

Seidman, D. 1975. *The Urban Arms Race: A Quantitative Analysis of Private Arming*. New Haven, Conn.: Yale University, Department of Political Science. Ph.D. dissertation.

Seidman, D., and M. Couzens. 1974. "Getting the crime rate down: Political pressure and crime reporting." *Law and Society Review*, **8**:457–493.

Seligman, M. E. P. 1975. *Helplessness: On Depression, Development, and Death*. San Francisco: Freeman.

Seligman, M. E. P., and J. Hager. 1972. *Biological Boundaries of Learning*. New York: Appleton-Century-Crofts.

Sellin, T. 1938. *Culture Conflict and Crime*. New York: Social Science Research Council, Bulletin No. 41.

Sellin, T. 1958. "Recidivism and maturation." *National Probation and Parole Association Journal*, **4**:241–250.

Sellin, T., and M. E. Wolfgang. 1964. *The Measurement of Delinquency*. New York: Wiley.

Seltzer, A. R., and E. Beller. 1969. "Perception of time related to moral judgment and moral conduct." Paper read at the annual meeting of the Eastern Psychological Association, Philadelphia.

Sesnowitz, M. 1972. "The returns to burglary." *Western Economic Journal*, **10**:477–481.

Sewell, W. H., et al. 1969. "The educational and early occupational attainment process." *American Sociological Review*, **34**:82–92.

Shannon, L. W. 1963. "Types and patterns of delinquency referral in a middle-sized city." *British Journal of Criminology*, **4**:24–36.

Shaw, C. R., and H. D. McKay. 1931. "Social factors in juvenile delinquency." National Commission on Law Observance and Enforcement, *Report on the Causes of Crime*, No. 13. Washington, D.C.: GPO.

Shaw, C. R., and H. D. McKay. 1942. *Juvenile Delinquency and Urban Areas*. Chicago: University of Chicago Press.

Sheehan, S. 1975. "Profiles: A welfare mother." *The New Yorker*, **51**:42–99 (September 29).

Sheehan, S. 1976. *A Welfare Mother*. Boston: Houghton Mifflin.

Sheldon, W. H. 1949. *Varieties of Delinquent Youth: An Introduction to Constitutional Psychiatry*. New York: Harper.

Sheth, H. 1961. *Juvenile Delinquency in an Indian Setting*. Bombay: Popular Book Depot.

Shils, E. 1972. *The Intellectuals and the Powers*. Chicago: University of Chicago Press.

Shinnar, S., and R. Shinnar. 1975. "The effects of the criminal justice system on the control of crime: A quantitative approach." *Law and Society Review*, **9**:581–611.

Shoham, S. 1966. *Crime and Social Deviation*. Chicago: Regnery.

Shoham, S. 1970. *The Mark of Cain: The Stigma Theory of Crime and Social Deviation*. New York: Oceana.

Shub, A. 1969. *The New Russian Tragedy*. New York: Norton.

Shulman, H. M. 1929. *The Study of Problem Boys and Their Brothers*. Albany: New York State Crime Commission.

Shulman, H. M. 1959. "The family and juvenile delinquency." In S. Glueck (ed.), *The Problem of Delinquency*. Boston: Houghton Mifflin.

Shumate, R. P. 1958. *Effect of Increased Patrol on Accidents, Diversion, and Speed*. Evanston, Ill.: Northwestern University, Traffic Institute.

Siegel, A. E. 1956. "Film mediated fantasy aggression and strength of aggressive drive." *Child Development*, **27**:365–378.

Siegel, A. E., and L. G. Kohn. 1959. "Permissiveness, permission, and aggression: The effect of adult presence or absence on aggression in children's play." *Child Development*, **30:**131–141.

Siegman, A. W. 1966a. "Effects of auditory stimulation and intelligence on time estimation in delinquents and nondelinquents." *Journal of Consulting Psychology*, **30:**320–328.

Siegman, A. W. 1966b. "Father absence during early childhood and antisocial behavior." *Journal of Abnormal and Social Psychology*, **71:**71–74.

Silver, M. 1974. *Punishment, Deterrence, and Police Effectiveness: A Survey and Critical Interpretation of the Recent Econometric Literature*. New York: Crime Deterrence and Offender Career Project.

Silverman, R. A. 1975. *The Reliability of Crime Statistics*. Edmonton: University of Alberta, Department of Sociology. Research prospectus.

Silverman, R. A., and J. J. Teevan, Jr. (eds.). 1975. *Crime in Canadian Society*. Toronto: Butterworth.

Simon, H. A. 1958. *Administrative Behavior: A Study of Decision-Making Processes in Administrative Organizations*. New York: Macmillan.

Simon, H. A. 1972. "Causation." In D. L. Sills (ed.), *International Encyclopedia of the Social Sciences*. New York: Macmillan.

Simon, R. J. 1975. *Women and Crime*. Lexington, Mass.: Heath.

Simon, R. J., and W. Shackelford. 1965. "The defense of insanity: A survey of legal and psychiatric opinion." *Public Opinion Quarterly*, **29:**411–430.

Skelly, W. 1974. "The role of private police and security forces in the law enforcement picture of Canada." Paper read at the Crime in Industry Seminar, Toronto.

Skinner, B. F. 1938. *The Behavior of Organisms*. New York: Appleton-Century-Crofts.

Skinner, B. F. 1953. *Science and Human Behavior*. New York: Macmillan.

Skinner, B. F. 1974. *About Behaviorism*. New York: Knopf.

Skogan, W. G. 1974. "The validity of official crime statistics: An empirical investigation." *Social Science Quarterly*, **55:**25–38.

Sluckin, W. 1965. *Imprinting and Early Learning*. Chicago: Aldine.

Smigel, E. O., and H. L. Ross (eds.). 1970. *Crimes against Bureaucracy*. New York: Van Nostrand Reinhold.

Smith, H. 1976. *The Russians*. New York: Quadrangle.

Smith, H. L. 1958. "A comparison of interview and observation measures of mother behavior." *Journal of Abnormal and Social Psychology*, **57:**278–282.

Smith, H. L., and H. Hyman. 1950. "The biasing effect of interviewer expectations on survey results." *Public Opinion Quarterly*, **14:**491–506.

Smith, K. J. 1965. *A Cure for Crime*. London: Duckworth.

Smith, R. A. 1961. "The incredible electrical conspiracy." *Fortune*, **63:**132–137 and *passim*; 161–164 and *passim*.

Snyder, C. R. 1958. *Alcohol and the Jew: A Cultural Study of Drinking and Society*. Glencoe, Ill.: Free Press.

Soares, L. M., and A. T. Soares. 1969. "Social learning and social violence." *Proceedings*, 77th annual meeting of the American Psychological Association. Washington, D.C.: The Association.

Soares, L. M., and A. T. Soares. 1970. "Social learning and disruptive social behavior." *Phi Delta Kappan*, 82–84 (October).

Solhaug, M. L. 1972. *Accuracy of "Bad Men" Stereotypes: A Comparison of Autostereotyping by Lawbreakers with Stereotyping by More Lawful Others*.

Edmonton: University of Alberta, Department of Sociology. M.A. dissertation prospectus.

Sollenberger, R. T. 1968. "Chinese-American child rearing practices and juvenile delinquency." *Journal of Social Psychology*, **74**:13–23.

Solomon, R. L. 1964. "Punishment." *American Psychologist*, **19**:239–253.

Solzhenitsyn, A. I. 1973. *The Gulag Archipelago, 1918–1956: An Experiment in Literary Investigation*. (Vols. I and II.) New York: Harper and Row.

Solzhenitsyn, A. I. 1975. "Words of warning to America." *U.S. News & World Report*, **79**:44–50 (July 14).

Sontag, L. W. 1963. "Somatopsychics of personality and body function." *Vita Humana*, **6**:1–10.

Sorel, G. 1908. *Reflections on Violence*. Reprinted 1950. Glencoe, Ill.: Free Press.

Sornberger, J. 1974. "Crime crackdown urged." *Edmonton Journal*, 1, 10 (December 28).

Sorokin, P. A. 1959. *Social and Cultural Mobility*. Glencoe, Ill.: Free Press.

Spinley, B. M. 1964. *The Deprived and the Privileged*. London: Routledge.

Spitz, R. A. 1946. "Hospitalism: A follow-up report." In R. S. Eissler et al. (eds.), *The Psychoanalytic Study of the Child*. (Vol. 2.) New York: International Universities Press.

Spitz, R. A. 1965. *The First Year of Life: A Psychoanalytic Study of Normal and Deviant Development of Object Relations*. New York: International Universities Press.

Srole, L., et al. 1962. *Mental Health in the Metropolis: The Midtown Manhattan Study*. (Vol. 1.) New York: McGraw-Hill.

Staats, A. W. 1968. *Learning, Language, and Cognition*. New York: Holt.

Staats, C. K., and A. W. Staats. 1957. "Meaning established by classical conditioning." *Journal of Experimental Psychology*, **54**:74–80.

Stacey, B. G. 1965. "Some psychological aspects of intergeneration occupational mobility." *British Journal of Social and Clinical Psychology*, **4**:275–286.

Statistical Abstracts of the United States. 1974. Washington, D.C.: U.S. Department of Commerce.

Statistics Canada. 1972. *Statistics of Criminal and Other Offences*. Ottawa: The Bureau.

Statistics Canada. 1973. *Statistics of Criminal and Other Offences*. Ottawa: The Bureau.

Statistics Canada. 1974a. *Crime and Traffic Enforcement Statistics, 1972–1973*. Ottawa: The Bureau.

Statistics Canada. 1974b. *Provincial Government Finance: Revenue and Expenditures (Estimates)*. Ottawa: The Bureau.

Statistics Canada. 1974c. *Uniform Crime Reporting Manual*. Ottawa: The Bureau.

Statistik Årsbok. 1970–1974. Stockholm: National Central Bureau of Statistics.

Statistischer Jahrbücher für die Bundesrepublik Deutschland. 1965–1974. Stuttgart/Mainz: Kohlammer.

Stein, A. H., et al. 1971. "Television content and young children's behavior." In J. P. Murray et al. (eds.), *Television and Social Behavior*. (Vol. 2: *Television and Social Learning*.) Washington, D.C.: GPO.

Stein, K. B., et al. 1968. "Future time perspective: Its relation to the socialization process and the delinquent role." *Journal of Consulting and Clinical Psychology*, **32**:257–264.

Stember, H., and H. Hyman. 1949–1950. "How interviewer effects operate through question form." *International Journal of Opinion and Attitude Research*, **3**:493–512.

Stephenson, R. M., and F. R. Scarpitti. 1968. "Negro-white differentials and delinquency." *Journal of Research in Crime and Delinquency*, **5**:122–133.

Stigler, G. J. 1970. "The optimum enforcement of laws." *Journal of Political Economy*, **78**:526–536.

Stigler, G. J. 1975. *The Citizen and the State: Essays on Regulation.* Chicago: University of Chicago Press.

Stinchcombe, A. L. 1964. *Rebellion in a High School.* Chicago: Quadrangle.

Stockwell, E. G. 1966. "Patterns of digit preference and avoidance in the age statistics of some recent national censuses." *Eugenics Quarterly*, **13**:205–208.

Stokols, D. 1972. "On the distinction between density and crowding: Some implications for future research." *Psychological Review*, **79**:275–277.

Stolz, S. B., et al. 1975. "Behavior modification: A perspective on critical issues." *American Psychologist*, **30**:1027–1048.

Stott, D. H. 1966. *Studies of Troublesome Children.* London: Tavistock.

Straus, M. A. 1962. "Deferred gratification, social class, and the achievement syndrome." *American Sociological Review*, **27**:326–335.

Sudman, S., and N. M. Bradburn. 1974. *Response Effects in Surveys: A Review and Synthesis.* Chicago: Aldine.

Sudnow, D. 1966. *Passing On.* Englewood Cliffs, N.J.: Prentice-Hall.

Surgeon General's Scientific Advisory Committee on Television and Social Behavior. 1972. *Television and Growing Up: The Impact of Televised Violence.* Washington, D.C.: GPO.

Sussman, F. B. 1959. *Law of Juvenile Delinquency.* New York: Oceana.

Sutherland, A. 1975. *Gypsies: The Hidden Americans.* New York: Free Press.

Sutherland, E. H. 1949. *White Collar Crime.* New York: Holt.

Sutherland, E. H., and D. R. Cressey. 1970. *Criminology.* (8th ed.) Philadelphia: Lippincott.

Sveri, K. 1960. *Kriminalitet og Older.* Stockholm: Almquist and Wiksell.

Swanton, J. W. 1973. *On the Use of Social Science: A Study in Inference.* Edmonton: University of Alberta, Department of Sociology. M.A. dissertation.

Szasz, T. S. 1957. "Commitment of the mentally ill: 'Treatment' or social restraint?" *Journal of Nervous and Mental Disease*, **125**:293.

Szasz, T. S. 1958. "Politics and mental health: Some remarks apropos of the case of Mr. Ezra Pound." *American Journal of Psychiatry*, **115**:508.

Szasz, T. S. 1961. *The Myth of Mental Illness: Foundations of a Theory of Personal Conduct.* New York: Hoeber-Harper.

Szasz, T. S. 1963. *Law, Liberty, and Psychiatry: An Inquiry into the Social Use of Mental Health Practices.* New York: Macmillan.

Szasz, T. S. 1974. "Our despotic laws destroy the right to self-control." *Psychology Today*, **8**:19–29, 127.

Taft, D. R. 1946. "The punishment of war criminals." *American Sociological Review*, **11**:439–444.

Talmon, Y. 1956. "The family in collective settlements." In *Transactions* of the Third World Congress of Sociology (Vol. 4.) London: International Sociological Association.

Tangri, S. S., and M. Schwartz. 1967. "Delinquency and the self-concept variable." *Journal of Criminal Law, Criminology, and Police Science*, **58**:182–190.

Tannenbaum, F. 1938. *Crime and the Community.* Boston: Ginn.

Tappan, P. W. 1947. "Who is the criminal?" *American Sociological Review*, **12**:96–102.

Taylor, I., et al. 1973. *The New Criminology: For a Social Theory of Deviance*. London: Routledge.

Taylor, I., et al. (eds.). 1975. *Critical Criminology*. London: Routledge.

Taylor, R. 1967. "Causation." In P. Edwards et al. (eds.), *The Encyclopedia of Philosophy*. New York: Macmillan.

Teahan, J. E. 1958. "Future time perspective, optimism, and academic achievement." *Journal of Abnormal and Social Psychology*, 57:379–380.

Teele, J. E., et al. 1966. "Teacher ratings, sociometric status, and choice-reciprocity of anti-social and normal boys." *Group Psychotherapy*, 19:183–197.

Teevan, J. J., Jr. 1972. "Deterrent effects of punishment: The Canadian case." *Canadian Journal of Corrections*, 14:68–82.

Terman, L. M., and M. H. Oden. 1947. *Genetic Studies of Genius: IV. The Gifted Child Grows Up*. Stanford, Calif.: Stanford University Press.

Terry, R. M. 1967. "Discrimination in the handling of juvenile offenders by social-control agencies." *Journal of Research in Crime and Delinquency*, 4:218–230.

Theis, S. van S. 1924. *How Foster Children Turn Out*. New York: State Charities Aid Association.

Thomas, A., et al. 1970. "The origins of personality." *Scientific American*, 223:102–109.

Thomas, A. E. 1972. "Community power and student rights." *Harvard Educational Review*, 42:173–216.

Thomas, C. W. n.d. "Are status offenders really so different? A comparative and longitudinal assessment." Mimeographed report No. 75-NI-99-0031 of the National Institute of Law Enforcement and Criminal Justice. Williamsburg, Va.: College of William and Mary.

Thomas, C. W. 1976. "Public opinion on criminal law and legal sanctions: An examination of two conceptual models." *Journal of Criminal Law and Criminology*, 67:110–116.

Thomas, W. I. 1937. *Primitive Behavior: An Introduction to the Social Sciences*. New York: McGraw-Hill.

Thomas, W. I., and D. S. Thomas. 1928. *The Child in America: Behavior Problems and Programs*. New York: Knopf.

Thompson, G. G., and C. W. Hunnicutt. 1944. "The effect of repeated praise or blame on the work achievement of 'introverts' and 'extroverts.'" *Journal of Educational Psychology*, 35:257–266.

Thompson, H. S. 1966. *Hell's Angels: A Strange and Terrible Saga*. New York: Random House.

Thompson, P. G. 1971. "Some factors in upward social mobility in England." *Sociology and Social Research*, 55:181–190.

Thornberry, T. P. 1973. "Race, socioeconomic status, and sentencing in the juvenile justice system." *Journal of Criminal Law and Criminology*, 64:90–98.

Thorngate, W. 1976. "Must we always think before we act?" *Personality and Social Psychology Bulletin*, 2:31–35.

Time. 1962. "Investigations: Decline and fall." 79:24–29 (May 25).

Time. 1964. "To catch a thief." 84:14 (October 2).

Time. 1965. "Crime: The man who fooled everybody." 85:24–25 (June 4).

Time. 1968. "The thin blue line." 92:39 (July 19).

Time. 1972. "*Time* citizens panel: The sour, frustrated and volatile voters." 99:22–23 (May 8).

Tittle, C. R. 1969. "Crime rates and legal sanctions." *Social Problems*, 16:409–423.

Tittle, C. R. 1975. "Labelling and crime: An empirical evaluation." In W. R. Gove (ed.), *Labelling of Deviance: Evaluating a Perspective*. New York: Wiley.

Tittle, C. R., and C. H. Logan. 1973. "Sanctions and deviance: Evidence and remaining questions." *Law and Society Review*, **7**:371–392.

Tittle, C. R., and A. R. Rowe. 1974. "Certainty of arrest and crime rates: A further test of the deterrence hypothesis." *Social Forces*, **52**:455–462.

Toby, J. 1950. "Comment on the Jonassen–Shaw and McKay controversy." *American Sociological Review*, **15**:107–108.

Toby, J. 1957. "The differential impact of family disorganization." *American Sociological Review*, **22**:505–512.

Toby, J. 1969. "Affluence and adolescent crime." In D. R. Cressey and D. A. Ward (eds.), *Delinquency, Crime, and Social Process*. New York: Harper.

Todorovich, A. 1970. "The application of ecological models to the study of juvenile delinquency in Belgrade." *International Review of Criminal Policy*, **28**:64–71. New York: United Nations.

Tomerlin, J. 1972. "Ralph Nader vs. Volkswagen: An evaluation of *The Volkswagen: An Assessment of Distinctive Hazards*." *Road and Track*, **23**:25–33.

Toro-Calder, J., et al. 1968. "A comparative study of Puerto Rican attitudes toward the legal system dealing with crime." *Journal of Criminal Law, Criminology, and Police Science*, **59**:536–541.

Trasler, G. 1962. *The Explanation of Criminality*. London: Routledge.

Tryon, R. C. 1967. "Predicting group differences in cluster analysis: The social area problem." *Multivariate Behavioral Research*, **2**:453–476.

Tuchman, B. W. 1972. *Notes from China*. New York: Collier.

Turk, A. T. 1966. "Conflict and criminality." *American Sociological Review*, **31**:338–352.

Turnbull, C. 1972. *The Mountain People*. New York: Simon and Schuster.

Turner, R. H. 1969. "The public perception of protest." *American Sociological Review*, **34**:815–831.

Turner, R. H. 1972. "Deviance avowal as neutralization of commitment." *Social Problems*, **19**:308–321.

Turner, S. 1969. "The ecology of delinquency." In T. Sellin and M. E. Wolfgang (eds.), *Delinquency: Selected Studies*. New York: Wiley.

United Nations. 1953. *Comparative Survey on Juvenile Delinquency*. Part V: *Asia and the Far East*. New York: United Nations.

United Nations. 1958a. *Comparative Survey of Juvenile Delinquency*. Part I: *North America*. New York: United Nations.

United Nations. 1958b. *Estudio Comparado Sobre Delincuencia Juvenil*. Parte III: *America Latina*. New York: United Nations.

United Nations. 1960. *Second United Nations Congress on the Prevention of Crime and the Treatment of Offenders*. Report Prepared by the Secretariat. New York: United Nations, Department of Economic and Social Affairs.

United Nations. 1965a. *Comparative Survey on Juvenile Delinquency*. Part V: *Middle East*. New York: United Nations.

United Nations. 1965b. *Third United Nations Congress on the Prevention of Crime and the Treatment of Offenders*. Report Prepared by the Secretariat. New York: United Nations, Department of Economic and Social Affairs.

United Nations. 1970. *Demographic Yearbook 1969*. New York: Statistical Office of the United Nations.

United Press International. 1973. "Contract bridge banished from socialist society" (January 27).

U.S. Department of Health, Education, and Welfare. 1963. *Illegitimate Births: United States, 1938–1957*. Washington, D.C.: GPO.

U.S. News & World Report. 1970. "Booming industry: Home safeguards." **59**:35 (October 26).

U.S. News & World Report. 1974a. "More and more vigilantes—legal and illegal." **76**:40–42 (February 4).

U.S. News & World Report. 1974b. "More and more vigilantes—legal and illegal." **76**:37–38 (May 6).

U.S. News & World Report. 1975a. "The American home under siege." **78**:41–42 (February 24).

U.S. News & World Report. 1975b. "Crimes by women are on the rise all over the world." **79**:50–51 (December 22).

U.S. News & World Report. 1975c. "Europe, too, has a crime wave: Burglary, kidnapping, terrorism." **79**:67–68 (July 28).

U.S. News & World Report. 1975d. "Violence in schools." **78**:37–40 (April 14).

U.S. News & World Report. 1976. "Terror in schools." **80**:52–55 (January 26).

Valentine, P. W. 1971. "D.C. crime reports: What they mean." *Washington Post* (October 26).

Vandenberg, S. G. 1966. "Contributions of twin research to psychology." *Psychological Bulletin*, **66**:327–352.

van den Haag, E. 1968. "On deterrence and the death penalty." *Ethics*, **78**:280–288.

van den Haag, E. 1975a. "The libertarian argument." *National Review*, **27**:729–731 (July 4).

van den Haag, E. 1975b. *Punishing Criminals: Concerning a Very Old and Painful Question.* New York: Basic Books.

van de Walle, E. 1966. "Some characteristic features of census age distributions in illiterate populations." *American Journal of Sociology*, **71**:549–555.

Vandivier, K. 1972. "The aircraft brake scandal." *Harper's Magazine*, **244**:45–52.

van Stolk, M. 1972. *The Battered Child in Canada.* Toronto: McClelland and Stewart.

Velez-Diaz, A., and E. I. Megargee. 1970. "An investigation of differences in value judgments between youthful offenders and non-offenders in Puerto Rico." *Journal of Criminal Law, Criminology, and Police Science*, **61**:549–553.

Velimesis, M. 1975. "The female offender." *Crime and Delinquency Literature*, **7**:94–112.

Verden, P., and D. Shatterly. 1971. "Alcoholism research and resistance to understanding the compulsive drinker." *Mental Hygiene*, **55**:331–336.

Vislick-Young, P. 1930. "Urbanization as a factor in juvenile delinquency." *Publications of the American Sociological Society*, **24**:162–166.

von Mises, L. 1960. "The resentment and the anti-capitalistic bias of American intellectuals." In G. B. Huszar (ed.), *The Intellectuals: A Controversial Portrait.* Glencoe, Ill.: Free Press.

von Mises, L. 1966. *Human Action: A Treatise on Economics.* (3d ed.) Chicago: Regnery.

von Mises, R. 1956. *Positivism: A Study in Human Understanding.* New York: Braziller.

von Neumann, J., and O. Morgenstern. 1947. *Theory of Games and Economic Behavior.* Princeton, N.J.: Princeton University Press.

Voss, H. L. 1963. "Ethnic differentials in delinquency in Honolulu." *Journal of Criminal Law, Criminology, and Police Science*, **54**:322–327.

Voss, H. L. 1966. "Socioeconomic status and reported delinquent behavior." *Social Problems*, **13**:314–324.

Votey, H. L., Jr., and L. Phillips. 1972. "An economic analysis of the deterrent effect of law enforcement on criminal activity." *Journal of Criminal Law, Criminology, and Police Science*, **63:**330–342.

Votey, H. L., Jr., and L. Phillips. 1974. "The control of criminal activity: An economic analysis." In D. Glaser (ed.), *Handbook of Criminology*. Chicago: Rand McNally.

Waldfogel, S. 1948. "The frequency and affective character of childhood memories." *Psychological Monographs*, **62:**1–39.

Waldo, G. P., and T. G. Chiricos. 1972. "Perceived penal sanction and self-reported criminality: A neglected approach to deterrence research." *Social Problems*, **19:**522–540.

Walker, N. 1971. *Crimes, Courts and Figures: An Introduction to Criminal Statistics*. Harmondsworth, England: Penguin.

Walker, N., et al. 1967. *The Violent Offender: Reality or Illusion?* Oxford: Blackwell.

Wallerstein, J. A., and C. J. Wyle. 1947. "Our law-abiding law-breakers." *Federal Probation*, **25:**107–112.

Wallis, C. P., and R. Maliphant. 1967. "Delinquent areas in the county of London: Ecological factors." *British Journal of Criminology*, **7:**250–284.

The Wall Street Journal. 1972. "And somebody stole our carpet and chairs." **86:**12 (June 19).

The Wall Street Journal. 1973. "SEC accuses *Los Angeles Times* publisher, oil promoter, others in $30 million fraud." **88:**5 (May 18).

The Wall Street Journal. 1975. "The golden fleece." **93:**16 (October 17).

The Wall Street Journal. 1976. "The cigaret tax lesson." **94:**12 (February 5).

Walters, R. H. 1967. "Nurturance and the intensity and timing of punishment." Public lecture. Edmonton: University of Alberta.

Walters, R. H., and L. Demkow. 1963. "Timing of punishment as a determinant of response inhibition." *Child Development*, **34:**207–214.

Walters, R. H., et al. 1962. "Enhancement of punitive behavior by audio-visual displays." *Science*, **136:**872–873.

Walters, R. H., et al. 1965. "Timing of punishment and the observation of consequences to others as determinants of response inhibition." *Journal of Experimental Child Psychology*, **2:**10–30.

Ward, R. H. 1971. "The labeling theory: A critical analysis." *Criminology*, **9:**268–290.

Warner, W. L. 1953. *American Life: Dream and Reality*. Chicago: University of Chicago Press.

Warner, W. L., and J. Abegglen. 1955. *Big Business Leaders in America*. New York: Harper and Row.

Warner, W. L., and P. S. Lunt. 1941. *The Social Life of a Modern Community*. New Haven, Conn.: Yale University Press.

Warriner, C. K. 1958. "The nature and functions of official morality." *American Journal of Sociology*, **64:**165–168.

Weaver, C. N., and C. L. Swanson. 1974. "Validity of reported date of birth, salary, and seniority." *Public Opinion Quarterly*, **38:**69–80.

Weaver, P. H. 1975. "The hazards of trying to make consumer products safer." *Fortune*, **92:**132–140.

Webster's New Collegiate Dictionary. 1976. (8th ed.) Springfield, Mass.: Merriam.

Weil, S. 1946. "War as an institution: Words and war." *Politics*, **3:**69–73.

Weil, S. 1952. *The Need for Roots*. Boston: Beacon Press.

Weinberg, J. 1968. "Causation." In P. P. Wiener (ed.), *Dictionary of the History of Ideas: Studies of Selected Pivotal Ideas*. New York: Scribner.

Weiner, N. L., and C. V. Willie. 1971. "Decision by juvenile officers." *American Journal of Sociology*, **77**:199–210.

Weiss, D. J., and R. V. Davis. 1960. "An objective validation of factual interview data." *Journal of Applied Psychology*, **44**:361–365.

Weissman. H. H. (ed.). 1969. *Justice and the Law in the Mobilization for Youth Experience*. New York: Association Press.

Wertheimer, M. 1955. "Figural aftereffect as a measure of metabolic deficiency." *Journal of Personality*, **24**:56–73.

Wessman, A. E., and D. F. Ricks. 1966. *Mood and Personality*. New York: Holt.

West, D. J. 1969. *Present Conduct and Future Delinquency*. London: Heinemann.

West, R. 1964. *The Meaning of Treason*. New York: Viking.

Wetzel, J. 1975. "Unemployment measurement and meaning." Paper read at the 30th annual meeting of the American Association for Public Opinion Research, Itasca, Ill.

Wheeler, L., and A. R. Caggiula. 1966. "The contagion of aggression." *Journal of Experimental Social Psychology*, **2**:1–10.

Wheeler, S., et al. 1968. "Agents of delinquency control: A comparative analysis." In S. Wheeler (ed.), *Controlling Delinquents*. New York: Wiley.

Whiting, J. M. W. 1944. "The frustration complex in Kwoma society." *Man*, **44**:113–121.

Whiting, J. M. W., and I. L. Child. 1953. *Child Training and Personality*. New Haven, Conn.: Yale University Press.

Wicker, A. W. 1969. "Attitudes versus actions." *Journal of Social Issues*, **25**:41–78.

Wicker, A. W. 1971. "An examination of the 'other variables' explanation of attitude-behavior inconsistency." *Journal of Personality and Social Psychology*, **19**:18–30.

Wicks, J. W., and E. G. Stockwell. 1975. "Age heaping in recent national censuses: An addendum." *Social Biology*, **22**:279–281.

Wiers, P. 1939. "Juvenile delinquency in rural Michigan." *Journal of Criminal Law and Criminology*, **30**:148–157.

Wiggins, N., and E. S. Kohen. 1971. "Man versus model of man revisited: The forecasting of graduate school success." *Journal of Personality and Social Psychology*, **19**:100–106.

Wilde, O. 1893. *Lady Windermere's Fan: A Play about a Good Woman*. London: Methuen.

Wilensky, H. L. 1964. "Mass society and mass culture: Interdependence or dependence?" *American Sociological Review*, **29**:173–197.

Wilkins, J. L., et al. 1974. "Personality type, reports of violence, and aggressive behavior." *Journal of Personality and Social Psychology*, **30**:243–247.

Wilkins, L. T. 1968. "The concept of cause in criminology." *Issues in Criminology*, **3**:147–165.

Wilkins, L. T. 1969. *Evaluation of Penal Measures*. New York: Random House.

Wilks, J., and R. Martinson. 1976. "Is the treatment of criminal offenders really necessary?" *Federal Probation*, **40**:3–9.

Williams, G. 1955. "The definition of crime." *Current Legal Problems*, **8**:107–130.

Williams, H. D. 1933. "A survey of pre-delinquent children in ten Middle Western cities." *Journal of Juvenile Research*, **17**:163–174.

Williams, J. A., Jr. 1964. "Interviewer-respondent interaction: A study of bias in the information interview." *Sociometry*, **27**:338–352.

Williams, J. D. 1967. "Eager investors drop more than $50 million as debts outrun New Jersey bus operator." *The Wall Street Journal*, **77**:1, 10 (October 23).

Williams, R. L. 1974. "Scientific racism and IQ: The silent mugging of the black community." *Psychology Today*, **7**:32–41, 101.

Willie, C. V., and A. Gershenovitz. 1964. "Juvenile delinquency in racially mixed areas." *American Sociological Review*, **29**:740–744.

Willing, M. K. 1971. *Beyond Conception: Our Children's Children*. Boston: Gambit.

Willmott, P. 1966. *Adolescent Boys in East London*. London: Routledge.

Wilson, E. O. 1975. *Sociobiology: The New Synthesis*. Cambridge, Mass.: Belknap Press.

Wilson, J. Q. 1968. "The police and the delinquent in two cities." In S. Wheeler (ed.), *Controlling Delinquents*. New York: Wiley.

Wilson, J. Q., et al. 1972. "The problem of heroin." *The Public Interest*, (29):3–28.

Winch, P. 1958. *The Idea of a Social Science and Its Relation to Philosophy*. London: Routledge.

Winter, J. A. 1970. "On the mixing of morality and politics: A test of a Weberian hypothesis." *Social Forces*, **49**:36–41.

Wirth, L. 1929. *The Ghetto*. Chicago: University of Chicago Press.

Withery, S. B. 1954. "Reliability of recall of income." *Public Opinion Quarterly*, **18**:197–204.

Witkin, H. 1965. "Psychological differentiation and forms of pathology." *Journal of Abnormal Psychology*, **70**:317–336.

Witkin, H., et al. 1962. *Psychological Differentiation*. New York: Wiley.

Wittgenstein, L. 1958. *Preliminary Studies for the "Philosophical Investigations," Generally Known as the Blue and Brown Books*. New York: Harper and Row.

Wolf, E. P. 1976. "Social science and the courts: The Detroit schools case." *The Public Interest*, (42):102–120.

Wolf, P. 1962. "Crime and social class in Denmark." *British Journal of Criminology*, **13**:5–17.

Wolf, P. 1965. "A contribution to the topology of crime in Denmark." In K. O. Christiansen et al. (eds.), *Scandinavian Studies in Criminology*. (Vol. 1.) London: Tavistock.

Wolfgang, M. E. 1958. *Patterns in Criminal Homicide*. Philadelphia: University of Pennsylvania Press.

Wolfgang, M. E. 1966. "Race and crime." In H. J. Sklare (ed.), *Changing Concepts of Crime and Its Treatment*. London: Pergamon.

Wolfgang, M. E. 1968. "Urban crime." In J. Q. Wilson (ed.), *The Metropolitan Enigma*. Cambridge, Mass.: Harvard University Press.

Wolfgang, M. E. 1974. "The social scientist in court." *Journal of Criminal Law and Criminology*, **65**:239–247.

Wolfgang, M. E., and F. Ferracuti. 1967. *The Subculture of Violence: Towards an Integrated Theory in Criminology*. London: Tavistock.

Wolfgang, M. E., R. M. Figlio, and T. Sellin. 1972. *Delinquency in a Birth Cohort*. Chicago: University of Chicago Press.

Wolfgang, M. E., and M. Riedel. 1973. "Race, judicial discretion, and the death penalty." *The Annals of the American Academy of Political and Social Science*, **407**:119–133.

Woodley, R. 1974. "How to win the soap box derby." *Harper's Magazine*, **249**:62–69.

Yankelovich, D. 1972. *The Changing Values on Campus: Political and Personal Attitudes of Today's College Students*. New York: Washington Square Press.

Yankelovich, D. 1974. *The New Morality: A Profile of American Youth in the 70's*. New York: McGraw-Hill.

Yarrow, M. R., et al. 1968. *Child Rearing: An Inquiry into Research and Methods*. San Francisco: Jossey-Bass.

Youell, K. J., and J. P. McCullough. 1975. "Behavioral treatment of mucous colitis." *Journal of Consulting and Clinical Psychology*, **43**:740–745.

Zax, M., et al. 1968. "Follow-up study of children identified early as emotionally disturbed." *Journal of Consulting and Clinical Psychology*, **32**:369–374.

Zeigarnik, B. 1927. "About the memorizing of completed and incompleted actions." *Psychologische Forschung*, **9**:1–86.

Zeitlin, M. 1967. *Revolutionary Politics and the Cuban Working Class*. New York: Harper and Row.

Zelnick, M. 1964. "Errors in the 1960 census enumeration of native whites." *Journal of the American Statistical Association*, **59**:437–459.

Zigler, E., and L. Phillips. 1965. "Psychiatric diagnosis and symptomatology." In O. Milton (ed.), *Behavior Disorders*. Philadelphia: Lippincott.

Zimring, F. E., and G. J. Hawkins. 1973. *Deterrence: The Legal Threat in Crime Control*. Chicago: University of Chicago Press.

Zirpins, W., and O. Terstegen. 1963. *Wirtschaftskriminalität, ihre Erscheinungsformen und ihre Bekämpfung*. Lübeck: Max Schmidt-Romhild.

Zunich, M. 1962. "Relationship between maternal behavior and attitudes toward children." *Journal of Genetic Psychology*, **100**:155–165.

Name Index

Name Index

Subject Index

Subject Index